Canadian Immigration and Refugee Law for Legal Professionals

SECOND EDITION

Lynn Fournier-Ruggles

CONTRIBUTORS
Peter McKeracher
Ana Rasmusson
Lavinia Inbar

2013
Emond Montgomery Publications
Toronto, Canada

Emond Montgomery Publications Limited
60 Shaftesbury Avenue
Toronto ON M4T 1A3
http://www.emp.ca/highered

Printed in Canada.

We acknowledge the financial support of the Government of Canada through the Canada Book Fund for our publishing activities.

The events and characters depicted in this book are fictitious. Any similarity to actual persons, living or dead, is purely coincidental.

Publishers, college division: Bernard Sandler and Sarah Gleadow
Developmental editor: Sarah Gleadow
Marketing manager: Christine Davidson
Director, sales and marketing, higher education: Kevin Smulan
Supervising editor: Jim Lyons
Copy editor and indexer: Paula Pike
Production editor: Andrew Gordon
Proofreader: Nancy Ennis
Cover and text designer and typesetter: Tara Wells
Cover image: © Ocean/Corbis

Library and Archives Canada Cataloguing in Publication

Fournier-Ruggles, Lynn
    Canadian immigration and refugee law for legal professionals / Lynn Fournier-Ruggles. — 2nd ed.

Includes index.
ISBN 978-1-55239-479-3

    1. Emigration and immigration law—Canada.   2. Refugees—Legal status, laws, etc.—Canada.   3. Canada. Immigration and Refugee Protection Act.   I. Title.

KE4454.F69 2013   342.7108'2   C2012-906053-4
KF4483.I5F69 2013

To the Three Ds, Willow and Jester,
and my mentor, Linda Pasternak

Contents

PART II

IMMIGRATION PROGRAMS

PART III

CITIZENSHIP

PART IV

REFUGEE LAW

PART VII

LEGAL PROFESSIONALS

Preface

The greatest challenge in writing a textbook about immigration and refugee law—an area of law rooted in rules and regulations—is ensuring its currency and utility. The *Immigration and Refugee Protection Act* (IRPA) is a framework piece of legislation, with many of the essential details—*how, how much*, or *how many*—and other important criteria contained in regulations, policy statements, and tribunal rules. Regulations may be amended without any parliamentary debate or consent. By adjusting immigration law through regulations, government can be responsive to fluctuations in the labour market, for example, or to national security and safety concerns.

Since the publication of the first edition of this textbook in late 2008, the Canadian government has not only made numerous changes to the regulations; it has also made major amendments to the *Immigration and Refugee Protection Act* that affect how cases are managed and processed under Canada's immigration and refugee systems. Perhaps one of the most profound changes was the granting of new and broader discretionary powers to the minister, including the authority to give instructions about the processing of applications. The government has also implemented a case differentiation strategy—even within the same classes of immigration and refugee applications—which gives preferential treatment to cases that, "in the opinion of the Minister, will best support the attainment of the immigration goals established by the Government of Canada" (IRPA, s. 87.3(2)).

The framework nature of immigration and refugee law requires legal professionals who specialize in it to frequently look for announcements of changes. The depth of knowledge about case law, regulatory details, and processing rules required by immigration and refugee specialists is outside the scope of this text. For students, however, the text sets the course and guides them through the complexities of the subject, concentrating on broader program descriptions.

Updates to the second edition of the text consider amendments from three bills in particular that make significant changes to Canada's immigration and refugee determination systems:

- Bill C-35, *An Act to Amend the Immigration and Refugee Protection Act* (formerly called the *Cracking Down on Crooked Immigration Consultants Act*) received royal assent on March 23, 2011 and came into force on June 30, 2011. The key change is in the regulation of immigration consultants, described in Chapter 12.

- Bill C-11, the *Balanced Refugee Reform Act* (BRRA), received royal assent on June 29, 2010, with some amendments coming into force at that time and others that were to come into force within two years after the date of royal assent. However, before changes could fully be implemented, the government introduced Bill C-31.

- Bill C-31, the *Protecting Canada's Immigration System Act* (PCISA), which received royal assent on June 28, 2012, introduced amendments to both the IRPA and the BRRA. Most of the changes that affect the inland refugee determination process are expected to come into force no later than June 28, 2014.

The first edition of the text offered detailed descriptions of application processes, forms, fees, and other important criteria; the second edition provides descriptions of the immigration and refugee programs, illustrative scenarios, and *general* application procedures. The text also includes numerous web links that enable you to find your way around the programs and learn how to stay up-to-date. If you wish to pursue studies in this subject or practise in this area of law, the text provides a solid foundation on which to build your knowledge of professional resources.

Acknowledgments

This text originated as a response to my desire to provide students with a textbook that will help them master the complexities of immigration and refugee law. Students in my classes are mostly interested in the human story—the story about a friend or relative who either has come to Canada or is in the process of immigrating here. With so little time in the classroom and so much to learn, the challenge is to present the law in a meaningful way that maintains student engagement and covers the vast curriculum.

I am grateful to reviewers and to students who provided both positive and instructive feedback in developing this second edition. With the second edition, I now have a better sense of what works pedagogically while engaging students' interest.

One serious omission from the first edition was the lack of any acknowledgment of the many contributors for their valuable work. I am grateful to Peter McKeracher (Durham College) for the early concept for the text and the first draft of the table of contents. Peter's contributions to the first edition are still evident in the coverage of citizenship, CSIC regulation, and the history of immigration and regulation sections.

I also wish to thank Lavinia Inbar (Fleming College) for her contribution on Chapter 1, and Lavinia Inbar and Elizabeth Strutt-MacLeod (St. Clair College) for providing reviews of the first edition that helped shape this edition.

I am especially grateful to Ana Rasmusson (ICCRC), who not only wrote part of Chapter 4, but also enriched it with the many scenarios. Her experience as a regulated immigration consultant added the right stuff to the mix of legal jargon. I had the opportunity to teach with Ana in the School of Legal and Public Administration at Seneca College, and am happy to be working with her on this project as the creator of the accompanying instructor's materials.

The folks at Emond Montgomery masterfully put all this good work together, especially Peggy Buchan, who worked with me on the first edition and whose voice has stayed with me throughout the second edition ("Just keep writing!"), and Sarah Gleadow, who guided me through the process of a second edition. Thanks are also due to Paula Pike, who copy-edited and indexed this edition; Nancy Ennis, who proofread galleys; and Tara Wells, who designed and typeset the text. I am sincerely grateful for their support and belief in this work.

Happy reading and learning.

Lynn Fournier-Ruggles, BA, MPPAL
Fall 2012

About the Author

Lynn Fournier-Ruggles, BA, MPPAL has a Bachelor of Arts (conc. Psychology) from the University of Ottawa (1983); a Master, Public Policy, Administration and Law from York University (2010); and a Graduate Diploma in Justice System Administration (York University, 2011). Lynn developed her knowledge of immigration and refugee law through acting in various capacities with the federal public service: Director, Operational Systems, Registrar, and Refugee Claims Officer (1989 to 1998, Immigration and Refugee Board); Case Presenting Officer (1989, Toronto Enforcement Branch, Employment and Immigration Canada); and Case Presenting Officer (1984 to 1989, Refugee Status Advisory Committee). She has been teaching in the School of Legal and Public Administration at Seneca College since 2001.

PART I

The Fundamentals of Immigration and Refugee Law

Programs Under the Canadian Immigration and Refugee System

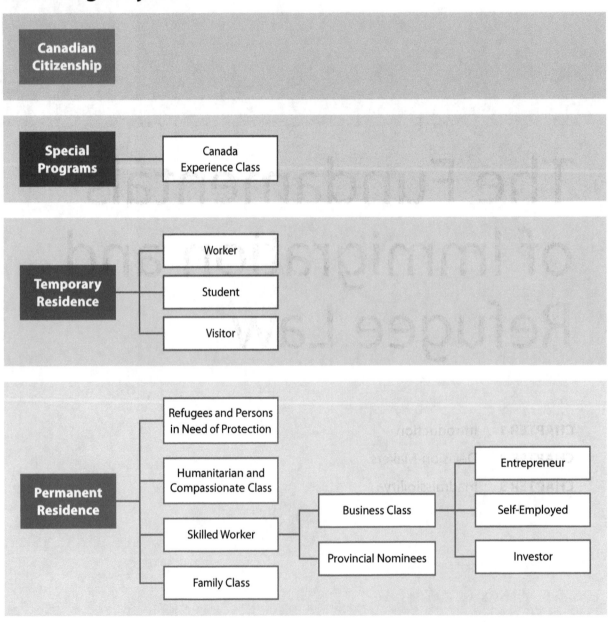

Canadian Citizenship

Special Programs
- Canada Experience Class

Temporary Residence
- Worker
- Student
- Visitor

Permanent Residence
- Refugees and Persons in Need of Protection
- Humanitarian and Compassionate Class
- Skilled Worker
- Family Class
- Business Class
  - Entrepreneur
  - Self-Employed
  - Investor
- Provincial Nominees

Introduction

1

LEARNING OUTCOMES

After reading this chapter you should be able to:

- List and describe the sources of immigration law.

- Find relevant immigration cases from the Immigration and Refugee Board, Federal Court, and Supreme Court of Canada.

- Find relevant sections from the *Immigration and Refugee Protection Act* and the IRP Regulations.

Introduction

Canada is a wealthy country with a highly developed social support system, a diverse population, and incredible natural resources. As a result, it is a highly attractive destination for people from around the world.

From an immigration law perspective, an individual's status in relation to Canada can be broken down into three types: **foreign national**, **permanent resident**, and **citizen**. Each status possesses its own set of rights.

Briefly, a "foreign national" is a person from another country who is neither a Canadian permanent resident nor a Canadian citizen. To gain entry to Canada, a foreign national requires permission from Canadian officials in the form of a **visa**, which permits the holder to enter Canada for a specific purpose either temporarily—to visit, to study, or to work—or permanently.

A foreign national with a temporary visa is a **temporary resident** who is coming to Canada for a short term and is not looking for a new permanent home (see Chapter 4.) Some foreign nationals, however, arrive without the proper authorization and they can be removed immediately unless they have arrived to seek protection and make a refugee claim (see Chapter 9.)

A foreign national who comes to Canada to live here permanently is a permanent resident. The rights of permanent residents to enter and remain in Canada are solely determined by the *Immigration and Refugee Protection Act* (IRPA) and its regulations (IRPR), which means that, under certain conditions, a permanent resident may lose that status and be forced to leave Canada (see Chapter 5).

For policy reasons, the government also creates special immigration programs, such as the Canada Experience class. This class is designed to facilitate the transition from temporary to permanent residence for those immigrants who acquire Canadian education and/or work experience.

A permanent resident, who follows all the rules can apply for Canadian citizenship, and when he or she obtains the status of citizen it gives him or her an unqualified right to enter, leave, and remain in Canada (see Chapter 6). This text examines the principles and processes of obtaining each of these status types.

Immigrant or Refugee?

The words "immigrant" and "refugee" do not mean the same thing. An immigrant is a person from another country who wishes to live in Canada permanently. A refugee is a person fleeing persecution, who comes to Canada to seek protection. Many refugees later choose to stay; but making Canada their permanent home is not their primary motivation for coming here. The term "immigration," however, is often used generally to include both immigrants and refugees.

History of Immigration Law in Canada

According to Citizenship and Immigration Canada (CIC), more than 15 million people have immigrated to Canada since Confederation in 1867. Canada's immigration scheme is founded on three pillars: economic, family, and refugee/humanitarian. These pillars are meant to balance Canada's economic self-interests with Canada's generosity and compassion to provide a safe haven to those in need from around the world.

Prior to the first *Immigration Act*, Canada's immigration rules were adapted from those of Great Britain.[1] For example, some provinces had enacted immigration laws primarily aimed at restricting the immigration of visible minorities. Historically, the ability for an alien to enter Britain was entirely dependent on the will of the King or Queen of England or officials appointed by the monarch. The power of the King or Queen to control immigration was gradually limited by statute law.

Patterns of Immigration

Immigration to what is now Canada predates the historical record. However, there are several scientific theories about the first migration to North America. Among them are the theories that stone-age hunters followed game from Siberia into Alaska across a land bridge that once spanned what is now the Bering Strait; a second theory proposes that Asian seafarers arrived by boats. Regardless of how or exactly when they arrived, these first migrants were probably the ancestors of Canada's First Nations peoples.

European immigration began in earnest in the early 17th century with French settlers and fur traders. The 18th century brought a wave of British loyalists leaving the newly formed United States of America. In the 19th century, a large number of immigrants came from Britain. In the 20th century, large numbers of immigrants began pouring in from just about everywhere, beginning with the first huge wave from continental Europe at the beginning of the century. This period of immigration in the 20th century is described in the CIC's publication *Forging Our Legacy: Canadian Citizenship and Immigration, 1900-1977* as follows:

> This huge influx of people represented a watershed in Canadian immigration history. From that time until today, Canada has never received the number of immigrants that it did in 1913, when over 400,000 newcomers arrived on Canadian soil. But throughout this century immigrants did continue to choose Canada as their new country, and a second great wave (the last one to date) occurred between 1947 and 1961. Although this wave, like the first, featured newcomers from continental Europe, southern Europe, especially Italy, and central Europe became much more important sources of immigrants. By contrast, immigration from Great Britain declined substantially from the earlier period (1900-1914).[2]

Although British immigration declined, British citizens still received preferential treatment over other immigrants. Various policies and laws restricted immigration from people considered to be the wrong colour or culture. Among the best-known examples of this institutionalized racism were the Chinese head tax and the *Chinese*

Immigration Act of 1923, which replaced the head tax but effectively shut down Chinese immigration until the Act's repeal in 1947.

When the Second World War erupted, anti-foreigner sentiment prevailed in Canada and many non-British people were interned, most famously the Japanese:

> In Canada itself, probably no group of people experienced as much hardship and upheaval as the Japanese Canadians. Their ordeal began on 8 December 1941, the day after the Japanese bombed Pearl Harbor. Within hours of that attack, Ottawa ordered that fishing boats operated by Japanese-Canadian fishermen be impounded and that all Japanese aliens be registered with the Royal Canadian Mounted Police. The worst blow was delivered on 25 February 1942. On that day, Mackenzie King announced in the House of Commons that all Japanese Canadians would be forcibly removed from within a hundred-mile swath of the Pacific coast to "safeguard the defences of the Pacific Coast of Canada." Thus began the process that saw a visible minority uprooted from their homes, stripped of their property, and dispersed across Canada. Japanese Canadians, unlike their counterparts in the United States, were kept under detention until the end of the war. After the conclusion of hostilities, about 4,000 of them succumbed to pressure and left Canada for Japan under the federal government's "repatriation" scheme. Of these, more than half were Canadian-born and two-thirds were Canadian citizens.[3]

After the Second World War, unlike after the First World War, the Canadian economy boomed, paving the way for more liberal immigration policies, including policies for the acceptance of European displaced persons and refugees. Although these policies were more liberal, non-white immigrants were still explicitly considered undesirable and fully a third of the postwar wave of immigrants were British.

In the mid-1960s, Canada's immigration policies finally began to change. Instead of basing the selection of immigrants on race and ethnicity, Canada adopted new selection criteria: education and skills. For the first time, significant numbers of non-British, non-European, non-white immigrants were being welcomed from Africa, Asia, Latin America, and the Caribbean. These more liberal immigration policies have continued to the present day.

Today, one out of every six Canadian residents was born outside Canada. Canada accepts proportionately more immigrants than any other country in the world, including the United States.

Governments generally plan for an annual immigration target of 1 percent of the total population for permanent residents. In reality, however, history shows that the numbers of immigrants fluctuate to respond to the economic, social, and labour market interests of the day. For example, the highest reported levels of immigration—as a percentage of Canada's population—were in 1911 with 331,288 (4.6% of the population) and peaked in 1913 with just over 400,000 immigrants (5.3%) and at one of its lowest levels of 0.3% in 1983 and 1984. In the past ten years, approximately 245,000 (about 0.7% of Canada's population) permanent residents on average were admitted to Canada in each year.[4]

In 2010, the government planned to admit between 240,000 and 265,000 new permanent residents in Canada; in fact, a total of 280,681 individuals were admitted as new permanent residents.[5]

Legislative History

The history of modern Canadian immigration is inextricably linked to the legislative history of immigration in Canada. Currently, the two most important pieces of legislation with respect to Canadian immigration law are the *Immigration and Refugee Protection Act* (IRPA) and the *Citizenship Act*. These are the two acts that guide decisions about who may come to Canada, and who may stay and enjoy all the rights of citizenship. The story of the predecessors to these statutes follows.

The *Immigration Act* of 1906 was a highly restrictive piece of legislation. It created a head tax for immigrants, barred many people from entering the country, and increased the government's power to deport:

> There had been laws since 1869 prohibiting certain kinds of immigration and since 1889 allowing designated classes of immigrants to be returned from whence they came. The 1906 Act differed in degree, significantly increasing the number of categories of prohibited immigrants and officially sanctioning the deportation of undesirable newcomers.[6]

The 1906 Act was followed by the *Immigration Act* of 1910. This Act was even more exclusionary than the 1906 Act, allowing Cabinet the authority to exclude "immigrants belonging to any race deemed unsuited to the climate or requirements of Canada." The 1910 Act also strengthened the government's power to deport such people as anarchists, on the grounds that they will contribute to the country's political and moral instability.[7]

The policy considerations behind these two statutes and the various related laws and immigration policies were, for the most part, to encourage British and American immigration to Canada, and to discourage all other groups. An amendment to the 1906 Act, in effect in 1908, sharply curtailed Asian immigration in particular. This amendment, known as the "continuous-journey regulation," required immigrants to travel to Canada by continuous passage from their countries of origin. This requirement was mostly designed to deter Indian and Japanese immigrants whose continuous passage to Canada was almost impossible.

Canada, however, needed cheap labour—people who were willing to work hard for low wages and under harsh conditions. The more desirable British and American immigrants were not willing to fill that need and although the Chinese who had worked on the building of the railroad had proven themselves willing and hardworking, the existing laws severely restricted their entry into the country. "Canadian industrialists therefore turned increasingly toward central and southern Europe for the semi-skilled and unskilled labourers needed to supply the goods and services required by the new settlers."[8]

Immigration from eastern, southern, and central Europe continued to swell Canada's population until just before the First World War. However, the decline of the Canadian economy and the subsequent war, which created increased suspicion and dislike of "foreigners," put the brakes on the boom in immigration. During the war, intolerance and harassment were suffered by those in Canada deemed "enemy aliens" because they originated from the now enemy countries. This was despite the fact that most of these so-called foreigners had settled in Canada and were contrib-uting members of Canadian society.

Not only did many Canadians treat these "enemy aliens" badly, the government itself acted against them—for example, by interning many in camps at the start of the war. The government also passed legislation that penalized "enemy aliens," most strikingly by passing the *Wartime Elections Act*:

> The *Wartime Elections Act*, invoked in the 1917 federal election, was perhaps the most extraordinary measure taken against enemy aliens. In addition to giving the federal vote to women in the armed forces and to the wives, sisters, and mothers of soldiers in active service (Canadian women as a whole had not yet won the right to vote in federal elections), the Act withdrew this right from Canadians who had been born in enemy countries and had become naturalized British subjects after 31 March 1902.[9]

These now disenfranchised, naturalized British subjects (Canadian citizenship did not yet exist) had fulfilled a three-year residency requirement so they were hardly newcomers. The *Naturalization Act*, passed in 1914, increased the residency requirement to five years. (British subjects did not have to be "naturalized" and ob-tained the full rights of Canadian nationals after only one year of residency.)

After the First World War, the economy suffered and the fear and dislike of for-eigners escalated. One of the defining events of this period of Canadian immigration history was the Winnipeg General Strike of 1919:

> The spiralling cost of living, widespread unemployment, and disillusionment with "the system" gave rise to a wave of labour unrest that rolled across the country in 1918 and 1919, intensifying fears of an international Bolshevik conspiracy. Noth-ing did more to inflame anti-foreign sentiment and heighten fears of revolution than the Winnipeg General Strike of May 1919.[10]

The government's legislative reaction was again to target so-called foreigners:

> Ultimately, the decisive intervention of the federal government brought about an end to the conflict. Persuaded that enemy aliens had instigated the strike, the gov-ernment succeeded in 1919 in amending the *Immigration Act*, to allow for their easy deportation. It then had ten strike leaders arrested and instituted deportation proceedings against the four who were foreign-born. When a protest parade on 21 June turned ugly, Royal North West Mounted Police charged the crowd, leaving one person dead and many others wounded. "Bloody Saturday," as it came to be called, led to the arrest and deportation of 34 foreigners and effectively broke the Winnipeg General Strike. But it would leave a long-lasting legacy of bitterness and unrest across Canada.[11]

The revised *Immigration Act* was further used to vigorously limit non-British immigration:

> The revised *Immigration Act* and the Orders in Council issued under its authority signalled a dramatic shift in Canadian immigration policy. Prior to the First World War, immigration officials had chosen immigrants largely on the basis of the

contribution that they could make to the Canadian economy, whereas now they attached more importance to a prospective immigrant's cultural and ideological complexion. As a result, newcomers from the white Commonwealth countries, the United States, and to a lesser extent the so-called preferred countries (that is, north-western Europe) were welcomed, while the celebrated "stalwart peasants" of the Sifton era were not, unless, of course, their labour was in demand.[12]

Whereas in 1923 the *Chinese Immigration Act* was enacted to prevent virtually all Chinese immigration, in 1922 the regulations of the *Immigration Act* were relaxed by the government of Mackenzie King, who over the next few years repealed most of the legislation preventing European immigration. However, during the Great Depression of the 1930s, government policy and legislation again were used to close the doors to non-British immigrants as well as to refugees, including Jewish refugees attempting to flee Nazi Germany. Many immigrants were barred from entry and tens of thousands who were in Canada were deported in those years. With the outbreak of the Second World War, fear and suspicion of foreigners escalated. Many were interned in camps, most famously the Japanese, many of whom had been born in Canada.

Besides being racist, Canadian immigration laws were sexist, well into the mid-20th century:

> Married women, for example, did not have full authority over their national status. Classified with minors, lunatics and idiots "under a disability," they could not become naturalized or control their national status as independent persons, except in very special circumstances.[13]

The *Canadian Citizenship Act*, which came into force in 1947, addressed some of these issues of racism and sexism. This was Canada's first citizenship statute. Before that, there was no Canadian citizenship as we understand it today. Prior to 1947, "Canadians" were British subjects. It wasn't until the *Canadian Citizenship Act* came into being that Canadians became citizens of their own country. The new statute also gave married women autonomy with respect to their status—the nationality of a married woman was no longer dependent on that of her husband.

> With the enactment of this revolutionary piece of legislation, Canada became the first Commonwealth country to create its own class of citizenship separate from that of Great Britain. … In a moving and historic ceremony, staged on the evening of 3 January 1947 in the Supreme Court of Canada chamber, 26 individuals were presented with Canadian citizenship certificates. Among them were Prime Minister William Lyon Mackenzie King, who received certificate 0001, and Yousuf Karsh, the internationally acclaimed Armenian-born photographer.[14]

A new *Immigration Act*, the first new such Act since 1910, was enacted in 1952. Although this Act included provisions designed to exclude non-whites, it also provided the government with the discretion—a discretion that it exercised—to admit large numbers of refugees and others who would otherwise have been inadmissible.

But the turning point in Canada's legislative history was probably the *Immigration Act* of 1976:

The *Immigration Act*, the cornerstone of present-day immigration policy, was enacted in 1976 and came into force in 1978. It broke new ground by spelling out the fundamental principles and objectives of Canadian immigration policy. Included among these are the promotion of Canada's demographic, economic, cultural, and social goals; family reunification; the fulfillment of Canada's international obligations in relation to the United Nations Convention (1951) and its 1967 Protocol relating to refugees, which Canada had signed in 1969; non-discrimination in immigration policy; and cooperation between all levels of government and the voluntary sector in the settlement of immigrants in Canadian society.[15]

Another important development was the creation of a new citizenship act—the *Citizenship Act*—which replaced the *Canadian Citizenship Act* and came into force in 1977. Amendments to the new Act have been made over the years, and it is still in force today. The new statute also addressed previous racist policies, particularly the different treatment received by "aliens" as opposed to those originating from Britain and the British Commonwealth (who would qualify for Canadian citizenship without being called before a judge for a hearing or taking the oath of allegiance in a formal ceremony):

> It was to rectify … anomalies and the unequal treatment accorded different groups of people that *An Act Respecting Citizenship* was first introduced in the House of Commons in May 1974. It received Royal Assent on 16 July 1976 and came into force, along with the Citizenship Regulations, on 15 February 1977. Henceforth, improved access and equal treatment of all applicants would be the guiding principles in the granting of Canadian citizenship.[16]

The new *Citizenship Act* provided equal rights and privileges, and equal obligations and duties, to Canadians, whether they were born in Canada or born elsewhere and acquired Canadian citizenship. It also permitted dual citizenship, allowing Canadians the citizenship benefits of Canada as well as another country.

Planning Immigration

Under s. 94 of the *Immigration and Refugee Protection Act* (IRPA), the minister is required to table an annual report to Parliament, which reports on the operations of the IRPA, and how Citizenship and Immigration Canada managed that year's immigration programs. This report includes:

- information on selection of foreign nationals including details on cooperation with the provinces;
- the number of foreign nationals who became permanent residents in the previous year, and projections for the future;
- the number of persons who entered Canada in the previous year under federal–provincial agreements;
- the number of persons who were given permanent resident status in the previous year for humanitarian and compassionate reasons, by the minister;

- the languages spoken by persons who became permanent residents;
- the number of times that immigration officers exercised the power to let in a person who would otherwise have been deemed inadmissible because the officers determined that the admission was justified; and
- a gender-based analysis of the impact of the IRPA.

The Management of Immigration and Refugee Programs

Canada's **immigration** management scheme is created by the IRPA, which was passed into law in 2001, and came into force on June 28, 2002, replacing the *Immigration Act* of 1976. Two federal government departments share responsibilities for administering this statute and its regulations: Citizenship and Immigration Canada (CIC) and the Canada Border Services Agency (CBSA). CIC and the CBSA have distinct responsibilities for the following general functions:

- admitting **immigrants** (permanent residents), and temporary residents such as foreign students, visitors, and temporary workers who enhance Canada's social and economic growth;
- resettling, protecting, and providing a safe haven for **refugees** and others who are in need of protection;
- helping newcomers adapt to Canadian society and become Canadian citizens; and
- managing access to Canada to protect the security, safety, and health of Canadians and the integrity of Canadian laws.

CIC also manages the Citizenship program and, since 2008, the Multiculturalism program.

Because there are many people wanting to come to Canada— on either a permanent or a temporary basis—CIC applies formal criteria to determine who will be permitted to enter. Generally, preference is given to those who are likely to make a positive contribution to the economy, or at the least not burden it. However, other factors, such as family reunification, and observing Canada's commitment to providing a safe refuge for people fleeing persecution, may also be considered regardless of a person's financial circumstances.

In general, Canada supports the entry of foreign nationals who

- have valuable skills needed by Canadian employers (for example, current practice gives priority to those skilled workers who have specialized abilities and a valid job offer);
- have the means, ability, and ambition to become entrepreneurs in Canada, or to extend the operation of existing, successful business enterprises to Canada;
- are the family members or dependants of immigrants; and
- have come to Canada for protection when fleeing persecution from their own government in their country of origin.

WEBLINK

For a copy of the most recent annual report to Parliament on immigration, visit the Citizenship and Immigration Canada website at www.cic.gc.ca/english/resources/publications/index.asp.

In general, Canada does not support the entry of foreign nationals who

- pose a threat to Canadian security;
- have a history of criminality or close connections to organized crime; or
- will likely pose a heavy burden on Canada's social support systems (for example, on the health care system) without contributing to the Canadian economy.

Sources of Immigration Law

Immigration in Canada is governed by both domestic law and international law.

Domestic law governing immigration includes the Constitution, the *Canadian Charter of Rights and Freedoms*, federal and provincial statutes and regulations, and case law. The primary sources of immigration law are the federal *Immigration and Refugee Protection Act* (IRPA), the regulations under that statute, and case law interpreting the statute and regulations. The *Citizenship Act* is another important federal statute that sets out the procedures for obtaining Canadian citizenship. Federal–provincial agreements governing immigration to a particular province are also considered domestic law.

International law—law that is ideally common to all nation-states—includes multinational treaties and conventions. Canada has signed a number of international agreements that affect our immigration rules—for example, the 1951 United Nations Convention Relating to the Status of Refugees and the accompanying 1967 Protocol Relating to the Status of Refugees, and the Convention on the Protection of Children and Cooperation in Respect of Inter-Country Adoption (Hague Convention). By signing these agreements, Canada has committed to structure our domestic law in a manner that is consistent with other like-minded countries.

Some of these treaties are multilateral involving many countries. Others relate to only a few specific countries—for example, the North American Free Trade Agreement (NAFTA), which contains specific provisions to facilitate temporary business entry among Canada, the United States, and Mexico.

Section 7 of the IRPA grants the minister of citizenship and immigration the power to enter into agreements with other countries or with certain international organizations. These agreements must be approved by the federal Cabinet and must be consistent with the purposes of the IRPA.

To some degree, international principles have been **codified** in our domestic law—such as the refugee provisions of the IRPA. The IRPA is the focal point for the study of immigration law in Canada, and it is thoroughly explored in this text. However, before examining the details of the IRPA and its regulations, it is useful to take a step back and survey Canada's wider legal landscape, which is composed of Canada's constitutional documents, case law (judge-made law), statutes and regulations, and government policy. Each component will be discussed in turn.

The Constitution Act, 1982

The **Constitution** is the supreme law of the land. It is the basic framework under which all other laws are created, and it establishes the basic principles to which all other laws must conform. Until 1982, Canada's Constitution was the *British North America Act* (later renamed the *Constitution Act, 1867*), a statute of England, and Canada's original and defining source of law. It set up the framework for Canada's democracy, but only England had the power to make constitutional amendments. The *Canada Act 1982* finally changed this, and brought the power to amend the Constitution home to Canada's Parliament. A truly Canadian Constitution was created with the *Constitution Act, 1982*, which contains both the *Constitution Act, 1867* and the *Canadian Charter of Rights and Freedoms*.

Division of Powers: Constitution Act, 1867

The *Constitution Act, 1867*, as Canada's supreme law, created a **federal system of government**, where it set out the law-making powers between the federal government and the provincial governments according to subject matter; these specific powers remain today. The federal government has jurisdiction over matters of national interest that affect all Canadians from coast to coast. The federal government also has law-making jurisdiction with respect to the territories. The provincial governments, on the other hand, have jurisdiction over local matters within their own provinces.

SECTION 91: FEDERAL POWERS

Federal powers are set out in s. 91 of the *Constitution Act, 1867*, and include the authority to regulate immigration, national defence, and criminal law. The basic rule governing the division of powers is that matters that require a national standard fall within the jurisdiction of the federal government. For example, immigration and refugee laws that govern who is permitted to enter and live in Canada are issues that affect Canada's status in the international community, which makes it important that the same legal standards are applied across the country.

SECTION 92: PROVINCIAL POWERS

Provincial powers are set out in s. 92 of the *Constitution Act, 1867*, and generally include authority over all matters of a local or private nature in the province, such as property, hospitals, schools, and child protection. In Canada, a large degree of legislative responsibility is delegated to the provinces. This means that there are many more provincial statutes, and accompanying regulations, than there are federal ones.

For example, s. 91(25) assigns jurisdiction over "naturalization and aliens," meaning immigration, to the federal government. For this reason, the *Immigration and Refugee Protection Act* and the *Citizenship Act* are both federal statutes. Section 92(13) assigns property and civil rights to the provincial governments. Accordingly, the Ontario *Residential Tenancies Act, 2006*, which deals with civil rights, is a provincial statute.

The federal government also has a **residual power** to make laws for "the peace, order and good government" of Canada in all matters that do not come within a provincial head of power. This means that any matters not specifically delegated to the provinces are matters over which the federal government has jurisdiction.

Occasionally, one level of government passes a law that appears to intrude on the jurisdiction of the other. Censorship is a good example of this. Controlling the sale of literature and images that may be offensive to some can be viewed as either a provincial concern (trade and commerce within a province), or a federal concern (obscenity as a criminal act).

Where someone alleges that a law is outside the jurisdiction (**ultra vires**) of the government that passed it, courts are often called on to settle the issue. If a law does not fit squarely into the camp of one or the other, the federal government takes jurisdiction, under the principle of **paramountcy**.

Examples of the Law-Making Powers of the Federal and Provincial Levels of Government

Federal Government Law-Making Powers by Subject Matter (Section 91)	Provincial Government Law-Making Powers by Subject Matter (Section 92)
• Interprovincial/international trade • National defence • Currency • Criminal law • Naturalization and aliens • Residual powers • Peace, order, and good government	• Property laws • Civil rights (contract, tort) • Hospitals • Matters of a local nature (local trade and public works) • Municipalities • Generally, all matters of a merely local or private nature in the province

SECTION 95: FEDERAL–PROVINCIAL AGREEMENTS

The *Constitution Act, 1867* makes a special provision for sharing power with respect to agriculture and immigration. With respect to immigration, s. 95 states that

> In each Province the Legislature may make Laws in relation to ... Immigration into the Province; and it is hereby declared that the Parliament of Canada may from Time to Time make Laws in relation to ... Immigration into all or any of the Provinces; and any Law of the Legislature of a Province relative to ... Immigration shall have effect in and for the Province as long and as far only as it is not repugnant to any Act of the Parliament of Canada.

In other words, a province may make laws in relation to the immigration of people into the province, provided that those laws are not inconsistent or in conflict with any federal law. Therefore, in the area of immigration, there are concurrent powers of legislation between the two levels of government, but if there is a conflict between federal and provincial legislation, it is the federal legislation that prevails, according to the principle of paramountcy.

CANADA–QUEBEC ACCORD

Canada and the province of Quebec have had immigration agreements since 1971; the most recent being the 1991 Canada–Quebec Accord. The Canada–Quebec Accord is the most significant and comprehensive immigration agreement between Canada and a province. From Quebec's perspective, two objectives are particularly important. Objective 2 states that, among other things, the Accord strives to maintain the preservation of Québec's demographic importance within Canada and the integration of immigrants to that province in a manner that respects the distinct identity of Québec.

Objective 4 states that

Québec has the rights and responsibilities set out in this Accord with respect to the number of immigrants destined to Québec and the selection, reception and integration of those immigrants.[17]

Under the Accord, Quebec has the sole responsibility for the selection of permanent residents and refugees outside Canada who wish to settle there. Because immigrants destined to Quebec must first apply to that province, most of the programs and processes examined in this text will have separate instructions unique to that audience and will not be discussed. Individuals who are successfully selected by Quebec are then referred to CIC, which tests for inadmissibility on the grounds of medical risk or burden, security threat, and criminality, because these are the same legal standards that are applied to all immigrants across the country. (The grounds of inadmissibility are discussed in Chapter 3 of this text.)

The federal government remains responsible for setting minimum national standards for the admission of all immigrants and visitors, and for the administrative function of processing applications and physical admission to Canada at ports of entry. Quebec may impose additional selection criteria for immigrants to Quebec, and is responsible for integrating immigrants into the community.

IMMIGRATION AGREEMENTS

The IRPA provides that the minister of CIC, with the approval of the Cabinet, may enter into agreements with the provinces and territories. Each province has one or more such agreements in place, tailored to meet its specific economic, social, and labour market needs and priorities. Furthermore, immigration agreements facilitate the exchange of information between the federal government and the provinces during the development of immigration programs and policies. For example, the Canada–Ontario Immigration Agreement, signed in 2005, provided that the federal government would transfer $920 million to the province over five years to assist with the integration of new immigrants, including language training.

Some agreements are comprehensive and cover a wide range of immigration issues. There are comprehensive agreements in place with British Columbia, Alberta, Saskatchewan, Manitoba, Ontario, Quebec, Nova Scotia, Prince Edward Island, and the Yukon.

Other agreements cover more specific issues—for example, the Provincial Nominee Program (British Columbia, Alberta, Saskatchewan, Manitoba, Ontario, New Brunswick, Prince Edward Island, Newfoundland and Labrador, the Northwest Territories, and the Yukon.) The Provincial Nominee Program allows a province or territory to nominate people as immigrants if the province believes that these people will contribute to the economic growth of the province. Here again, because provincial programs have their own criteria, these will not be examined in this text.

The Annual Report to Parliament on Immigration is generally a good source to check for current federal-provincial agreements. Students who are interested in a specific provincial agreement or program are advised to search that province's website for specific information or to go to the Citizenship and Immigration Canada website: http://www.cic.gc.ca/english/resources/publications/annual-report-2011/section3.asp.

The Canadian Charter of Rights and Freedoms

The *Canadian Charter of Rights and Freedoms* (the Charter) is part of the Constitution of Canada—*Constitution Act, 1982*. It was designed to help accomplish one of the most important constitutional functions—to express the fundamental values and principles of our society. Canada prides itself on being a free and democratic society that protects the welfare of its members. The Charter reflects that pride by providing a mechanism to balance individual freedoms with the need to protect society's more vulnerable members.

Rights and freedoms protected by the Charter include the following:

- fundamental freedoms, including freedom of expression (s. 2(b)) and freedom of religion (s. 2(a));
- mobility rights (s. 6), such as the rights Canadian citizens have to enter, remain in, and leave Canada;
- legal rights, such as the right to life, liberty, and security of the person (s. 7) and the right to an interpreter at a hearing (s. 14);
- right to equality (s. 15); and
- language rights, such as the right to use any one of the two official languages (English and French) in a court proceeding (s. 19) or when obtaining services from the federal government (s. 20(1)).

The Charter provides in s. 1 that government legislation and actions cannot infringe on these rights and freedoms unless the infringement can be reasonably justified in a free and democratic society. Therefore, the Charter has two important effects:

1. If any law or government policy contravenes the terms of the Charter, that law or policy may be declared unconstitutional and of no force and effect by a court or administrative tribunal.

2. Any action of an agent or representative of any level of government that contravenes any right or freedom protected in the Charter can be challenged in the courts.

The precise scope of the Charter's application has been a matter of debate and litigation. Although it is clear that the Charter applies to the content and effects of government law and to the nature and effects of government action, it has sometimes been difficult to define what is meant by "government" action. Many organizations and regulated industries in Canada have some connection to government, and there have been many cases argued that turn on whether the actions of a quasi-governmental organization is government action.

Unregulated private activity is not intended to be subject to the Charter. The purpose of the Charter is to set limits on what the government can do to protect minority rights in a democracy where the majority elects the government. Because the Charter applies only with respect to *government* activity or decisions, the protection of equality rights with respect to *non-governmental* activities has also been codified in human rights legislation.

The purpose of human rights legislation is similar to the purpose of the Charter, but its scope stretches beyond government to regulate the actions of landlords, employers, and providers of goods and services—whether they be individuals, businesses, or private institutions. For example, if an apartment building owner refuses to rent to people with children, this type of discrimination would be addressed by human rights legislation.

REASONABLE LIMITS ON RIGHTS AND FREEDOMS

Section 1 of the Charter provides that all its rights and freedoms are subject to "such reasonable limits prescribed by law as can be demonstrably justified in a free and democratic society." Each time a court considers whether a law is in violation of the Charter, it must consider whether the law imposes a reasonable limit as described in s. 1. A law will be struck down only when both of the following conditions exist:

1. the law violates a right or freedom; and
2. the law cannot be justified as a reasonable limit in the particular circumstances.

For example, freedom of expression may be curtailed by the duty of society to protect children from being exploited in pornography. In many instances the courts will conclude that although a right or freedom was violated, this violation was justifiable.

SELECTED CHARTER CASES

The reasons of the Supreme Court of Canada in the following four cases exemplify the power of the Charter to shape the law in Canada.

◇ Andrews v. Law Society of British Columbia

The Supreme Court first ruled on the equality provisions set out in s. 15 of the Charter in 1989, in *Andrews v. Law Society of British Columbia*, where it was held that the Law Society of British Columbia's requirement that lawyers be Canadian citizens violated s. 15 of the Charter. The wording of s. 15(1) is as follows:

> Every individual is equal before and under the law and has the right to the equal protection of the law without discrimination and, in particular, without discrimination based on race, national or ethnic origin, colour, religion, sex, age or mental or physical disability.

The Court held that the grounds of discrimination listed in s. 15 were not exhaustive, and analogous grounds, such as "citizenship," were also covered. The respondent Andrews was a British subject and permanent resident in Canada. He met all the requirements for admission to the British Columbia Bar except that of Canadian citizenship. When he was refused admission, he successfully challenged the citizenship requirement on the ground that it violated his right to equality.

As the first s. 15 case, *Andrews* gave us the foundational analysis for Charter challenges involving equality. The Supreme Court held that s. 15 provides every individual a guarantee of equality before and under the law, as well as the equal protection and equal benefit of the law without discrimination. The Court expanded the scope of the right to equality by rejecting an equality test—known as the "similarly situated should be similarly treated" test—which was used by the lower court for interpreting s. 15. This approach permitted distinctions, such as with respect to citizenship, provided that all non-citizens were treated the same, and all citizens were treated the same.

Instead, the Supreme Court held that discrimination is a distinction based on grounds relating to the personal characteristics of the individual or group, which has the effect of imposing disadvantages not imposed on others. Distinctions based on personal characteristics attributed to an individual solely on the basis of association with a group will rarely escape the charge of discrimination, while those based on an individual's merits and capacities will rarely be so classed. This guarantee is not a general guarantee of equality; its focus is on the application of the law. The effect of the impugned distinction or classification on the complainant must also be considered.

The Court noted that citizenship may be properly required for certain legitimate reasons; however, it concluded that barring an entire class of persons from certain forms of employment, solely on the ground of a lack of citizenship status and without consideration of educational and professional qualifications or the other attributes or merits of individuals in the group, infringes s. 15 equality rights.

Note that although *Andrews* held that s. 15 of the Charter prohibited discrimination against permanent residents, discrimination in some circumstances will be tolerated, either because it is justifiable under s. 1 of the Charter, or because the Charter itself makes a distinction between citizens and non-citizens—for example, only citizens may vote in elections. Also, the IRPA legitimately discriminates against non-citizens with respect to the right to live in Canada permanently and not be deported.

◇ Singh v. Minister of Employment and Immigration

Singh is an important case for two reasons: (1) it clarifies who is protected under the Charter, and (2) it sets out the procedural requirements for fairness. In *Singh* the Supreme Court of Canada considered whether s. 7 of the Charter applied to the adjudication of refugee claims, as set out in the former *Immigration Act* of 1976, and, if so, whether those procedures denied the s. 7 requirement of fundamental justice.

The wording of s. 7 is as follows:

> Everyone has the right to life, liberty and security of the person and the right not to be deprived thereof except in accordance with the principles of fundamental justice.

The *Singh* case actually involved a number of claims by six appellants each of whom made separate and unrelated claims to Convention refugee status. Under the former refugee determination scheme, a refugee claimant was examined under oath by a senior immigration officer—a public servant in the federal Department of Employment and Immigration. A transcript was made of the examination under oath and sent to the Refugee Status Advisory Committee (RSAC) for a paper review and recommendation to the minister. The minister, acting on the advice of the RSAC, determined in each case that the claimants were not Convention refugees. Each of the appellants then applied to the Immigration Appeal Board (IAB), a quasi-judicial tribunal, for a redetermination of their claims. The IAB refused their applications on the basis that the board did not believe that there were "reasonable grounds to believe that a claim could, upon the hearing of the application, be established" and consequently no hearing into their claims would be held.

Although none of the appellants were Canadian citizens, the Court found that they were entitled to the protection of s. 7, which the Court held applied to "every human being who is physically present in Canada and by virtue of such presence amenable to Canadian law." Thus, the Supreme Court extended Charter protection to any persons in Canada, regardless of whether they have any legal right to be here.

The Court found that the denial of the right of a refugee claimant not to "be removed from Canada to a country where his life or freedom would be threatened" amounted to a deprivation of security of the person within the meaning of s. 7.

The Court determined that, at a minimum, the concept of fundamental justice in s. 7 includes the notion of procedural fairness. The procedural scheme under the former *Immigration Act* for refugee determinations was not in accordance with fundamental justice, because the hearings were based only on written submissions. The Court held that "where a serious issue of credibility is involved, fundamental justice requires that credibility be determined on the basis of an oral hearing." Only an oral hearing would be adequate in such circumstances to fairly assess a refugee claimant's credibility.

The Court further held that failure to provide an oral hearing was not reasonable or justifiable, and therefore could not be saved under s. 1. As a result of the *Singh* decision, the former refugee determination system was replaced by the current Immigration and Refugee Board (IRB), which holds quasi-judicial oral hearings for refugee claimants who are in Canada.

◇ Canada (Minister of Employment and Immigration) v. Chiarelli

Section 7 was raised again in *Canada (Minister of Employment and Immigration) v. Chiarelli* to challenge the former *Immigration Act* of 1976, but this time unsuccessfully. In *Chiarelli* the Court ruled that non-citizens (except refugees) do not have the same unqualified right to enter and remain in Canada as Canadian citizens. Sections 27(1)(d)(ii) and 32(2) of the *Immigration Act* of 1976 required that deportation be ordered for persons convicted of an offence carrying a maximum punishment of five years or more, without regard to the circumstances of the offence or the offender. Chiarelli, a permanent resident, immigrated with his family as an adolescent, and was declared inadmissible on the ground of criminality and ordered deported.

Chiarelli's criminal record classified him such that he was barred from admission to Canada, and the minister was authorized to issue a certificate dismissing Chiarelli's appeal. In other words, Chiarelli was not accorded the usual right to appeal, where all the circumstances of the case are considered regarding the deportation order.

Chiarelli argued that these provisions were contrary to the s. 7 principles of fundamental justice. However, the Supreme Court of Canada held the following:

> [I]n determining the scope of the principles of fundamental justice as they apply to this case, the Court must look to the principles and policies underlying immigration law. The most fundamental principle of immigration law is that non-citizens do not have an unqualified right to enter or remain in the country.

The Court noted the distinction between citizens and non-citizens recognized in the Charter—only citizens are accorded the right "to enter, remain in and leave Canada" under s. 6(1). Additionally, the Court held the following:

> [T]here has never been a universally available right of appeal from a deportation order on "all the circumstances of the case." Such an appeal has historically been a purely discretionary matter. Although it has been added as a statutory ground of appeal, the executive has always retained the power to prevent an appeal from being allowed on that ground in cases involving serious security interests.

But, more to the point, with regard to the s. 7 requirement of fundamental justice, the Court held that

> Parliament has the right to adopt an immigration policy and to enact legislation prescribing the conditions under which non-citizens will be permitted to enter and remain in Canada. It has done so in the *Immigration Act*. ... [N]o person other than a citizen, permanent resident, Convention refugee or Indian registered under the *Indian Act* has a right to come to or remain in Canada. ... One of the conditions Parliament has imposed on a permanent resident's right to remain in Canada is that he or she not be convicted of an offence for which a term of imprisonment of five years or more may be imposed. This condition represents a legitimate, non-arbitrary choice by Parliament of a situation in which it is not in the public interest to allow a non-citizen to remain in the country. ... [T]he personal circumstances of individuals who breach this condition may vary widely. The offences ... also vary in gravity, as may the factual circumstances surrounding the commission of a particular offence. However there is one element common to all persons who fall within the class of permanent residents described in the s. 27(1)(d)(ii). They have all deliberately violated an essential condition under which they were permitted to remain in Canada. In such a situation, there is no breach of fundamental justice in giving practical effect to the termination of their right to remain in Canada. In the case of a permanent resident, deportation is the only way in which to accomplish this. There is nothing inherently unjust about a mandatory order. ... It is not necessary, in order to comply with fundamental justice, to look beyond this fact to other aggravating or mitigating circumstances.

Thus, in a nutshell, while s. 7 of the Charter does provide minimum procedural protections, it generally does not shield non-citizens from deportation.

◇ Suresh v. Canada (Minister of Citizenship and Immigration)

In the case of *Suresh v. Canada (Minister of Citizenship and Immigration)*, the Court again addressed the issue of deportation, but with the additional element that the person was a Convention refugee who faced a risk of torture if deported. In this case, inadmissibility was a result of membership in a terrorist organization.

Suresh came to Canada from Sri Lanka and was recognized as a Convention refugee and applied for landed immigrant status (now called permanent resident status). He was ordered deported on security grounds, based on the opinion of the Canadian Security Intelligence Service that he was a member and fundraiser for the Liberation Tigers of Tamil Eelam, an organization engaged in terrorist activity in Sri Lanka, and whose members were subject to torture in Sri Lanka.

Section 53 of the *Immigration Act* of 1976 permitted deportation of persons who had been engaged in terrorism or were members of terrorist organizations, and who also posed a threat to the security of Canada, "to a country where the person's life or freedom would be threatened." The question was raised as to whether such deportation violated the procedural protection found under s. 7 of the Charter.

The Court held that while s. 53 did not infringe the Charter, deportation to face torture is generally unconstitutional, and some of the procedures followed in Suresh's case did not meet the required constitutional standards. Therefore, he was entitled to a new deportation hearing:

> [T]he procedural protections required by s. 7 in this case do not extend to the level of requiring the Minister to conduct a full oral hearing or a complete judicial process. However, they require more than the procedure required by the Act under s. 53(1)(b)—that is, none—and they require more than Suresh received.

In terms of the larger question of whether to deport a refugee when there is a risk that this would subject the refugee to torture, the Court held that it was a matter of balancing interests:

> Canadian jurisprudence does not suggest that Canada may never deport a person to face treatment elsewhere that would be unconstitutional if imposed by Canada directly, on Canadian soil. To repeat, the appropriate approach is essentially one of balancing. The outcome will depend not only on considerations inherent in the general context but also on considerations related to the circumstances and condition of the particular person whom the government seeks to expel. On the one hand stands the state's genuine interest in combatting terrorism, preventing Canada from becoming a safe haven for terrorists, and protecting public security. On the other hand stands Canada's constitutional commitment to liberty and fair process. This said, Canadian jurisprudence suggests that this balance will usually come down against expelling a person to face torture elsewhere.

So, although generally it would be a violation of the Charter to deport a refugee where there were grounds to believe there was a substantial risk of torture, the Court left open the possibility that in an exceptional case such deportation might be justified.

Case Law

Case law is judge-made law. The ability of courts to create law as well as interpret it is significant, as demonstrated in the Charter cases described above. Case law also includes the **common law,** which is a body of legal principles and rules that can be traced back to Britain. The common law is law that has evolved from decisions of English courts going back to the Norman Conquest. Some would say English common law began with King Henry II who was crowned shortly after the Norman conquest, and who created principles of law that were to be "common" to all free men in England. This is similar to the concept of **customary international law**, where customs and practice take on legal significance over time. Common-law principles still apply in Canada with respect to areas of law that are not fully codified by statute, such as contract law and tort law. As underscored by the Charter cases examined above, the common-law rules of procedural fairness—developed in the common law through judicial review—play a huge role in immigration law.

Case law also includes tribunal and judicial decisions that interpret the Constitution, statutes, and regulations. To achieve predictability and consistency, by treating similar cases in a similar manner, our courts make decisions in accordance with **precedent**. "Rules" created by judges in legal decisions bind the decision-makers in future decisions, at least where those decisions turn on the same or similar facts. The decisions of higher-level courts (provincial courts of appeal, or the Supreme Court of Canada) must be respected and followed in lower-level courts unless the facts of the new case before the lower court differ substantially. Tribunal decisions, however, are not binding across different tribunals or within the same tribunal. See the discussion of tribunals and the role of administrative law in the box on pages 26-27.

Statutes and Regulations

Statutes, such as the IRPA, are written "codes" of law, also called legislation, which typically deal with a particular subject matter—for example, immigration, criminal law, child protection, and income tax. Many statutes are accompanied by **regulations**, which fill in the details on how the law is to be implemented.

Statutes are created by a legislature—either by the federal Parliament in Ottawa or the provincial or territorial legislatures in each of the provinces or territories. The legislature is the elected arm of government and is accountable to the voters. Provided that constitutional principles are not violated, such as those found in the *Charter of Rights and Freedoms*, a legislature can change the rules developed over time in case law, by using clear language in a statute. Also, courts may make decisions about how to interpret and apply legislation, especially when the wording in a statute is vague or ambiguous or may have changed over time; the effect of proper interpretation of statutory provisions can make broad changes to the operation of a law.

Many statutes, including the IRPA and the *Citizenship Act*, authorize the creation of regulations, which provide the practical details of how the statute is to be implemented. Regulations are sometimes described as being "created under statutes." They are a subordinate form of legislation, drafted by the staff of the Cabinet of the governing party. Unlike statutes, regulations need not be approved and passed by the legislature.

Regulations tend to be practical and can include lists, schedules, diagrams, forms, and charts. The information contained in regulations

WEBLINK

It is easy to access statutes and regulations online, but it is important to ensure that you are using a website that maintains official versions of the legislation, updated regularly. The Canadian Legal Information Institute (CanLII) website contains up-to-date versions of statutes and regulations for the federal, provincial, and territorial governments, as well as extensive case law. Visit the Canadian Legal Information Institute at www.canlii.org.

is just as important as that found in the primary legislation—the statute or act. If a statute has regulations made under it, the regulations will be found published in their own volumes separate from the statute, and will be revised according to the same schedule as the statute itself. However, regulations cannot exist independently without a parent statute. For a regulation to lawfully exist, it must have a parent statute that contains a provision designating regulation-making authority. If no such provision exists, no regulations may be enacted.

Policy

Policies explain the operation of legislation and regulation. Government **policy** is not law; however, it is a very important source of guidance and direction. How the law is actually applied in practice often evolves as a matter of government policy, especially where the law leaves room for discretion in administrative decision making. Policies can be formal or informal, and they can be written or unwritten. They can also have a wide range of objectives, such as promoting fairness and prioritizing the government's use of resources. For example, it is policy that CIC gives priority to processing and finalizing applications within six months for those applying under the family class for spouses, common-law and conjugal partners, and dependent children.[18]

The objectives and operation of government policy must be in compliance with legislation and regulations. If policies are found to operate in a way that is inconsistent with legislation or regulations, they must not be applied. Government policy documents are often made available to the public on government websites.

The Immigration and Refugee Protection Act: Overview

The *Immigration and Refugee Protection Act* (IRPA) and its Regulations (IRPR) are referred to on a regular basis throughout this text, and for that reason it will be useful to examine this legislation briefly in order to become familiar with their structure and content. In contrast to many of Canada's earlier laws, the current legislative framework for immigration is based on non-discriminatory principles and is grounded in the values enshrined in the Charter. The current immigration act, the *Immigration and Refugee Protection Act*, came into force on June 28, 2002, replacing the *Immigration Act* of 1976. The IRPA introduced new provisions designed to increase national security and public safety, balanced with provisions intended to make it simpler for admissible persons to enter Canada.

The IRPA provides a framework for the operation of our immigration and refugee systems, setting out general rules and principles, the rights and obligations of permanent and temporary residents and protected persons, and key enforcement provisions. The regulations under it provide the specific details needed for its implementation and operation. The regulations change relatively frequently, and immigration consultants and other legal professionals must monitor information sources such as the Citizenship and Immigration Canada website (www.cic.gc.ca) on a regular basis.

The IRPA is divided into parts, and these parts are subdivided into divisions and then sections and subsections. A table of contents for the IRPA is produced in the box below.

IRPA Table of Contents

Sections 1 to 10: These sections set out the short title of the Act, provide definitions and objectives, and give the minister authority to appoint officers, make regulations, and set up international and provincial agreements.

Part 1: Immigration to Canada	Part 2: Refugee Protection
Division 1: Requirements Before Entering Canada and Selection	Division 1: Refugee Protection, Convention Refugees and Persons in Need of Protection
Division 2: Examination	Division 2: Convention Refugees and Persons in Need of Protection
Division 3: Entering and Remaining in Canada	Division 3: Pre-removal Risk Assessment
Division 4: Inadmissibility	Part 3: Enforcement
Division 5: Loss of Status and Removal	Part 4: Immigration and Refugee Board
Division 6: Detention and Release	Part 5: Transitional Provisions, Consequential and Related Amendments, Coordinating Amendments, Repeals and Coming into Force
Division 7: Right of Appeal	
Division 8: Judicial Review	
Division 9: Protection of Information	Schedule: Sections E and F of Article 1 of the United Nations Convention Relating to the Status of Refugees
Division 10: General Provisions	

IRPA Objectives

The IRPA sets out separate objectives for the provisions regarding immigrants and the provisions regarding refugees. The objectives offer important guidance to immigration officers, the Immigration and Refugee Board, and the courts with respect to how the statute should be applied and interpreted.

With respect to immigration, the objectives of the IRPA, set out in s. 3(1), can be summarized as follows:

- maximize the social, cultural, and economic benefits of immigration;
- enrich and strengthen the social and cultural fabric of Canadian society, while respecting the federal, bilingual, and multicultural character of Canada;
- support and assist the development of minority official languages communities in Canada;
- support the development of a strong and prosperous Canadian economy, in which the benefits of immigration are shared across all regions of Canada;
- reunite families in Canada;
- integrate permanent residents into Canada, while recognizing mutual obligations for new immigrants and Canadian society;

- support consistent standards and prompt processing;
- facilitate the entry of visitors, students, and temporary workers for purposes such as trade, commerce, tourism, international understanding, and cultural, educational, and scientific activities;
- protect the health and safety of Canadians and maintain the security of Canadian society;
- promote international justice and security by fostering respect for human rights and by denying access to Canadian territory to persons who are criminals or security risks; and
- cooperate with the provinces to better recognize the foreign credentials of permanent residents.

With respect to refugees, the objectives of the IRPA, set out in s. 3(2), can be summarized as follows:

- recognize that the priority of the IRPA is to save lives and protect displaced and persecuted persons;
- fulfill Canada's international legal obligations with respect to refugees and affirm the commitment to international efforts to assist with resettlement;
- grant fair consideration to those who come to Canada claiming persecution;
- offer a safe haven to persons with a well-founded fear of persecution based on race, religion, nationality, political opinion, or membership in a particular social group, as well as those at risk of torture or cruel and unusual treatment or punishment;
- establish fair and efficient procedures that will maintain the integrity of the Canadian refugee protection system, while upholding Canada's respect for the human rights and fundamental freedoms of all human beings;
- support the self-sufficiency and the social and economic well-being of refugees by facilitating reunification with their family members in Canada;
- protect the health and safety of Canadians and maintain the security of Canadian society; and
- promote international justice and security by denying access to Canadian territory to persons, including refugee claimants, who are security risks or serious criminals.

The IRPA also contains a section (s. 3(3)) that directs all decision-makers to interpret and apply the IRPA in a manner that

- furthers the domestic and international interests of Canada;
- promotes accountability and transparency by enhancing public awareness of immigration and refugee programs;
- facilitates cooperation among the government of Canada, provincial governments, foreign states, international organizations, and non-governmental organizations;

- ensures that decisions taken under the IRPA are consistent with the Charter, including its principles of equality and freedom from discrimination and the equality of English and French as the official languages of Canada;
- supports the government's commitment to enhancing the vitality of the English and French linguistic minority communities in Canada; and
- complies with international human rights instruments to which Canada is signatory.

The structure and mandate of the Immigration and Refugee Board of Canada—an administrative tribunal—is created by the IRPA. The IRB has four divisions: the Immigration Division, the Immigration Appeal Division, the Refugee Protection Division, and the Refugee Appeal Division. Within these divisions, members perform the following functions: hold admissibility hearings to determine whether individuals may enter or remain in Canada; hold detention reviews; hear and decide appeals on immigration matters (such as removal orders, sponsorship refusals, and residency requirements); and decide refugee claims made by individuals in Canada. IRB decisions may be subject to judicial review by the Federal Court of Canada.

The Role of Administrative Law

Administrative law is a branch of public law concerned with the legal rules and institutions used to regulate and control the conduct of the state in its relations with citizens. Much of immigration law is administrative law because immigration law governs how government administrators and employees (that is, public servants) exercise the decision-making powers granted to them under the IRPA. In administrative law, administrative decisions may be made quickly and routinely, depending on the requirements of the statute, such as by a visa officer who issues a temporary resident visa to a foreign national. Or, administrative decisions may be quasi-judicial where a hearing before an impartial decision-maker is held. Often decisions start out as routine, but an applicant who is denied the right or benefit sought may challenge the decision, and it will be reheard, usually by an independent board or tribunal such as a law society or the Immigration and Refugee Board.

Generally, **administrative tribunals** require a greater degree of procedural fairness than do routine administrative decisions made by staff, and they function in a similar manner to courts, with both sides making arguments and providing evidence to the decision-maker. At the least, the person seeking a decision is entitled to be heard—that is, to know the reasons for the decision and to be given an opportunity to respond. However, this does not necessarily extend to the right to a full oral hearing with the submission of evidence, examination, and cross-examination of witnesses and arguments similar to a trial. The degree of procedural fairness required depends on the wording of the statute in question.

Whether a decision is administrative or quasi-judicial (with a hearing before a tribunal), the decision must be fair—based on the relevant criteria and made by an unbiased decision-maker. An advantage of administrative tribunals is that hearing procedures are generally much less formal than court procedures, and matters can be resolved more quickly.

Administrative decisions may also be judicially reviewed by a divisional court. On judicial review, the court considers whether the tribunal acted within its jurisdiction (according to the statute and regulations), whether it exercised its discretion in a reasonable manner, and whether its procedures were fair.

This is different from an appeal, which reconsiders the legal merits of the decision. On appeal, a court may overturn a decision if the decision was based on an erroneous interpretation or application of the law. In other words, the decision was "wrong."

Decisions of administrative tribunals may be appealed to a court only if expressly permitted by the statute that creates and governs that tribunal. The rationale for limiting appeals of tribunal decisions is that essentially an appeal involves replacing a tribunal's decision with a court's decision. This undermines one of the advantages of tribunals—their expertise in their particular subject area. It is a principle of administrative law that deference should be given to administrative decisions by government officials and tribunals, because they possess expertise in the particular regulatory regime—such as immigration and refugee law.

The Citizenship Act

The *Citizenship Act* does not discriminate between citizens by birth and immigrants who obtain citizenship, nor does it discriminate between men and women, or among people of different nationalities or race. All citizens share the same rights and privileges, such as the right to vote and hold office, and all share the same obligations and duties. Most notably, the *Citizenship Act* permits dual citizenship, allowing Canadians the benefits of citizenship of another country as well as Canada.

With a few exceptions, such as the children of diplomats, all persons born in Canada are Canadian citizens. Children born outside Canada who have at least one Canadian parent are automatically citizens as well.

The *Citizenship Act* is divided into eight parts, as shown in the table of contents reproduced in the box below.

The *Citizenship Act* currently has two regulations: the *Citizenship Regulations, 1993* and the *Foreign Ownership of Land Regulations*. The Act is explored in more detail in Chapter 6.

Citizenship Act Table of Contents

Sections 1 and 2: These sections set out the short title and definitions.

Part I: The Right to Citizenship

Part II: Loss of Citizenship

Part III: Resumption of Citizenship

Part IV: Certificate of Citizenship

Part V: Procedure

Part VI: Administration

Part VII: Offences

Part VIII: Status of Persons in Canada

Schedule: Oath or Affirmation of Citizenship

Interpretation Tools

Immigration Regulations and Rules

Regulations under the IRPA are made by the Cabinet and must be published in the *Canada Gazette* along with a regulatory impact analysis statement. These explanatory notes are helpful in determining how the regulations are to be applied, and cover the following points:

- description of the regulation, including its purpose and function;
- alternatives to the regulation that were considered;
- benefits and costs to the public of the regulation;
- consultations that took place with interested parties and the public in the drafting of the regulation;
- compliance and enforcement issues;
- gender-based analysis of the impact of the regulation; and
- contact person.

There are numerous regulations under the IRPA, covering a variety of subject areas. The largest is the *Immigration and Refugee Protection Regulations*, which consist of 21 parts and provide detailed guidance regarding the application of the IRPA, including definitions of family relationships, details setting out the criteria for applying to the various permanent and temporary resident programs, definitions of classes of refugees, and procedures for detentions, release, removals, and appeals. As you study the different temporary and permanent resident programs, you will undoubtedly become familiar with a number of these regulations.

Other regulations include the following:

- *Alejandra Flores Velasquez Immigration Exemption Regulations* (S.O.R./91-693);
- *Order Designating the Minister of Citizenship and Immigration as the Minister Responsible for the Administration of That Act* (S.I./2001-120);
- *Order Setting Out the Respective Responsibilities of the Minister of Citizenship and Immigration and the Minister of Public Safety and Emergency Preparedness Under the Act* (S.I./2005-120); and
- *Protection of Passenger Information Regulations* (S.O.R./2005-346).

Citizenship Regulations

Similar to the regulations described above, citizenship regulations set out the detail for processing citizenship applications. For example, the specific criteria for granting, renouncing, or resuming Canadian citizenship is provided, as well as criteria for the citizenship test; you will also find the oath of citizenship, procedures for citizenship ceremonies, and fees for becoming a citizen.

Policy Instruments

As noted above, policy fills in the gaps left out of a statute or its regulations, and is intended to promote consistency, fairness, and transparency. Most policy develops and evolves over time on an informal basis, as certain procedures that work well become accepted policy. Policy may also be formalized through a variety of policy instruments that codify informal policy or create new policy. Both Citizenship and Immigration Canada (CIC) and the Immigration and Refugee Board (IRB) use a variety of policy instruments, as described below.

Consider the following types of CIC policy instruments:

1. *Policy notes.* Policy notes are memoranda used to address issues that are temporary in nature or that are limited to a specific region.

2. *Program manuals.* The minister of citizenship and immigration Canada publishes operational manuals to guide the activities of immigration and citizenship officers. Officers consult these manuals when applying the IRPA, the *Citizenship Act*, and their accompanying regulations; likewise, immigration practitioners should consult these documents when advising clients. The existing manuals can be found online at http://www.cic.gc.ca/english/resources/manuals/index.asp and are as follows:

   • Citizenship Policy (CP);

   • Enforcement (ENF);

   • Temporary Foreign Workers Guidelines (FW);

   • Immigration Legislation (IL);

   • Information Sharing (IN);

   • Inland Processing (IP);

   • Reference (IR);

   • Overseas Processing (OP); and

   • Protected Persons (PP).

   Keep in mind that although the operational manuals are important, they are merely policy and do not have the force of law. Therefore, if a provision of a manual is inconsistent with the provisions of the IRPA or its regulations, it will not be valid.

3. *Operational bulletins.* Occasionally, operational bulletins are issued to deliver urgent or one-time-only instructions to staff to be used on a one-time or temporary basis while the program and policy manuals are updated, or to issue urgent instructions to officers. There can be a number of bulletins that are issued each month by the minister, so it is advisable to check these to see whether the processing of a given application will be affected. Both current and archived operational bulletins can be found under "Operational Bulletins" on the CIC website at http://www.cic.gc.ca/english/resources/manuals/bulletins/2012/index.asp.

Immigration and Refugee Board: Tribunal Rules and Policy Instruments

Tribunal **rules** are regulations that establish practices and procedures for the processing and presentation of cases. They are generally binding, like any other regulations, unless they specifically provide otherwise. The Rules are authorized by s. 161(1) of the *Immigration and Refugee Protection Act*, and include the following examples:

- Adjudication Division Rules (S.O.R./93-47);
- Immigration Appeal Division Rules (S.O.R./2002-230);
- Immigration Division Rules (S.O.R./2002-229); and
- Refugee Protection Division Rules (S.O.R./2002-228).

Consider the following policy instruments of the IRB:

1. *Chairperson's guidelines.* The chairperson's guidelines are authorized by s. 159(1)(h) of the *Immigration and Refugee Protection Act* to provide guiding principles for resolving cases and to further the government's strategic objectives. The chairperson of the Immigration and Refugee Board is permitted to make guidelines and identify decisions as important precedents, to better enable members of the IRB to carry out their duties. The chairperson's guidelines are not mandatory, but decision-makers are required to justify cases of non-compliance. The following eight guidelines existed as of August 2012:
    - Guideline 1: Civilian Non-Combatants Fearing Persecution in Civil War Situations;
    - Guideline 2: Guidelines on Detention;
    - Guideline 3: Child Refugee Claimants: Procedural and Evidentiary Issues;
    - Guideline 4: Women Refugee Claimants Fearing Gender-Related Persecution;
    - Guideline 5: Providing the PIF and No PIF Abandonment in the Refugee Protection Division (the PIF is the personal information form that is completed for a refugee applicant);
    - Guideline 6: Scheduling and Changing the Date or Time of a Proceeding in the Refugee Protection Division;
    - Guideline 7: Concerning Preparation and Conduct of a Hearing in the Refugee Protection Division; and
    - Guideline 8: Guideline on Procedures with Respect to Vulnerable Persons Appearing Before the Immigration and Refugee Board of Canada.

    The guidelines can be found online at http://www.irb-cisr.gc.ca/eng/brdcom/references/pol/guidir/Pages/index.aspx.

2. *Jurisprudential guides.* The jurisprudential guides are authorized by s. 159(1)(h) of the *Immigration and Refugee Protection Act*. Their purpose is to facilitate consistency in decision making with regard to similar cases. A

jurisprudential guide reiterates the reasoning of the IRB in a specific decision so that it can be applied in other similar cases. The jurisprudential guides are not mandatory, but decision-makers are required to justify non-compliance with the guides in cases with similar facts.

3. *Persuasive decisions.* Persuasive decisions are decisions identified by the head of the division, such as the Refugee Protection Division, as being well reasoned. Decision-makers are encouraged to follow the same reasoning in their own decisions. Unlike with the jurisprudential guides, decision-makers are not required to justify the choice not to follow persuasive decisions.

4. *Policies.* Policies are formal statements explaining the details of new IRB initiatives, such as outlining roles and responsibilities. A few examples of policies are as follows:

   - Policy for Handling IRB Complaints Regarding Unauthorized, Paid Representatives (April 2008);
   - Policy on Oral Decisions and Oral Reasons (September 2003)—reaffirms that delivery of decisions and reasons orally, at the conclusion of a hearing, is normal practice for the IRB; and
   - Policy on the Use of Jurisprudential Guides (March 2003)—governs the exercise of the chairperson's authority to identify a decision as a jurisprudential guide.

5. *Chairperson's instructions.* Chairperson's instructions provide formal direction to individual IRB staff. They are more narrow and specific than the policies described above.

KEY TERMS

administrative tribunal, 26

case law, 21

citizen, 4

codified, 12

common law, 21

Constitution, 12

customary international law, 22

federal system of government, 13

foreign national, 4

immigrants, 11

immigration, 11

paramountcy, 14

permanent resident, 4

policy, 23

precedent, 22

refugees, 11

regulations, 22

residual power, 13

rules, 30

statutes, 22

temporary resident, 4

ultra vires, 14

visa, 4

REVIEW QUESTIONS

History of Immigration Law in Canada

1. List and provide one historical highlight from each of Canada's immigration statutes.

2. List and provide one historical highlight from each of Canada's citizenship statutes.

Sources of Immigration Law

1. What are the key federal statutes and regulations used in Canada for immigration, refugee, and citizenship matters?

2. Why is immigration a federal responsibility?

3. Give an example of how the federal government shares its federal powers related to immigration with the provinces and territories.

4. Are permanent residents, temporary residents, and refugees protected by s. 7 of the *Canadian Charter of Rights and Freedoms*? If yes, why? If no, why not?

5. Which Supreme Court decision holds that the concept of fundamental justice includes the notion that procedural fairness requires that where credibility is at issue, it must be determined on the basis of an oral hearing?

The Immigration and Refugee Protection Act and Its Regulations

This section of the chapter described the Act, its regulations, and other instruments that you will need as part of your professional toolkit.

1. Find and briefly summarize the following sections of the IRPA:

   • Section 2

   • Sections 8 and 10

   • Section 11

   • Section 12

   • Section 14

   • Section 15

   • Section 16

   • Section 18

   • Section 19

2. Find the section of the IRPA that requires the minister to table an annual report to Parliament.

Administrative Law

1. What is administrative law?

2. What is a judicial review?

The Citizenship Act and Its Regulations

1. Find the section of the *Citizenship Act* that defines who is a Canadian citizen.

2. Find the section of the *Citizenship Act* that details the requirements for citizenship.

3. Where in the *Citizenship Act* does the citizenship oath appear?

EXERCISE

Find the most recent *Annual Report to Parliament on Immigration* and determine the following:

- the government's plan to admit permanent residents by category,
- the government's plan to admit temporary residents, and
- the government's plan to admit protected persons as permanent residents.

NOTES

1. For a description of the history of immigration law, see D. Galloway, *Immigration Law* (Concord, ON: Irwin Law, 1997), chapter 1.
2. Citizenship and Immigration Canada, *Forging Our Legacy: Canadian Citizenship and Immigration, 1900–1977*, October 2000, http://www.cic.gc.ca/english/resources/publications/index.asp.
3. Ibid.
4. Citizenship and Immigration Canada, "Canada—Permanent Residents as a Percentage of Canada's Population, 1860 to 2010 Historical Highlights," *Facts and Figures: Immigration Overview—Permanent and Temporary Residents*, 2011, at 2, http://www.cic.gc.ca/english/pdf/research-stats/facts2010.pdf.
5. Citizenship and Immigration Canada, *Annual Report to Parliament on Immigration 2011*, October 27, 2011, s. 2, at 16, http://www.cic.gc.ca/english/pdf/pub/annual-report-2011.pdf.
6. Supra note 2.
7. Ibid.
8. Ibid.
9. Ibid.
10. Ibid.
11. Ibid.
12. Ibid.
13. Ibid.
14. Ibid.
15. Ibid.
16. Ibid.
17. Gouvernement du Québec, Ministère des relations avec les citoyens et de l'immigration, *Canada–Québec Accord Relating to Immigration and Temporary Admission of Aliens*, March 2000, at 2, http://www.micc.gouv.qc.ca/publications/pdf/Accord_canada_quebec_immigration_anglais.pdf.
18. Citizenship and Immigration Canada, "Processing Priorities," in *Operation Procedures: OP 1*, August 16, 2012, s. 5.14, http://www.cic.gc.ca/english/resources/manuals/op/op01-eng.pdf.

REFERENCES

Andrews v. Law Society of British Columbia. [1989] 1 S.C.R. 143.

Canada (Minister of Employment and Immigration) v. Chiarelli. [1992] 1 S.C.R. 711.

Canadian Charter of Rights and Freedoms. Part I of the *Constitution Act, 1982.* R.S.C. 1985, app. II, no. 44.

Citizenship Act. R.S.C. 1985, c. C-29.

Constitution Act, 1867. 30 & 31 Vict., c. 3 (UK).

Constitution Act, 1982. R.S.C. 1985, app. II, no. 44.

Convention Relating to the Status of Refugees. 189 U.N.T.S. 150, entered into force April 22, 1954. http://www2.ohchr.org/english/law/refugees.htm.

Gouvernement du Québec. Ministère des relations avec les citoyens et de l'immigration. *Canada–Québec Accord Relating to Immigration and Temporary Admission of Aliens.* March 2000. http://www.micc.gouv.qc.ca/publications/pdf/Accord_canada_quebec_immigration_anglais.pdf.

Immigration and Refugee Protection Act. S.C. 2001, c. 27.

Immigration and Refugee Protection Regulations. S.O.R./2002-227.

Singh v. Minister of Employment and Immigration. [1985] 1 S.C.R. 177.

Suresh v. Canada (Minister of Citizenship and Immigration). 2002 SCC 1, [2002] 1 S.C.R. 3.

RECOMMENDED READING

Knowles, Valerie. *Strangers at Our Gates: Canadian Immigration and Immigration Policy, 1540–1990*, rev. ed. (Toronto: Dundurn Press, 2007).

Malarek, Victor. *Haven's Gate: Canada's Immigration Fiasco* (Toronto: Macmillan of Canada, 1987).

Decision-Makers

2

LEARNING OUTCOMES

After reading this chapter you should be able to:

- Identify key federal organizations involved in deciding immigration, citizenship, and refugee protection matters.

- Distinguish the role and function of Citizenship and Immigration Canada (CIC), the Canada Border Services Agency (CBSA), the Immigration and Refugee Board (IRB), the Federal Court, and the Supreme Court.

- Identify the divisions of the Immigration and Refugee Board and distinguish the jurisdiction and function of each of those divisions.

- Distinguish the decision-making roles of the minister of CIC, the minister of Public Safety and Emergency Preparedness, minister's delegates, and decision-makers in the IRB, including the chairperson and members.

- Understand the basis in law for decision making.

Introduction

Take a look in the government section of your phone book or try a web search to answer some of these questions:

- Who do you contact about how to have a client released from immigration detention?
- Who do you contact if your client's sponsorship of a family member has failed—Citizenship and Immigration Canada (CIC) or the Immigration and Refugee Board (IRB)?
- Who is responsible for removing people who should not be in Canada—CIC, the IRB, or the Canada Border Services Agency (CBSA)?
- If your application to sponsor a family member is refused, do you file an appeal with the board, the Federal Court, or the Supreme Court?

Canadian immigration and refugee laws and related processes are complex and subject to frequent changes. A client may have "a file" with more than one organization, so determining which organization to contact depends on the issues in each case and how much progress has been made in the application and in the decision-making processes.

In Chapter 1 we learned about the various sources of law that are applied to manage the complexities of Canadian immigration. There is one more piece of the puzzle to add: the role of decision-makers in immigration and refugee matters. Who makes decisions on cases? What decision-making powers do they have? Where do they get that authority? In this chapter, we look briefly at the following three levels of decision making and the related organizations involved in immigration and refugee protection matters:

1. the "minister," including officers, for Citizenship and Immigration Canada, Public Safety and Emergency Preparedness PSEP), and one of its agencies, the Canada Border Services Agency;
2. the four divisions of the Immigration and Refugee Board and tribunal decision-makers; and
3. the courts.

We learn about who, within each of those organizations, has the statutory authority for making decisions, where they get their jurisdiction to make decisions, and what relationships exist among the three levels of decision making.

Ministers Responsible for Immigration and Refugee Matters

Section 4 of the *Immigration and Refugee Protection Act* (IRPA) divides responsibility for immigration and refugee functions between two ministers:

- the minister of Citizenship and Immigration Canada (CIC), and
- the minister of Public Safety and Emergency Preparedness (PSEP).

Note that the minister of CIC's title is Minister of Citizenship, Immigration and Multiculturalism. The Department of Public Safety and Emergency Preparedness is now called Public Safety Canada. We use the former titles in this text because that is the way they are referenced in the relevant legislation.

The following descriptions of ministerial authority relate to either the minister of CIC or PSEP, unless otherwise specified.

Ministerial Authority and Decision-Making Powers

The minister of Citizenship and Immigration heads CIC, which is responsible for general areas of immigration and citizenship, including the following:

- immigration policy development, including guidance to staff in carrying out their functions and applying legislation;
- an annual immigration plan, which sets out the target numbers for immigration;
- immigration programs related to temporary and permanent immigration;
- the settlement and integration of newcomers to Canada;
- the resettlement of refugees; and
- most policies related to admissibility.

The minister of Public Safety and Emergency Preparedness heads PSEP and has the policy lead for immigration enforcement functions, such as those carried out by the Canada Border Services Agency. Those functions include the management and operation of Canada's borders, including the following:

- arrests,
- detentions,
- removals, and
- port-of-entry functions.

The IRPA grants broad regulatory power to Cabinet through the **governor in council** to make rules and regulations in the form of **orders in council**. This enables the government to respond quickly to adapt the Act's broad provisions to changing circumstances. As noted in Chapter 1, regulations set out standards and criteria for the purpose of selecting qualified applicants and cover a broad number of definitions. For example, the regulations stipulate the dollar amount for processing the different kinds of visa applications for permanent and temporary resident visas. Regulations also identify the various categories within the economic classes of immigrants and set out specific criteria within each class; these criteria too can be changed. By an order in council, the regulations can easily be amended to change the amount payable for processing the application (s. 5) or to add or to repeal a class of permanent resident.

The minister of CIC is required to table proposed regulations before each House of Parliament (the House of Commons and the Senate) so that they can be referred to the appropriate committee of that House when those proposals relate to the following provisions:

- examinations;
- rights and obligations of permanent and temporary residents;
- status documents;
- loss of status and removal, detention, and release;
- examination of eligibility to refer a refugee claim;
- the principle of *non-refoulement*; and
- transportation companies (s. 5(2)).

The proposed regulation need only be tabled once; it does not have to be presented to each House of Parliament again, even if it has been altered (s. 5(3)). As a result, amendments can be made without further examination by Parliament.

The IRPA empowers the minister to make decisions on a variety of matters. We will learn the basis in law for this authority, including the minister's power to delegate specific powers and decisions to others.

Immigration Policy and Administrative Functions

The minister of CIC is responsible for immigration policy development and immigration processes. Did you ever wonder who decides whether Canada should accept fewer or more immigrants? This is an area of responsibility of the minister of CIC, who, in consultation with the provinces, is responsible for setting the annual targets, including the number and types of foreign nationals who may come to Canada either as temporary or permanent residents.

The minister of CIC must table the annual immigration plan before Parliament on or before the first of November in each year, following consultations with the provinces, which, at a minimum, estimate the number of permanent residents to be admitted each year (see Chapter 1). The minister also determines the requirements for foreign nationals such as the minimum standards they must meet in order to qualify as permanent residents. An example of this is the "pass mark" for skilled workers discussed in Chapter 5, Permanent Entry.

Each minister also has specific administrative authorities under the regulations to the IRPA. For example, the minister of PSEP can designate ports of entry and their dates and hours of operation.

Ministerial Discretion

In 2008, IRPA s. 87.3 was amended to expand the discretionary powers of the minister. The minister of CIC has the power to issue instructions to officers—through the issuance of Operational Bulletins (see Chapter 1)—that directly affect the daily work of citizenship and immigration officers (C&I officers) and Canada Border Services officers (CBSA officers) in their handling of cases:

The processing of applications and requests is to be conducted in a manner that, in the opinion of the Minister, will best support the attainment of the immigration goals established by the Government of Canada. (s. 87.3(2))

These instructions, which reflect a change in policy and/or the regulations, are not debated in Parliament; they are published in the *Canada Gazette*. Note that there are new instructions added or updated and others that expire on a frequent basis. It is therefore important for immigration legal professionals to check CIC's website for updated operational bulletins for changes to programs, application criteria, and processing procedures. These legislative amendments give the minister powers to issue instructions to staff that categorize, prioritize, or even determine the number of applications and requests that are to be processed (s. 87.3(3)).

Under Canadian immigration law, the minister decides whether a person is allowed to enter (is admissible) or is to be removed from Canada (see Chapter 3). The minister also has the discretionary power to grant temporary and permanent resident status to foreign nationals on the basis of humanitarian and compassionate grounds. This may apply both to those who wish to come to Canada and to those who wish to remain here but are inadmissible for technical, medical, or criminal reasons.

For example, you may have read or heard about cases in the news where a child is in need of life-saving surgery that is not available in the child's home country. How is it that the child may come to Canada for medical treatment, if she is not healthy enough to pass the required medical examination? This is an example of the minister of CIC exercising discretionary powers to allow entry. Although the child does not meet the statutory requirements for admission to Canada, the reasons for seeking entry to Canada are compelling enough for the minister to grant temporary authorization. The minister may issue a temporary resident visa—formerly known as a "minister's permit"—which is valid for a specified and limited period of time, and which can also be cancelled.

Security Certificates

A security certificate may be issued in exceptional circumstances against a permanent resident or foreign national for removal purposes when there is reason to believe that the person poses a security threat and there is information that needs to be protected for security reasons. The purpose of the security certificate is to ensure that the government's classified information remains confidential: this has the effect of closing proceedings and ensuring the non-disclosure of certain information that could seriously harm the government's ability to protect its citizens.

On February 13, 2008, Bill C-3, *An Act to Amend the Immigration and Refugee Protection Act (Certificates and Special Advocates)*, received royal assent. This was in response to the 2007 Supreme Court ruling in *Charkaoui v. Canada* that additional safeguards should be incorporated into the security certificate process to better protect the rights of individuals subject to a certificate. As a result, a **special advocate** must be appointed to act on behalf of a person who is subject to a closed security certificate hearing process to protect his or her interests.

Where in the case of a removal of a permanent resident or foreign national there is information that needs to be protected for security reasons and reason to believe that the person poses a security threat, both the minister of PSEP and the minister of CIC must personally sign a security certificate. Because of the lack of transparency and public accountability inherent in a closed process, this power must not be delegated under s. 77(1) of the IRPA.

The certificate is then referred to the Federal Court, where a judge hears evidence in the absence of the person named to protect national security or the safety of any person in a closed security certificate hearing. The judge will also hear evidence from the person named in the certificate. If the judge decides that the certificate is reasonable, then the certificate automatically becomes a removal order (IRPA, s. 80).

Delegation of Authority

Through the "Designation of Officers and Delegation of Authority" instrument signed by the minister of CIC and updated regularly, most of the powers vested in the minister by the IRPA in relation to the application of the law are delegated to officers; the instrument includes a description of the duties and powers of officers granted to those persons working for CIC, the CBSA, and other agencies. The instrument also contains a section that sets out those authorities that have not been delegated. There is a separate designation and delegation-of-authority instrument signed by the president of the CBSA for those authorities that are under the specific mandate of the minister of Public Safety and Emergency Preparedness, such as those related to designating officers as peace officers.

The minister's **delegation of authority** to others is necessary, given the sheer volume of immigration cases. The IRPA allows for certain ministerial powers, duties, requirements, and authorities to be delegated, to ensure that Canada's immigration, refugee protection, and citizenship programs can be delivered efficiently. Generally, the minister may **designate** persons wherever the word "officer" is used in the Act or its regulations with respect to a power, duty, requirement, or authority. Each minister (of CIC or PSEP) may designate **officers** to carry out certain provisions of the Act and its regulations with regard to their respective mandates, and may delegate their powers. An officer is a public servant who has been given specific powers and has been designated by the minister to carry out specific duties under the IRPA. There are several types of officers, including visa officers, examining officers, senior immigration officers, immigration officers, and CBSA officers. The minister also has the authority to designate certain RCMP officers to carry out immigration functions at certain ports of entry, and to delegate the authority to carry out physical and mental examinations to "panel physicians" (formerly known as designated medical officers). The minister's delegation of authority must be made in writing and must specify the powers and duties of officers (IRPA, ss. 6(1) and (2)).

Officers

As noted above, officers are public servants who, for our purposes, work either for CIC or the CBSA. CIC officers are responsible for the delivery of the immigration program at Canadian missions abroad, and at national, regional, and local offices across Canada. Officers who work for CIC hold a number of positions and carry out a variety of duties, including the following:

- processing applications for temporary residence (such as authorizations for visitors, students, and temporary workers), permanent residence, refugee resettlement, and citizenship;
- providing settlement and integration services for newcomers;
- conducting research;
- reporting and analyzing international migration and refugee and social policy trends used for formulating government policy; and
- developing policy and programs.

Officers who work for the CBSA carry out a variety of duties related to immigration, including the following:

- examining people at ports of entry;
- detaining those people who may pose a threat to Canada; and
- removing people who are inadmissible to our country, including those involved in terrorism, organized crime, war crimes, or crimes against humanity.

Under the IRPA, officers have the power to examine people, perform search and seizures, and exercise the powers of a **peace officer**. Presented below is a general overview of officers' authorities both outside Canada and within.

Note that in an officer's decision-making role, he or she must follow the principles of natural justice, including the right to be heard and impartiality. It is up to whomever examines a person or an application, including evidence and documents, to make the decision. In certain processes, however, one officer may read, hear, and evaluate all the pertinent information and then submit a report to another officer who makes the decision. This exception to the rule in administrative law—one who hears must decide—is allowed as long as the decision-maker takes all the information into account. More on an officer's authority to make decisions on applications is provided in later chapters.

Before Entry: Examination on Application

Generally, a person seeking to come to Canada must apply for and obtain permission—a visa—before appearing at a port of entry. Under Canadian immigration law, this permission comes from the minister who decides whether a person is allowed to enter (that is, "is not inadmissible"). In practice, however, the decision making related to reviewing an application is delegated from the minister to an officer who is working outside Canada in a visa office.

When a person wishes to come to Canada, he must apply for temporary or permanent residence, usually before arriving. The application may be made abroad or at a port of entry, such as at the border or at an airport. It may be made orally or in writing depending on a number of factors described in later chapters.

Oral applications are made, for example, when a person landing at an airport asks to make a refugee claim, or a US citizen at the Canada–US border asks to enter Canada. Written applications may be made using forms provided by CIC, including applications for temporary or permanent residence. Applications are considered complete when all the instructions for completing the forms have been followed and all supporting documents have been submitted to the appropriate office.

Whether the person applies abroad or at a port of entry, the application must be assessed by an officer who is authorized to make a decision (IRPA, s. 15(1)). The officer decides whether the person qualifies under an immigration program, such as the Family Class or Skilled Worker program, and whether the person has the right to enter Canada. Generally, the officers who work abroad and assess applications, at visa offices or consulates, are called **visa officers**; CBSA officers working at ports of entry, such as the Canada–US border, airports, or harbours, may have titles such as border services officer or enforcement officer.

Visa officers typically review written applications, ensure their completeness, and evaluate the information. They may also interview applicants. CBSA officers, on the other hand, typically carry out their duties orally through examination procedures by questioning the person to elicit information—for example, about citizenship, residency, intention, employment, and length of stay at a port of entry.

Consider the case of Sanjay Patel, a citizen of India who wishes to apply for Canadian permanent residence under the Economic class as a Skilled Worker. The process to review Sanjay's application and examine him in order to grant him a permanent resident visa involves several officers who each have distinct decision-making authority. For example, Sanjay's application may initially be reviewed and screened in Canada to ensure it is complete and meets certain minimum standards; the application will then be forwarded to a visa officer who will review it along with additional documentation and decide whether Sanjay meets the regulatory definition of a federal Skilled Worker and whether there are any grounds of admissibility that would bar Sanjay from Canada. The details of the application procedures for specific immigration programs are explored in later chapters, including the Patel scenario under the federal Skilled Worker class in Chapter 5.

Examination at Port of Entry

After Sanjay obtains his permanent resident visa, he will be examined at the port of entry by yet another officer who has the authority to admit him as a permanent resident. Section 28 of the *Immigration and Refugee Protection Regulations* provides that all persons who seek to enter Canada are deemed to be making an application and are therefore subject to an examination. Officers can compel an applicant to answer questions; to provide relevant documents, photographs, and fingerprints; and to submit to medical examinations. Officers act in an adjudicative capacity, which means they must be unbiased in their assessments and evaluations. They render binding decisions after reviewing and considering information received as evidence.

SEARCH AND SEIZURE

Some officers are delegated the authority to search and seize; however, these powers may be exercised only when the officer has **reasonable grounds** to believe that a person who is trying to enter Canada has done any of the following:

- concealed his identity;
- hidden documents that are relevant to his admissibility; or

- concealed documents that may have been used for the purpose of smuggling or trafficking of persons.

The *Canadian Charter of Rights and Freedoms*, in s. 8, provides that all persons in Canada, including foreign nationals, have the right to be secure against unreasonable search or seizure. Therefore, an officer may only exercise search and seizure powers if that officer has reasonable grounds to believe that one of the above criteria has been met. Reasonable grounds are a set of facts and circumstances that would satisfy an ordinarily cautious and prudent person and are more than mere suspicion.

Provided that there are reasonable grounds, an officer is authorized under the IRPA to conduct the following types of searches:

- search person, luggage, and personal effects (s. 139(1));
- board and inspect vessels to carry out a search (s. 15(3));
- seize vehicles and other items or assets used in relation to an immigration offence or to ensure compliance with the Act and its regulations; and
- seize documents that were fraudulently or improperly obtained or used, or likely to be fraudulently or improperly used, such as fraudulent passports (ss. 139 and 140).

Consider the following case of an examination at the port of entry where officers exercise their authority for search and seizure:

> A female traveller from the United States, Martina Vidi, is stopped at the Peace Arch border crossing from Washington into British Columbia. The CBSA officer has reasonable grounds to believe that Martina is concealing her identity. The officer instructs Martina to pull her car into a separate lane and advises Martina that he wishes to conduct a search. Martina complies. The search involves the examination of all of her belongings: her purse, her briefcase, two suitcases, other personal effects, and her car. The officer's search is for the purpose of detecting documents or evidence that relate to Martina's identity, her admissibility, and any potential offences under the IRPA. She is asked to empty her pockets and to remove her jacket for examination. There is no physical contact between the officer and Martina, and no force or constraint is used in the search.

In the scenario above, Martina consented to the search, but if a person for some reason refuses to be searched, or behaves in any manner that puts the officer's safety at risk, the officer may detain the person and compel compliance with the search. However, detaining the person triggers the right to be advised of one's right to counsel. Section 10 of the Charter requires that all persons being arrested or detained, including anyone submitting to an involuntary personal search, must be advised of the reason for the detention and of the right to retain and instruct counsel without delay.

After Entry: Enforcement

Certain CIC and CBSA officers—such as those bearing the titles Citizenship and Immigration Officer (C&I), Detentions; Citizenship and Immigration Officer,

Enforcement; Citizenship and Immigration Officer, Port of Entry; Border Services Officer; and Case Presenting Officer[1]—have the authority and powers of a peace officer to arrest and detain permanent residents or foreign nationals pursuant to s. 138(1) of the IRPA. The authorization is generally given to the "title" relevant to the type of work performed.

Officers have the authority to **arrest** a permanent resident or foreign national who they believe has or may have breached the IRPA, and may **detain** him if the person poses a danger to the public, if his identity is in question, or if there is reason to believe that the person will not appear for an immigration proceeding. Officers may also detain a permanent resident or foreign national at a port of entry if

- it is necessary for the completion of an examination, and
- there are reasonable grounds to believe that the person is inadmissible for reasons of security or for violating human or international rights.[2]

Generally, an officer must have a warrant to arrest and detain a permanent resident, foreign national, or protected person (IRPA, s. 55(1)). However, the IRPA makes an exception in s. 55(2) for the arrest and detention without a warrant of a foreign national:

(a) who the officer has reasonable grounds to believe is inadmissible and is a danger to the public or is unlikely to appear for examination, an admissibility hearing, removal from Canada, or at a proceeding that could lead to the making of a removal order by the Minister under subsection 44(2); or

(b) if the officer is not satisfied of the identity of the foreign national in the course of any procedure under this Act.

Recall our scenario involving Martina Vidi:

Suppose that Martina disagrees to the search or behaves in any manner that puts her or the officer's safety at risk. The officer has the authority to detain her without a warrant, and her detention compels her to comply with the search. Of course, this is predicated on the fact that the officer had reasonable grounds to believe that Martina was concealing her identify. At this point, Martina must be advised of her right to counsel.

As peace officers, CIC and CBSA officers have the authority to apply for and obtain search warrants under ss. 487 to 492.2 of the *Criminal Code* and to execute warrants for arrest and detention. Generally, an officer applies for a search warrant to obtain information to establish a person's identity, locate a person wanted on an immigration arrest warrant, or obtain evidence related to an immigration investigation. An officer who wants to apply for a search warrant must make an application to a judge or justice of the peace, who issues the warrant.

Removal

After being admitted to Canada, some permanent residents and foreign nationals may do something (for example, commit a criminal act) or fail to do something (for example, renew a visitor's visa) that makes them "inadmissible." (Inadmissibility matters are more thoroughly explored in Chapter 3.) When such cases come to the attention of an officer, the law allows for the removal of such individuals. Generally, the minister (or, more practically, his or her delegate) will review a written report and decide whether to remove the person or whether there needs to be a hearing.

On the other hand, when an officer has reason to believe that a permanent resident or foreign national who is already in Canada has become inadmissible, the officer writes an "admissibility report" to be reviewed by the minister. The minister is authorized under s. 44(2) to take one of the following actions:

- allow the person to stay in Canada, if the minister concludes that the report is not well founded;

- issue a removal order, if the minister concludes that the report is well founded and that it falls within the jurisdiction of the officer who wrote the report; or

- refer the case to the Immigration Division of the Immigration and Refugee Board, if the minister concludes that the report is well founded, but that it does not fall within the jurisdiction of the officer who wrote it.

Consider the following scenario relating to the minister's authority to make decisions that could lead to a foreign national's removal from Canada. In this scenario, the minister's authority has been delegated to officers, who carry out the immigration functions.

Jose Rodriguez came to Canada to visit his uncle Juan, who owns a small restaurant. One of Juan's employees quit suddenly so he asked Jose to come and work for him until he can find a replacement. Jose agreed and over a period of several weeks worked as a waiter and bus boy, and even helped out in the kitchen. His uncle paid him cash for his services. Jose was allowed entry to Canada as a temporary visitor but had no authorization to work. He is now considered to be in a state of non-compliance—namely, not in possession of a work authorization—and is now inadmissible. Jose came to the attention of immigration officials, and an officer "wrote a report" against him.

In Jose's case, the minister (or, in practice, the minister's delegate) will review the officer's admissibility report and make a decision that ultimately can lead to Jose's removal from Canada. This process is explored in detail in Chapter 10.

Minister Responsible for Citizenship Matters

In addition to the immigration and refugee portfolios, the minister of Citizenship and Immigration also has authority over citizenship. In the same way that the IRPA confers immigration functions, s. 2(1) of the *Citizenship Act* allows for citizenship functions to be assigned to the appropriate member of Cabinet, which is currently the minister of CIC. These functions include the following:

- granting Canadian citizenship to new Canadians,
- providing documentation of citizenship to citizens, and
- promoting Canadian citizenship.

Under s. 23 of the *Citizenship Act*, the minister may delegate those powers, in writing, to those responsible for applying the law. As a matter of policy, the power to determine citizenship status and to grant, retain, renounce, or resume citizenship is delegated only to those applying the law—for example, citizenship judges, who must be Canadian citizens.[3] Citizenship judges are appointed by the governor in council.

Similar to the IRPA, the *Citizenship Act* grants broad regulatory power to Cabinet through the governor in council to make rules and regulations in the form of orders in council.

The minister of CIC is required to table proposed regulations before each House of Parliament (the House of Commons and the Senate) so that they can be referred to the appropriate committee of that House.

The proposed regulation need only be tabled once, however, as it does not have to be presented to each House of Parliament again, even if it has been altered (s. 27.1(3)). As a result, amendments can be made without further examination by Parliament. The minister has the authority to prescribe the form of citizenship applications, certificates, and other documents.

Immigration and Refugee Board

Structure of the IRB

Established in 1989, the **Immigration and Refugee Board (IRB)** is a federal administrative tribunal that conducts admissibility hearings, detention reviews, immigration appeals, refugee protection hearings, and refugee appeals. It is sometimes called the "board" or by the name of one of its four tribunals, also known as divisions:

- the Immigration Division (ID),
- the Immigration Appeal Division (IAD),
- the Refugee Protection Division (RPD), and
- the Refugee Appeal Division (RAD).

An organizational chart for the IRB and its four divisions is provided below.

Each division performs specialized functions, such as adjudicating immigration matters and appeals or deciding claims for refugee protection. The IRB reports to Parliament through the minister of CIC; the minister is represented by officers from either CIC or the CBSA who may appear before the divisions as a party to one of its proceedings. However, the board functions independently from government and, like all tribunals, is expected to exercise its role in an impartial manner.

The board is composed of a chairperson, numerous members who preside over hearings and make decisions, and tribunal staff who support the decision-makers and the tribunal's operations. The board has a dual accountability structure in which the decision-makers are responsible to the chairperson through their respective managers—namely, a deputy chairperson, assistant deputy chairperson, and coordinating

Structure of the Immigration and Refugee Board

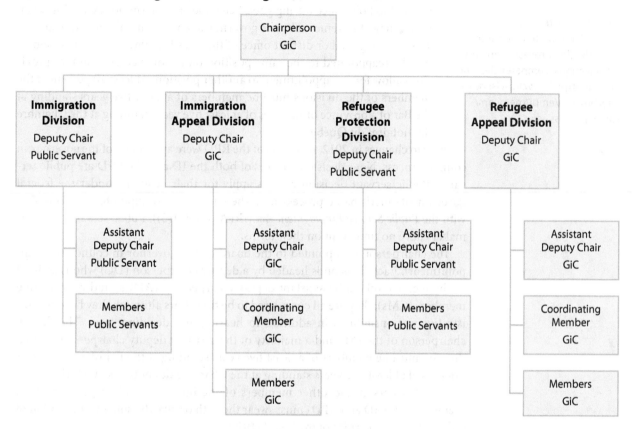

members—and the public servants who are responsible to separate managers—namely, the executive director, director general, regional director, and registrar. "Member" is the term used by each tribunal to denote the role of the decision-maker in immigration and refugee cases.

On June 28, 2012, Bill C-31, the *Protecting Canada's Immigration System Act*, received royal assent and amended the IRPA, with some amendments coming into force at that time and others that will come into force probably over the next two years. The amendments to the IRPA had the effect of changing the structure of the IRB (see the organization chart above), significant changes to the appointment of decision-makers, as well as many of the processes and timelines related to refugee matters (examined in Chapter 9.)

Decision-makers are appointed to their roles in two different ways based on the area of specialization: by the governor in council process or as public servants.

The governor in council (GiC) appoints members to two of the board's tribunals: the Immigration Appeal Division and the Refugee Appeal Division.[4] The selection process includes the review and selection of qualified candidates by the Selection Advisory Board (SAB), which is chaired by the IRB's chairperson and composed of at least seven members. The SAB makes recommendations to the minister of CIC, who recommends appointments to the governor in council. The minister is responsible for managing all GiC appointments within his portfolio. Members are appointed to hold office during good behaviour for a term not exceeding seven years, subject to removal by the governor in council at any time for cause, to serve in a regional or district office of the board (IRPA, s. 153(1)). Members may be reappointed to the same position or, in some cases, statutory provisions allow for a reappointment to another position. At least 10 percent of the members of the divisions must be members of at least five years standing at the Bar of a province or notaries of at least five years standing at the Chambre des notaires du Québec.

Prior to changes in 2012, members of the RPD were appointees of the governor in council process. Now, decision-makers of both the ID and the RPD are public servants. Public servant decision-makers apply for their positions under the federal government's merit-based process and, when qualified, are appointed in accordance with the *Public Service Employment Act* (IRPA, s. 169.1(2)). Public servant decision-makers have no time limit on their terms.

The chairperson is appointed to the board by the governor in council (GiC appointment). Each division is headed by a deputy chairperson (DC) who is assisted in the regional offices by assistant deputy chairpersons (ADCs) and coordinating members (CMs); they are all considered to be **members** although they have administrative responsibilities in addition to hearing and deciding cases. The deputy chairperson of the IAD and a majority of the assistant deputy chairpersons of that division must be members of at least five years standing at the Bar of a province or notaries of at least five years standing at the Chambre des notaires du Québec.

The chairperson and other members of the board (including public servant members in the ID and RPD) must swear the oath or give the solemn affirmation of office set out in the rules of the board (IRPA, s. 152.1).

The chairperson is appointed to the board by the governor in council (GiC appointment). As illustrated in the organization chart above, each division is headed by a deputy chairperson (DC) who is assisted in the regional offices by assistant deputy chairpersons (ADCs) and coordinating members (CMs); they are all considered to be members although they have administrative responsibilities in addition to hearing and deciding cases. The ID does not have CMs.

Generally, members hear and decide cases without additional formal responsibilities.

Chairperson's Powers

The chairperson is the IRB's chief executive officer and has a range of statutory powers for the management of decision-makers, including the authority to supervise and direct the work of the board, to designate coordinating members to the IAD and the RAD, to assign members to the IAD and RAD, and, with the approval of the governor in council, to assign an IAD or an RAD member to work in another regional or district office for up to 120 days to satisfy operational requirements (IRPA, s. 159(1)(c)).

The chairperson can delegate certain powers to the deputy chairs, the ADCs, or other members, including CMs, only in relation to the IAD and the RAD. For example, the chairperson may delegate to an IAD member powers in relation to the RAD, and may delegate to an RAD member powers in relation to the IAD.

The chairperson's powers in relation to the RPD cannot be delegated to an ID member and vice versa; powers in relation to the ID or the RPD may only be delegated to the DC, the ADCs, or other members, including CMs, of that division.

The chairperson also has the authority to issue guidelines to decision-makers and to identify any of the board's decisions as jurisprudential guides (IRPA, s. 159(1)). As well, the chairperson has the exclusive authority to make the rules of practice and procedure for the tribunal; these powers may not be delegated (IRPA ss. 159(1) and 161).

The role of deputy chairperson is to oversee the management of decision-makers. With the exception of the power to make the rules of practice and procedure, the chairperson's authority may be delegated to a board member.

Members' Powers

As noted above, decision-makers at the IRB, in all divisions, are called members. Members are selected for their expertise and their experience in a variety of fields including but not limited to general law, immigration, refugee law, and human rights.

Members have the power and authority of a commissioner appointed under Part I of the *Inquiries Act*. These powers include the power to summon witnesses and require them, under oath, to give evidence, orally or in writing, and to produce documents. Members may do anything they consider necessary to achieve a full and proper hearing. They may also choose to conduct hearings by telephone or by video conference, and may determine whether a hearing will be held in public or in private. Members have the authority to designate a representative in cases involving a minor or a person who is unable to appreciate the nature of the proceedings.

Should a person fail to appear for her hearing, the member assigned to hear the case has the statutory power to determine that the hearing has been abandoned. The member may also refuse a withdrawal by an applicant and make a finding of abuse of process. Members in all divisions of the IRB have the power to apply the Charter, and may declare a specific section of the IRPA inoperative if they find it to be in violation of a Charter right.

The IAD is a court of record, and has an official seal (IRPA, s. 174.); this division of the IRB has all the powers, rights, and privileges vested in a superior court of justice.

The Board's Four Divisions

Each of the board's four divisions has jurisdiction to hear and decide specific types of cases. Each division is supported by its own tribunal rules that set out its practices and procedures so that those who appear before the tribunal (that is, the parties and their counsel), members, and tribunal staff have clear and consistent direction about how to present or process a case. What follows is a brief description of each division's decision-makers and jurisdiction. Details of the procedures of each are described in later chapters.

Immigration Division (ID)

Members of the ID are not bound by any legal or technical rules of evidence; they may receive and base their decision on any evidence they consider credible and trustworthy (IRPA, s. 173). Members of the ID are responsible for hearing and deciding matters regarding the following:

- admission or removal of permanent residents and foreign nationals, and
- review of immigration detentions.

Admissibility hearings involve a determination of whether a person should be allowed to enter or remain in Canada or ordered removed from Canada. In our earlier example of Jose, who was caught working without a work permit, the matter will likely be referred for a hearing before a member of the ID. At the hearing, the minister, represented by a hearings officer, will argue the case against Jose. The member will hear both sides of the case, and decide Jose's status in Canada.

Members review the reasons for detention under the IRPA and determine whether there are sufficient reasons to continue the detention of a person who is detained or to release the person. Using our example, Jose can be detained if the minister's representative makes a case that there is a risk that Jose won't appear for his admissibility hearing. At the detention review, Jose will appear before a member of the ID to argue his release while the hearings officer will argue against his release or ask that certain conditions to be imposed on a release order.

Immigration Appeal Division (IAD)

Members of the IAD have jurisdiction to hear and decide four types of appeals, as follows:

- sponsorship appeals from Canadian citizens and permanent residents whose applications to sponsor close family members to come to Canada have been refused;
- removal order appeals from permanent residents, foreign nationals with a permanent resident visa, and protected persons who have been ordered removed from Canada;
- loss-of-permanent-residence appeals by a permanent resident against a decision made outside Canada on residency obligation under s. 28; and
- minister's appeals from the minister responsible for the CBSA, who may appeal a decision made by the ID at an admissibility hearing.

There are certain immigration matters where a person has a statutory right to appeal decisions to the IAD. Section 63 of the IRPA provides those appeal rights to sponsors, visa holders, permanent residents, protected persons, and the minister against a decision by the ID.

In hearing appeals, IAD members are not limited to reviewing findings of fact at the first hearing. Appeals are hearings *de novo*, which means starting afresh, and the IAD must receive any additional evidence, and base its decision on its own assessment of the evidence—including credibility of witnesses—even if the strict rules of evidence have not been met.[5] IAD hearing procedures are explored in greater detail in Chapter 10.

Let's return to our scenario concerning Juan and his nephew Jose:

> Because of all the problems that Juan, the restaurant owner, had in hiring his nephew Jose, he has encouraged his wife, Marie, to help out more at the restaurant. But this requires Marie to put their two children in daycare. As a Canadian citizen, she decides to sponsor her mother, Ana, with the plan that Ana will look after the children while Marie works in the restaurant. The sponsorship is refused. What recourse does Marie have now?

Permanent residents and Canadian citizens, like Marie in the example above, have the right to appeal the decision to refuse their sponsorship applications to the IAD. A member of the IAD will hear and decide the appeal. In this example, the appellant Marie will present her case, and a hearings officer will represent the minister at the appeal hearing as the respondent. As noted earlier, the IAD is the only division that has "all the powers, rights and privileges vested in a superior court." Members may swear in and examine witnesses, and may issue orders for the production and inspection of documents (IRPA, s. 174(2)).

Refugee Protection Division (RPD)

With the coming into force of the IRPA in June 2002, the Convention Refugee Determination Division was renamed the Refugee Protection Division. Members of the RPD are responsible for hearing refugee claims made by persons in Canada and determining whether the claimants are refugees.

Refugee hearings are generally informal and non-adversarial. Members of the RPD are not bound by any legal or technical rules of evidence; they may receive and base their decision on any evidence they consider credible and trustworthy. They may inquire into any matter that they consider relevant to the establishment of a well-founded claim. Furthermore, members may take **judicial notice** of any facts, information, or opinion within the division's specialized knowledge (IRPA, s. 170). Judicial notice is a rule in the law of evidence that allows a fact to be accepted as true without supporting evidence if the truth of that fact is so well known that it cannot be refuted. Refugee hearings are discussed in greater detail in Chapter 9.

Refugee Appeal Division (RAD)

Although the IRPA provides that an unsuccessful refugee claim may be appealed to the Refugee Appeal Division, this division has only recently been operative. When the IRPA came into force in June 2002, the sections that created the RAD (ss. 110 and 111) were not proclaimed into law. Amendments to the IRPA in 2012 provide that an unsuccessful refugee claim may be appealed to the Refugee Appeal Division, by the claimant or the minister, not later than 15 working days after the day on which the person or the minister receives written reasons for the decision (proposed Regulations, s. 159.95(1)). The appeal may be made:

- on a question of law, of fact, or of mixed law and fact,
- against a decision of the RPD to allow or reject a claim for refugee protection, or
- against a decision of the RPD regarding an application for cessation or vacation (IRPA, s. 110(1)).

Members of the RAD—like members of the RPD—are not bound by any legal or technical rules of evidence; they may receive and base their decision on any evidence they consider credible and trustworthy. They may inquire into any matter that they consider relevant to the establishment of a well-founded claim. Furthermore, members may take judicial notice of any facts, information, or opinion within the division's specialized knowledge (IRPA, s. 171).

Courts

Matters involving the IRPA and the *Citizenship Act* may come before the courts by way of judicial review or appeal. Judicial review provides the means for the courts to oversee administrative decisions, such as those made by the minister, members of the IRB, and citizenship judges. Although the courts defer to the expertise of administrative tribunals, and generally accept their findings of fact, on judicial review the court will determine whether the administrative decision-making process was fair and was based on the appropriate legal considerations.

Appeals from lower court decisions consider whether the decision-maker erred in its interpretation of the law, or in its application of the law to the facts. Findings of fact, such as the credibility of a witness, are not generally reconsidered on appeal—only points of law are argued.

Because the IRPA and the *Citizenship Act* are federal laws, the courts with jurisdiction over the interpretation and application of these statutes are the federal courts. The trial court is the Federal Court, and the appeal court is the Federal Court of Appeal. If a significant legal issue is in question, decisions of the Federal Court of Appeal may be appealed to the final decision-maker in Canada—the Supreme Court of Canada.

Federal Court and Federal Court of Appeal

The Federal Court has jurisdiction to review decisions, orders, and other administrative actions made by the IRB, CIC, the CBSA, and citizenship judges. In this way the courts exercise a supervisory role. Judicial review may be sought by either party—the individual or the minister—provided that an application for leave to the Federal Court is made within the statutory time limit of 60 days after receiving the disputed decision. A Federal Court judge will either grant or deny leave for judicial review. The IRB may also refer any question of law, jurisdiction, or practice to the Federal Court at any stage of a proceeding.

The Federal Court derives its authority from s. 18.1(3) of the *Federal Courts Act*. On judicial review of an IRB decision, the Federal Court may do any of the following:

- send the matter back for redetermination by a different member or panel,
- quash the IRB decision and substitute its own decision, or
- uphold the IRB decision.

If a party is dissatisfied with a decision of the Federal Court, leave for appeal may be sought from the Federal Court of Appeal. However, s. 74(d) of the IRPA provides that an appeal may be made only if the court certifies that a serious question of general importance is involved, and states the question. The appeal then deals only with this particular question.

In citizenship matters, the minister of CIC and the applicant both have the right to appeal a citizenship judge's decision for adult grant, retention, renunciation, and resumption applications. The Federal Court may do any of the following:

- allow the appeal and substitute its own decision;
- allow the appeal and send the matter back for redetermination by a different citizenship judge;
- allow the appeal and send the matter back for redetermination by the same citizenship judge;
- dismiss the appeal;
- dismiss the appeal, but send the matter back for a reconsideration to the original citizenship judge;
- dismiss the appeal, but send the matter back for a reconsideration to a new citizenship judge; or
- dismiss the appeal, but send the matter to the minister for his or her use of discretion.

The decision of the Federal Court is final and no further appeals are allowed.

Non-lawyers, such as immigration consultants and paralegals, are not authorized to represent clients in Federal Court or the Federal Court of Appeal (see s. 11 of the *Federal Courts Act* and rule 119 of the *Federal Courts Rules*). In appropriate cases, non-lawyers who are representing immigration or refugee clients should explain the judicial review process and refer their clients to an immigration lawyer. For self-represented litigants, the Federal Court provides information on "Court Process and Procedures" online at http://cas-ncr-nter03.cas-satj.gc.ca/portal/page/portal/fc_cf_en/Process.

Supreme Court of Canada

The Supreme Court of Canada is the final court of appeal from all other Canadian courts, on all subject matters. Before a case can reach the Supreme Court of Canada, all other avenues of appeal must first be exhausted.

A party who is not satisfied with a Federal Court of Appeal decision has the right to seek leave to appeal to the Supreme Court of Canada, under s. 40(1) of the *Supreme Court Act*. The Supreme Court of Canada may grant leave to appeal only if the case involves a question of public importance, if it raises an important issue of law or mixed law and fact, or if the matter is, for any other reason, significant enough to be considered by the country's Supreme Court.

APPENDIX

A summary of the various decision-makers discussed in this chapter, their functions, and their responsibilities and activities is provided in the table below.

Immigration and Refugee Decision-Makers

Decision-makers	Organization	Function	Responsibility or activity
Minister and designated or delegated officers	CIC	Immigration	Responsible for • immigration policy development • annual immigration plan • temporary residents immigration processes • permanent residents immigration processes • settlement and integration of newcomers to Canada • pre-removal risk assessments • most policies related to admissibility
Minister and designated or delegated officers	PSEP/CBSA	Immigration/ Enforcement	Responsible for • management and operation of Canada's borders and port-of-entry functions • arrests • detentions • removals • background checks of immigration applicants
Minister only	CIC PSEP/CBSA	Enforcement	Responsible for • signing security certificates • referring security certificates to the Federal Court
Minister and designated or delegated officers	CIC	Refugee protection	Responsible for • the resettlement of refugees • admissibility of refugee claimants in Canada • determinations of eligibility
Minister and designated or delegated officers	PSEP/CBSA		Responsible for • background checks of refugee claimants • removal of refugee claimants where a "danger opinion" exists
Minister and designated or delegated officers	CIC Citizenship Commission	Citizenship	Citizenship program and policy
Member	IRB: Immigration Division	Immigration	Hears and decides • admissibility hearings for persons who are inadmissible to or removable from Canada • detention review hearings into the reasons for detention of persons under the IRPA Issues removal orders in complex cases

Decision-makers	Organization	Function	Responsibility or activity
Member	IRB: Immigration Appeal Division	Immigration	Hears and decides appeals against • the minister's decision to refuse a sponsorship application (sponsorship appeal) • a removal order decision by a member of the ID or the minister from a permanent resident, foreign national with a permanent resident visa, or protected person who has been ordered removed from Canada (removal order appeal) • an immigration officer's decision that a permanent resident has lost his permanent resident status (loss-of-permanent-residence appeal) • an appeal from the minister responsible for the CBSA, who may appeal a decision made by the ID at an admissibility hearing (minister's appeal) Note: The IAD does not hear appeals against a removal order for a person who is a security threat or war criminal, has committed crimes against humanity, is involved in organized crime, or is a serious criminal, because that person has no right of appeal.
Member	IRB: Refugee Protection Division		Hears claims made by persons in Canada and determines whether or not the claimants are refugees
Member	IRB: Refugee Appeal Division		Hears appeals from failed refugee claimants from the Refugee Protection Division
Citizenship Judge	Citizenship Commission		Decides citizenship applications for: • grant of citizenship • retention of citizenship • renunciation of citizenship • resumption of citizenship
Judge	Federal Court		• Decides reasonableness of a security certificate • Conducts judicial review
Judges	Federal Court of Appeal		Hear appeals from the Federal Court
Judges	Supreme Court of Canada		Hear and decide an appeal only if • the case involves a question of public importance, • the case raises an important issue of law or mixed law and fact, or • the matter is, for any other reason, significant enough to be considered by the country's Supreme Court

KEY TERMS

REVIEW QUESTIONS

Ministers Responsible for Immigration and Refugee Matters

1. Which ministers are authorized by the IRPA to carry out immigration and refugee functions? Can you name them?

2. Provide an example of a minister's authority that cannot be delegated.

3. Provide examples of an officer's duties related to the examination of an application.

4. Under what circumstances can an officer exercise her search and seizure powers?

5. Can an officer arrest and detain an individual under the IRPA without a warrant?

Minister Responsible for Citizenship Matters

1. Which minister is responsible for citizenship functions?

2. Which statute provides this authorization?

Immigration and Refugee Board

1. What are decision-makers at the IRB called?

2. Members of which divisions are appointed by the governor in council?

3. Which members are public servants?

Courts

1. In which court is a judicial review conducted?

2. If a party is not satisfied with the decision of the Federal Court, can that party appeal to the Supreme Court of Canada?

NOTES

1. For a complete list of officers by title, refer to "Instrument of Designation and Delegation" signed by the minister of CIC on August 15, 2012 (designations and delegations are updated regularly), http://www.cic.gc.ca/english/resources/manuals/il/il3-eng.pdf.

2. Canada Border Services Agency, "Fact Sheet: Arrests and Detentions," August 2009, http://cbsa-asfc.gc.ca/media/facts-faits/menu-eng.html.

3. Citizenship and Immigration Canada, "CP 2: Decision-Making," in Citizenship Policy (CP), March 21, 2007, s. 1.5, http://www.cic.gc.ca/english/resources/manuals/cp/index.asp.

4. Prior to legislative changes, members of the Refugee Protection Division were also appointed by the governor in council.

5. Kahlon v. Canada (Minister of Employment and Immigration) (1989), 7 Imm. L.R. (2d) 91, 97 N.R. 349 (F.C.A.).

REFERENCES

Canada. Bill C-11, An Act to Amend the Immigration and Refugee Protection Act and the Federal Courts Act (short title Balanced Refugee Reform Act), 40th Parl., 3rd sess., 59 Eliz. II, 2010, assented to June 29, 2010. http://www.parl.gc.ca/HousePublications/Publication.aspx?Language=E&Mode=1&DocId=4644728&File=14.

Canada. Bill C-31, An Act to Amend the Immigration and Refugee Protection Act, the Balanced Refugee Reform Act, the Marine Transportation Security Act and the Department of Citizenship and Immigration Act (short title Protecting Canada's Immigration System Act), 41st Parl., 1st sess., 60-61 Eliz. II, 2011–2012, assented to June 28, 2012. http://www.parl.gc.ca/HousePublications/Publication.aspx?Docid=5697417&file=4.

Canada. "Regulations Amending the Immigration and Refugee Protection Regulations, Regulatory Impact Analysis." Canada Gazette, Part I: Notices and Proposed Regulations, vol. 145, no. 12, March 19, 2011.

Canada Border Services Agency. "About the CBSA," June 7, 2011. http://www.cbsa-asfc.gc.ca/agency-agence/menu-eng.html.

Canada Border Services Agency. Designation and Delegation by the Minister of Public Safety and Emergency Preparedness Under the Immigration and Refugee Protection Act and Immigration and Refugee Protection Regulations—Amendment, October 2012. http://www.cbsa-asfc.gc.ca/agency-agence/delegation/irpa-lipr_2012-02_amd-mod-eng.html.

Canada Border Services Agency. "Fact Sheet: Arrests and Detentions," August 2009. http://www.cbsa-asfc.gc.ca/media/facts-faits/007-eng.html.

Citizenship Act. R.S.C. 1985, c. C-29.

Citizenship and Immigration Canada. "Citizenship and Immigration Canada: Serving Canada and the World." Catalogue no. Ci51-99/2003.

Citizenship and Immigration Canada. "ENF 9: Judicial Review," in *Enforcement (ENF)*, January 30, 2006. http://www.cic.gc.ca/english/resources/manuals/enf/enf09-eng.pdf.

Citizenship and Immigration Canada. "Instrument of Designation and Delegation," August 15, 2012. http://www.cic.gc.ca/english/resources/manuals/il/il3-eng.pdf.

Citizenship and Immigration Canada. "IP 1: Temporary Resident Permits," in *Inland Processing (IP)*, June 19, 2007. http://www.cic.gc.ca/english/resources/manuals/ip/ip01-eng.pdf.

Citizenship and Immigration Canada. "Coming into Force of Bill C-35, An Act to Amend the Immigration and Refugee Protection Act (Authorized Representatives)," *Operational Bulletin* 317, June 30, 2011. http://www.cic.gc.ca/english/resources/manuals/bulletins/2011/ob317.asp.

Coakeley, Simon. "New Developments in the Refugee Determination System." Immigration and Refugee Board of Canada, presentation to the Canadian Council for Refugees, Hamilton, May 26, 2011. http://www.irb-cisr.gc.ca/Eng/media/newsnouv/2011/Pages/ccrsn.aspx.

Criminal Code. R.S.C. 1985, c. C-46.

Federal Courts Act. R.S.C. 1985, c. F-7.

Federal Courts Immigration and Refugee Protection Rules. S.O.R./93-22.

Federal Courts Rules. S.O.R./98-106.

Immigration and Refugee Protection Act. S.C. 2001, c. 27.

Immigration and Refugee Protection Regulations. S.O.R./2002-227.

Immigration Division Rules. S.O.R./2000-229.

Inquiries Act. R.S.C. 1985, c. I-11.

Public Safety Canada. "Security Certificates," February 15, 2012. http://www.publicsafety.gc.ca/prg/ns/seccert-eng.aspx.

Public Service Employment Act. S.C. 2003, c. 22.

Supreme Court Act. R.S.C. 1985, c. S-26.

Treasury Board of Canada Secretariat. "Section 3: Supplementary Information," in *DPR 2004-2005: Immigration and Refugee Board*, October 26, 2005. http://www.collectionscanada.gc.ca/webarchives/20060120064254/http://www.tbs-sct.gc.ca/rma/dpr1/04-05/irb-cisr/irb-cisrd4509_e.asp.

Inadmissibility 3

LEARNING OUTCOMES

After reading this chapter you should be able to:

- Describe the general provisions for applying for a visa.

- Describe the general provisions for entering Canada.

- Describe how temporary residents and permanent residents can lose their status.

- Identify the eight grounds of inadmissibility to Canada under the *Immigration and Refugee Protection Act*.

- Understand when exemptions to these grounds of inadmissibility apply.

- Describe the three types of decisions that may be used by officers to identify persons who are inadmissible on the ground of membership in a group that engages in espionage, subversion, or terrorism.

- Describe the four types of decisions that may be used by officers to identify persons who are inadmissible on the ground of violating human or international rights.

- Distinguish among the three types of domestic crime that may make a person inadmissible to Canada: serious criminality, criminality, and organized criminality.

- Understand that different government agencies may be involved in assessing inadmissibility.

Introduction

Managing permanent and temporary immigration to Canada is a difficult balancing act. On the one hand, immigration policies may aim to facilitate immigration to attract a skilled workforce, reunite families, encourage students and visitors to stay on a temporary basis, and protect refugees and persons in need of protection. On the other hand, immigration law and policy reform are often tied with national security, especially since 9/11, or in response to Canada's economic health. Consequently, there are rules to exclude some individuals, and controls to deny access to people who would pose a heavy burden on health and social services or a risk to the health and safety of Canadians.

These competing goals are reflected in the stated objectives of immigration law, particularly ss. 3(1)(a) and (h) of the *Immigration and Refugee Protection Act* (IRPA) as follows:

> (a) to permit Canada to pursue the maximum social, cultural and economic benefits of immigration; ...
>
> (h) to protect the health and safety of Canadians and to maintain the security of Canadian society.

The task of balancing competing demands is reflected in the processing of applications of prospective temporary and permanent residents: an officer must assess a person's application to decide whether the applicant is *eligible* (that is, meets specific program criteria) and is *not inadmissible*. The officer may accept the application and issue a visa or refuse it, thus denying access to Canada.

In this chapter, we examine the general requirements for obtaining a visa for temporary and permanent immigration. The various classes and subclasses of immigration are described in detail in Chapter 4, Temporary Entry; Chapter 5, Permanent Entry; Chapter 8, Refugee and Humanitarian Resettlement Program; and Chapter 9, In-Canada Refugee Determination Process. After the foreign national has proved he is eligible under the specific criteria, he may nevertheless be barred from entering Canada because of inadmissibility; or after being admitted, he may be removed from Canada because of inadmissibility. Therefore, the chapter will also outline and discuss the grounds of **inadmissibility**.

Generally, inadmissibility applies to all applicants in the same manner, regardless of the class or subclass under which they are requesting entry to Canada. For this reason, this chapter on inadmissibility precedes those dealing with program eligibility requirements. We examine the eight grounds of inadmissibility set out in the IRPA as follows:

1. security risk (s. 34);
2. human or international rights violations (s. 35);
3. serious criminality (s. 36(1)), criminality (s. 36(2)), and organized criminality (s. 37);
4. health reasons (s. 38);

5. financial reasons—that is, inability to provide for oneself or dependants (s. 39);
6. misrepresentation (s. 40);
7. failure to comply with the IRPA (s. 41); and
8. inadmissible family member (s. 42).

General Rules

The first hurdle that a foreign national faces when applying to come to Canada is obtaining permission as either a temporary or permanent resident. This involves meeting the eligibility requirements for one of the numerous classes or subclasses under which a foreign national may apply, such as visitor, member of the Family class, or refugee, to name just a few. Note that an applicant for entry must first establish eligibility under the relevant class or subclass before an officer will consider inadmissibility. This is because the background checks that are required to verify that an applicant is not inadmissible, such as police record checks, medical examinations, and other investigations, may be costly and time consuming. Because so many applicants will fail to meet the eligibility requirements, it is more efficient to consider inadmissibility only after eligibility is confirmed.

Only Canadian citizens and registered (status) Indians have the absolute right to enter Canada and remain here. Everyone else must seek permission before they are allowed to enter Canada to live here either on a temporary or permanent basis.

> ### What Is Your Residency Status?
> - Canadian citizen
> - Registered under the *Indian Act*
> - Permanent Resident
> - Temporary Resident
> - Convention Refugee
> - Protected Person
> - Temporary Permit Holder
>
> Depending on your residency status, you have different rights and obligations.

Prior to Entry: Application for a Visa

According to IRPA s. 2, a **foreign national** is a person who is not a Canadian citizen or a permanent resident and includes a stateless person. Such a person who wishes to live temporarily or permanently in Canada must submit to an application and approval process and obtain a visa (for example, a **temporary resident visa (TRV)**, such as a visitor visa, a study permit, a work permit, or a permanent resident visa) before coming to Canada (although some foreign nationals from "visa-exempt" countries coming as temporary residents are excluded from this requirement—see Chapter 4).

Section 11 of the IRPA obliges all foreign nationals to apply before entering Canada. For most foreign nationals, obtaining a visa involves a formal, written application procedure, and, generally, includes medical examinations and background checks for identity, criminality, and security. Generally, the purpose of requiring foreign nationals to obtain a visa is to stop those who are not eligible or who are inadmissible from entering Canada before they travel, rather than to wait until they arrive at a port of entry and then incur the expense of removal.

Foreign nationals must apply *before* entering Canada to an officer for a visa or other document and satisfy the officer that they are:

- **eligible** and
- not **inadmissible**. (IRPA, s. 11)

An applicant has a duty to tell the truth as required pursuant to s. 16 of the IRPA and to produce any relevant evidence, including photographs and fingerprints. A visa is issued only when the officer is satisfied that the applicant meets the requirements of the IRPA and its regulations, specifically s. 22 of the IRPA and related sections of the IRP Regulations, which require that the applicant has

- fulfilled certain obligations;
- met the criteria for the particular class of permanent or temporary resident that he has applied under; and
- shown that he is not inadmissible.

Obligations of Applicant

- Answer truthfully all questions at an examination by an officer.
- Show a visa, and other documents, on request.
- Provide photographic and fingerprint evidence.
- Submit to a medical examination on request. (IRPA, s. 16)

Generally, an officer may refuse to issue a visa for one of two reasons:

- the applicant does not meet the eligibility criteria for the particular class of permanent or temporary resident; or
- the applicant (or any family member) is inadmissible.

General Application Requirements

There are basic criteria that must generally be met for all applicants for any of the classes of permanent and temporary resident visas. A visa may be issued only if, on examination, the foreign national establishes that he

- has used the appropriate IRPA application documents for the particular class and subclass of resident and completed them (generally, incomplete applications are neither processed nor returned for completion);
- has applied to the appropriate office in accordance with the requirements of the IRPA;
- has paid the required processing fees and other fees as applicable;
- holds a passport or similar document that may be used to enter the country that issued it, or another country;

- meets the medical examination requirements contained in the IRP Regulations; and

- is not inadmissible.

Each of these criteria is considered in more detail in the chapters that follow.

Fees

Applicants are required to pay processing fees. The current processing fees for each type of application for permanent and temporary visa and permit can be found in the *Fee Schedule for Citizenship and Immigration Services* on the CIC website at http://www.cic.gc.ca/english/information/fees/fees.asp.

Because the processing fee is intended to cover the costs of processing the application and not the decision, processing fees are non-refundable even if the application is refused.

Applicants should be prepared to pay additional fees to third parties for medical examinations; fees to translate documents; fees to a representative such as a lawyer, licensed paralegal, or regulated immigration consultant; and, for example, any transportation costs.

Applicants for permanent residence must also include a right to permanent residence fee (RPRF) with their application for each adult. This fee is refundable if the application is refused.

Medical Examinations

Medical examinations are required for applicants who seek permanent residence, including their dependants regardless of whether or not they are accompanying the applicant. For those seeking temporary residence, there are many medical examination exemptions; these are discussed in Chapter 4. Generally, however, a medical examination is required for those who intend on working in occupations where the protection of public health is essential—such as occupations in the health services—or that require close contact with other persons. A medical examination is also required if the foreign national resided, sojourned, or lived in a "designated country or territory" during the year immediately preceding the date of applying for entry to Canada.

Medical examinations must be performed by **panel physicians** (formerly known as designated medical officers).

Port-of-Entry Arrival: Examination

The events of September 11, 2001 refocused efforts on protecting the country against terrorists, at times lessening the openness and efficiency of cross-border movement that travellers previously enjoyed. These efforts are reflected in the functions of the Canada Border Services Agency (CBSA). CBSA officers decide who is allowed to enter Canada, who should be detained under the IRPA, and who should be removed. Even when a permanent or temporary resident visa is obtained, it is not a guarantee of admission to Canada. Section 18 of the IRPA authorizes the examination of all travellers at ports of entry, including Canadian citizens, registered Indians, permanent residents, permanent resident visa holders, temporary resident visa holders, and foreign nationals. A change of circumstances between the time of acquiring a permanent resident or temporary resident visa and the time of arrival in Canada, or additional available information on security concerns, could result in applicants being refused entry or having certain conditions or restrictions placed on their admission. In other words, a visa allows a person to travel to a Canadian port of entry for permanent residence or to visit, work, or study in Canada, but does not in itself grant admission to Canada to carry out those activities.

Right to Enter Canada

Canadian citizens and registered Indians

- unqualified right to enter and remain in Canada. (IRPA, s. 19(1))

Permanent residents must prove their status (IRPA, s. 19(2))

- right to enter and remain subject to conditions (IRPA, ss. 27, 28)
- may be removed if they become inadmissible.

Temporary residents

- authorized to enter and stay on a temporary basis. (IRPA, s. 29)

Section 19(1) of IRPA states that Canadian citizens and persons registered under the *Indian Act* have an automatic right to enter and remain in Canada. Anyone else who wishes to do so must

- obtain permission to enter Canada, as either a temporary or permanent resident; and
- satisfy an officer that she is not inadmissible.

Ports of entry generally have two, separate control points. If you have ever travelled outside Canada, you have experienced the interview at the first control point, or primary inspection line, on your return to Canada. The primary inspection line is where CBSA officers conduct the initial interview of travellers and carry out a mix of immigration and customs activities. Here, they perform the basic duties of checking your identity and your immigration status, and asking about your travel and about any goods you may be bringing into the country.

The examining officer must be satisfied that a foreign national is not inadmissible in order to allow that person to come into Canada. CBSA officers attempt to balance their duty to prevent entry by problem individuals with the goal of allowing other travellers to move easily through the checkpoint. An officer may refer a person for a secondary examination if she believes that a more thorough interview is required. The purpose of the secondary interview is to confirm the identity of the traveller, verify documents such as passports and permits, and gather information to make an informed decision regarding admissibility.

Permanent Residents

Permanent residents arriving at a port of entry who already have status (as compared with applicants who are seeking status) must undergo an examination to satisfy the CBSA officer that they have not lost their status or become inadmissible since acquiring their permanent resident status (IRPA, s. 19(2)). An officer verifies the person's permanent resident card and whether the residency obligation to live in Canada (that is, two years in each five-year period) was met, and checks for inadmissibility (for example, a criminal conviction). If the officer is satisfied that the permanent resident has complied with the conditions of permanent residency and has not become inadmissible, then the officer must allow entry.

Permanent Residence Visa Holders

Visa officers issue permanent resident visas for applicants (and any family members who are accompanying them) under the various categories of permanent residence as a precondition to permanent entry (IRPA, s. 21). Successful applicants may travel to Canada—with confirmation of permanent residence documents or a permanent residence visa—but must undergo a further examination by an officer at the port of entry before being admitted and allowed to remain in Canada (see Chapter 5, Permanent Entry). They must also show a valid passport and other essential documents (for example, a list of all the household and personal items they are bringing into Canada), and proof of funds and assets.

A CBSA officer verifies whether there have been any changes since the issuance of the visa by the visa officer, and that the document holders are not inadmissible. For example, the CBSA officer confirms the applicant's identity; checks that medical examinations are still valid; and verifies that the applicant has enough money to cover living expenses (such as rent, food, clothing, and transportation), if applicable, for a six-month period.

If the CBSA officer is satisfied that the applicant and any accompanying family members are not inadmissible, the officer is required to allow the person entry as a permanent resident. Conditions may be imposed, or there may be a requirement that a medical condition be monitored. Non-compliance with conditions could result in inadmissibility and removal.

Temporary Resident Visa Holders

Foreign nationals living in certain countries require a visa to enter Canada, even on a temporary basis. Visa officers issue temporary resident visas (TRVs) in three categories: visitor, student, and temporary worker, as described in Chapter 4, Temporary Entry.

Like the permanent resident visa, a temporary resident visa authorizes a person to board an airplane or ship to travel to Canada; however, the final decision to allow a person to come into Canada is made at the port of entry (IRPA, s. 22). Temporary residents must undergo an interview at the port of entry to confirm identity, verify admissibility, review any visa restrictions (such as expiration of a work permit or prohibition against work), confirm that medical examinations if required are still valid, and verify that they have enough money to cover living expenses for the duration of the temporary stay. They must show a valid passport and other essential documents, such as proof of funds and assets, a letter of invitation for visitors, a letter of confirmation for foreign students, and a return ticket. If the officer is satisfied that the foreign national and any accompanying family members are not inadmissible, then the officer is required to allow entry.

Conditions may be imposed—for example, the CBSA officer may confirm that a visitor may not work or study, and must leave before the temporary resident visa has expired. Admission as a temporary resident requires compliance with any conditions; non-compliance could result in removal.

Temporary Resident Permit Holders

At times it is not workable to conduct an examination for inadmissibility right away. This may arise as a result of such circumstances as lateness in the day or the unavailability of an interpreter. In such cases, an officer may issue a **temporary resident permit (TRP)** and notice to appear, according to ss. 23 and 24 of the IRPA. This allows the person to enter Canada temporarily so that an examination or an admissibility hearing can be held at a later time.

The person is consequently allowed to enter Canada but is compelled to appear for her immigration proceeding, which may be an examination or a hearing. The temporary resident is permitted to move freely within Canada; however, Citizenship and Immigration Canada (CIC) must be notified of any change in address.

In some cases, a TRP may be issued to an applicant who has been found inadmissible. However, the TRP may be issued to an inadmissible applicant only where the grounds of inadmissibility are technical or medical, or where they concern the applicant's criminal history. In addition, the officer must find compelling reasons to issue the TRP, while weighing the risks to Canada or Canadians (this is discussed further in Chapter 4.)

Another example of a situation where a person may be issued a TRP is if there are sufficient humanitarian and compassionate grounds, such as the admission of a child to undergo life-saving surgery. Although the child would normally be found inadmissible for medical reasons, an exception may be made if the surgery is not available in the child's country of citizenship and if the medical bills are paid through charitable donations.

No Right of Appeal

There is no right to appeal the refusal of an application for either a permanent or temporary resident visa to the Immigration and Refugee Board. The applicant may seek leave for a judicial review at the Federal Court. If an applicant who was refused admission believes that the refusal was discriminatory and without bona fide justification, the applicant may file a complaint under the *Canadian Human Rights Act* (see Chapter 11).

Grounds of Inadmissibility

The IRPA sets out eight grounds of inadmissibility, the first five of which are the most serious reasons for being denied entry to or being removed from Canada (that is, ss. 34 to 37). For these grounds, an officer must have **reasonable grounds** to believe that an applicant is inadmissible (that is, security risk, human or international rights violations, serious criminality, criminality, and organized criminality.) "Reasonable grounds" is a lower standard of proof than the civil standard, which is the **balance of probabilities**.

Border Watch Line

In 2011, the government created a publicly accessible "wanted by the CBSA" list, which consists of the names and photographs of people who CBSA has reasonable grounds to believe are security risks; have committed or were complicit in war crimes, crimes against humanity, or genocide; have committed or are complicit in serious criminality or organized crimes; or who are wanted for removal. To view the "Border Watch Line" go to the CBSA website at http://www.cbsa-asfc.gc.ca/wc-cg/menu-eng.html.

The eight grounds of inadmissibility are generally considered below.

1. Security Risk (Section 34)

A permanent resident or foreign national may be found inadmissible on security grounds for several reasons, according to s. 34(1) of the IRPA, as follows:

- espionage or subversion against a democratic government, institution, or process;
- subversion by force of any government;
- terrorism;
- being a danger to the security of Canada; or
- violence that would or might endanger the lives or safety of persons in Canada.

The terms "espionage," "subversion," "democratic," and "terrorism" are not defined in the IRPA or its regulations. However, CIC's *Enforcement (ENF)* operations manual provides the following definitions:[1]

- *Espionage* is the practice of spying. It is the gathering of information in a surreptitious manner and involves secretly seeking out information, usually from a hostile country, to benefit one's own country.
- *Subversion* is the practice of overturning or overthrowing; it seeks to accomplish change by illicit means or for improper purposes related to an organization. Subversion need not be by force.

- *Democratic* describes government by the people, especially where the people hold the supreme political power.
- *Terrorism* is defined as activities directed toward or in support of the threat or use of acts of violence against persons or property for the purposes of achieving a political objective; an act intended to cause death or serious bodily injury to a civilian, or to any other person not taking an active part in hostilities in a situation of armed conflict, when the purpose of such act, by its nature or context, is to intimidate a population or to compel a government or an international organization to do or to abstain from doing any act.

Membership in a Group That Engages in Espionage, Subversion, or Terrorism

A person may be found inadmissible for her own activities or for belonging to an organization that engages in espionage, subversion, or terrorism. There are three types of decisions that may be used by officers as evidence of "a conclusive finding of fact" that a person is a member of such an organization. These decisions are listed in s. 14 of the *Immigration and Refugee Protection Regulations* (IRP Regulations), as follows:

- an Immigration and Refugee Board (IRB) determination that a foreign national or permanent resident has engaged in terrorism;
- an IRB determination that a person is a person referred to in section F of article 1 of the Convention Relating to the Status of Refugees (Refugee Convention)—that is, a person excluded from refugee protection for committing crimes against peace, war crimes, or a crime against humanity; or
- a court decision under the *Criminal Code* concerning the commission of a terrorism offence.

In deciding whether a terrorism offence has been committed, the courts look to the *Criminal Code*'s definition of **terrorist group** in s. 83.01, which reads in part:

> (a) an entity that has as one of its purposes or activities facilitating or carrying out any terrorist activity …
> and includes an association of such entities.

Reliance on the decisions of the IRB and the courts saves the time and expense of rehearing the issue of membership.

Identifying Security Threats

Officers rely on security screening checks as important tools for identifying known security threats. The many documents that an applicant must provide when applying for permanent or temporary residence offer important information about the applicant's identity, relationships, financial history, work and school activities, and background.

Officers may also consult police and intelligence reports and records of criminal convictions and previous dealings with Canadian immigration if these resources are available. When the identity of a person cannot be confirmed in Canada, fingerprints and photographs are taken and are used not only to identify the person but also to conduct background checks with international authorities. In cases where a security certificate has been issued against a person, this fact alone is considered conclusive proof that a person is inadmissible.

Terrorist List

Under the *Anti-terrorism Act*, the minister of Public Safety and Emergency Preparedness (PSEP) can create a list of entities that

- have knowingly carried out, attempted to carry out, participated in, or facilitated a terrorist activity; or
- knowingly acted on behalf of, at the direction of, or in association with an entity that has knowingly carried out, attempted to carry out, participated in, or facilitated a terrorist activity.

An entity is placed on the list on the recommendation of the minister of public safety to the governor in council. The current list of terrorist entities can be found on the department website at http://www.publicsafety.gc.ca/prg/ns/le/index-eng.aspx.

Exemptions

In rare cases, a person who is found to have engaged in one or more of the activities listed in s. 34(1) may nevertheless be able to satisfy the minister that being in Canada would not be detrimental to the national interest. This decision is at the discretion of the minister and may not be delegated.

Inadmissible on Security Grounds: The Case of Ernst Zundel

The infamous case of Ernst Zundel, a Holocaust denier, is a real-life Canadian case about a person who was found inadmissible on security grounds and removed from Canada. A German national, Zundel first came to Canada in 1958 when he was 19 years old. He lived here until 2000 never having obtained Canadian citizenship as his application was refused. During the 1980s, Zundel became well known as a Holocaust denier and disseminator of Nazi material. His company, Samisdat Publishers, produced the pamphlet "Did Six Million Really Die?" and the book *The Hitler We Loved and Why*, which led to criminal charges.

In the late 1990s, Zundel faced a complaint before the Canadian Human Rights Commission for spreading hatred against Jews on his website, but left Canada for the United States in 2000 before the hearing was completed. Zundel returned to Canada in 2003 when he was deported from the United States for overstaying. Around the same time, Germany issued a warrant for his arrest on hate charges.

On May 1, 2003, the solicitor general of Canada and the minister of citizenship and immigration signed a security certificate stating that Mr. Zundel was a danger to the security of Canada. Zundel was alleged to be inadmissible on the security grounds of "engaging in acts of terrorism, being a danger to the security of Canada, engaging in acts of violence that would or might endanger the lives or safety of persons in Canada or being a member of a group that there are reasonable grounds to believe has or will engage in acts of espionage, subversion or terrorism."[2]

Zundel was detained. As required when a security certificate is issued, the matter went before the Federal Court for approval. On February 24, 2005, Justice Blais of the Federal Court of Canada found the security certificate to be reasonable and stated in his decision:

> Mr. Zundel has associated, supported and directed members of the Movement who in one fashion or another have sought to propagate violent messages of hate and have advocated the destruction of governments and multicultural societies. Mr. Zundel's activities are not only a threat to Canada's national security but also a threat to the international community of nations. Mr. Zundel can channel the energy of members of the White Supremacist Movement from around the world, providing funding to them, bringing them together and providing them advice and direction."[3]

The security certificate issued against Zundel was conclusive proof that Zundel was inadmissible and the removal order against him could be enforced. He had no appeal rights because of the serious grounds of inadmissibility. Zundel was deported to Germany, where upon his arrival he was arrested and charged with 14 counts of inciting racial hatred. In February 2007, Zundel was sentenced to a five-year term in prison. He was released on March 1, 2010.

2. Human or International Rights Violations (Section 35)

Permanent residents and foreign nationals who have committed violations of human or international rights outside Canada are inadmissible. Specifically, s. 35 of the IRPA lists the following prohibited activities and conditions:

- committing an offence referred to in ss. 4 to 7 of the *Crimes Against Humanity and War Crimes Act*, while outside Canada;
- being a **prescribed senior official** in the service of a government that, in the opinion of the minister, engages in or has engaged in terrorism, systematic or gross human rights violations, genocide, a war crime, or a crime against humanity within the meaning of ss. 6(3) to (5) of the *Crimes Against Humanity and War Crimes Act*; or
- being a person, other than a permanent resident, whose entry or stay in Canada is restricted pursuant to a decision, resolution, or measure of an international organization of states, of which Canada is a member, that imposes sanctions on a country against which Canada has imposed or has agreed to impose sanctions in concert with that organization or association.

The terms "crimes against humanity," "genocide," and "war crime" are defined in the *Crimes Against Humanity and War Crimes Act* at s. 4(3):

- **Crimes against humanity** include murder, extermination, enslavement, deportation, imprisonment, torture, sexual violence, persecution, or any other inhumane act or omission that is committed against any civilian population or any identifiable group and that, at the time and in the place of its commission, constitutes a crime against humanity according to customary international law or conventional international law or by virtue of its being criminal according to the general principles of law recognized by the community of nations, whether or not it constitutes a contravention of the law in force at the time and in the place of its commission.

- **Genocide** means an act or omission committed with intent to destroy, in whole or in part, an identifiable group of persons, as such, that, at the time and in the place of its commission, constitutes genocide according to customary international law or conventional international law or by virtue of its being criminal according to the general principles of law recognized by the community of nations, whether or not it constitutes a contravention of the law in force at the time and in the place of its commission.

- **War crime** means an act or omission committed during an armed conflict that, at the time and in the place of its commission, constitutes a war crime according to customary international law or conventional international law applicable to armed conflicts, whether or not it constitutes a contravention of the law in force at the time and in the place of its commission.

Prescribed senior officials are referenced in s. 35(1)(b) as members of governments that the minister of PSEP has authority to designate as perpetrators of terrorism, systematic or gross human rights violations, genocide, war crimes, or crimes against humanity. The minister may add and remove countries from the list, so it changes from time to time.[4] Consider the following examples of designated governments:

- the Bosnian Serb regime between March 27, 1992 and October 10, 1996;
- the Siad Barré regime in Somalia between 1969 and 1991;
- the former military governments in Haiti between 1971 and 1986, and between 1991 and 1994 except the period from August to December 1993;
- the former Marxist regimes of Afghanistan between 1978 and 1992;
- the governments of Ahmed Hassan al-Bakr and Saddam Hussein in power since 1968;
- the government of Rwanda under President Habyarimana between October 1990 and April 1994, as well as the interim government in power between April 1994 and July 1994;
- the governments of the Federal Republic of Yugoslavia and the Republic of Serbia (Milosevic) between February 28, 1998 and October 7, 2000;
- the Taliban regime in Afghanistan from September 27, 1996 to December 22, 2001; and
- the Government of Ethiopia under Mengistu Haile Mariam from September 12, 1974 to May 21, 1991.

War Crimes Program

Canada became a signatory to the Rome Statute of the International Criminal Court on December 18, 1998 and established the War Crimes Program in 1998 to address crimes against humanity and war crimes committed during the Second World War. The program now includes more recent cases that stem from conflicts in the former Yugoslavia, Rwanda, or Iraq and that involve not only war crimes but also crimes against humanity or genocide.

The objective of the program is to deny safe haven in Canada to persons involved in war crimes, crimes against humanity, or genocide. The CBSA, CIC, the Department of Justice, and the RCMP are partners in the program, and they work together to deny visas or entry to Canada, develop policy, investigate crimes, prosecute war criminals in Canada, and assess cases.

A finding of inadmissibility under s 35 of the IRPA has far-reaching implications for an individual:

- A refugee claimant may be excluded from protection and/or have his claim suspended for an admissibility hearing;
- A Canadian citizen may have her citizenship revoked by the government under the *Citizenship Act* for obtaining her Canadian citizenship through misrepresentation, fraud, or for knowingly concealing material circumstances; or
- A fugitive may be transferred to another state under the *Extradition Act*, when the Canadian government responds to a request from a foreign state or tribunal.

Identifying Rights Violators

There are four types of decisions that may be used by officers as evidence of "a conclusive finding of fact" that a person has committed human or international rights violations. These decisions are listed in s. 15 of the IRP Regulations, as follows:

- a UN-established international tribunal decision;
- an IRB determination that a foreign national or permanent resident has committed a war crime or a crime against humanity;
- an IRB determination that a foreign national or permanent resident is a person referred to in section F of article 1 of the Refugee Convention—that is, a person excluded from refugee protection for committing crimes against peace, war crimes, or a crime against humanity; or
- a court decision under the *Criminal Code* or the *Crimes Against Humanity and War Crimes Act*.

As with the determination of security risks, reliance on the decisions of these bodies saves the time and expense of rehearing the issue. A security certificate issued against a person can also be used as conclusive proof that a person is inadmissible for violating human or international rights.

Exemptions

As with security threats, in rare cases a person who is found to have engaged in one or more of the activities listed in s. 35 may nevertheless be able to satisfy the minister of PSEP that being in Canada would not be detrimental to the national interest. This decision is at the discretion of the minister and may not be delegated.

3. Serious Criminality (Section 36(1)), Criminality (Section 36(2)), and Organized Criminality (Section 37)

Sections 36(1), (2), and (3), and 37 all deal with criminality. **Criminality** refers to domestic crime, as opposed to crimes against humanity or war crimes as proscribed by international law.

When a person is convicted of an offence outside Canada, it is necessary to compare the elements of Canadian law with those of the foreign jurisdiction to determine whether the person is inadmissible. The particular law under which the person was convicted in the foreign country is not relevant. Rather, what matters is the Canadian offence that matches the criminal act committed. The officer must establish that the foreign offence contains the essential elements of the offence in Canada to show that it is equivalent to the foreign offence. The officer can compare foreign law and foreign court documents and examine the person at the admissibility hearing.

The intent of CIC's policy is "first and foremost to deny entry into Canada and thereby prevent Canadian territory being used as a safe haven by persons who are subject to a criminal proceeding in a foreign jurisdiction; or are fleeing from such proceedings."[5]

Criminal charges that are dropped, or result in a not-guilty verdict, will not cause inadmissibility. However, if a person has been charged with a crime and the trial is still under way, the person may be inadmissible pending the results of the trial.

There are three categories of criminality: serious criminality (s. 36(1)), criminality (s. 36(2)), and organized criminality (s. 37). These are described below.

Serious Criminality (Section 36(1))

Serious criminality is a ground of inadmissibility for both foreign nationals and permanent residents. Generally, the offence must be punishable by a maximum of ten years' imprisonment to qualify. However, this depends on whether the offence was committed in or outside Canada and, if outside Canada, whether the person was convicted. These three subcategories of serious criminality are described below:

- *Convicted in Canada:* The person was convicted in Canada of an offence punishable by a maximum term of imprisonment of at least ten years, or of an offence for which a term of imprisonment of more than six months was imposed.
- *Convicted outside Canada:* The person was convicted of an offence that, if committed in Canada, would constitute an offence punishable by a maximum term of imprisonment of at least ten years.

- *Committed an act outside Canada*: The person committed an act that is an offence in the place where it was committed and that, if committed in Canada, would constitute an offence punishable by a maximum term of imprisonment of at least ten years.

If a permanent resident or foreign national is convicted of a serious crime while living in or visiting Canada, the minister alleges inadmissibility. Ordinarily, an officer receives information of the conviction from the court.

EXEMPTIONS

A person found inadmissible by reason of serious criminality may be exempted and permitted to enter or remain in Canada if pardoned or acquitted for the offence committed. With respect to such offences committed outside Canada, the person is exempt if rehabilitated.

These exemptions apply in the same way for the grounds of criminality and organized criminality. These exemptions are outlined in detail in the sections below.

Criminality (Section 36(2))

Whereas grounds of serious criminality apply to both foreign nationals and permanent residents, grounds of criminality apply only to foreign nationals. Permanent residents cannot be found inadmissible on the basis of this lesser threshold of criminality.

There are four subcategories of criminality under s. 36(2), but before describing these subcategories, it is necessary to understand the terminology of Canada's *Criminal Code*. The Code distinguishes among three kinds of offences, as follows:

- **Summary conviction offences:** Less serious offences such as speeding, with a maximum sentence of six months and prosecuted using streamlined procedures in a provincial court.
- **Indictable offences:** More serious offences such as murder, with longer periods of imprisonment and more complex prosecution procedures.
- **Hybrid or dual procedure offences:** Offences for which the Crown prosecutor chooses to proceed either by summary conviction or by indictment, in light of the circumstances of the alleged offence. An example is impaired driving.

For immigration purposes, a hybrid or dual procedure offence is "deemed to be an indictable offence, even if it has been prosecuted summarily" (IRPA, s. 36(3)(a)). The four subcategories of criminality are as follows:

- *Convicted in Canada*: The person was convicted in Canada of an offence punishable by way of indictment, or of two summary conviction offences not arising out of a single occurrence.
- *Convicted outside Canada*: The person was convicted outside Canada of an offence that, if committed in Canada, would constitute an indictable offence, or of two summary conviction offences not arising out of a single occurrence that, if committed in Canada, would constitute offences.

- *Committed an act outside Canada:* The person committed an act outside Canada that is an offence in the place where it was committed and that, if committed in Canada, would constitute an indictable offence.

- *Committed an act on entering Canada:* The person committed, on entering Canada, a summary conviction offence prescribed by regulations.

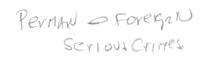

EXEMPTIONS

The IRPA provides a few exemptions to inadmissibility on the ground of criminality, and Canada will admit persons who have been pardoned or acquitted, or, if otherwise inadmissible because of offences committed outside Canada, are either deemed to be rehabilitated or have satisfied the minister that they are rehabilitated. Each of these exemptions is considered below:

1. **Pardon**: A pardon may be granted under the *Criminal Code*, resulting in the offence being deemed not to have occurred. A person who is pardoned from the offence at issue is exempt from inadmissibility. A foreign pardon must be equivalent to a pardon in Canada. This applies regardless of whether the offences occurred in or outside Canada.

2. **Acquittal**: An acquittal, or finding of not guilty, also exempts a person from inadmissibility. This applies regardless of whether the offences occurred in or outside Canada.

3. **Deemed rehabilitated**: A person whose conviction occurred outside Canada may be deemed rehabilitated, thereby removing the ground of criminal inadmissibility, if the following criteria under s. 18(2) of the IRP Regulations are met:

   a. at least ten years have elapsed since the completion of the sentence imposed (such as probation, prison term, fines, or restitution);

   b. the conviction is not considered serious in Canada;

   c. the conviction did not involve any serious property damage, physical harm to any person, or any type of weapon; and

   d. the offence committed would be punishable in Canada by a maximum term of imprisonment of less than ten years.

   Even if ten years have passed, the person seeking entry to Canada must disclose the conviction and should provide evidence that no further offence has occurred.

4. **Individual rehabilitation**: Unlike the deeming provision described above, to be considered for individual rehabilitation, one must apply. To be eligible, a person must show that at least five years have passed since the completion of the sentence imposed (such as prison term, suspended sentence, fines, or probation), and that the conviction equates to a hybrid or indictable offence in Canada. Applications must be submitted to a Canadian visa office, where the visa officer considers all relevant factors to approve or refuse the application.

Consider the following case scenarios regarding exemptions to inadmissibility on the ground of criminality under s. 36(2).

- Sovann, a Cambodian national, is interested in applying for a student permit to complete a two-year culinary program offered at the University of British Columbia. Sovann is concerned that he may be inadmissible on the ground of criminality. In 1989, Sovann was convicted in the United States of "driving while impaired." Sovann did not serve any time in prison and he has no other convictions. In the United States, this may be prosecuted as a misdemeanour offence, often under a state motor vehicle law or municipal law. However, in Canada, impaired driving is a criminal offence under the *Criminal Code* and is listed as a hybrid offence.

  Sovann may be deemed rehabilitated when more than ten years have elapsed since the payment of his fine in 1989. He must, because his offence is equivalent to a hybrid offence under Canadian law, apply at the Canadian visa office for individual rehabilitation at the time he submits his visa application. If his application is accepted, Sovann will be allowed to enter Canada, provided that he complies with the eligibility criteria for a student permit.

- Juanita, a Colombian national, would like to apply for a temporary resident visa to attend her sister's wedding in Canada. Juanita is concerned that she may be criminally inadmissible to Canada. Juanita was convicted of shoplifting in April 2001 and was sentenced to one year's probation and required to attend counselling. She has no other convictions. The elements of Juanita's offence in her home country are equivalent to an offence (informally known as "theft under") in the *Criminal Code*. It is a hybrid offence that could be prosecuted either summarily or by indictment.

  Unfortunately for Juanita, she is inadmissible to Canada because hybrid offences are deemed indictable for immigration purposes. However, under s. 36(3)(c), Juanita is eligible to apply for rehabilitation after April 2007, which is five years after the completion of the imposed sentence. Because probation is considered part of a sentence or a conviction, Juanita must count five years from the end of the probation period, which was April 2002.

- Kelly and Alicia are friends from Trinidad and Tobago. They both want to apply for temporary resident visas to Canada. Each of them is concerned that she may be criminally inadmissible to Canada. Kelly was convicted of a crime on June 18, 2003, and received a jail sentence of three months. Alicia was convicted of driving under the influence on April 3, 2003 and had her driver's licence taken away from her for three years.

  Kelly may apply for rehabilitation five years after the end of the sentence imposed. If Kelly's three-month jail sentence ended September 18, 2003, Kelly was eligible to apply for rehabilitation on September 18, 2008, as long as no other terms were imposed on her sentence.

  Alicia's sentence ended on April 3, 2006. Because five years must elapse from the end date of the suspension or the date her driver's licence is reinstated, Alicia was eligible to apply for rehabilitation on April 3, 2011.

Those not eligible for deemed rehabilitation or individual rehabilitation, because neither five nor ten years have elapsed since the completion of the sentence, may apply at a visa office for a TRP. A TRP will be issued only in compelling circumstances, as described later in this chapter.

An applicant may request that an officer review the details of his case and assess inadmissibility on the ground of criminality. The applicant must fill out an application for rehabilitation and check off the box "for information only." There is no fee for this type of application, although the processing usually takes several months.

Organized Criminality (Section 37)

Both permanent residents and foreign nationals may be found inadmissible for being members of an organized crime group under s. 37 of the IRPA.

Specifically, this section applies when the permanent resident or foreign national

- is a member of an organization that is believed on reasonable grounds to be or to have been engaged in activity that is part of a pattern of criminal activity planned and organized by a number of persons acting in concert in furtherance of the commission of an indictable offence or in furtherance of the commission of an offence outside Canada that, if committed in Canada, would constitute an indictable offence, or engaging in activity that is part of such a pattern; or
- is, in the context of transnational crime, engaged in activities such as people smuggling, trafficking in persons, or money laundering.

There must be proof of membership and of a pattern of criminal activity that is planned and organized by persons acting in concert to find a person inadmissible under this ground.

According to the *Enforcement (ENF)* manual, officers typically wait for the courts to decide the organized criminality charges before considering inadmissibility.[6] However, in cases where local authorities are not pursuing formal charges, officers may investigate and report the person as inadmissible if organized criminal activity is uncovered.

Foreign nationals who have received a sentence of two years or more in Canada for committing a serious crime are denied access to the refugee determination system.

On June 28, 2012, Bill C-31, *An Act to Amend the Immigration and Refugee Protection Act, the Balanced Refugee Reform Act, the Marine Transportation Security Act and the Department of Citizenship and Immigration Act* (short title, *Protecting Canada's Immigration System Act*) received royal assent. Amendments to the IRPA restrict access to the refugee determination system for foreign nationals who committed serious crimes in or outside Canada (IRPA, s. 101(2)(a) and (b)).

EXEMPTIONS

A refugee claimant whose only involvement with a criminal organization was to facilitate travel to Canada to make the refugee claim is exempt from inadmissibility. It would be unfair to return a person at risk whose only involvement with crime was necessary for survival, and such a person would not pose a risk of further criminality in Canada.

Any person found inadmissible on the ground of organized criminality may also be exempt from inadmissibility if the minister is satisfied that the person's presence in Canada would not be detrimental to the national interest.

Human Smuggling and Trafficking

Human Smuggling

Those who are engaged in human smuggling do so for a material gain by facilitating the illegal entry of foreign nationals. Human smuggling is criminal when it is carried out for the purpose of profit rather than for saving lives. It is particularly challenging for the government to discern whether the person being smuggled is an economic migrant duped by unscrupulous agents into paying large sums of money to gain entry to Canada, or whether he is a legitimate refugee who could not otherwise travel on a commercial carrier with false documents.

A foreign national or permanent resident charged with human smuggling must have knowingly organized, induced, aided, or abetted the entry into Canada of another person who does not have the right to enter because that person is not in possession of a visa or passport. Human smuggling is a criminal offence with penalties dependent on the number of people who are smuggled into Canada. For smuggling fewer than ten persons, a smuggler may be convicted by summary offence and fined up to $100,000 or to a term of imprisonment of not more than two years, or to both; or may be convicted of an indictable offence with a fine of up to $500,000 or to a term of imprisonment of not more than 10 years, or to both for a first offence. It is an indictable offence to smuggle ten or more persons and a smuggler can be fined up to $1,000,000 or to life imprisonment, or to both (IRPA, s. 117).

Human Trafficking

Human trafficking involves the exploitation of people, although victims are not necessarily foreign nationals because trafficking has been known to occur entirely within our borders. Section 118 of IRPA provides that the human traffickers must have knowingly "organized" (defined as recruiting, transporting, receiving, or harbouring) the entry into Canada of another person or persons; and done so by means of abduction, fraud, deception or use or threat of force or coercion.

With respect to either adults or children, it is an indictable offence under the *Criminal Code* to recruit, transport, transfer, receive, hold, conceal, or harbour a person, or exercise control, direction, or influence over a person's movements for the purpose of exploiting or facilitating the exploitation of that person (s. 279.01). Exploitation means (Dept. of Justice, 2011):

- causing a person to provide labour or a service (for example, sexual services, any kind of work including drug trafficking and begging) by engaging in conduct that could reasonably be expected to cause the victim to believe that their safety, or the safety of someone known to them, would be threatened if they did not provide that labour or service; or
- causing a person to have an organ or tissue removed, by means of deception or the use or threat of force or of any other form of coercion.

The IRPA sets out the aggravating factors that the court must consider in decid-ing penalties for human trafficking, including the treatment of the victim and whether the victim was harmed or killed during the trafficking operation; whether the operation was for the benefit or in association with a criminal organization; and the amount of profit realized (IRPA, s. 120).

Inadmissible on Grounds of Organized Criminality: The Case of the Domotor Family

Consider the case of the Domotor family in what is called Canada's largest proven human trafficking case.

In April 2012, Ferenc Domotor Sr., considered to be the kingpin of the organiz-ation, was sentenced to nine years in prison after pleading guilty to charges of human trafficking, fraud, conspiracy, and organized crime before the Ontario Su-perior Court of Justice. The human trafficking ring comprised his wife, Gyongi Kolompar, and 21-year-old son, Ferenc Domotor Jr., who each received sentences ranging from time served to five years; Attila Kolompar, who plead guilty to two counts of conspiring to traffic humans and defrauding Hamilton's welfare system; and other extended family members (who were still at large at the time of writing.) The Domotor family recruited as many as 19 victims from Hungary, who were brought to Canada against their will, had their passports taken away, held in base-ments, and forced to work in construction jobs with little or no pay. The victims were counselled to claim refugee status and apply for social assistance.

The Domotors came to Canada from Hungary in 1998 and claimed refugee status; by 2000 they were permanent residents. As a result of their sentences, they will become inadmissible and, consequently, face deportation.

CBC News, "Hamilton Human Trafficking Kingpin Sentenced to 9 Years," April 3, 2012, http://www.cbc.ca/news/canada/story/2012/04/03/hamilton-human-trafficking.html; and Global News, "Leader of Largest Human Trafficking Ring in Canadian History Sentenced to 9 Years," April 3, 2012, http://www.globalnews.ca/leader+of+largest+human+trafficking+ring +in+canadian+history+sentenced+to+9+years/6442614008/story.html.

4. Health Grounds (Section 38)

Only foreign nationals may be inadmissible for reasons of health. Permanent resi-dents already accepted and living in Canada cannot later be found inadmissible if they develop a medical condition. Once permanent resident status is granted, health concerns arising later will not result in inadmissibility. Generally, applicants for tem-porary residence must undergo a medical examination if applying to stay in Canada for six months or longer or if there is an occupational basis (for example, health field workers, teachers, caregivers).

A foreign national who applies for temporary or permanent residence and who suffers from a health condition may be inadmissible according to s. 38(1) of the IRPA if the health condition

- is likely to be a danger to public health, such as a communicable disease;
- is likely to be a danger to public safety, such as a mental condition that causes unpredictable or violent behaviour; or

- might reasonably be expected to cause excessive demand on health or social services, such as a condition that requires ongoing expensive medical treatment.

  "Excessive demand" is defined in the regulations and generally means that the anticipated costs for health or social services would likely exceed the average Canadian per capita costs over a period of five years for such services; or that the foreign national would likely add to the waiting lists for such services and as such would likely create a delay for Canadians and permanent residents and could increase the rate of mortality or morbidity.

The first two conditions are not limited to a person's physical condition, but also extend to a psychological incapacity that may create a danger to the health or safety of persons living in Canada.

Sexually transmitted viruses and diseases, such as human immunodeficiency virus (HIV) and syphilis, pose a danger to public health or safety only if there is evidence that the person engages in high-risk behaviour, such as sharing contaminated needles or engaging in unprotected sex, and the person is refusing to cooperate with public health authorities. This is in contrast to a disease such as tuberculosis: if it is active (and contagious), it is generally grounds for inadmissibility, mainly because it can be transmitted easily through coughing or sneezing. A person with inactive tuberculosis cannot transmit the disease and may be admitted into Canada, provided that regular medical follow-ups are undertaken to ensure that the disease continues to be inactive.

Persons who are HIV-positive may pass the first two health considerations only to be refused on the third consideration of excessive demand on health or social services. The current guidelines for assessing HIV cases state that any applicant receiving antiretroviral therapy (ARV) is inadmissible because of excessive demand.

Medical Examination

As part of the application process, permanent residence applicants and their dependants (whether they are coming to Canada or not) must undergo a medical examination at their own expense. Temporary residence applicants may also be required to do this, depending on factors such as country of origin, length of stay, and type of activity in Canada.

Additionally, a temporary residence applicant who normally would be exempt from the medical examination may be required to submit to one if an officer suspects illness or a medical condition that could render the applicant medically inadmissible. A suspicion may be raised if the applicant appears to be sick, or if questioning by the officer reveals that the applicant was recently discharged from the hospital or is taking medication for a serious illness. The medical examination may be conducted as part of a port-of-entry examination—for example, when a temporary resident is seeking admission.

The medical examination must include the following:

- a physical and mental examination;
- a review of past medical history, laboratory tests, and diagnostic tests; and
- a medical assessment of records.

Those applicants who pass their medical examinations are issued a medical certificate that is usually valid for 12 months.

Only a panel physician (formerly known as designated medical practitioner), a physician designated by CIC, is authorized to carry out a medical assessment. The panel physician considers the following factors:

- the nature, severity, and probable duration of any health impairment from which the person is suffering;
- the danger of contagion;
- any unpredictable or unusual behaviour that may create a danger to public safety; and
- the supply of social or health services that the person may require in Canada and whether the use of such services will deprive Canadian nationals of these services (for example, the risk of a sudden incapacity).

A person may overcome inadmissibility and be admissible as a temporary resident if she is seeking medical treatment, provided that the medical treatment will not create excessive demand on health services.

The panel physician prepares a medical profile based on the test results and gives an opinion about whether the person is admissible, inadmissible, or requires **medical surveillance**. A designation of medical surveillance does not bar a person from admission; rather, it provides for monitoring. For example, an applicant's inactive tuberculosis must be checked periodically to ensure that it does not become active and contagious.

The panel physician's report is provided to the visa officer, who, in accordance with s. 20 of the IRP Regulations, must follow the medical opinion. The visa officer notifies the applicant if there is a finding of inadmissibility to give the applicant the opportunity to reply and provide further documentation, within a reasonable period of time, before rendering a final decision.

Exemptions

In some circumstances, foreign nationals who intend to stay in Canada for six months or longer are exempt from the requirement to submit to a medical examination if they are one of the following:

- a person entering Canada with the purpose of carrying out official duties, unless they seek to engage or continue in secondary employment in Canada;
- a family member of an accredited foreign representative under s. 186(b) of the IRP Regulations, unless that family member seeks to engage or continue in employment in Canada;
- a member of the armed forces of a country that is a designated state for the purposes of the *Visiting Forces Act* who is entering or is in Canada to carry out official duties, other than a person who has been designated as a civilian component of those armed forces, unless that member seeks to engage or continue in secondary employment in Canada;

- a family member of a protected person, if the family member is not included in the protected person's application to remain in Canada as a permanent resident; or

- a non-accompanying family member of a foreign national who has applied for refugee protection outside Canada.

Although Family-class spouses; common-law partners; or children of sponsors, Convention refugees, and protected persons must undergo medical examinations for health and public safety reasons, they cannot be found inadmissible on the basis of excessive demand on health or social services. Also, persons who are likely to be refused on the basis of excessive demand may avoid inadmissibility by having a satisfactory financial arrangement to cover the cost of the treatment and related expenses. For example, a person seeking to enter Canada for medical treatment would normally be inadmissible unless the visa officer was satisfied that the person could pay all associated costs for the medical treatment, including travel and accommodation.

5. Financial Reasons (Section 39)

A foreign national who applies for temporary or permanent residence must satisfy the visa officer of his ability to both be self-sufficient and support any dependants in Canada, physically and legally, pursuant to s. 39 of the IRPA.

At the time of processing an application abroad, the visa officer assesses the person's financial resources as well as any arrangements in place, such as job offers, and the person's potential employability. Upon the applicant's arrival in Canada, an officer verifies that the person has sufficient funds to cover the temporary stay, that adequate arrangements for care and support (not involving social assistance) are in place, or, in the case of an applicant seeking to establish permanent residence, that the person has employment or that his funds are sufficient for six months.

Exemption

Convention refugees and protected persons who apply for permanent residence in Canada are exempted by the IRPA from inadmissibility as a result of financial grounds.

6. Misrepresentation (Section 40)

According to s. 16 of the IRPA, applicants are required to answer truthfully all questions and produce all relevant documents at the examination. Failure to do so could result in inadmissibility.

There are four situations of misrepresentation described in s. 40, but before we examine them it is worthwhile to consider the definitions of the following terms as stated in the *Enforcement (ENF)* operations manual:

- **Misrepresentation** (also referred to as false pretences): "Misstating facts to obtain money, goods, benefits or some other thing desired by a person who might otherwise not be entitled to it."

- **Withholding**: [T]o hold back from doing or taking an action; to keep (within); to refrain from granting, giving, allowing or 'letting it be known.' A person can misrepresent themselves by being silent just as easily as a person who actively states a 'mistruth.' A person who refuses or declines to answer a question, preferring instead to allow outdated or false information to be accepted as current or true information, is engaging in the activity of misrepresentation."

Keeping those definitions in mind, consider the four situations of misrepresentation, as follows:

1. A permanent resident or foreign national is inadmissible on the ground of misrepresentation for directly or indirectly misrepresenting or withholding material facts relating to a relevant matter that induces or could induce an error in the administration of the IRPA.

   For example, a person who provides false identity documents to conceal her identity or to falsify a relationship would be found inadmissible on this ground. Persons found inadmissible while outside Canada may be banned for two years. Persons found inadmissible while in Canada may be banned from the date that the removal order is enforced, in accordance with s. 40(2)(a) of the IRPA.

   Under s. 22 of the IRP Regulations, refugee claimants are exempted from inadmissibility on this ground if the disposition of the claim is pending, as are protected persons.

2. A permanent resident or foreign national is inadmissible on the ground of misrepresentation for being or having been sponsored by a person who is found to be inadmissible for misrepresentation.

   The consequence is a two-year ban. Also, according to s. 64(3) of the IRPA, the sponsor loses the right to appeal unless the sponsored person is the sponsor's spouse, common-law partner, or child.

3. A permanent resident or foreign national is inadmissible on the ground of misrepresentation on a final determination to **vacate** a decision to allow the claim for refugee protection by the permanent resident or the foreign national.

   This refers to a refugee claimant who commits a misrepresentation in order to acquire Canada's protection. The Refugee Protection Division (RPD) has the authority to vacate a refugee determination under s. 109(1) of the IRPA if it finds that the decision was obtained as a result of directly or indirectly misrepresenting or withholding material facts relating to a relevant matter. The consequence of such a finding is that the refugee claim is deemed rejected and the decision conferring refugee protection is vacated, or nullified, according to s. 109(3).

   Currently, the **notice of decision** by the Refugee Protection Division of the IRB (RPD) to vacate the claim is sufficient evidence of such a determination.

4. A permanent resident or foreign national is inadmissible on the grounds of misrepresentation on ceasing to be a citizen under s. 10(1)(a) of the *Citizenship Act*, in the circumstances set out in s. 10(2) of that Act.

If a person loses Canadian citizenship because of misrepresentation, the officer obtains a letter confirming that the person has ceased to be a citizen from CIC, which has the responsibility for processing citizenship applications and maintaining citizenship records.

As with all other grounds of inadmissibility, a finding of misrepresentation may be made by visa officers to deny visas to applicants abroad, by port-of-entry officers to deny entry into Canada, as well as by officers in Canada to remove a person already admitted.

Consider the following case scenarios.

- A vehicle with four individuals arrives at a Canadian port of entry and the driver is asked whether all the occupants in the car are Canadian citizens. The driver replies, "yes." One of the passengers is a foreign national and remains silent.

  In this scenario the driver misrepresented the foreign national, and the foreign national withheld material facts by remaining silent. Both are grounds for inadmissibility.

- An individual appears at a Canadian port of entry to claim refugee status. The individual is using someone else's passport, but advises the officer that he used this passport for the purposes of leaving his country because his life was in danger.

  Normally, an individual who is using a false identity would be inadmissible to Canada on the basis of misrepresentation. However, the IRPA exempts persons who have claimed refugee protection if a determination of their claim is pending. This is an important exemption because without some degree of subterfuge, refugees may not be able to escape from the countries they are fleeing.

- A representative for a temporary residence applicant provides false information regarding the applicant's educational credentials. The applicant is truly unaware that the representative submitted false documentation until the officer brings this anomaly to the applicant's attention.

  Misrepresentation is extended to those who may not be aware of a misrepresentation or whose actions or lack of actions were unintentional but resulted in misrepresentation. In the present case, the applicant is responsible for ensuring that the application is truthful and the supporting documents are genuine. The applicant could therefore be inadmissible for misrepresentation for submitting false documents even though he was not the one who fabricated the evidence.

Exemptions

Under s. 22 of the IRP Regulations, the misrepresentation provisions do not apply to protected persons and persons who have claimed refugee protection, provided that a disposition regarding their claim is pending. Additionally, under s. 176 of the

IRP Regulations and s. 21 of the IRPA, misrepresentation provisions do not apply to those abroad who are family members of protected persons.

7.   Failure to Comply with the IRPA (Section 41)

The ground of "non-compliance with the IRPA" is a catch-all covering contraventions of immigration law and regulations that are not captured by other grounds of inadmissibility. This section provides for the refusal of admission, and it is especially useful for enforcement of conditions or obligations that may be imposed on temporary and permanent residents. A non-compliance allegation is not a stand-alone allegation—it must be coupled with a specific requirement found elsewhere in the IRPA or the IRP Regulations with which the person has failed to comply.

Examples of failure to comply include the failure to do the following:[8]

- appear for an examination;
- appear for an admissibility hearing;
- obtain the written authorization of an officer to return to Canada (required by s. 52(1) of the IRPA for a person who has been excluded);
- hold the relevant temporary or permanent visa under s. 20 of the IRPA (for example, a visitor or student who engages in employment without a work visa);
- leave Canada by the end of the period authorized for their stay as required by s. 29(2) of the IRPA (for example, a person who overstays her authorized visit); or
- abide by s. 29(2) of the IRPA to comply with any condition set out in s. 184 of the IRP Regulations (for example, members of a crew such as those on a ship who must leave Canada within 72 hours after they cease to be a member of the crew).

The most common reason for inadmissibility is arriving at a port of entry without a valid visa as required by s. 11 of the IRPA and ss. 6 and 7 of the IRP Regulations.

8.   Inadmissible Family Member (Section 42)

A person may be inadmissible as a result of the inadmissibility of family members. Under s. 42, a foreign national, other than a protected person, is inadmissible on the ground of an inadmissible family member if

- the accompanying family member or, in prescribed circumstances, the non-accompanying family member, is inadmissible; or
- the foreign national is an accompanying family member of an inadmissible person.

A visa officer assesses the foreign national's application, including information provided about dependants, such as background and medical records, to determine whether they are inadmissible. According to s. 23 of the IRP Regulations, a foreign national thus may be inadmissible because of the inadmissibility of a dependant, even if the dependant is not accompanying the foreign national to Canada. The policy reason for this provision is forward looking: a non-accompanying dependant today could be tomorrow's sponsored applicant.

Assessing Inadmissibility

The minister of Citizenship and Immigration Canada is responsible for most policies related to admissibility. Visa officers who work abroad assess an applicant's admissibility. The minister of PSEP is responsible for policy regarding inadmissibility on the grounds of security, organized criminality, and violation of human or international rights. The Canada Border Services Agency (CBSA)—an agency of Public Safety Canada, formerly the Department of Public Safety and Emergency Preparedness—investigates foreign nationals and permanent residents for immigration violations, and has the authority to arrest, detain, and remove those who do not have a right to enter or stay in Canada.

Several immigration agencies may be involved in identifying inadmissible foreign nationals, depending on the place and circumstances. For example, CBSA works with the Royal Canadian Mounted Police (RCMP), local police authorities, and other agencies in carrying out investigations and removals. Consider the four different processes for determining inadmissibility:

1. A CIC visa officer may refuse to issue a visa to a person who makes an application for permanent or temporary entry while outside Canada, barring the person from coming to Canada.

2. At a port of entry, a CBSA officer may refuse entry and issue a removal order to any of the following:
   - a person who is a returning permanent resident with a permanent resident card;
   - a new permanent resident with a confirmation of permanent resident visa;
   - a foreign national with or without a temporary resident visa; or
   - a refugee claimant.

3. A CBSA officer may find that a permanent or temporary resident who is already in Canada becomes inadmissible after admission to Canada, and issues a removal order or writes an "admissibility report" to be reviewed by the minister. The minister may issue a removal order or refer the case to the Immigration Division of the Immigration and Refugee Board.

4. The Immigration Division may hold an **inadmissibility hearing** for cases referred to it by the minister (usually of PSEP), at which time a permanent or temporary resident may be found inadmissible, and a removal order issued. Additionally, the Immigration Appeal Division hears immigration appeals, including those against certain decisions on admissibility.

These processes are discussed fully in Chapters 10 and 11.

KEY TERMS

acquittal, 75

balance of probabilities, 67

crimes against humanity, 71

criminality, 73

deemed rehabilitated, 75

eligible, 62

foreign national, 61

genocide, 71

hybrid or dual procedure offences, 74

inadmissibility, 60

inadmissibility hearing, 86

inadmissible, 62

indictable offences, 74

individual rehabilitation, 75

medical surveillance, 81

misrepresentation, 82

notice of decision, 83

panel physician, 63

pardon, 75

prescribed senior official, 70

reasonable grounds, 67

summary conviction offences, 74

temporary resident permit (TRP), 66

temporary resident visa (TRV), 61

terrorist group, 68

vacate, 83

war crime, 71

withholding, 83

REVIEW QUESTIONS

1. List and briefly describe the eight grounds of inadmissibility under the IRPA.

2. Provide an example of an action or condition that would render a person inadmissible under s. 34(1) of the IRPA.

3. What are the differences between s. 34(1) and s. 35(1) of the IRPA? Give examples.

4. Is failing to comply with the IRPA a ground for inadmissibility? Where is this section found in the Act?

5. In what situation is a person an inadmissible family member under the IRPA? Which section of the Act deals with this issue?

NOTES

1. Citizenship and Immigration Canada, "ENF 1: Inadmissibility," in *Enforcement (ENF)*, August 8, 2008, s. 3, at 6-8, http://www.cic.gc.ca/english/resources/manuals/enf/enf01-eng.pdf.

2. *Zundel v. Canada*, 2004 FCA 145, [2004] 3 F.C.R. 638.

3. *Zundel, Re*, 2005 FC 295, at para. 112.

4. Citizenship and Immigration Canada, "ENF 2: Evaluating Inadmissibility," in *Enforcement (ENF)*, s. 6.4, April 12, 2012, http://www.cic.gc.ca/english/resources/manuals/enf/enf02-eng.pdf.

5. Ibid., at s. 3.5.

6. Ibid., at s. 4.2.

7. Ibid., at s. 9.2.

8. These examples are taken from CIC's *Enforcement (ENF)* operations manual, supra note 1, at 28.

REFERENCES

Canada. Bill C-11, *An Act to Amend the Immigration and Refugee Protection Act and the Federal Courts Act* (short title: *Balanced Refugee Reform Act*), 40th Parl., 3rd sess., 59 Eliz. II, 2010, assented to June 29, 2010. http://www.parl.gc.ca/HousePublications/Publication.aspx?Language=E&Mode=1&DocId=4644728&File=14.

Canada. Bill C-31, *An Act to Amend the Immigration and Refugee Protection Act, the Balanced Refugee Reform Act, the Marine Transportation Security Act and the Department of Citizenship and Immigration Act* (short title: *Protecting Canada's Immigration System Act*), 41st Parl., 1st sess., 60-61 Eliz. II, 2011–2012, assented to June 28, 2012. http://www.parl.gc.ca/HousePublications/Publication.aspx?Docid=5697417&file=4.

Canada Border Services Agency, Citizenship and Immigration Canada, Department of Justice, and Royal Canadian Mounted Police. *Canada's Program on Crimes Against Humanity and War Crimes: 12th Report, 2008–2011*. http://www.cbsa-asfc.gc.ca/security-securite/wc-cg/wc-cg2011-eng.html.

CBC News. "Hamilton Human Trafficking Kingpin Sentenced to 9 Years," April 3, 2012. http://www.cbc.ca/news/canada/story/2012/04/03/hamilton-human-trafficking.html.

Citizenship Act. R.S.C. 1985, c. C-29.

Criminal Code. R.S.C. 1985, c. C-46.

Department of Justice. "Information Sheet for Law Enforcement," August 3, 2012. http://www.justice.gc.ca/eng/fs-sv/tp/is-fr.html.

Global News. "Leader of Largest Human Trafficking Ring in Canadian History Sentenced to 9 Years," April 3, 2012. http://www.globalnews.ca/leader+of+largest+human+trafficking+ring+in+canadian+history+sentenced+to+9+years/6442614008/story.html.

Immigration and Refugee Protection Regulations. S.O.R./2002-227.

Indian Act. R.S.C. 1985, c. I-5.

Visiting Forces Act. R.S.C. 1985, c. V-2.

PART II

Immigration Programs

Chart of Temporary Resident Classes

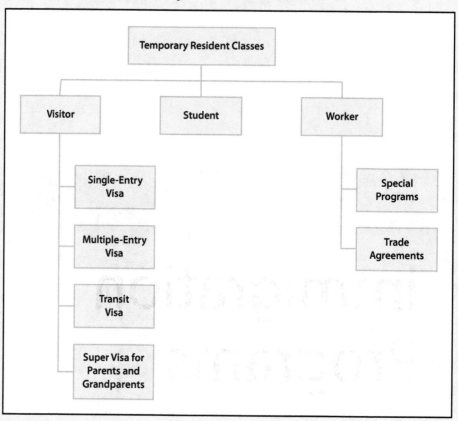

Temporary Entry

4

LEARNING OUTCOMES

After reading this chapter you should be able to:

- Differentiate among the classes of temporary residents: visitors, students, and workers.

- Describe the general provisions for applying for a temporary resident visa.

- Understand the general obligations of temporary residents.

- Describe how temporary residents can lose their status.

- Describe the general requirements and application processes for the visitor class, student class, and worker class.

- Explain the rights and obligations of Canadian employers in relation to temporary resident employees.

- Have a general understanding of the international agreements that apply to the temporary entry of business workers.

- Describe the Live-In Caregiver Program, including the responsibilities of Canadian employers under the program.

- Understand the difference between a temporary resident visa and a temporary resident permit.

- Explain the criteria for obtaining a temporary resident permit.

Introduction

We usually think about immigration to Canada as a permanent change that a person makes to seek opportunities and a better standard of living, escape poverty or violence, or reunite with family. However, another important type of immigration exists: temporary immigration. Canada's temporary immigration program allows thousands of people each year to visit, study, or work in Canada while providing benefits to our economy.

Temporary residents are foreign nationals who are permitted to enter and remain in Canada for a specified period of time. Temporary residents must leave Canada by the end of the period authorized for their stay. They may re-enter Canada only if their authorization provides for re-entry.

There is no definition of "temporary immigration," "temporary residence," or "temporary resident" in the *Immigration and Refugee Protection Act* (IRPA). The IRPA instead stipulates that all foreign nationals must apply for and obtain a visa before appearing at a port of entry (s. 11). Temporary residence is a prescribed category of residency in the IRP regulations (Part 9) in which there are three classes:

- visitors,
- students, and
- workers.

Temporary resident permit (TRP) holders are a separate class of residence and will be discussed at the end of this chapter.

A clear distinction is made among each class on the basis of the activity that the foreign national intends to undertake while in Canada temporarily, such as visiting, studying, or working.

According to the *Annual Report to Parliament on Immigration 2011*, temporary immigration is permitted to contribute to "Canada's economic development by filling gaps in the labour market, enhancing trade, purchasing goods and services, and increasing cultural and people-to-people links."[1] In 2010, Citizen and Immigration Canada (CIC) processed applications (new and extensions) from over one million people seeking temporary resident visas as tourists and business visitors to Canada, and issued **visitor visas**, permits, and extensions to 920,412 persons; admitted 182,276 temporary foreign workers, who filled skill gaps in the domestic labour market; and permitted entry to 96,000 foreign students.[2]

What would happen if people stopped coming to Canada? Consider the economic impact of the 2003 outbreak of SARS (severe acute respiratory syndrome), which not only kept tourists away but also kept international students and business workers at home. Temporary resident programs are vital to Canada's prosperity. At the same time, Canada's immigration policy recognizes that it is important to balance the need to attract foreign nationals and process applications efficiently with the need to protect Canadians by denying access to those who pose a criminal or security threat and those who abuse our system by not leaving at the end of their permitted stay. These goals are reflected in the following immigration objectives in s. 3(1) of the IRPA:

(g) to facilitate the entry of visitors, students and temporary workers for purposes such as trade, commerce, tourism, international understanding and cultural, educational and scientific activities;

(h) to protect the health and safety of Canadians and to maintain the security of Canadian society; [and]

(i) to promote international justice and security by fostering respect for human rights and by denying access to Canadian territory to persons who are criminals or security risks.

This chapter considers the general requirements for all temporary residents and distinguishes some of the specific requirements for each of the categories of temporary residence. It discusses the overriding restrictions that deny temporary access to Canada, such as admissibility criteria. Also discussed are the obligations and conditions that must be fulfilled by temporary residents after admission to Canada. The government creates special programs for students and workers. In addition, there are agreements between the federal and provincial/territorial governments that also permit the creation of special programs for workers; although a sample and general discussion of special programs is provided, please note, that they are too numerous to identify and discuss fully in this text.

The Importance of Keeping Informed

You should monitor information sources such as the Citizenship and Immigration Canada website for up-to-date information about temporary resident programs and the related application processes: the IRP Regulations contain the details about temporary residents—including the classes (such as students and visitors), related eligibility criteria, and exemptions—which are subject to frequent change. Moreover, the minister's operational bulletins are updated frequently and provide important information about processing applications.

Generally, a foreign national who wishes to reside temporarily in Canada must submit to an application and approval process and obtain a temporary resident visa before coming to Canada. However, foreign nationals from "visa-exempt" countries are excluded from this requirement, as are those with special status (see "Exemptions" below).

Temporary Resident Visas

Generally, foreign nationals may not enter Canada to remain on a temporary basis without first obtaining a temporary resident visa (TRV), unless they are exempt from visa requirements, according to s. 7 of the *Immigration and Refugee Protection Regulations* (IRP Regulations). A TRV is an official document issued, or a stamped impression made on a document, by an officer from a Canadian visa office or a regional processing centre such as a Canadian consulate, embassy, or high commission outside Canada that processes immigration applications. Note that not all consulates or embassies process immigration applications and some also have different processing procedures.

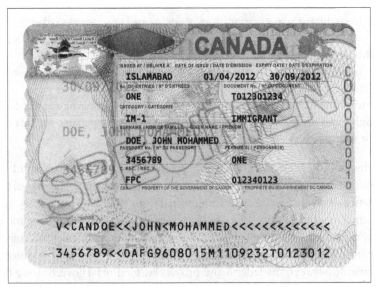

Source: *Temporary Residence Visa.* Reproduced with the permission of the Minister of Public Works and Government Services Canada, 2012.

The TRV is placed in the applicant's passport to identify the holder as a person who may become a temporary resident upon admission to Canada.

A TRV is not to be confused with a temporary resident permit (TRP), which is issued by an officer only in special cases, and is discussed at the end of this chapter.

For most foreign nationals, obtaining a TRV involves a formal, written application procedure. For those who are exempt, an oral application at the port of entry is sufficient. In both situations, an applicant has a duty to tell the truth as required pursuant to s. 16 of the IRPA and to produce any relevant evidence, including photographs and fingerprints. A TRV is issued only when the officer is satisfied that the applicant meets the requirements of the IRPA and its regulations, specifically s. 22 of the IRPA and s. 179 of the IRP Regulations, which require that the applicant has

Application accepted

- fulfilled certain obligations;
- met the criteria for the particular class of temporary resident that he has applied under; and
- shown that he is not inadmissible.

Applications for a TRV may be refused for any of the following reasons:

Application refused

- the applicant does not meet the eligibility criteria for the particular class of temporary resident;
- the applicant (or any family member) is inadmissible on the grounds of security risk, human or international rights violations, criminality, organized criminality, health risk, financial reasons, misrepresentation, or non-compliance with the IRPA, or because of an inadmissible family member (see Chapter 3, Inadmissibility); or
- the officer is not satisfied that the applicant will leave by the end of his stay.

TRV Exemptions

Although the general rule is that all foreign nationals who seek temporary residence require a TRV before arriving at a port of entry, the regulations grant exceptions to this rule. Some persons may be exempt on the basis of nationality, possession of certain documents, or purpose of the entry:

- *Nationality.* Citizens of numerous countries, including Australia, France, and Britain or citizens of a British overseas territory do not require a temporary resident visa to enter Canada. Nor do nationals of the United States or permanent residents of the United States. Section 190(1) of the IRP Regulations provides a full list of nationality exemptions.

- *Documents.* Foreign nationals do not require a TRV to enter Canada if they hold particular documents, which include a diplomat's passport, a passport or travel document issued by the Holy See, a national Israeli passport, or certain Hong Kong passports. Section 190(2) of the IRP Regulations provides a full list of exemptions based on the applicant's documents.

Current IRP Regulations Online

The list of countries may change at any time, so it is important to consult the most current version of the IRP Regulations or the CIC website at http://www.cic.gc.ca/english/visit/visas.asp. For quick reference, the CIC website provides a list of countries and territories whose citizens require visas in order to enter Canada as visitors. This detail in the regulations allows the minister to quickly add or remove countries (by way of an order in council) in response to changing trends. For example, in 1997, the Canadian government imposed visa requirements on the Czech Republic in response to a trend of a rising number of Romany people from that country who travelled to Canada as visitors, then overstayed to make refugee claims, the majority of which were refused. To stem the flow of citizens from the Czech Republic, visa requirements were imposed. Ten years later, however, in October 2007 Canada lifted the visa imposition for Czech nationals wanting to visit Canada for fewer than 90 days. This was in response to pressure from the European Commission to lift requirements on eight, then new, European Union member nations, including the Czech Republic. Similarly, a more recent example occurred when, in July 2009, the minister imposed a visa restriction for citizens of Mexico because of an increase in refugee claims from that country.

- *Purpose of entry.* Foreign nationals may be exempted from the TRV requirement if they are members of a transportation crew, are airplane passengers landing in Canada for refuelling, or have come to Canada for an interview with a US consular officer regarding re-admission to the United States. Section 190(3) of the IRP Regulations provides a full list of exemptions based on the applicant's purpose of entry.

TRV Conditions

Temporary residents must comply with any conditions imposed under s. 183 of the IRP Regulations. There are general conditions that are automatically imposed on all TRVs that are issued, such as the requirement:

- to leave by the end of the authorized period of stay; and
- not to study or work without the appropriate permit.

A temporary resident's passport or travel document will be stamped at the port of entry to record the date by which she must leave Canada. Other terms and conditions may be noted depending on the class of temporary resident.

The officer at the port of entry authorizes the foreign national's entry as a temporary resident and will remind her of these conditions. If the officer has any doubts about the temporary resident's intention to live up to the general terms and conditions of admission, a security deposit may be imposed (see Chapter 10).

General TRV Application Requirements

According to s. 179 of the IRP Regulations, there are basic criteria that must generally be met for all classes of TRVs: all visitors, workers, and students seeking a TRV. A TRV may be issued only if an examination establishes that the foreign national

- has used the application documents that the IRPA requires for the particular temporary resident class;
- has applied to the appropriate office in accordance with the requirements of the IRPA;
- will leave Canada by the end of the period authorized for staying in Canada;
- has paid the required processing fees;
- holds a passport or similar document that may be used to enter the country that issued it, or another country;
- meets the medical examination requirements contained in s. 30 of the IRP Regulations;
- meets the requirements applicable to the temporary resident class; and
- is not inadmissible.

Each of these criteria is considered in more detail below.

Application Documents

A foreign national is deemed to have applied for a TRV as a member of the visitor, worker, or student class by submitting a number of forms and documents that support the application. The following list is an example of what might be required:

- a completed application form (for example, IMM 5257 for visitors, IMM 1294 for students, or IMM 1295 for workers);

- a statutory declaration of common-law union form (IMM 5409), if applicable;
- a cost-recovery processing fee receipt (form IMM 5401), which indicates that the cost-recovery processing fee has been paid to an approved financial institution;
- a valid passport or travel/identity document, unless the foreign national is exempt from passport and travel document requirements under s. 52(1) of the IRP Regulations;
- recent passport-size photos for each family member (the name of the person should be written on the back of each photo);
- proof of custody and/or a letter of consent from the custodial parent where a child under 16 years of age is either travelling alone, without proper identification, or with adults other than a sole custodial parent or guardian; and
- proof of current immigration status if the foreign national is not a citizen of the country in which she is applying (more information in this area is provided in the following section).

Applicants may also be required to provide other documents to convince the officer that they intend to return to their country of residence at the end of the period authorized for their temporary stay, such as a letter from an employer indicating that the applicant is expected to return.

Finally, there are also specific documents required for each type of TRV, as discussed later in this chapter.

Place of Application

Applicants *outside* Canada seeking a TRV as a student or worker are required to submit their application to the visa office that is responsible for serving one of the following jurisdictions:

- a country in which the applicant was lawfully admitted; or
- the applicant's country of nationality (or if the applicant is stateless, her country of habitual residence).

However, applicants already *in* Canada who are seeking authorization to study or work, or a renewal, are required to submit their application to a case processing centre, such as CPC-V in Vegreville, Alberta; a Centralized Intake Office; or, electronically, through the CIC website (check the CIC website for current information because the place of application may change depending on the department's operational requirements).

The following list provides further clarification of the persons who are eligible to apply for a TRV or to vary or cancel the conditions imposed on entry to Canada:

- foreign nationals and their family members holding valid work or study permits;
- foreign nationals and their family members holding temporary resident permits valid for a minimum of six months;

- refugee claimants subject to an unenforceable removal order;
- protected persons who are the subject of humanitarian and compassionate considerations, spouses or common-law partners in Canada, and live-in caregivers who have been determined eligible for permanent resident status;
- persons whose study permits were authorized by a visa office abroad, where the permit was not issued at a port of entry; or
- family members of athletes on a Canadian-based team, media representatives, members of the clergy, or military personnel assigned to Canada (IRP Regulations, s. 215).

Consider the following scenario:

> Rose, a Colombian national, is currently working in Arizona as a live-in caregiver for the British ambassador to the United States. Rose is 32 years old, speaks fluent English, and obtained a university degree in Colombia. After completing her education in Colombia, Rose moved to Arizona in order to care for the ambassador's three children. She has now worked for the ambassador for five years.
>
> The ambassador is soon moving back to London, but has told Rose that the new Canadian ambassador would like to employ Rose in Ottawa. Rose has worked problem-free for the ambassador in Arizona although she was never authorized to work in the United States and she did not enter the United States legally. Rose would like to apply for a work permit in Los Angeles under the Live-In Caregiver Program.

Unfortunately for Rose, she may not apply within the United States because s. 11(2) of the IRP Regulations prohibits her from doing so. Rose was not lawfully admitted to the United States at any time; therefore, she has no right to apply in Los Angeles. Rose must submit her application in her country of nationality, Colombia.

On the other hand, a business person from India spending a day or two in France may apply for a Canadian TRV in Paris, as long as he was lawfully admitted to France; or a Pakistani student studying in Singapore may apply for a TRV and a study permit at the visa office there.

Section 11(2) is applicable only to persons who are physically present in the country in which they were lawfully admitted. For example, s. 11(2) will not permit a Peruvian national who is physically in Peru to make a TRV application by mail to the Canadian visa office in New York City.

Consider another scenario:

> Maria is a dual citizen of Mexico and Argentina. Maria is currently living in the United Kingdom; she entered the United Kingdom legally but then lost her immigration status because she failed to extend her work permit. Maria would like to apply for a TRV to Canada, but she is unsure where she can submit her application.

Maria is entitled to submit her application to the Canadian visa office in either Mexico or Argentina, where she will be required to attend an interview, because

Maria is a citizen of both countries. Alternatively, Maria may submit her application to the Canadian visa office in London, because she was lawfully admitted to the United Kingdom. The fact that she lost her immigration status afterward does not exclude her from submitting her application to the visa office in London.

Intention to Leave Canada

A foreign national must satisfy an officer that he will leave Canada at the end of the period authorized for the temporary stay, according to s. 20(1)(b) of the IRPA. An officer relies on certain factors to determine whether an applicant intends to remain in Canada illegally, claim refugee status, or otherwise seek to remain in Canada, and thus not abide by the requirement to leave Canada at the end of the period authorized for his temporary stay:

1. whether the applicant has family or economic ties to the country of residence;

2. whether the applicant has the financial capability to be self-sufficient while in Canada;

3. the applicant's immigration status in the country of residence;

4. the economic and political situation of the applicant's country of residence; and

5. any other obligations or responsibilities that the applicant may have in the country of residence.

These factors are considered in more detail below; however, it is important to keep in mind that a foreign national who has a **dual intent** of becoming a permanent resident is not necessarily precluded from becoming a temporary resident. Provided that the visa officer is satisfied that the foreign national has the capacity and willingness to leave Canada by the end of the period authorized for his stay, a TRV may not be denied simply because the foreign national intends to apply for permanent status, according to s. 22 of the IRPA. For example, a person who has already submitted an application for permanent residence as a provincial nominee (described in Chapter 5) may wish to visit Canada for the purpose of an "exploratory visit" while awaiting the processing of that application.

The foreign national must satisfy both the officer abroad and the officer at the port of entry that he has the ability and willingness to leave Canada at the end of the temporary period authorized. Therefore, the fact that a foreign national has been issued a visa does not in itself grant admission to Canada. Under s. 180 of the IRP Regulations, the foreign national must not only meet the requirements for issuance of the visa at the time it is issued, but also continue to meet these requirements at the time of the examination on entry into Canada.

1. FAMILY AND ECONOMIC TIES

The officer examines whether the applicant has any family living in the country of residence, and whether the family will be accompanying the applicant to Canada. If the applicant does not have family in the country of residence or if the family lives outside the country of residence, the applicant will be deemed to not have family ties in the country of residence. This may lead the officer to believe that the applicant is less likely to be motivated to return there.

The officer also examines the applicant's employment status and financial stability in his country of residence. The officer determines whether the applicant is employed and, if so, the amount of the salary. Has the applicant's employer approved a request for leave, and is the employer expecting the applicant to return to the job? This would suggest a genuine intention to return. The officer also considers whether the applicant owns any property in the country of residence and, if so, the value of the property. Significant holdings, particularly a family home, suggest an intention to return to the country of residence.

2. FINANCIAL SELF-SUFFICIENCY

The applicant must prove that there are sufficient funds to cover living expenses for the applicant and any dependants while they are in Canada, and that there will be funds remaining to pay for the return trip home at the end of the temporary stay. The amount of money that an applicant needs varies according to the circumstances of the visit, such as how long the applicant will stay and whether the applicant will stay in a hotel or with friends or relatives. The following is a list of supporting documents that could be included as evidence of an applicant's financial resources:

- bank statements or deposit books that show accumulated savings, for both applicant and spouse;
- letters of employment, providing the name of the employer, the applicant's position/occupation, the date that the employment commenced, and annual earnings, for both applicant and spouse; and
- evidence of assets in the country of residence, such as deeds and car ownership, for both applicant and spouse.

In the event that the applicant lacks the means of self-support, but a host or family member in Canada is willing to provide adequate support for the applicant while in Canada, the officer examines the ability of the host or family member to do so. In such cases the following documents and evidence may be enclosed in support of the application:

- a letter of invitation from the host or family member in Canada, including a description of the financial assistance offered, such as accommodation, transportation costs, and medical costs;
- to prove the host or family member's income, either her last two Canada Revenue Agency Notice of Assessments, or a letter from her employer indicating her position, date employment commenced, and annual earnings; and
- evidence of the size of the host's or family member's family in Canada to ensure that sufficient income, known as the minimum necessary income, is available to support all dependants. The minimum necessary income is determined by reference to an annual Statistics Canada measure called the low income cut-off (LICO).

Letter of Invitation

A letter of invitation from the Canadian citizen or permanent resident host is helpful to the person applying for temporary residence. It may be a notarized letter setting out important information about the host such as her name, date of birth, contact information, status in Canada, occupation, and the number of persons residing in the host's household, and a promise to support the temporary resident during his stay. The letter must also include similar information about the person being invited, including his name and contact information, his relationship to the host, the expected length of the visit, and arrangements for accommodation while in Canada.

3. IMMIGRATION STATUS

The officer examines the applicant's immigration status in the country of residence. Section 11(2) of the IRP Regulations gives TRV applicants great flexibility to apply to come to Canada from any country as long as they were lawfully admitted and they remain physically present in that country during the processing of their applications.

Note, however, that there are situations where applicants are able to rely successfully on s. 11(2), but their applications are less likely to succeed because they lack credibility on the basis that the applicants will leave Canada at the end of the period authorized for their stay. Consider a citizen of the Bahamas who enters the United States legally but then overstays the period authorized for his temporary stay. Section 11(2) permits this Bahamian applicant to apply for a Canadian TRV at a visa office in the United States, because he was lawfully admitted to the United States—even though he is no longer entitled to be there. However, the fact that he overstayed his visa in the United States may undermine his efforts to convince the officer that he will not do the same if he is granted a Canadian TRV.

4. ECONOMIC AND POLITICAL CONDITIONS

The officer examines the economic and political situation in the applicant's country of residence. This is necessary because even if ties to the home country are strong, unstable economic or political conditions may cause a change of mind about returning home.

5. OTHER OBLIGATIONS AND RESPONSIBILITIES

The officer may consider any other obligations or responsibilities that the applicant has in the country of residence if they are clearly disclosed during the examination. This may include personal responsibilities, such as caring for an aged parent, or business obligations to partners or employees. It is important to remember that the onus to provide sufficient evidence to support the applicant's case rests on the applicant. Failure to provide supporting documentation may result in the application for a TRV being refused.

Processing Fees

Applicants for TRVs and permits are required to pay processing fees. Processing fees vary for a single-entry TRV, multiple-entry TRV, transit visa, study permit, and work permit. There is no fee for a TRV if a work or study permit is issued at the same time.

The easiest way to find the current processing fees for each type of and permit, can be found in the "Fee Schedule for Citizenship and Immigration Services" on the CIC website at: http://www.cic.gc.ca/english/information/fees/fees.asp.

Processing fees are non-refundable even if the application is refused; the fee is for the costs of processing the application, not for the decision. However, in certain circumstances, applicants for a TRV may be exempt from paying the processing fee.

The following visitor class applicants are exempt from paying the processing fee:

- foreign nationals applying for transit visas;
- persons who are issued courtesy visas as long as the person is listed in s. 296(2) of the IPR Regulations;
- diplomats, who are always fee-exempt, whether the purpose of the visit is official or not;
- members of the armed forces who comply with the *Visiting Forces Act*;
- members of the clergy and religious groups; and
- competitors such as coaches, judges, team officials, medical staff, or members of a national or international sports organizing body participating in the Pan-American Games, or as a performer participating in a festival associated with any of those Games.[3]

The following student class applicants are exempt from paying the processing fee:

- foreign nationals who have been determined to be Convention refugees or members of a designated class prior to their arrival in Canada, and their family members;
- foreign nationals in Canada whose claim to be Convention refugees has been deemed admissible but has not yet been decided by the Refugee Protection Division, and their family members;
- diplomats accredited to Canada or another country, consular officers, representatives or officials of a foreign country, and their family members (for example, a dependent son of an accredited diplomat posted in Morocco who intends to study in Canada);
- students seeking renewal of their study permits who have become temporarily destitute through circumstances totally beyond their control or the control of any person on whom they are dependent for financial resources; and
- foreign nationals who are in Canada or who are coming into Canada under an agreement between Canada and a foreign country or an arrangement entered into with a foreign country by the government of Canada that provides for reciprocal educational opportunities (for example, participants in the Canada–US Fulbright Program).[4]

Passport and Travel Documents

The details of what documents are acceptable and what documents are unacceptable are set out in s. 52 of the IRP Regulations. Foreign nationals seeking to become temporary residents must hold a passport or travel document that is valid for the period authorized for their stay. Such documents, including certain passports, travel documents, identity documents, and *laissez-passers* (travel permits from the United Nations), are listed in s. 52(1) of the IRP Regulations.

There is also a list of individuals exempt from this requirement, provided in s. 52(2):

(a) citizens of the United States; ...

(c) residents of Greenland seeking to enter Canada from Greenland;

(d) persons seeking to enter Canada from St. Pierre and Miquelon who are citizens of France and residents of St. Pierre and Miquelon;

(e) members of the armed forces of a country that is a designated state for the purposes of the *Visiting Forces Act* who are seeking entry in order to carry out official duties, other than persons who have been designated as a civilian component of those armed forces;

(f) persons who are seeking to enter Canada as, or in order to become, members of a crew of a means of air transportation and who hold an airline flight crew licence or crew member certificate issued in accordance with International Civil Aviation Organization specifications;

(g) persons seeking to enter Canada as members of a crew who hold a seafarer's identity document issued under International Labour Organization conventions and are members of the crew of the vessel that carries them to Canada.

The validity of a TRV does not outlast the validity of a passport. Therefore, if the applicant's passport will soon expire, it should be renewed before the applicant applies for a TRV.

Medical Examinations

Medical examinations are required for applicants who will work in occupations where the protection of public health is essential. Regardless of the intended period of stay in Canada, a foreign national who is seeking to work in Canada in an occupation that is related to health services, or that requires close contact with other persons, must undergo a medical examination.

Such persons include schoolteachers, domestic workers, day nursery employees, clinical laboratory workers, medical students admitted to Canada to attend university, and physicians on short-term locums, because they may involve close contact with people for more than three hours per day and/or a risk of exchange of body fluids. Additionally, agricultural workers from designated countries and territories[5] are required to undergo a medical examination.

A medical examination is also generally required in the following situations, regardless of any public health concerns:

- the foreign national is seeking entry into Canada, or applying for a renewal of a work or study permit or authorization to remain in Canada, as a temporary resident for a period in excess of six consecutive months, including an actual or proposed period of absence from Canada of less than 14 days; or

- the foreign national resided or sojourned for six or more consecutive months in a designated country or territory during the one year immediately preceding the date of seeking entry to Canada.

Medical examinations must be performed by designated panel physicians. Furthermore, medical exams should be done at least two months before the expiry of the temporary resident's work or study permit, to avoid processing delays.

In certain circumstances, a foreign national seeking to stay in Canada for six months or longer may be exempt from the medical examination requirement. Section 30(2) of the IRP Regulations lists the following exempt persons:

- a person entering Canada with the purpose of carrying out official duties, unless that person seeks to engage or continue in secondary employment in Canada;
- a family member of an accredited foreign representative, as listed in s. 186(b) of the IRP Regulations, unless that family member seeks to engage or continue employment in Canada;
- a member of the armed forces of a country that is a designated state for the purposes of the *Visiting Forces Act* who is entering or is in Canada to carry out official duties, other than a person who has been designated as a civilian component of those armed forces, unless that member seeks to engage or continue in secondary employment in Canada;
- a family member of a protected person, if the family member is not included in the protected person's application to remain in Canada as a permanent resident; or
- a non-accompanying family member of a foreign national who has applied for refugee protection outside Canada.

Examination at Port of Entry

As noted in chapter 3, even when a TRV is obtained, it is not a guarantee of admission to Canada. All people seeking to come to Canada, including temporary residents, must be examined by an officer according to s. 18 of the IRPA. Therefore, when the applicant arrives at a Canadian port of entry seeking admission, an officer from the Canada Border Services Agency (CBSA) makes the decision whether or not to allow it. A change of circumstances between the time of acquiring a TRV and the time of arrival in Canada, or additional information available, could result in the applicant being refused entry. In other words, a TRV allows a person to travel to a Canadian port of entry in order to visit, work, or study in Canada, but does not in itself grant admission to Canada to carry out those activities.

No Right of Appeal

There is no right to appeal the refusal of an application for a TRV, study permit, or work permit to the Immigration and Refugee Board. The applicant may seek leave for a judicial review at the Federal Court. If an applicant who was refused admission believes that the refusal was discriminatory and without bona fide justification, the applicant may file a complaint under the *Canadian Human Rights Act*.

Status Change or Extension of a Temporary Resident Visa

Once entry has been granted, a temporary resident may not change status without permission. Doing so would be a violation of the IRPA, causing inadmissibility, and could result in removal. For example, under ss. 186 and 187 of the IRP Regulations, a temporary resident holding a TRV issued under the visitor class, is not allowed to work in Canada without a work permit; and under ss. 188 and 189, a temporary resident generally may not study without a study permit. Similarly, a temporary worker may not change jobs, and some international students may not change their approved type of educational institution without first applying to have the conditions amended.

A foreign national who wishes to change the type of visa or to change a condition must first apply to CIC, while still in status at least 30 days before the visa expires. There is an online application option available. The following are examples of the type of documentation that must be submitted (note that processing procedures change, so it is prudent to verify this on the department's website):

- a completed application to change conditions, extend the stay, or remain in Canada form (IMM 1249) for applicants in Canada who wish to change their type of visa, or to change the conditions imposed upon entry;
- a statutory declaration of common-law union form (IMM 5409), if applicable;
- a use of a representative form (IMM 5476), if applicable;
- a document checklist form (IMM 5558); and
- a cost-recovery processing fee receipt form (IMM 5401), which indicates that the cost-recovery processing fee of $75 has been paid to an approved financial institution.

Processing may take 30 days or more in some cases.
The applicant should also provide the following:

- an explanation of why he wishes to stay in Canada longer;
- proof of identity;
- proof of current status in Canada (a valid and current visa);
- evidence of how he will support himself and any dependants in Canada; and
- a purchased ticket or funds set aside to prove an intention to leave Canada, and any other details including date and type of transportation.

Under s. 183(5) of the IRP Regulations, as long as the temporary resident applies to renew his status before it expires, status is retained until a decision is rendered on the application. If the applicant has a study or work visa and applies to extend the visa before it expires, he has the right to continue to study or work under the same conditions while in Canada.

Loss and Restoration of Temporary Resident Status

A temporary resident may lose temporary resident status under s. 47 of the IRPA. This can happen where a temporary resident becomes inadmissible, such as by overstaying the authorized period of stay. If found to be inadmissible, the temporary resident loses that status and may be removed from Canada. The enforcement process is discussed in Chapter 10.

When a visitor, worker, or student loses status or the status expires as a temporary resident and the foreign national has not left Canada, an application may be made to have it reinstated or restored within 90 days after temporary resident status is lost. If the 90 days have passed, the person must leave Canada.

A restoration of status may be granted only in cases where the temporary resident continues to comply with the initial requirements for the stay in Canada after failing to comply with one or more of the subsequent requirements by

- remaining in Canada longer than the period authorized for her stay, but no longer than 90 days;
- changing the type of studies, educational institution, location of studies, or times and periods of studies, without applying to change these conditions on her study permit, if they were specified on her study permit as conditions; or
- changing employers, type of work, or location of work, without applying to change the conditions, if they were specified on her work permit.

Therefore, a temporary resident whose temporary resident status has expired is not eligible to apply for an extension but may apply for restoration of status, provided that the 90-day period has not passed. There is no guarantee that the application for restoration of status will be approved, because every application is assessed on its own merits. Therefore, the submissions should include an explanation for the failure to comply with the requirements of the TRV, and as much supporting evidence as possible.

Additionally, a foreign national may not apply for restoration of status if the loss of status resulted from non-compliance with conditions for which a six-month ban may be imposed. Section 200(3)(e)(i) of the IRP Regulations provides that

> (3) [a]n officer shall not issue a work permit to a foreign worker if …
> (e) the foreign national has engaged in unauthorized study or work in Canada or has failed to comply with a condition of a previous permit or authorization unless
> (i) a period of six months has elapsed since the cessation of the unauthorized work or study or failure to comply with a condition.

Consider the following scenario:

Robert is working in Canada with a work permit and he is seeking an extension. Robert's work permit expired three weeks ago but he has continued to work in Canada. Robert did not intend to violate any conditions imposed on his work permit, but he thought that he would be receiving a reminder from CIC regarding the renewal.

To which case processing centre (CPC) should Robert send his application? What will Robert's status be if the CPC contacts Robert's employer and discovers that he was working after the work permit expired?

According to the Act, Robert may not be issued a new work permit unless a period of six months has elapsed from the date of the violation.

Furthermore, under s. 306 of the IRP Regulations, a completed application and the appropriate restoration fee (a $200 fee as of July 2012) must be submitted. The restoration fee is in addition to the TRV fee, which must be paid again. The documents that must be submitted are the same as those listed above.

Visitor Class

The visitor class is the most straightforward of the temporary resident classes. It includes travellers, tourists, vacationers, and family members and friends of Canadians who wish to come here for short periods of time. Visitors contribute significantly to the Canadian economy, and it is important to welcome them with a minimum of red tape, while ensuring security and safety.

The foreign national must satisfy the officer that he will comply with all the restrictions imposed by the visitor visa. Generally, visitors are not allowed to work or study in Canada unless they are authorized to do so under the IRP Regulations. In many cases, a work or study permit is required (as described below).

There are exceptions to this rule, too. Certain categories of workers do not require work permits to work in Canada (for example, business workers under NAFTA) and, in certain circumstances, visitors are allowed to study in Canada without first obtaining a study permit (for example, taking a program such as English if it is less than six months in duration).

Processing time guidelines suggest that foreign nationals should apply for a visitor visa at least one month before the intended departure date, but it is important to check the CIC website for the most up-to-date processing times.

There are four types of visitor visas:

1. **Single-entry visa.** A single-entry visa allows a foreign national to enter Canada only once, usually for no longer than six months. An exception exists for repeated entries into Canada from the United States or St. Pierre and Miquelon, provided that the foreign national does not enter another country in between visits.

2. **Multiple-entry visa.** A multiple entry visa allows a foreign national to enter Canada from another country multiple times during the validity of the visa. The maximum validity period that a multiple-entry visa can be issued is matched to the maximum validity of the length of the passport, up to ten years, minus one month.[6]

3. **Transit visa.** A transit visa is required for travel through Canada to another country by anyone who would need a TRV to enter Canada and whose flight will stop here for less than 48 hours. The foreign national is required to show travel tickets.

4. **Super Visa.** Since December 1, 2011, foreign nationals who are the parents or grandparents of a Canadian citizen or a permanent resident can apply for the Parent and Grandparent Super Visa.

Parent and Grandparent Super Visa

The Parent and Grandparent Super Visa was created to replace the lengthy sponsorship processing for permanent residence so that family members can be reunited (under the family class sponsorship program—see Chapter 5). With the Super Visa, the foreign national is allowed to re-enter Canada for up to two years without the need to renew her visa.

Specific to the Super Visa is the requirement that all applicants undergo a medical examination and buy Canadian medical insurance coverage for at least one year that provides a minimum coverage of $100,000 with coverage for health care, hospitalization, and repatriation, and is valid for re-entry. Applicants must also provide proof of the parent or grandparent relationship to the Canadian citizen or permanent resident (for example, birth certificate, baptismal certificate, or other official document that names the applicant as a parent or grandparent). The applicant can include a spouse or common-law partner in the application, but cannot include any dependants.

The Canadian citizen or permanent resident child or grandchild in Canada must provide a written commitment of financial support, including a letter of invitation that sets out the living arrangements, care, and support for the duration of the stay in Canada. Similar to the requirement to sign an undertaking in the sponsorship process (see Chapter 5), the child or grandchild must establish that they meet a minimum income threshold according to the low income cut-off (LICO) table. Therefore, the letter of invitation must include details of the number of members in the family unit ("sponsoring" child or grandchild, spouse and dependants, and the visiting parents and/or grandparents) and the number of people residing in the household including current sponsorships.

Consider the following scenario:

Michele, a Canadian permanent resident and her husband John, a Canadian citizen have two young children, Kara and Matthew. Michele has returned to work full-time and wishes her parents could move to Canada to live with them to help care for the children. Michele's parents, Teresa and Enrique, are healthy and energetic and like the idea of being able to spend time with their grandchildren and to help out, but they are not sure they want to permanently move from their home in Mexico. The Super Visa would allow Teresa and Enrique to visit for up to two years.

Michele needs to prepare a letter of invitation that proves that she can provide care and support for her parents in addition to her family. Michele must show that she meets or exceeds the minimum income threshold as set out in a current LICO table. In order to determine the amount of income that Michele should have:

Calculate the size of Michele's family as follows:

4 Michele, John, Kara & Matthew	+ 2 Teresa & Enrique	= 6 Total # of persons
Use the LICO table to determine the minimum necessary income for 6 persons		
Minimum necessary income: $53,808		

Additionally, Michele will have to provide supporting documentation to prove she has sufficient financial resources, such as a copy of her most recent notice of assessment, Option C printout from her latest tax return from Canada Revenue Agency, or a copy of her most recent T1 or T4.

The LICO table is updated each year but looks like the following example, which was effective from January 1 to December 31, 2012.

Size of family unit	Minimum necessary income
1 person (Michele)	$22,637
2 persons	$28,182
3 persons	$34,646
4 persons	$42,065
5 persons	$47,710
6 persons	$53,808
7 persons	$59,907
For each additional person more than 7	$6,099

Student Class

Consider the value of international students who bring with them new ideas and a global perspective. One reason why studying in Canada may be an attractive option for the foreign student is the possibility of future permanent residence. For example, under the federal skilled worker class of permanent residence (discussed in Chapter 5), an applicant receives credit for Canadian post-secondary education under the point system. To attract and retain Canadian-educated foreign students, the government created the Canadian experience class in 2008 (discussed later in this chapter).

Foreign students are a prescribed class of persons who may obtain temporary resident status and who have been issued study permits or who are authorized by the IRP Regulations to study. A student is defined in the IRP Regulations as "a person who is authorized by a study permit or these Regulations to engage in studies in Canada and who is studying or intends to study in Canada," and studies are defined as "studies undertaken at a university or college, or any course of academic, professional or vocational training" (IRP Regulations, s. 1(1)).

A study permit is a written authorization issued to foreign students authorizing them to engage in studies in Canada. The following sections consider the criteria and overview of the application process for foreign students.

Criteria for a Study Permit

A foreign national who wishes to study in Canada must obtain a study permit unless she qualifies for an exemption (discussed below under the heading "Study Permit Exemptions"). Generally, if the program of study is six months or less, a study permit is not required.

A foreign national may be issued a study permit according to s. 216(1) of the IRP Regulations if an examination establishes that the foreign national meets the basic criteria applicable to all temporary resident applicants, as well as the criteria specific to students.

Visa officers look at many factors before deciding whether an applicant qualifies for a study permit. In addition to presenting the application form and basic documents that must be provided in support of all TRV applications, such as passport and travel documents (unless exempt), proof of immigration status, passport-size photos, and cost-recovery processing fee, applicants must also

- present a letter of acceptance from the educational institution where they intend to study;
- be able to pay the tuition fees for the course or program that they intend to pursue;
- be able to financially support themselves and any family members who are with them during their period of study;
- be able to cover the transportation cost for themselves and any family members to and from Canada;
- pass the CIC medical examination, if required;[7] and
- receive a Certificat d'acceptation du Québec (Quebec Certificate of Acceptance, or CAQ) if they intend to study in Quebec.

Not everybody is required to submit a letter of acceptance from an educational institution. For example, under s. 219(2)(a) of the IRP Regulations, accompanying family members of a student or a worker are exempt from the acceptance-letter requirement. Additionally, under ss. 219(2)(b) and 219(3), students whose study

Letter of Acceptance

The **letter of acceptance** is a key document that must be included in the application. The following list of items, although not mandatory, should be included in the letter of acceptance to increase the chances of approval of the application for a study permit:

- the full name, date of birth, and mailing address of the student;
- the course of study for which the student was accepted;
- the estimated duration or date of completion of the course;
- the date on which the selected course of study begins;
- the last date on which a student may register for a selected course;
- the academic year of study that the student will be entering;
- whether the course of study is full time or part time;
- the tuition fee;
- any conditions related to the acceptance or registration, such as academic prerequisites, completion of a previous degree, and proof of language competence;
- clear identification of the educational institution, usually confirmed through its letterhead; and
- where applicable, licensing information for private institutions, usually confirmed through letterhead.[8]

permits will expire in less than 90 days are not required to submit a letter of acceptance from an educational institution when applying for an extension. The extension may be issued only for a validity period of 90 days starting the day that the students receive written notification from their educational institutions of successful completion of their studies.

All applicants for study permits destined to a Quebec educational institution at the primary, secondary, college, or university level must obtain a Certificat d'acceptation du Québec issued by the Ministère des Relations avec les citoyens et de l'Immigration du Québec (MRCIQ) before being eligible for a study permit, even for part-time courses or for courses delivered by private institutions.

Because education is within the jurisdiction of each province, CIC makes it clear in its information guides to international students that it is up to the student to inquire about the quality of the schools in which they intend to enroll.

A study permit will not be issued for preschool, kindergarten, courses of general interest or self-improvement, distance learning courses, or audited courses attended without credit.

Application

The instruction guide (IMM 5269) and application forms are available online at http://www.cic.gc.ca/english/information/applications/student.asp.

The application package generally includes the following key forms; however, it is important to check for updates on the CIC website:

- Application for a Study Permit Made Outside of Canada form (IMM 1294)
- Schedule 1—Application for Temporary Resident Visa (IMM 5257);
- Use of a Representative form (IMM 5476), if applicable; and
- Document checklist for a study permit form (IMM 5483).

Other forms must be completed as applicable: Statutory Declaration of Common-Law Union form (IMM 5409); Family Information (IMM 5645); and the Custodian Declaration Form (IMM 5646) for minor children studying in Canada.

Generally, processing times can range from between 1 month and 16 months.

Post-secondary international students may transfer between programs of study and institutions without applying for a change to the conditions of their study permit. Consider the following scenario:

> Claudia from Costa Rica wishes to attend the University of Toronto to obtain a B.Sc. degree in mathematics. Claudia wishes to submit the minimum number of documents required in order to be issued her study permit.

The documents that must accompany Claudia's application for a study permit are proof of acceptance into the B.Sc. program at the University of Toronto, which is an accredited educational institution; a passport, because Costa Rica is no longer on the list of visa-exempt countries; and proof of funds to pay for the program and to support herself while in Canada.

> Claudia changes her mind after beginning her studies at the University of Toronto. She now wants to conclude her degree in mathematics at the University of British Columbia but doesn't know whether she needs to apply for a change to the conditions of her study permit.

Claudia is permitted to continue studying because she will take the same degree at another accredited university.

Health Insurance

Although the issuance of the study permit does not require proof of private health insurance, student applicants must obtain private health insurance prior to their arrival in Canada because provincial health insurance coverage varies depending on the province of destination. For example, Saskatchewan and the Northwest Territories extend immediate coverage to foreign students while British Columbia, Alberta, Ontario, and Nova Scotia extend health coverage only after various waiting periods. For Quebec-destined students, health insurance may be a precondition to the issuance of the CAQ.

Place of Application

Some foreign nationals are permitted to apply for a student visa at a Canadian port of entry, such as United States nationals or persons who have been lawfully admitted to the United States for permanent residence, and residents of Greenland and St. Pierre and Miquelon. Nevertheless, these foreign nationals must comply with the requirements applicable to the student class, pursuant to s. 216(1) of the IRP Regulations. CIC is modernizing its government services to include online applications; some applicants can now submit their applications for study permits online (see the CIC website for further details.)

Study Permit Extensions

A foreign national may apply for the renewal of her study permit if the following conditions are met:

- the renewal application was made before the expiry of the current study permit (processing time guidelines suggest that the application for renewal should be made at least 30 days before the expiry date of the current study permit);
- all conditions imposed on entry into Canada have been complied with;
- the foreign national is in good standing at the educational institution, in accordance with s. 217(1) of the IRP Regulations; and
- the foreign national is in compliance with the eligibility criteria for a study permit pursuant to s. 216.

Because it may take some time to process a renewal, a foreign national is allowed to continue studying in Canada with an expired study permit if the following conditions are met:

- the renewal application was made before the expiry of the current study permit;
- the foreign national has remained in Canada since the expiry of the study permit; and
- the foreign national continues to comply with the conditions, other than the expiry date, set out on the expired study permit, in accordance with s. 189 of the IRP Regulations.

Consider the following scenario:

> Lara is an international student attending Seneca College in Toronto. Lara applied for the renewal of her study permit two weeks before it expired. Unfortunately, Lara has not yet received a decision regarding her application for renewal and her student visa has expired. What would you advise Lara to do?

Under ss. 186(u) and 189 of the IRP Regulations, Lara has *implied status* and has the right to continue studying under the same conditions as long as she remains in

Canada. Consequently, the original study permit continues to be valid until a decision is made and Lara is notified (IRP Regulations, s. 183(5)).

Study Permit Exemptions

Not everyone is required to obtain a study permit in order to study in Canada. Foreign nationals are exempt from the requirement of a study permit if they fall under one of the following categories:

- family members and members of the private staff of diplomats or foreign accredited representatives (IRP Regulations, s. 188(1)(a));
- persons seeking to study a short-term program of study of six months or less (s. 188(1)(c)) unless they are seeking to work on campus;
- members of the armed forces of a country designated for the purposes of the *Visiting Forces Act*, even if they want to study for more than six months (IRP Regulations, s. 188(1)(b)); or
- minor children in Canada, other than children of a temporary resident not authorized to work or study, who intend to study at the preschool, primary, or secondary level (IRPA, s. 30(2)). However, it is important to clarify that minor children applying outside Canada do require a study permit.

Consider the following case scenario:

> Carlos, a Mexican priest, has been granted temporary resident status for a period of one year for the purpose of assisting a congregation. During this time, Carlos would like to enroll in a four-month language-training course, and once he completes that course, he would like to engage in a four-month religious studies course. Does Carlos require a study permit?

Carlos may complete the two courses without a study permit because each course of study is less than six months in duration and can be completed within the original period of stay authorized upon entry—namely, one year.

However, if Carlos wants to enroll in another short-term course of an additional four months, this would exceed the period of temporary resident status authorized upon his entry. In that case, Carlos must apply for an extension of his temporary resident status. However, the reason for his request for an extension must be to continue assisting the congregation, and not for the purpose of completing the course. Carlos would likely be granted an extension of his temporary resident status and could then enroll in the short-term course without a study permit.

Minors

In some cases, minor children do not need a study permit to study in Canada. These cases include:

- minor children attending kindergarten;
- minor children who are refugees or refugee claimants, or whose parents are refugees or refugee claimants; and
- minor children who are already in Canada with parents who are allowed to work or study in Canada, and who want to attend preschool, primary, or secondary school.

When minor children studying in Canada without a permit reach the age of majority (turn 18 or 19 depending on the province or territory), they must apply for a permit if they want to continue studying.

In some cases, parents may choose to send their child to Canada on his own for the purpose of studying. In situations where a minor is travelling alone, the length of time a study permit is valid is as follows:

- Minor children in grades 1 through 8: the study permit is normally valid for one year.
- Minor children in grades 9 through 12, or attending a post-secondary institution: the study permit is normally valid for the length of time of studies, plus 90 days.
- Minor children studying in Quebec: the study permit is valid for the same length of time as their *Certificat d'acceptation du Québec*—CAQ (certificate of acceptance).

If a minor child is with parents who have long-term study or work permits, the child's study permit should be valid for the same length of time as:

- the parents' permits;
- the child's passport, if it expires before the parents' permits; or
- the CAQ, if studying in Quebec.

Study Permit Restrictions

A study permit is a written authorization issued to foreign students that authorizes them to engage in studies in Canada,[9] subject to certain restrictions. An officer may impose, vary, or cancel conditions on the study permit. These conditions may include one or more of the following:

- type of studies or course that the foreign national may take;
- educational institution that the foreign national may attend;
- location of studies;
- time and period of studies;
- time and place at which the foreign national shall report for medical examination or observation;
- time and place at which the foreign national shall report for the presentation of evidence in compliance with applicable conditions;

- duration of stay in Canada; or
- prohibition of engaging in employment, except for students attending an accredited educational institution on a full-time basis, who are in possession of a valid and subsisting study permit and who are allowed to work on campus without a work permit (IRP Regulations, s. 186(f)).

Work for Foreign Students

Although CIC requires foreign students to arrive in Canada with sufficient funding for the duration of their study period, many students find the need to earn extra income. This need is recognized in the IRPA and IRP Regulations, which provide that foreign students may work while pursuing post-secondary education in Canada in certain circumstances. In some cases, a work permit is not required, as in the case of a student who works on campus. In others, a permit is required, as in the case of a student who works off campus or one who is enrolled in postgraduate studies or a co-op program. Each of these situations is discussed below.

Work Not Requiring a Permit (On Campus)

A foreign national in Canada on a valid study permit is authorized to work on campus without a work permit, provided that the student is enrolled full-time at a public or other authorized post-secondary institution, and that the student maintains full-time status at the institution (IRP Regulations, s. 186(f)).

"On campus" is defined as the employment facilities within the boundaries of the campus. The student may work only on the campus of the educational institution at which she is registered. In the event that the school has more than one campus, the student may work at a different location, provided that it is within the same municipality. The student may not work at campuses outside the municipality (IRP Regulations, s. 186(f)).

Students working as graduate assistants, teaching assistants, or research assistants are considered to be within the scope of "on-campus" employment, provided that the students have been recommended by officials of their department; the work to be performed is directed by a department head or a faculty member; and the work takes place in a research institute or program in an affiliated hospital or research unit.

Consider the following case scenario:

> Sara has obtained a temporary resident visa and will visit Canada in September. Upon arriving, Sara wants to enroll in a five-month, full-time, postgraduate linguistics certificate program offered by Humber College. Sara also intends to work on campus to further assimilate the Canadian culture.

Recall that s. 188(1)(c) of the IRP Regulations states that a foreign national may study in Canada without a study permit if the duration of the program is six months or less. However, this exemption does not apply to a foreign national who wishes to work on campus. In the present case, Sara should be advised that although she does not need a study permit to study in the five-month course at Humber College, she does need a study permit to work on campus.

Work Requiring a Permit (Off Campus)

There are two situations in which a foreign student may be eligible to work off campus, as follows:

1. *They have become destitute through circumstances beyond their control.* Students may apply for a work permit if, by reason of circumstances beyond their control, they become temporarily destitute according to s. 208 of the IRP Regulations. Such circumstances may include war, upheaval, or collapse of the banking system in the home country.

   These students may be granted an **open work permit**, which allows the student to work for any employer for a specific period of time. Usually, the time period coincides with the duration of the current term of study, rather than with the duration of the entire program or with the duration of the study permit.

2. *They are enrolled as full-time students at a post-secondary educational institution that participates in the Off-Campus Work Permit Program.* A student may apply for an off-campus work permit if the student is attending a publicly funded post-secondary institution that has signed an agreement to participate in the program with its provincial or territorial government. The list of participating institutions can be found on the CIC website at http://www.cic.gc.ca/english/study/institutions/participants.asp.

   These students are required to comply with the following criteria to qualify for an off-campus work permit. They must:

   - hold a valid study permit;
   - be enrolled in a participating institution;
   - have full-time student status for at least 6 months of the 12 months preceding the application for a work permit;
   - have maintained satisfactory academic standing; and
   - have signed a form authorizing the institution, the province, and CIC to share the student's personal information in order to confirm that the above criteria are met.[10]

Furthermore, students are not eligible to apply for a work permit under this program if they

- have a partial or full scholarship or award from the Canadian Commonwealth Scholarship Program, from the Government of Canada Awards Program funded by the Department of Foreign Affairs and International Trade (DFAIT), or from an award or internship program funded by the Canadian International Development Agency (CIDA);
- are registered in programs that consist either exclusively or primarily of an English-as-a-second-language or French-as-a-second-language (ESL/FSL) program;

- have completed their studies and are no longer considered as full time; or
- have previously held an off-campus work permit and failed to maintain their eligibility under the program or failed to comply with the terms and conditions of their work or study permit.[11]

Consider the following scenarios:

> Melissa is a student in the science and technology program at Capilano University in British Columbia. Melissa is interested in obtaining an off-campus work permit but is unsure when she will be eligible to submit her application. Melissa began full-time studies in September and continued through the end of February (with the exception of the Christmas break). During this time, she has maintained good grades.

Melissa will be eligible for a work permit in March because she has been enrolled in full-time studies from September to February, which equals six months, she continues to be enrolled in full-time studies, and she has maintained satisfactory academic standing at the time of her application.

> Melissa's friend George, a fellow student at the university, is also interested in applying for an off-campus work permit, and he would like to know when he will be eligible to apply for one. George was enrolled in full-time studies from January until the end of April. He took four months off for summer break, and resumed full-time studies in September.

George will not be eligible to apply for a work permit until he has completed a full six months of studies. George studied full time from January until the end of April, and then resumed full-time studies in September after taking a four-month break. George will be eligible to apply in November, because January to April equals four months, and September to October equals two months, which totals six months.

Students who have obtained a work permit may only work part time—a maximum of 20 hours per week—off campus while school is in session. Students are allowed to extend that to full-time work only when the school is in a scheduled break, such as winter or spring break.

However, the legislation does not prohibit students from working both 20 hours per week off campus and 20 hours per week on campus. This legislative oversight may threaten a student's ability to continue full-time studies and to maintain satisfactory academic standing as required to remain eligible for the program.[12]

Work Requiring a Permit (Postgraduate Work Permits)

Foreign nationals currently in possession of a valid study permit and about to graduate from a post-secondary institution may apply for a postgraduate open work permit under the Post-Graduation Work Permit Program (PGWPP).[13] An open work permit enables the foreign national to seek and accept employment, and to work for any employer for a specified period of time. An open work permit also exempts the foreign national from the requirement of obtaining a confirmation from Human Resources and Social Development Canada (HRSDC), which is generally required to obtain a work permit. More information about open work permits and HRSDC is provided below under the heading "Worker Class."

A foreign national seeking to obtain a postgraduate work permit/open work permit must meet the following criteria:

- the student must have graduated from a post-secondary institution from a program of at least eight months' duration;
- the student must still be in possession of a valid study permit upon submission of a postgraduate work permit; and
- the application for a postgraduate work permit must be submitted within 90 days of receiving a written confirmation from the institution indicating that the academic program was successfully completed, such as a transcript or notice of graduation.

Careful consideration must be given to the transition from off-campus work permit to postgraduate work permit. If the study permit is set to expire within the 90-day period, the student must apply for a "bridging extension" to her valid study permit prior to applying for a postgraduate work permit. Once granted, the postgraduate work permit may be valid for a period not longer than that in which the graduating student studied at a Canadian post-secondary institution, and may not exceed three years.

Additionally, when a graduating student is in possession of a valid off-campus work permit, the student may continue to use this work permit in the 90 days following the date of graduation. This off-campus work permit may also be used to commence postgraduate work until the postgraduate work permit is issued.[14]

Once the one-year postgraduate work permit expires, the student must apply for a labour market opinion (also referred to as an LMO or HRSDC confirmation) to maintain work permit status. The LMO is discussed below under the heading "Worker Class."

Work Requiring a Permit (Co-op Work Program)

Students whose work experience is an essential and integral component of their program of study may be eligible for a work permit under a co-op or internship program. To be eligible, the following conditions must be met:

- the student must be in possession of a valid study permit;
- the student's intended employment must be an essential part of the program of study in Canada;
- the employment must be certified as part of the academic program by a responsible academic official of the institution;
- the student's co-op or internship employment may not form more than 50 percent of the total program of study; and
- the student must not be a medical intern or extern, nor a resident physician (except in veterinary medicine).[15]

Note that international students, scholars, and scientists may also be eligible to obtain work permits for work related to a research, educational, or training program. These work permits are issued under specific programs funded by the Canadian International Development Agency, the International Development Research Centre of Canada (IDRC), Atomic Energy of Canada Ltd., the National Research Council of Canada (NRC), and the Natural Sciences and Engineering Research Council of Canada (NSERC).[16]

Worker Class

Foreign temporary workers contribute to Canada's economy by filling labour market shortages and boosting trade. This section will focus on the general eligibility requirements for a foreign national who wishes to work temporarily in Canada, including the process for vetting the job offer, and the responsibilities of Canadian employers. Finally, we describe some of the various foreign worker programs available to foreign nationals.

"Work" is defined under s. 2 of the IRP Regulations as "an activity for which wages are paid or commission is earned, or that is in direct competition with the activities of Canadian citizens or permanent residents in the Canadian labour market."

Under ss. 194 to 196 of the IRP Regulations, foreign nationals who wish to work temporarily in Canada are part of the worker class of temporary residents and are generally required to have a genuine job offer to obtain a work permit, unless exempt under s. 186. Generally, part of the process for obtaining a work permit is to first obtain a job offer from a Canadian employer.

It is important that a foreign national understand his rights so he is not exploited or abused, and that he be aware of his responsibilities when working in Canada.

Unfortunately, there have been instances where human traffickers exploit foreign workers by enticing them with false promises of work and exaggerated wages and living conditions and permanent immigration. Human trafficking operations include recruiting, transporting, harbouring, and controlling foreign nationals in other ways. As previously discussed in Chapter 3, exploitation causes a person to provide labour or a service (for example, sexual services, any kind of work including drug trafficking, and begging) by engaging in conduct that could reasonably be expected to cause the victim to believe that their safety, or the safety of someone known to them, would be threatened if they did not provide that labour or service (Dept. of Justice, 2011).

Employers are not allowed to:

- prevent the foreign worker from leaving the work site after work;
- remove a passport or work permit;
- abuse physically, sexually, or psychologically;
- threaten the foreign worker that something bad will happen to them or a family member; or
- coach the worker into misleading Immigration and other Canadian authorities.

Information about foreign worker rights can be found on the CIC website. The temporary worker program relies on the cooperation of three key departments, as follows:

- CIC (to, for example, process applications);
- Human Resources and Social Development Canada/Service Canada (HRSDC/SC) (for example, employer compliance review; labour market opinion, letter of confirmation); and
- the Canada Border Services Agency (for example, port-of-entry examinations and admitting foreign nationals).

Generally, a foreign national seeking to work in Canada is required to comply with a three-tiered process involving each of these departments, as follows, in this order:

1. their employer must undergo an employer compliance review and obtain a positive labour market opinion (LMO) and confirmation from HRSDC/SC;
2. obtain a work permit (and temporary visa if applicable) from a visa office (see the discussion earlier in this chapter); and
3. enter Canada only after an examination by a CBSA officer at the port of entry (see the discussion in Chapter 3).

Cumulative Duration

As of April 1, 2011, a new regulation establishes the maximum allowable cumulative time that a temporary foreign worker can work in Canada. The policy decision to limit prolonged periods of time to work in Canada was implemented to prevent situations where a temporary foreign worker sets down roots in Canada and loses ties with and is reluctant to return to his country of origin. The maximum cumulative duration is currently set at a total of four years, and generally must be followed by a period of four years in which the temporary foreign worker is no longer eligible to work in Canada (IRP Regulations, s. 200(3)(g)).

Criteria for a Work Permit

The criteria used to determine eligibility for a work permit are based mainly on the same factors discussed earlier, which are applicable to all temporary residents—namely, intention to leave Canada at the end of the authorized temporary stay; possession of a passport; compliance with the medical examination requirements (IRP Regulations, s. 30); and not inadmissible. In addition, under s. 200 of the IRP Regulations, the foreign worker must satisfy the specific requirements related to the worker class, which include the following:

- a genuine offer to work in Canada from a Canadian employer (IRP Regulations, s. 203);
- approval of the employment offer by HRSDC/SC (unless exempted); and

WEBLINK

Information sources on foreign workers' rights

Temporary Foreign Workers—Your Rights and the Law is available at http://www.cic.gc.ca/english/work/tfw-rights.asp. This site contains links to federal, provincial, and territorial employment standards, and information on eligibility for employment insurance.

- compliance with the requirements of the job in Canada, such as education, training, and experience.

Generally, to be eligible for a work permit, a temporary foreign worker must show she has access to sufficient funds to cover her living expenses. Exceptions include refugee claimants subject to an unenforceable removal order, students who have become temporarily destitute, and temporary resident permit holders as long as their permits are valid for at least six months (IRP Regulations, s. 200).

It is important to note that a work permit does not guarantee admission to Canada. The temporary foreign worker must meet the requirements for issuance of the work permit at the time the visa is issued, and must continue to meet these requirements at the time of arrival at the port of entry where the examination by a CBSA officer takes place, (IRP Regulations, s. 180). Therefore, a temporary foreign worker may be refused at the port of entry if she does not comply with the requirements for issuance of the work permit (for example, if she is inadmissible on the ground of criminality), regardless of whether she has obtained a genuine job offer.

Application

In addition to the documents required to support any TRV application (for example, an application form, the cost-recovery processing fee, passport and travel documents —unless exempted by s. 52(1) of the IRP Regulations—proof of immigration status, and passport-size photos), an applicant must provide documents and forms specifically relevant to the worker class, including

- an Application for Work Permit Made Outside Canada (IMM 1295);
- a Schedule 1—Application for Temporary Resident Visa (IMM 5257— Schedule 1);
- a "genuine job offer," and/or job contract from the temporary foreign worker's prospective employer;
- a copy of the HRSDC/SC positive LMO, unless the occupation or category is exempt; and
- background documents showing qualifications and experience (for example, trade/apprenticeship certificate or education credential) as evidence that she meets the requirements for the job (IRP Regulations, s. 200(3)(a)).

If the application is for Quebec, the foreign worker must also provide a copy of the Quebec Certificate of Acceptance (Certificat d'acceptation du Québec—CAQ).

Place of Application

The general rule is that a foreign worker must apply outside Canada for a work permit; however, there are situations where a work permit may be obtained at the port of entry or within Canada (IRP Regulations, ss. 198 and 199).

The following persons must apply outside Canada:

- all persons who require a TRV;
- seasonal agricultural workers;

- live-in caregivers;
- all persons who require a medical examination, unless valid medical examination results are available at the time of entry; and
- international youth exchange program participants other than US citizens or US permanent residents, unless approved by the responsible visa office (that administers the DFAIT-granted quota) abroad (Canadian experience class exemption code C21).[17]

Unless they are identified in the above list of persons who must apply outside Canada, the following persons may apply at a port of entry:

- all nationals or permanent residents of the United States and residents of Greenland and St. Pierre and Miquelon (contiguous territories);
- persons whose work does not require HRSDC confirmation; and
- persons whose work requires HRSDC confirmation, as long as the confirmation has been issued before the worker seeks to enter.[18]

Additionally, the following persons are eligible to apply for a work permit within Canada:

- holders of valid work or study permits and their family members;
- members of a crew;
- religious members, provided that they have a positive LMO;
- students applying for postgraduate work permits;
- holders of temporary resident permits that are valid for a minimum of six months and their family members;
- refugee claimants and persons subject to an unenforceable removal order;
- in-Canada applicants and their family members who are deemed eligible for permanent resident status, which includes live-in caregivers, spouses, or common-law partners; protected persons, and persons who qualify on humanitarian and compassionate grounds;
- persons whose work permits were authorized by a visa office abroad, where the permit was not issued at a port of entry;
- Mexican citizens admitted to Canada as temporary residents, who may apply for a work permit under any NAFTA category; and
- US citizens admitted as visitors, who may apply in Canada under the professional or intra-company transferee NAFTA categories only (IRP Regulations, s. 199).

A foreign worker may be accompanied by a spouse or common-law partner and dependent children. The family members do not need to complete separate applications, but they must be named and included either as accompanying or non-accompanying family members in the foreign worker's application. However, in the event that accompanying family members want to work in Canada, they must apply for separate work permits and must meet the same standards, including the HRSDC confirmation if applicable. They may, however, benefit from applying for their work permit from within Canada.

Genuine Job Offer

The applicant must have a genuine job offer from a Canadian employer and, generally, a written contract—signed by both the applicant and the employer—setting out the details of employment that includes the following information:

- transportation to Canada from applicant's country to the location of work in Canada;
- medical insurance coverage provided from the date of arrival until eligible for provincial health insurance;
- workplace safety insurance coverage for the duration of the employment;
- all recruitment fees, including any amount payable to a third-party recruiter or agents hired by the employer;
- job duties;
- hours of work;
- wages;
- accommodation arrangements if applicable (including room and board);
- holiday and sick leave entitlements; and
- termination and resignation terms;

As proof of a genuine job offer from a Canadian employer, the applicant must obtain a copy of the LMO confirmation letter that was provided to the potential employer.

Labour Market Opinion

Human Resources and Skills Development Canada/Service Canada (HRSDC/SC) has the responsibility to confirm that the job offer conforms to current rules and regulations. Employers must submit their job offer to the HRSDC/SC so that the genuineness of the job offer to a foreign worker, and an employer compliance review can be assessed based on four factors:

1. The employer is actively engaged in the business.
2. The job offer is consistent with the needs of the employer.
3. The employer is reasonably able to fulfill the terms of the job offer.
4. The employer has complied with federal/provincial/territorial laws regulating employment in the province/territory where the worker will be employed.

The HRSDC/SC provides a **labour market opinion (LMO)**, which is an opinion to an immigration officer regarding whether the issuance of a work permit to a foreign worker will have either a neutral or positive effect on Canada's economy.

Several factors, such as wages, working conditions, the availability of Canadians or permanent residents to do the work, and the skills and knowledge transfer and job creation that may result from employing a foreign worker are considered. These factors are considered in more detail below under the heading "Factors." The LMO is typically given for a specific period of time, and the work permit issued will co-incide with that period. Renewal of a work permit beyond the specified period will likely require a new LMO.

Generally, Canadian employers who wish to employ a foreign worker must obtain an HRSDC confirmation from HRSDC before the foreign worker may apply for a work permit from CIC. There are, however, a number of important exemptions and special programs, explained later in this chapter, which may apply in particular industries or circumstances to permit circumvention of the requirement of obtaining an HRSDC confirmation.

FACTORS

Unless an exemption applies, the HRSDC/SC considers several factors when assessing an employment offer, including the following:

1. *Verification of the employment offer.* Verification that the employment offer is genuine must be provided.

2. *Recruitment efforts.* The employer must demonstrate reasonable efforts to hire Canadians or permanent residents for the position, before offering it to a foreign worker. The onus is on the employer to prove that there were no Canadians available for the position, or that Canadian applicants could not be trained for the position in a reasonable amount of time.

3. *Union consultation.* All relevant unions and professional associations must be consulted with respect to the potential employment of a foreign worker, and letters of consent from them must be attached to the application for the LMO. Additionally, the employment of the foreign worker must not adversely affect the settlement of any labour dispute in progress or the employment of any person involved in that dispute.

4. *Job creation.* A position that is likely to help job creation or job retention for Canadian citizens or permanent residents has a greater chance of being approved.

5. *Transfer of skills.* Workers who are likely to transfer skills and knowledge for the benefit of Canadians or permanent residents are favoured.

6. *Labour shortages.* Consideration will be given to whether the worker is likely to fill a labour shortage in the Canadian market because of a skills shortage.

7. *Wages and working conditions.* The wages and working conditions offered must be sufficient to attract Canadian citizens or permanent residents and retain them in that work. Jobs offering less than adequate remuneration will not be approved. Temporary foreign workers have the same rights and protections as Canadian workers under applicable federal/provincial

employment standards and labour laws, and are paid at the same rate that a Canadian worker would be paid for the same job. However, in April 2012 the HRSDC announced a new wage structure that considers pay of up to 15 percent below the average wage for an occupation in a specific region as long as employers demonstrate that the wage is consistent with that of Canadian workers based on Statistics Canada data. The provinces and territories have primary responsibility for establishing and enforcing health and labour standards, such as safe working conditions, for all workers, including temporary foreign workers.

It is crucial that the employer's submissions include information regarding the above factors, such as details about recruitment efforts and their results, and a detailed explanation of how the company would benefit from the foreign worker's employment—with respect to profitability, employee skills, and positive spillover effects on Canadians.

EMPLOYER COMPLIANCE REVIEW

Service Canada conducts a review of the employer's history as an employer:

- to provide better protection to vulnerable temporary foreign workers against abusive employers and third-party agents;
- to increase employer accountability and compliance with terms and conditions of their job offer made to foreign nationals; and
- to restrict the use of temporary foreign workers to short-term situations.

The review is conducted to determine whether, over the past two years, the employer has reasonably respected the terms of past job offers, particularly with regard to wages, working conditions, and employment in a job that was substantially the same as those listed in the offer of employment. To demonstrate compliance, employers should keep a record of all documentation in order to facilitate the process for subsequent LMO applications. Employers may be asked to provide:

- payroll records,
- time sheets,
- a job description,
- the temporary foreign worker's work permit, and
- proof of registration with provincial/territorial workplace safety.

For employers of temporary foreign workers of lower levels of formal training, or hired under the Seasonal Agricultural Worker Program or the Live-In Caregiver Program (discussed below), the following additional information is required:

- transportation costs,
- accommodation information, and
- private health insurance coverage (if applicable).

The employer has the opportunity to justify any discrepancies. If the employer does not pass the review, he will not be able to hire any foreign temporary workers for two years and will be named on CIC's List of Ineligible Employers—Temporary Foreign Worker Program website http://www.cic.gc.ca/english/work/list.asp.

MINIMUM ADVERTISING REQUIREMENTS

Employers seeking to hire workers are required to show that they have conducted ongoing recruitment efforts—for example, they will have advertised on recognized Internet recruitment sites; in trade journals, newsletters, or national newspapers; or by consulting unions or professional associations. Alternatively, they will have advertised on the government of Canada's national Job Bank (or the equivalent in Saskatchewan, Newfoundland and Labrador, or the Northwest Territories) for a minimum of 14 calendar days, during the 3 months prior to applying for an LMO.

For lower-skilled occupations (NOC C and D) minimum advertising efforts may also include advertising in weekly or periodic newspapers, journals, newsletters, national/regional newspapers, ethnic newspapers/newsletters, or free local newspapers; advertising in the community—for example, posting ads for two to three weeks in local stores, community resource centres, churches, or local regional employment centres; and advertising on Internet job sites (for example, union, community resource centres, or ethnic group sites).

Consider this scenario:

> Kevin, a British national, is a specialized programmer of tool and die machines. He received a job offer from a Canadian company that is looking to fill a labour shortage in its workforce. The company has submitted an application to HRSDC. In its application, the company has documented the labour shortage in Canada and described its employment offer, which is consistent with Canadian standards and wage rates. Additionally, the company has argued that Kevin's recruitment will result in the transfer of new skills and knowledge to the Canadian market and labour force, which will enable it to hire and train additional Canadian workers.
>
> Unfortunately, Kevin is criminally inadmissible to Canada, because he was convicted of a crime two days after the employer submitted the application to HRSDC. Will HRSDC refuse the employer's application?

The employer's application to HRSDC will most likely be approved, provided that the hiring of Kevin meets all the LMO requirements.

However, the inadmissibility of Kevin as a foreign worker to Canada on criminal grounds may result in a refusal of his work permit by CIC. It is important to understand that HRSDC's role is to review the job's proposed wages and working conditions, the availability of Canadians or permanent residents to do the work in question, the skills and knowledge transfer, and the job creation for the benefit of Canadians or permanent residents that may result from confirming the employment of a foreign worker. Assessing an applicant's inadmissibility is outside the scope of the HRSDC's official duties.

Open Permits

In some cases, an open work permit may also be available. An open work permit has the advantage of not being job-specific; thus, a foreign national with an open work permit may work for any Canadian employer, without first having a confirmed offer of employment. An open work permit may carry some restrictions, such as the length of time that the foreign worker may work in Canada, the location of where the foreign worker may work, or the type of occupation.

The following persons may be eligible to apply for an open work permit:

- live-in caregivers who have met the requirements for permanent residence (IRP Regulations, s. 113);
- members of the spouse or common-law in Canada class (IRP Regulations, s. 124);
- spouses or common-law partners of foreign representatives and family members of military personnel;
- spouses or common-law partners of foreign workers whose work is at a level that falls within NOC skill levels O, A, or B;
- spouses or common-law partners of work permit holders who have been nominated for permanent residence by a province, irrespective of the skill level of the principal applicant's occupation;
- destitute students;
- persons who are deemed to be Convention refugees or persons in need of protection (IRPA, s. 95(2));
- persons for whom eligibility or admissibility requirements have been waived under humanitarian and compassionate grounds and who, as such, are eligible to become permanent residents (IRPA, s. 25(1));
- family members of the above who are in Canada; and
- international students who have graduated from a Canadian post-secondary institution.

If the foreign national requires a TRV to enter Canada, the open work permit will be issued for the same length of time. The application for an open work permit can be made prior to arrival to Canada, at the port of entry, or after arrival.

Work Permit Conditions

A work permit is a written authorization to work in Canada issued by an officer. Generally, it is based on a specific position with a specific employer, and is subject to one or more of the following conditions:

- type of employment in which the foreign worker may work;
- employer for whom the foreign worker may work;
- location where the foreign worker may work; and
- length of time the foreign worker may work.

In the event that the foreign worker seeks to engage in work with a different employer, a new HRSDC confirmation will be required, unless the occupation is HRSDC-exempt (IRP Regulations, s. 52(1)). This is in addition to the requirement to obtain a new work permit.

Work Permit Extensions

As with the general procedures described earlier in this chapter regarding extensions to TRVs, a foreign worker may apply for the renewal of a work permit. The foreign worker must, however, comply with the following conditions:

- the renewal application was made before the expiry of the current work permit (processing time guidelines suggest that the foreign worker should apply for a renewal at least 30 days before the expiry date); and
- the foreign worker has complied with all conditions imposed on entry into Canada.

It is important to note that a foreign worker is allowed to continue working in Canada under the conditions of an expired work permit if the following conditions are met:

- the renewal application was made before the original work permit expired;
- the foreign worker has remained in Canada since the expiry of the work permit; and
- the foreign worker continues to comply with the conditions, other than the expiry date, set out in the expired work permit (IRP Regulations, s. 186(u)).

A work permit becomes invalid when it expires or when a removal order that is made against the permit holder becomes enforceable (IRP Regulations, s. 209).

Work Permit Exemptions

Not everyone is required to obtain a work permit in order to work in Canada (IRP Regulations, s. 186). Some categories of workers who are exempt from needing a temporary work permit include the following:

- business visitors;
- diplomats;
- foreign athletes;
- military personnel;
- crew members;
- clergy;
- performing artists;
- public speakers;
- news reporters;

- expert witnesses, examiners, and evaluators; and
- students engaging in part-time work on campus.

Special Programs and International Agreements

The IRP Regulations provide for issuing work permits for certain occupations that are included in special programs that may make acquiring the LMO much quicker. These programs are created by s. 204 of the IPR Regulations as follows:

(a) an international agreement between Canada and one or more countries, other than an agreement concerning seasonal agricultural workers;

(b) an agreement entered into by one or more countries and by or on behalf of one or more provinces; or

(c) an agreement entered into by the Minister with a province or group of provinces under subsection 8(1) of the Act.

Whenever possible, the Canadian employer should seek an exemption from HRSDC approval, or an appropriate special program, because the HRSDC process may be lengthy and there is no assurance of success.

A sampling of some of the programs available to foreign workers are discussed below.

Academics Program

HRSDC and CIC, in cooperation with universities, degree-granting colleges, and unions representing Canadian academics, set out the criteria for the Academics Program. It was created with the purpose of assisting degree-granting, post-secondary educational institutions in Canada to meet their staffing and teaching needs by seeking internationally the best-qualified and most suitable candidates for full-time academic staff positions.

Prior to the hiring of a foreign academic for a position in Canada, the institution must obtain a positive LMO and:

- complete the foreign academic recruitment summary outlining the educational institution's hiring decision and providing summaries of Canadian applicants verified by the vice-president or other senior academic official of the educational institution; and

- complete a yearly summary report on recruitment practices for Canadian academics and results.[19]

The Academics Program does not extend to community colleges unless they are affiliated with a university and their students are able to obtain degrees, nor does it apply to the Collèges d'enseignement général et professionnel (Cégep) in Quebec.

The IRPA includes a variety of foreign academics who, while required to obtain a work permit, are exempt from obtaining an LMO, as follows:

- postdoctoral fellows and research award recipients;
- leaders in various fields;

- guest lecturers and visiting professors;
- citizens of the United States and Mexico appointed as professors under the university, college, and seminary levels of the North American Free Trade Agreement (NAFTA); and
- citizens of Chile appointed as professors under the Canada–Chile Free Trade Agreement.[20]

Additionally, the following foreign academics are exempt from obtaining both an LMO and a work permit:

- academic consultants and examiners, provided that they are eminent individuals seeking entry to evaluate academic programs or research proposals;
- graduate assistants, provided that they are considered to be within the scope of on-campus employment; and
- self-funded researchers, provided that they comply with the business visitor's criteria.

Seasonal Agricultural Worker Program

The **Seasonal Agricultural Worker Program (SAWP)** permits the entry of foreign nationals to work in specific on-farm primary agriculture commodity sectors such as fruits, vegetables, greenhouses, nurseries, apiary products, tobacco, sod, flowers, Christmas trees, and certain animal commodities. SAWP was developed by HRSDC and CIC in cooperation with agricultural producers and a number of foreign countries including Mexico and several Commonwealth Caribbean countries (for example, Anguilla, Antigua and Barbuda, Barbados, Dominica, Grenada, Jamaica, Montserrat, St. Kitts-Nevis, St. Lucia, St. Vincent, and Trinidad and Tobago.)[21]

Employers can hire agricultural workers for a maximum duration of eight months between January 1 and December 15 of the same year.

SAWP currently operates in British Columbia, Alberta, Saskatchewan, Manitoba, Ontario, Quebec, New Brunswick, Nova Scotia, Prince Edward Island, and Newfoundland and Labrador, and meets the needs of specific agricultural commodity sectors.

Prior to hiring a foreign worker under SAWP, a Canadian employer must meet the following criteria:

- demonstrate efforts to hire Canadian agricultural workers or unemployed Canadians through HRSDC and provincial employment programs;
- prepare a human resources plan explaining the efforts to find Canadian workers, eight weeks before the start of the work;
- offer the foreign worker the same wages paid to Canadian agricultural workers doing the same work;
- pay for the foreign worker's airfare to and from Canada (a portion of this cost can be recovered through payroll deductions);
- provide free seasonal housing to the foreign worker that has been approved by the appropriate provincial/municipal body;

- pay the immigration visa cost-recovery fee for the worker (this fee or a portion of this fee can be recovered through payroll deductions);
- ensure that the foreign worker is covered by workers' compensation;
- ensure that the foreign worker is covered under private or provincial health insurance during his stay in Canada; and
- sign an employment contract outlining wages, duties, and conditions related to the transportation, accommodation, health, and occupational safety of the foreign worker.[22]

CIC will issue a work permit of no more than eight months, provided that the foreign worker meets the work permit's eligibility criteria pursuant to s. 200 of the IRP Regulations.

Stream for Lower-skilled Occupations

In July 2002, HRSDC first introduced a stream for lower-skilled occupations as a pilot project for hiring foreign workers in occupations that require lower levels of formal training (NOC C and D), called the **Low Skill Pilot Project (LSP)**. Today, the main objective of the program is to meet the labour market demand for temporary foreign workers in jobs that are listed in parts C and D of the National Occupational Classification, which includes labourers, cleaners, cashiers, and drivers.

Foreign workers must have at least a high school diploma or two years of job-specific training to qualify under the LSP, while employers must agree to do the following in order to qualify:

- pay the full transportation costs for the foreign worker to Canada from the country of origin;
- cover all recruitment costs related to hiring the foreign worker;
- ensure that affordable and suitable accommodation is available for the foreign worker;
- provide temporary medical insurance coverage for the duration of the employment;
- register the foreign worker with the provincial workers' compensation/ workplace safety insurance plan;
- sign an employment contract; and
- demonstrate continued efforts to recruit and train Canadian workers.[23]

There is no prohibition against spouses and dependent children accompanying a foreign worker to Canada for the 24 months of work; however, questions may be raised about the applicant's bona fides and ability to support dependants while in Canada. Furthermore, spouses of workers admitted under the pilot project are not eligible for an open work permit and children may be required to pay international student rates to attend school.

The Live-In Caregiver Program

Canada has had programs for the recruitment and employment of foreign care-givers for a number of decades beginning with the Foreign Domestic Movement Program (1980 to 1992), which enabled caregivers—mostly women—to apply for what was then called landed-immigrant status after living in their employers' houses for a minimum of two years. The program was created to address the shortage of caregivers in Canada. The current Live-In Caregiver Program (LCP) is a variation of the former program, which introduced new criteria for education and skills. There is now a requirement for the caregiver to have the equivalent of a Canadian Grade 12 education supplemented with domestic training.

The attraction for the temporary foreign worker is that she becomes eligible to apply for permanent residence once she has completed two years, or the equivalent of 3,900 hours of work, within a four-year period. However, the program does not allow family members to accompany the caregiver until she has fulfilled her time, thereby leading to family separation for a minimum period of two years (but usually more.) Another concern about the program is the requirement to live in the em-ployer's home, which can create a greater possibility for sexual abuse and labour exploitation.

The LCP applies only to the care of

- children aged 18 or under,
- an elderly person aged 65 or older, or
- a person with a disability.

It is important to distinguish the LCP from other categories of persons who may perform a domestic or care-giving function, such as the following:

- *Participants in an international youth exchange program.* This is a reciprocal exchange program that enables youth to engage in short-term work or study activities in Canada. Participants may find work as a nanny or mother's helper.
- *Diplomatic staff.* Employees of diplomatic staff, such as domestic workers, may enter Canada as accredited members of a diplomat's suite.

These categories are not part of the LCP; therefore, the persons who apply under them are not eligible to apply for permanent residence in Canada.

The employer must meet the specific HRSDC requirements for the LCP, and the applicant must meet the specific LCP requirements as outlined below.

EMPLOYER REQUIREMENTS

The LCP applies only to caregivers who live in the home of the person for whom they are caring. This is the case even if the home is not the employer's residence. For example, an employer may hire a live-in caregiver to look after an elderly parent who lives at a separate address. It is also possible for a live-in caregiver to reside in two different locations in circumstances where the caregiver will care for a child whose parents share custody. In this instance, both locations should be disclosed to

HRSDC. It is also acceptable under the LCP for one parent to act as the employer even though the children live with the other parent.

The employer must employ the live-in caregiver on a full-time basis and must provide a private and furnished room with a lock for the exclusive use of the caregiver.

To obtain an HRSDC confirmation, an employer must satisfy the following requirements:

- submit an LMO to HRSDC (as described earlier in this chapter);
- submit a contract (SC-EMP 5093; see the weblink on page 135), signed by both the employer and live-in caregiver, which sets out the following information:
  - The employer's responsibility for mandatory employer-paid benefits:
    ◇ transportation to Canada from the live-in caregiver's country to the residence where she will be working in Canada;
    ◇ medical insurance coverage from the date of her arrival until she is eligible for provincial health insurance;
    ◇ workplace safety insurance coverage for the duration of her employment; and
    ◇ all recruitment fees, including any amount payable to a third-party recruiter or agents hired by the employer.
  - the caregiver's job duties (for example, details about the number and ages of children, etc.);
  - the caregiver's hours of work (and details about anticipated overtime);
  - the caregiver's wages;
  - accommodation arrangements (for example, room and board);
  - holiday and sick leave entitlements; and
  - terms that address termination and resignation.

Quebec employers must apply for a Certificat d'acceptation du Québec (Quebec Certificate of Acceptance, or CAQ) from the Ministère de l'Immigration et des Communautés culturelles in addition to applying for an LMO.

In most provinces, an employer is required to advertise the live-in caregiver position to find qualified Canadians or permanent residents. Advertisements in newspapers are not the only type of acceptable recruitment available—also valid are flyers, networking, recruitment agencies, friends, and local and ethnic newspapers. If an employer has published an ad in a language other than English or French, a translation should be enclosed with the LMO application.

An employer is permitted to seek candidates who possess desired skills, such as the ability to speak in a language other than English or French, or to cook. However, such preferences are not weighted by the officer when assessing an application under the LCP.

Live-in caregivers must obey the restrictions imposed by the LCP. For example, a live-in caregiver may not work for more than one employer at a time. Additionally, a live-in caregiver may not work for a health agency or labour contractor, or work in daycare or foster care.

It is acceptable for an employer to make an offer of employment to a live-in caregiver for less than 12 months. However, if this is the case, the employer will most likely be contacted by HRSDC to find out why, because CIC generally issues the work permit for a minimum duration of one year.

In the event that the live-in caregiver changes employers, the new employer must obtain a new HRSDC confirmation, the new employer and live-in caregiver must sign an employment contract, and the live-in caregiver must apply for a new work permit.

WEBLINK

Useful LCP Weblinks
The Live-In Caregiver Program
Employment Contract Template available online at: http://www.cic.gc.ca/english/work/caregiver/sample-contract.asp.

Service Canada provides the actual application forms and a guide online at: Contract Template—Live-in Caregiver Program http://www.servicecanada.gc.ca/eforms/forms/sc-emp5498%282011-09-005%29e.pdf.

Guide for Completion of Employment Contract Template—Live-in Caregiver Program http://www.servicecanada.gc.ca/eforms/forms/sc-emp5498%282011-09-001%29e-guide.pdf.

ELIGIBILITY CRITERIA

The criteria set out by CIC for an LCP applicant includes educational, training, and language requirements, which must be met by foreign live-in caregivers seeking to qualify for the LCP. Specifically, the requirements for applicants who wish to work outside Quebec are as follows:[24]

1. *Educational requirement.* Successful completion of the equivalent of Canadian secondary school.

2. *Training/work experience requirement.* Either the training requirement or the work experience requirement below:

   - Training requirement—successful completion of six months of full-time classroom training in the field or occupation related to the job in question. (Full time is considered at least 25 to 30 hours per week of educational instruction.) Additionally, the training must be in a classroom setting; therefore, correspondence courses are not acceptable.

   - Work experience requirement—completion of at least 12 months of full-time paid employment, including at least six months of continuous employment with one employer, in the related field or occupation (for example, in a daycare, hospital, or senior citizen home), within three years immediately prior to the day on which the person submits an application for a work permit to a visa office.

3. *Language proficiency requirement.* The ability to read, listen, and speak English or French at a level sufficient to communicate effectively in an unsupervised setting, such as to respond to emergency situations by contacting a doctor, an ambulance, the police, or the fire department, answer the door and the telephone, and administer medication. In the event that the officer is not convinced that the applicant has sufficient language proficiency, the officer may request an interview.

4. *Mandatory employment contract.* The employer must forward the original employment contract to the applicant. As noted earlier, the contract must

be signed by both the employer (not by the employer's representative or another employee on behalf of the employer) and by the live-in caregiver. Furthermore, the employment contract must be consistent with provincial employment standards.

Live-in caregivers seeking to work in Quebec need only 6 months of work experience in the related occupation, as opposed to the 12 months of experience outlined above. However, the live-in caregiver is required to obtain a Quebec Certificate of Acceptance before applying for the work permit, and the employer is required to facilitate access to French courses outside regular working hours.

The applicant must follow the procedures for applying for a work permit (as discussed earlier), including proof of her educational credentials (the equivalent of Canadian secondary school graduation) and proof of training (diploma and transcripts) or proof of work experience (letters of reference from previous employers), and she must undergo a medical examination.

Consider the following scenario related to paid work experience:

> Maria, a Filipino national, is seeking to apply for a work permit under the LCP. Maria has obtained a job in Canada as a live-in caregiver to care for a Canadian employer's two minor children. The employer has obtained the required LMO.
>
> Maria would like to know whether she is eligible to obtain a work permit under the LCP. Maria has 17 years of work experience as a caregiver taking care of her own three children at home. She has a high level of English proficiency and has completed a high school program. Would Maria qualify for a work permit?

Unfortunately for Maria, her work experience does not comply with the requirements set out by the LCP, because her work experience is not paid work experience. Although there may be situations where the applicant is employed as a live-in caregiver by a relative, applicants must satisfy the officer that they were actually paid for work performed.

Consider the following scenario on required documents:

> Boupha, a Cambodian national, submitted her application for a work permit under the LCP to the Canadian embassy in Bangkok. Boupha completed a college diploma in physiotherapy and then completed seven months of full-time training for live-in caregivers in a classroom setting, within the past year.
>
> Boupha has included in her work permit application all of the requisite documents that establish her experience in accordance with the requirements of the IRPA and the IRP Regulations. In addition, Boupha is including the documents that the Canadian employer forwarded to her, these being the HRSDC confirmation and the employment contract signed by the Canadian employer's legal representative. Boupha signed the employment contract prior to submitting her application to the Canadian embassy. Finally, Boupha also included the identity documents and police clearances for her and all members of her family. Boupha would like to know whether her application is complete.

Section 8.2 of "OP 14: Processing Applicants for the Live-In Caregiver Program" in the CIC operations manual *Overseas Processing (OP)* sets out the documents required for LCP applications. It specifically provides that the employment contract must be signed by both the employer and by the applicant. It is not sufficient that the contract was signed by the legal representative of her employer.

PERIOD OF VALIDITY OF WORK PERMIT

Because a live-in caregiver's work permit is valid for only one year at a time, it must be renewed every year to maintain eligibility under the LCP. The work permit may be extended up to a maximum of four years, during which time the two years of full-time employment to qualify for permanent residence must be completed. The four-year extension was established to give the live-in caregiver flexibility to compensate for periods of unemployment, illness, vacation, or maternity leave.

In the event that the live-in caregiver continues to work for the same employer and is seeking to renew her work permit, there is no need for a new LMO. She must submit the following documents:

- a letter from the employer stating that the live-in caregiver will continue to be employed full time for another year; and
- a new employment contract extending the original employment contract for another year.

In the event that a live-in caregiver is between jobs and has not yet found a new employer, the live-in caregiver may apply for a **bridge extension**. A bridge extension is an interim work permit valid for a period of two months, which gives the live-in caregiver the opportunity to find a new employer within that period.

PLACE OF APPLICATION

Applicants seeking an initial work permit under the LCP must submit their applications to a visa office abroad. This may be a little confusing, because applicants already in Canada with a TRV are entitled to submit an application in Canada for work permits and renewals, study permits, and live-in caregiver's applications for permanent residence in Canada.[25] However, applicants seeking an initial work permit under the LCP must apply outside Canada, regardless of whether they are in Canada with a TRV.

Consider the following scenario on where to apply for an LCP permit:

Julie is a student completing a six-month live-in caregiver program at Humber College. Julie will graduate from this program in May 2009 and would like to submit her application for a work permit under the LCP soon after completing the program. She would also like to eventually become a permanent resident of Canada. Julie is unsure where to submit her application for a work permit.

Julie must submit her application for a work permit to the visa office that corresponds to her country of nationality. Applicants seeking an initial work permit under the LCP must submit their applications outside Canada to qualify under the LCP and therefore be eligible for permanent residence in Canada. Consequently, if Julie submits her application to a case processing centre in Canada, she will not qualify under the LCP and will not be eligible for permanent residence in Canada. Julie, however, may apply for extensions of her work permit in Canada and, once she is eligible for permanent residence, she may submit her application without having to leave Canada.

APPLYING FOR PERMANENT RESIDENCE

Family members may not accompany live-in caregivers to Canada. Even when an employer agrees that a family member may reside with the caregiver in the employer's residence, there are no guarantees that any subsequent employer would agree to the same terms.[26] To mitigate the harsh consequences of this to many caregivers who leave their own children behind, the LCP allows caregivers and their family members to apply for permanent residence after the live-in caregiver has fulfilled the terms of the LCP—24 months of authorized full-time employment or a total of 3,900 hours of authorized full-time employment, within the 4 years of arrival to Canada.

Live-in caregivers applying for permanent residence may request **parallel processing** for some or all of their family members residing in or outside Canada.[26] Alternatively, live-in caregivers may sponsor family members at a later date after becoming permanent residents themselves.

Additionally, a live-in caregiver who has received first-stage approval (approval in principle) of the permanent resident application is entitled to apply for an open work permit. This allows the live-in caregiver to accept employment and to work for any employer for the time period specified on the work permit.

Business Workers

Significant Benefit

Consistent with ss. 204 to 208 of the IRP Regulations, senior managers, executives, and individuals with specialized knowledge may apply for a work permit without having first obtained an HRSDC confirmation, provided that their presence in Canada will result or is likely to result in a **significant benefit** to Canada. The meaning of "significant" equates to important or notable.

When assessing requests for work permits based on significant social or cultural benefits, immigration officers are required to consider the impact that the foreign worker would have on Canada's labour market and economy. If an individual's work in Canada is likely to produce a significant social or cultural benefit, then "the balance of practical considerations argues for the issuance of a work permit in a time frame shorter than would be necessary to obtain an HRSDC opinion."[27]

Officers rely on the following objective measures when assessing whether a foreign worker's presence in Canada will result in a significant social or cultural benefit:

- the foreign worker's degree;
- whether the foreign worker has significant full-time experience in the occupation sought (ten or more years of experience);
- awards and accolades conferred on the foreign worker;
- membership in organizations requiring excellence of its members;
- whether the foreign worker has judged or critiqued others' work in the field of specialty;
- scientific or scholarly contributions in the field; and
- publications authored by the foreign national in academic or industry publications.

Business Visitors and Professionals

A **business visitor** is a foreign worker who seeks to engage in international business activities in Canada without directly entering the Canadian labour market (IRP Regulations, s. 187(1)). Thus, the business visitor's primary source of remuneration is outside Canada, and the principal place of business and actual place of accrual of profits remains predominantly outside Canada. For example, a foreigner who wants to enter Canada for the purpose of purchasing Canadian goods for a foreign business is a business visitor, as is a foreigner who wants to enter Canada for the purpose of receiving training by a Canadian parent of the corporation that employs the foreign worker outside Canada.

In contrast, a **business person** is someone who seeks entry through some sort of pre-arrangement—for example, as a salaried employee under a personal contract with a Canadian employer or through a contract with the professional's employer in the home country. The business person class includes foreign workers who are seeking to enter Canada under an international agreement such as NAFTA or GATS (see "International Free Trade Agreements" below).

Consider the following scenario:

> Maps & Software Inc. is a US company that manufactures marine maps and computer software. Maps & Software Inc. does not have any subsidiaries or affiliates in Canada. The company is interested in sending three of its employees to Toronto to conduct research for a new mapping software device that will assist mariners in navigating Lake Ontario. Once research is finalized, the three employees are to return to the United States with their findings; once the product is manufactured, it will be available to anyone who wants to purchase it. Are the three employees required to obtain work permits?

In this case, the three employees of the US company are not required to obtain work permits, for the following reasons: there is no Canadian employer contracting for their services; the US company will be the direct beneficiary of the foreign workers' efforts; and the employees' source of remuneration for the work performed remains outside Canada. Consequently, the three workers satisfy the business visitor's criteria which exempts them from having to obtain a work permit. Additionally, because they are US nationals, they can apply for the business visitor's visa at the port of entry.

Members of the clergy are not required to obtain a work permit to work in Canada. Pursuant to s. 186(l) of IRP Regulations:

> [a] foreign worker may work in Canada without a work permit … as a person who is responsible for assisting a congregation or group in the achievement of its spiritual goals and whose main duties are to preach doctrine, perform functions related to gatherings of the congregation or group or provide spiritual counselling.

However, they are required to ask for a **visitor's record** at the port of entry. Consider the following scenario:

> Larry, a US national who lives in Utah, has recently been hired by a Canadian church to serve as its minister for the upcoming year. Larry has been given contradictory information regarding whether he needs a work permit. Some have said that everyone who works in Canada needs a work permit, and others have told him that members of the clergy may work without a work permit in Canada. Which opinion is correct?

Larry needs to request a visitor's record from the port of entry reflecting the one-year duration of his clergy work in Canada. However, he will not need a work permit because work done during the course of a legitimate business visit is considered exempt work.

Performing artists are also exempt from obtaining a work permit, provided that they are not in an employment relationship with a Canadian organization or business that has contracted them for their services in Canada. For example, singers performing at a private event are exempt from obtaining a work permit, whereas bands performing at bars or clubs or actors performing in a Canadian-based production are not exempt from obtaining a work permit.[28]

Intra-Company Transfers

The **intra-company transfer** category was designed to assist multinational businesses to move executives temporarily, when required for business purposes. It applies to executives who would not necessarily provide a significant benefit to the social, cultural, or economic threads of Canadian life, and therefore would not qualify under the significant benefit category.

The intra-company transfer category permits "international companies to temporarily transfer qualified employees to Canada for the purpose of improving management effectiveness, expanding Canadian exports, and enhancing the competitiveness of Canadian entities in overseas markets."[29] In other words, the admission of an intra-company transferee to Canada is subject to the relationship between the Canadian and foreign company. The intra-company transferee will be admitted for the purpose of assisting in the operations of a foreign company's Canadian parent, subsidiary, branch, or affiliate company.

To qualify as an intra-company transferee exempt from obtaining an LMO, a foreign worker must

- seek entry to undertake employment in Canada for a multinational business that is or will be doing business in both Canada and in the foreign country;[30]
- assume a position in an executive, senior managerial, or specialized knowledge capacity;
- have been employed in a similar full-time position for a minimum of one year in the three years prior to coming to Canada; and
- comply with all immigration requirements for temporary entry.

Additionally, the foreign worker must submit the following documentation:

- confirmation of her continuous employment (full time, not accumulated part time) with the enterprise outside Canada for one year within the three-year period immediately preceding the date of application;
- an outline of her position in an executive or managerial capacity or one involving specialized knowledge, including title, place in the organization, and job description;
- an outline of her position in Canada, including title, place in the organization, and job description;
- in the case of a foreign national possessing "specialized knowledge," evidence that the person has such knowledge and that the position in Canada requires it;
- an indication of her intended duration of stay; and
- a description of the relationship between the enterprise in Canada and the enterprise in the foreign country and, on request, evidence of this, such as annual reports, articles of incorporation, financial statements, partnership agreements, and business tax returns.

There are no restrictions on which country the foreign executive is from. Consider the following scenario:

Ernesto, an Italian executive with San Pelligrani, a renowned bottled-beverage company, is being transferred to run San Pelligrani's Canadian subsidiary. The company relationship qualifies San Pelligrani under the affiliate definition in the intra-company transfer category. The Canadian office employs 350 people.

Ernesto has worked as an executive with San Pelligrani in Italy for the past 15 years. He is in good health and has no criminal record. Ernesto would like to submit the bare minimum in documentation for the intra-company transfer work permit application. What is Ernesto required to submit?

Ernesto's application requires only a company support letter and the fees for the work permit. The letter from the foreign company is crucial because it will support the fact that Ernesto has come from an executive position; that he will be moving into a similar role in the Canadian office; and that the corporate relationship between the foreign entity and the Canadian entity exists and complies with the IRP Regulations.

As was discussed earlier, an LMO is not needed because intra-company transferees in the executive category do not require HRSDC approval. Rather, they are LMO-exempt as per s. 205 of the IRP Regulations. A copy of the applicant's university degree is also unnecessary because the educational background of the applicant in the executive transfer category is not required. Indeed, the executive need not have graduated from high school. Rather, he must hold an executive position in the company abroad, be coming to occupy an executive position in the Canadian affiliate, and have worked for the company for at least one year in the past three years in an executive or senior managerial role.

Executives and senior managers are permitted to renew their initial intra-company transfer work permits up to a maximum of seven years. Specialized knowledge workers may renew their work permits up to a maximum of five years. After the maximum period is reached, the foreign worker must leave Canada and the Canadian labour market for at least one year. When the year is over, the foreign worker may reapply and begin the cycle again.

MERGERS AND ACQUISITIONS

If the multinational company that employs the foreign worker is subject to a corporate merger or acquisition,[31] the corporate relationship between the foreign business and the Canadian business may be affected. Because this is a critical component of the foreign worker's eligibility under this category, a merger or acquisition may have consequences for a foreign worker who currently possesses a work permit under the intra-company transfer category.

If it can be established that a qualifying relationship between the foreign and Canadian businesses[32] continues to exist, even though there have been changes in ownership internally, the foreign worker may still qualify as an intra-company transferee. The Canadian company need only document the corporate restructuring with CIC. This would be the case if the foreign and Canadian companies remained related through a common parent company that held the shares of both subsidiaries.

However, if the entities no longer meet the requirements for this relationship, then any foreign intra-company transferee currently working for the Canadian entity would not qualify to continue working for the new entity. The foreign worker will be required to obtain either a new work permit under another LMO-exempt category (if possible) or an LMO in order to obtain a work permit. Foreign workers must address the issue as soon as possible with CIC to avoid any risk of misrepresentation and, in a worst-case scenario, risk of the foreign worker being barred from entry to Canada.

Where the employee's position has changed only in name, but all other duties remain the same, eligibility for a work permit is not affected. An amendment of the work permit may be all that is needed. However, where the responsibilities have changed, eligibility may require reassessment. The foreign worker must be in an executive, senior managerial, or specialized knowledge position to continue qualifying for the intra-company transfer work permit. If the foreign worker's job description has changed such that she is no longer eligible, an application must be made for a new work permit.

Consider the following scenario:

> Robert holds a work permit as an intra-company transferee. Because of a merger transaction, Robert's position changed, but the description of his duties remained the same. The merger transaction did not affect the corporate relationship between the Canadian entity and the foreign entity.

Robert's eligibility is not affected; however, he should seek an amendment to his work permit to reflect the change.

Finally, in all cases it is important to assess whether the corporate relationship between the Canadian entity and foreign entity continues to be valid. Is the Canadian employer still doing business, either directly or through a parent, branch, affiliate, or subsidiary, in another country to which the employee can reasonably be expected to be transferred at the end of his assignment in Canada?

International Free Trade Agreements

According to s. 204 of the IRP Regulations, a foreign national may be issued a work permit without an LMO to perform work in Canada pursuant to an international agreement between Canada and one or more countries. Among the international agreements to which Canada is a signatory are the North American Free Trade Agreement (NAFTA) and the General Agreement on Trade in Services (GATS), the Canada–Chile Free Trade Agreement, the Canada–Peru Free Trade Agreement, and the Canada–Colombia Free Trade Agreement. We will briefly examine two of these agreements—NAFTA and GATS.

NORTH AMERICAN FREE TRADE AGREEMENT

The North American Free Trade Agreement (NAFTA), arguably the most important agreement for those practising US and Canadian immigration law, was created to facilitate trade among its three signatory countries: Canada, the United States, and Mexico. NAFTA facilitates trade as well as the movement of persons involved in the trade of goods or services. Business people covered by NAFTA are not required to obtain an LMO and can gain quicker, easier, temporary entry into Canada.

NAFTA covers three categories of foreign workers: business visitors, professionals, and intra-company transferees. It is important not to confuse "intra-company transfer," a category discussed earlier, with the intra-company transferee category under NAFTA, which applies only to citizens of Mexico and the United States.

From a Canadian immigration perspective, a business visitor under NAFTA refers to citizens of the United States or Mexico who seek to engage in international business activities related to research and design; growth, manufacturing, and production;

marketing; sales; distribution; after-sales service; and general service.[33] Because business visitors are restricted from entering the Canadian labour market and their primary source of remuneration must remain outside Canada, they are not required to obtain an LMO or a work permit. However, business visitors must apply at the port of entry for a visitor's record and must comply with the usual admissibility requirements for temporary entry.

A **professional** under NAFTA refers to a citizen of the United States or Mexico who has pre-arranged employment[34] with a Canadian employer and whose occupation is listed in the 60-plus occupations/professions covered by NAFTA. Such professions include accountants, computer systems analysts, engineers, management consultants, and technical writers. Professionals must be qualified to work, as evidenced by degrees, diplomas, professional licences, accreditation or registration, and must comply with existing immigration requirements for temporary entry.

The professional must be qualified to provide professional services in Canada; therefore, both the qualifications of the individual and the position in Canada must be considered. For example, a lawyer must be seeking to enter Canada as a lawyer and not as a paralegal. Alternatively, a paralegal cannot be admitted to work as a lawyer unless the applicant is also qualified as a lawyer as indicated in the Minimum Education Requirements and Alternative Credentials List in appendix 1603.D.1 of NAFTA.

Additionally, an individual must be seeking to enter Canada to work in a position for which he possesses the required qualifications. For example, a physiotherapist cannot be admitted to Canada to be a corporate executive, because physiotherapy is his field of qualification.

The list of Minimum Education Requirements and Alternative Credentials provides more than 60 professions and their equivalent minimum educational requirements and alternative credentials to assess the qualifications of foreign professionals.[35]

On initial entry, the professional is given work permit status for a maximum duration of one year. Extensions are also issued for up to one year, provided that the individual continues to comply with the requirements for professionals.

The professional category does not allow self-employment in Canada. However, responding to unsolicited inquiries about services that the professional may be able to perform, or establishing an office from which to deliver pre-arranged services to clients, does not constitute self-employment.

The **intra-company transferee** is the third category under NAFTA. As mentioned previously, it is different from the intra-company transfer category under the IRPA because it applies only to citizens of Mexico and the United States (whereas that category under the IRPA applies to foreign nationals from any country). However, because of the harmonization of IRPA and NAFTA provisions, there are now no differences in entry requirements and work permit durations.

Citizens of the United States or Mexico whose employment pertains to an executive or managerial capacity or one involving specialized knowledge for an enterprise in the United States or Mexico that has a parent, branch, subsidiary, or affiliate relationship with a Canadian company may qualify. The executive is required to have been continuously employed in a similar position outside Canada for one year in the previous three-year period. Like all other visitors, intra-company transferees must also comply with existing immigration requirements for temporary entry.

Consider the following scenario:

> Ricardo, a Mexican citizen, arrives at a Canadian port of entry to apply for a work permit. On arrival, he advises the CBSA officer that he has been offered employment by the Canadian subsidiary of a Mexican company where he worked as a senior marketing manager from May 2007 until he left approximately two months ago.

Ricardo may be granted a work permit because he qualifies as a NAFTA intra-company transferee pursuant to LMO exemption CEC T24 under s. 204(a)(i) of the IRP Regulations. Ricardo is a Mexican citizen who has worked for the Mexican parent company in a managerial capacity for more than one year in the three-year period preceding the presentation of his application for adjudication.

Both professionals and intra-company transferees may alternatively be admitted under the general service provision of the business visitor category, if they are not seeking to enter the Canadian labour market and their primary source of remuneration remains outside Canada—in other words, if they meet the business visitor criteria.

GENERAL AGREEMENT OF TRADE IN SERVICES

The General Agreement on Trade in Services (GATS) is similar to NAFTA in several respects, including the categories under which a foreign worker may apply and the fact that such categories are HRSDC-exempt.

Under GATS, each of the 155 member nations has made individual commitments to member signatories concerning trade in services in specific market sectors. Additionally, GATS has set out unique rules for the entry of professionals.

A **GATS professional** refers to a person who seeks to engage in an activity at a professional level in a designated profession, and who meets the following criteria:

- possesses citizenship of a member nation, or the right of permanent residence in Australia or New Zealand;
- has an occupation that falls within the definition of an eligible GATS profession;
- works as part of a short-term services contract obtained by a company in another member nation; and
- has the necessary academic credentials and professional qualifications, which have been duly recognized, where appropriate, by the professional association in Canada.[36]

The list of GATS professional occupations and their equivalent requirements can be found in appendix D of "FW 1: Foreign Worker Manual" in the CIC operations manual *Temporary Foreign Workers Guidelines (FW)*.[37]

GATS professionals are not permitted to work in service sectors that relate to education, health services, culture, and sports services. Visas are restricted to a maximum duration of 90 days; thus, extensions beyond the 90 days are not permitted under the GATS professional category.[38]

WEBLINK

As of May 10, 2012, the World Trade Organization website listed 155 member nations. The current list of member nations is available at http://www.wto.org/english/thewto_e/whatis_e/tif_e/org6_e.htm.

Canadian Experience Class

The Canadian experience class allows certain foreign students who are graduates of a Canadian post-secondary institution and possess professional, managerial, and skilled Canadian work experience to apply for permanent residence. Changes to the IRPR created the Canadian experience class (CEC) in 2008 as a prescribed "class of persons who may become permanent residents on the basis of their experience in Canada and who intend to reside in a province other than the Province of Quebec" (IRRP, s. 87.1). This class was created so that graduates from post-secondary institutions and temporary foreign workers with Canadian experience can transition to permanent residence status.

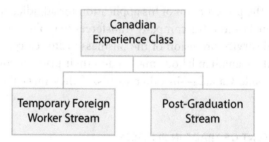

To qualify, a temporary foreign resident must have maintained her status within the 24 months before applying for permanent residence.

If the applicant was a student, then after having graduated with a diploma, degree, or trade from a Canadian post-secondary institution, she must have acquired at least 12 months of full-time work experience, or the equivalent in part-time work experience, in one or more occupations that are listed in Skill Type 0 Management Occupations or Skill Level A or B of the *National Occupational Classification* matrix.

To qualify for permanent residence, the temporary foreign worker must prove that she has gained work experience

- of at least 24 months of full-time work experience, or the equivalent in part-time work experience;

- in one or more occupations that are listed in Skill Type 0 Management Occupations or Skill Level A or B of the *National Occupational Classification* matrix; and

- acquired within the past 36 months.

In either situation, the applicant must demonstrate a language proficiency that corresponds to the *Canadian Language Benchmarks 2000* for the English language or the *Niveaux de compétence linguistique canadiens 2006* for the French language. The specific benchmarks are set out at s. 87.1(2) in the IRP Regulations according to the applicants work experience.

Applications under this class follow similar procedures as all other applications for permanent residence discussed in Chapter 5.

Temporary Resident Permit

A foreign national may be barred from entering Canada as a temporary resident, either because of inadmissibility or because of a failure to meet the requirements of the IRPA. Sometimes it is still possible to enter Canada with a **temporary resident permit (TRP)**, formerly known as a "minister's permit." TRPs are issued for a limited period of time and may be cancelled at any time.

It is important to ensure that all other options for temporary entry are thoroughly explored before applying for a TRP. For example, in a case of inadmissibility because of criminality, has the person since been deemed rehabilitated or pardoned and therefore become admissible?

Consider the following situations where the granting of a TRP may be appropriate:

1. *Medical treatment.* A foreign national wishes to come to Canada for pre-arranged medical treatment, but is inadmissible on health grounds. In this instance an officer may consider whether the treatment is unavailable in the home country, the cost of the treatment, and how the medical costs will be covered. Unless the foreigner is suffering from a communicable or contagious disease, and precautions cannot guarantee that there will be no threat to anyone en route or in Canada, a TRP may be issued.

2. *Minor crimes.* A foreign national wishes to come to Canada as a visitor, but is inadmissible on the ground of criminality. A TRP may still be issued if the following are true: the offence was minor (did not involve drugs, physical violence, or damage to property); there are no more than two convictions; there is no pattern of criminal behaviour; the individual has completed all sentences; and there is a high probability that the individual will successfully settle in Canada without committing further offences. However, it will be necessary to demonstrate a compelling need for admission to Canada, even if the offence was minor and all other conditions were met. For example, the foreigner may be seeking entry to Canada in order to visit a dying parent.

In contrast, cases that may not warrant favourable consideration include cases of an inadmissible sponsored parent needing medical treatment who has other children or family members in the home country to provide care, or a criminally inadmissible spouse with a risk of violence or repeat offence. Additionally, TRPs are not granted to those who want to restore their temporary resident status as a visitor, student, or worker when their status has expired.

Application Criteria

A foreign national who is inadmissible, or does not meet the requirements of the IRPA, may be eligible for a TRP and become a temporary resident if an officer is of the opinion that, according to s. 24(1), admission is justified in the circumstances. Whether or not to grant the TRP is at the discretion of the officer, who measures the risk posed by the foreign national to Canadians and Canadian society against the foreign national's need for admission (or in some situations the need to remain in Canada, if previously admitted). The foreign national's circumstances must be compelling and sufficient to overcome inadmissibility.

The TRP may be cancelled at any time. However, it is important to note that it remains valid until any one of the following events occurs:

- the permit is cancelled under s. 24(1) of the IRPA;
- the permit holder leaves Canada without obtaining prior authorization to re-enter Canada;
- the period of validity specified on the permit expires; or
- a period of three years elapses from the permit's date of validity (IRP Regulations, s. 63).

A TRP carries privileges greater than those accorded to visitors, students, and workers. For example, foreign workers holding a TRP are allowed to submit applications inland for a work or study permit, and may have access to health or other social services.

Additionally, TRP holders may be eligible for permanent residence as long as they remain continuously in Canada on a permit for at least three years and do not become inadmissible on other grounds. Therefore, permit holders must be cautious about a break in continuity, which may affect their eligibility for permanent residence. A break in continuity occurs when permit holders, without authorization for re-entry, leave Canada, or when they neglect their responsibility to seek an extension of their status prior to the expiry of their permit. It is therefore recommended that permit holders do not leave Canada unless their TRP specifically authorizes re-entry, and that they apply for an extension of their status at least 30 days before the permit expires.

Place of Application

TRPs are issued at both Canadian ports of entry and CIC inland offices, whereas temporary resident extensions are only issued inland.

A foreign national outside Canada wishing to apply for a TRP must do so at the visa office. The visa office will assess the application and refuse it or approve it. If approved, the TRP will be issued at the port of entry, when the approved person arrives in Canada. The visa office does not issue the TRP itself.

Therefore, a foreign national outside Canada may apply at the port of entry or visa office for a TRP. Depending on the circumstances, an officer at a port of entry may agree to consider this type of application. However, it is generally not advisable to apply at the port of entry, given that an officer always reserves the right to refuse entry and may require the person to leave immediately. Although processing times at a visa office can take several months, this route may be safer than taking the risk of appearing at a port of entry.

If the officer approves the TRP, the duration of the permit will be determined on the basis of the facts and circumstances presented by the applicant. For example, a person seeking to enter Canada for a short business trip will be issued a TRP that is valid for the duration of that trip and no longer.

Consider the following scenario where the applicant was admitted lawfully and then her status as a temporary resident expired:

> Cecilia is seeking an extension of her work permit. She continues to work, even though her work permit expired a week ago. Unfortunately, Cecilia forgot to send her application for renewing her work permit to a case processing centre before it expired. An inadmissibility finding is made against Cecilia on the basis of her violating Canadian immigration laws by working without a valid work permit. What does Cecilia have to do to obtain a new work permit?

When there has been an inadmissibility finding, a TRP is required to enter or stay in Canada, no matter what type of inadmissibility (IRPA, s. 24(1)). Note that Cecilia should not apply for an extension because her work permit has already expired. Additionally, Cecilia is not eligible to apply for restoration of status because she has been found inadmissible. Thus, the fact that 90 days have not passed since the expiration of her work permit is irrelevant (IRP Regulations, s. 182).

Designated Foreign Nationals

To curtail abuse of and limit access to Canada's immigration and refugee systems, Bill C-31 (*Protecting Canada's Immigration System Act*, which received royal assent on June 28, 2012) amended the IRPA with provisions to differentiate between those who follow the appropriate application procedures and those who do not. A foreign national who arrives as part of a group that has been designated as an irregular arrival by the minister (pursuant to IRPA, s. 20.1(1)) is a **designated foreign national** (IRPA, s. 20.1(2)).

The IRPA restricts the application for a TRP by a designated foreign national until after five years of becoming designated (IRPA, s. 24(5)); or

- from the final determination on a refugee claim; or
- from the final determination of an application for protection.

Moreover, an application can be refused by an officer if the designated foreign national failed to comply with conditions.

APPENDIX

The following box provides a reference list of important definitions and topics that relate to temporary entry to Canada.

Reference for Temporary Entry to Canada

Provision	IRPA and IRP Regulations
Definition, application	IRPA s. 22
Obligations—general	IRPA ss. 20 and 29
Obligations—work, study	IRPA s. 30
Loss of status	IRPA s. 47
Temporary resident authorization (visa)	IRPA s. 22 and IRP Regulations ss. 179 to 185
Definitions: "study permit," "work"	IRP Regulations ss. 1 and 2
General entry requirements	IRP Regulations s. 7
Place of application	IRP Regulations s. 11(2)
Medical examinations	IRP Regulations s. 30
Deposit or guarantee	IRP Regulations s. 45
Passport and visa exemptions	IRP Regulations ss. 52 and 190
Employer requirements, offences	IRPA ss. 124, 125, and 126; IRP Regulations s. 203(15)
Workers—no permit	IRP Regulations ss. 186 and 187
Students—no permit	IRP Regulations ss. 188 and 189
TRV exemptions	IRP Regulations s. 190
Visitor class	IRP Regulations ss. 191 to 193.5
Worker class	IRP Regulations ss. 194 to 209
Students: applications, permits, restrictions	IRP Regulations ss. 210 to 222

KEY TERMS

bridge extension, 137
business person, 139
business visitor, 139
designated foreign national, 149
dual intent, 99
GATS professional, 145
intra-company transfer, 140
intra-company transferee, 144
labour market opinion (LMO), 124

letter of acceptance, 111
Low Skill Pilot Project (LSP), 132
multiple-entry visa, 107
open work permit, 117
parallel processing, 138
professional, 144
Seasonal Agricultural Worker
  Program (SAWP), 131
significant benefit, 138

single-entry visa, 107
Super Visa, 108
temporary resident permit (TRP), 147
transit visa, 108
visitor visas, 92
visitor's record, 140

REVIEW QUESTIONS

1. What kind of documents can an applicant who wants to visit Canada provide to prove that she will leave at the end of the authorized stay?

2. What is a TRV?

3. Name the different types of Canadian TRVs and briefly describe their use.

4. What are the application requirements for a foreign national who is applying for a Super Visa?

5. What does the visa officer consider when processing an application for a TRV?

6. Under which conditions can temporary residents lose their status and privilege?

7. To change the terms and conditions of their authorization or extend their stay, what must temporary residents do?

8. Describe the main document that a person must submit in order to obtain a student visa.

9. List the specific terms and conditions listed on a work visa.

10. Some business visitors may enter Canada more easily under the provisions of trade agreements with Canada. Name two such agreements and describe them briefly.

11. What is the maximum allowable cumulative time that a temporary foreign worker can work in Canada?

12. What is a positive LMO and which department is responsible for its issuance?

NOTES

1. Citizenship and Immigration Canada, *Annual Report to Parliament on Immigration 2011*, October 27, 2011, s. 2, at 19, http://www.cic.gc.ca/english/pdf/pub/annual-report-2011.pdf.

2. Ibid.

3. Fees and exemptions are established in the *Immigration and Refugee Protection Regulations* and thus subject to change. The list of exemptions is found at s. 296.

4. Citizenship and Immigration Canada, "OP 12: Students," in *Overseas Processing (OP)*, December 15, 2008, s. 5.13, http://www.cic.gc.ca/english/resources/manuals/op/op12-eng.pdf.

5. Designated countries or territories are those that have been determined to have a higher incidence of serious communicable disease than Canada. The list of designated countries/territories includes most countries with the exception of countries in Western Europe, the United States, Australia, New Zealand, and Japan. The list of designated countries/territories is available on the CIC website at http://www.cic.gc.ca/english/information/medical/dcl.asp.

6. Citizenship and Immigration Canada, "Ten-Year Multiple-Entry Visa: Better Use of Government Resources and Easier Travel to Canada," *News Release*, July 20, 2011, http://www.cic.gc.ca/english/department/media/releases/2011/2011-07-20.asp.

7. Foreign students must meet the same medical requirements as those that apply to all temporary residents to Canada.

8. Supra note 4, s. 5.6.

9. Ibid., s. 5.1.

10. Ibid., s. 5.23.

11. Ibid.

12. Citizenship and Immigration Canada, "Study in Canada: Off-Campus Work Permit Program and the Electronic Notification System," July 2011, http://www.cic.gc.ca/english/study/institutions/guide-dir.asp#part3_1.

13. As of April 21, 2008, for the first time, international students can apply to obtain an open work permit under the Post-Graduation Work Permit Program (PGWPP), with no restrictions on the type of employment and no requirement for a job offer.

14. Supra note 4, s. 5.24.

15. Citizenship and Immigration Canada, *Guide 5580—Applying for a Work Permit—Student Guide*, August 30, 2012, http://www.cic.gc.ca/english/information/applications/guides/5580ETOC.asp#coop.

16. Ibid.

17. Citizenship and Immigration Canada, "FW 1: Foreign Worker Manual," in *Temporary Foreign Workers Guidelines (FW)*, June 15, 2012, s. 5.23, http://www.cic.gc.ca/english/resources/manuals/fw/fw01-eng.pdf.

18. Ibid.

19. Human Resources and Social Development Canada, "Temporary Foreign Worker Program: Hiring Foreign Academics in Canada," April 25, 2012, http://www.hrsdc.gc.ca/eng/workplaceskills/foreign_workers/academic.shtml.

20. Ibid.

21. Human Resources and Social Development Canada, "Temporary Foreign Worker Program: Seasonal Agricultural Worker Program," July 30, 2012, http://www.hrsdc.gc.ca/eng/workplaceskills/foreign_workers/sawp.shtml.

22. Ibid.

23. Human Resources and Social Development Canada, "Temporary Foreign Worker Program: Stream for Lower-Skilled Occupations," August 23, 2012, http://www.hrsdc.gc.ca/eng/workplaceskills/foreign_workers/questions-answers/general.shtml#01noc.

24. Citizenship and Immigration Canada, "OP 14: Processing Applicants for the Live-In Caregiver Program," in *Overseas Processing (OP)*, October 27, 2010, s. 8.3, http://www.cic.gc.ca/english/resources/manuals/op/op14-eng.pdf.

25. Citizenship and Immigration Canada, "IP 4: Processing Live-In Caregivers in Canada," in *Inland Processing (IP)*, January 19, 2011, s. 5.2, http://www.cic.gc.ca/english/resources/manuals/ip/ip04-eng.pdf.

26. Ibid, s. 5.8.

27. Supra note 17, s. 5.29.

28. Ibid., s. 5.8.

29. Ibid., s. 5.31A.

30. There must be a qualifying business relationship between the Canadian and foreign company. Furthermore, the companies must be "doing business," which means "regularly, systematically, and continuously providing goods and/or services by a parent, branch, subsidiary, or affiliate in Canada and the foreign country, as the case may be" (ibid., s. 5.31B).

31. A merger is "the joining together of two entities into a single entity called a surviving entity; the surviving entity assumes all of the assets and liabilities of the merged entities—that is, it purchases the stock, assets and liabilities of the other entities, absorbing them into one corporate structure." An acquisition is "the takeover of the controlling interest of one entity by another and both entities retain their legal existence after the transaction" (supra note 17, appendix I).

32. The terms and conditions of the intra-company transferee's work permit will continue to be valid if the Canadian employer is still doing business either directly or through a parent, branch, affiliate, or subsidiary in another country to which the employee can reasonably be expected to be transferred at the end of his or her assignment in Canada (supra note 17, appendix I).

33. Supra note 17, appendix G, s. 1.8.

34. Evidence of pre-arranged employment includes a signed contract with a Canadian enterprise; evidence of an offer of employment from a Canadian employer; or a letter from the American or Mexican employer on whose behalf the service will be provided to the Canadian enterprise. Professionals seeking self-employment in Canada are excluded.

35. Supra note 17, appendix G, s. 3.8.

36. Supra note 17, appendix D.

37. Supra note 17.

38. Ibid.

REFERENCES

Canadian Human Rights Act. R.S.C. 1985, c. H-6.

Citizenship and Immigration Canada. "FW 1: Foreign Worker Manual," in *Temporary Foreign Workers Guidelines (FW)*, June 15, 2012. http://www.cic.gc.ca/english/resources/manuals/fw/fw01-eng.pdf.

Citizenship and Immigration Canada. "IP 4: Processing Live-In Caregivers in Canada," in *Inland Processing (IP)*, January 19, 2011. http://www.cic.gc.ca/english/resources/manuals/ip/ip04-eng.pdf.

Citizenship and Immigration Canada. "IP 6: Processing Temporary Resident Extensions," in *Inland Processing (IP)*, March 29, 2006. http://www.cic.gc.ca/english/resources/manuals/ip/ip06-eng.pdf.

Citizenship and Immigration Canada. "Ten-Year Multiple-Entry Visa: Better Use of Government Resources and Easier Travel to Canada." *News Release*, July 20, 2011. http://www.cic.gc.ca/english/department/media/releases/2011/2011-07-20.asp.

Citizenship and Immigration Canada. "OP 12: Students," in *Overseas Processing (OP)*, December 15, 2008. http://www.cic.gc.ca/english/resources/manuals/op/op12-eng.pdf.

Citizenship and Immigration Canada. "OP 14: Processing Applicants for the Live-In Caregiver Program," in *Overseas Processing (OP)*, October 27, 2010. http://www.cic.gc.ca/english/resources/manuals/op/op14-eng.pdf.

Citizenship and Immigration Canada. "Changes to Human Resources and Skills Development Canada's Labour Market Opinion Confirmation Letters," *Operational Bulletin* 310, May 31, 2011. http://www.cic.gc.ca/english/resources/manuals/bulletins/2011/ob310.asp.

Citizenship and Immigration Canada. "Fourth Set of Ministerial Instructions: Temporary Pause on Family Class Sponsorship Applications for Parents and Grandparents," *Operational Bulletin* 350, November 4, 2011. http://www.cic.gc.ca/english/resources/manuals/bulletins/2011/ob350.asp.

Citizenship and Immigration Canada. "Parents and Grandparents Extended Stay Temporary Resident Visa (Super Visa) and Authorized Period of Extended Stay." *Operational Bulletin* 357, December 1, 2011. http://www.cic.gc.ca/english/resources/manuals/bulletins/2011/ob357.asp.

Citizenship and Immigration Canada, RDM. *Facts and Figures 2010*. July 30, 2012. http://www.cic.gc.ca/english/resources/statistics/menu-fact.asp.

Human Resources and Skills Development Canada. "Government of Canada Announces a More Efficient and Responsive Temporary Foreign Worker Program." News release, April 25, 2012.

Immigration and Refugee Protection Act. S.C. 2001, c. 27.

Immigration and Refugee Protection Regulations. S.O.R./2002-227.

Visiting Forces Act. R.S.C. 1985, c. V-2.

Permanent Entry

5

LEARNING OUTCOMES

After reading this chapter you should be able to:

- Describe the general provisions for applying for permanent residence.

- Explain the general rights and obligations of permanent residents.

- Describe how an individual can lose their permanent resident status.

- Explain and be able to differentiate the eligibility requirements for a permanent resident applicant in each of the classes and subclasses of permanent entry.

- Explain the mutual rights and obligations of sponsorship.

- Explain the purpose of the National Occupational Classification system and be able to find the code for an occupation.

- Use the point system to calculate points.

Introduction

Immigration to Canada is beneficial to both Canada and newcomers to our country: in the *Annual Report to Parliament on Immigration 2011*, the minister of citizenship and immigration reminds us that Canada is a country built by immigrants.[1] The government recognizes the need for maintaining a strong and skilled labour force to support our economy's development. Our aging population and low birth rate mean that Canada must look to immigration to fill our labour shortages. Moreover, because other countries are experiencing similar challenges, Canada must remain competitive in the global marketplace in order to attract workers with the right skill sets to contribute significantly to our economy.

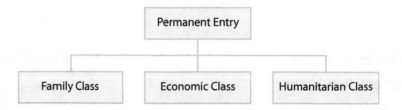

The management of immigration programs includes balancing the need to attract newcomers with the need to protect Canadians by denying access to people who pose a health, criminal, or security threat, and those who would abuse our immigrant or refugee systems. In studying the various immigration programs, you will find examples of this balancing act. On the one hand are programs designed to attract newcomers who can contribute to Canada, and on the other hand are overriding restrictions that deny access.

A foreign national who wishes to reside in Canada must go through a lengthy application process and a complex approval process. Nevertheless, the time and associated financial costs of applying have not discouraged the thousands of people who apply and are accepted as permanent residents each year.

Immigration levels are typically set as a range; the range of 240,000 to 265,000 is maintained for 2012 for the sixth consecutive year. In 2010, Canada exceeded this range and admitted 280,681 permanent residents in the following classes:[2]

- *Family class:* 60,220 were sponsored and admitted as permanent residents (21 percent of the total permanent resident admissions) because of their family relationship to Canadian citizens and permanent residents;
- *Economic class:* Members of this class made up the largest proportion of total immigration to Canada. This class includes skilled workers, business people, provincial or territorial nominees, and live-in caregivers, with 67 percent of the total (186,913);
- *Refugees and protected persons:* Members of this group made up 8.8 percent (24,696); and
- *Persons admitted on humanitarian and compassionate grounds:* Members of this group made up 3.2 percent (8,845).

Acquiring the status of Canadian permanent residence is a step closer to becoming a Canadian citizen. This chapter explores the requirements and rules of eligibility that apply to all permanent resident applicants. It also explores those requirements particular to the family class; economic class; subclasses; and, finally, permanent residency based on humanitarian and compassionate considerations, which may apply in rare circumstances.

Permanent resident status under the Refugee and Humanitarian Resettlement Program is described in Chapter 8. Those who make refugee claims in Canada must first apply for Convention refugee status or the status of "protected person" before they can apply for permanent residence. These processes are discussed in Chapter 9.

General Provisions

With the enactment of the *Immigration and Refugee Protection Act* (IRPA) in 2002, the term **permanent resident** came into use, replacing the former term, "landed immigrant." Both terms carry the same meaning. The IRPA distinguishes between permanent residents and temporary residents. A permanent resident has more rights than a temporary resident—such as a visitor, business traveller, or student—but fewer rights than a Canadian citizen.

Permanent Resident Visas

Before applying for Canadian citizenship, a foreign national must obtain **permanent resident status**. A person with permanent resident status enjoys most of the same rights and responsibilities as Canadian citizens guaranteed under the *Canadian Charter of Rights and Freedoms*, such as the right to live, work, and study in Canada and the legal obligation to pay taxes and respect Canadian laws. However, a permanent resident may not run for political office and may not vote—these privileges are reserved for citizens. Furthermore, although s. 27 of the IRPA gives permanent residents the absolute right to enter and remain in Canada, they must comply with statutory requirements or risk having their status revoked, the consequence of which generally leads to their removal.

Under s. 6 of the IRP Regulations, all foreign nationals who wish to make Canada their permanent home must obtain a **permanent resident visa**. The permanent resident visa allows the foreign national to travel to Canada and, after a successful examination at a port of entry, to enter Canada as a permanent resident. To obtain the visa, the IRP Regulations require a foreign national to submit an application under a specific immigration program in one of the four basic classes of permanent residence (s. 70(2)), as is appropriate to the situation.

The IRP Regulations also require that all applications for permanent residence be made in writing (s. 10). Applications are available on the CIC website and must be completed by the principal applicant and include all information about her dependants. Forms can be filled out online and saved for future completion. There are specific forms related to the appropriated class of immigration as well as generic forms such as the Generic Application Form for Canada (IMM 0008), available at

Source: *Confirmation of Permanent Residence.*
Reproduced with the permission of the Minister of
Public Works and Government Services Canada, 2012.

http://www.cic.gc.ca/english/pdf/kits/forms/IMM0008ENU_2D.pdf
to be used for all classes of permanent residence.

The IRP Regulations also stipulate that counsel (anyone assisting
with the application and charging a fee for services) must be an *authorized representative* and must provide contact information in the
application (s. 10(2)) (see Chapter 12, Regulating the Practice of Immigration and Refugee Law).

The foreign national's application is assessed by an **immigration
visa officer** (a public servant working in a Canadian consulate or
visa office abroad), who assesses the application against eligibility
and inadmissibility criteria, and then may issue the permanent resident visa.[3]

After a foreign national meets all immigration criteria, she is
permitted to travel to Canada with a confirmation of permanent residence document (COPR) (see the figure on this page) and permanent
resident visa in hand; however, she is not yet considered to have
permanent resident status until admitted as such to Canada. Permanent resident status is acquired on the date of the foreign national's
admission to Canada, formerly known as the landing date. On arrival
at the port of entry, the foreign national is examined by an officer
who decides whether to admit the person as a permanent resident.
Generally, the officer examines the person to confirm her intention to
establish permanent residence in Canada, and to confirm that there
is nothing new, such as an invalid medical examination or expired
permanent resident visa, that would make the foreign national or her
family members inadmissible (IRP Regulations, s. 70(1)).

Fees

There are a number of expenses associated with an application for permanent residence, including two fees payable to CIC:

1. An *"application" fee related to the specific class of permanent residence application:* Fees are charged to assess applications and these fees are non-refundable and subject to change.

2. *The right of permanent residence fee (RPRF):* This fee must be paid before a permanent resident visa is issued. The RPRF must be paid for the principal applicant and other family members. Generally, dependants are exempt from paying this fee. This fee is also subject to change—for example, the fee was set at $975 for years and then it was reduced to $490 in 2006.

Because fees are subject to change, check the CIC website for a current schedule of fees: http://www.cic.gc.ca/english/information/fees/fees.asp or the list of fees contained within the instruction guides as part of the application package.

Permanent Resident Card

Once in Canada, a permanent resident uses the **permanent resident card (PR card)**[4] to show proof of immigration status. The PR card is a wallet-sized plastic card that is mailed to the person after arrival in Canada, provided that CIC is informed of the person's correct address within 180 days of her arrival. The PR card must be renewed every five years.

Source: *Permanent Residence Card.* Reproduced with the permission of the Minister of Public Works and Government Services Canada, 2012.

The CIC website provides instructions and a guide on how to apply for a renewal or replacement card. The application must be sent to one of CIC's case processing centres (CPCs) (for example, in Sydney, Nova Scotia) together with a processing fee.

According to the IRP Regulations, the PR card is considered to be property of the Crown (s. 53(2)) and can be revoked if any of the following events occur:

- a new card is issued;
- the permanent resident becomes a Canadian citizen or loses permanent resident status;
- the PR card is lost, stolen, or destroyed; or
- the permanent resident dies (ss. 59(2) and 60).

Generally, a permanent resident may apply for citizenship after accumulating three years of residence in Canada. This process is fully explored in Chapter 6, Citizenship.

Loss of Permanent Resident Status

Unlike citizenship, permanent residence is technically not "permanent" because a person can lose this status. Section 2(1) of the IRPA defines a permanent resident as a person who has acquired permanent resident status and has not subsequently lost it under s. 46.

Section 46 sets out four ways in which persons may lose their permanent residence status:

1. if they become Canadian citizens;
2. if they fail to comply with the residency obligations under s. 28 of the IRPA;
3. if a removal order made against them comes into force; or
4. if a final determination is made that they are not refugees or not entitled to protection.

1. Becoming a Canadian Citizen

A person who becomes a Canadian citizen is no longer a permanent resident. Citizenship includes all the rights of permanent residence, plus additional rights. Chapter 6 explains in detail the process for becoming a Canadian citizen; generally, a permanent resident must be a resident of Canada for at least three years (1,095 days) in the past four years (1,460 days). Days spent in Canada as a temporary resident may be counted toward the residency requirements.

2. Residency Obligations

A person can lose permanent resident status by failing to fulfill residency obligations. Although a permanent resident is not required to spend all of his time in Canada, generally he must physically reside here for 730 days out of every five years, according to s. 28 of the IRPA. There are some exceptions to the residency obligation. In certain circumstances, time outside Canada may be counted as equivalent to days in Canada, according to s. 28(2)(a). These circumstances exist where permanent residents reside as follows:

- outside Canada while accompanying a Canadian citizen who is their spouse or common-law partner or, in the case of a child, their parent;
- outside Canada while employed on a full-time basis by a Canadian business or in the federal public administration or the public service of a province; or
- outside Canada while accompanying a permanent resident who is their spouse or common-law partner or, in the case of a child, their parent and who is employed on a full-time basis by a Canadian business or in the federal public administration or the public service of a province.

A person who loses permanent resident status because of failure to meet residency obligations (IRPA, s. 46(1)(b)) may appeal to the Immigration Appeal Division of the Immigration and Refugee Board (IRB).[5]

3. Removal Order

A person who is subject to a removal order as a result of inadmissibility can lose permanent resident status. Generally, an allegation of inadmissibility is reviewed on its merits by an immigration official delegated by the minister of public safety and emergency preparedness, who, according to s. 44(2) of the IRPA, decides whether to allow the person to remain in Canada or to refer the case to the Immigration Division of the Immigration and Refugee Board for a decision on admissibility and removal. The grounds of inadmissibility, such as security and criminality issues, are discussed in detail in Chapter 3, Inadmissibility; removal hearings are discussed in Chapter 10, General In-Canada Enforcement and Removal Procedures. A decision made at an admissibility hearing may be appealed to the Immigration Appeal Division (discussed in Chapter 11.)

4. Final Determination That a Person Is Not a Refugee or Is Not Entitled to Protection

A person who becomes a permanent resident following a determination that she is a Convention refugee or a person in need of protection may lose permanent resident status and be removed from Canada if fraud or misrepresentation was involved in her refugee claim. Misrepresentation may involve false statements and documents, as well as omissions, such as failing to disclose a relevant fact. In such situations, the minister makes an application to the Refugee Protection Division under s. 109 of the IRPA to vacate the original decision because of fraud or misrepresentation. An application to vacate a decision is a request to the division to "do away with" the original decision to grant protection. The division, on a final determination, may decide to vacate the original decision for refugee protection, which consequently also leads to the loss of the person's permanent residency.

Canada–Quebec Accord

Under the Accord, Quebec has the sole responsibility for the selection of permanent residents and refugees outside Canada who wish to settle there. Immigrants destined to Quebec must first apply to that province and meet Quebec's selection criteria. Applications from individuals who successfully meet the province's eligibility criteria are then forwarded to CIC, which tests for inadmissibility on each of the grounds because these are the same legal standards that are applied to all immigrants across the country. This way, the responsibility for immigration remains with the federal government for the administrative function of processing applications and physical admission to Canada at ports of entry.

Family Class

As discussed in Chapter 1, one of the stated objectives of Canadian immigration policy is to facilitate family reunification (IRPA, s. 3(1)(d)). Under the family class program, Canadians and permanent residents may sponsor their close family members. Features of the program include:

- a modern definition of "family" that includes common-law and same-sex partners;

- the age to sponsor a relative is as young as 18 years of age;
- the definition of "dependent child" includes children under 22 years of age;
- adoption provisions—keeping with the principle of the "best interests of the child"—that lead directly to citizenship for the adoptee;
- a provision for "in-Canada" class sponsorship;
- the length of the sponsorship requirement ranges from three to ten years, depending on the relationship to the sponsor;
- spouses and dependants under 22 are exempt from the medical grounds of inadmissibility (for example, those grounds related to a medical condition placing excessive demand on health and social services); and
- there is no right to appeal in cases where the family member was found inadmissible for reasons of security, human or international rights violations, serious criminality, or organized criminality.

Sponsorship Under the Family Class

The family class program includes two separate processes, as follows:

1. **Sponsorship application process:** A sponsor or sponsorship applicant is a person in Canada who wants to reunite with a family member. There is a separate application and approval process for becoming a sponsor. According to s. 13(1) of the IRPA, a sponsor must be a Canadian citizen or permanent resident, and must meet other criteria such as financial requirements.

2. **Permanent residence application process:** The permanent residence applicant is the foreign national who wishes to live in Canada as a permanent resident, according to s. 12(1) of the IRPA. The applicant must meet

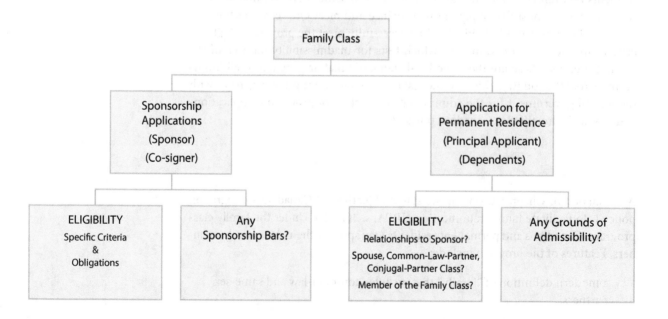

the regulatory definition of a "member of the family class" as well as specific criteria to qualify for permanent residence; in addition to meeting the eligibility criteria, the applicant must not be inadmissible. The application and approval are separate but related processes from the sponsor. A person applying to be sponsored for permanent residence is called the "principal applicant."

Both these processes must be successfully completed before an applicant may become a permanent resident under the family class. Consider the following case scenario:

> Gary is a 48-year-old Canadian citizen. He has been divorced for several years, and lives in Toronto, Ontario where he shares custody of his two children: Thomas, 9, and Samantha, 7. Ellie is a 45-year-old citizen of the United States with two daughters: 17-year-old Amanda and 12-year-old Martha. Ellie's husband, Paul, died when Martha was a baby.
>
> Gary met Ellie through Paul years ago when they were all undergraduates at Cornell University in New York. After Ellie and Paul were married, they remained close friends with Gary, who moved back to Canada after graduation. Gary's job required him to travel frequently to the United States, so it was easy to maintain his friendship with Ellie throughout the years, even after Paul died. After Gary divorced, his relationship with Ellie became intimate, leading to a marriage proposal and a legal marriage. Even though Gary could seek a job transfer to the United States through his company, he doesn't want to relocate there because he would lose joint custody of his two school-aged children. Ellie, however, is more flexible about where she can live and is even welcoming a chance to start a new life with Gary. Together, they decided that Gary should sponsor Ellie and the girls as permanent residents so they can all live as a family in Canada. Does Gary meet the legal requirements to sponsor Ellie and her children? Do Ellie and her children, Amanda and Martha, qualify for sponsorship?

To answer these questions, we will examine the various elements of the family class program, including a review of provisions of the IRPA and its regulations. We will learn about the two separate but interrelated processes for sponsoring a person to Canada and for applying as a permanent resident under the family class.

Throughout the text, we refer to "immigration officers" and "visa officers." The sponsor's application is processed in Canada by an immigration officer, who is a public servant working at a case processing centre (CPC). The sponsored person's application for permanent residence is processed abroad by a visa officer. Visa officers are Canadian public servants who work at Canadian missions abroad and perform multiple duties, including assessing applications from foreign nationals who wish to become permanent residents.

For the sake of simplicity, we will focus on the sponsorship of a spouse and dependent children, as in our scenario. However, where the requirements are different for sponsoring other members of the family class, they are explained.

Sponsors

Family class immigration involves sponsorship by a qualifying individual—the sponsor. A successful sponsorship includes many elements, but hinges on the relationship of the permanent resident applicant to the sponsor. In agreeing to enter into a sponsorship relationship, the sponsor makes the legal commitment to provide the basic living expenses of the family member being sponsored—called an undertaking—for a prescribed period of time. The list of persons who may be sponsored include the following:

- spouses, common-law partners, and conjugal partners;
- dependent children;
- children intended for adoption;
- parents, grandparents, and their dependent children;
- brothers, sisters, nephews, nieces, or grandchildren if they are either orphaned, not a spouse or common-law partner, and under 18; and
- any relative if the sponsor is alone in Canada and has none of the above family members to sponsor.

Eligibility Requirements of the Sponsor

The process of sponsoring a person for permanent residence begins with the sponsor—in our scenario, Gary. The framework is found in s. 13(1) of the IRPA, and further details are provided in the regulations. The sponsor must be either a Canadian citizen or permanent resident who is at least 18 years old, must reside in Canada, and must file an application to sponsor a member of the family class (see below under the heading "Sponsorship Kits and Applications for Permanent Residence"), according to s. 130(1) of the IRP Regulations. Furthermore, a sponsor is not eligible to sponsor a spouse or partner if he has an existing sponsorship undertaking for a previous spouse or partner and the period of that undertaking has not ended (IRP Regulations, s. 117(9)(b)).

Reside in Canada

Generally, the sponsor must reside in Canada. An exception is made where a *Canadian citizen* residing outside Canada satisfies immigration officials that he will resume residence in Canada once the sponsored person becomes a permanent resident. This allows a Canadian citizen whose work may require him to live outside Canada for a period of time to begin the sponsorship process. However, permanent residents, while living abroad, may not sponsor.

Bars to Sponsorship

Gary meets the age, status, and residence requirements of the definition of a sponsor. He must, however, meet other conditions to satisfy immigration officials that he will be able to carry out his obligations as a sponsor.

Just as a bank will conduct a credit check to ensure you have the ability to repay a loan, the government wants to limit the risk of a sponsor defaulting on his obligations. Sponsorship requires Gary to provide the basic living expenses for Ellie and her children; therefore, he must prove there is nothing that would prevent him from fulfilling this commitment. The immigration officer who processes Gary's application must be satisfied that there is nothing in Gary's history, such as criminality, that would make him a risk for sponsorship.

Certain activities, as set out in s. 133 of the IRP Regulations, would bar Gary from sponsorship. A person may not sponsor or be a co-signer[6] if any of the following bars to sponsorship exist:

- *The person is subject to a removal order.* The IRPA requires permanent resident sponsors to reside in Canada. A person subject to a removal order is at risk of not being able to fulfill this obligation.

- *The person has been detained in any penitentiary, jail, reformatory, or prison.* Such a person has no ability to provide financial support.

- *The person has been previously convicted of a specified offence.* These offences include a sexual offence (or an attempt or threat to commit such an offence), either in Canada or abroad, against anyone, or an offence resulting in bodily harm (including threats to or attempts at doing so) against a relative. This bar addresses concerns that a sponsored family member could be at risk of sexual abuse or family violence.[7] A history of such offences within five years of the sponsorship application bars the sponsor unless he was pardoned or acquitted. For convictions outside Canada, the sponsor must show rehabilitation or acquittal.

- *The person is in default of spousal or child support payments ordered by a court in or outside Canada.* A sponsor who is in default of a court-ordered or court-registered support obligation must first resolve this matter with the local provincial or territorial authorities to remove this bar.

- *The person is in default of a debt[8] owed under the IRPA.* Sponsorship includes signing a legally binding contract with the minister of CIC. As long as there is an unpaid debt, the minister will not enter into another legal contract with a person who is in default of payment.

- *The person is not an undischarged bankrupt under the Bankruptcy and Insolvency Act.* A bankrupt person is considered a poor financial risk.

- *The person is in receipt of social assistance other than for reasons of disability.* A sponsor who receives social assistance cannot provide for his own basic necessities, let alone those of others. Only under exceptional circumstances may this bar be waived under humanitarian and compassionate grounds.

- *The person is in default of a previous sponsorship undertaking.* Such a person is considered to be a poor risk because he has not previously honoured a legal, financial obligation with the minister of CIC.

- *Five-year requirement.* A permanent resident or a naturalized Canadian citizen who has previously sponsored a spouse or partner, may not sponsor a new spouse or partner. There is a bar of a five-year period from sponsoring.

An amendment to the regulations was made to curb abuse of the spouse/ partner sponsorship program by foreign nationals who would enter into a relationship of convenience for immigration purposes (IRP Regulations, s. 130, SOR/2012-20, s. 1.).

Gary read about all the conditions he must meet to be a sponsor, and has determined that there is nothing that would bar him from sponsoring Ellie. When Gary signs his completed application form, he will be consenting to specific obligations: an undertaking with the minister of CIC and a sponsorship agreement with Ellie.

Undertaking

According to the IRP Regulations, a sponsor must make a formal three- to ten-year commitment to become financially responsible for the family members, depending on the sponsorship relationship and the age of the family members being sponsored. This commitment is called an undertaking and is included in the sponsor's application form—Application to Sponsor, Sponsorship Agreement and Undertaking (IMM 1344). The undertaking part of the application form is the legal contract with the minister of citizenship and immigration.

The basis for this requirement is two-fold. First, the sponsor's function is to ensure that relatives receive the support they need to establish themselves in Canada so that they will not become a financial burden on the community and require social assistance. By signing the undertaking, the sponsor agrees to repay the Canadian government for any social assistance payments made to the sponsored family members.

When Gary signs the undertaking, he is entering into a binding contract with the minister of citizenship and immigration. As the sponsor, he remains obligated to provide basic requirements regardless of any change in circumstances, such as a marital breakdown, unemployment, or even the death of Ellie. Gary agrees to provide Ellie, the sponsored person, and Amanda and Martha, Ellie's family members, with basic necessities, including food, clothing, shelter, dental care, eye care, and other health needs not covered by public health services, from the day they enter Canada until the end of the specified period of the undertaking.

The undertaking takes effect the day that Ellie is admitted to Canada as a permanent resident. Generally, the duration of the undertaking is for ten years, but there are exceptions depending on the relationship of the person being sponsored and can vary with the age of a dependent child, as follows:

- a three-year commitment for a spouse, common-law partner, or conjugal partner of the sponsor;
- ten years or age 25, whichever comes first, for a dependent child who is less than 22 years of age and is the child of the sponsor, or the sponsor's spouse, or common-law or conjugal partner;
- three years for a dependent child who is 22 years of age or older and is the child of the sponsor or the sponsor's spouse, or common-law or conjugal partner; and
- for anyone else, ten years.

Duration of Undertakings

Person Being Sponsored	Term of Undertaking	
Spouse, common-law partner, and conjugal partner	3 years	
Dependent child of the sponsor, or Dependent child of the sponsor's spouse, common-law partner, or conjugal partner *and under 22 years of age* at date of becoming a permanent resident	10 years or age 25, whichever comes first	
	Years of age:	Maximum duration:
	Infant to 15	10 years
	16 years	9 years
	17 years	8 years
	18 years	7 years
	19 years	6 years
	20 years	5 years
	21 years	4 years
Dependent child of the sponsor, or Dependent child of the sponsor's spouse, common-law partner, or conjugal partner *and 22 years of age* at date of becoming a permanent resident	3 years	
Any other person (i.e., parents, grandparents, dependent children of sponsor's parents)	10 years	

According to the above table, the duration of the undertaking for Gary to sponsor Ellie and each of her daughters is as follows:

- Ellie is Gary's spouse; therefore, the duration of the undertaking for Ellie is for three years from the date that she arrives in Canada as a permanent resident.

Gary's obligations toward Amanda and Martha (the dependent children of his spouse, Ellie) are tied to their economic dependency and their ages, and therefore are longer in duration. The girls will both be under 22 years of age on the date of becoming permanent residents, so Gary would calculate his undertaking to be 10 years or when the girls reach the age of 25, whichever comes first, as follows:

- Amanda is 17 years old. If she is 17 when she becomes a permanent resident, the duration of Gary's undertaking with the minister of CIC will be for 8 years: 17 years old + 8 years undertaking = 25 years old.
- Martha is 12 years old. If she is 12 when she becomes a permanent resident, the duration of Gary's undertaking with the minister of CIC will be for the full 10 years: 12 years old + 10 years undertaking = 22 years old.

DEFAULT OF SPONSORSHIP

What happens to the sponsorship undertaking if, say, Gary becomes unemployed and can no longer afford to pay the basic necessities for Ellie and her daughters? Or Gary and Ellie divorce and Gary is simply unwilling to support them? If Ellie and her daughters start to collect social assistance, Gary, the sponsor, is deemed to have defaulted on the undertaking and either the provincial or federal government may recover the cost of providing social assistance. Gary is liable for the sponsorship debt and will not be allowed to sponsor other family members until he has repaid to the government all of the social assistance payments. Section 132 of the IRP Regulations obligates a sponsor to reimburse the Crown in right of Canada or a province for the cost of every benefit provided as social assistance to the sponsored family member during the term of the undertaking. The undertaking sets out the obligations of the sponsor, the duration of the undertaking, and the consequences of the default.

The undertaking is binding notwithstanding any change in the sponsor's personal circumstances, even if the permanent resident becomes estranged from the sponsor for any reason, including marriage fraud.[9] Until recently, there was no protection for a Canadian citizen or permanent resident who was duped into a marriage in exchange for permanent residence by a foreign national who had no intent of living in a relationship with the sponsor. In 2012, the government introduced a new regulation to address marriage fraud that would place a condition on the sponsored permanent resident to live together "in a legitimate relationship for two years following receipt of their permanent resident status."[10]

Sponsorship Agreement

In addition to the undertaking with the minister of CIC, Gary must also enter into an agreement with Ellie. This sponsorship agreement is separate from the undertaking but related because its purpose is to set out the mutual obligations and rights of the sponsor and the sponsored person.

The sponsorship agreement is part of the sponsor's application form. After Gary signs it, he sends it to Ellie so that she has the opportunity to read it and understand her rights and responsibilities. The document makes it clear that the undertaking remains in effect notwithstanding events such as the granting of citizenship or a change in circumstances, such as marital breakdown.

Unfortunately, not all sponsored persons are aware of their rights. Some women, for reasons such as poor language skills, poor education, and cultural norms, are vulnerable to a range of domestic abuse including physical and financial control, isolation, and violence. A woman may stay in a relationship under threat of deportation because she is unaware of her rights and believes that she must remain in an abusive relationship or face deportation. This is false.

To address this issue, the sponsorship agreement provides the following:

> Sponsored persons and/or their family members who are being abused or assaulted by their sponsors should seek safety away from their sponsors even if this means they will have to apply for social assistance benefits. A sponsor cannot force Citizenship and Immigration Canada to remove you from Canada.

Let's suppose that Gary and Ellie separate or divorce: Gary would continue to be financially responsible for Ellie (if this happens within the three years of his undertaking) and for the girls (also for the duration of his undertaking). Ellie and her children would not be forced to leave Canada as some sponsored persons are led to believe: they have the right to remain in Canada because they are permanent residents.

Sponsors of all ages, and sponsored persons of at least 22 years of age, must sign the sponsorship agreement part of the sponsor's application form. If the sponsored person is a spouse, common-law partner, or conjugal partner, then that person, regardless of age, must sign the agreement.

Gary the sponsor and Ellie the spouse will both sign the application. Amanda and Martha are both under the age of 22 and therefore will not sign the document. The sponsorship agreement part of Gary's application form provides details of Gary's obligations to support Ellie and her girls during the period of the undertaking by providing basic requirements such as food, shelter, clothing, and medical care. The agreement also provides that Ellie is obligated to make reasonable efforts to provide necessities for herself and her children.

Financial Requirements

Generally, sponsors must show that they have the financial means to provide for all their family members, including those already residing in Canada and those they intend to sponsor. The minimum necessary income requirement is published annually by Statistics Canada in **low income cut-off (LICO)** levels. The general rule is that sponsors must prove that they can meet the minimum "LICO test" in order to be eligible to sponsor members of the family class.

EXCEPTIONS

The LICO financial obligations do not apply to all relatives. Excepted persons are set out in s. 133(4) of the IRP Regulations, and include the following:

- a spouse, common-law partner, or conjugal partner;
- a dependent biological child, where the child has no dependent children of her own;
- a child under the age of 18 who the sponsor intends to adopt in Canada; or
- a child under the age of 18 where the sponsor is a guardian of the child.

Although the sponsor is not required to meet the LICO test for these cases, he must still complete a financial evaluation using CIC's Financial Evaluation form (IMM 1283).

In our scenario, Gary is exempt from the LICO test because he is sponsoring his spouse and her dependants.

LOW INCOME CUT-OFF TEST

The applicable LICO level is based on urban areas of 500,000 inhabitants or more, regardless of where the sponsor lives. The sponsor's income must generally come from Canadian sources with two exceptions:

- sponsors who commute from Canada to work in the United States may use their US employment income, provided that it is declared as income on their Canadian income tax return; and

- sponsors living in Canada, who declare income from foreign sources on their Canadian income tax returns, may use this foreign income to meet the financial requirements for sponsorship.

Sponsors must provide their latest Notice of Assessment (Option C print-out) from the Canada Revenue Agency to report total income, as referenced in s. 133(1)(j)(i) of the IRP Regulations and shown on line 150 of the notice of assessment.

Fast forward to a time after Ellie's sponsorship is approved. Gary successfully sponsored Ellie and she now has status as a Canadian permanent resident. Ellie wishes to sponsor her fifteen-year old brother, Edward. Ellie's parents died and Edward is considered orphaned. Edward is obviously not Ellie's spouse—and so she will be required to pass the LICO test.[11]

HOW TO CALCULATE LICO

The LICO level is determined on the basis of the total number of family members. In sponsorship situations, the number of family members includes all members of a sponsor's own family and all sponsored persons and their family members, including family members listed as non-accompanying.

Generally, the LICO table is updated each year, so look for effective dates. The annual LICO tables can be found on the CIC website. The sample LICO table reproduced below is effective until December 31, 2012.

Consider this example, in which Ellie decides to sponsor her brother:

The size of Ellie's family unit is equal to 7 as follows:

- Ellie must count herself (1),
- her 2 children (2), and
- her spouse, Gary (1),
- Gary's 2 children (2), and
- the number of people being sponsored—Ellie's brother, Edward (1).

The total number of persons to be included in the family unit is equal to 7, assuming that all 4 children are dependants.

If we use the LICO table provided below as an example, Ellie must show that she has an annual income of at least $59,907. Any income Ellie earns in Canada is reported in her notice of assessment (Option "C" print-out) from her income tax return for the past 12 months; this is how she proves that she meets the minimum to qualify on financial grounds to sponsor her mother. If Ellie has not earned enough money, she can ask Gary to act as a *co-signer* to make up the financial gap, provided that their pooled resources meet the minimum income requirement of $59,907.

Low Income Cut-Off (LICO) Table for 2012

Size of family unit	Minimum necessary income
1 person (the sponsor)	$22,367
2 persons	$28,182
3 persons	$34,646
4 persons	$42,065
5 persons	$47,710
6 persons	$53,808
7 persons	$59,907
More than 7 persons, for each additional person, add	$6,099

Source: Citizenship and Immigration Canada website, Basic Income Required at http://www.cic.gc.ca/english/information/applications/guides/5256ETOC .asp#incometables.

CO-SIGNER

When a sponsor does not have the necessary financial means to be a sponsor, she may take on a **co-signer** to make up the difference financially. Consequently, the co-signer must also sign the sponsor's application form that includes the undertaking. A co-signer must meet the following criteria:

- be either the spouse or common-law partner of the sponsor;
- meet the same eligibility requirements as the sponsor; and
- assume the same obligations as the sponsor.

Together the sponsor and co-signer become **jointly and severally liable** if there is a default. This means that either of them may be required to pay the full amount, should the other lack funds to contribute—the obligation is not divided in half.

Assume that when Ellie sponsors her brother, she asks her spouse, Gary, to act as a co-signer because she does not have sufficient funds to pass the LICO test. In this situation, both Ellie and Gary become jointly responsible for the undertaking and sponsorship of Edward.

Members of the Family Class

Foreign nationals who are sponsored as members of the family class are not assessed on their ability to support themselves. They obtain their permanent residence status on the sole basis of being in a familial relationship with a sponsor; they are not required to meet the financial or other selection requirements which are imposed on other classes of immigrants. It is therefore important for the sponsor and the applicant to show that a bone fide relationship exists between them. Part of the eligibility requirements of sponsorship is to demonstrate that the sponsored person and their dependants are members of the family class as defined in the IRP Regulations. Note that a "member of the family class" is not the same as a "family member." How you would define your family may not fit with the definitions in the regulations as we will explore in this section.

In our scenario, Ellie is seeking to come to Canada as a permanent resident along with her dependent children—Amanda and Martha. In order to do so, she and her daughters must meet the definition of "members of the family class" as set out in the IRP Regulations.

Individuals who wish to come to Canada permanently may choose to apply under the family class program because they have family in Canada with whom they wish to be reunited and who are willing to act as their sponsor, as in Ellie's case. Members of the family class may include the following, according to s. 117(1) of the IRP Regulations:

- spouses and common-law or conjugal partners 16 years of age or older;
- fathers or mothers;
- grandfathers or grandmothers;
- dependent children, including children adopted overseas;[12]
- orphan children under 18 to be adopted in Canada, if they are the sibling, niece or nephew, or grandchild of the sponsor; and
- children under 18 to be adopted in Canada.

Sponsors who do not have a closely related family member who is either a Canadian citizen or a permanent resident, or a relative who could be sponsored as a member of the family class, may sponsor one distant relative regardless of age or relationship. Unlisted relatives include independent children, aunts, uncles, nieces, nephews, and cousins. This does not work in reverse—that is, if a relative is the only one living abroad and all his relatives are in Canada but he does not meet the definition of member of the family class, he cannot be sponsored.

The IRP Regulations also create a class for sponsored spouses or common-law partners in Canada (s. 123) and their dependent children, if the spouse or common-law partner has legal temporary status in Canada, such as a visitor, student, or business worker.

A person who applies for permanent residence under the family class program must not only have an eligible sponsor but must also meet the regulatory definition of a member of the family class and fulfill other requirements, as follows:

- be able to prove identity, age, and relationship to the sponsor and other family members, whether those family members are accompanying or not;
- be admissible to Canada, including family members, whether they are accompanying or not; and
- have a valid and subsisting passport or travel document.

Relationship to the Sponsor

Applicants for permanent residence must provide proof of their age and identity by providing birth certificates and identity documents. Canadian immigration policy also places the onus on the applicant to establish the nature of the relationship to the sponsor, as defined in the IRP Regulations.

For relationships such as marriages, common-law partnerships, and conjugal partnerships, a person must show that the relationship to the sponsor is genuine and includes the existence of a conjugal relationship. Immigration visa officers are trained to look for *relationships of convenience* or *bad-faith relationships* and, according to ss. 4 and 4.1 of the IRP Regulations, can refuse an application if they have evidence that an applicant entered into a relationship for the purpose of immigrating to Canada.

It is important to know the kind and variety of documentation one must provide to establish the bona fides of a relationship. In the case of biological relatives, such as parents, grandparents, siblings, and children, if no documentary evidence exists to support the relationship, applicants may be required to produce DNA evidence.

Spousal Relationships

The definition of a "spouse" under the IRPA includes a married spouse, common-law partner, conjugal partner, and same-sex partner. Under previous immigration law, a person could sponsor another person to which he or she was engaged to be married. However, it was difficult to assess whether the engagement would actually result in a marriage, and, consequently, when the current IRPA came into force, this ground for sponsorship was eliminated. If the applicant for permanent residence is engaged to be married, he or she must wait until after the marriage to apply as a spouse, or may apply as a common-law partner if the couple lived together continuously for at least 12 months.

CONJUGAL RELATIONSHIPS

An important feature of any of these relationships is that there exists a conjugal relationship. The term conjugal is traditionally used to describe marriage and, for immigration purposes, extends to marriage-like relationships (see the text box below for features of a conjugal relationship.)

"Conjugal" is not defined in the IRPA or the IRP Regulations; however, CIC provides direction to visa officers in assessing the conjugal nature of a relationship in their operations manuals. Officers must look beyond the presence of a physical relationship and consider the following features:[13]

- a significant degree of attachment, both physical and emotional;
- a mutual and continuing commitment to a shared life together; and
- emotional and financial interdependency.

In considering conjugal partnerships visa officers consider:

- whether the relationship is monogamous;

- whether the relationship is of some permanence—namely, a minimum duration of one year; and
- whether mutual interdependence exists between the partners.

A conjugal relationship must be similar to a marriage-like relationship where the couple can demonstrate that, over time, they have exclusive and emotional ties to one another and have made a commitment to each other.

CIC's operations manual "OP 2" provides a more detailed examination of the characteristics and assessment of conjugal relationships. Visa officers are directed on how to assess whether a couple may be considered to be in a conjugal relationship and cautioned to assess each case separately to take account of cultural differences and whether local laws or customs might discourage parties from freely admitting the existence of the relationship.

What follows is a general discussion of each category of a spouse who may be sponsored and some of the particular considerations that apply to each in establishing the relationship to the sponsor.

Characteristics of All Conjugal Married and Unmarried Relationships

- Mutual commitment to a shared life;
- Exclusive—people cannot be in more than one conjugal relationship at a time;
- Intimate—commitment to sexual exclusivity;
- Interdependent—physically, emotionally, financially, and socially;
- Permanent—long-term, genuine, and continuing;
- Present themselves as a couple ("Here's my other half!");
- Regarded by others as partners; and
- Care for children together (if there are children).

SPOUSE

According to s. 117(9) of the IRP Regulations, a spouse must be at least 16 years of age, legally married, and not otherwise married to someone else to qualify for sponsorship. A marriage that takes place outside Canada must be legal in the country where it took place and also conform to Canadian law (IRP Regulations, s. 2). The onus of proving the marriage's validity rests on the applicant (IRPA, s. 16(1)).

A same-sex spouse who is a Canadian citizen or a permanent resident qualifies for family class sponsorship, provided that the marriage took place in Canada and within the time frame allowed for each particular province. For example, in Ontario, the marriage must have taken place on or after June 10, 2003, and in British Columbia, on or after July 8, 2003.[14]

Telephone marriages (where one member of the couple is not physically present but participates by telephone), proxy marriages (where one member of the couple is not present and has named another person to represent him or her as the proxy), and tribal marriages (marriages carried out according to tribal custom) are considered legal marriages for immigration purposes if these marriages are legally recognized according to the law of the place where they occurred.

In our scenario concerning Ellie, she must provide documentary evidence that she and Gary were free to marry and entered into a legal marriage. She will provide a certified copy of Paul's death certificate to prove that she was widowed and Gary will provide a certified copy of his divorce decree as evidence that he was divorced. Ellie will also provide a certified copy of her marriage certificate to Gary to show that their marriage was a legal marriage in the country where it took place.

COMMON-LAW PARTNER

A "common-law relationship" is defined in s. 1 of the IRP Regulations as "in relation to a person, an individual who is cohabiting with the person in a conjugal relationship, having so cohabited for a period of at least one year." Temporary absences notwithstanding, in order for the person in the common-law relationship to qualify for sponsorship, the year of living together must be a continuous 12-month period, and cannot be intermittent periods that add up to one year.

Common-law relationships may be either opposite-sex or same-sex. The relationship must be genuine and not for purposes of acquiring immigration status. The applicant must have a valid passport or travel document, and must generally satisfy admissibility requirements.

The common-law partner must be separated from any spouse or previous common-law partner for at least one year, and must be able to prove this.

One of the key issues that arises in determining whether a relationship meets the common-law definition is whether the relationship is conjugal. (See the features of a conjugal relationship in the text box above.)

Applicants for permanent residence must provide documentation with their application to show they are known as a couple, such as documents showing that they have combined their affairs and set up their household together in one home. This could include the following:

- joint bank accounts or credit cards;
- joint ownership of a home;
- joint residential leases;
- joint rental receipts;
- joint utilities (electricity, gas, and telephone);
- joint management of household expenses;
- proof of joint purchases, especially for household items; and
- correspondence addressed to either person or both people at the same address.

CONJUGAL PARTNER

Section 2 of the IRP Regulations defines a "conjugal partner" as "in relation to a sponsor, a foreign national residing outside Canada who is in a conjugal relationship with the sponsor and has been in that relationship for a period of at least one year." This category was created for those who might have applied as common-law partners but who did not live together continuously for one year, usually because of legal or social obstacles. These obstacles include the following:

- an immigration barrier, such as where the applicant and/or sponsor were denied long-term stays in each other's country;
- a person's marital status, such as where one partner is married to someone else and living in a country where divorce is not possible; or
- a person's sexual orientation, where the partners are in a same-sex relationship but same-sex marriage is not permitted in the country of the applicant.

Canadian immigration policy on conjugal partners assumes that if a Canadian and a foreign national could get legally married or could live together and thereby establish a common-law relationship, this is what they would have done before submitting the sponsorship and immigration applications. In other words, this category is considered an exception that applies only when marriage or common-law partnership was not an option in the particular circumstances.

Although no legal document such as a marriage certificate exists, the conjugal partners should be able to provide other types of evidence of their significant commitment to each other, such as the following:

- insurance policies or estates showing they have named each other as beneficiaries;
- documents showing they hold joint ownership of possessions; and
- documents showing they hold joint expenses or share income.

EXCLUDED RELATIONSHIPS

An applicant for permanent residence applying as the sponsor's spouse, common-law partner, or conjugal partner is excluded as a member of the family class, according to ss. 5 and 117(9) of the IRP Regulations, if any of the following circumstances exist:

1. the applicant is under 16 years of age; or
2. the sponsor is already sponsoring a spouse, common-law partner, or conjugal partner, and the undertaking has not ended; or
3. the sponsor is the spouse of another person; or
4. the sponsor is a spouse who has lived separate and apart from the applicant for at least one year and either
   a. the sponsor is the common-law partner of another person or the conjugal partner of another foreign national, or
   b. the applicant is the common-law partner of another person or the conjugal partner of another sponsor; or
5. the applicant was a non-accompanying family member of the sponsor and was not examined when the sponsor previously applied to Canada as a permanent resident.

RELATIONSHIPS OF CONVENIENCE

The sponsorship of a spouse, common-law partner, or conjugal partner is barred where the relationship between the sponsor and the applicant exists only for immigration purposes.

A "relationship of convenience" is a relationship that is entered into for the sole purpose of gaining permanent residence, described as a bad-faith relationship in s. 4 of the IRP Regulations. A feature of a bad-faith relationship may be a new relationship or a relationship of convenience formed after a previous relationship was dissolved for the purpose of entering into the relationship of convenience.

With respect to new relationships, case law has held that there are two elements, both of which have to be present to bar sponsorship. In other words, the applicant only needs to negate one. The two elements are as follows:

- the applicant must have gone into the marriage primarily for the purpose of coming to Canada as a family class member; and
- the applicant lacked the intention to permanently reside with the sponsoring spouse.

Consider the following scenario:

> Donna, a 53-year-old divorced Canadian citizen, goes on vacation to a Caribbean island with her girlfriends and meets Grant, a 30-year-old scuba instructor. She spends most of her time during the next two weeks with Grant and learns all about how difficult life is for him on the island. He asks for her help to immigrate to Canada and promises her a large sum of money, which he can get from his uncle. Donna had "the best time of her life" while on vacation but isn't looking for a long-term commitment. She doesn't know anything about immigration to Canada but, from what Grant tells her, the system seems unfair to men like Grant. She figures, what harm is there in helping out such a young, talented, good-looking guy as Grant? Together they work out a scheme to get married so that Grant can come to Canada as her spouse and she can make a little bit of money to renovate her house: a win–win situation. They marry on the eve of Donna's return to Canada.

In assessing Grant's application for permanent residence under the family class, the visa officer will consider the following issues as set out in s. 12 of CIC's operations manual "OP 2":

Officers may need to closely examine evidence that a marriage took place. Photographs or other documents used as evidence of a marriage can be altered. Marriage certificates and other documents may be fraudulent.

In some instances, home visits may be used to establish cohabitation in the case of a marriage or common-law relationship.

Some factors that may be considered and that are common to marriage, common-law relationships, and conjugal partner relationships are as follows:

- Do the spouses or common-law or conjugal partners have a good knowledge of each other's personal circumstances, background, and family situation?

- What is the immigration status of the applicant and the timing of the marriage, common-law relationship, or conjugal-partner relationship?
- Is there evidence that both parties have planned their immigration or immigration of the foreign born spouse/common-law partners or conjugal partner jointly and over a period of time?
- Is there a history of multiple marriages, divorces, common-law relationships, or conjugal partner relationships?
- Have previous relationships clearly ended and does the period of separation seem reasonable in the circumstances?
- Do the applicants speak a common language?

In cases where the new relationship is not genuine, the sponsor and applicant may not share a common language and may have no plans to reside together. As well, one may have made some kind of payment to the other for the inconvenience. Although Donna and Grant have a valid and legal marriage, their age difference, their quick marriage, and their lack of knowledge of each other's personal circumstances would certainly raise a red flag and be questioned by the immigration officer.

Officers are also warned to consider whether relationships have been dissolved in order to facilitate immigration. Section 12.5 of "OP 2" gives the following direction:

> In addition to persons who may enter into relationships of convenience for the sake of acquiring any status under the Act, officers must be conscious of persons who "conveniently" dissolve their marriages or common-law partnerships and then subsequently resume them for the sake of facilitating immigration—that is, persons in marriage-like relationships who fraudulently declare that their relationship is dissolved in order to facilitate their own or another person's immigration application and later attempt to sponsor that person. R4.1 [s. 4.1 of the IRP Regulations] provides officers the means to refuse applications where persons have dissolved a relationship in bad faith in order to acquire any status under the Act.

Although neither Donna nor Grant dissolved any marriages or common-law partnerships in this scenario, you can see how such circumstances would also attract in-depth investigation by the visa officer. Part of the information each must provide in their applications is their history of previous marriages and common-law partnerships.

In the scenario involving Gary and Ellie, where both partners were in previous relationships, the visa officer would be interested in not only the documentary evidence that Gary is divorced but also the duration of his relationship with Ellie. By looking at the timing of Gary's divorce together with the timing of his subsequent marriage to Ellie, as well as the long-term relationship that existed before the marriage, the officer would determine that the motive to marry was not purely for immigration purposes.

To deter marriages of convenience, the government has established new rules for sponsorship. In October 2012, new regulations were introduced that place a condition on acquiring permanent residence status for a foreign national who is a sponsored spouse or partner.[15] The applicant for permanent residence under the family class is required to live together with their sponsor in a legitimate relationship for two years from the date of becoming a permanent resident. If the condition is not met, permanent residence status may be revoked from the foreign national and lead to removal from Canada. As a further deterrence to marriage fraud or fraudulent common-law relationships, the regulations also include the possibility of criminal charges against the sponsored person.

Other Relationships

Dependent Children

One of the major changes brought in by the IRPA was raising the age for a dependent child from 19 to 22. The definition of a "dependant" in s. 2 of the IRP Regulations is technical and should be read carefully. In summary, it means a biological child (provided that the child was not adopted by a person other than the spouse or common-law partner of the parent), or an adopted child of the parent, where the child is in one of the following situations of dependency:

- under age 22 and single (no spouse or common-law partner);
- a full-time student and substantially dependent on a parent for financial support since before age 22, or since becoming a spouse or common-law partner (if this happened before age 22); or
- financially dependent on a parent since before age 22 because of a disability.

Using our scenario concerning Gary and Ellie, Ellie's daughters Amanda (aged 17) and Martha (aged 12) both meet the regulatory definition of a dependant. The lock-in age is on the day that the case processing centre receives Gary's sponsorship application and the required processing fees. The sponsorship process can be lengthy, so the ages of Martha and Amanda will be "frozen in time" for the full duration of the time that it takes to process the sponsorship and applications for permanent residence: starting on the day that Gary submits his sponsorship application in Canada to the date of the issuance of the permanent resident visas by the visa office at the port of entry.

Dependants over the age of 22 may still qualify as dependants if they are substantially dependent on their parents for financial support and must either be full-time students enrolled in an accredited post-secondary institution or have a physical or mental disability. Applicants must provide evidence to prove this, such as school or medical records. In assessing applications, visa officers are encouraged to raise questions such as the following:

- Is the schooling a dominant activity in the life of the student?
- What is the attendance record?
- What grades were achieved?
- Can the student discuss with some knowledge the subjects being studied?
- Has a genuine effort been made to assimilate the knowledge in the courses being studied?

Should the conclusion be reached that the primary purpose of undertaking the program of study is for immigration purposes, officers are directed to deny the application for that child (s. 14.2 of "OP 2").

The applicant must also demonstrate with supporting documentation the degree of dependence. Officers inquire into the costs of study and the living arrangement of the child. For a student living apart from the parents, the parents are expected to show payment of room and board. Students who pay a significant portion of their own educational and living costs, or who may be receiving student loans or financial assistance from another source, may not meet the definition.

Adopted Children

Under the family class provisions of the IRP Regulations, a child must be related to the sponsor by a blood relationship or by adoption. An adoption by definition severs a child's legal relationship to the biological parents (s. 3(2)). Severance from the biological parents means that an adopted child may not sponsor the biological parents or grandparents in the future.

In all cases of adoption, the genuine and informed consent of the biological parents must be provided. If both parents are alive, both should give consent. In the event that only one parent gives consent to an adoption, visa officers must be satisfied that the second parent has no legal rights with respect to the child.

To sponsor an adopted child for permanent residence, there are two processes to complete:

- the adoption process; and
- the sponsorship process or citizenship process.

There are separate adoption processes and conditions depending on whether the sponsor is adopting a child from outside or from within Canada and whether the child is over age 18.

ADOPTION PROCESS OUTSIDE CANADA

International adoption is complex because of social welfare laws, immigration laws, and the laws of the child's country. The IRP Regulations provide for the adoption abroad of children both under 18 years of age and children over 18 years of age (if they also meet the definition of a dependant).

Adoptions of children under 18 years of age must be in the best interests of the child, according to s. 117(2) of the IRP Regulations. If the foreign adoption was not in the best interests of the child, the child shall not be considered a member of the family class. To meet the "best interests" test, the following requirements listed in s. 117(3) must be met:

- a competent authority conducted or approved a home study of the adoptive parents;
- before the adoption, the child's parents gave their free and informed consent to the child's adoption;

- the adoption created a genuine parent–child relationship, and not a relationship of convenience for immigration purposes;
- the adoption was in accordance with the laws of the place where the adoption took place;
- the adoption was in accordance with the laws of the sponsor's country of residence;
- if the sponsor lived in Canada at the time that the adoption took place, the competent authority of the child's province of intended destination stated in writing that it does not object to the adoption;
- if the adoption was subject to the Hague Convention on Adoption, the competent authority of the country where the adoption took place and the province of destination both stated in writing that they approved the adoption as conforming to the convention; and
- if the adoption was not subject to the Hague Convention on Adoption, there is no evidence that the adoption is for the purpose of child trafficking or undue gain within the meaning of the convention.

The "best interests of the child" principle is recognized by the international community as a fundamental human right of every child, and is also entrenched in article 3 of the United Nations *Convention on the Rights of the Child*. Article 1 of the convention defines a child as any person under the age of 18, unless an earlier age of majority is recognized by a country's law.

Article 3 elaborates on the meaning of "best interests" and provides that signatory states, including Canada, must ensure such protection and care as is necessary for a child's well-being, taking into account the rights and duties of parents, legal guardians, or other individuals legally responsible, and, to this end, shall take all appropriate legislative and administrative measures.

The *Convention on the Protection of Children and Co-operation in Respect of Inter-Country Adoption* (the Hague Convention), referenced in the IRP Regulations, provides minimum standards and procedures for adoptions between countries. It is intended to end unethical adoption practices and promote cooperation between countries. The Hague Convention puts in place procedures that minimize the chance of exploitation of children, birth parents, or adoptive parents during the adoption process.

The Hague Convention requires the central adoption authority in both the child's destination country and country of current residence to agree to the child's adoption. Canada and all provinces and territories follow the requirements of the Hague Convention. If the child to be adopted is from a signatory state to the Hague Convention, the adoption must follow the convention's rules. In other words, no private adoptions may take place for a child from a signatory state. In Canada, a CIC officer must approve the sponsorship before the adoption is completed.

The Hague Convention requires that the authorities in the child's country of origin ensure that

- the child is legally free for adoption;
- the birth parents have consented to the adoption in the child's best interests and understand the consequences for their parental rights; and

- the decision to place a child for adoption is not motivated by any financial gain.

The Hague Convention requires that the authorities in Canada—namely, Human Resources and Social Development Canada (HRSDC), Child, Family and Community Division—ensure the following:

- the adoptive parents are eligible and suitable to adopt; and
- the appropriate authorities have decided that the child will be allowed to enter and live permanently in Canada.

The CIC website directs sponsors/adoptive parents to links to access a list of countries that are parties to the Hague Convention, and provinces and territories in Canada that have implemented the Convention. Canadian adoptive parents must also obtain the approval of the province in which they live. There are several specific requirements that must be successfully met by prospective adoptive parents, as follows:

1. **Home study.** A home study is an assessment of the prospective parents with respect to their suitability to adopt. It is undertaken by provincial or territorial authorities, and generally carried out by an accredited social worker. The home study is comprehensive, and an important precondition to an adoption. It is also required for immigration purposes under s. 117(1)(g)(ii) of the IRP Regulations.

2. **Letter of no-involvement.** A letter of no-involvement may be accepted instead of a home study where a private adoption takes place outside Canada and in a state that is not a signatory to the Hague Convention. It may also be accepted in cases where an adoption is finalized abroad prior to the adopted child's arrival in Canada. The purpose of the letter of no-involvement is to inform the visa office that an adoption order, which is in accordance with the laws of the jurisdiction where the adoption took place, will be recognized by the adopting parents' province or territory of residence.[16]

3. **Letter of no-objection.** A letter of no-objection is a written statement from the province or territory where the child will live, stating that the province or territory does not object to the adoption (IRP Regulations, ss. 117(1)(g)(iii)(B) and 117(3)(e)).

4. **Letter (or notice) of agreement.** A letter or notice of agreement is required in Hague Convention adoption cases, indicating that the province and adoptive parents agree to the adoption (IRP Regulations, ss. 117(1)(g)(ii) and 117(3)(f) and (g)). It is sent by the receiving provincial or territorial authorities to the visa office, with a copy to the central authority of the adopted child's country of residence.

ADOPTION PROCESS INSIDE CANADA

For in-Canada adoptions, s. 117(1)(g) of the IRP Regulations sets out the following conditions for membership in the family class:

- the child must be under the age of 18;
- there must be no evidence that the adoption is for the purpose of acquiring any privileges or status under the IRPA;
- if the adoption was subject to the Hague Convention on Adoption, the competent authority of the country in which the child lives and the province of destination of that child must have stated in writing that they approve the adoption as conforming to the convention; and
- if the adoption was not subject to the Hague Convention on Adoption, the child must have been placed for adoption in the country in which he or she lives or is legally available for adoption and there must be no evidence that the adoption is for the purpose of child trafficking or undue gain within the meaning of the convention, and the competent authority of the child's province of intended destination must have stated in writing that it does not object to the adoption.

ADOPTIONS OF CHILDREN OVER 18

Adopted children over the age of 18 must be considered a dependant as defined in the IRP Regulations. For an adopted child over the age of 18, in order to be considered a member of the family class, the following circumstances must exist:

- the adoption must have been in accordance with the laws of the place where the adoption took place and, if the sponsor resided in Canada at the time of the adoption, the adoption must have been in accordance with the laws of the province where the sponsor then resided, if any, that applied in respect of the adoption of a child 18 years of age or older;
- a genuine parent–child relationship must have existed at the time of the adoption and existed before the child reached the age of 18; and
- the adoption must not have been primarily for the purpose of acquiring a status or privilege under the IRPA.

Regardless of whether the adoption is outside or inside Canada, or if the adoptee is older than 18 years, a visa officer must be satisfied the adoption creates a genuine parent–child relationship, and not a relationship of convenience entered into for the sole purpose of gaining permanent residence. Section 4 of the IRP Regulations refers to this kind of relationship as a bad-faith relationship, and excludes adoption where the relationship between the sponsor and the adopted child exists only for immigration purposes. The sponsorship will not be approved if a visa officer concludes that the purpose of the adoption is to gain admission to Canada.

Guardianship

The intent of the guardianship provisions was to provide a mechanism to sponsor an orphaned or abandoned child who would not otherwise meet the criteria of a "member of the family class," and who lived in a country where adoption is unavailable.

However, the guardianship provisions of the IRP Regulations were not implemented when those regulations came into force in June 2002, but rather were delayed to allow the provinces and territories time to conduct feasibility studies. The result was that the provinces and territories informed CIC that they would not participate in the implementation of the guardianship provisions, making implementation impossible.

The regulations relating to guardianship were subsequently repealed in 2005, and amended such that CIC will continue to deal with immigration cases where children in need of care are brought into families through guardianships. Officers examine these situations case by case and, where humanitarian and compassionate reasons exist, use their discretion to allow these children into Canada.[17]

Specified Orphaned Relatives

Siblings, including half and step siblings, nephews, nieces, and grandchildren, may also be admitted as sponsored relatives if they meet all the following criteria according to s. 117(1)(f) of the IRP Regulations:

- they are orphaned;
- they are not a spouse or common-law partner; and
- they are under 18.

Generally, the sponsorship for orphaned relatives who are under 18 years of age follows the same procedures as for adopted children under 18 years of age, provided they are unmarried and not in a common-law relationship. As in adoption cases, a visa officer must obtain the written consent of the appropriate authorities in the country of residence of the child, before the child may be removed from that country. Written consent of any legal guardians must also be obtained.

Officers are directed to counsel sponsors to obtain legal guardianship of the child upon the child's arrival in the province of residence to ensure that the sponsor has legal obligations toward the sponsored child, according to s. 73 of the operations manual "OP 3."

Under the provisions of the former Act, the Federal Court of Appeal held that a visa officer did not have to consider whether the biological father was alive or not, if he was not married to the mother and there had been no declaration of parentage.[18]

Applying for Permanent Residence Under the Family Class

Sponsorship Kits and Applications for Permanent Residence

Sponsorship kits can be obtained online from the CIC website or from a CIC call centre. All kits come with extensive guides that describe the forms in each kit, the supporting documentation that must be submitted, and the addresses for mailing. There are specific sponsoring kits, tailored to different family situations, so it is important to select the appropriate application package. For example, there are two different application packages for applicants outside Canada depending on the relationship to the sponsor:

- one for a "spouse, common-law partner, conjugal partner or dependent child," and
- the other for sponsoring "any other family member."

Both kits contain the sponsor's application package, the permanent resident's application package, and region-specific instructions (for example, for submitting police certificates, photographs, and other details). Another sponsorship kit is for temporary residents in Canada who are applying for permanent residence under the "spouse or common-law partner in Canada" class.

A Canadian or permanent resident sponsor under the in-Canada class must meet the same requirements as a sponsor under the "spouse, common-law partner, conjugal partner or dependent child" class; however, the sponsor does not have any right to appeal a rejected application.

Calculating Fees

As discussed earlier under general provisions, there are a number of expenses associated with an application for permanent residence. In the case of a sponsorship application, the fees payable to CIC include the following:

- Sponsor's application fee—because the sponsor must be assessed for eligibility to sponsor (approximately $75).
- Application for permanent residence fee (approximately $475 for applicants over 22, and significantly less for children).

In our scenario involving Gary and Ellie, the processing fees adds up to $850, as shown in the table below:

Sponsorship Application Fees

Person	Type of Application	Fee
Gary—sponsor	Sponsorship application	$75
Ellie—principal applicant (over 22 years of age, married to the sponsor)	Permanent residence application	$475
Amanda—accompanying family member (under 22 years of age, not married or in a common-law relationship)	Permanent residence application	$150
Martha—accompanying family member (under 22 years of age, not married or in a common-law relationship)	Permanent residence application	$150
Total application fees		$850

In addition to the application fees, there is a right of permanent residence fee (RPRF) for Ellie's permanent residence (recall that dependent children of the applicant are exempt.) For our scenario, the fee is $490, as shown in the table below:

Right of Permanent Resident Fee

Person	Right of Permanent Residence Fee
Ellie, principal applicant	$490
Amanda, dependant of principal applicant	$0
Martha, dependant of principal applicant	$0
Total Right of Permanent Residence Fee	$490

Therefore, together, the application and RPRF fees total $1,340 ($850 + $490) for Gary, Ellie, and Ellie's daughters. These fees do not cover the cost of medical examinations, or any criminal or background checks.

Decisions on Applications for Permanent Residence Under the Family Class

The possible outcomes of CIC decisions with respect to both sponsorship applications and permanent resident applications, and the rights of appeal of sponsors and applicants, are described in this section. The outcomes of adoption processes are also discussed.

Decision—Sponsor Applications

In our scenario, Gary sent his Application to Sponsor, Sponsorship Agreement and Undertaking (IMM 1344) to Ellie to sign. Ellie must complete her application package, gather all her supporting documents, and send them to Gary. After all his forms are completed and signed and he has gathered all supporting documentation, Gary will send the packages to a centralized case processing centre in Mississauga, Ontario for processing. A Canadian immigration officer will assess Gary's sponsorship application to verify that Gary meets all the requirements, as follows:

- the sponsor meets the regulatory definition and is eligible to sponsor;
- the applicants for permanent residence are members of the family class; and
- the application for permanent residence is complete, including fees.

The immigration officer's decision will result in one of a number of possible outcomes, as follows:

1. *Sponsor is ineligible—elect to end processing.* If the immigration officer finds that Gary is an ineligible sponsor, Gary may choose to end the process by checking in box 1 of the Application to Sponsor, Sponsorship Agreement and Undertaking (IMM 1344), "To withdraw your sponsorship," and all processing fees (less $75) will be repaid. The immigration officer will close the file.

Ellie's application will not be assessed. Gary has no right to appeal to the immigration officer's decision.

2. *Sponsor is ineligible—elect to pursue application.* If the immigration officer finds that Gary is an ineligible sponsor, Gary may choose to pursue the matter at the next level, by checking box 1, "To proceed with the application for permanent residence," on his Application to Sponsor, Sponsorship Agreement and Undertaking (IMM 1344). The immigration officer will then transfer the application for permanent residence and the negative decision (that is, the officer's finding of ineligibility) to the nearest visa office where Ellie, the principal applicant, resides. Gary has the right to appeal to the Immigration Appeal Division of the Immigration and Refugee Board.

3. *Sponsor is ineligible because sponsored person is not a member of the family class.* If the immigration officer finds that Gary is ineligible because Ellie, the principal applicant, is not a member of the family class, Gary may accept this finding and elect to discontinue processing. However, if Gary does not accept the finding and elects to pursue the matter, the officer will send her decision to the visa office. Gary's right to appeal to the Immigration Appeal Division of the IRB is maintained.

4. *Sponsor is eligible.* Finally, if the immigration officer finds that Gary is eligible, the immigration officer's written decision and Ellie's application for permanent residence are forwarded to the appropriate visa office for further processing.

Decision—Permanent Residence Application

In processing applications under the family class program, a visa officer reviews the application for permanent residence to ensure that the applicants (Ellie and her daughters, for example) do indeed meet the regulatory definition as members of the family class and that they have an eligible sponsor. The visa officer does the following:

- examines the supporting documents to ascertain the applicants' identity, age, and relationship to the sponsor and other family members (whether or not those family members are accompanying them to Canada);
- examines their passports or travel documents to determine whether they are valid; and
- determines whether the applicants are inadmissible (including family members, whether or not they are accompanying them or not to Canada), according to any of the grounds of inadmissibility, described in Chapter 3.

Ellie might be called to appear for an interview with a visa officer. However, although visa officers have the authority to interview applicants, they generally waive interviews unless there is a need to confirm the applicant's identity or the relationship to the sponsor, or to address questions related to admissibility.

If all the requirements are met, the visa officer issues a confirmation of permanent residence (COPR) document and permanent resident visa to travel to Canada as a permanent resident. The names of non-accompanying family members are included on the visa of the principal applicant. (In our scenario, Ellie does not have any other dependants.) Ellie and her daughters must travel to Canada before the expiry date on their visas, where they will be examined at the port of entry.

If one or more of the requirements are not met, and Ellie's application for permanent residence is refused by the visa officer, a **refusal letter** is sent to her setting out the grounds for the refusal—that is, the reasons why the application for permanent residence was rejected. This written record can then be used as the basis of an appeal. The visa office mails a copy of the refusal letter, together with a notice of appeal, to Gary, the sponsor. The notice informs the sponsor of his right to appeal under s. 63 of the IRPA.

Right to Appeal

Appeal procedures are discussed in Chapter 11, Appeals. Below is a brief explanation of when sponsorship appeals are permitted.

APPEALS PERMITTED BY SPONSOR

A sponsor who is found to be ineligible to sponsor may appeal to the Immigration Appeal Division. Sometimes a sponsor may be ineligible because he does not meet the eligibility criteria—for example, something bars him from sponsorship. The sponsor may also appeal the decision of the visa officer if the applicant for permanent residence (the person being sponsored) is not eligible. For example, a visa officer may find the application incomplete, that the relationship is one of convenience, or that the family member is inadmissible.

APPEALS NOT PERMITTED BY SPONSOR

Sponsorship appeals are not permitted in the following cases:

1. *Ineligible sponsor—spouse or common-law partner in Canada.* Appeal rights for "in-Canada" applications are different from those for appeals of sponsorship cases abroad. When a sponsor does not meet the requirements of the "spouse or common-law partner in Canada class," as defined in s. 130(1) of the IRP Regulations, then it follows that the applicant for permanent residence does not have an eligible sponsor. The application for permanent residence is therefore refused, and the applicant for permanent residence is advised by the case processing centre of the reasons for the refusal and directed to leave Canada or risk removal action.

   In this case, neither the sponsor nor the applicant for permanent residence has a right to appeal to the Immigration Appeal Division. However, the applicant for permanent residence may apply for a judicial review within 30 days after the date of refusal.

2. *Inadmissible applicant.* There are no appeal rights for applicants for permanent residence if they are found inadmissible on the most serious grounds of inadmissibility. Sponsors generally do not have the right to appeal under s. 64 of the IRPA when a family member applicant is found to be inadmissible on

the grounds of security, violating human or international rights, serious criminality, or organized criminality. (For a full description of these grounds, refer to Chapter 3.)

Adoption Process: Permanent Residence

Adoptive parents may apply to sponsor their child for permanent residence if

- the adopted child is coming to Canada to live right after the adoption takes place; or
- one or both parents are Canadian citizens or permanent residents.

The adopted person does not meet the requirements for the immigration process if

- the adopted person is not going to Canada to live right after the adoption takes place; or
- the adopted person is an adult adoptee living outside Canada and not returning to Canada to live right after his or her application is approved.

Before a permanent resident visa under the family class is issued for an adopted dependent child or orphan,[19] the sponsor must provide a statement in writing confirming knowledge of information regarding any medical condition of the child or orphaned person. This is intended to safeguard against the abandonment of the child by prospective parents, by ensuring that they are aware of, and equipped to deal with, any health or medical conditions before the adoption is complete and the child is issued a COPR document and permanent resident visa to travel to Canada (IRP Regulations, s. 118).

Adoption Process: Citizenship Process

Until recently, a child adopted by Canadian citizens did not automatically become a Canadian citizen, but instead arrived in Canada with a permanent resident visa and was admitted as a permanent resident. The parents then had to apply for citizenship on behalf of the child.

However, a new process introduced on December 23, 2007 allows an adopted child to apply for Canadian citizenship without first becoming a permanent resident, if the adoption was by a Canadian citizen after February 14, 1977. Adoptive parents may apply for citizenship on behalf of their adopted child if all the following criteria are met:[20]

- at least one adoptive parent is, or was, a Canadian citizen when the adoption took place;
- the adoption severs (or severed) all ties with the adopted person's legal parents; and
- the adoption was or will be completed outside Canada (except for Quebec).

The adopted person does not meet the requirements for the citizenship process if any of the following factors exist:

- neither parent was a Canadian citizen when the adoption took place;
- the adoption took place before February 15, 1977;
- the adoption did not fully sever all ties with the child's legal parents;
- the adoption will be completed in Canada; or
- a probationary period is to be completed in Canada before a final adoption order is issued from the child's birth country.

Economic Classes

Immigration under the economic classes fulfills one of the stated objectives of Canada's immigration policy: to "permit Canada to pursue the maximum social, cultural and economic benefits of immigration" (IRPA, s. 3(1)(a)). Foreign nationals who acquire permanent residence under an economic class category help to develop the Canadian economy and fill labour market shortages with their skills, knowledge, expertise, and other assets.

As noted earlier, the economic class comprises 67 percent of the total permanent immigration to Canada, including spouses and dependants. This class includes skilled workers, business people, provincial or territorial nominees, the Canadian experience class, and live-in caregivers. Within this group, the majority were admitted as federal skilled workers.[21]

Section 12(2) provides the legal basis for selecting foreign nationals as members of the economic class on the basis of their ability to become economically established in Canada. The government creates the classes or programs, the details of which are found in the regulations. This allows the government to be responsive to labour shortages and the need for economic development.

The following chart shows all the classes and subclasses as currently found in the IRP Regulations.

For each class and subclass there are specific eligibility requirements that must be met, as well as application processing procedures: both of which may change either through a change in the regulations or as a result of ministerial instructions. This part of the chapter focuses on three traditional streams within the economic class:

- federal skilled workers (outside Quebec);
- provincial and territorial nominees; and
- members of the business class (entrepreneurs, self-employed persons, and investors).

Separate rules apply to skilled workers who intend to reside in Quebec. Because of the Canada–Quebec Accord, Quebec has sole responsibility for determining the selection criteria and for integrating skilled workers. Skilled workers who are destined for Quebec must obtain a Certificat de sélection du Québec (Quebec certificate of selection) from that province. However, issues of inadmissibility and the issuance of the permanent resident visa remain federal responsibilities.

For the Canadian experience class and the Live-In Caregiver Program, permanent residence status is acquired by first meeting the eligibility requirements as a temporary resident; these programs were discussed in Chapter 4. The general provisions

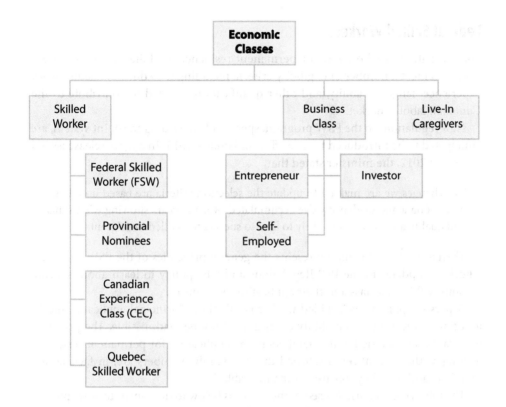

of applying for permanent residence (as discussed earlier in this chapter) are generally relevant.

What follows is a closer examination of the requirements for each of the main economic classes.

The reader should take note that the eligibility criteria and processing procedures in all economic classes are in the process of change. CIC has been criticized for the lengthy processing times for all applications for permanent residence. Therefore, as part of the minister's commitment to reduce the backlog of applications and processing times, he has issued a number of ministerial instructions that affect how applications are processed. The federal skilled worker class (FSW), for example, has undergone a number of changes in processing requirements that began 2008:

- minimum requirements must be met or applications will be returned;
- caps that limit the number of applications by occupation for applications without arranged employment are imposed;
- applications submitted prior to 2008 that have not been processed are suspended;
- as of July 1, 2012, a temporary suspension of all new applications except from those who have arranged employment has taken effect; and
- in August 2012, proposed regulatory changes to the point system were introduced.

The business class, too, is under review and is undergoing an administrative pause while implementing program amendments.

Federal Skilled Workers

Foreign nationals who apply for permanent residence as skilled workers are expected to meet a number of eligibility criteria including the education, skills, work experience, language ability, and other qualifications needed to contribute to the Canadian labour market.

New regulations to the FSW program, specifically regarding the point system, are anticipated to be introduced to take effect in January 2013. In a news release issued in August 2012, the minister stated that

> The changes we are making to update the selection criteria are based on a large body of data and evidence we've accumulated over the years showing what skills and qualifications are most likely to lead to success for skilled immigrants.[22]

Therefore, the following represents the general principles of the FSW program. Check for updates to the IRP Regulations and CIC policy to learn about specific streams within this class and their application procedures.

A person applying as a skilled worker is called the "principal applicant" and in addition to meeting the eligibility criteria must not be inadmissible. The principal applicant may include family members in the application for permanent residence as long as the visa officer is satisfied that the family members are, in fact, family members and that they too are not inadmissible.[23]

The following scenario is used in the sections below to demonstrate how "points" are assessed for permanent residence as a skilled worker:

Sanjay Patel was born in Ahmedabad, Gujarat on the west coast of India in 1980. His mother tongue is Gujarati. He learned English at school and he speaks, understands, reads, and writes fluently. He was exposed to French briefly as a young boy when his parents worked in the kitchen at a French consulate and he can still answer simple questions in French.

Sanjay attended primary school at the Municipal School Harda from 1985 to 1993, then attended Sadhana Higher Secondary School from 1993 to 1997. He worked in various restaurants as a dishwasher, busboy, and kitchen helper until 2001 when he decided to go back to school to become a chef. He enrolled in a four-year degree program to obtain a bachelor's degree in hotel and tourism management at the Gujarat Institute of Hotel Management. In 2005, he married Anita a month after he graduated, and he has worked in the food service sector since that time. Anita completed a four-year bachelor's degree in 2005 and worked as an English teacher until the birth of their son, Sanjit, in 2007. Two years later, Priya, their daughter, was born. Anita has not returned to work.

Sanjay's first job after obtaining his degree was as a cook in a local restaurant. In his spare time, he also ran his own business, catering medium-sized business functions. His reputation for good-quality food and service brought him to the attention of the famous Chef de cuisine, Julian, who talked Sanjay into joining his prestigious restaurant, Saffron, as a sous-chef in 2009. A year later, Sanjay moved up into a supervisory position as a chef, with the promise of rising to the position of manager.

In 2011, Sanjay escorted Julian to an international competition hosted by the Canadian Culinary Institute of the Canadian Federation of Chefs, in Vancouver, British Columbia. Although the competition was a gruelling two weeks of hard work, Sanjay got his first "taste" of Canada.

Paul Pierre, a renowned Toronto chef, noticed Sanjay at the competition. Sanjay was invited to spend an additional week in Toronto to check out the restaurant scene with Paul Pierre. Paul Pierre offered Sanjay the posting of food services manager at his new restaurant, Taj. Sanjay fell in love with the cosmopolitan city and sees this as his chance to finally realize his dream of running an upscale Indian-fusion restaurant, and provide a good life for his family.

Sanjay does not know anything about immigrating to Canada, but thinks he would have to apply under the federal skilled worker class. Is Sanjay Patel a good candidate for immigrating as a permanent resident with his family? We consider this question in the sections below.

Requirements for Federal Skilled Workers

"Skilled workers" are a class of persons selected "on the basis of their ability to become economically established in Canada and who intend to reside in a province other than the Province of Quebec," according to s. 75 of the IRP Regulations. In our scenario, Sanjay Patel is destined for Toronto, Ontario.

To be successful in his application for permanent residence as a skilled worker, Sanjay, as the principal applicant, must first meet the minimal work experience requirements, pursuant to the IRP Regulations at s. 75(2):

- he must possess a minimum of one year of continuous full-time, paid work experience within the past ten years in a management occupation or in an occupation normally requiring university, college, or technical training as set out under skill type 0 or skill level A or B of the National Occupational Classification (NOC) matrix (as described below); and
- his occupation must not be considered a restricted occupation;

If Sanjay meets the minimal requirements, his application will be assessed further by a visa officer to ensure that he meets additional selection criteria:

- he has sufficient points to meet or exceed the pass mark under the point system (discussed below under the heading "Point System"); and
- he is self-supporting upon arrival (based on a job offer or sufficient settlement funds).

Finally, Sanjay and his family members must not be inadmissible, as described in Chapter 3, Inadmissibility.

NATIONAL OCCUPATIONAL CLASSIFICATION

What is "a management occupation or an occupation normally requiring university, college, or technical training as set out under skill type 0 or skill level A or B?" Occupations are classified according to Canada's NOC system. It provides consistency and

WEBLINK

To view the complete NOC matrix online, including the list of occupations in each major group, visit the NOC website at http://www5.hrsdc.gc.ca/NOC/English/NOC/2011/Welcome.aspx.

information about the education credentials, training, and job duties for an occupation. The NOC 2011 is used by Citizenship and Immigration Canada to differentiate among occupations and skill levels, with respect to prospective immigrants in the skilled worker class, for example.

The NOC is developed by Human Resources and Social Development Canada (HRSDC) in partnership with Statistics Canada and is used by a variety of technicians from economists and business analysts to career counsellors. It is a standardized system that provides formal definitions for more than 40,000 job titles into 500 occupational group descriptions. Each occupation is coded according to the type and level of skill required to perform the work. It is a tool for understanding the world of work by describing duties, skills, interests, aptitudes, educational requirements, and work settings.

The NOC is organized in a matrix format to show the relationship between skill types and skill levels. There are nine skill types (coded by the digits 1 through 9) that are listed across the top of the matrix, and a tenth skill type (coded with 0) that occupies the first row of the matrix. There are four skill levels (A through D) that appear on the left side of the matrix. To demonstrate the organization of the NOC, an outline of the matrix is shown below with only the skill types and skill levels included. To see the complete matrix, go to http://www5.hrsdc.gc.ca/NOC/English/NOC/2011/Matrix.aspx.

NOC Matrix

	1 Business, Finance and Administration Occupations	2 Natural and Applied Sciences and Related Occupations	3 Health Occupations	4 Occupations in Education, Law and Social, Community and Government Services	5 Occupations in Art, Culture, Recreation and Sport	6 Sales and Service Occupations	7 Trades, Transport and Equipment Operators and Related Occupations	8 Natural Resources, Agriculture and Related Production Occupations	9 Occupations in Manufacturing and Utilities
0 Management Occupations									
Skill Level A									
Skill Level B									
Skill Level C									
Skill Level D									

Source: * http://www5.hrsdc.gc.ca/NOC/English/NOC/2011/Occupations.aspx?val=4. ** http://www5.hrsdc.gc.ca/NOC/English/NOC/2011/Occupations.aspx?val=8.

Occupations at skill type 0 require a relevant university degree, professional designation, college diploma or other management training, and proven management experience.

The four skill levels refer to the type of education or training needed to perform the work, as follows:

- Skill level A: university;
- Skill level B: college/technical school or apprenticeship training;
- Skill level C: high school/on-the-job training; and
- Skill level D: short demonstration training.

Generally, each matrix cell is called a major group, and consists of a list of specific occupations. Under the skilled worker class, applicants for permanent residence must have at least one year of continuous full-time, paid work experience within the past ten years that is either in the category of skill type 0 or in skill level A or B.

To assist applicants to find their occupation in the NOC, CIC directs applicants to the HRSDC website, where applicants can view the complete NOC matrix and descriptions of specific occupations.

For example, consider the field "Paralegal and Related Occupations," found within major group 42 in the matrix and coded in the NOC as 4211. For "Paralegal and Related Occupations," the NOC provides a lead statement to describe the work performed, job titles in this occupational field (for example, independent paralegal, law clerk, legal assistant, and legal researcher), and duties, as well as the employment requirements.

Let's take a closer look at the NOC code. The first digit of an occupational code designates the skill type. Skill type refers to the type of work performed and the field of training or experience normally required for entry into the occupation, including the educational area of study and employment. The skill type is intended to identify employment sectors on the basis of the ten broad occupational areas from 0 through 9.

In our example of code 4211, the first digit in the code is 4, corresponding to skill type 4, "Occupations in Social Science, Education, Government Service and Religion."

The second digit of the occupational code indicates the skill level: 1 corresponds to skill level A, 2 corresponds to skill level B, and so on.

If a skilled worker applicant has work experience in the category of skill level A, this means that she has experience in a professional occupation, requiring a relevant university degree, professional designation, or two-year college diploma, and several years of directly related experience.

If a skilled worker applicant has work experience in the category of skill level B, this means that she has experience as a technician or technologist. Occupations at skill level B typically require two to five years of apprenticeship training and apprenticeship or trades certification, and several years of directly related work experience.

In our example of code 4211, the second digit in the code is 2, corresponding to skill level B, which requires college/technical school or apprenticeship training.

Recall our scenario. Would Sanjay Patel meet the minimum work experience requirements of having at least one year of continuous full-time paid work experience within the past ten years of the date of application that is in the category of skill type 0, or skill level A or B, according to the NOC? The easiest way to find out is to go to the HRSDC website at http://www5.hrsdc.gc.ca/NOC/English/NOC/2011/Welcome.aspx and click on the Occupational Structure menu item in the left-hand column. Click on the links for the appropriate skill type, "6 Sales and service occupations" and "0 Management occupations" to search for Sanjay's job title. "Chefs" (code 6321) and "Restaurant and food service managers" (code 0631) are listed. Then click on the link to read a description of the duties for jobs in these fields. We find that Sanjay's job title is listed and the duties described are a match with the work he performed. We also know from the scenario that he has been working full time as a manager since 2010. He therefore exceeds the minimum requirement of work experience in an occupation that is listed in the NOC.

Point System

Canada has used a point-based system to assess skilled workers since 1967, when it was first introduced into immigration regulations. Under the *Immigration Act* of 1976, skilled workers were known as "independent applicants," because they were not financially reliant on sponsors or the government for their settlement.

The point system was designed to improve consistency and fairness by reducing discretion and the potential for discrimination in selecting immigrants. Under the point system, immigration officers assign points up to a fixed maximum in each of several categories. The minister is authorized to set the pass mark, or "minimum number of points required of a skilled worker," under s. 76(2) of the IRP Regulations. Such authority allows the minister to amend the pass mark when there are changes in the Canadian economic and social landscape or when there are changing demands for prospective immigrants. For the first time since the enactment of the IRPA in 2002, the point system has undergone amendments that came into effect early in 2013. The 2013 point system favours younger applicants who are proficient in one or both of Canada's official languages. Generally, the point system changes affect the weight and number of points in the selection factors that include:

- giving higher priority to younger workers by changing the points for age;
- placing more emphasis on fluency in official languages by establishing new minimum official language proficiency thresholds and increasing points for language;
- increasing points for Canadian work experience and reducing points for foreign work experience;
- simplifying the process for those who have arranged employment; and
- awarding points for an applicant whose spouse has fluency in official languages and Canadian experience.

In addition to meeting minimum requirements, the principal applicant must achieve a passing score on the selection grid.

The pass mark is the minimum-required total out of a possible 100 points for six selection factors. The current pass mark is 67 points, and because it is in the regulations, that pass mark can be increased or decreased without being debated in the House of Commons.

Federal skilled workers are assessed according to six selection factors set out in ss. 78 to 83 of the IRP Regulations as follows:

1. education;
2. language proficiency in English and French;
3. experience;
4. age;
5. arranged employment; and
6. adaptability.

Points are allocated to the principal applicant with a view to select applicants who possess attributes that will lead to their becoming economically established.

When regulations were originally introduced in 2002, 70 out of 100 possible points were spread over only three factors—education, language skills, and work experience—to show the importance of these factors in the selection of skilled workers. Almost a decade later, the point system is changing to offset the barriers that well-educated newcomers face today in becoming economically established: there is a greater emphasis on the selection of foreign nationals who possess some fluency in Canada's official languages, who are younger, who have Canadian experience, and who are well educated—for a weighting of 80 points out of 100. Compare the old and new points for selection factors:

Selection factor	Points: 2002–2012	Points: 2013
Education	maximum 25	maximum 25
Language proficiency in official languages	maximum 24	maximum 28
Work experience	maximum 21	maximum 15
Age	maximum 10	maximum 12
Arranged employment	maximum 10	maximum 10
Adaptability	maximum 10	maximum 10
Total	100	100
Pass mark	67	67

A grid of the selection factors is part of the self-assessment worksheet that is provided to applicants in the CIC instruction guide "Application for Permanent Residence: Federal Skilled Worker Class" (IMM EG7000). Below is a brief description of each of the selection factors.

EDUCATION FACTOR

The visa officer awards points for education in a range from 0 points to 25 points, generally based first on the number of years of completed full-time or full-time-equivalent studies and then second on the applicant's educational credentials.

The following terms are defined in the IRP Regulations as follows:

- **Full-time studies:** A program of study leading to an educational credential, consisting of at least 15 hours of instruction per week during the academic year.
- **Full-time equivalent:** In reference to part-time or accelerated studies, the period that would have been required to complete those studies on a full-time basis.
- **Educational credential:** Any diploma, degree, or trade or apprenticeship credential issued on completion of a program of study or training at an educational or training institution recognized by the authorities responsible for registering, accrediting, supervising, and regulating such institutions in the country of issue (s. 73).

Credential and number of years of education	Points: 2002–2012
No secondary school diploma obtained and the applicant has no trade or apprenticeship educational credentials	0
Secondary school educational credential (e.g., diploma)	5
One-year post-secondary educational credential, other than a university credential, and at least 12 years of completed full-time or full-time-equivalent studies	12
One-year post-secondary educational credential, other than a university educational credential, and at least 13 years of completed full-time or full-time-equivalent studies	15
One-year university educational credential at the bachelor's level, and at least 13 years of completed full-time or full-time-equivalent studies	15
Two-year post-secondary educational credentials, other than a university educational credential, and at least 14 years of completed full-time or full-time-equivalent studies	20
A university educational credential of two years or more at the bachelor's level, and at least 14 years of completed full-time or full-time-equivalent studies	20
Three-year post-secondary educational credential, other than a university educational credential, and at least 15 years of completed full-time or full-time-equivalent studies	22
Two or more university educational credentials at the bachelor's level and at least 15 years of completed full-time or full-time-equivalent studies	22
University educational credential at the master's or doctoral level and at least 17 years of completed full-time or full-time-equivalent studies	25

Source: "OP-6B Federal Skilled Workers—Applications received on or after June 26, 2010," s. 9.2, p. 27. http://www.cic.gc.ca/english/resources/manuals/op/op06b-eng.pdf.

Changes to the regulations measure the education selection factor as follows:

Credential	Points: 2013
Secondary school educational credential (e.g., diploma)	5
One-year post-secondary credential	15
Two-year post-secondary credential	19
Three-year or longer post-secondary credential	21
Two or more post-secondary credentials, one of which is a three-year or longer post-secondary credential	22
Master's level or professional degree	23
Doctoral level	25

Source: Canada Gazette. Regulations Amending the Immigration and Refugee Protection Regulations. Archived, Vol. 146, No. 33, August 18, 2012. http://gazette.gc.ca/rp-pr/p1/2012/2012-08-18/html/reg2-eng.html.

Educational credentials are not measured according to Canadian standards; rather, visa officers assess how they are considered locally. Professional degrees, such as medical and law degrees, may be considered first-level degrees (bachelor's degrees) or second-level degrees (graduate degrees), depending on the country. For example, a bachelor of laws degree in the United Kingdom is a first-level degree, because students require no university credits to enter law school. The same degree in Canada is a second-level degree, because students require a minimum number of university credits before applying to law school. For assessing educational credentials, Officers are instructed to consider how local authorities consider professional degrees, in the CIC's *Overseas Processing (OP)* operations manual.[24]

How many points would Sanjay Patel score for education? The calculations for years of study are as follows:

Overview of Sanjay Patel's Education

From	To	Institution	City/country	Degree/diploma held
2001	2005	Gujarat Institute of Hotel Management	Gujarat, India	Bachelors degree, hotel & tourism management
1993	1997	Sadhana Higher Secondary School	Mumbai, India	Secondary school diploma
1985	1993	Municipal School Harda	District Harda Madhya Pradesh, India	Primary school

Given the above dates:

- 8 years full-time: attendance at primary school;
- 4 years full-time: attendance at Sadhana Higher Secondary School
- 4 years full-time: four-year degree

Sanjay's total is 16 years full-time studies.

Sanjay Patel has a four-year university degree, which matches the category "A university educational credential of two years or more at the bachelor's level" and has 16 years of full-time studies so he exceeds the 14 years of full-time study requirement: under the 2002–2012 point system, he would be assessed as having 20 points. You cannot award him more points for his years of study because he does not have the requisite educational credential under the original point system. Under the 2013 regulations, however, Sanjay would receive 21 points because he has a four-year bachelor degree.

LANGUAGE PROFICIENCY

As of June 26, 2010, all applicants in the FSW category are required to submit the results of a language proficiency test (that is, the International English Language Testing System (IELTS), Canadian English Language Proficiency Index Program (CELPIP) for English or Test d'Evaluation du Français (TEF) for French) even if they are from an English- or French-speaking country. The ability to communicate proficiently in one or more of Canada's official languages is another quality that is highly valued in the selection of skilled workers. The principal applicant must first consider which of the two official languages, English or French, he is most proficient in and select it as his first Canadian official language on the application form.

Visa officers do not assess language proficiency; they award points based either on language test results or other evidence provided by the applicant. According to s. 79(2) of the IRP Regulations, the applicant's proficiency is assessed on the basis of benchmarks referred to in Canadian Language Benchmarks 2000 (CLB) for the English language and *Niveaux de compétence linguistique canadiens 2006* for the French language, in four abilities: speaking, listening, reading, and writing.

It is important for the applicant to make the distinction between "first" and "second" official language, because more points are awarded for proficiency in the first official language.

Under the 2002–2012 point system, a maximum 16 points are awarded for proficiency in the first official language, and a maximum 8 points for ability in the second official language, as shown in the tables below, which are based on ss. 79(2)(a), (b), and (c) of the IRP Regulations.

Under the 2013 point system, as previously discussed, there is a greater emphasis placed on the applicant's fluency; therefore, changes to the regulations will require the applicant to meet the minimum level of basic language proficiency in each of the four abilities (speaking, listening, reading, and writing). Basic ability can be described as the ability to

- understand the main points and important details of a conversation;
- write routine business correspondence; and
- be able to participate in small group discussions and express opinions and reservations about a topic.

In the case where the applicant has language abilities in a second official language, 4 points are awarded if his proficiency meets or exceeds benchmark level 5 in each of the four language skill areas.

Point System, 2002–2012: First Official Language Ability

Proficiency	Benchmark	Speak	Listen	Read	Write
High	8 or higher	4	4	4	4
Moderate	6 or 7	2	2	2	2
Basic	4 or 5	1-2*	1-2*	1-2*	1-2*
No	3 or lower	0	0	0	0

* 1 or 2 is matched to the test results.

Point System, 2002–2012: Second Official Language Ability

Proficiency	Benchmark	Speak	Listen	Read	Write
High	8 or higher	2	2	2	2
Moderate	6 or 7	2	2	2	2
Basic	4 or 5	1-2*	1-2*	1-2*	1-2*
No	3 or lower	0	0	0	0

* 1 or 2 is matched to the test results.

Changes to the regulations would measure the **language** selection factor as follows:

Point System, 2013: First Official Language Ability (24 Points)

Proficiency	Benchmark	Speak	Listen	Read	Write
High	8 or higher	6	6	6	6
Moderate	6 or 7	5	5	5	5
Basic	4 or 5	4	4	4	4

Minimum language requirements: applicant must achieve the Basic level of fluency in each ability.

In the case where the applicant has language abilities in a second official language, 4 points are awarded if his proficiency meets or exceeds benchmark level 5 in each of the four language skill areas.

Point System, 2013: Second Official Language Ability (4 Points)

Proficiency	Benchmark	Speak	Listen	Read	Write
High	4	1	1	1	1
Moderate	6 or 7	1	1	1	1
Basic	4 or 5	1	1	1	1
No	3 or lower	0	0	0	0

Returning to our scenario, how many points would Sanjay Patel score for language proficiency? Sanjay would select English as his first official language, because his English skills are stronger than his French skills. He is proficient in all four abilities with respect to English, and his score is therefore the highest possible: 16 points under the 2002–2012 system or 24 points under the 2013 point system.

Sanjay can answer simple questions in French, which requires the basic ability to understand and speak, so he probably would receive 1 point each under the speak and listen categories, for a total of 2 points for French.

Therefore, Sanjay's total language score would be 18 points under the 2002–2012 system or 26 under the 2013 point system.

WORK EXPERIENCE

The visa officer awards points based on the principal applicant's full-time or full-time-equivalent paid work experience that occurred within the past ten years of the date of the application for permanent residence. According to s. 80(7) of the IRP Regulations, full-time work means at least 37.5 hours of work per week.

The applicant must show past performance of the main and essential duties of the occupation as described in the NOC to meet the regulatory definition of work experience. Furthermore, that work experience must be in the category of skill type 0, or skill level A or B, according to the NOC. Therefore, the principal applicant must provide the four-digit NOC code that corresponds to the occupation indicated on her application form.

Under the 2002–2012 point system, the visa officer awards up to a maximum of 21 points as follows (IRP Regulations, s. 80(1)):

Years of experience within the ten years preceding the date of application

	Less than one	One	Two	Three	Four or more
Points	0	15	17	19	21

Under the 2013 point system, the visa officer awards up to a maximum of 15 points as follows:

Years of experience within the ten years preceding the date of application

	Less than one	One	Two	Three	Four or more
Points	0	9	11	13	15

Finally, the work experience may not be in an occupation that is considered a restricted occupation. According to s. 73 of the IRP Regulations, the minister has the authority to restrict an occupation on the basis of labour market demands and consultations with HRSDC, the provinces, and other organizations. There are currently no designated restricted occupations.

How many points would Sanjay Patel score for work experience? Sanjay would provide a detailed account of his work history setting out the from-and-to dates, the employers, locations, and the title of the positions held along with the classification of the occupation according to the NOC, and the number of hours worked. Based on the case scenario, we know the following.

Assessment of Work Experience

From	To	Employer	City/ Country	Position	NOC Skill Level	Hours per week
2005	2009	Local restaurant	India	Sous-chef	6321	37.50
2005	2009	Self-employed	India	Caterer/ Business owner	0631	? part-time
2009 2010	Today	Saffron Restaurant	India	Chef/ Manager	6321 0631	50.00

Sanjay performed the duties of manager (code 0631) on a full-time basis since 2009. This amounts to more than four years of experience. Therefore, he would probably be assessed with the full 21 points under the 2002–2012 system but only 13 or 15 points under the 2013 point system (depending on today's date).

AGE

Points based on age are awarded according to s. 81 of the IRP Regulations.

Under the 2002–2012 point system, the visa officer may award a maximum of 10 points to a principal applicant who is 21 years of age but less than 50 years of age. For every year younger than 21 or every year older than 49, 2 points are subtracted, to a maximum of 10 points, as follows:

Years of age	Points, 2002–2012
21 or older but less than 50	10
20 or 50	8
19 or 51	6
18 or 52	4
17 or 53	2
Less than 17 or 54 years of age or older	0

Under the 2013 point system, the visa officer may award a maximum of 12 points to a principal applicant who is 18 years of age but less than 36 years of age. For every year older than 36, 1 point is subtracted, as follows:

Years of age	Points, 2013
18 or older but less than 36	12
36	11
37	10
38	9
39	8
40	7
41	6
42	5
43	4
44	3
45	2
46	1
Under 18 years of age or 47 years of age or older	0

How many points would Sanjay Patel score for age? He was born in 1980. He falls within the range for maximum points; therefore, he would receive the full 10 points under the 2002–2012 point system but would score more points under the new system—the full 12 points—because he is still under 36 (presuming today's date is before 2016).

ARRANGED EMPLOYMENT

There is no change to the number of points to be awarded under the proposed 2013 regulations. "Arranged employment" is an offer of employment in Canada for an indeterminate term, meaning that it is open-ended and not a fixed term such as six months. The visa officer may award 10 points if the principal applicant provides proof of an approved offer of employment, according to s. 82 of the IRP Regulations. However, the occupation must be listed in skill type 0 or skill level A or B of the NOC matrix. Furthermore, the officer will assess whether the applicant is able to perform and is likely to accept and carry out the employment.

Proof of a job offer is obtained from HRSDC. The 10 points are awarded if the applicant satisfies one of the following four conditions:

1. The applicant is already in Canada as a temporary resident, holds a valid work visa, is currently working in the job, and has a valid job offer for an indeterminate basis for that same job if the applicant is accepted as a skilled worker.

2. The applicant is already in Canada as a temporary visitor under one of the international treaties for business visitors (such as the North American Free Trade Agreement), is working in the job, and has a valid job offer for an indeterminate basis for that same job if the applicant is accepted as a skilled worker.

3. The applicant does not intend on working in Canada before becoming a permanent resident and has an approved job offer for an indeterminate basis if the applicant is selected as a skilled worker.

4. The applicant is already in Canada as a temporary resident, holds a valid work visa or is a temporary visitor under one of the international treaties for business visitors, and has a valid job offer for an indeterminate basis for another job if the applicant is accepted as a skilled worker.

How many points would Sanjay Patel score for arranged employment? If Toronto chef Paul Pierre follows through with his job offer of executive chef, he must apply for an "arranged employment opinion" (AEO) from the Human Resources and Skills Development Canada (HRSDC)/Service Canada office. When assessing a job offer, HRSDC/Service Canada considers

- that the category of the occupation matches the majority of duties in the NOC;
- the wages and working conditions;
- the genuineness of the offer and the employer's history (see Chapter 4 for a description); and
- that the offer is for a full-time, permanent job that is non-seasonal.

If the approval is obtained, Sanjay will be assessed as having an arranged employment, for a total of 10 points. Without the HRSDC AEO, no points will be awarded.

ADAPTABILITY

Adaptability encompasses a variety of factors that are likely to benefit the applicant's chances of successful integration into Canadian society. These may include education, previous work or study in Canada, and arranged work, as they relate to the applicant and/or the applicant's partner. If the applicant's partner is likely to integrate well into Canadian life, this will assist the applicant to do likewise. Other support networks such as relatives in Canada may also increase the applicant's chances of successful integration.

The five elements for which the applicant may accumulate up to a maximum of 10 points, according to s. 83 of the IRP Regulations, are as follows:

Point System, 2002–2012: Adaptability

Element	Description	Points
1. Educational credentials of spouse or common-law partner	The visa officer evaluates the spouse or common-law partner's educational credentials as if that person were the principal applicant, as follows: • if the spouse or common-law partner would receive 25 points, the principal applicant receives 5 points • if the spouse or common-law partner would receive 20 or 22 points, the principal applicant receives 4 points • if the spouse or common-law partner would receive 12 or 15 points, the principal applicant receives 3 points	3-5
2. Previous study in Canada	The principal applicant or his accompanying spouse or common-law partner completed a program of full-time study of at least two years' duration at a post-secondary institution in Canada, by the age of 17 or older under a study permit, whether or not the person obtained an educational credential	5
3. Previous work in Canada	The principal applicant or his accompanying spouse or common-law partner has at least one year of full-time work in Canada under a valid work permit	5
4. Family relationships in Canada	The principal applicant or his accompanying spouse or common-law partner is related to a Canadian citizen or permanent resident who is a parent, grandparent, child, grandchild, child of a parent, sibling, child of a grandparent, aunt/uncle, or grandchild of a parent, niece, or nephew	5
	The principal applicant's spouse or common-law partner is a Canadian citizen or permanent resident living in Canada	5
5. Arranged employment	The principal applicant was awarded points under the arranged employment factor	5

Under the new adaptability grid, no points are awarded for the spouse's education. There is instead emphasis on previous Canadian education and work experience for the applicant and accompanying spouse, even if an academic credential was not achieved.

Point System, 2013: Adaptability

Element	Description	Points
1. Language proficiency of spouse or common-law partner	In either official language of at least benchmark level 4 for all the four language skill areas	5
2. Previous study in Canada by the principal applicant	Full-time study of at least two academic years in a program of at least two years in duration whether or not the skilled worker obtained an educational credential	5
3. Previous study in Canada by the spouse or common-law partner	Full-time study of at least two academic years in a program of at least two years in duration whether or not the accompanying spouse or common-law partner obtained an educational credential for completing a program in Canada	5
4. Previous work in Canada by the principal applicant	For any previous period of full-time work under a work permit or under s. 186 of at least one year in Canada in an occupation that is listed in Skill Type 0 Management Occupations or Skill Level A or B	10
5. Previous work in Canada by the spouse or common-law partner	For any previous period of full-time work under a work permit or under s. 186 of at least one year in Canada in an occupation that is listed in Skill Type 0 Management Occupations or Skill Level A or B	5
6. Family relationships in Canada	The principal applicant or his accompanying spouse or common-law partner is related to a Canadian citizen or permanent resident who is a parent, grandparent, child, grandchild, child of a parent, sibling, child of a grandparent, aunt/uncle, or grandchild of a parent, niece, or nephew	5
	The principal applicant's spouse or common-law partner is a Canadian citizen or permanent resident living in Canada	5
7. Arranged employment	If the principal applicant was awarded points under the arranged employment factor	5

How many points would Sanjay Patel score for adaptability? The scenario does not provide much information about Anita Patel, but let's assume that her bachelor's degree was a four-year degree. Under the 2002–2012 point system, Sanjay would receive 4 points under adaptability for the educational credentials of his spouse.

Neither of the Patels studied or worked in Canada, and there is no information about relatives in Canada. However, Sanjay arranged employment for himself, for an additional 5 points. Therefore, the total number of points earned by Sanjay for adaptability under the 2002–2012 point system would be 9 points.

Under the 2013 point system, there would be no credit for Anita's degree. Sanjay would only acquire additional points if he had arranged employment for a possible 5 points.

WORKSHEET

Use this table for your assessment of the case scenario of Sanjay Patel or another one provided by your instructor.

Begin by checking the regulations for the most up-to-date number of points, then add them as the maximum number of points in the column next to the selection factor.

Sanjay Patel's overall total number of points for all factors exceeds the pass mark of 67.

Worksheet

Selection factor	Maximum number of points	Your reason for assessment				Points awarded
Education						
Language proficiency	1st official language	S	L	R	W	
	2nd official language	S	L	R	W	
Work experience						
Age						
Arranged employment						
Adaptability						

Settlement Funds

According to s. 76 of the IRP Regulations, the applicant must show proof of sufficient settlement funds, unless employment has been arranged. The settlement funds must be enough to support the applicant and any dependants, and are assessed according to the applicant's family size using 50 percent of Statistics Canada's most current LICO for urban areas with populations of 500,000 or more.

The easiest way to determine the requisite amount of funds is to consult the CIC website or to refer to the Application for Permanent Residence: Federal Skilled Worker Class Instruction Guide (IMM EG7000), which contains a grid outlining the minimum amount required to settle based on family size. You can also refer to the LICO table provided earlier in this chapter.

Because Sanjay Patel arranged employment for himself, he would be exempt from the requirement of settlement funds. Without the job offer, he would have calculated the amount of settlement funds required for a family of four, including himself, his wife, and their two children; found the matching minimum amount from the LICO table; and divided it in half (which represents the amount of settlement funds for six months).

Application Procedures for Federal Skilled Workers

Foreign nationals interested in applying as skilled workers are encouraged to first use a self-assessment tool available on the CIC website, entitled "Skilled Worker Self-Assessment." The self-assessment tool identifies how the applicant's skills and experience would be evaluated on an actual application. Applicants who score below the passing grade can consider which areas they can most easily upgrade, such as education or language skills. The self-assessment tool can also help couples decide which of them should be the principal applicant, based on who has more points.

Generally, applicants mail their applications to a Canadian centralized intake office (CIO) where an officer checks for completeness, makes sure the appropriate fees are paid, and determines whether the applicant has met the minimum requirements and any other processing criteria set out in ministerial instructions. If the immigration officer is satisfied that the applicant meets the criteria to process the application, it is forwarded to the appropriate Canadian visa office located in the applicant's country of residence.

The application kit consists of a guide, several forms, and other information, as follows:

- the Application for Permanent Residence: Federal Skilled Worker Class Instruction Guide (IMM EG7000) with detailed instructions for completing the necessary forms;
- a Generic Application for Permanent Residence in Canada form (IMM 0008);
- a Schedule A: Background/Declaration form (IMM 5669 Schedule 1);
- a Schedule 3: Economic Classes form (IMM 0008 Schedule 3);
- an Additional Family Information form (IMM 5406); and
- a Use of a Representative form (IMM 5476), if the applicant uses a representative to complete the application.

In our scenario, restaurant owner Paul Pierre has to formalize the offer of employment by going to HRSDC to obtain the AEO. After he obtains the AEO, he provides Sanjay Patel with the letter of offer. The letter of offer, AEO, and other supporting documentation are required for Sanjay's application package, including status and marriage documents, language test results, academic credentials, and proof of employment.

If the application is deemed complete, an officer at the CIO in Canada assesses it to determine whether it is eligible for processing by a visa office. If so, the application package is sent to the visa office where an officer will assess the application for eligibility and inadmissibility. Sanjay and his family will be notified about submitting to a medical examination and any other matter. Sometime thereafter, a visa officer may invite the applicant for a personal interview in order to finalize the assessment and render a decision regarding the application.

Decisions

Federal skilled worker class applications are decided by visa officers, who determine eligibility by examining supporting documents to ascertain the applicant's identity, whether they meet the requirements of the point system (for example, age, educational and work credentials, language test results), relationship to family members, and verifying the validity of passports or travel documents. Although visa officers have the authority to interview applicants, they generally waive interviews unless there is a need to clarify information or address questions related to admissibility.

Visa officers review the application to ensure that the selection criteria are met, and that the applicant and family members are not inadmissible. If the application is refused on the basis of the eligibility criteria, the visa officer issues a refusal detailing the number of points awarded for each selection factor and the reasons for refusal.

If all the requirements are met and the application is accepted, the visa officer issues a visa to travel to Canada as a permanent resident and a confirmation of permanent residence document (COPR) and permanent resident visa. The names of non-accompanying family members are also included on the visa of the principal applicant. The principal applicant and all accompanying family members must travel before the expiry date on their visas.

Upon arrival at the port of entry, the principal applicant and all accompanying family members present their permanent residence visa to an officer at the port of entry and are subject to examination. The applicant must also present two copies of a detailed list of all personal and household items brought, and the value of each item, and two copies of an additional list of items that are arriving later, and the value of each item.

Generally, the officer counsels the new permanent residents about their rights and responsibilities as permanent residents, advises them about obtaining provincial health insurance and social insurance numbers, and officially welcomes them to Canada.

Applicants who already reside legally in Canada, such as temporary residents with legal work authorizations, are directed to present themselves, with permanent resident visas to a CIC location to finalize processing as permanent residents.

Right to Appeal

There are no appeal rights extended to a foreign national whose application for permanent residence as a skilled worker is rejected.

Provincial Nominees

The minister is authorized by s. 8 of the IRP Regulations to sign agreements with the provinces, and to coordinate and implement immigration policies and programs. Individuals—who are nominated by a province—"may become permanent residents on the basis of their ability to become economically established in Canada" (ss. 87(1) and (2)). Provincial nominee programs (PNPs) can generally provide quicker entry into Canada for qualified workers and experienced business professionals who wish to settle as permanent residents in a particular province.

Provincial Nominees

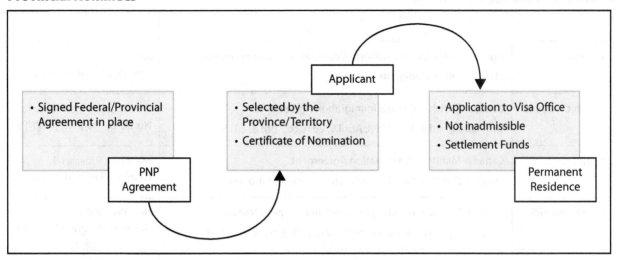

The PNP provides the provinces with the benefits of targeted recruiting and selection of foreign nationals who can contribute to meeting the local labour market and economic needs of each particular province, such as filling a skills shortage or attracting specialized occupational skills. Unlike the FSW program, provincial nominee programs may include the selection of semi- or low-skilled professions and they do not have to be assessed on the six selection factors.

The province must first enter into an agreement with the federal government to establish a provincial nominee program, because the responsibilities are shared between these two levels of government according to s. 87 of the IRP Regulations. The agreements allow the provinces to conduct their own recruiting and selection of foreign nationals who are nominated and must then undergo an inadmissibility assessment by CIC—the federal government.

See the table on the next page for provincial agreements and nominee programs in place to date.

Application Procedures for a Provincial Nominee Program

There are two applications involved when applying to be a provincial nominee:

- an application to the province for nomination; and
- an application to a federal visa officer for permanent residence.

The criteria for nomination varies from province to province. Each province has its own application package, which must be submitted with related documentation and appropriate fees. The province nominates the individual, together with any spouse or common-law partner and dependent children, for permanent residence on the basis of that person's ability to contribute knowledge and skills to become economically established in that province.

An applicant who meets the province's selection criteria is notified by letter, so that he may begin the second stage of the application process. The province also issues a certificate of nomination and notifies CIC officials at the appropriate visa office.

Provincial Nominee Agreements

Province	Agreement	Nominee program
Alberta	Agreement for Canada–Alberta Cooperation on Immigration May 11, 2007 to indefinite	Alberta Immigrant Nominee Program (AINP)
British Columbia	Canada–British Columbia Immigration Agreement Original signed in May 1998; April 9, 2010 to April 8, 2015	British Columbia Provincial Nominee Program (BCPNP)
Manitoba	Canada–Manitoba Immigration Agreement Original signed in October 1996; June 6, 2003 to indefinite	Manitoba Provincial Nominee Program (MPNP)
New Brunswick	Canada–New Brunswick Agreement on Provincial Nominees Original signed in February 1999; March 29, 2005 to Indefinite	New Brunswick Provincial Nominee Program (NBPNP)
Newfoundland and Labrador	Canada–Newfoundland and Labrador Agreement on Provincial Nominees September 1, 1999; November 22, 2006 to indefinite	Newfoundland and Labrador Provincial Nominee Program (NLPNP)
Northwest Territories	Canada–Northwest Territories Agreement on Provincial Nominees August 5, 2009 to indefinite	Northwest Territories Nominee Program (NTNP)
Nova Scotia	Agreement for Canada–Nova Scotia Co-operation on Immigration September 19, 2007 to indefinite	Nova Scotia Nominee Program (NSNP)
Ontario	Canada–Ontario Immigration Agreement November 21, 2005 to November 21, 2010; one year extension of the agreement expired March 31, 2011	Provincial Nominee Program (PNP)
Prince Edward Island	Agreement for Canada–Prince Edward Island Co-operation on Immigration Original signed March 29; June 13, 2008 to indefinite	Prince Edward Island Provincial Nominee Program (PEI PNP)
Saskatchewan	Canada–Saskatchewan Immigration Agreement Original signed in March 1998; May 7, 2005 to indefinite	Saskatchewan Immigrant Nominee Program (SINP)
Yukon	Agreement for Canada–Yukon Co-operation on Immigration Original signed April 2, 2001; February 12, 2008 to indefinite	Yukon Provincial Nominee Program (YNP)

Source: Adapted from Minister of Public Works and Government Services Canada, *Annual Report to Parliament on Immigration 2011*, 2011, Table 7: Federal-Provincial/Territorial Agreements Currently in Force, page 24.

Each province has a time frame for submission of the application for permanent residence to the visa office. Generally, the nominated applicant submits the application package together with the certificate of nomination and the appropriate fees to the CIO in Canada.

The application kit consists of a guide, several forms, and other information, as follows:

- the Application for Permanent Residence: Guide for Provincial Nominees Instruction Guide (IMM EP7000);
- the Generic Application Form for Canada (IMM 0008);
- a Schedule A: Background/Declaration form (IMM 5669);
- a Schedule 4: Economic Classes—Provincial Nominees form (IMM 0008);
- an Additional Family Information form (IMM 5406); and
- a Use of a Representative form (IMM 5476), if the applicant uses a representative to complete the application.

As of July 2012, applicants in the PNP category who are applying for jobs in semi- or low-skilled professions are required to submit the results of a language proficiency test (that is, the IELTS and CELPIP for English, or TEF for French) even if they are from an English- or French-speaking country. The ability to communicate proficiently in one or more of Canada's official languages is another quality that is highly valued in the selection of new immigrants.

The certificate of nomination is required for the visa officer assessment along with the applicant's forms and other supporting documentation, including status and marriage documents, language test results, medical examination, and police checks. A nomination by the province does not guarantee that the applicant will be granted permanent residence—the final decision rests solely with CIC.

Decisions

Applications for permanent residence by members of the provincial nominee class are decided by visa officers. The officer evaluates the nominated applicant's ability to become economically established in Canada, according to s. 87(3) of the IRP Regulations, and also assesses inadmissibility. Although visa officers have the authority to interview applicants, they generally waive interviews unless there is a need to clarify information or address questions related to admissibility.

If all the requirements are met and the application is accepted, the visa officer issues a visa to travel to Canada as a permanent resident and a confirmation of permanent residence document (COPR) and permanent resident visa. The names of non-accompanying family members are also included on the visa of the principal applicant. The principal applicant and all accompanying family members must travel before the expiry date on their visas.

Business Class

The third stream of permanent residence immigration in the economic class is the business class, which in turn comprises three subcategories:

- entrepreneurs,
- investors; and
- self-employed persons.

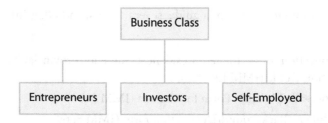

The business class allows for the immigration of experienced business persons who can stimulate national and regional economic development in Canada with their financial capital and business knowledge. The business class represents only a small part of overall immigration: in 2010, 10 percent of new permanent residents (and their spouses and dependants) were admitted as business immigrants.[25]

Business class applicants are selected primarily on the basis of their ability to create jobs for themselves and other Canadians. Requirements vary depending on the subcategory.

We examine the eligibility requirements for each of the subclasses, and the modified point system applicable to all business class applicants, below. As with all immigrants, the usual admissibility requirements also apply to business class applicants and their family members.

Eligibility Requirements

The entrepreneur and investor subcategories are the most similar to each other—pursuant to s. 88(1) of the IRP Regulations, both require two years of *business experience*, a minimum net worth, and an agreement with CIC.

To satisfy the requirement of business experience, the entrepreneur or investor must show that she managed a qualifying business for at least two years in the previous five years.

A qualifying business is one with operating income (income from the sale of goods or services), rather than only passive investment income such as interest, dividends, or capital gains. Additionally, the applicant is required to present documentary evidence of any two of the following:

- the percentage of equity multiplied by the number of full-time job equivalents is equal to or greater than two full-time job equivalents per year;
- the percentage of equity multiplied by the total annual sales is equal to or greater than $500,000;
- the percentage of equity multiplied by the net income in the year is equal to or greater than $50,000; and
- the percentage of equity multiplied by the net assets at the end of the year is equal to or greater than $125,000.

A *full-time job equivalent* means two or more part-time jobs that add up to 1,950 hours of paid employment annually.

Point System for the Business Class

The point system is modified for business class applicants to include only five selection criteria, as set out in s. 102 of the IRP Regulations:

- age,
- education,
- language proficiency in English and French,
- experience, and
- adaptability.

Business Class Point System

Selection factor	Maximum points
Age	10
Education	25
Language	24
Business experience 5 years—35 points 4 years—30 points 3 years—25 points 2 years—20 points	35
Adaptability Business exploration trip to Canada—6 points (Entrepreneur & Investor) Participation in federal–provincial business immigration initiatives—6 points (Entrepreneur & Investor) Education of spouse or common-law partner—3 to 5 points (Self-Employed) One year full-time work in Canada—5 points (Self-Employed) Two years full-time post-secondary studies in Canada—5 points (Self-Employed) Family member in Canada—5 points (Self-Employed)	6

Age, education, and language proficiency are all measured in the same manner as for skilled workers. However, assessments of experience and adaptability vary depending on whether the applicant is applying as an entrepreneur, investor, or self-employed person. All business class applicants, regardless of subclass, must achieve a score of at least 35 points out of 100. Note that the eligibility requirements for business class applicants were under review at the time of writing; check the most current regulations to remain up to date.

Applications

The application kits are available on the CIC website, and generally consist of a guide, several forms, and other instructions.

Applicants mail their completed packages to a CIO (for example, Sydney, Nova Scotia), which controls the number of applications processed and checks for their completeness.

If the application is deemed complete, it is sent for the processing queue to the visa office, which sends the applicant a letter of receipt with the visa office file number so that the applicant can track the progress of the case online.

Visa officers examine the application to ensure that the applicant meets the statutory requirements and selection criteria: they examine the person's business and financial background, evaluate the soundness of business plans in Canada, and make sure the applicant's wealth was not obtained illegally.

Settlement Funds

Business class applicants must show they have sufficient funds to support themselves and their family members, because they do not receive any financial support from the Canadian government. Generally, an applicant who has met the net worth requirements for the entrepreneur or investment categories will have sufficient settlement funds.

Entrepreneur Class

The entrepreneur immigration program is intended to attract experienced business people who can operate and potentially grow their businesses here in Canada. The requirements for eligibility are therefore related to this objective. CIC has suspended the processing of any new applications indefinitely (check the CIC website for updates). What follows is a brief overview of the regulatory requirements for this class, before the program was suspended in July 2011.

An "entrepreneur," as set out in s. 88(1) of the IRP Regulations, must:

- have two years of business experience, as defined above;
- have a legally obtained minimum net worth of at least $300,000; and
- agree to follow the conditions for entrepreneurs after arrival in Canada (see below).

The entrepreneur must demonstrate a net worth of at least $300,000 Canadian (this amount is under review by the minister). The net worth is calculated by subtracting all debts and liabilities (including those of a spouse or common-law partner) from the fair market value of all assets (including those of a spouse or common-law partner).

The entrepreneur must also demonstrate that all net worth was accumulated through legal means, such as employment income, business income, investment income, and inheritance. It may be necessary to prove this with documents that trace the sources of the money, such as pay slips, income tax returns, and business financial statements. This provision is very important to prevent those involved in organized crime from setting up shop in Canada.

CONDITIONS

To ensure that the entrepreneur follows through with plans to operate a business in Canada, the permanent resident status of the entrepreneur and any family members is subject to terms and conditions. The entrepreneur immigration program is the only program of the three in the business class where conditions apply.

Conditions are set out in the IRP Regulations at ss. 98(1) to (5) and are subject to change. At the time of writing, however, the following conditions are imposed within three years of becoming a permanent resident:

- The entrepreneur must own at least one-third of a business in Canada and actively manage it for one year.
- The entrepreneur must create at least one full-time job equivalent (1,950 hours of paid employment) for a Canadian citizen or permanent resident (other than the entrepreneur and dependants).
- The entrepreneur must report regularly to CIC to show compliance.

CIC provides counselling and monitoring to entrepreneurs to ensure compliance with the program. The entrepreneur is provided with a counselling and monitoring guide along with the visa for the principal applicant and each of the dependants. The guide provides the details for reporting requirements and other documents (for example, a mail-in card used for the first reporting period, a form to vary or cancel the terms and conditions, and a list of federal and provincial business immigrant contacts who can help the entrepreneur comply with conditions).

The reporting requirements are as follows:

- First report period (within six months of becoming a permanent resident)— provide CIC with contact information, such as address and telephone number.
- Second report period (within 18 to 24 months of becoming a permanent resident)—provide evidence of efforts to meet the conditions.
- Third report period (final time, within three years of becoming a permanent resident)—provide evidence that the conditions were met.

The conditions are removed once the entrepreneur sets up a significant business venture, hires at least one employee, and provides evidence of being actively involved in managing the business.

Investor Class

The Immigrant Investor Program (IIP) was first established in 1986 to allow applicants to gain permanent residence by making a substantial investment in the Canadian economy. Essentially, the investor provides an interest-free loan to the government of Canada. The investment is government-guaranteed and is repaid in full, without interest, after five years. CIC has suspended the processing of any new applications indefinitely (check the CIC website for updates). What follows is a brief overview of the regulatory requirements for this class, before the program was suspended in July 2012.

To be eligible for the investor class, applicants must satisfy the definition of "investor" set out in s. 88(1) of the IRP Regulations. According to this definition, applicants must meet the following requirements:

- have two years of business experience, as defined above;
- have a net worth of at least $1.6 million; and
- enter into a written subscription agreement to invest $800,000.

SUBSCRIPTION AGREEMENT

The investor enters into a legally binding contract called the "subscription agreement" with CIC. The agreement sets out the operation and administration of the program. The applicant must pay $800,000 directly to the receiver general of Canada before the permanent resident visa is issued. The investment is non-refundable after the visa is issued and is locked in for five years.

CIC issues the investor a debt obligation (that is, the IIP promissory note). It advises the investor of the provincial distribution of her $800,000 investment, and states that the redemption date will be sent to her when the investment funds are dispersed to the province. At the end of the five-year period, the investor presents the IIP promissory note for repayment of her investment.

Federal Self-Employed Persons Class

To be eligible for the self-employed class, applicants must satisfy the definition of "self-employed person" set out in s. 88(1) of the IRP Regulations. According to this definition, applicants must generally have relevant experience and the intention and ability to be self-employed and make a significant contribution to specified economic activities in Canada.

RELEVANT EXPERIENCE

"Relevant experience" is not the same as "business experience" (as required for entrepreneurs and investors). Self-employed applicants must instead have experience that involves at least two years of the following:

- cultural activities,
- athletics, or
- purchase and management of a farm.

Citizenship and Immigration Canada's *Overseas Processing (OP)* operations manual provides the following examples to assist visa officers in assessing relevant experience in cultural activities or athletics: music teachers, painters, illustrators, film makers, freelance journalists, choreographers, set designers, and coaches and trainers. Management experience includes theatrical or musical directors and impresarios.[26]

INTENTION AND ABILITY

The self-employed applicant must demonstrate the intention and ability to establish a business that will, at a minimum, create employment for himself and that will make a significant contribution to the Canadian economy. There are no conditions imposed to set up the self-employed business (unlike the entrepreneur class) and there is no minimum financial investment (unlike both the entrepreneur and investor classes).

Humanitarian and Compassionate Considerations Class

Most applicants for permanent residence fall within either the family class or economic class; however, there are sometimes situations that "just don't fit" the criteria, yet are compelling cases for permanent residence. These exceptional cases may be considered under the class of humanitarian and compassionate considerations (H & C).

The H & C class provides the minister (or delegated immigration officer) with the discretion to grant permanent or temporary residence to applicants who would otherwise not be able to meet statutory and regulatory criteria.

Generally, those who apply in Canada under the H & C class are doing so as a final attempt to remain here, often after having made an unsuccessful attempt to gain refugee status.

The Canadian Council for Refugees, a non-profit organization that advocates for the rights of immigrants and refugees, claims that many of the H & C class applicants for permanent residence fall under the following categories:[27]

- refugees who were refused status because of flaws in the determination system;
- survivors of human trafficking;
- family members of refugees or permanent residents;
- stateless persons;
- victims of domestic violence who left a family sponsorship because of the violence;
- persons whose removal from Canada would involve a serious rights violation, such as lack of treatment for a serious medical condition;
- persons from countries to which Canada generally does not deport because of a situation of generalized risk (moratorium countries);
- persons who have been continuously in Canada for several years;
- persons who have integrated in Canada, socially, culturally, and with family;
- persons who have worked for some time on temporary worker programs, notably as seasonal agricultural workers.

H & C applications are one of the more subjective processes in immigration matters. Decision making is based solely on documentation submitted by the applicant, and the decision-maker has broad discretion when considering the reasons and circumstances of the application. The onus is on the applicant to prove that she would face hardship if she were removed or had to leave Canada. Generally, the hardship must be a hardship that is beyond the applicant's control and is undeserved. There are no definitions in the IRPA or its regulations for the terms "humanitarian" and "compassionate," so the minister or delegated officer must use discretion in deciding applications.

Moreover, an officer may exempt an applicant from the requirements of the IRPA and its regulations for inadmissibility except for reasons of health, serious criminality, human rights violations, organized crime, and security.[28] These discretionary provisions are intended to allow for the approval of deserving cases that were not specifically anticipated when the IRPA was drafted.

H & C applications are not meant as an alternative means of immigration and are intended only for extraordinary cases: the processing of applications is lengthy and the success rate is minimal. Permanent residence applications made under H & C considerations are approved on an exceptional basis and their acceptance rate is low compared with other types of permanent residence applications. For example, only 3.1 percent (8,736) of the total permanent residents admitted to Canada in 2010 were H & C applicants.[29] It may take years before a decision is made and there is no right of appeal from an unsuccessful H & C application.

Bearing in mind that H & C cases are generally unique, complex, and favourably decided only on an exceptional basis, the purpose of this section is to provide a general overview of H & C cases. The examples provided are not conclusive as successful types of cases; they are merely examples used to help explain the information.

Section 25 Criteria

The H & C criteria as set out in s. 25 of the IRPA infuse a degree of flexibility into an otherwise rigid and bureaucratic system. Section 25 offers an opportunity to those whose failure to qualify under any other class is causing significant distress because of individual circumstances. This section allows the minister or delegate to use discretionary power to grant status to foreign nationals where there are strong humanitarian and compassionate reasons for doing so. This may apply to both those who wish to come to Canada and those who wish to remain here, but who are inadmissible for technical, medical, or criminal reasons.

Specifically, s. 25(1) of the IRPA provides that on *the written request of* "a foreign national who is inadmissible or does not meet the requirements of the Act," or at s. 25.1(1) on *the Minister's own initiative* the minister may

> examine the circumstances ... and may grant ... permanent resident status or an exemption from any applicable criteria or obligation of this Act if the Minister is of the opinion that it is justified by humanitarian and compassionate considerations ... taking into account the best interests of a child directly affected.

Section 25.2(1) of the IRPA provides that the minister may grant permanent resident status or an exemption if the minister is of the opinion that it is justified by public policy considerations.

Consider the following examples where normal eligibility requirements are not met, and where a person might ask to be considered for H & C reasons:

- excluded family members, under s. 117(9)(d) of the IRP Regulations;
- non-biological children who are separated from their only family, which is in Canada;
- parents and siblings of child refugees in Canada;
- other family members of persons in Canada where there are specific humanitarian concerns (for example, a situation of generalized risk); and
- a person whose spouse, a Canadian citizen or permanent resident, can afford to sponsor the applicant; however, it would be an unusual and undeserved and disproportionate hardship for the person to leave Canada in order to apply for sponsorship under the family class.

Two criteria specifically requiring consideration in the determination of an H & C application, according to s. 25, are the *best interests of a child* directly affected by the decision; or *public policy* considerations. Both are examined briefly below. It is important to keep in mind that it is the responsibility of the applicant to satisfy the officer that sufficient factors exist to warrant an exemption from the regular admission criteria. Officers will not return the application to ask for further information, so it is very important that all relevant evidence to support one or both of the two criteria is submitted initially.

Child's Best Interests

The minister must consider the best interests of any child who is directly affected by the decision because of the child's relationship to the applicant. In determining the child's best interests, the minister must consider the following issues:

- the child's emotional, social, cultural, and physical welfare;
- the child's age;
- the child's level of dependency on the applicant;
- the degree of the child's establishment in Canada;
- the child's links to country of origin or previous residence;
- the child's medical issues or special needs;
- the child's educational needs; and
- matters related to the child's gender.[30]

This provision applies regardless of whether the child is a Canadian citizen or foreign national. In other words, the best interests of a child who has no right to be in Canada must also be considered, if such a child is directly affected by the decision regarding the applicant. For example, how is it in the best interests of the child to remain in Canada as opposed to being removed to her home country? Are there family members in the home country to return to or will the child be separated from relatives remaining in Canada? Are the living conditions, education opportunities, and health care better or worse in the home country?

Public Policy

The minister has the authority to respond to public demands through the creation of new categories for permanent residence or "public policy" cases. Consider the following examples:

1. *Resumption of Canadian citizenship:* The resumption of Canadian citizenship is a class of permanent residence established specifically for former Canadian citizens who lost their Canadian citizenship inadvertently as minors, because a parent lost his or her citizenship.

2. *Vietnamese living in the Philippines:* Vietnamese living in the Philippines without status since the 1970s, with close family members in Canada, were recently admitted. In a news release dated March 7, 2008, the minister of CIC explained that applications by members of this group received by December 31, 2007 were considered on a priority basis by immigration officers, who examined each on a case-by-case basis to decide whether the applications warranted exemption from the statutory requirements and qualified for humanitarian and compassionate considerations.[31]

Public policy cases differ from other H & C cases because once a new category is created, all cases that fit the category are likely to be accepted.

Applying Under the Humanitarian and Compassionate Class

Note that the H & C class is not intended as a parallel process to refugee determination. Refugee claimants (see Chapter 9) may not submit an application for permanent residence for H & C considerations while their refugee claims are still in process. Generally, a failed refugee claimant may not apply within the past 12 months following a decision by the Refugee Protection Division or the Refugee Appeal Division or if they withdrew their claim.

Designated foreign nationals (see Chapter 10) may not apply for H & C for at least five years after the day of their designation, or if there is a refugee claim or an appeal pending before a division of the Immigration and Refugee Board, or if there is a decision pending on an application for a Pre-removal Risk Assessment.

For those who may apply, their application is assessed on its own merits: officers consider the humanitarian and compassionate considerations for each application on the individual basis of the applicant's personal circumstances.

A written request for an H & C exemption must accompany either an application to remain in Canada as a permanent resident or, in the case of a foreign national outside Canada, an application for a permanent resident visa (IRP Regulations, s. 66). It must be made by the principal applicant and, where applicable, by the following family members:

- spouse or common-law partner (if that person is in Canada and is not a permanent resident or a Canadian citizen); and
- any dependent children who are 18 years of age or older and are not permanent residents or Canadian citizens.

A person who has a removal order against him may apply for permanent residence for humanitarian and compassionate considerations, but the application will not delay removal from Canada. The applicant must leave on or before the date stated in the removal order, while the application is in process.

The application guide provided by CIC cautions that it can take as long as several years to process an application in the H & C category. The onus is on the applicant to put forth any and all H & C factors and to satisfy the decision-maker that there are grounds for an exemption. The guide therefore comes with a warning that CIC will not ask for additional information because the onus is on the applicant to "list any and all factors you wish to have considered at the time you submit your application."

Place of Application

Like other permanent residence applications, most public policy H & C applications are made from outside Canada.[32] Generally, a foreign national does not have the right to apply for permanent residence from within Canada. However, such applications are allowed by exemption under s. 25 of the Act if the applicant lives in Canada and would experience unusual and undeserved or disproportionate hardship if she were required to leave.[33]

The inconvenience of leaving an established life in Canada and moving elsewhere in order to apply for permanent residence in the normal manner is not considered an unusual and undeserved hardship. According to department policy, an "unusual and undeserved hardship" is a situation unanticipated by the IRPA or the regulations that results from circumstances beyond the applicant's control.[34]

"Disproportionate hardship" is defined as hardship that has a "disproportionate impact on the applicant due to their personal circumstances."[35] This may be the case, for example, if there is no home or support system to which to return in the applicant's country of origin.

Steps

Generally, in-Canada H & C applications are assessed in the following order:

Step 1: An immigration officer (or visa officer in the case of applications made outside Canada) assesses the eligibility of the applicant under the permanent resident category (such as family class or skilled worker) in which she applied.

Step 2: If the applicant does not meet the requirements, the officer must decide whether to exempt the applicant from the requirement of applying outside Canada for H & C considerations. For example, if an applicant did not have sufficient points to meet the selection criteria under the federal skilled worker class, and there was a written submission from the applicant for H & C considerations, the visa officer could, instead of rejecting the application, review the case to decide whether there are grounds to exempt the applicant from this requirement.

Step 3: If the applicant is exempted from the requirement to apply outside Canada, CIC will issue a letter informing the applicant of this and setting out requirements such as a medical examination and criminality check.

Step 4: The application for permanent residence will be processed to assess admissibility on the basis of criteria such as financial, medical, criminality, prior misrepresentation, or inadmissible family member (IRPA, ss. 36 to 42). There are exceptions made for protected persons, who are not generally removed from Canada because of their special status.

Step 5: If the applicant is not found to be inadmissible, she will receive a notice to appear for a final interview, at which the immigration officer will review the application for H & C considerations to decide whether to exempt the applicant from the requirements of ss. 70(1)(a), (c), and (d) of the IRP Regulations. If the application is rejected, the applicant will receive a letter with instructions to confirm her departure, and removal proceedings will commence if necessary.

Decisions on applications made outside Canada are made in a similar manner, but steps 3 and 4 are skipped.

Application Kit and Forms

Generally, applications made from outside Canada do not require specific forms. The foreign national applies for a permanent resident visa under one of the existing three classes (that is, family class, skilled worker class, or business class), and submits a written request for consideration on humanitarian and compassionate grounds. If the visa officer determines that the applicant does not meet the requirements of the class of permanent residence, the officer makes an H & C determination.

An exception is the public policy to facilitate immigration to Canada of certain members of the Vietnamese community in the Philippines, for example, who do not have permanent resident status but have close family members in Canada. Forms for applicants and sponsors relating to this public policy are available from CIC.

Applications made from inside Canada require substantially more paperwork, because the applicant has the additional burden of proving that unusual and undeserved, or disproportionate, hardship would result if he were forced to leave Canada in order to apply. An application kit can be obtained online from the CIC website at www.cic.gc.ca/english/information/applications/handc.asp or from a CIC call centre, and it includes the following:

- the Applying for Permanent Residence from Within Canada: Humanitarian and Compassionate Considerations Instruction Guide (IMM 5291);
- an Application for Permanent Residence from Within Canada—Humanitarian and Compassionate Considerations form (IMM 5001);
- a Supplementary Information—Humanitarian and Compassionate Considerations form (IMM 5283);
- an Instruction Guide (IMM 5291);
- a Use of a Representative form (IMM 5476);
- an Authority to Release Personal Information to a Designated Individual form (IMM 5475); and
- a Document Checklist: Humanitarian and Compassionate Considerations form (IMM 5280).

The guide describes the required forms and supporting documentation that must be submitted for in-Canada applications. The key document for setting out humanitarian and compassionate grounds is the Supplementary Information form (IMM 5283). Completing this form with as much detail as possible is essential. It is relied on by the officer to decide whether there are grounds for exempting the applicant. Consider the following review of the relevant boxes in the Supplementary Information form, together with examples borrowed from MOSAIC:[36]

BOX 7: "EXPLAIN THE HUMANITARIAN AND COMPASSIONATE REASONS THAT PREVENT YOU FROM LEAVING CANADA."

Although box 7 is not very large, the applicant must provide as much detail as possible to demonstrate that she would suffer unusual and undeserved or disproportionate hardship if forced to leave Canada and return to her country of origin. Supporting written arguments and other documents, such as letters and medical reports, can be attached.

Examples of hardship where the applicant cannot return to the country of origin are the following:

- the government of the country of origin does not recognize the applicant as one of its citizens;
- there is a complete breakdown of the infrastructure in the country of origin and there is no government in charge;
- the applicant or a family member would suffer medical hardship and might die because medical treatment is not available in the home country; or
- in the case of a female applicant, she would face specific difficulties.

The cost and inconvenience of applying for permanent residence outside Canada is not considered a hardship.

BOX 8: "[C]LEARLY INDICATE IN YOUR APPLICATION THE SPECIFIC EXEMPTION(S) YOU ARE REQUESTING; AND ... PROVIDE ALL DETAILS RELATED TO THIS REQUEST, INCLUDING THE REASONS WHY YOU SHOULD BE GRANTED AN EXEMPTION ON HUMANITARIAN AND COMPASSIONATE GROUNDS."

Where an applicant or family member is inadmissible, such as for criminality, misrepresentation, health, or financial reasons, the applicant must state the specific exemption sought, because CIC will not ask for this information.

BOX 9: "IF APPLICABLE, DESCRIBE THE CIRCUMSTANCES OF YOUR FAMILY AND OTHER RELATIONSHIPS THAT WOULD SUPPORT YOUR HUMANITARIAN AND COMPASSIONATE APPLICATION."

In addition to other factors, CIC also considers the willingness of a family member or close relative in Canada to sign an undertaking of assistance to support the applicant's application for permanent residence. This type of sponsorship may be used as an important consideration when the applicant is not self-sufficient in Canada.

In such cases, the applicant must also submit the following sponsorship forms with the application:

- an Application to Sponsor and Undertaking form (IMM 1344A); and
- a Document Checklist—Sponsor form (IMM 5287).

BOX 10: "IF APPLICABLE, CONSIDERING THE BEST INTEREST OF THE CHILD, PROVIDE INFORMATION ON ANY CHILD AFFECTED BY THIS DECISION."

The immigration officer must consider whether the applicant's child or children would face hardship if they were to return to the applicant's home country. The child's ties to Canada will be considered, such as whether the child was born in Canada, attends school here, or has ever been to the applicant's home country.

The applicant can submit evidence in the form of an opinion letter to demonstrate how the child or children would be affected by having to leave Canada. Opinion letters about the negative mental or physical effects on children from experts such as school counsellors, health workers, physicians, social workers, or psychologists can help to support the application for humanitarian and compassionate considerations.

BOX 11: "HOW HAVE YOU ESTABLISHED YOURSELF IN CANADA?"

CIC officials consider the following examples as evidence of establishment in Canada:

- the amount of time lived in Canada;
- language skills in English and/or French and efforts to improve them;
- efforts to improve education and skills while in Canada;
- the number of family members and relatives legally in Canada;
- the amount of contact with family in Canada;
- marriage to a permanent resident or a Canadian citizen;
- Canadian-born children;
- contacts in Canada, other than family; and
- community involvement (religious or non-religious) and volunteer work performed.

Evidence that does not show establishment in Canada, and that might instead demonstrate the opposite, includes the following examples:

- the amount of time spent collecting welfare;
- the amount of contact with family in the applicant's home country (having many close relatives in the applicant's home country suggests no hardship on return);
- assets abroad; and
- children still living in the applicant's home country.

Evidence that the applicant is financially self-supporting in Canada includes documents such as letters from past and present employers, pay stubs, income tax assessments, mortgage statements, and bank statements. The evidence should support the existence of a reliable income stream and all assets owned.

**BOX 13: "INDICATE ANY OTHER INFORMATION YOU WANT TO
              HAVE CONSIDERED IN YOUR APPLICATION."**

The applicant may provide positive reference letters affirming her integrity and responsibility, from employers, schools, volunteer organizations, the religious community, and others.

Those applying under the s. 25.2 public policy provision because they lost their Canadian citizenship as minors must use the Request for Exemption from Permanent Resident Visa Requirement form (IMM 5001).

All applications for permanent residence within Canada for H & C considerations, along with supporting documentation, must be sent to a case processing centre in Canada (for example, Backlog Reduction Office, Vancouver).

Expenses and Fees

The expenses and fees for applying for a permanent resident visa under H & C considerations are the same as those for applying normally for permanent residence. Expenses include the cost of medical examinations, legal fees, fees for police certificates, and fees to obtain documents. The two fees payable to CIC are the application or processing fee, which is non-refundable, and the right of permanent residence fee. However, the IRPA allows for an exemption (ss. 25(1.1); 25.1(2); 25.2(2)).

Loans may be available for the right of permanent residence fee, but not for the application fee, and the applicant must show an ability to repay the loan. Fees payable to CIC can be paid online or at a designated financial institution and the fees receipt (form IMM 5401) must accompany the application forms (IRP Regulations, s. 295). Because fees are subject to change, check the CIC website regularly to keep up to date.

Decisions on Humanitarian and Compassionate Applications

If an applicant provides sufficient evidence of H & C considerations to satisfy a visa officer, she may be exempted from the normal requirements for applying in a particular immigration class. However, before the permanent resident visa may be issued, the visa officer must be satisfied that the applicant is not inadmissible. If the applicant, or any family member, is inadmissible, the application must be rejected.

This may result in a catch-22: an applicant seeks H & C consideration because she would not otherwise be able to obtain a permanent resident visa, and although the application is accepted on the basis of H & C considerations, the application may ultimately be rejected because of inadmissibility. This explains, in part, why H & C applications take so long to process and why so few are successful.

Although the visa officer may exempt the applicant from eligibility criteria, the officer does not have the authority to waive inadmissibility. Only the minister may waive inadmissibility on grounds related to security, human or international rights violations, and organized criminality.

Reasons for a refusal are not automatically provided, because there is no statutory obligation to do so. However, an applicant may write to CIC to request reasons.

As mentioned above, applicants have no right to appeal refused applications for permanent residence on humanitarian and compassionate grounds. However, an application for leave for judicial review may be filed with the Federal Court within 30 days after the date of refusal.

APPENDIX

The boxes below summarize the relevant provisions in the IRPA and IRP Regulations for the three main classes of permanent residents discussed in the chapter.

Reference for Family Class

Provision	IRPA and IRP Regulations
Objective relating to family reunification	IRPA s. 3(1)(d)
Sponsor does not meet requirements	IRPA s. 11(2)
Selection of members of family class	IRPA, s. 12(1)
Rights and obligations to sponsor a family member	IRPA, s. 13(1)
Inadmissible family member	IRPA, s. 42
Right to appeal family class refusal	IRPA, s. 63(1)
Exception to excessive demand	IRPA, s. 38(2) and IRP Regulations, s. 24
Definitions	IRP Regulations, ss. 1, 2
Relationships of convenience	IRP Regulations, s. 4
Definition of a member of the family class	IRP Regulations, s. 117
Adoptions	IRP Regulations, s. 117
Who may sponsor	IRP Regulations, s. 130
Sponsorship criteria	IRP Regulations, s. 133

Reference for Humanitarian and Compassionate Classes

Provision	IRPA and IRP Regulations
H & C considerations	IRPA, ss. 25, 25.1
Public policy	IRPA, s. 25.2
Best interests of the child	IRPA, s. 25
Application in writing	IRP Regulations, s. 66
Application outside Canada	IRP Regulations, s. 67
Application in Canada	IRP Regulations, s. 68
Accompanying family members	IRP Regulations, s. 69

Reference for Skilled Worker and Business Classes

Provision	IRPA and IRP Regulations
Economic class	IRPA, s. 12(2)
Skilled worker class	IRP Regulations, Part 6, Division 1
Minimum requirements	IRP Regulations, s. 75(2)
Minimum points required	IRP Regulations, s. 76(2)
Selection grid for skilled workers	IRP Regulations, ss. 78 to 83
Settlement funds requirement	IRP Regulations, s. 76
Business class	IRP Regulations, Part 6, Division 2
Entrepreneurs and self-employed persons	
Definitions	IRP Regulations, s. 88
Selection criteria	IRP Regulations, ss. 102, 78, 79, 81, 103, 104, 105
Minimum points to pass	IRP Regulations, s. 108
Conditions—Entrepreneur	IRP Regulations, s. 98
Self-employed person defined	IRP Regulations, s. 102
Units of assessment, self-employed person	IRP Regulations, ss. 78, 79, 81, 103(2)
Investors	
Definitions	IRP Regulations, s. 88
Minimum requirements	IRP Regulations, s. 91

KEY TERMS

co-signer, 171

educational credential, 198

full-time equivalent, 198

full-time studies, 198

home study, 182

immigration visa officer, 158

jointly and severally liable, 171

language, 201

letter (or notice) of agreement, 182

letter of no-involvement, 182

letter of no-objection, 182

low income cut-off (LICO), 169

permanent residence application process, 162

permanent resident, 157

permanent resident card (PR card), 159

permanent resident status, 157

permanent resident visa, 157

refusal letter, 188

sponsorship application process, 162

REVIEW QUESTIONS

1. Canadians believe that people who immigrate to Canada will establish themselves more easily if their family supports them. Find the three objectives of the Family Class program as stated in the IRPA.

2. Define the following terms found in the IRPA:
   - family member
   - common-law partner
   - dependent child
   - marriage

3. Who may be a sponsor?

4. What are the obligations of sponsors?

5. What are the applicable fees for sponsorship?

6. What is an undertaking?

7. What is the sponsorship agreement and who signs it?

8. Provide an example of a condition or situation that would bar a person from being a sponsor or co-signer.

9. What does the acronym LICO stand for?

10. Who is exempt from the minimum income test?

11. What is the rationale behind business class immigration, from Canada's point of view?

12. What is a qualifying business?

13. In what way is the point system for the business class different from the point system for the federal skilled worker class?

14. What are the three subcategories of business class applicants?

15. Which subcategory of business class applicant must meet conditions? What are they?

16. Which subcategory of business class applicant could be considered "buying a ticket to Canada"? What are the pros and cons of this type of immigration?

17. In the examples provided under the heading "Application Kit and Forms" on pages 224 to 227, discuss what factors could lead to successful outcomes on H & C considerations or why the applications would be rejected.

NOTES

1. Citizenship and Immigration Canada, *Annual Report to Parliament on Immigration 2011*, October 27, 2011, s. 2, at 19, http://www.cic.gc.ca/english/resources/publications/annual-report-2011/index.asp.

2. Ibid., at 17.

3. Canada also allows applications for permanent residence from individuals in Canada whose refugee claims have been accepted. These persons receive Convention refugee status or are recognized as persons in need of protection by the Immigration and Refugee Board. As well, applications for permanent residence are permitted for persons who have been granted protection through the pre-removal risk assessment program. Those who are protected through these programs may apply for permanent residence for themselves and their dependants or close family members (whether they are in Canada or abroad). More information about these programs is provided in Chapter 9.

4. Under the former *Immigration Act* of 1976, permanent residents, known as "landed immigrants," held an IMM 1000 document in their passports as proof of status. A person landed before June 2002 and under the former Act must now apply to CIC for a PR Card.

5. Section 63(4) reads: "A permanent resident may appeal to the Immigration Appeal Division against a decision made outside of Canada on the residency obligation under section 28."

6. For the purpose of sponsorship, a co-signer can only be the spouse or common-law partner of the sponsor to help meet income requirements of sponsoring members other than the spouse or common-law or conjugal partner by pooling resources; if the co-signer is a common-law partner, the relationship must have existed for at least one year to qualify.

7. For a list of applicable sexual offences and applicable offences that equate to family violence, see Citizenship and Immigration Canada, "IP 2: Processing Applications to Sponsor Members of the Family Class," in *Inland Processing (IP)*, appendix E, p. 62. February 28, 2011, http://www.cic.gc.ca/english/resources/manuals/ip/ip02-eng.pdf.

8. Such debts include transportation, adjustment assistance, admissibility or Right of Permanent Residence Fee loan, a deposit or guarantee of performance of an obligation, and removal costs of a foreign national.

9. See *Canada (Attorney General) v. Mavi*, 2011 SCC 30, [2011] 2 S.C.R. 504, http://scc.lexum.org/en/2011/2011scc30/2011scc30.html.

10. CIC, "Conditional Permanent Residence Proposed to Deter Marriages of Convenience," *News Release*—March 9, 2012. http://www.cic.gc.ca/english/department/media/releases/2012/2012-03-09.asp.

11. On November 4, 2011, the government announced a temporary pause on sponsorships of parents and grandparents, and created a special temporary visa: see Chapter 4, Temporary Entry.

12. For clarification about dependent children, see *Dhillon v. Canada (Minister of Employment & Immigration)* (1990), 14 Imm. L.R. (2d) 138 (Ref. Bd.).

13. Section 5.25 of CIC's "OP 2: Processing Members of the Family Class" ("OP 2"), http://www.cic.gc.ca/english/resources/manuals/op/op02-eng.pdf.

14. The time frames for the other provinces and territories as set out in s. 5.40 of "OP 2" are: Quebec (on or after March 19, 2004); Yukon (on or after July 14, 2004); Manitoba (on or after September 16, 2004); Nova Scotia (on or after September 24, 2004); Saskatchewan (on or after November 5, 2004); Newfoundland (on or after December 21, 2004); New Brunswick (on or after July 4, 2005); all other provinces or territories (on or after July 20, 2005).

15. "Regulations Amending the Immigration and Refugee Protection Regulations," *Canada Gazette*, archived, vol. 146, no. 10, March 10, 2012.

16. Citizenship and Immigration Canada, "OP 3: Adoptions," s. 5.4, p. 6, in *Overseas Processing (OP)* ("OP 3"), April 2009, http://www.cic.gc.ca/english/resources/manuals/op/op03-eng.pdf.

17. "Regulations Amending the Immigration and Refugee Protection Regulations," *Canada Gazette*, vol. 139, no. 2, January 8, 2005.

18. *Lindo v. Canada (Minister of Employment & Immigration)*, [1988] 2 F.C. 396, 91 N.R. 75 (C.A.).

19. A person referred to in the IRP regulations, ss. 117(1)(f) and (g).

20. Citizenship and Immigration Canada, "Intercountry Adoption," November 21, 2011, http://www.cic.gc.ca/english/immigrate/adoption/index.asp.

21. Citizenship and Immigration Canada, *Annual Report to Parliament on Immigration 2011*, supra note 1.

22. "News Release—Revised Federal Skilled Worker Program Unveiled, Ottawa," August 17, 2012, http://www.cic.gc.ca/english/department/media/releases/2012/2012-08-17.asp.

23. See ss. 33 to 43 of the IRPA for all inadmissible classes.

24. Citizenship and Immigration Canada, "OP 6: Federal Skilled Workers," in *Overseas Processing (OP)*, s. 10.2, April 24, 2008, and the recent procedures in "OP 6B Federal Skilled Workers—Applications received on or after June 26, 2010," at s. 9.2.

25. Citizenship and Immigration Canada, *Annual Report to Parliament on Immigration 2011*, supra note 1.

26. Citizenship and Immigration Canada, "OP 8: Entrepreneur and Self-Employed," in *Overseas Processing (OP)*, s. 11.3, August 7, 2008, http://www.cic.gc.ca/english/resources/manuals/op/op08-eng.pdf.

27. Canadian Council for Refugees, "Issues for Roundtable, 26-27 March 2006" (no date), http://ccrweb.ca/H&CMarch2006.html.

28. Citizenship and Immigration Canada, "IP 5: Immigrant Applications in Canada Made on Humanitarian or Compassionate Grounds," in *Inland Processing (IP)*, s. 4.2, May 12, 2008, updated April 2011, http://www.cic.gc.ca/english/resources/manuals/ip/ip05-eng.pdf.

29. Supra note 1.

30. Supra note 28, s. 5.19.

31. Diane Finley, "Government of Canada Welcomes Vietnamese People Living Without Status in the Philippines" (news release), March 7, 2008, http://www.cic.gc.ca/english/department/media/releases/2008/2008-03-07b.asp.

32. Unless the applicants are members of the live-in caregiver class, the spouse or common-law partner in Canada class, or the protected temporary residents class in accordance with s. 72(2) of the IRP Regulations.

33. Supra note 28, s. 5.1.

34. Ibid., s. 5, for a discussion about assessing hardship.

35. Ibid.

36. MOSAIC is a multilingual non-profit organization that addresses issues affecting immigrants and refugees. These examples are taken from "A Guide to Humanitarian and

Compassionate Applications," March 2004, http://www
.mosaicbc.com/sites/all/files/18/A%20Guide%20to
%20Humanitarian%20and%20Compassionate
%20Applications.pdf.

REFERENCES

Canada Gazette. Regulations Amending the Immigration and Refugee Protection Regulations, archived, vol. 146, no. 33, August 18, 2012. http://gazette.gc.ca/rp-pr/p1/2012/2012-08-18/html/reg2-eng.html.

Canadian Charter of Rights and Freedoms. Part I of the *Constitution Act, 1982*. R.S.C. 1985, app. II, no. 44.

Canadian Council for Refugees. Fact Sheet for Nationals of Moratoria Countries Without Permanent Status in Canada, July 2007. http://ccrweb.ca/documents/infosheetmoratoria.pdf.

Citizenship and Immigration Canada. *Annual Report to Parliament on Immigration 2011*. http://www.cic.gc.ca/english/resources/publications/annual-report-2011/index.asp.

Citizenship and Immigration Canada. "Five-Year Sponsorship Bar for Persons Who Were Sponsored to Come to Canada as a Spouse or Partner." *Operational Bulletin* 386, March 2, 2012. http://www.cic.gc.ca/english/resources/manuals/bulletins/2012/ob386.asp.

Citizenship and Immigration Canada. "Revised Federal Skilled Worker Program Unveiled." News release, August 17, 2012. http://www.cic.gc.ca/english/department/media/releases/2012/2012-08-17.asp.

Citizenship and Immigration Canada. "IP 2: Processing Applications to Sponsor Members of the Family Class," February 28, 2011. http://www.cic.gc.ca/english/resources/manuals/ip/ip02-eng.pdf.

Citizenship and Immigration Canada. "IP 5: Immigrant Applications in Canada Made on Humanitarian or Compassionate Grounds," May 12, 2008, updated April 2011. http://www.cic.gc.ca/english/resources/manuals/ip/ip05-eng.pdf.

Citizenship and Immigration Canada. "IP 8: Spouse or Common-Law Partner in Canada Class," in *Inland Processing (IP)*, October 16, 2006. http://www.cic.gc.ca/english/resources/manuals/ip/ip08-eng.pdf.

Citizenship and Immigration Canada. "OP 2: Processing Members of the Family Class," in *Overseas Processing (OP)*, November 14, 2006. http://www.cic.gc.ca/english/resources/manuals/op/op02-eng.pdf.

Citizenship and Immigration Canada. "OP 3: Adoptions," *Overseas Processing (OP)*, April 2009. http://www.cic.gc.ca/english/resources/manuals/op/op03-eng.pdf.

Citizenship and Immigration Canada. "OP 4: Processing of Applications Under Section 25 of the IRPA," in *Overseas Processing (OP)*, July 28, 2008. http://www.cic.gc.ca/english/resources/manuals/op/op04-eng.pdf.

Citizenship and Immigration Canada. "OP 6: Federal Skilled Workers—Applications received before February 27, 2008," in *Overseas Processing (OP)*, April 24, 2008. http://www.cic.gc.ca/english/resources/manuals/op/op06-eng.pdf.

Citizenship and Immigration Canada. "OP 6B: Federal Skilled Workers—Applications Received On or After June 26, 2010," March 22, 2012. http://www.cic.gc.ca/english/resources/manuals/op/op06b-eng.pdf.

Citizenship and Immigration Canada. "Determine Your Eligibility—Sponsor Your Spouse, Partner or Children," October 3, 2012. http://www.cic.gc.ca/english/immigrate/sponsor/spouse-apply-who.asp.

Human Resources and Skills Development Canada. "Welcome to the National Occupational Classification 2011," June 27, 2012. http://www5.hrsdc.gc.ca/noc/english/noc/2011/welcome.aspx.

Immigration and Refugee Protection Act. S.C. 2001. c. 27.

Immigration and Refugee Protection Regulations. S.O.R./2002-227.

United Nations General Assembly. *Convention on the Rights of the Child*, November 20, 1989, United Nations, Treaty Series, vol. 1577, p. 3. http://www2.ohchr.org/english/law/crc.htm.

PART III

Citizenship

CHAPTER 6   Citizenship

Citizenship

6

LEARNING OUTCOMES

After reading this chapter you should be able to:

- Assess whether a client is eligible to apply for Canadian citizenship.

- Explain to a client the steps that must be taken in order to obtain citizenship.

- Describe the methods of becoming a Canadian citizen.

- Complete the citizenship application form for a client who wishes to become a Canadian citizen.

- Describe how Canadian citizenship may be lost.

Introduction

Citizenship is an important element in the makeup and identity of Canadian society. The rules of citizenship are designed to make sure that all people recognized as citizens, and granted citizenship, have significant ties to Canada. Some controversy still exists about these rules, and proposals to amend them have been made over the past years.

Many Canadians are citizens as a result of being born here. Others are citizens because one of their parents is a Canadian citizen. Most of this chapter is about a third category of Canadians—those who were formerly foreign nationals, but have since acquired Canadian citizenship as the result of a process called **naturalization**. In 2010, Citizenship and Immigration Canada (CIC) processed 153,644 applications for citizenship, resulting in 143,329 individuals becoming Canadian citizens.[1] The top ten countries of origin of new citizens for 2011 were India, Philippines, the People's Republic of China, Pakistan, the United States, Iran, England, South Korea, Colombia, and Romania.

A person is not a citizen of Canada merely because he has lived here for an extended period of time. For example, a person born outside Canada to parents who were not Canadian citizens could enter Canada, either legally or illegally, as a two-year-old child, spend an entire lifetime in Canada, yet not be a Canadian citizen. To become a Canadian citizen, a foreign national must first be admitted to Canada as a permanent resident, spend several years in Canada, and then apply to become a citizen.

This chapter describes how citizenship is conferred by place of birth or parentage, as well as how it may be actively sought by a foreign national. The process of acquiring citizenship is described in some detail. The chapter also discusses the process of renouncing citizenship and the situations in which citizenship may be revoked. Finally, the chapter examines recent amendments to the *Citizenship Act* in the areas of adoptions and restoration of citizenship.

International Law

International law allows a sovereign country such as Canada the power to decide whom to recognize as citizens and as nationals. The term "national" is a broader term than "citizen." It may include persons who are not citizens, but who have rights and obligations such as those given to Canadian permanent residents. International law also permits countries to establish rules and requirements regarding how citizenship may be acquired by **foreign nationals**.[2] **Citizenship** endows a person "with the full political and civil rights in the body politic of the state."[3] These may include the right to vote and hold political office. Citizenship may also carry potential obligations, such as military service.

In Canada, permanent residents have a right to enter and remain in Canada as long as they maintain their permanent resident status, but, unlike Canadian citizens, they are not permitted to vote or hold political office.

A **stateless person** is not recognized by any nation as being its national; therefore, such a person has no residency rights in any country. Statelessness is addressed in article 15 of the *Universal Declaration of Human Rights*, as follows:

1. Everyone has the right to a nationality.

2. No one shall be arbitrarily deprived of his nationality nor denied the right to change his nationality.

The objective of this article is to encourage nations to take responsibility for their people and thus reduce statelessness.

Special rights of entry are accorded to anyone registered as an Indian under the *Indian Act*. Such a person may enter Canada, even if not a citizen or permanent resident, according to s. 19(1) of the *Immigration and Refugee Protection Act* (IRPA). This special status is granted in recognition of the fact that the traditional homelands of some North American First Nations groups straddle both the United States and Canada, and to protect the right of First Nations people to move freely on these traditional homelands.

Legislative History

Canada's *Citizenship Act* (1977) defines who is deemed a citizen at birth, and how foreign nationals may acquire citizenship through the naturalization process. A person is a citizen if born in Canada, or born outside Canada to a parent who is a Canadian citizen.

However, prior to 1947, Canada did not have its own citizenship act and instead relied on British law. There was legally no such thing as Canadian citizenship. Both native-born and naturalized citizens were British subjects. The rules determining who was a British subject also applied in Canada to determine the equivalent of citizenship for Canadians. Since 1947, the law has evolved with a series of Canadian citizenship statutes.

In Canada, the three time periods of importance are the following:

- pre-1947: British law applied
- 1947–1977: *Canadian Citizenship Act* in force[4]
- 1977–present: *Citizenship Act* (1977) enacted, replacing the *Canadian Citizenship Act*.

Our first citizenship act, the *Canadian Citizenship Act*, came into force January 1, 1947, and thus for applications after this date Canadian law applied and replaced British law. Each time the law changed, the new rules applied only to future, prospective citizens, so the former law may be applicable for citizenship applications. An example of this is that under the 1947 *Canadian Citizenship Act*, Canadian citizens who were not "natural-born" lost their citizenship if they resided outside Canada for a period of six consecutive years. ("Natural-born" Canadian citizens include those who are born either in Canada or outside Canada if, at the time of birth, one parent is a Canadian citizen.) This period was increased to ten years during the 1950s, and repealed altogether in 1967. However, some people had already lost their Canadian citizenship, in many cases unknowingly.[5] Recent amendments to the current *Citizenship Act* (see below, "Amendments") provide a remedy for such situations by restoring citizenship to people considered as "formerly lost Canadians."

The *Canadian Citizenship Act* was replaced, effective February 14, 1977, with a new *Citizenship Act*, which continues to govern citizenship applications. This new Act introduced several major changes, including the recognition of dual citizenship for Canadians and a reduction of the residency period needed to apply for citizenship.

Amendments

Policy decisions to amend immigration law rules, including rules relating to citizenship, are often controversial. The decisions as to who will be recognized as a citizen of Canada involve fundamental policy choices about the nature of Canada. There have been a number of controversial issues with respect to the recognition of citizenship, including the treatment of foreign children adopted by Canadian parents.

Two bills that received royal assent to amend the *Citizenship Act* include:

- Bill C-14, *An Act to Amend the Citizenship Act (adoption)*, which addresses adoptions (royal assent given on June 22, 2007); and
- Bill C-37, *An Act to Amend the Citizenship Act*, which gives Canadian citizenship to those who have lost or never had Canadian citizenship because of outdated provisions in existing and former legislation (royal assent given on April 17, 2008).[6]

Both new laws took effect on April 17, 2009.

Citizenship Commission

The Citizenship Commission is an administrative tribunal within CIC that consists of citizenship judges with offices across Canada. Citizenship judges' authorities and responsibilities are derived from the *Citizenship Act* and the *Citizenship Regulations*. **Citizenship judges** are independent, quasi-judicial decision-makers who have the authority to decide citizenship applications.

CIC provides the Citizenship Commission with administrative, financial, and human resources services; however, it maintains an arm's-length relationship on decision-making matters related to citizenship in order to ensure the independence of citizenship judges.

The Citizenship Commission is responsible for the following functions:

- deciding citizenship applications;
- administering the oath of citizenship and stating the rights and responsibilities of Canadian citizenship to new citizens;
- maintaining the integrity of the citizenship process; and

- promoting citizenship by working with school boards, service clubs, multi-cultural groups, and other community organizations.

According to the *Citizenship Act*, there are four types of citizenship applications for which citizenship judges make decisions:

- grant of citizenship, involving the conferral of citizenship on a non-citizen (s. 5(1));
- retentions, involving confirmation of citizenship of children of a Canadian parent (s. 8);
- renunciations, involving the termination of citizenship (s. 9(1)); and
- resumptions, involving the recommencement of a terminated citizenship (s. 11(1)).

Most of these applications are decided by judges on the basis of a file review. However, when a judge finds that more information is required to make a decision, the applicant is invited to attend a hearing before that judge.

Attributes of Citizenship

Right to Enter and Remain in Canada

Every citizen has a right to enter and remain in Canada, according to s. 19 of the IRPA and s. 6 of the *Charter of Rights and Freedoms*. This means that a Canadian border services officer may not refuse admission to Canada at a port of entry if the officer is satisfied that the person is a Canadian citizen. Also, a Canadian citizen generally cannot be subject to removal or deportation from Canada.

These rights of citizenship are subject to reasonable limits, such as the power of an officer to detain a Canadian citizen subject to an arrest warrant. Similarly, although Canada may not banish or exile citizens, it may apprehend and extradite a citizen to face criminal charges in another country, according to the *Extradition Act*.

The Supreme Court examined the process of extradition in the case of *United States of America v. Cotroni* and confirmed that the process is in compliance with s. 6(1) of the Charter. However, the Court provided the following caution:

> Of course, the authorities must give due weight to the constitutional right of a citizen to remain in Canada. They must in good faith direct their minds to whether prosecution would be equally effective in Canada, given the existing domestic laws and international cooperative arrangements. They have an obligation flowing from s. 6(1) to assure themselves that prosecution in Canada is not a realistic option.[7]

Extradition powers are important to prevent Canada from becoming an attractive place for fugitives.

Also, although Canada may not order citizens to leave the country, it may revoke a Canadian citizenship that was obtained by fraud, misrepresentation, or concealment of important facts. Once citizenship is revoked, removal from Canada may be ordered.

Multiple Citizenships

Canada has permitted **multiple citizenships** since the *Citizenship Act* was enacted in 1977. Canada allows a person who becomes a citizen of Canada to retain any previous citizenship. This is subject to the law of the other country, which may choose to revoke the citizenship of those who obtain citizenship elsewhere, such as in Canada.

Right to Vote and Hold Office

Every citizen of Canada has the right to vote in provincial and federal elections and to be qualified to be a member of Parliament or the provincial Parliament, according to s. 3 of the Charter. Like all Charter rights and freedoms, these rights are also subject to reasonable limits, such as minimum voting age requirements. Our *Citizenship Act* makes no distinction between persons who are born citizens and persons who acquire citizenship through naturalization (s. 6). A naturalized citizen has all the rights that a citizen who was born in Canada or born to Canadian parents has. However, not all countries extend full political rights to naturalized citizens. For example, a naturalized citizen of the United States is prohibited from becoming president—only people born in the United States may become president.

Becoming a Citizen

The two most common principles of citizenship are the following:

- **Jus soli:** *Jus soli* is citizenship based on the land of birth. At birth, a person is automatically granted citizenship of the country in which she was born.
- **Jus sanguinis:** *Jus sanguinis* is citizenship based on blood ties. At birth, a person is automatically granted citizenship of the country where one of the parents is a citizen. If the parents are citizens of separate or multiple countries, the child is granted citizenship of both or all of those countries.

Countries tend to adopt one or both of these principles, or some variation, as the basis for conferring citizenship. Other approaches used by some nations are to grant citizenship to foreign nationals who marry one of their citizens.[8] In addition, most countries allow immigrants to apply for citizenship through the process of naturalization.

The Canadian *Citizenship Act* allows for all three methods of becoming a citizen—namely, being born in Canada, being born outside Canada to a Canadian citizen, and naturalization. Each method is described below.

Being Born in Canada

Generally, any person born in Canada is automatically a Canadian citizen. This is according to s. 3(1) of the *Citizenship Act* (1977), and follows the principle of *jus soli*, or citizenship by soil. The rule applies even if neither parent is a Canadian citizen, and even if one or both parents are in Canada illegally.

Some locations outside Canada are deemed to be in Canada for the operation of the rule, including Canadian ships and aircraft registered in Canada. Persons born on these vessels are Canadian citizens according to s. 2(2) of the *Citizenship Act* (1977).

An exception to the rule that birth in Canada confers Canadian citizenship applies to a person who, at the time of his birth, is the child of a foreign national who is in Canada as the representative of a foreign government or an international agency. Such persons are deemed not to be Canadian citizens, according to s. 3(2) of the *Citizenship Act* (1977).

Being Born Outside Canada to a Canadian Citizen

A person born outside Canada is a Canadian citizen if one parent is a Canadian citizen at the time of the birth. This follows the principle of *jus sanguinis*, or citizenship by blood. The rule applies even if the baby's only connection with Canada is having a parent who is a Canadian citizen and even if the baby never resides in or even visits Canada. Often, such a baby is automatically a citizen of the country of birth as well. Canadian law allows such a person to retain Canadian citizenship unless she takes steps to renounce it.

This raises an issue with respect to the continuation of citizenship for second and subsequent generations born outside Canada. Canadian citizenship could potentially be passed on for generations, even when connection with Canada is non-existent. Canada would be obliged to admit these persons to Canada automatically, and to offer them the assistance of Canadian overseas services such as embassies and consulates.

Changes to the Citizenship Act (Bill C-37, *An Act to amend the Citizenship Act*, http://www.canadavisa.com/canada-immigration-discussion-board/bill-c37-an-act-to-amend-the-citizenship-act-t12150.0.html;msg46284#msg46284, came into effect on April 17, 2009) remove the requirement to register and retain citizenship by age 28. People born before April 17, 2009, and who are second- or subsequent-generation Canadians born abroad, retain their existing Canadian citizenship, according to s. 3(4). They must still apply for a citizenship certificate because they are subject to the retention requirement. CIC notified these individuals by letter advising them of the steps to take before their 28th birthday in order to retain Canadian citizenship.

The rule limits citizenship by descent to one generation for people born after the rule came into effect, on April 17, 2009. This means that a child born abroad to a parent who derived her citizenship from a Canadian parent who was also born abroad will no longer automatically become a Canadian citizen, according to s. 3(3).[9] Children born to Canadian parents in the first generation outside Canada will only be Canadian at birth if:

- one parent was born in Canada; or
- one parent became a Canadian citizen by immigrating to Canada and was later granted citizenship through naturalization.

Retaining Citizenship for Second- and Subsequent-Generation Canadians Born Outside Canada

John Smith was born in Calgary, Alberta in 1958. He moved to Australia in 1978 because of a job, and lived the rest of his life there. His son, Bob Smith, born in Australia in 1979, is a Canadian citizen by descent because his father was a Canadian citizen. Bob Smith lived his entire life in Australia, and had no connection with Canada. Bob's son, Roger Smith, was born in Australia in 2010.

Before the changes to the *Citizenship Act* (1977), second- and subsequent-generation Canadians born outside Canada on or after February 15, 1977 to a Canadian parent who was also born outside Canada were allowed to apply to retain Canadian citizenship before age 28; otherwise, the chain would be broken and Canadian citizenship would be lost. Citizenship is now limited to only the first generation for children born outside Canada on or after April 17, 2009.

The CIC website states that these changes were necessary to "protect the value of Canadian citizenship for the future."

An exception is provided for:

people who are born to a Canadian parent working abroad in or with the Canadian Armed Forces, the federal public administration or the public service of a province, unless the parent is a locally engaged person, according to the new section 3(5). For such people, citizenship is automatic at birth even though the person is a second or subsequent generation Canadian born abroad.[10]

Cutting off citizenship by descent after the first generation of Canadians born abroad will result in some offspring of Canadians born abroad in the future being stateless. Therefore, amendments include a provision for a mandatory grant of citizenship to a person who was born outside Canada after the provision comes into force and to a parent who was Canadian at the time of the person's birth if, at the time that the person applies for Canadian citizenship, the person

- is less than 23 years old;
- has resided in Canada for at least three years during the four years immediately before the date of the application for citizenship;
- has always been stateless; and
- has not been convicted of various listed national security offences.[11]

Being Born Outside Canada: Adoptions by a Canadian Citizen

Bill C-14 amended the *Citizenship Act* by eliminating distinctions in the way that the *Citizenship Act* treats foreign-born children adopted by Canadian citizens and biological children born abroad to Canadian citizens. Whereas a child born of Canadian parents outside Canada is automatically a Canadian citizen, a foreign child adopted by Canadian citizens did not automatically become a Canadian citizen upon adoption. Instead, an application had to be made for the child to become a permanent resident first, and only then could an application for citizenship be made. The amendments now allow a foreign-born child adopted by a Canadian citizen after February 14, 1977 to access citizenship without requiring that the child first becomes a permanent resident.

Section 3 of the *Citizenship Act* states that adopted children who attain citizenship without first obtaining permanent resident status are Canadian citizens. Citizenship may now be granted to a minor child who is being adopted by a Canadian citizen, or to an adopted child of at least 18 years of age, provided that the adoption satisfies the following conditions:

- it is in the best interests of the child;
- it creates a genuine parent–child relationship;
- it was not primarily for the purpose of acquiring citizenship or immigration status;
- it was legal in the place of adoption; and
- it was legal in Canada or the country of residence of the Canadian citizen if the Canadian citizen was not resident in Canada.

This same rule applies in the case of the legal adoption of a person 18 years of age or older, provided that a parent–child relationship was established prior to the child becoming 18, and the adoption was not primarily for the purpose of immigration.

The *Citizenship Act* now provides for the governor in council to make regulations providing for the factors to be considered in determining whether these requirements have been met.

Section 5 of the *Citizenship Act* applies to adopted children who are minors and also to those who are at least 18 years of age; amendments provide that, subject to certain conditions, the minister shall grant citizenship to children who are adopted abroad after February 14, 1977. The adoption must satisfy the following conditions:

- a genuine parent–child relationship must be established before the person is 18 years old as well as at the time of adoption;
- the adoption was not primarily for the purpose of acquiring citizenship or immigration status;
- the adoption was legal in the place of adoption; and
- the adoption was legal in Canada or the country of residence of the Canadian citizen if the Canadian citizen was not resident in Canada.

There is also a special provision for adoptions that are under the jurisdiction of Quebec. Adoptions in Quebec are considered finalized when the child is physically in Quebec and residing with the adoptive parents. Under Quebec law, the authority responsible for international adoptions must confirm in writing that the adoption complies with Quebec law so that Canadian citizenship can be granted to children adopted abroad before the adoption is officially approved by the Court of Quebec.

Adoption is also discussed in Chapter 5, Permanent Entry.

Naturalization

Naturalization is the legal process that transforms a permanent resident into a Canadian citizen. In order to be naturalized the permanent resident must apply for citizenship. Most of these applications are decided by judges on the basis of a file review. However, when a judge finds that more information is required to make a decision, the applicant is invited to attend a hearing before that judge.

Permanent residents who wish to obtain Canadian citizenship must meet certain criteria. They must

- be admitted to Canada as a permanent resident;
- be at least 18 years old or be included with the application of a parent who is over 18 years old;
- make an application for citizenship;
- pay fees;
- provide photos;
- have lived in Canada for at least three years (1,095 days) out of the four years prior to applying for citizenship;
- not be under a removal order or declared to be a threat to security or a member of an organized crime group;
- show an adequate knowledge of English or French;
- demonstrate an understanding of the responsibilities of a citizen and pass the citizenship test; and
- take the citizenship oath.

An applicant who is physically or mentally unable to comply may have the following requirements waived for compassionate reasons:[12]

- the citizenship test;
- competence in English or French; and
- the citizenship oath.

In these circumstances, medical documentation must be provided that outlines the applicant's condition and how it prevents the applicant from fulfilling the obligations.

Naturalization Process

Numerous steps must be taken when applying for Canadian citizenship. Some steps, such as the payment of fees, are relatively straightforward. However, many applicants require advice and assistance with other steps in the naturalization process. For example, documents must be provided to support the application, and, if the originals are not in English or French, they must be translated into one of those official languages. An affidavit must be sworn by the translator stating that the translation is a true one.[13]

Other steps, such as demonstrating sufficient time spent residing in Canada, may be complex and require legal advice and guidance from counsel.

Proof of Identity and Age

The applicant for Canadian citizenship must be 18 years of age or over. The applicant must provide proof of his identity and age. Specifically, the applicant must do the following:

- present two identity documents, such as a passport, health insurance card, and Canadian driver's licence;
- establish age by filing a birth certificate or other evidence that shows the date and place of birth; and
- disclose any version of his name that has been used. It is not unusual for permanent residents to use Canadianized versions of their names, and these names must be reported on the application.

Application Form, Fees, and Photos

The applicant must complete the approved citizenship application form, CIT 0002, which must not be postdated. After three months, the form will be considered stale-dated, and will have to be redone.

An applicant must pay the fees fixed by regulation and provide photos that conform to the size and other dimensions specified by regulation.

The fees include a $100 non-refundable processing fee for all applicants and a $100 right of citizenship fee that is payable if the applicant is 18 years or older.

Photos must be signed on the back by both the photographer and the applicant. The applicant's signature on the photograph must match the signature on the application. Head coverings must be removed for the photo unless for the purpose of religious observance.

WEBLINK

A list and the amount of the fees required for a citizenship application can be found on the CIC website at http://www.cic.gc.ca/english/information/fees/fees.asp.

Proof of Residency

According to s. 5(1) of the *Citizenship Act*, to satisfy the citizenship judge that sufficient residency was achieved, the applicant must meet three conditions of residency as follows:

1. *Lawful admittance to Canada as a permanent resident.* The applicant must file her Canadian immigration record/paper (such as the Record of Landing (IMM 1000)), Confirmation of Permanent Residence (IMM 5292), which was obtained from CIC when permanent residency was granted, and a copy of both sides of the Permanent Resident Card. This shows entitlement to enter Canada. (It is also important to establish accumulation of the required residency period in Canada.)

2. *No loss of permanent residency.* The applicant's permanent residency must not be invalidated by a failure to maintain the connection with Canada or by an order to leave Canada. A connection with Canada is not maintained if the person is not resident in Canada for two years out of every five-year period (loss of permanent resident status is discussed in Chapter 5, Permanent

Entry). Permanent resident status is also lost if a removal order is made because the person has become inadmissible and the appeals of that order have been exhausted (IRPA, s. 28). This could occur if the permanent resident engaged in criminal activity, for example.

3. *Residence in Canada.* Under s. 5(b) of the *Citizenship Act*, the applicant must prove residency in Canada for at least three years (1,095 days) in the past four years (1,460 days). Days spent in Canada as a temporary resident count as half days for satisfying the residency requirements. The IRPA and its regulations make it clear that certain periods of time spent in Canada may not be included in the period counted toward residency, including time spent incarcerated in a penal institution or jail, on probation, or on parole, according to s. 21 of the *Citizenship Act* (1977).

The requirement of **residence in Canada** is complicated by the fact that the *Citizenship Act* does not specify whether actual physical presence in Canada is required or whether it is sufficient to establish a life in Canada and to treat Canada as a home base while spending time outside the country.

Case law is divided as to whether actual physical presence in Canada is required. In many cases, judges have held that once a person is resident in Canada he may be absent from Canada for periods of time provided that the pattern and length of absences from Canada are not significant enough to show that Canadian residence has been abandoned. This allows time spent outside Canada for a vacation or business trip to count toward the requirement. Consider the court's reasoning in *Re Papadogiorgakis*, at 213-214:

> It seems to me that the words "residence" and "resident" in paragraph 5(1)(b) of the new *Citizenship Act* are not as strictly limited to actual presence in Canada throughout the period as they were in the former statute but can include, as well, situations in which the person concerned has a place in Canada which is used by him during the period as a place of abode to a sufficient extent to demonstrate the reality of his residing there during the material period even though he is away from it part of the time. …
>
> A person with an established home of his own in which he lives does not cease to be resident there when he leaves it for a temporary purpose whether on business or vacation or even to pursue a course of study. The fact of his family remaining there while he is away may lend support for the conclusion that he has not ceased to reside there. The conclusion may be reached, as well, even though the absence may be more or less lengthy. It is also enhanced if he returns there frequently when the opportunity to do so arises.

The residency requirement was further explored in *Re Koo*, where the Federal Court Trial Division identified the following indicia of residency:

- The applicant was physically present in Canada for a long period prior to absences, which occurred before the application for citizenship.
- The applicant's immediate family and dependants (and extended family) are resident in Canada.

- The applicant's pattern of physical presence in Canada indicates returning home rather than merely visiting.
- The extent of the physical absences was limited. (If an applicant is only a few days short of the 1,095-day total, deemed residence is more likely to be found than if those absences were extensive.)
- The applicant's physical absence is caused by a clearly temporary situation, such as a posting as a missionary abroad, a course of study abroad as a student, temporary employment abroad, or time spent accompanying a spouse who has accepted employment abroad.
- The quality of the connection with Canada is more substantial than that which exists with any other country.

Evidence to support residency includes the following:

- ownership of residential property in Canada;
- bank accounts in Canada;
- club or association memberships;
- membership in a provincial health insurance plan;
- travel documents and receipts showing frequent return trips to Canada;
- presence of family in Canada;
- income tax returns filed in Canada;
- car registration in Canada;
- a provincial driver's licence;
- registered retirement savings plan; and
- payroll deductions.[14]

Other judges reviewing appeals of citizenship application cases have taken the position that actual physical presence in Canada is required and that the applicant must show that he has been physically present in Canada for at least 1,095 days during the past four years. The need for physical presence in Canada was described in *Re Pourgashemi*, at 260:

It is clear that the purpose of paragraph 5(1)(c) is to insure that everyone who is granted precious Canadian citizenship has become, or at least has been compulsorily presented with the everyday opportunity to become, "Canadianized." This happens by "rubbing elbows" with Canadians in shopping malls, corner stores, libraries, concert halls, auto repair shops, pubs, cabarets, elevators, churches, synagogues, mosques and temples—in a word wherever one can meet and converse with Canadians—during the prescribed three years. One can observe Canadian society for all its virtues, decadence, values, dangers and freedoms, just as it is. That is little enough time in which to become Canadianized. If a citizenship candidate misses that qualifying experience, then Canadian citizenship can be conferred, in effect, on a person who is still a foreigner in experience, social adaptation, and often in thought and outlook.

The court attempted to reconcile these conflicting opinions in *Re Mui*, as follows:

I agree in principle with some decisions of this Court which, given special or exceptional circumstances, do not require physical presence in Canada for the entire 1095 days. However, it is my view that an extended absence from Canada during the minimum period of time, albeit temporary, as in the present case, is contrary to the purpose of the residency requirements of the Act. Indeed, the Act already allows a person who has been lawfully admitted to Canada for permanent residence not to reside in Canada during one of the four years immediately preceding the date of that person's application for Canadian citizenship.

The contradictory rules provided in these cases create a challenge for citizenship officers and citizenship judges who must make decisions about citizenship applications. In an effort to provide some direction, the *Citizenship Policy (CP)* operations manual instructs officers as follows:

If you determine that all the absences of the applicant fall within the allowable exceptions, you must then assess if the applicant was outside of Canada, in total, for a longer period of time than he or she was in Canada.

Given that the purpose of the residence requirement is to ensure that the applicant for citizenship can become familiar with Canada and become integrated into Canadian society, it follows that the longer the absences of the applicant, the more difficult it will be for the Minister to be convinced that the applicant meets the residence requirement. This is true even if the reasons for the absences seem to fall entirely within the exceptional circumstances described above.

Another way to consider the "majority rule" is to keep in mind that, for citizenship purposes, a person can only have one residence at any given time. Therefore, if a person is spending a lot of time in another country (in effect, residing there), that person cannot, at the same time, "maintain residence in Canada." If the citizenship judge approves an application where the applicant has been outside Canada the majority of the time (in other words, has been outside Canada for more time than in Canada), the citizenship judge's complete file on the applicant must then be referred to Case Management Branch for possible appeal by the Minister. Include your analysis of why the applicant does not appear to meet the residence requirement.[15]

In other words, the officer refers cases for review and possible appeal where the applicant was granted citizenship despite being physically out of the country for more than half the time of residency. This rule applies even if the absences were deemed by the judge to fall within the six categories set out in the *Koo* case.

The CIC website provides a **residency calculator** so that applicants can ensure they are not submitting applications too early. To be eligible for Canadian citizenship, an applicant must meet residency requirements for the four years preceding the date of application. The applicant must have lived in Canada for at least three years (1,095 days) out of the four years (1,460 days) preceding the application. At least two years of this must be as a permanent resident.

When calculating time in Canada the following rules apply:

- only the four years preceding the date of the application are taken into account;

- each day spent in Canada before the applicant became a permanent resident counts as half a day, up to a year;
- each day spent in Canada after the applicant became a permanent resident counts as one day; and
- generally, time spent serving a sentence for an offence in Canada is not counted.

In cases where there were fewer than 1,095 days of physical presence in Canada, only a citizenship judge may determine whether residency requirements were met. Consider the following scenario:

Grant, a citizen of Germany, came to Canada on September 1, 2009 on a student visa for post-secondary studies. He met and married a fellow classmate, Faye, on September 1, 2011. He applied for permanent resident status from within Canada (by being sponsored by Faye) and received that status on September 1, 2012. What is the first date that Grant can apply for Canadian citizenship?

Keeping in mind that Grant became a permanent resident on September 1, 2012 and that Grant must have lived in Canada for at least three years (1,095 days) out of the four years (1,460 days) preceding the application, the calculation is as follows:

Each day that Grant lived in Canada as a student in the 2 years prior to his becoming a permanent resident counts for $\frac{1}{2}$ day, up to a maximum of one year:

September 1, 2010 to September 1, 2012 = 730 days × $\frac{1}{2}$
= 365 countable days

Grant needs a minimum of 2 years as a permanent resident, so count forward 2 years from the date he became a permanent resident:

September 1, 2012 to September 1, 2014 = 2 years = 730 countable days

Total countable days: 365 + 730 = 1,095

The first day that Grant can apply is September 2, 2014.

Admissibility

An applicant for citizenship must not be under a removal order. (For information about contesting removal orders, see Chapter 10, General In-Canada Enforcement and Removal Procedures. An applicant must also not be a declared threat to security or a member of an organized crime group. For information about declarations as a security threat or a member of an organized crime group, see Chapter 3, Inadmissibility.

If applicable, any such ground of inadmissibility must be disclosed. However, the citizenship judge may recommend to the minister that the discretion to grant citizenship in the face of these problems be exercised, according to s. 5(4) of the *Citizenship Act*, as follows:

In order to alleviate cases of special and unusual hardship or to reward services of an exceptional value to Canada, and notwithstanding any other provision of this Act, the Governor in Council may, in his discretion, direct the Minister to grant citizenship to any person and, where such a direction is made, the Minister shall forthwith grant citizenship to the person named in the direction.

Before the citizenship judge will make such a recommendation to the minister, the judge will need to be convinced that either the case is one of special and unusual hardship or the applicant rendered services of exceptional value to Canada.

Language Test

The applicant for citizenship must demonstrate an adequate knowledge of one of Canada's two official languages. Applicants between the ages of 18 and 54 are expected to be able to carry out simple everyday conversations in either English or French, and to carry out basic activities such as shopping, banking, and taking public transit. Applicants who fail the written language test are given the opportunity for an oral interview with a citizenship judge, during which the applicant's ability to engage in a conversation will be directly assessed. The judge will consider whether the applicant can respond to instructions, fill out a simple form, and talk about personal experiences. On the recommendation of a citizenship judge, the minister may, under s. 5(3)(a) of the *Citizenship Act*, waive this requirement on compassionate grounds, and does so routinely for older persons.

Canada's Citizenship Week

In 2006, CIC launched the first Citizenship Week to promote citizenship. Citizenship Week is an annual event celebrating the value of citizenship, and promoting the privileges and responsibilities of being a Canadian citizen. Canada celebrated the 65th anniversary of Canadian citizenship in 2012. For more information about Citizenship Week as well as other reasons to celebrate Canada, visit the CIC website and click on the "Citizenship Week" link, at http://www.cic.gc.ca/english/celebrate/index.asp.

Citizenship Test

WEBLINK

To learn more about the citizenship test and to see more sample questions, visit the CIC website at http://www.cic.gc.ca/english/citizenship/cit-test.asp.

Changes to the *Citizenship Regulations* in 2010 set out procedures for an updated citizenship test. CIC revised the citizenship test as "part of overall efforts at CIC to strengthen the value of citizenship and to emphasize the integrity of the testing process."[16] The citizenship test focuses on building awareness of Canadian values and history, institutions that shape Canada, and the rights and responsibilities associated with Canadian citizenship.

The applicant for citizenship must display civic literacy through an adequate broad knowledge of Canada and of the rights and responsibilities of Canadian citizenship as outlined in s. 15 of the *Citizenship Regulations*. Applicants are generally required to take a citizenship test measuring knowledge of national symbols of Canada and a general understanding in the following areas:

- the chief characteristics of Canadian political and military history;
- the chief characteristics of Canadian social and cultural history;
- the chief characteristics of Canadian physical and political geography;
- the chief characteristics of the Canadian system of government as a constitutional monarchy; and
- other characteristics of Canada.

Applicants must also have a general understanding of:

- participation in the Canadian democratic process;
- participation in Canadian society, including volunteerism, respect for the environment, and the protection of Canada's natural, cultural, and architectural heritage;
- respect for the rights, freedoms, and obligations set out in the laws governing Canada; and
- other responsibilities and privileges of citizenship.

The test is waived for applicants over age 55 or under the age of 18.

To assist with preparations for the test, CIC provides the citizenship study guide online, called "Discover Canada: The Rights and Responsibilities of Citizenship." Information about the test is available on the CIC website along with sample study questions, at http://www.cic.gc.ca/english/citizenship/cit-sample.asp.

The applicant receives a notice to appear for a citizenship test, indicating the date, time, and place of the test.

Testing takes place at local CIC offices. Applicants have 30 minutes to complete the multiple-choice test and to correctly answer 15 questions out of 20 or higher to receive a passing mark on the citizenship test. For those applicants who fail the test, they must appear for an oral interview/hearing before a citizenship judge.

Citizenship Oath

When an applicant meets the basic requirements for citizenship and has passed both the language and citizenship tests, she receives a notice to appear to take the oath of citizenship. All applicants over the age of 14 must take the oath of citizenship. The oath of citizenship is administered at a special ceremony presided over by a citizenship judge.

The citizenship oath as set out in the schedule to the *Citizenship Act* reads as follows:

> I swear (*or* affirm) that I will be faithful and bear true allegiance to Her Majesty Queen Elizabeth the Second, Queen of Canada, Her Heirs and Successors, and that I will faithfully observe the laws of Canada and fulfil my duties as a Canadian citizen.

Historically, such an oath would be taken holding a Bible. In recognition of the rights of religious freedom enshrined in our legal system, this is no longer required. Applicants with a religious or other objection to swearing an oath are given the option of affirming rather than swearing the oath. Applicants who choose to swear the oath are given the option of holding the holy book of their choosing when taking the oath. Furthermore, all applicants must be seen to be taking the oath. Applicants who wear a face covering must remove the face covering for the oath-taking portion of the ceremony so they can be seen taking it.[17]

Applications for Minors

According to s. 5(2) of the *Citizenship Act*, a citizenship application for a minor may be completed by the parents (biological or adoptive), legal guardians, or other persons legally entitled to have custody of the child. A minor is a person who is not yet 18. A minor child between 14 and 18 years of age is expected to also sign the application, unless he has a mental disability. In addition to the information provided in the application that accompanies an adult's application, the following additional items must be provided:

- Evidence establishing that the minor child is the child of a citizen. Acceptable documents include birth certificates showing the names of the parents, adoption orders, parents' passports showing the names of the children, and IMM 1000 or Confirmation of Permanent Residence forms listing parents' names for children who entered Canada as refugees.[18]
- If the applicant is not a birth or adoptive parent of a citizen, evidence establishing that the applicant has legal custody of the child. Acceptable documents include a court order or written agreement.

Steps After Application Submitted

Once the applicant has completed the application for citizenship, she must mail it to the Case Processing Centre (CPC) in Sydney, Nova Scotia, where the following steps[19] occur:

Step 1: The CPC reviews the application to ensure the following:

- it is complete;
- the fee is paid; and
- all information is included.

Step 2: The CPC reviews the documents submitted with the application—for example, the Confirmation of Permanent Residence or the Record of Landing (IMM 1000).

Step 3: The CPC directs the applicant to the CIC website to study "Discover Canada: The Rights and Responsibilities of Citizenship," at http://www.cic.gc.ca/english/resources/publications/discover/index.asp.

Example of a Citizenship Certificate [front]

Example of a Citizenship Certificate [back] with the Oath of Citizenship

Source: *Canadian Citizenship Certificate*. Reproduced with the permission of the Minister of Public Works and Government Services Canada, 2012.

Step 4: The CPC forwards the application to the following for background checks to ensure admissibility:

- Immigration Canada (CIC), to check for an immigration record;
- the RCMP, to check for a criminal record; and
- the Canadian Security and Intelligence Service, to check for a security record.

Step 5: The CPC prepares and sends a package of information to the CIC office nearest to the applicant.

Step 6: The CIC office sends the applicant a notice to appear for a citizenship test.

Step 7: If necessary, an interview with a citizenship judge is arranged to review residency issues, literacy, or possible prohibitions.

Step 8: If the citizenship judge approves citizenship, the applicant is invited to a citizenship ceremony by way of a notice to appear to take the oath of citizenship.

Step 9: A citizenship ceremony is held, where the applicant takes the oath of citizenship. As of February 1, 2012, the plastic wallet-sized citizenship certificate was replaced with a letter-sized paper citizenship certificate. This new certificate is a legal status document issued to new citizens and anyone applying for their proof of citizenship; although it does not include a photo of the Canadian citizen, it does contain a unique number and basic information (that is, name, date of birth, and gender) that allows the government to electronically validate the certificate to reduce instances of fraud. New citizens must wait at least two business days after their ceremony to apply for a Canadian passport. (Any citizen of Canada may apply for a certificate of citizenship as proof of his Canadian citizenship, according to s. 12 of the *Citizenship Act*.)

Step 10: The applicant's completed file is microfilmed and stored.

Step 11: If the citizenship judge refuses citizenship, the applicant may reapply or appeal to the Federal Court. Only a lawyer, not an immigration consultant, may represent an applicant at the Federal Court.

Restoration of Citizenship

Under former legislation, there are several reasons why people either lost their citizenship or were never recognized as Canadian citizens. Bill C-37, *An Act to Amend the Citizenship Act* addresses these situations as follows:

- it permits certain persons who lost their Canadian citizenship for specified reasons to have their citizenship restored from the time it was lost;
- it permits certain persons who, born outside Canada to a Canadian parent, did not acquire Canadian citizenship for specified reasons to become Canadian citizens from the time of their birth;
- it provides that certain persons born outside Canada to a Canadian parent who was himself or herself born outside Canada do not acquire Canadian citizenship; and
- it provides for a grant of citizenship, on application, to persons who have always been stateless and meet other specified conditions.[20]

Bill C-37 also addressed the issue of "Lost Canadians." Lost Canadians are individuals who have been residing most of their lives in Canada and had a reasonable but mistaken belief they were Canadian citizens. They either ceased to be citizens at some point or never were Canadian citizens. Generally, lost Canadians only discovered they were not Canadian citizens when they applied for a certificate of Canadian citizenship or other document. In the past, a person who lost Canadian citizenship had to apply for a resumption of citizenship. Amendments to the *Citizenship Act* under Bill C-37, allow for citizenship to be granted or restored retroactively to most, but not all, lost Canadians.

The amendments to the *Citizenship Act* give citizenship to the following kinds of lost Canadians:

- people naturalized to Canada who subsequently lived outside the country for more than ten years prior to 1967 and lost their citizenship; and
- people born abroad to a Canadian parent before the current *Citizenship Act* came into effect on February 15, 1977.

The amendments also give citizenship to "former lost Canadians":

- people who lost their citizenship between January 1, 1947 and February 14, 1977 because they or one of their parents acquired the nationality or citizenship of another country; and

- second- and subsequent-generation Canadians born abroad since the current *Citizenship Act* came into effect on February 15, 1977. Furthermore, relief is provided for the anticipated situations where these amendments will result in some offspring of Canadians born abroad being stateless.

Renouncing and Revoking Citizenship

For administrative efficiency, applications to retain, renounce, and resume citizenship are decided by the senior citizenship judge.

Citizenship may be lost only for the reasons specified in the *Citizenship Act*—namely, renunciation and revocation.

Renouncing Citizenship

Renouncing citizenship means that a citizen actively takes steps to terminate citizenship. A Canadian citizen who is no longer resident in Canada may renounce her Canadian citizenship. A person may be motivated to do this if Canadian citizenship prevents entitlement to an advantage or benefit in another country.

For example, the Canadian-born newspaper magnate Conrad Black, when he had the opportunity to become a British peer and sit in the British House of Lords, actively sought to renounce his Canadian citizenship. Black wanted to be granted a peerage by the Queen of England, an honour that has been bestowed on other wealthy Canadian newspaper owners in the past. A constitutional convention prevented the Queen from granting such a peerage to a Canadian citizen without the approval of the prime minister of Canada. The prime minister refused permission, and his refusal was upheld by the Ontario Court of Appeal in *Black v. Canada (Prime Minister)*. However, Black, as a resident of England, was allowed to renounce his Canadian citizenship so that the Queen could grant the peerage, and Black ceased to be a Canadian citizen in 2001.

The decision to renounce his Canadian citizenship has created an unusual problem for Black. In 2007, he was convicted of three counts of fraud and one count of obstruction of justice in a US court. After having served a 42-month sentence, Black wanted to return to Canada, but could not do so because he no longer had any right to enter Canada: he had to apply for a temporary resident permit as a foreign national. Black has stated that he intends to apply for Canadian citizenship in the future.

A person may also need to renounce his Canadian citizenship if he wishes to become a citizen of another country that does not allow dual citizenship.

Note that Canadian citizenship may not be renounced by a resident in Canada for the purpose of avoiding an obligation falling on Canadian citizens, such as military duty in the event of conscription.

Resuming Citizenship

An individual who wishes to resume Canadian citizenship, must apply and be eligible to do so by meeting the following requirements:

- have been a Canadian citizen;
- have become a permanent resident of Canada after losing Canadian citizenship; and
- have lived in Canada as a permanent resident for at least one year immediately before applying.

Certain individuals are not eligible if:

- their Canadian citizenship was revoked;
- they were convicted of an indictable offence or an offence under the *Citizenship Act* in the three years before application;
- they are currently charged with an indictable offence or an offence under the *Citizenship Act*;
- they are in prison, on parole, or on probation;
- they are under a removal order; or
- they are under investigation for, are charged with, or have been convicted of a war crime or a crime against humanity.

Application packages to resume citizenship are available on the CIC website.

Revoking Citizenship

Revoking citizenship means that the Canadian government takes steps to remove a person's citizenship. Revocation is done by Cabinet through an order in council.

Revocation proceedings may be applied to citizenship granted by any method under the Act, if it comes to light that either the person's admission to Canada for the prerequisite period of residence or the citizenship application itself involved at least one of the following:

- fraud;
- false representation (misrepresentation); or
- knowing concealment of material circumstances.

In September 2012, the minister announced that, following investigations, steps have begun to revoke the citizenship of up to 3,100 citizens who obtained it fraudulently.[21]

For example, if it can be shown that a person's documents indicating place of birth or parentage were falsified in order to claim citizenship by place of birth, or through a birth parent, then the citizenship of that person could be revoked. Likewise, a person who applies to retain citizenship on the basis of having a substantial connection with Canada and who files false documents showing educational time spent in Canada could have her citizenship revoked.

Often, the cases dealing with revocation of citizenship do not clearly define which of the three reasons is the basis for the revocation. This is because the facts that give rise to revocation may be described as fraudulent, a false representation, and a knowing concealment of material circumstances.

The operation of these provisions was illustrated in the case of Helmut Oberlander, in which the government revoked Oberlander's citizenship because he lied about his participation in war crimes when he applied to come to Canada. During the Second World War, although there was no evidence that he took part in the killings, Mr. Oberlander worked as a translator for a Nazi police unit that killed 23,000 persons in the Ukraine during the years 1941 to 1943. He immigrated to Canada in 1954. This was considered a material issue because Canada was not admitting persons involved in atrocities during the Second World War. The government did not take action until 2001 almost 50 years after Oberlander entered Canada.

An example of citizenship being revoked because of fraud would be a case where an applicant with a criminal record forges documents to support the application. The applicant could obtain and try to use forged certificates showing he had no criminal record.

The evidentiary requirements for proving fraud are stricter than those for proving false representation or knowing concealment of material circumstances, as was illustrated in *Minister of Citizenship v. Odynsky*. In order to establish fraud, it is not sufficient to simply show that a person did an action such as making a false statement—it must be shown that there was some mental element involved in the activity such as an intention to get around the restrictions in the system.

In the *Odynsky* case, the government could not prove fraud but was able to show both knowing concealment of a material circumstance and the making of a false representation. Odynsky was forced to act as a guard in a concentration camp during the Second World War. He did not reveal this fact when he applied to come to Canada in 1949, and he became a Canadian citizen in 1955. It was not proven that Canadian officials asked about his actions during the war when he made his application; therefore, his omission was not fraudulent. However, by omitting this fact, he rendered his application untrue, and thus it was a false representation. In addition, the circumstances were material because Canada would not have admitted him if he had admitted he was a concentration camp guard, and he knew he was not fully revealing this information.

Note that to prove knowing concealment of a material circumstance it does not have to be shown that the person knew the circumstances were material. Furthermore, the person does not have to know about the criteria being applied by the Canadian authorities in assessing his application.

The mere fact of making a false representation is sufficient even without the presence of a mental element. Thus, in the *Odynsky* case, the government did not have to prove that Mr. Odynsky intentionally did not reveal his service during the war in order to circumvent the application process. Once it showed that the statement was false, this was sufficient. Finally, the courts have indicated that the false statement cannot be merely a technical or minor error in order for citizenship to be revoked.[22]

WEB LINK

The Canadian government provides a Fraud Tip Line in Canada at 1-888-242-2100 (in Canada only, 8:00 a.m. to 4:00 p.m. local time, Monday through Friday) or http://www.cic.gc.ca/english/information/protection/fraud/report.asp to report cases involving false representation, fraud, or knowingly concealing material in the citizenship process.

KEY TERMS

REVIEW QUESTIONS

1. List the three basic methods by which a person may become a Canadian citizen.

2. List and describe the requirements that must be satisfied for a person to become a citizen of Canada through the process of naturalization.

3. List and describe the reasons why a person may lose Canadian citizenship.

4. What are the functions of a citizenship judge?

5. In what situation will time spent in Canada not be counted toward satisfying the residency requirement for citizenship?

NOTES

1. Citizenship and Immigration Canada, *Annual Report to Parliament on Immigration 2011*, October 27, 2011, s. 2, at 19, http://www.cic.gc.ca/english/pdf/pub/annual-report-2011.pdf.

2. See general texts on public international law such as J.G. Castel, *International Law* (Toronto: Butterworths, 1976) and I. Brownlie, *Principles of Public International Law*, 6th ed. (Oxford: Oxford University Press, 2003).

3. G.H. Hackworth, *Digest of International Law* (Washington, DC: US Government Printing Office, 1942), vol. 3 at 1, cited in Castel, supra note 2, at 431.

4. This Act provided that persons born outside Canada to Canadian fathers were Canadian citizens, but persons born outside Canada to Canadian mothers had to naturalize. The overt sexism of this provision was overturned by the Supreme Court of Canada in the case of *Benner v. Canada (Secretary of State)*, [1997] 1 S.C.R. 358.

5. Penny Becklumb, Law and Government Division, Legislative Summary: Bill C-37: An Act to Amend the Citizenship Act, January 9, 2008, http://www.parl.gc.ca/About/Parliament/LegislativeSummaries/bills_ls.asp?lang=E&ls=c37&Parl=39&Ses=2&source=library_prb.

6. The CIC website provides an online guide entitled, "Am I a Canadian Citizen Under the New Law?," April 15, 2009, http://www.cic.gc.ca/english/citizenship/rules/index.asp.

7. *United States of America v. Cotroni; United States of America v. El Zein*, [1989] 1 S.C.R. 1469.

8. See Patrick Weil, "Access to Citizenship: A Comparison of Twenty-Five Nationality Laws," presentation given October 28, 2002 as part of the Metropolis Presents series, http://canada.metropolis.net/events/metropolis_presents/eu_speakers/weil2_e.htm.

9. Becklumb, supra note 5.

10. Ibid. at 10.

11. Ibid. at 10-11.

12. *Citizenship Act*, s. 5(3); Citizenship and Immigration Canada, "CP 7: Waivers," in *Operational Manuals—Citizenship Policy (CP)*, July 27, 2006, http://www.cic.gc.ca/english/resources/manuals/cp/cp07-eng.pdf.

13. Citizenship and Immigration Canada, "CP 12: Documents," in *Operational Manuals—Citizenship Policy (CP)*, June 16, 2008, http://www.cic.gc.ca/english/resources/manuals/cp/cp12-eng.pdf.

14. *Re Koo*, [1993] 1 F.C. 286 (T.D.); see also *Nakhjavani v. Canada (Secretary of State)* (1987), 13 F.T.R. 107, [1987] 2 Imm. L.R. (2d) 241.

15. Citizenship and Immigration Canada, "CP 5: Residence," in *Operational Manuals—Citizenship Policy (CP)*, June 11, 2010, http://www.cic.gc.ca/english/resources/manuals/cp/cp05-eng.pdf; see s. 5.10, extensive absences.

16. Citizenship and Immigration Canada, Operational Bulletin 244B—February 25, 2011, "Amendment to Operational Bulletin 244: Amendments to the Citizenship Regulations and Updated Guidelines Regarding the Citizenship Test," Annex B—Attachment to test and hearing notices, http://www.cic.gc.ca/english/resources/manuals/bulletins/2011/ob244B.asp#annB.

17. For a discussion about the citizenship ceremony and the taking of the oath, see Citizenship and Immigration Canada, "CP 15: Guide to Citizenship Ceremonies," in *Operational Manuals—Citizenship Policy (CP)*, December 21, 2011, s. 6, http://www.cic.gc.ca/english/resources/manuals/cp/cp15-eng.pdf.

18. Citizenship and Immigration Canada, supra note 15, s. 1.3.

19. Adapted from Citizenship and Immigration Canada, "CP 1: Citizenship Lines of Business," in *Operational Manuals—Citizenship Policy (CP)*, April 17, 2009, s. 2.15, http://www.cic.gc.ca/english/resources/manuals/cp/cp01-eng.pdf.

20. Becklumb, supra note 5.

21. Citizenship and Immigration Canada, "Canadian Citizenship Not for Sale: Minister Kenney Provides Update on Residence Fraud Investigations," news release, September 10, 2012, http://www.cic.gc.ca/english/department/media/releases/2012/2012-09-10.asp.

22. *Canada (Minister of Multiculturalism and Citizenship) v. Minhas* (1993), 66 F.T.R. 155; 21 Imm. L.R. (2d) 31 (F.C.T.D.).

REFERENCES

An Act to Amend the Citizenship Act. S.C. 2008, c. 14 (formerly Bill C-37).

An Act to Amend the Citizenship Act (adoption). S.C. 2007, c. 24 (formerly Bill C-14).

Black v. Canada (Prime Minister). (2001), 54 O.R. (3d) 215 (C.A.).

Canadian Charter of Rights and Freedoms. Part I of the *Constitution Act, 1982.* R.S.C. 1985, app. II, no. 44.

Citizenship Act. R.S.C. 1985, c. C-29.

Citizenship and Immigration Canada. "Amendment to Operational Bulletin 244: Amendments to the Citizenship Regulations and Updated Guidelines Regarding the Citizenship Test," *Operational Bulletin 244–B*, February 25, 2011. http://www.cic.gc.ca/english/resources/manuals/bulletins/2011/ob244B.asp#annB.

Citizenship and Immigration Canada. "CP 2: Decision-Making," in *Citizenship Policy (CP)*. March 21, 2007. http://www.cic.gc.ca/english/resources/manuals/cp/cp02-eng.pdf.

Citizenship and Immigration Canada. "CP 3: Establishing Applicant's Identity," in *Citizenship Policy (CP)*. August 20, 2012. http://www.cic.gc.ca/english/resources/manuals/cp/cp03-eng.pdf.

Citizenship and Immigration Canada. "CP 4: Grants," in *Citizenship Policy (CP)*. August 7, 2009. http://www.cic.gc.ca/english/resources/manuals/cp/cp04-eng.pdf.

Citizenship and Immigration Canada. "CP 9: Loss, Resumption, Renunciation, Revocation," in *Citizenship Policy (CP)*. April 17, 2009. http://www.cic.gc.ca/english/resources/manuals/cp/cp09-eng.pdf.

Citizenship and Immigration Canada. "CP 10: Proof of Citizenship," in *Citizenship Policy (CP)*. January 28, 2005. http://www.cic.gc.ca/english/resources/manuals/cp/cp10-eng.pdf.

Citizenship and Immigration Canada. "CP 11: Search of Records," in *Citizenship Policy (CP)*. June 8, 2010. http://www.cic.gc.ca/english/resources/manuals/cp/cp11-eng.pdf.

Citizenship and Immigration Canada. "CP 13: Administration," in *Citizenship Policy (CP)*. January 17, 2008. http://www.cic.gc.ca/english/resources/manuals/cp/cp13-eng.pdf.

Citizenship and Immigration Canada. "CP 14: Adoption," in *Citizenship Policy (CP)*. April 19, 2012. http://www.cic.gc.ca/english/resources/manuals/cp/cp14-eng.pdf.

Citizenship Regulations. S.O.R./93-246.

Extradition Act. S.C. 1999, c. 18.

Immigration and Refugee Protection Act. S.C. 2001, c. 27.

Indian Act. R.S.C. 1985, c. I-5.

Koo, Re. [1993] 1 F.C. 286, 1992 CanLII 2417 (T.D.).

Kuruvila, Elizabeth. "Legislative Summary: Bill C-14: An Act to Amend the Citizenship Act (adoption)." Parliament of Canada, Law and Government Division, May 29, 2006, revised September 24, 2007. http://www.parl.gc.ca/About/Parliament/LegislativeSummaries/bills_ls.asp?lang=E&ls=c14&Parl=39&Ses=1&source=library_prb.

Minister of Citizenship v. Odynsky. [2001] F.C.J. no. 286 (T.D.).

Mui, Re. (1996), 105 F.T.R. 158.

Papadogiorgakis, Re. [1978] 2 F.C. 208, 88 D.L.R. (3d) 243 (T.D.).

Pourgashemi, Re. (1993), 62 F.T.R. 122, 19 Imm. L.R. (2d) 259.

United States of America v. Cotroni; United States of America v. El Zein. [1989] 1 S.C.R. 1469.

Universal Declaration of Human Rights. G.A. res. 217A (III), U.N. Doc A/810 at 71 (1948).

PART IV

Refugee Law

Refugees and Protected Persons

7

LEARNING OUTCOMES

After reading this chapter you should be able to:

- Identify relevant international treaties pertaining to refugees and human rights and describe the role of international agencies with regard to those treaties.

- Understand the criteria for determining refugee status.

- Describe the inclusion, exclusion, and cessation elements of the definition of a Convention refugee.

- Understand the criteria for granting protection to persons in need of protection.

- Understand Canada's obligations toward refugee claimants.

- Identify relevant sections of the *Immigration and Refugee Protection Act* as they relate to refugees and persons in need of protection.

Introduction

Millions of people around the world leave their home countries each year, driven by war, political or religious oppression, natural disaster, environmental destruction, and poverty. Are they all **refugees**? Do they all need protection? Does Canada treat people fleeing from humanitarian crises, such as the 1994 genocide in Rwanda, the same as victims of natural disasters, such as those left homeless in South Asia by the tsunami that struck in December 2004? Although it is common place to label these people "refugees," under international and Canadian law this label has a precise meaning. The legal definition distinguishes those who are *genuine* or *bona fide* refugees from those who are economic migrants—that is, people in search of better living and economic conditions. This chapter examines the international agreements that are the legal basis for Canada's granting refugee status and providing protection, introduces the principle of *non-refoulement*, and provides a general overview of Canada's role in refugee protection. By the end of this chapter you will be able to answer the questions, "Who are Convention refugees and protected persons?" and "How do they receive Canada's protection?"

International Conventions

A **convention**, "covenant," or "treaty" is an agreement that obliges countries under international law to conform to its provisions. Countries bind themselves through **ratification**, or by signing the agreement, which is a confirmation of the commitment to abide by the agreement. When a country ratifies or accedes to an agreement, that country becomes known as a state party to the agreement and is thereafter legally bound to the obligations imposed by the agreement.

Generally in United Nations (UN) agreements, there are provisions for independent monitoring bodies to supervise implementation of and compliance with the obligations and responsibilities of state parties. The relevant international conventions and their related monitoring bodies are described below.

In Canada, the basis in law for determining refugee status is found in the following UN refugee treaties:

- the 1951 *Convention Relating to the Status of Refugees*; and
- the 1967 *Protocol Relating to the Status of Refugees*.

Canada is also a state party to treaties respecting human rights, and the following UN international agreements provide the basis in law for granting human rights protection:

- the 1984 *Convention Against Torture and Other Cruel, Inhuman or Degrading Treatment or Punishment*, and
- the 1966 *International Covenant on Civil and Political Rights*.

The United Nations High Commissioner for Refugees and the Refugee Convention

The UN High Commissioner for Refugees (UNHCR) was created in 1950 by the UN General Assembly to ensure the protection of refugees and provide assistance to them. The UNHCR is an international agency responsible for supervising the refugee determination process and safeguarding the rights of refugees. In addition to providing international legal protection for refugees, the UNHCR promotes international refugee agreements and provides programs and funding to assist refugees with the following:

- **voluntary repatriation** (voluntary return to home country) if conditions improve there;
- integration into the country of refuge; or
- **resettlement** in a third country.

The Refugee Convention, formally known as the 1951 *Convention relating to the Status of Refugees*, is the major legal foundation on which the UNHCR's work is based. It was originally created to help the hundreds of thousands of people displaced in Europe after the Second World War, and future refugees—but for a limited period of time. The framers of the 1951 Convention did not expect refugee issues to be a major international problem on an ongoing basis, and consequently the UNHCR was only given a three-year mandate to help the post–Second World War refugees. It was hoped that it would then cease operations.

Instead, the refugee crisis spread—from Europe in the 1950s to Africa in the 1960s and then to Asia. In 1967 the UN General Assembly adopted the 1967 *Protocol Relating to the Status of Refugees* to strengthen the 1951 Convention so that it would continue to operate to the benefit of future waves of refugees. The 1967 Protocol removed the earlier time limit of three years and the geographical restrictions that had limited the Convention's mandate to resettling European refugees uprooted by the Second World War.

The Convention and its Protocol provide the framework of principles for Canada's refugee determination system. These instruments define a "Convention refugee," describe our legal obligations toward refugees, set out the basic procedures for refugee determination, and describe the basic entitlements and obligations of refugees as well as the role and authority of the monitoring body—the UNHCR.

In 1969, Canada ratified the 1951 Convention and the related 1967 Protocol, thus cementing the obligation to establish a refugee status determination system and upholding the principle of *non-refoulement*. This is notable because, prior to 1969, Canada had no legal process in place for protecting refugees. After ratifying the Convention, however, Canada began accepting refugees on a number of special programs. However, it wasn't until passage of the 1976 *Immigration Act* that Canadian law could fulfill its international obligations by distinguishing between the immigrant and refugee classes, and implementing a process to determine refugee status.

WEBLINK

For more information about the UNHCR, and about refugees around the world. http://www.unhcr.org. The website for UNHCR in Canada is www.unhcr.ca.

UNHCR in Canada

Today, the UNHCR still maintains its authority to supervise the refugee status determination process. In Canada, the UNHCR has a branch office located in Ottawa and employs legal officers in cities throughout the country to monitor compliance with international refugee law to ensure that refugee claimants' rights are protected. Some practical examples of the UNHCR's work in Canada include observing refugee protection hearings and making recommendations to the Canadian government on refugee issues.

Principle of Non-Refoulement

An important principle of refugee law, called the **principle of *non-refoulement***, is reflected in the way in which Canada manages refugee claims. Translated, *non-refoulement* means "no return." The principle of *non-refoulement* is a rule of international law that obliges countries to provide protection to refugees against return to the country where they face a risk of persecution, or where their life or freedom would be threatened because of their race, religion, nationality, membership in a particular social group, or political opinion.[1]

Canada is committed to the principle of not returning a refugee to the country of origin. The protection against *refoulement* applies in situations where a refugee claimant is awaiting a decision; where refugee status is granted; and where, under a deportation order, an individual's life or human rights are threatened unless an exclusion applies under international law (discussed below under the heading "Exclusions"). Canada does not expel refugee claimants while their claims are in process, and consequently claimants are allowed to remain in Canada until their claims are settled.

Definition of a Convention Refugee

Canada has adopted almost verbatim the three parts of the 1951 "Convention refugee" definition in the IRPA, with the following three clauses:

1. *Inclusion clause:* defines the criteria for who is a refugee, such as a well-founded fear of persecution by reason of religion (s. 96).
2. *Exclusion clause:* defines who is not a refugee, such as people who commit war crimes (s. 98).
3. *Cessation clause:* defines when a person no longer enjoys the protection of the Convention—that is, when refugee protection ceases (s. 108).

Inclusion

IRPA defines a **Convention refugee** as follows:

> A Convention refugee is a person who, by reason of a well-founded fear of persecution for reasons of race, religion, nationality, membership in a particular social group or political opinion,

(a) is outside each of their countries of nationality and is unable or, by reason of that fear, unwilling to avail themself of the protection of each of those countries; or

(b) not having a country of nationality, is outside the country of their former habitual residence and is unable or, by reason of that fear, unwilling to return to that country.

Refugee claimants who meet all the inclusion elements of the definition of a Convention refugee will be granted refugee status. Therefore, it is important to identify each of the elements of the definition and understand how they are used in the decision-making process. There are four elements that form the positive basis for meeting the criteria of inclusion, as follows:

1. alienage;

2. a well-founded fear;

3. persecution; and

4. the nexus—that is, persecution under one of the five grounds in the IRPA.

A refugee claimant must meet all of the elements of inclusion in order for her claim to be accepted. What follows is a general explanation of the four inclusion elements.

1. Alienage

First, the claimant must establish alienage. **Alienage** occurs when a person is outside the country of her nationality or citizenship. If a person cannot establish a nationality or has no citizenship, alienage occurs when the person is outside a country considered to be the former habitual residence. Generally, people have an expectation of protection from their government, and it is only when their government is either unable or unwilling to protect them that they need to seek protection from another country.

Furthermore, the Convention refugee definition requires that the claimant make a claim against the country of nationality. If the claimant has citizenship in more than one country, then she must establish a claim against each of those countries. Consider the following scenario.

WEBLINK

The UNHCR's *Handbook on Procedures and Criteria for Determining Refugee Status* (1979, re-edited January 1992) is recommended reading for an in-depth study of these elements. http://www.unhcr.org/3d58e13b4.html.

Let's consider, by way of example, the fictitious case of Ariana. Ariana is a citizen of Bovoria, an impoverished country with no universities and few prospects for women. Ariana's father is a prominent businessman in Bovoria who wants to give his daughter every opportunity to be self-sufficient, so he decides to send her outside Bovoria to study. Ariana pursues a degree in political science at the National University of Vonburg in the neighbouring country of Furtania. She is outspoken about student rights and is a regular contributor of cartoons to the student newspaper. She is detained by Furtanian authorities for three days for participating in an anti-government rally and is subsequently harassed for the publication of her cartoons, which have been deemed too political. When her cartoons are denounced by the government-run Furtanian press, Ariana fears for her life there and flees the country without completing her degree, and travels to Canada where she will make a refugee claim.

One of the first elements that Ariana must establish in making her refugee claim in Canada is the element of alienage. In seeking protection, Ariana must prove that she cannot avail herself of the protection of any of her countries of nationality (or former habitual residence, if she did not have a nationality). Ariana, like all other refugee claimants, must provide documentary evidence of her citizenship (or multiple citizenships), usually by providing a birth certificate, national identity card, or passport.

Ariana has Bovorian citizenship, so Furtania does not qualify as "a former habitual residence," despite her time spent there. Furthermore, Ariana is not a citizen of Furtania and enjoys the protection of her country of nationality, Bovoria, so she is not able to claim protection in Canada against Furtania. The element of alienage cannot be established and Ariana's claim is rejected.

2. Well-Founded Fear

In considering each refugee claim, a member of the Refugee Protection Division will assess whether the refugee claimant's fear is well founded. There is both an objective and subjective component to this test. The objective component considers whether the fear is reasonable in the circumstances, and considers the circumstance in which the fear arises, such as the conditions in the country of origin. The subjective component considers the personal perspective of the claimant—does the claimant actually experience fear? The following scenario sets out two cases to show how the element of **well-founded fear** can be individualized.

Kairat and Ravil are both citizens of the fictitious country of Zarkhanistan, a country where young males between the ages of 18 and 33 have been arbitrarily arrested and detained in the context of the "war on terror." Some detainees have disappeared and others have been sentenced to death and executed. Young men are typically targeted in the southern part of the country. Kairat arrived in Canada directly from Zarkhanistan six months ago, just after a raid in his neighbouring village that resulted in a total sweep of unmarried males. One of Kairat's relatives has been missing since the raid. Ravil arrived in Canada around the same time as Kairat; however, he has been out of Zarkhanistan for the past 12 years working on a cruise ship. His contract has now expired and he wants to settle down, but he is concerned about the unstable situation in his home country.

In this scenario, both Kairat and Ravil will make refugee claims, and despite the fact that their claims may share certain similarities, the decisions in their cases will be made on the basis of their independent accounts, experiences, and circumstances. It is possible that one claim may be accepted while the other is rejected. This is because each claim will be decided on its own merits. The outcomes may be different because each claimant, who will have the opportunity to present his own story both orally and in writing, will submit separate and individualized evidence to a member of the RPD. Furthermore, the members who hear their cases are independent of each other, and they will each consider both the objective and subjective bases of the claims. The outcomes will depend on the merits of each case, including whether the information that the claimants provide is credible and trustworthy.

OBJECTIVE COMPONENT

To establish that a claim is well founded, there must be an objective component—a valid reason for the fear, such as known human rights violations and other pertinent background information. Therefore, a claimant should support his allegations with documentary evidence of the prevailing country conditions, as reported in reliable country-of-origin reports, human rights reports, newspaper articles, medical reports, and other personal documentation, and as testified to by witnesses.

In our example, Kairat and Ravil would likely present similar objective evidence about their country of origin, Zarkhanistan. The objective component requires that each claim be assessed in the context of the prevailing conditions in the country of origin. This kind of generalized information can be obtained by researching current and credible information about the country, typically including:

- whether the country of origin is in the midst of political upheaval, war, or generally unsettled conditions;
- the country's human rights record; and
- whether the government is able and willing to protect its citizens.

It is generally accepted that if a claimant has suffered persecution in the past, he continues to be at risk and therefore needs the protection of the UN Refugee Convention. However, it is not necessary for a claimant to have suffered past harm to fear it in the future. That is why the definition is forward looking—the decision-maker must look to the future to consider whether there is a serious possibility of a risk in returning the claimant to his country of origin. Is there a serious possibility that the claimant would risk persecution if returned today or tomorrow? Have the conditions in the claimant's country changed? Would Ravil, who has been out of Zarkhanistan for many years, face persecution if he were to return there? Does he fit the government's profile of a potential terrorist? Is he likely to be perceived to be a threat?

SUBJECTIVE COMPONENT

The subjective component of a well-founded fear considers the claimant's individual state of mind and fearfulness. The subjective basis will depend on the claimant's own background and experiences, as well as those of family and close associates. To support the subjective basis for a refugee claim, the claimant must make a credible case for future risk, and should provide evidence of past persecution, if any, by submitting documentary evidence such as medical or psychological reports. In practice, it is not always possible to provide independent evidence; most often, it is the claimant's written and verbal statements that provide insight into his state of mind.

The subjective component, therefore, is unique to each claimant. Let's suppose that Kairat's claim was accepted and Ravil's claim was rejected, even though the prevailing country conditions—the objective component—are the same. Why might the outcomes be different? The difference in their claims may be due in part to the subjective component of their alleged fear.

The RPD member will also assess whether the claimant's fear is valid and will be interested in the chronology of events that led him to make a claim for protection. Did the claimant delay leaving his country of origin when the fear arose? Did he delay making a claim or did he make a claim at the first possible opportunity? In our scenario, Kairat shows evidence of a valid fear: he lived next to a village where men like him were arrested; one of his relatives "disappeared"; and he left and sought refuge immediately when danger was imminent. Ravil, on the other hand, left the country 12 years ago to seek work on a ship, and in all his travels he never sought protection until after his contract expired. This may raise a suspicion that he is not genuinely fearful, but instead is seeking better economic conditions.

3. Persecution

A refugee claimant's well-founded fear must relate to persecution. The term **persecution** is not defined in the 1951 Convention or in the IRPA; however, Canadian courts provide some parameters for defining it. Generally, to qualify as persecution, an act or series of acts must present a serious harm—a threat to life or physical freedom, or other persistent and serious violations of human rights.

Under the 1951 Convention, a refugee claimant is not entitled to protection from legitimate prosecution by his country of origin. However, for the prosecution to be legitimate, the laws and the legal processes must not violate fundamental human rights. Someone who fled her country to avoid a trial and punishment for having committed a criminal act such as robbery or murder is not "persecuted," provided that she would have been given a fair trial and fair treatment.

However, if a claimant faces prosecution for committing an act that is protected by international human rights standards—for example, the practice of his religion—this may be tantamount to persecution. In this case, the "crime" is the exercise of a fundamental right; therefore, the claimant is fleeing persecution. Even if the crime is legitimate, issues of persecution could be raised if the claimant was not given access to a fair and impartial trial, or if the punishment was unduly severe—such as torture, or execution for a minor offence.

In some cases, the refugee claimant's fear is based on acts of discrimination or harassment. Although an individual act of discrimination or harassment on its own would usually not substantiate a case for persecution, a series of acts taken cumulatively may amount to persecution. This could be the case if the acts are perpetrated by the government or by government agents, or if the acts are perpetrated by individuals outside the government, and the government takes no steps to provide protection against them. Consider the following scenario, where discrimination and harassment occurred with repetition and persistence, and thus cumulatively amounted to persecution.

Mr. K is a 35-year-old male member of the ethnic minority in his country. For much of his life he has been the victim of attacks. His teachers discouraged him and verbally abused him as a child, and he had difficulty finding employment—all because of his ethnic background. He eventually found work in a factory, where he endured physical assaults by co-workers. His employer was not interested in his problems and the police refused to investigate, stating that it was a personal matter. He joined an organization that worked peacefully to improve the working and living conditions of his ethnic community; this organization, however, was perceived by the authorities as a threat to local peace. Since joining the organization, Mr. K has frequently been stopped by the police on his way home from meetings, taken into detention, beaten, and released. This has been going on for several years. The detentions have become more frequent and longer, and the beatings more severe. The authorities are not interested in stopping the violence and are sometimes the perpetrators. Other members of Mr. K's ethnic community have similar complaints.

To determine whether the element of persecution exists, the RPD takes into consideration the agents of persecution. Agents of persecution are those individuals who carry out the acts of persecution. Authorities of the claimant's country of origin are **state agents**, such as the police or members of the military, and their acts are generally sanctioned or authorized by the government or by legislation. Discrimination and harassment by state agents amounts to persecution if these actions are persistent and serious.

Members of the militia who violate human rights, or members of the majority ethnic or religious groups, rebels, guerrillas, drug or warlords, etc., who commit serious acts of discrimination or other targeted harmful acts are known as **nonstate agents**. When persecution is carried out by non-state agents, the claimant must prove that the government knowingly tolerates the acts, or is unwilling or unable to provide effective protection from those acts.

In the case of Mr. K, the agents of persecution were both state agents (the police) and non-state agents (teachers and co-workers). The police refused to assist Mr. K when he reported physical assaults by co-workers; therefore, it is possible that these assaults could be considered acts of persecution.

4. The Nexus: Persecution Under One of the Five Grounds in the IRPA

Much like Canadian human rights legislation prohibits discrimination based on prohibited grounds, the IRPA sets out five grounds of persecution. The five grounds, enumerated in the definition of a Convention refugee, are as follows:

a. race,

b. religion,

c. nationality,

d. membership in a particular social group, and

e. political opinion.

To determine whether the persecution falls under one of the enumerated grounds, the RPD considers the following questions: Does the persecutor perceive the claimant to be a member of a certain race, nationality, religion, or particular social group or to hold a certain political opinion? Is there a reasonable chance of persecution because of that perception? It is not necessary that the perception be accurate, only that the persecutor may act on it. Therefore, it is important for the claimant to provide as much information as possible about the context of the persecution.

A. RACE

A claimant may have a well-founded fear of persecution on the basis of his race, which is understood to mean his ethnic group. Examples may include discriminatory hiring practices by government, exclusion from public education, segregation, and discriminatory taxation. The claimant must establish that persecution was suffered as a result of race. Evidence should include examples of how the claimant was targeted, what harm was suffered, whether the claimant's race is a minority group, and the general treatment of members of that group.

B. RELIGION

Claimants may be persecuted on the basis of religion because they are members of a religious minority or sect. The laws of the country may prohibit joining or worshipping in a particular religious community. In that case, the claimant must establish that he is a member of the particular religious group by detailing such things as whether he is a practising or non-practising member, whether his religious group is legally recognized in his country, and how members of that religious group are generally treated.

Alternatively, a country may prohibit the practice of any religion, and ban any religious instruction or practice. In that case, even members of a majority religion may be persecuted.

C. NATIONALITY

Nationality encompasses not only a person's citizenship, but also a person's ethnic or linguistic group, and so may sometimes overlap with race. Examples of persecution based on nationality include genocide, torture, rape, and discrimination against members of a minority or low-caste clan.

D. MEMBERSHIP IN A PARTICULAR SOCIAL GROUP

According to the UNHCR, a particular social group "normally comprises persons of similar background, habits or social status."[2] The Supreme Court of Canada in *Canada (Attorney General) v. Ward* classified "particular social group" as consisting of three distinct categories of groups:

- "groups defined by an innate, unchangeable characteristic" (which might include claims based on a person's gender, linguistic background, sexual orientation, family, or caste);

- groups "whose members voluntarily associate for reasons so fundamental to their human dignity that they should not be forced to forsake the association" (which might include claims from members of human rights organizations or trade union activists); and

- groups "associated by a former voluntary status, unalterable as a result of its historical permanence" (which expresses the idea that "one's past is an immutable part of the person").

Some examples of persons suffering persecution on the basis of membership in a particular social group include women who face rape or other forms of violence by government agents, women who face female genital mutilation or forced marriage, homosexuals who face violence, and members of trade unions who face violence.

E. POLITICAL OPINION

A person may express a political opinion by words or actions—for example, by participating in anti-government demonstrations, distributing literature, or speaking out in public. However, a person who does not articulate a political opinion may still be identified by the government as an opponent—for example, by failing to attend pro-government rallies or join a government party. To prove the case, the claimant has to explain the significance of his actions or inactions, whether he was identified by the government, and how the government would likely react if he were returned to his country of origin. In assessing the claim, the RPD member asks: "Does the government consider the claimant's actions to be political?"

If a claimant belongs to a political party or group, it is important that he provide evidence of how his membership, activities, and opinions brought him to the attention of authorities or are the basis of a future risk. The claimant should be able to explain why the government would perceive the failure to do something, such as join a political party, as a political act. Documentary proof such as membership cards may also be useful.

Refugee Sur Place

What is a **refugee *sur place***? A refugee *sur place* is someone who did not flee her country as a refugee when she first left, but later requires legal protection. In this situation, the person becomes a refugee while in a foreign country as a result of a change in government while the person is away from home, or some other change in circumstance. International law, specifically the UN Refugee Convention, does not require that a person is a refugee at the time of leaving the country of origin. If an occurrence gives rise to a well-founded fear of persecution while the person is in another country, the person may be deemed a refugee *sur place*.

Human Rights Conventions

The *Immigration Act* of 1976 created the legal basis for a refugee determination system in Canada. Prior to the enactment of the *Immigration and Refugee Protection Act* in June 2002, however, refugee claims were assessed only within the scope of the

Refugee Convention's technical definition of a refugee. Decision-makers had no jurisdiction to assess claims beyond that definition. Consequently, a claim could be rejected if the person did not fit the limited definition of a Convention refugee, even if the person faced a threat or risk of threat to life or freedom.

The IRPA significantly broadened the scope of refugee protection and filled in gaps for protection. The new statute did not eliminate the importance of the definition of a Convention refugee, but rather, expanded its protection to foreign nationals to include "persons in need of protection" who face individualized risk of death, torture, or cruel and unusual treatment or punishment—that is, those who are in refugee-like situations but for whom the Refugee Convention does not apply.

Let's first take a look at the human rights Conventions that provide the basis for considering refugee claims of "**persons in need of protection**."

Convention Against Torture

Torture is an extreme human rights violation. The 1984 *Convention Against Torture and Other Cruel, Inhuman or Degrading Treatment or Punishment* (CAT) provides a definition of torture, bans torture, and makes it illegal under all circumstances—including under state emergency and external threats.

Signatories to this Convention agree to exercise the principle of *non-refoulement*: a host country may not expel, return, or extradite a person to another country where there are substantial grounds for believing that a person in need of protection would be in danger of being subjected to torture. As a signing state to the CAT, Canada has also agreed to take into account the human rights record of the person's country when making the decision to return him.

The CAT consists of 33 articles, which became effective in June 1987. Canada was one of the original 20 states to ratify this Convention. To monitor the implementation and compliance of the CAT, a ten-member Committee Against Torture was created. States that are party to the Convention must report to the committee one year from becoming signatories, and must submit a report to the committee every four years thereafter for review and recommendation.

International Covenant on Civil and Political Rights

The 1966 *International Covenant on Civil and Political Rights* (ICCPR) serves to codify a person's core human rights, which are non-derogable. **Non-derogable rights** are rights that must be respected and cannot be taken away from an individual or suspended for any reason, even in a time of crisis. These include the right to life and freedom from torture.

By contrast, **derogable rights** are those that may be temporarily suspended, as by a state during emergencies. For example, freedom of movement may be restricted during war or a natural disaster. The ICCPR permits a state to temporarily suspend derogable rights in cases of public emergency; however, it must not discriminate between groups. For example, Canada's internship of Japanese Canadians during the Second World War would not be permitted under this exception, because it singled out Canadians of Japanese descent.

The ICCPR provides for the inherent right to life; the right to recognition everywhere as a person before the law; and the right to freedom of thought, conscience, and religion, including freedom to have or to adopt a religion or belief of one's choice. It forbids torture or cruel, inhuman, or degrading treatment or punishment; involuntary servitude; and arbitrary arrest or detention.

The ICCPR is based on the *Universal Declaration of Human Rights* (UDHR), the first international statement to use the term "human rights." The ICCPR, the UDHR, and another international legal instrument, the *International Covenant on Economic, Social and Cultural Rights* (ICESCR), are known collectively as the International Bill of Rights. In March 1976, the ICCPR became international law. Two months later, it was ratified by Canada. The UN Human Rights Committee was established to monitor ICCPR compliance.

Canada also became a party to the *Second Optional Protocol to the International Covenant on Civil and Political Rights, Aiming at the Abolition of the Death Penalty* in November 2005. The Second Optional Protocol has the objective of protecting the right to life through abolition of the death penalty and obliges state parties to take all necessary measures to abolish the death penalty within their jurisdictions.

IRPA: Persons in Need of Protection

IRPA extends the scope of protection beyond the Convention refugee definition to persons in need of protection who face individualized risk of death, torture, or cruel and unusual treatment or punishment.

A refugee claimant who is found to be a person in need of protection enjoys the same rights as those claimants who are granted protection under the Refugee Convention, including the right to apply for permanent residence.

The definition of "person in need of protection" in s. 97 of the IRPA confirms Canada's international obligation to protect refugees under the 1984 *Convention Against Torture and Other Cruel, Inhuman or Degrading Treatment or Punishment*, and the 1966 *International Covenant on Civil and Political Rights*. Section 97 reads as follows:

> (1) A person in need of protection is a person in Canada whose removal to their country or countries of nationality or, if they do not have a country of nationality, their country of former habitual residence, would subject them personally
>> (a) to a danger, believed on substantial grounds to exist, of torture within the meaning of Article 1 of the Convention Against Torture; or
>> (b) to a risk to their life or to a risk of cruel and unusual treatment or punishment if
>>> (i) the person is unable or, because of that risk, unwilling to avail themself of the protection of that country,
>>> (ii) the risk would be faced by the person in every part of that country and is not faced generally by other individuals in or from that country,
>>> (iii) the risk is not inherent or incidental to lawful sanctions, unless imposed in disregard of accepted international standards, and
>>> (iv) the risk is not caused by the inability of that country to provide adequate health or medical care.

(2) A person in Canada who is a member of a class of persons prescribed by the regulations as being in need of protection is also a person in need of protection.

The elements of this definition are considered in more detail below.

Country of Nationality or of Former Habitual Residence

Similar to the concept of alienage for the Convention refugee definition, it is generally accepted that nationality refers to citizenship. A refugee claimant must prove that there is a risk of torture (or risk to life or cruel and unusual treatment or punishment) upon return to the country of citizenship. If the claimant has more than one nationality, the claimant must prove that there is a risk of torture upon return to any of those countries of citizenship. If the claimant does not have a country of citizenship, then a claim must be established against the country of former habitual residence.

Risk

Even if there is current and credible information to establish that torture is practised in the refugee claimant's country of origin, the refugee claimant must nevertheless demonstrate that, on a **balance of probabilities**,[3] she would be personally subjected to a danger of torture if returned. The claimant must present evidence of this personal risk—it will not be enough to establish that widespread torture occurs in the country.

The claimant may also be denied refugee status under the IRPA under the following conditions:

- refuge exists within some parts of the country;
- the risk is part of lawful sanctions, such as punishment for a crime; or
- the risk is a result of inadequate health or medical care.

Refugee protection is intended for the truly desperate; therefore, claimants who are able to find safe haven in pockets of their own country are expected to go there. The IRPA also denies refugee protection in circumstances where the floodgates would open up to large populations—such as where all citizens of a country are at risk of torture, or where poverty on a national scale precludes health or medical care. Under those conditions, other types of interventions such as diplomatic, military, and humanitarian aid are considered more appropriate.

Grounds

The two grounds for claiming to be a person in need of protection are danger of torture (s. 97(1)(a)) and risk to life or of cruel and unusual treatment or punishment (s. 97(1)(b)).

DANGER OF TORTURE

Torture is considered an extreme violation of human rights. A major principle articulated in article 5 of the *Universal Declaration of Human Rights* is that people should be free from torture or cruel, inhuman, or degrading treatment or punishment.

Article 1 of the CAT sets out the definition of torture as follows:

> For the purposes of this Convention, the term "torture" means any act by which severe pain or suffering, whether physical or mental, is intentionally inflicted on a person for such purposes as obtaining from him or a third person information or a confession, punishing him for an act he or a third person has committed or is suspected of having committed, or intimidating or coercing him or a third person, or for any reason based on discrimination of any kind, when such pain or suffering is inflicted by or at the instigation of or with the consent or acquiescence of a public official or other person acting in an official capacity. It does not include pain or suffering arising only from, inherent in or incidental to lawful sanctions.

There are three essential elements to this legal definition of torture,[4] which answer the questions "what," "who," and "why," as follows:

- *What was done?* Did the act result in severe physical or psychological pain or suffering?
- *Who did it?* Was the act intentionally inflicted by a state agent or public official, such as state police or secret security forces?
- *Why was it done?* Was the act carried out for the purpose of intimidation, deterrence, coercion, control, revenge, punishment, or information gathering?

The refugee claimant must prove, on a balance of probabilities, all three of these elements. For example, if a claimant could prove that physical pain was inflicted for the purpose of intimidation, but could not prove that the government was behind it or turned a blind eye to it, the claimant would be denied refugee status on the basis of torture. Consider the following scenario:

> Ms. W was a journalist for a national newspaper and wrote a critical piece about election fraud that exposed the criminal activities of top elected officials. She was arrested by the Secret Service shortly after her story was released. Ms. W was detained in a darkened cell, placed in metal restraints, and subjected to beatings and electric shock treatment during prolonged periods of interrogation about her sources, which she refused to name. She was extremely weakened by the time her interrogators dumped her by the roadside one night with a warning to stick to "fashion and entertainment reporting" or her children would "disappear." Shortly afterward, Ms. W, her husband, and her children fled the country. She continues to suffer from her physical injuries and post-traumatic stress disorder. She is making a refugee claim under s. 97 on the basis of having been tortured and the future risk to her life and the lives of her family.

WEBLINK

You can find an in-depth discussion of torture and some examples in *The Torture Reporting Handbook* at www.essex.ac.uk/torturehandbook.

Under the Convention definition of torture, all three elements of torture were met: Ms. W suffered severe physical and psychological pain as a result of the incident; it was intentionally inflicted by state agents; and the purpose was punishment and intimidation.

The Canadian Centre for Victims of Torture

WEBLINK

For more information, see the Canadian Centre for Victims of Torture at www.ccvt.org.

The Canadian Centre for Victims of Torture (CCVT) provides services to immigrants and refugees who have experienced torture. These services include language training, job search assistance, referrals to other professionals and agencies, translation, and counselling. The CCVT is a non-profit, registered charitable organization and is considered a pioneer in the rehabilitation of survivors of torture. Based in Toronto, the centre works with the community to help survivors integrate into Canadian society and to raise awareness of the continuing effects of torture and war.

RISK TO LIFE OR RISK OF CRUEL AND UNUSUAL TREATMENT OR PUNISHMENT

The terms **risk to life** and **risk of cruel and unusual treatment or punishment** are not defined in the IRPA. However, these terms are customarily understood to refer to ill-treatment causing suffering that is less severe than torture. These acts are intentional and intended to cause significant physical, mental, and psychological pain or suffering. Consider the following scenario:

Mr. X was a journalist for a major independent newspaper in his home country. He was investigating a story about international monetary transactions and uncovered a corruption scheme by senior government officials. On several occasions (for example, on his way home from work; on his way to the market; and on his way to a friend's house, within a block from his home), Mr. X has been attacked and threatened by thugs wearing masks. He claims they are members of the national intelligence service, which he says is attempting to censor him. It is well documented that journalists, some of whom were Mr. X's colleagues, have been unlawfully detained for their criticisms of corrupt government officials. The attacks against newspaper publishers and journalists have started to escalate. Mr. X believes that even if he were to move to another city or the countryside, there is still a risk to his life or a risk of cruel and unusual treatment or punishment, so he has fled his country.

Mr. X was the victim of acts that were intentional and intended to cause significant physical and mental suffering, so a claim under s. 97(1)(b) on the basis of risk to life or of cruel and unusual treatment or punishment is appropriate. Note, however, that the harm suffered by Mr. X was less severe than that suffered by Ms. W and that it is less clear whether the masked thugs were state agents, so a claim under s. 97(1)(a) may be less likely to succeed.

The table below summarizes and compares the international conventions we have discussed in the chapter.

International Conventions

Legal instrument	Key feature	Supervised by	Year ratified by Canada	Refugee status	Protected persons
1951 *Convention Relating to the Status of Refugees*	Defines a Convention refugee	UNHCR	1969	✔	
1967 *Protocol Relating to the Status of Refugees*	Removes timelines and geographical limitations of 1951 Convention	UNHCR	1969	✔	
1984 *Convention Against Torture and Other Cruel, Inhuman or Degrading Treatment or Punishment* (CAT)	Defines torture and makes it illegal under all circumstances	Committee Against Torture	1984		✔
1966 *International Covenant on Civil and Political Rights* (ICCPR)	Codifies non-derogable and derogable human rights	UN Human Rights Committee	1976		✔
Second Optional Protocol to the International Covenant on Civil and Political Rights, Aiming at the Abolition of the Death Penalty	Abolishes the death penalty	UN Human Rights Committee	2005		✔

Exclusions

The IRPA provides for instances where refugee protection must not be conferred (s. 98): this is known as "exclusion."

Even where a refugee claimant meets all the elements of the refugee definition (IRPA, s. 96) or all the elements of a person in need of protection (IRPA, s. 97), he may nevertheless be returned to his country of origin if any of the following exclusions apply:

- the claimant has protection elsewhere;
- the claimant is likely guilty of persecuting others;
- the claimant is likely guilty of a serious non-political crime; or
- the claimant is likely guilty of acts contrary to the purposes and principles of the United Nations.

These exclusions are set out in sections E and F of article 1 of the *Convention Relating to the Status of Refugees*, and are included in a schedule to the IRPA. The sections are reproduced below:

E. This Convention shall not apply to a person who is recognized by the competent authorities of the country in which he has taken residence as having the rights and obligations which are attached to the possession of the nationality of that country.

F. The provisions of this Convention shall not apply to any person with respect to whom there are serious reasons for considering that:

(a) He has committed a crime against peace, a war crime, or a crime against humanity, as defined in the international instruments drawn up to make provision in respect of such crimes;

(b) He has committed a serious non-political crime outside the country of refuge prior to his admission to that country as a refugee;

(c) He has been guilty of acts contrary to the purposes and principles of the United Nations.

These exclusions apply to refugee claimants under both ss. 96 and 97 of the IRPA as provided in s. 98, which states the following:

Under Canadian law, when a person is found to meet the criteria described in section E or F of Article 1 of the Refugee Convention, he will not be granted Convention refugee status or protections as a person in need of protection.

Claims for refugee status are to be made only as a last resort, by those who have no other options and by those who are innocent victims. Drafters of the Convention, and of the IRPA, were mindful of the potential for misuse of refugee laws by those who wish to emigrate for economic or personal reasons. They also wanted to prevent refugee laws from offering protection to those who actually perpetrated acts of torture against others. Under some circumstances, such as civil war, atrocities are often committed by individuals on each side of the conflict. Refugee laws are not intended to offer asylum to anyone guilty of such acts.

Protection of Another Country

Article E of the exclusion clause refers to a refugee claimant who has taken residence in another country or territory and has the protection of that country or territory. In that case, the claimant is not in need of Canada's protection. If a claimant has the option of living safely elsewhere, even if it is economically difficult and not the claimant's preference, she is expected to do so.

War Crimes and Crimes Against Humanity

Article 1F(a) refers to a refugee claimant for whom there are serious reasons to believe that he has committed war crimes or **crimes against humanity**, such as crimes relating to genocide, slavery, torture, apartheid, or terrorist activities. Such a person is considered undeserving of the protection of the Refugee Convention and should be tried in an international court for the alleged crimes, not awarded safe asylum in a host country such as Canada. There are also practical concerns with respect to how such a person might behave in Canada, and whether he would facilitate or perpetrate those crimes within Canadian borders.

Serious Non-Political Crime

Article 1F(b) refers to a refugee claimant for whom there are serious reasons to believe that she has committed serious **non-political crimes**. Again, such a person is considered undeserving of the protection of the Refugee Convention, and admitting her would raise practical concerns about criminal behaviour in Canada that could endanger Canadians. Although there is no list of serious crimes in the Refugee Convention, a serious non-political crime is understood to be an act committed for personal reasons or gain with no political end or motive involved. Generally, this would encompass the more serious crimes included in the Canadian *Criminal Code*, such as assault, murder, theft, and fraud. Petty crimes such as shoplifting and trespassing would likely not qualify as "serious" enough to justify the exclusion of an otherwise legitimate refugee claim.

Acts Contrary to United Nations Principles

Article 1F(c) refers to a refugee claimant for whom there are serious reasons to believe that he is guilty of committing acts that breach the purposes and principles of the United Nations. Such a person is considered undeserving of the protection of the Refugee Convention. The Charter of the United Nations lists the four purposes of that organization[5] as follows:

1. to maintain international peace and security;
2. to develop friendly relations among nations based on respect for the principle of equal rights and self-determination;
3. to achieve international cooperation in solving international socio-economic and cultural problems; and
4. to harmonize the actions of nations in the attainment of these common ends.

For example, a refugee claimant who engages in acts of international terrorism that constitute a threat to international peace and security would be excluded from *non-refoulement* protection under article 1F(c) because such acts are contrary to the purposes and principles of the United Nations. The UNHCR, in its *Guidelines on International Protection: Application of the Exclusion Clauses—Article 1F of the 1951 Convention Relating to the Status of Refugees*, cautions the following in guideline 17:

> Given the broad, general terms of the purposes and principles of the United Nations, the scope of this category is rather unclear and should therefore be read narrowly. Indeed, it is rarely applied and, in many cases, Article 1F(a) or 1F(b) are anyway likely to apply. Article 1F(c) is only triggered in extreme circumstances by activity which attacks the very basis of the international community's coexistence. Such activity must have an international dimension. Crimes capable of affecting international peace, security and peaceful relations between States, as well as serious and sustained violations of human rights, would fall under this category. ... [I]t would appear that in principle only persons who have been in positions of power in a State or State-like entity would appear capable of committing such acts. In cases involving a terrorist act, a correct application of Article 1F(c) involves an

assessment as to the extent to which the act impinges on the international plane—in terms of its gravity, international impact, and implications for international peace and security.

Cessation of Protection

Refugee protection is not intended to be permanent. Article 1C of the United Nations *Convention Relating to the Status of Refugees* includes a **cessation clause**. This clause provides the framework for when protection may lawfully cease under s. 108 of the IRPA.

Section 108 provides that a claim for refugee protection shall generally be rejected, and a person is not a Convention refugee or a person in need of protection, where that person has done any of the following:

- voluntarily "reavailed" herself of the protection of the country of nationality—for example, by returning to live there;
- voluntarily reacquired her nationality—for example, by applying for a passport;
- acquired a new nationality and is enjoying the protection of the country of that new nationality; or
- voluntarily re-established herself in the country of former habitual residence on which the claim to refugee protection was based (where the refugee has no country of citizenship).

The cessation clause also provides that a person is not a refugee if the reasons for the claim in the first place have ceased to exist, such as when the country conditions in the country of origin have stabilized. Section 108 does provide one exception to this, in the rare cases where a refugee has been so traumatized by her experiences that she refuses to trust the protection of the country of origin when it is offered. To satisfy this exception to the cessation criteria, the refugee must establish compelling reasons arising out of previous persecution, torture, ill-treatment, or punishment for refusing to return home after conditions have improved.

You may be wondering how the cessation clause is important to Canadian immigration law. A person with Convention refugee status, for example, is allowed to remain in Canada and can apply for permanent residence status. In cases where a removal order is issued against a permanent resident, the minister can execute the order; however, if that permanent resident also has Canada's protection, then because of the principle of *non-refoulement*, that person cannot be removed to their country of origin. Thus, where refugee status has previously been granted, the burden of proof is on the minister to show that the protection should cease. Under the Refugee Protection Division Rules, the minister must apply in writing to the RPD, and must disclose any evidence to the refugee. If the RPD makes an order for cessation of refugee status or protection, then the principle of *non-refoulement* would no longer apply. It should be noted that very few applications for cessation are made to the RPD.

Canada's Scope of Protection

Canada offers protection to the world's displaced people through three programs, which are described briefly below and more thoroughly in other chapters. The authority to provide refugee protection comes from IRPA, which sets out three distinct ways (s. 95):

1. abroad, through the selection of foreign nationals who apply for permanent or temporary residence when they have already been determined to be a Convention refugee or a person in similar circumstances (s. 95(a));

2. in Canada, through the determination by the Refugee Protection Division of the Immigration and Refugee Board that a foreign national is a Convention refugee or a person in need of protection (s. 95(b)); or

3. in Canada, through an administrative decision on an application in certain cases prior to removal

From this authority, the grant of protection is carried out under three programs.

Protection Programs

In previous chapters, you learned about how individuals are selected to come to Canada as permanent residents: the rigorous criteria and the complicated, expensive, and time-consuming application processes in order to meet statutory requirements. Canada's immigration programs are managed so as to control the flow of immigration through such means as established immigration levels, application criteria, enforcement procedures, and admissibility criteria. Generally, we know who is coming to Canada before they arrive because they have had to seek prior approval from the Canadian government. This is not always the case for refugees. Although, the government selects some refugees through the Refugee and Humanitarian Resettlement program, Canada must also manage spontaneous arrivals (see below), of which only some are considered as genuinely in need of our protection.

Refugee and Humanitarian Resettlement Program

Canadian officials from missions abroad work with the UNHCR and various non-governmental organizations (NGOs) to identify refugees and persons in refugee-like situations from abroad who are in need of resettlement. CIC is the federal department responsible for this program. Refugees who arrive in Canada under this program arrive as permanent residents, and are either given financial assistance by the government or are assisted through private sponsorship. The program is described in detail in Chapter 8, Refugee and Humanitarian Resettlement Program.

The Refugee Challenge: Spontaneous Arrivals and Overstayers

Unlike immigrants, some refugees are not selected. Refugees who arrive at our borders without having been subject to any immigration assessment processes and without prior approval are considered to be spontaneous arrivals. Generally, these people would be turned away but for the fact they are asking for Canada's protection by seeking asylum here. Given that the criteria for a successful refugee claim does not include any of the usual criteria for immigrating (that is, ability to speak English or French, ability for self-sufficiency, future contribution to the economy, ability to integrate, or family ties), there can be much suspicion as to the individual's motivation for arriving here.

Consequently, refugees are often portrayed as illegal migrants and abusers of the immigration process or are criticized for using the back door to gain entry, especially if they come from democratic countries. Some people have the perception that refugees are queue jumpers, bogus claimants, and a burden on our social support systems. No doubt there is some abuse of the system by illegal migrants and the human smugglers who help them get to Canada. And some foreign nationals who do not otherwise qualify for temporary or permanent residence do try to manipulate the refugee system to their advantage. Besides undermining the efficiency of the refugee determination process in Canada, access to the process creates a plethora of problems for immigration officials following a failed application. Invariably, those claimants who are refused refugee status or protection can exercise a right to apply to other processes (for example, the Pre-Removal Risk Assessment Program or for a judicial review to the Federal Court) convinced that they can delay their removal and continue to enjoy the benefits of living in Canada for several years.

In response to this, there have been legislative amendments that give the minister the power to designate certain countries the government considers to be non-refugee producing as "designated countries of origin."[6] New policies and procedures are being implemented to deter those who are considering using Canada's refugee determination process for immigration rather than for protection purposes. For example, the process for a claimant from a designated country of origin would be quicker, and failed claimants would not have the same post-determination rights as those from refugee-producing countries, and consequently could be removed from Canada much sooner.

But for those who genuinely seek protection, their motivation or intent is rooted in suffering, rather than a desire for economic betterment. Unlike immigrants, who make a considered decision to leave their homelands, refugees do not have a choice: they are forced to flee because of some serious risk to their life or because they are victims of human rights abuses, and they cannot safely return home. The fundamental difference, therefore, between a refugee and an immigrant or an illegal immigrant is that a refugee needs protection, which is not provided by their government of the country of origin.

The UNHCR defines asylum as "the right to be recognized as bona fide refugees and receive legal protection and material assistance." Therefore, in keeping with our legal obligation, Canada generally allows strangers who ask for legal protection to enter the country, then extends basic civil and legal rights and will not return them until it is proved whether they need longer-term protection.

Another part of our formal commitment to identifying and protecting refugees is Canada's legal obligation to respect the basic rights of refugee claimants by enabling them to live normal lives. Consequently, refugee claimants are provided with work authorizations and have access to financial, legal, and medical assistance if required. As well, their children are allowed to attend public school.

Finally, Canada's commitment includes a refugee determination system. The process for deciding who is and who is not a genuine refugee is complex and can be lengthy because each case must be decided individually and on its own merits. Until a decision is made about the claim, the individual is called a **refugee claimant**.

The challenge is that we do not know whether that person knocking at Canada's door is indeed a refugee until her case has been decided by a member of the RPD who has the specialized knowledge and training to make that determination.

In-Canada Refugee Determination Process

The in-Canada refugee determination process is for refugees who make claims for refugee protection status at the Canadian border or from an immigration office inland. While the entire process includes the involvement of CIC and the Canada Border Services Agency (CBSA), the mandate to decide refugee claims rests exclusively with the Immigration and Refugee Board (IRB) through its Refugee Protection Division (RPD) and the Refugee Appeal Board. The participation, role, and mandate of each of these organizations are very specific, and this partially explains why the process is so complex and often misunderstood. This program is discussed in greater detail in Chapter 9, In-Canada Refugee Determination Process.

Pre-Removal Risk Assessment Program

Claimants in Canada who are unsuccessful in arguing their case for refugee status, and who claim to face a risk if they are returned to their country of origin, may apply to have that risk assessed. Until recently, CIC was responsible for this program. Legislative changes have transferred the authority to evaluate the risk of return and decide applications to the Refugee Protection Division. This program is discussed further in Chapter 9, In-Canada Refugee Determination Process.

KEY TERMS

alienage, 267

balance of probabilities, 276

cessation clause, 282

convention, 264

Convention refugee, 266

crimes against humanity, 280

derogable right, 274

nationality, 272

non-derogable right, 274

non-political crimes, 281

non-state agent, 271

persecution, 270

person in need of protection, 274

principle of *non-refoulement*, 266

ratification, 264

refugee, 264

refugee claimant, 285

refugee *sur place*, 273

resettlement, 265

risk of cruel and unusual treatment or punishment, 278

risk to life, 278

state agent, 271

torture, 277

voluntary repatriation, 265

well-founded fear, 268

REVIEW QUESTIONS

Introduction

1. What is the fundamental difference between an immigrant and a refugee?

2. Describe in your own words the principle of *non-refoulement*.

3. What is a refugee *sur place*?

International Conventions

1. Name the two international instruments that are the basis for determining refugee status in Canada.

2. Name the two international human rights instruments that are the basis for protecting persons in need of protection in Canada.

3. List the ways that the UNHCR, as the main agency offering international legal protection for refugees, helps the world's uprooted peoples.

Canada's Programs

1. What three ways does Canada provide protection to refugees?

2. What is the name of the IRB division that has exclusive jurisdiction to hear and decide refugee claims in Canada?

Scope of Protection

1. What are the three clauses of the Convention refugee definition that have been adopted in the IRPA?

2. What are the five grounds of persecution contained in the definition of a Convention refugee?

3. Under what sections of the IRPA can a refugee claimant ask for protection when the Refugee Convention definition does not fit the claimant's situation?

Exclusions

On what grounds may a person be excluded from *non-refoulement* protection?

Cessation of Protection

In what situations does refugee protection cease to apply under the IRPA?

DISCUSSION QUESTION

Discuss why refugee protection is not intended to be a permanent status.

NOTES

1. *Convention Relating to the Status of Refugees*, 189 U.N.T.S. 150 (entered into force April 22, 1954), art. 33(1).

2. *Handbook on Procedures and Criteria for Determining Refugee Status Under the 1951 Convention and the 1967 Protocol Relating to the Status of Refugees*, HCR/IP/4/Eng/REV.1, re-edited, Geneva, January 1992, UNHCR 1979.

3. *Li v. Canada (Minister of Citizenship and Immigration)* (2005), 249 D.L.R. (4th) 306 (F.C.A.).

4. Camille Giffard, *The Torture Reporting Handbook*, Human Rights Centre, University of Essex, 2000. http://www.essex.ac.uk/torturehandbook/handbook.

5. See *Charter of the United Nations*, October 24, 1945, U.N.T.S. XVI, chapter I, article 1, for the full text of these purposes.

6. The passage of Bill C-11 (*Balanced Refugee Reform Act*, which received royal assent on June 29, 2010) and Bill C-31 (*Protecting Canada's Immigration System Act*, which received royal assent on June 28, 2012), resulted in amendments to the IRPA. Many of the changes affect the inland refugee determination process, and are expected to come into force no later than June 28, 2014. These changes include, for example, new powers that allow the minister to designate certain countries of origin so as to limit access to the refugee appeal process.

REFERENCES

Balanced Refugee Reform Act. S.C. 2010, c. 8 (formerly Bill C-11).

Canada (Attorney General) v. Ward. [1993] 2 S.C.R. 689, 103 D.L.R. (4th) 1, 20 Imm. L.R. (2d) 85 at 692 and 739.

Canada. "Regulations Amending the Immigration and Refugee Protection Regulations, Regulatory Impact Analysis." *Canada Gazette, Part I: Notices and Proposed Regulations*, vol. 145, no. 12, March 19, 2011.

Canadian Heritage. "Background Information, International Covenant on Civil and Political Rights," November 2005. http://www.pch.gc.ca/ddp-hrd/docs/pacon/101-eng.cfm.

Coakeley, Simon. "New Developments in the Refugee Determination System: Presentation to the Canadian Council for Refugees, Hamilton," May 26, 2011. http://www.irb-cisr.gc.ca/Eng/media/newsnouv/2011/Pages/ccrsn.aspx.

Convention Against Torture and Other Cruel, Inhuman or Degrading Treatment or Punishment. G.A. res. 39/46, annex, 39 U.N. GAOR Supp. (no. 51) at 197, U.N. Doc. A/39/51 (1984), entered into force June 26, 1987.

Criminal Code. R.S.C. 1985, c. C-46.

Department of Justice. "Canada's Accession to the United Nations Second Optional Protocol to the International Covenant on Civil and Political Rights, Aiming at the Abolition of the Death Penalty," November 2005. http://canada.justice.gc.ca/en/news/nr/2005/doc_31756.html.

Human Rights Web. *A Summary of United Nations Agreements on Human Rights*. Created July 8, 1994, last edited January 25, 1997. http://www.hrweb.org/legal/undocs.html.

Immigration and Refugee Protection Act. S.C. 2001, c. 27.

Immigration and Refugee Protection Regulations. S.O.R./2002-227.

International Covenant on Civil and Political Rights. G.A. res. 2200A (XXI), 21 U.N. GAOR Supp. (no. 16) at 52, U.N. Doc. A/6316 (1966), 999 U.N.T.S. 171, entered into force March 23, 1976.

Legal Services, Immigration and Refugee Board. *Consolidated Grounds in the Immigration and Refugee Protection Act: Persons in Need of Protection—Danger of Torture*, May 15, 2002. http://www.irb-cisr.gc.ca/eng/brdcom/references/legjur/Pages/ProtectTorture.aspx.

Legal Services, Immigration and Refugee Board. *Consolidated Grounds in the Immigration and Refugee Protection Act: Persons in Need of Protection—Risk to Life or Risk of Cruel and Unusual Treatment or Punishment*. http://www.irb-cisr.gc.ca/eng/brdcom/references/legjur/Pages/ProtectLifVie.aspx.

Legal Services, Immigration and Refugee Board. *Interpretation of the Convention Refugee Definition in the Case Law*. December 31, 2010. http://www.irb-cisr.gc.ca/eng/brdcom/references/legjur/Pages/Def2010.aspx.

United Nations High Commissioner for Refugees. *Guidelines on International Protection: Application of the Exclusion Clauses—Article 1F of the 1951 Convention Relating to the Status of Refugees*, HCR/GIP/03/05, 4 September 2003. http://www.unhcr.org/3f7d48514.html.

United Nations High Commission for Refugees. *Handbook on Procedures and Criteria for Determining Refugee Status Under the 1951 Convention and the 1967 Protocol Relating to the Status of Refugees*, HCR/IP/4/Eng/REV.1, re-edited, Geneva, January 1992, UNHCR 1979. http://www.unhcr.org/publ/PUBL/3d58e13b4.pdf.

United Nations High Commissioner for Refugees. *Refugee Status Determination: Identifying Who Is a Refugee—Self-Study Module 2*, September 1, 2005. http://www.unhcr.org/publ/PUBL/43144dc52.pdf.

Universal Declaration of Human Rights, G.A. res. 217A (III), U.N. Doc A/810 at 71 (1948).

RECOMMENDED READING

Canadian Heritage. Human Rights Program. http://www.pch.gc.ca/ddp-hrd/index-eng.cfm. Describes the UN human rights system, UN instruments, and how Canada is involved in this area; provides a glossary of specialized terms and weblinks to related sites.

Office of the United Nations High Commissioner for Human Rights. http://www.ohchr.org/EN/Pages/WelcomePage.aspx.

Statutes of the United Nations

Convention Relating to the Status of Refugees. 189 U.N.T.S. 150, entered into force April 22, 1954. http://www2.ohchr.org/english/law/refugees.htm.

Protocol Relating to the Status of Refugees. 606 U.N.T.S. 267, entered into force October 4, 1967. http://www2.ohchr.org/english/law/protocolrefugees.htm.

Convention Against Torture and Other Cruel, Inhuman or Degrading Treatment or Punishment. Can. T.S. 1987 no. 36; G.A. res. 39/46 (annex, 39 U.N. GAOR Supp. (no. 51) at 197, U.N. Doc. A/39/51 (1984)). http://www2.ohchr.org/english/law/cat.htm.

International Covenant on Civil and Political Rights. G.A. res. 2200A (XXI), 21 U.N. GAOR Supp. (No. 16) at 52, U.N. Doc. A/6316 (1966), 999 U.N.T.S. 171, entered into force March 23, 1976. http://www2.ohchr.org/english/law/ccpr.htm.

Universal Declaration of Human Rights. G.A. res. 217A (III) U.N. Doc. A/810 at 71 (1948). http://www.un.org/Overview/rights.html.

Human Rights Organizations

Amnesty International. An international organization whose mission is to conduct research and promote action to prevent human rights abuses. http://www.amnesty.org.

Canadian Council for Refugees. A non-profit umbrella organization that promotes the rights and protection of refugees, both in Canada and internationally. Composed of organizations that aid in the settlement, sponsorship, and protection of refugees and immigrants. http://ccrweb.ca.

Human Rights Watch. An organization dedicated to protecting the human rights of people around the world and investigating human rights violations. http://www.hrw.org.

Country-Specific Sources for Research Purposes

Amnesty International Report 2012. http://thereport.amnesty.org.

Human Rights Watch Country Reports. http://www.hrw.org/publications/reports.

US State Department Country Reports on Human Rights Practices. http://www.state.gov/j/drl/rls/hrrpt.

Refugee and Humanitarian Resettlement Program

8

LEARNING OUTCOMES

After reading this chapter you should be able to:

- Understand Canada's role in the resettlement of refugees.

- Identify the organizations involved in refugee resettlement.

- Define the different classes of refugees under the resettlement program.

- Describe the eligibility criteria for applying for resettlement.

- Describe the inadmissibility assessment that forms part of the resettlement application process.

- Understand the role and obligations of different types of sponsors of refugees.

- Describe the kinds of assistance available to refugees who apply for resettlement.

Introduction

Canada offers protection to the world's displaced people through the Refugee and Humanitarian Resettlement Program. The program is intended to protect refugees and people in refugee-like situations for the following purposes:

- to address humanitarian needs;
- to meet international responsibilities; and
- to respond to international crises.

The Refugee and Humanitarian Resettlement Program applies only to those refugees who are located outside Canada, such as those who have sought temporary refuge in camps across the border from their war-torn countries. The program is managed by Citizenship and Immigration Canada (CIC). Canadian officials from missions abroad work with the United Nations High Commission for Refugees (UNHCR) and various non-governmental organizations (NGOs) to identify refugees and persons in refugee-like situations who are in need of resettlement.

Note that the Refugee and Humanitarian Resettlement Program does not apply to refugee claimants seeking a status determination while already inside Canada. Refugee claimants who have found their own way here are subject to different procedures, which are examined in Chapter 9, In-Canada Refugee Determination Process.

The program is part of a broader international effort led by the UNHCR to find durable solutions for refugees. A **durable solution** is a lasting solution, and in the context of refugee law generally means one of the following:

- *voluntary repatriation:* voluntary return to the home country because it is safe to do so;
- *local integration:* integration in the country of refuge; or
- *resettlement:* resettlement in a third country such as Canada, where a participating state provides legal and physical protection that should eventually lead to citizenship.

Consider the following scenario:

Dumo Akuak's husband was killed a year ago by a land mine, and she was left with five young children to support. One night, she was awakened by the screams of neighbours. She smelled fire and could make out flames in the dark. Was the village under attack by soldiers? Rebels? Dumo was not sure because both sides had been involved in a conflict in this region of Solaria for the past year. Dumo shouted out to her children and together they fled into the night wearing only light sleepwear. The family hid in the bush and waited until dawn. There was nothing left of their home. She tried to shield her children's eyes from the hacked-up bodies that lay on the side of the road. Dumo and her children set out for the border of a neighbouring country, hoping to find safety. They walked for days, and along the way met others who had lost their homes, parents, spouses, and children.

By the time they reached the border, Dumo and her family had not eaten in days; the children were so weak they could not even cry. Somehow Dumo found her way to a temporary camp; but it soon filled up. Dumo waited in line for hours to register for shelter; life had become one long line-up for water, food rations, and news. The family lived in limbo, with no status in the new country; they could not work legally and the children were not allowed to attend school. Life was on hold as they spent the next year living in a temporary tent city as refugees. The family waited for the day when they could safely return home.

When a refugee does not have the option, in the foreseeable future, of either returning home or integrating into the country fled to, the only durable solution for a safe and viable new life is resettlement in a third country. Resettlement offers protection to those who need it, and Canada shares in the responsibility of resettling refugees for whom resettlement is the appropriate durable solution.

Canada has been providing humanitarian assistance to people fleeing conflicts and persecution in their homeland since the end of the Second World War. There are only a small number of states that participate in the UNHCR's resettlement program—the number was only recently increased to 25 from 16. Canada is traditionally ranked among the top-three countries participating in the program.[1] This country has a history of accepting large numbers of persecuted and displaced persons, including refugees from the following countries:

- Hungary, in the 1950s;
- Czechoslovakia, in the 1960s;
- Chile, Uganda, and Vietnam, in the 1970s;
- the former Yugoslavia, in the late 1990s;
- Sudan and Somalia, in 2003;
- the Karen refugees (from Myanmar), in 2006;
- the resettlement of 230 Tibetans from Northern India under the Tibetan Refugee Program in 1972, and 1,000 Tibetans from the state of Arunachal Pradesh in India, over a period of five years beginning in 2010;
- the resettlement of over 550 Afghan nationals beginning in 2009 under a special immigration measures program for those who supported the Canadian mission to Kandahar and faced extraordinary and individualized risk as a result of that work; and
- most recently, Bhutanese refugees from Nepal, between 2008 and 2012.

Refugees who resettle in Canada need a lot of support to adapt to their new home and become self-sufficient. A significant feature of the Refugee and Humanitarian Resettlement Program is that it allows private groups to sponsor refugees. Sponsorship is an important feature of the program, which provides financial and other resources to refugees. Generally, refugees who are resettled in Canada become permanent residents upon their arrival and this may lead to citizenship.

Targets

The minister of CIC reports on the number of refugees who have resettled in the prior year, in the annual **immigration resettlement plan**. As we learned in Chapter 2, the minister tables this plan every year, and includes the number and types of foreign nationals who can come to Canada as permanent residents. Included in this plan are Canada's targets for resettlement by class of refugee.

These targets are established through consultations both within the CIC and between the CIC and provincial governments, Canadian non-governmental organizations, and the UNHCR. Funding is then allocated to visa offices on the basis of projected resettlement needs.

Under the government's plan to reform immigration and refugee policies, the government announced that it will continue the tradition of resettling refugees.

This chapter provides an overview of Canada's Refugee and Humanitarian Resettlement Program, including the various types of sponsorship and settlement assistance available.

Important Organizations

There are many organizations, agencies, and people who assist refugees in their quest for a durable solution. Three of the most important organizations are described below.

United Nations High Commissioner for Refugees

A person seeking to apply to resettle in Canada is required under s. 150(1) of the *Immigration and Refugee Protection Regulations* (IRP Regulations) to provide an **undertaking** or a referral from a recognized referral organization. Currently, the only referral organization recognized by the Canadian government is the UNHCR. The UNHCR's responsibilities include finding solutions to refugee problems, including resettling refugees in Canada. UNHCR selects refugees—often those involved in protracted situations—when local integration in the host country is not a viable or feasible solution. The role of the UNHCR is to assess each refugee's situation and identify to CIC those cases for which resettlement is the only durable solution. Cases where the UNHCR deems there are risks to the refugee's life, liberty, safety, health, or fundamental human rights in the country of refuge, are typically referred. The UNHCR provides a letter or document to a Canadian visa office, which serves as documentary proof of the referral.

Citizenship and Immigration Canada

CIC is the federal department responsible for the selection process for refugees and persons in refugee-like situations from abroad (with the exception of Quebec, which has its own resettlement process under the Canada–Quebec Accord). Visa officers receive referrals from the UNHCR or named referrals from private sponsors as well as applications for resettlement from those in need of resettlement. They assess, evaluate, and decide the outcome of the applications on the basis of whether the applicant for resettlement meets Canadian statutory eligibility and admissibility requirements.

In assessing applications, visa officers place emphasis on the following principles, which are articulated in the objectives of s. 3(2) of the *Immigration and Refugee Protection Act* (IRPA):

- to recognize that Canada's refugee program is about saving lives and offering protection to persecuted and displaced persons;
- to facilitate rapid refugee family reunification;
- to develop relationships with partners, such as sponsors; and
- to accelerate the processing of urgent and vulnerable protection cases.

CIC works with the International Organization for Migration (IOM) to coordinate the refugee's travel and resettlement arrangements.

International Organization for Migration

Established in 1951, the **International Organization for Migration (IOM)** is an intergovernmental organization that assists in the resettlement of displaced persons, refugees, and migrants and works closely with governmental, intergovernmental, and non-governmental partners. Canada is a founding member and a full member of the IOM and works with the organization in resettlement cases.

The IOM organizes and makes arrangements for the transfer of refugees, displaced persons, and other individuals in need of international migration services to receiving countries. It also arranges counselling and performs medical examinations or screens medical documents for refugees. In several locations around the world, the IOM assists refugees in language training, reception, and the integration process before they arrive in Canada through an in-depth Canadian Orientation Abroad (COA) program, which serves "to reduce their levels of anxiety while increasing the overall chances of successful integration, and empowering them to adapt more rapidly to the day-to-day demands of their new life."[2]

Classes of Refugees

There are two main classes of refugees covered by the Refugee and Humanitarian Resettlement Program: the Convention refugees abroad class and the humanitarian-protected persons abroad class.[3] The country of asylum class is a prescribed subclass under the humanitarian-protected persons abroad class. The definitions and criteria for each are provided in the IRP Regulations.

Convention Refugees Abroad Class

As the name suggests, refugees under the Convention refugees abroad class must first be granted that status under the Convention by the UNHCR. Refugees, however, must apply for resettlement outside Canada (this is a different process from the one for those arriving in Canada, as discussed in Chapter 9), and it must be established that no other durable solution (such as voluntary repatriation or integration in the host country of refuge) other than resettlement is viable.

To qualify for resettlement as members of the Convention refugees abroad class, individuals must posses the necessary financial resources to resettle. Many, however, do not have such resources, so part of the qualifying criteria requires that financial assistance be available to them to support themselves and their dependants through government assistance or private sponsorship (described later in this chapter.)

Humanitarian-Protected Persons Abroad Class

The humanitarian-protected persons abroad class includes persons who are not Convention refugees but who are in refugee-like situations.

Country of Asylum Class

The country of asylum class includes individuals who have fled their countries and who are the victims of war or the massive violations of human rights. Section 147 of the IRP Regulations defines members of the country of asylum class as individuals who "have been, and continue to be, seriously and personally affected by civil war, armed conflict or massive violation of human rights." In this context, "seriously and personally affected" refers to a sustained and effective denial of basic human rights. Additionally, to qualify as refugees for resettlement under this class, individuals must

- be outside all of their countries of nationality and/or habitual residence;
- apply for resettlement when outside Canada; and
- be in need of resettlement because no other durable solution other than re-settlement is viable for them.

Applicants for resettlement under this class must have a private sponsor or have their own financial means to support themselves and their dependants. In certain situations, they may qualify for a joint assistance sponsorship if they also qualify as a special needs case, described below.

Special Needs Cases

All types of special needs refugees must be members of the Convention refugees abroad or humanitarian-protected persons abroad classes. The label "special needs" means that there is special consideration of these cases, including priority processing and a deviation from the routine assessment eligibility criteria. Two categories of special needs cases are defined in s. 138 of the IRP Regulations: urgent protection cases and vulnerable persons cases. These cases are given special consideration because they involve refugees in greater need of protection or in more immediate danger.

In assessing applications for special needs cases, the visa officer gives more weight to the need for protection than to the refugee's ability to settle in Canada. In these cases, the criteria are not applied as strictly, and individuals may be accepted despite having limited settlement prospects, because the overriding concern is their safety.

All special needs cases are exempt from the requirement under s. 139(1)(g) of the IRP Regulations to successfully establish.

Special needs cases usually require expedited processing. The visa officer issues a protected temporary resident visa in situations like these to allow the refugee to travel to Canada prior to the completion of the admissibility assessment process. The admissibility assessment, regarding medical, security, and criminality concerns (as discussed in Chapter 3, Inadmissibility) is completed after the refugee is in Canada. While awaiting the finalization of their application they hold the status in Canada as protected temporary residents, which is a prescribed class under the IRP Regulations (s. 151.1). When the applicant passes the assessment, the refugee may then apply for permanent residence from within Canada.

Urgent Protection Program

A person in **urgent need of protection** is defined in s. 138 of the IRP Regulations as someone whose life, liberty, or physical safety is under immediate threat and who, if returned to his country of nationality or former habitual residence, is likely to be killed or subjected to violence, torture, sexual assault, or arbitrary imprisonment.

When the UNHCR identifies an emergency case to a visa office where a refugee is in need of urgent protection because of immediate threats, the Urgent Protection Program (UPP) allows Canada to respond. Resettlement in urgent protection cases is undertaken as a priority where there is no other way to guarantee the security of the person concerned.

Vulnerable Cases

The term "**vulnerable**," as defined in s. 138 of the IRP Regulations, describes a person with a greater need of protection than other applicants for protection abroad, because of the person's particular circumstances that give rise to a heightened risk to their physical safety.

For example, a visa officer may identify as vulnerable a female refugee who is at risk of rape or sexual abuse because she does not have the protection of a family or support network. Similarly, victims of torture who are in need of medical treatment may be deemed vulnerable.

Women at Risk Program

The UNHCR identifies refugee women who are in dangerous situations and refers them for resettlement. The **Women at Risk Program** is designed to offer resettlement to women who are members of the Convention refugees abroad or humanitarian-protected persons abroad class so that they may be admitted to Canada even if they do not meet the normal regulatory standard of "ability to establish" themselves. Furthermore, although inadmissibility on the grounds of security risk, violating human or international rights, serious criminality, organized criminality, and health risk or burden is still assessed, policies and procedures are in place to assess these grounds less stringently. For example, in the assessment of inadmissibility on criminality grounds, it is a matter of policy that officers do not require refugees to submit police certificates or certificates of no criminal conviction from their home country because of the risk of alerting authorities in their country of alleged persecution. Instead, officers may request police certificates from countries of temporary asylum. Also, under s. 38(2) of the IRPA, women at risk are exempted from inadmissibility on the ground of creating excessive demand on Canada's health care system.

In times of conflict, it is often civilian women who suffer violence, abuse, and exploitation. Women in these circumstances generally require additional assistance re-establishing themselves. They often are unable to meet the eligibility requirement of having the potential to become self-sufficient in the short or medium term. Women refugees face special, gender-based problems and can be at risk for a multitude of reasons, including the following:

- *They are alone.* A woman may have lost her husband, may not have the protection of a male relative or family members, and may be isolated because of the stigma of being raped or abused.
- *They lack basic skills.* A woman may be illiterate, and may lack the knowledge or experience necessary for dealing with local authorities.
- *They face health concerns.* A woman and her children may face exacerbated health problems as a result of living in refugee camps or as a result of conflict, famine, war-related injuries, or lack of medical attention.
- *They are vulnerable.* A woman and her children may be vulnerable to violence, sexual abuse, and sexual exploitation, and may have experienced harassment by local authorities or even by members of her own community.
- *They face barriers to resettlement.* A woman may have a minimal level of education, limited job skills, or heavy child-care responsibilities.

A woman who has been identified as "at risk" requires help in starting a new life. Generally, a woman who is resettled under this program requires a joint assistance sponsorship, described below, and needs a longer period to become integrated and established in Canada.

The Application for Refugee Resettlement

Refugees in need of resettlement must apply for permanent residence under the program at a Canadian high commission, embassy, or consulate outside their home country. The Canadian government sponsors some refugees and works closely with non-governmental organizations, such as refugee groups, religious communities, and ethnic associations, in sponsoring refugees for resettlement in Canada.

Applicants must meet the general criteria for permanent residence set out in s. 139 of the IRP Regulations unless they qualify for an exemption. These criteria include the requirement in s. 139(1)(g) that

if the foreign national intends to reside in a province other than the Province of Quebec, the foreign national and their family members included in the application for protection will be able to become successfully established in Canada.

Exemptions are made in special needs cases, discussed above under the heading "Special Needs Cases."

An application for refugee resettlement must be accompanied by a referral from the UNHCR or by an undertaking for private sponsorship. Applications are submitted to a Canadian high commission, embassy, or consulate outside the refugee's home country. For refugees destined to Quebec, they require a Certificat de sélection du Québec[4] along with the required documentation.

Copies of documents must be translated and certified. In situations where the refugee applicant cannot provide all the necessary documentation, such as if the documents are not available from her homeland or don't exist, an explanation is required. Failure to explain why documents are missing will result in rejection of the application as incomplete.

There are no application or processing fees for refugees applying for permanent residence under this program, and the refugee applicant receives a letter of confirmation with a file number once the visa office receives the application.

The refugee applicant must meet the statutory requirements for admissibility to Canada, which apply to almost all new immigrants, and the statutory requirements for eligibility under the Refugee and Humanitarian Resettlement Program.[5]

Eligibility

The refugee applicant must be eligible for resettlement under the Refugee and Humanitarian Resettlement Program, which means they must

1. be referred by the UNHCR[6] or by an undertaking by a private sponsor (IRP Regulations, s. 150(1); and

2. meet the regulatory definition of one of the following:

   • a member of the Convention refugees abroad class; or
   • a member of the country of asylum class.

A Canadian visa officer decides whether the applicant falls into one of the classes of refugees and is eligible under the program, which includes meeting selection criteria and not being inadmissible. A visa officer generally holds an interview to supplement the refugee's application and supporting documentation. If the applicant is found to be ineligible, the application is rejected. If, on the other hand, the refugee is found eligible, than she must undergo further screening for admissibility.

Individuals whose applications have previously been rejected may not reapply unless they can show that their circumstances have changed or that they have new information that was not available in their previous application. Also, an applicant is not eligible if

• she already has the protection of another country and is allowed to live in that country;
• she has integrated into the host country; or
• she can safely return home.

Admissibility

Just like any applicant for permanent residence, there are a number of checks that an applicant must pass to establish that she is "not inadmissible." (Inadmissibility is described in detail in Chapter 3.) The visa officer considers the information along with the documents provided in the application and the interview, and determines whether the refugee applicant is inadmissible. Some refugee applicants do not have to meet the normal requirement for being self-sufficient because they are exempted from financial inadmissibility by s. 139(3) of the IRP Regulations.

The following is a very brief overview of four of the grounds of inadmissibility as they relate to this program:

1. *Medical inadmissibility.* Canada normally bars someone who is inadmissible for health reasons because of a health condition that is likely to be a danger to public health, a health condition that is likely to be a danger to public safety, or a health condition that might reasonably be expected to cause excessive demand on health or social services. Refugee applicants, however, are exempted from the "excessive demand" grounds by s. 139(4) of the IRP Regulations. Nevertheless, all refugee applicants and their dependants must undergo medical examinations for health and public safety reasons. They must pass a medical examination to ensure that no medical condition exists that is likely to be a danger to Canadian public health or safety. The examination is carried out by a **panel physician** (a local physician), who is authorized to perform a medical examination by the Canadian government.

   If a refugee applicant cannot afford to pay for the medical examination, a loan may be issued under the provisions of the Immigration Loans Program, described below. In countries where the IOM is arranging travel for the refugees, the IOM may also arrange and prepay medical examinations. The IOM usually covers the cost of medical examinations for those refugees who are referred by the UNHCR. Canada later reimburses the IOM for costs incurred on behalf of refugees resettled to Canada.

2. and 3. *Serious criminality grounds* and *criminal checks.* The refugee applicant is not required to submit a police certificate from the country from which he is fleeing, and Canada does not contact organizations or individuals that could place the refugee applicant or family members in danger. However, a police certificate may be requested from any host country that granted the applicant temporary asylum.

4. *Security or violation of human or international rights.* A refugee applicant can be inadmissible on security grounds because of her own activities or those of an organization to which she belongs outside Canada, where the activities are related to espionage, subversion, and terrorism or are considered to be a danger to the security of Canada or which might endanger the lives or safety of persons in Canada. An applicant can also be found inadmissible if she has been convicted of, or has committed, crimes against humanity (for example, extermination, enslavement, imprisonment, torture, sexual violence, or persecution committed against any civilian population), genocide, or war crimes.

Applicants who held positions with the government or military regimes that participated in war crimes or crimes against humanity are inadmissible as a risk to security. Likewise, individuals who belong to organizations that espouse violence, such as terrorist groups, are also inadmissible.

If an applicant is found inadmissible, his application is rejected.

Selection Factors and the Admissibility Interview

Refugees who seek protection when already in Canada cannot be subjected to immigration selection criteria, unless they are first sent back to their country of nationality or former habitual residence. Obviously, this would not be an appropriate response to those claiming to have fled persecution and violence. However, applicants for permanent residence under the Refugee and Humanitarian Resettlement Program are not yet in Canada, and a process of selection is necessary to ensure that the number of refugees admitted does not exceed the resources available for their absorption in Canada.

There are a number of methods of selection, such as by order of application ("first come, first served"), by need, or by ability to become self-sufficient. The Refugee and Humanitarian Resettlement Program first emphasizes need and the ability to become self-sufficient, although once applicants are in the system, they are processed in the order received. Need may take priority over other considerations when an applicant falls within one of the special needs categories of urgent protection, vulnerable cases, or women at risk. For example, the selection factors with respect to self-sufficiency are not applied as strictly in cases identified by a visa officer as special needs because the overriding concern is protection.

Applicants that do not fall within a special needs category are assessed on the basis of their ability to become self-sufficient within three to five years of their arrival in Canada. To determine the likelihood of the applicant's attaining self-sufficiency, the visa officer considers a modified version of the factors measured by the formal point system of skills and adaptability that is applied to skilled workers in the economic class (see Chapter 5). Refugees are interviewed as part of the selection process, and the following factors are considered:

- education;
- work experience and qualifications;
- language abilities in English or French; and
- suitability factors such as a support network of family connections or a sponsor.

Although these factors are similar to those used in the formal point system, the threshold for refugees is much less onerous. Also, CIC's guidelines for assessing refugee applicants instruct the visa officer to assess the refugee's qualities that "assist in integration" such as personal characteristics of "initiative, resourcefulness, ingenuity, perseverance or other characteristics."[7]

To illustrate the process by which the selection factors are evaluated, we return to our example of Dumo Akuak, an Inka refugee from Solaria:

The UNHCR came in contact with Dumo and her family in a refugee camp located in a neighbouring country to Dumo's. A UNHCR protection officer assessed Dumo's situation and determined that resettlement was the only durable solution. Furthermore, because Dumo is a single woman with five children, the officer concluded that hers was an urgent case.

To serve as documentary proof of the UNHCR's referral, a refugee referral form would then be sent to a Canadian visa office. The form includes the refugee claim and information about the family. The family would then submit an application for permanent residence, along with their referral, to the Canadian embassy located in the capital of the host country.

In the host country, a Canadian visa officer would assess Dumo's application. In some cases, visa officers travel to camps to interview refugee applicants, and in other cases, interviews are held at the embassy or consulate.

In Dumo's case, the interview was held in person at the visa office to determine the family's admissibility and the appropriate refugee class, and to assess Dumo's ability to become self-sufficient in Canada as a permanent resident. An interpreter was provided at the interview.

The interview is used to establish identity, settlement plans, and the ability to be self-supporting. When assessing Dumo, the visa officer would ask many questions and consider many factors.

The visa officer determined that Dumo and her family were not personally subjected to persecution in their country of origin and therefore did not meet the regulatory definition of persons under the Convention refugees abroad class. However, because of their ethnic and religious background, there was a reasonable chance, given the genocide in their country of origin, that they were at risk should they be returned there.

The visa officer also determined that even if the Akuak family were not Convention refugees, they met the requirements for the country of asylum subclass of the humanitarian-protected persons abroad class. They had fled their country as a result of war and human rights violations. They had been seriously and personally affected—their home was destroyed and their lives threatened.

Before permitting Dumo to resettle in Canada under the Refugee and Humanitarian Program, the visa officer would consider the following criteria:

- *No other durable solution.* The host country was not willing or able to take Dumo and her children permanently, and they would be at risk if returned to their home country. Resettlement was the only viable and durable solution.

- *Self-sufficiency.* Normally, Dumo would have had to demonstrate to the visa officer that she had the potential to become self-sufficient within three to five years and not burden Canada by depending on social assistance after that time period. To assess Dumo's earning potential, the visa officer asked about her level of education, work experience and training, language skills, and whether she had any family in Canada. Dumo had a grade 8 education, and her work experience was limited to fieldwork for a neighbouring farm and her own small garden. She spoke broken English, and had no known family in Canada. Furthermore, she would have to take care of a large family on her own. However, the visa officer was impressed by the speed with which Dumo was learning English and by her resourcefulness in taking care of her five children under such terrible circumstances.

- *Private sponsor or financial means.* Dumo had neither a private sponsor nor the financial means to support herself and her five children.
- *Inadmissibility.* The visa officer also found that Dumo was not inadmissible to Canada on security and criminality grounds.

Dumo had come this far, but might have been rejected by Canada. Fortunately for her, the visa officer determined that she qualified for government assistance as a special-needs case. The UNHCR referral identified her for the Women at Risk Program as a woman alone, without the protection of a male relative, and particularly vulnerable because of her five young dependent children. As a result, her poor outlook for self-sufficiency in three to five years was given less weight, and she was entitled to a joint assistance sponsorship. She was also able to defer medical examinations for her and the children, necessary to confirm their admissibility, until after they arrived in Canada.

Because Dumo and her family were destined to a country very different from their own, the officer believed she was a good candidate for the **Canadian Orientation Abroad (COA) program** to help her integrate into Canadian society. This program is conducted in partnership with the IOM and consists of learning modules that last from one to five days. Topics include an introduction to Canada, the settling-in period, employment, rights and responsibilities, climate, finding a place to live, living in a multicultural society, cost of living, family life, education, communications, and adaptation to Canada. She would attend the sessions before travelling to Canada.

Forms and Documents

An Application for Permanent Residence in Canada form (IMM 0008) is the generic form used to apply for permanent residence. Each refugee applicant over 18 years of age must submit it along with other forms that the department creates. Here are examples of some of the forms that have been required in the past:

- Background/Declaration form specifically created for refugees outside Canada;
- Use of a Representative form;
- Military Service Details form; and
- Supplementary Information form.

WEBLINK

All forms are available on the CIC website and include general guidelines for completing them—As of April 30, 2012, the guide entitled *Guide 6000 Convention Refugees Abroad and Humanitarian-Protected Persons Abroad* can be found at http://www.cic.gc.ca/ english/information/ applications/conref.asp.

There are many additional documents that applicants must also provide with their application forms, such as the following:

1. photos of each refugee applicant;
2. identity and civil status documents for each refugee applicant:
   - copy of birth certificate;
   - copy of marriage, divorce, annulment, or separation certificates;
   - copies of death certificates of family members; and
   - children's information—copy of birth certificate, adoption papers, proof of custody papers, etc.;
3. background documents for each refugee applicant (where applicable):
   - completion of military service card and military records;
   - membership cards (for social, political, vocational, and cultural organizations);
   - educational certificates, diplomas, school-leaving certificates;
   - trade/apprenticeship certificates; and
   - letters of reference from past employers;
4. travel documents for each refugee applicant:
   - copy of passport,
   - copy of national identity document, and
   - copy of UNHCR registration card or national refugee registration document;
5. proof of settlement funds (if self-supporting) including financial statements, and proof of assets; and
6. copy of the UNHCR referral or sponsorship undertaking (if privately sponsored).

There may be other documents required that are case or country specific. Generally, visa offices require that documents be translated into English or French.

Decision

The final decision as to whether to accept or reject a refugee applicant for resettlement is made by the visa officer, after a consideration of both the admissibility and eligibility criteria. Those accepted for resettlement are issued a confirmation of permanent residence and at the time of arrival in Canada are generally granted permanent resident status. They enjoy the same rights accorded to all permanent residents, and are eligible to apply for Canadian citizenship.

Applicants who are refused admission to Canada as refugees are informed of this decision and sent a letter outlining the reasons for the refusal. The IRPA does not specifically provide for a direct appeal of the visa officer's decision. However, the refused refugee applicant may seek leave for judicial review before the Federal Court of Canada.

Financial and Resettlement Support

Refugees and their families who are in need of resettlement and who do not have sufficient resources of their own may obtain support from a number of sources, as follows:

- the Canadian government, through the Government-Assisted Refugee (GAR) program;
- Canadian citizens and permanent residents, individually or in groups, through the Private Sponsorship of Refugees Program; or
- both the Canadian government and private sponsors, through the Joint Assistance Sponsorship (JAS) program.

The **Government-Assisted Refugee (GAR) program** applies only to the sponsorship of members of the Convention refugees abroad class, including special needs cases. Private sponsorship applies to all categories of refugees.

Government-Assisted Refugee (GAR) Program and Resettlement Assistance Program (RAP)

As the name suggests, government-assisted refugees are sponsored or supported by the Canadian or Quebec governments, generally through the Resettlement Assistance Program (RAP). Immigration loans and temporary health care may also be available.

Each year, the government of Canada plans for the resettlement of a number of refugees from abroad, and supports these refugees through the **Resettlement Assistance Program (RAP)**.

The RAP provides both financial and immediate essential services to government-assisted refugees, who require help integrating into their new community on their road to self-sufficiency and independence. Part of the eligibility requirements for resettlement, as noted above, is the ability to be self-supporting or to become self-supporting within 12 months of arrival (that is, posses the ability to find employment based on language and skills). Consider the following types of assistance available under the RAP:

- *Financial assistance.* The refugee's personal assets, as described in the application, are considered when assessing the need for financial assistance. The amount of income support is guided by provincial social assistance rates for food and shelter, and covers the most basic needs for up to 12 months after arrival in Canada, or up to an additional 24 months for refugees identified as special needs cases. This money may be used for food, clothing, accommodation, basic household goods and furniture, and incidentals such as soap and toothpaste.
- *Settlement assistance.* Unlike refugees who are privately sponsored, government-assisted refugees have no integration assistance from members

of the community. Therefore, from the moment they arrive, they will require assistance and so will be provided with reception at the airport, transportation, temporary accommodation and meals, and winter clothing if needed. They receive assistance locating permanent housing and are provided with household furnishings and basic necessities. They receive help completing essential paperwork, such as that concerning medical insurance, social insurance numbers, and child tax benefits. Furthermore, they receive language training, employment training, and vocational training, which are usually administered by Human Resources and Social Development Canada.

Settlement services are delivered by service provider organizations (SPOs), which consist of individuals, non-profit organizations, agencies serving immigrants, community groups, businesses, provincial and municipal governments, and educational institutions that receive funding from CIC.

Under RAP, settlement officers in Canada have authority to convert government-assisted refugees with special needs to the joint assistance sponsorship category after their arrival in Canada because they have determined that it will take longer for some refugees to adapt to resettlement and become self-sufficient.

Joint Assistance Sponsorship (JAS)

There are certain types of refugees who are not likely to become independent after only 12 months of living in Canada. Consider the following examples:

- women at risk;
- refugees who are severely traumatized by torture;
- large families of refugees;
- refugees who lived in refugee camps for extended periods; and
- refugees with medical conditions.

The **Joint Assistance Sponsorship (JAS) program** was designed to accommodate these kinds of situations. It is a hybrid of the GAR program and private sponsorship programs. The JAS program extends the normal sponsorship commitment of 12 months up to 24 months for special needs refugees, or 36 months in exceptional cases because of the extra care required for special needs cases.

Under the JAS program, the responsibilities for sponsorship are shared between CIC and private sponsors (see the discussion of private sponsors below). CIC provides the financial assistance necessary to meet basic resettlement costs such as food, shelter, clothing and essential household goods. The private sponsor provides the human contact of ongoing guidance, orientation to the community, and help with language skills and job searches, and friendship.

The IRP Regulations also allow for private sponsorships to be extended in exceptional circumstances (for example, when the refugee needs more time to resettle) and therefore the sponsor agrees to the extension and to divide the responsibilities of sponsorship with the government.

Other Government Programs

Immigration Loans

The **Immigration Loans Program (ILP)** is a special federal fund available to indigent refugees and immigrants who qualify by demonstrating both the need for the loan as well as the potential to repay it after arrival in Canada. Under the ILP, loans may be available to cover the cost of transportation to Canada, travel documents, immigration medical examinations, the right of permanent residence fee, and assistance loans to cover expenses such as housing rental and utilities.

Interest is charged at a rate set each January by the Department of Finance. However, members of the Convention refugees abroad and humanitarian-protected persons abroad classes may have a period of one to three years during which they will not be charged interest on their ILP loans. Also, under certain circumstances loan repayment may be deferred for up to two years, and special needs refugees (urgent protection, vulnerable cases, and women at risk) may be granted financial assistance in the form of a contribution that does not have to be repaid.

Interim Federal Health Program

Resettled refugees are eligible for provincial health coverage, generally within 90 days of arrival in the province or territory in which they reside. In the interim, the federal government provides essential and emergency health care coverage to refugees in need of assistance through the **Interim Federal Health Program (IFHP)**, administered by CIC. The IFHP provides health care coverage, public health or public safety health care coverage, or coverage of the immigration medical examination, on a temporary basis, to resettled refugees, refugees and protected persons, refugee claimants, rejected refugee claimants, and certain persons detained under the IRPA. Health care coverage is provided in Canada only if it is deemed to be of an urgent (that is, for an injury or illness that poses an immediate threat to a person's life, limb, or a bodily function) or essential (for example, illness, injury, or labour and delivery) nature. Health care may include:

- hospitalization;
- services by a medical professional (for example, a physician or a registered nurse);
- laboratory, diagnostic, and ambulance services; and
- immunization and medication only if required to prevent or treat a disease that poses a risk to public health or to public safety.

Private Sponsorship Programs

Private individuals often agree to sponsor relatives or members of their own communities. However, sometimes individuals or groups simply want to help others. Consider the following scenario:

Kim-Ly was only four when she, her parents, and two brothers fled the oppressive communist regime in Vietnam and arrived in Canada in 1980. She was one of 9,000 Indochinese "boat people" sponsored under Canada's newly created private sponsorship program. Kim-Ly's family settled in a small town in Ontario, the same community as the local church group that had sponsored her family. They were safe and in a new land now. They were the only Vietnamese family in town but that didn't matter to the community: people welcomed her family into their parish and their hearts. Kim-Ly recalls that there were always people around to help the family learn the intricacies of the English language, ensure they had the proper clothes for chilling winters, and take them to local fairs, Thanksgiving dinners, and pancake breakfasts. Kim-Ly's father, a former schoolteacher, eventually opened his own vegetable and flower shop in town. He became what people consider "independent" or "self-sufficient." Kim-Ly's mother stayed home to care for Kim-Ly, her two brothers, and a sister born here. Kim-Ly started junior kindergarten shortly after her arrival; eventually she earned a college diploma and then moved to the city to pursue a career in fashion.

On one of her recent visits to her parents' home, Kim-Ly became curious about her homeland and what led to her family's departure. Her parents had refused to speak about atrocities they suffered and witnessed. She doesn't have any memories of "back home"—Canada is the only home she knows. However, Kim-Ly did have frequent, horrible nightmares as a child and sometimes still wakes at night for no apparent reason. There is a great sadness behind her father's eyes that no one ever talks about. She remembers that her mother used to cry often. She probably suffered from bouts of depression from missing her relatives who were killed. Kim-Ly knows that her life was saved by the kind people who sponsored her family. She laments to her mother that there seem to be so many people in the world today who deserve the same help that she and her family received. Her mother peers over her glasses at Kim-Ly and says, "So why don't you sponsor a refugee? One at a time you can make a difference, Kim-Ly." Her voice trails off. Could she, Kim-Ly, really do that? Sponsor someone? She is excited ... but where to start?

The private sponsorship of refugees is the hallmark of Canada's refugee resettlement program, because it opens the door to a greater number of refugees and helps them to adapt to their new community. Sponsorship is considered a three-way commitment among the Canadian government, the sponsor, and the refugee.

Sponsors enter into a legal contract, called an undertaking, with the Canadian government, whereby they agree to be responsible for income support and medical costs for one year after the arrival of the refugee(s) they are sponsoring, and so much more. For example, sponsors help to find accommodation and basic household items, help the family adjust to their new community, and orient them to resources and services available in the community. This may involve assistance with basic activities such as banking, registering children for school, taking public transportation, shopping, and searching for a job. Sponsors may also help enroll adult refugees in English- or French-language classes, and with anything else that needs to be done to promote their self-sufficiency as soon as possible within the first 12 months of arrival.

Types of Private Sponsorship

Although sponsoring one refugee or an entire family can be rewarding, it requires some effort and there is much to do before the refugee arrives. In our example, Kim-Ly may or may not know whom to sponsor or from which part of the world. There are two ways to identify whom to sponsor for resettlement, as follows:

1. *Sponsor-referred cases.* The sponsor may know of a particular refugee or refugee family from contacts abroad or in Canada, and can identify them to CIC. For this reason, sponsor-referred cases are also known as **named cases**.

   Sponsors may know refugees through friends, relatives, or religious and community organizations. Often these cases involve refugees with relatives in Canada. Sponsor-referred sponsorships are meant to promote and facilitate family reunification, where refugee applicants meet the eligibility criteria of one of the refugee classes.

2. *Visa office-referred cases.* The sponsor may not personally know a refugee or a refugee family, and instead may be matched up by the visa office. For this reason, visa office-referred cases are also known as **unnamed cases**. Instead of identifying a specific refugee, the sponsor submits to CIC a Request for a Refugee Profile form, and CIC refers the request to the CIC Matching Centre. The sponsor then receives from CIC information that includes a description and profile about the refugee's family, community affiliation, language and work skills, and any special needs to determine whether the match is suitable for the sponsor.

Would-be sponsors must also determine their level of involvement in the sponsorship. Kim-Ly must decide whether she wants to be solely responsible for the sponsorship, or whether she would prefer to join a community group and share the responsibilities. Perhaps she would prefer to forgo responsibility altogether and simply donate money to an organization with experience in sponsoring refugees. CIC provides a Refugee Sponsorship Training Program to groups that are seriously interested in private sponsorship of refugees in need of resettlement. The following is an overview of the three types of private sponsorship groups and their general requirements.

GROUP OF FIVE

Kim-Ly may decide to form a **Group of Five (G5)** with four or more other people she knows. Any group of five or more individuals, each from at least five different households, may join together to sponsor one or more refugees, provided that each member also meets the following requirements:

- be at least 18 years of age;
- be a Canadian citizen or permanent resident;
- live in the community where the refugees are expected to settle;
- not be in default on any other sponsorship undertaking; and

- have the necessary resources, such as financial, material, and social, to guarantee support for the full duration of the sponsorship, usually up to a 12-month period.

G5 sponsors are usually one-time sponsors who get together to respond to a special situation. In our example, Kim-Ly could form her group with friends, coworkers, or members of her family who belong to different households.

The five households must show that they can afford to support the refugees they intend to sponsor through a financial assessment and by providing a detailed plan for the refugees' settlement in the community. The individual members of the G5 act as guarantors: they ensure that the necessary support is provided for the full duration of the sponsorship, usually the refugee's first 12 months in Canada.

If Kim-Ly chooses to form a G5, she will need to assess the financial resources of each potential member of the group. Once the group is formed, it must start saving or raising funds. Kim-Ly's group then applies to CIC using the Group of Five sponsorship application kit: they should start the process as Group of Five sponsors. They will then complete a Sponsor Assessment form and an Undertaking/Application to Sponsor—Groups of Five form. The G5 must also research and write a settlement plan and financial plan.

COMMUNITY SPONSORS

Community sponsor sponsorship is open to organizations, associations, and corporations that meet the following requirements. They must

- demonstrate the financial capacity to fulfill the sponsorship by raising funds, if necessary;
- demonstrate the ability to provide necessary emotional and social supports, organizing members to take on various roles; and
- be based in the community where the refugee family is expected to live.

Kim-Ly may join an existing community sponsor, or may initiate the formation of a new group interested in sponsoring refugees. Generally, these groups are formed because a person in the community knows of a refugee, such as a relative, who needs to be resettled. That person approaches a community or faith-based organization to request its participation in the sponsorship. Several groups may come together as co-sponsors to form the sponsorship group. For example, if Kim-Ly belongs to a church near her home, regularly attends the local Vietnamese cultural centre, and is a member of her college's women's alumni association, she could approach one or more of these organizations to solicit their participation.

The composition of the community sponsor group will depend on a number of factors: the amount of money that the group can raise; how much each potential member can commit to donate; and how much each potential member can assist in the settlement of the refugees for the full duration of the sponsorship. All members of the community sponsor group are named in the undertaking with the minister of CIC; therefore, all members are held legally responsible for the sponsorship. One member, however, must be identified as the contact person. By signing the undertaking, the members are subject to any collection action by CIC should they breach the conditions of their financial obligations.

SPONSORSHIP AGREEMENT HOLDERS AND THEIR CONSTITUENT GROUPS

In contrast to community sponsors, **sponsorship agreement holders (SAHs)** are established, incorporated organizations. They have signed a sponsorship agreement with the minister of CIC (or with the Quebec government) to facilitate the sponsorship process. There are many SAHs across Canada ranging from religious organizations to ethnocultural groups and other humanitarian organizations. SAHs may undertake sponsorships on an ongoing basis and are completely responsible for managing sponsorships under their agreements.

Examples of organizations that have signed sponsorship agreements with the minister of CIC include national faith-based organizations such as the United Church of Canada, the Governing Council of the Salvation Army, the Canadian Unitarian Council, and the Presbyterian Church in Canada; and ethnocultural groups such as the Afghan Women's Counselling and Integration Community Support Organization and the Canadian International Immigrant and Refugee Support Association. For a list of Sponsorship Agreement Holders see the CIC website at http://www.cic.gc.ca/english/refugees/sponsor/list-sponsors.asp.

SAHs may sponsor refugees directly, or sponsorships may be undertaken indirectly through a local **constituent group (CG)**, which sponsors the refugees under the SAH agreement. For example, a local congregation of a national faith-based organization may apply to its head office to become recognized as a CG so that it can sponsor a refugee.

Each SAH sets its own criteria for recognizing CGs and is responsible for managing and training any CGs belonging to it. A CG must be authorized in writing by the SAH to act on its behalf to sponsor refugees for resettlement. CGs are usually located in the community where the refugees are destined to live.

In our example, Kim-Ly might find that her local parish or congregation is already a CG, has experience sponsoring refugees, and is already in the process of sponsoring a family. Kim-Ly could therefore approach the organization and volunteer to raise funds, serve as a greeter, or provide some other ongoing assistance to the refugee after arrival in Canada.

Obligations of Refugee Sponsorship

Refugees are responsible for becoming self-sufficient in 12 months or less from the date of arrival. This is a relatively short span of time, considering that many refugees come here with limited or no ability to speak, read, or write in English or French; minimal education; and psychological issues as a result of trauma suffered in their homeland. In exceptional circumstances, the length of the sponsorship may be extended up to 36 months, but only with the consent of the sponsor.

The obligations of sponsors are also onerous. The sponsorship application, together with the sponsorship undertaking, is a legally binding contract between the sponsor and the minister of CIC. The minister of CIC can collect the financial obligation should the signees default in their undertaking and may refuse any future applications for sponsorship. Sponsoring groups undertake to work alongside refugees in order to ensure that they have the necessary support to integrate into life in Canada and to become independent. Consider the following examples of the responsibilities of sponsors:

- *Reception services.* Meeting the refugee upon arrival in the community and giving them an orientation to the community and life in Canada, which includes providing information about public transit, community resources, libraries, and volunteer and settlement agencies.
- *Accommodation.* Locating suitable accommodation, basic furniture, and other household essentials.
- *Access to education.* Arranging language training such as that provided by the Language Instruction for Newcomers to Canada program, or other basic training, and enrolling children in school or daycare.
- *Employment.* Assisting with resumé writing, skills training, and job searches.
- *Financial orientation.* Explaining where and how to shop, bank, budget, etc.
- *Financial support.* Arranging for payment of rent, utilities, telephone, groceries, local transportation, clothes, and household supplies.
- *Assistance and support.* Completing forms, such as health insurance, social insurance, and child tax benefits forms; helping the refugee understand the rights and responsibilities of being a permanent resident; explaining local laws; helping the refugee find a physician and dentist; and providing ongoing friendship and emotional support.

The commitment to sponsor a refugee may be substantial in terms of both financial resources and time and energy. Fortunately, potential sponsors may choose from the several options described above, depending on what they have to give—money or time—and the degree of commitment they are comfortable making.

SETTLEMENT PLAN

A **settlement plan** details the sponsor's commitment to provide the sponsored refugees with the following:

- basic financial support, such as money for lodging and food; and
- care, such as showing them how to register their children in school and providing a network of support and orientation.

The settlement plan is the framework for facilitating the newcomer's independence. It serves as a guide to members of the sponsoring group, and allocates responsibilities for each of the many tasks involved. The settlement plan must be submitted with the sponsor's application.

Sponsorship Application Process

Anyone interested in becoming a sponsor should begin by reading the "Guide to the Private Sponsorship of Refugees Program," available on the CIC website at http://www.cic.gc.ca/english/resources/publications/ref-sponsor/index.asp. The guide provides information about sponsorship opportunities and processes.

If the sponsor does not have a particular refugee in mind, a match form may be requested from CIC.

There is a separate sponsorship application kit for each type of private sponsorship—namely, G5, community sponsor, and SAH/CG. Generally, the sponsoring group must submit the application, an undertaking, and a financial and settlement plan to its local CIC branch. The sponsorship kits for all categories of private sponsorship can be found on the CIC website, including the guide, the application and undertaking, the requirements for a settlement plan, financial assessment forms, and document checklist. The CPC Winnipeg is responsible for processing sponsorship applications.

The sponsorship application is assessed by CIC to determine whether the applicant for sponsorship meets the eligibility criteria, and to ensure that there is no bar to the applicant becoming a sponsor. Such bars to application include being in default of a child support obligation or involvement in certain criminal offences and immigration violations, as described in s. 156(1) of the IRP Regulations. If the applicant for sponsorship is approved, CIC sends an approval letter to the sponsor and provides information about how long it will take to process the refugee's application.

The refugee application is then processed by the appropriate visa office. As explained earlier, this begins with an assessment by a visa officer, which involves an interview, medical examination, and criminal and security checks. If the refugee application is approved, the refugee receives a visa to travel to Canada for permanent residence. Travel arrangements are generally made through the IOM. The sponsor receives a **notice of arrival** with information about the refugee's arrival in Canada.

KEY TERMS

Canadian Orientation Abroad (COA) program, 301

community sponsor, 308

constituent group (CG), 309

durable solution, 290

Government-Assisted Refugee (GAR) program, 303

Group of Five (G5), 307

Immigration Loans Program (ILP), 305

immigration resettlement plan, 292

Interim Federal Health Program (IFHP), 305

International Organization for Migration (IOM), 293

Joint Assistance Sponsorship (JAS) program, 304

named cases, 307

notice of arrival, 311

panel physician, 298

Resettlement Assistance Program (RAP), 303

settlement plan, 310

sponsorship agreement holder (SAH), 309

undertaking, 292

unnamed cases, 307

urgent need of protection, 295

vulnerable, 295

Women at Risk Program, 295

REVIEW QUESTIONS

1. What is the role of the UNHCR in refugee resettlement to Canada?

2. Briefly describe the Convention refugees abroad class.

3. Briefly describe the country of asylum class.

4. How does a refugee apply for resettlement?

5. The Government-Assisted Refugee Program is for special needs refugees. Briefly describe the types of special needs cases that qualify and describe the features of the program.

6. Briefly list the categories of private sponsorship.

7. Briefly describe the process to sponsor a refugee and identify the sponsor's responsibilities.

8. What is the Joint Assistance Sponsorship program?

NOTES

1. United Nations High Commissioner for Refugees, *2010 Global Trends*, at 17, http://www.unhcr.org/4dfa11499.html, and Frequently Asked Questions About Resettlement, 2012, http://www.unhcr.org/4ac0873d6.html.

2. International Organization for Migration, "Concrete Benefits for Refugees," *Canadian Orientation Abroad: Helping Future Immigrants Adapt to Life in Canada*, http://www.iom.int/jahia/Jahia/canadian-orientation-abroad.

3. Under refugee policy reform, the government repealed the sections of the regulations that prescribed the subclass "source country" (ss. 148 and 149 of the regulations) on October 7, 2011. The source country class and the accompanying list of prescribed countries were for individuals who were in refugee-like situations, but who remained in their country of nationality.

4. This certificate is issued to an applicant who meets Quebec's provincial selection criteria.

5. The procedures manual for visa officers acknowledges that the number of applications processed and finalized is based on the available resources of the visa office to do so. A pre-screening process helps to identify special needs cases for priority processing; however, it appears that backlogs occur for other applications and, consequently, processing times can extend into years.

6. There are "direct access" cases. In exceptional cases, a person can have direct access to the program, through self-referral, when the minister has identified a specific geographic area as having a high number of refugees. For example, recent programs include the resettlement of Karen refugees living in remote camps in Thailand, beginning in 2006, and the resettlement of up to 5,000 Bhutanese refugees beginning in 2008.

7. Citizenship and Immigration Canada, "OP 5: Overseas Selection and Processing of Convention Refugees Abroad Class and Members of the Humanitarian-protected Persons Abroad Classes," 2009-08-13, ss. 13.09 to 13.13, http://www.cic.gc.ca/english/resources/manuals/op/op05-eng.pdf.

REFERENCES
Legislation and Regulations
Immigration and Refugee Protection Act

Immigration and Refugee Protection Act. S.C. 2001, c. 27.

Part 1: Immigration to Canada—Division 4—Inadmissibility, ss. 34 to 38.

Part 2: Refugee Protection—Division 1—Refugee Protection, Convention Refugees and Persons in Need of Protection, ss. 95(1)(a), 99(1) and (2) (governed by Part 1: ss. 11(1), 12(3), 13(2) and (3)).

Immigration and Refugee Protection Regulations

Immigration and Refugee Protection Regulations. S.O.R./2002-227.

Part 8: Refugee Classes—Division 1—Convention Refugees Abroad and Humanitarian-Protected Persons Abroad:
   Definition—general, s. 138
   Definition—Convention refugees abroad class, ss. 144 and 145
   Definition—humanitarian-protected persons abroad class, s. 146
   Member of the country of asylum class, s. 147
   Application procedures, referral, s. 150

Part 8: Refugee Classes—Division 2—Convention Refugees Abroad and Humanitarian-Protected Persons Abroad:
   Sponsorship, ss. 152, 153, and 156
   "Special needs," defined, s. 157

General

Citizenship and Immigration Canada. *Annual Report to Parliament on Immigration 2011.* http://www.cic.gc.ca/english/resources/publications/annual-report-2011/index.asp.

Citizenship and Immigration Canada. *Guide to the Private Sponsorship of Refugees Program*, 2003. http://www.cic.gc.ca/english/pdf/pub/ref-sponsor.pdf.

Citizenship and Immigration Canada. IP 3—In-Canada Processing of Convention Refugees Abroad and Members of the Humanitarian-Protected Persons Abroad Classes—Part 4, updated October 7, 2011. http://www.cic.gc.ca/english/resources/manuals/ip/ip03-part4-eng.pdf.

Citizenship and Immigration Canada. "Repeal of the Source Country Class of Humanitarian-Protected Persons Abroad," *Operational Bulletin* 346, October 7, 2011. http://www.cic.gc.ca/english/resources/manuals/bulletins/2011/ob347.asp.

Citizenship and Immigration Canada. "OP 5—Overseas Selection and Processing of Convention Refugees Abroad Class and Members of the Humanitarian-Protected Persons Abroad Classes," August 13, 2009. http://www.cic.gc.ca/english/resources/manuals/op/op05-eng.pdf.

Citizenship and Immigration Canada. "Application for Refugee Sponsorship: Community Sponsors," December 1, 2011. http:www.cic.gc.ca/english/refugees/sponsor/community-how.asp.

Citizenship and Immigration Canada. "Application for Refugee Sponsorship: Group of Five," December 1, 2011. http://www.cic.gc.ca/english/refugees/sponsor/groups.asp.

Citizenship and Immigration Canada. "Application for Refugee Sponsorship: Sponsorship Agreement Holders and Constituent Groups," December 1, 2011. http://www.cic.gc.ca/english/information/applications/private.asp.

Citizenship and Immigration Canada. "Request for a Refugee Profile," December 1, 2011. http://www.cic.gc.ca/english/information/applications/ref-profile.asp.

International Organization for Migration. "Canadian Orientation Abroad: Helping Future Immigrants Adapt to Life in Canada." http://www.iom.int/jahia/Jahia/canadian-orientation-abroad.

UNHCR. "Resettlement: A New Beginning in a Third Country," 2001–2012. http://www.unhcr.org/pages/4a16b1676.html.

UNHCR. "Frequently Asked Questions About Resettlement," 2012. http://www.unhcr.org/4ac0873d6.html.

In-Canada Refugee Determination Process

9

LEARNING OUTCOMES

After reading this chapter you should be able to:

- Identify the main federal organizations involved in the in-Canada refugee determination process.

- Describe front-end processing and the application eligibility criteria.

- Summarize the main activities of the Refugee Protection Division in processing claims.

- Identify important timelines in the refugee determination process.

- Identify the key forms used by refugee claimants.

- Explain a refugee claimant's rights and responsibilities.

- Explain the role and responsibilities of participants in the refugee hearing process.

- Describe post-determination options available to the refugee claimant.

Introduction

In Chapter 7 you learned that Canada, as a signatory to the 1951 *Convention Relating to the Status of Refugees* and its protocol (Refugee Convention), cannot return Convention refugees to territories where they face persecution on the basis of their race, religion, nationality, membership in a particular social group, or their political opinions. As well, the 1984 *Convention Against Torture, and Other Cruel and Inhuman or Degrading Treatment or Punishment* (Convention Against Torture), is embedded in domestic law and practice to provide protection to "persons in need of protection" who face an individualized risk of death, torture, or cruel and unusual treatment.

In Chapter 1, you also read about how the *Canadian Charter of Rights and Freedoms* is part of the legal framework for immigration and refugee law in Canada and how the 1985 *Singh* decision (*Singh v. Minister of Employment and Immigration*) is a significant Supreme Court decision in Canadian refugee law, particularly in establishing the standards of procedural fairness.

Can you imagine the challenge decision-makers face in attempting to distinguish between someone who has a choice to leave her homeland and someone who is forced to flee, especially if the pervading country conditions include conflict, violence, and poverty? Recall that everyone who presents themselves at a port of entry must have the legal permission to enter Canada: either they have a right to enter and remain because of their Canadian citizenship or permanent resident status, or they have authorization to enter temporarily as a temporary resident, business visitor, or student.

What happens when a person arrives at the border who does not fit into one of these classes, and asks for Canada's protection? Refugees who have not been selected for settlement (as discussed in Chapter 8) come to Canada seeking protection from being returned to a country where they are at risk. If protection is granted, this may lead to granting the right to remain permanently in Canada.

Refugee claimants who arrive as "spontaneous arrivals" have not gone through any immigration assessment processes and have no approval from Canadian authorities prior to their arrival: protection is granted *later* by the tribunal without regard to the refugee's origin, ability to speak English or French, ability for self-sufficiency, future contribution to the economy, ability to integrate, or family ties. You could say it goes against the grain because refugees select Canada and, by doing so, immigration enforcement officials must make exceptions to their regular procedures for protecting Canada's borders, and for other officials who provide social services. Consequently, refugees are oftentimes portrayed as illegal migrants who abuse the immigration process and are criticized for using "back-door strategies" to gain entry. Some people have the perception that refugees are "queue jumpers" or "bogus claimants" or "illegals" who take advantage of Canada's generosity by being "a burden on our social systems." Some refugee claimants do, in fact, take advantage of our refugee determination system. However, the motivation or intent of genuine refugees who arrive at our borders is rooted in an overriding desire to escape human rights violations rather than for economic betterment. Unlike immigrants who make a considered decision to leave their homelands, refugees do not have such a choice: they are forced to flee because of some serious risk to their lives or because they are victims of human rights abuses and cannot safely return home. The fundamental difference, therefore, between an "illegal migrant," "immigrant," or "economic migrant" and a refugee is that a refugee *needs* protection. Note too that a "failed" refugee claimant is not necessarily a person who is trying to cheat the Canadian system. He may have left his country, rife with violence and poverty; however, his personal situation and individual experiences do not meet the legal requirements for acquiring refugee status and Canada's protection.

Canada's immigration policies must be mindful of the necessary balance between achieving our humanitarian and legal commitments to protect refugees and protecting Canadians by denying access to those who pose a criminal or security threat. It is therefore worth noting the objectives of the Canadian refugee system, set out in s. 3(2) of the IRPA:

> (a) to recognize that the refugee program is in the first instance about saving lives and offering protection to the displaced and persecuted;
>
> (b) to fulfil Canada's international legal obligations with respect to refugees and affirm Canada's commitment to international efforts to provide assistance to those in need of resettlement;
>
> (c) to grant, as a fundamental expression of Canada's humanitarian ideals, fair consideration to those who come to Canada claiming persecution;
>
> (d) to offer safe haven to persons with a well-founded fear of persecution based on race, religion, nationality, political opinion or membership in a particular social group, as well as those at risk of torture or cruel and unusual treatment or punishment;
>
> (e) to establish fair and efficient procedures that will maintain the integrity of the Canadian refugee protection system, while upholding Canada's respect for the human rights and fundamental freedoms of all human beings;
>
> (f) to support the self-sufficiency and the social and economic well-being of refugees by facilitating reunification with their family members in Canada;
>
> (g) to protect the health and safety of Canadians and to maintain the security of Canadian society; and
>
> (h) to promote international justice and security by denying access to Canadian territory to persons, including refugee claimants, who are security risks or serious criminals.

Bill C-11, the *Balanced Refugee Reform Act* (BRRA), received royal assent on June 29, 2010, with major amendments to the refugee determination system that were scheduled to come into force on June 29, 2012. However, before these changes could be fully implemented, the government introduced Bill C-31, the *Protecting Canada's Immigration System Act* (PCISA), which received royal assent on June 28, 2012, resulting in amendments to both the IRPA and the BRRA. Most of the changes that affect the inland refugee determination process are expected to come into force no later than June 28, 2014. Consequently, at the time of writing this textbook, the new Refugee Protection Division Rules have yet to be amended and not all new procedures have been fully implemented. This chapter, therefore, provides an overview of how backlog cases (those claims made prior to June 28, 2012) are processed, and an overview of the new refugee determination system.

We consider the general process for making a claim for refugee protection and examine the major steps that a refugee claimant takes during the determination process, the decision that is made about the claim, and the post-determination options. This process involves three main organizations, as follows:

- Citizenship and Immigration Canada (CIC) and its officials, whose role in the process primarily relates to immigration;
- the Canada Border Services Agency (CBSA), whose role in the process primarily relates to enforcement and security functions; and
- the Immigration and Refugee Board (IRB), specifically the Refugee Protection Division (RPD), which processes the refugee claims and makes the determination about refugee status, and the newest tribunal—the Refugee Appeal Division (RAD)—which decides appeals from failed refugee claimants.

As you learn about the process, you will no doubt recall cases you heard or read about where failed refugee claimants are still fighting removal years later or where some refugees have long waits to determine their status. It is beyond the scope of this text to describe every possible circumstance. However, we will set out how the procedures are generally expected to be carried out. Typically a refugee claim goes through three stages of assessment and processing:

- the front-end stage includes the initial application for a refugee claim and the assessment of the claimant's eligibility (CIC, CBSA);
- the refugee determination stage, where the claim is heard and decided at the tribunal (RPD); and
- the post-determination stage in which the claimant's refugee status is decided (RAD, CIC, Federal Court).

Stages of the Refugee System

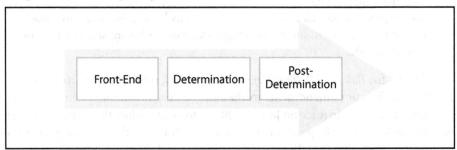

Case Differentiation

The people who make refugee claims in Canada have different motivations for doing so: there are those who are genuinely in need of protection, those who wish to leave their country of origin to improve living conditions for themselves and their family members, and those who would endeavour to circumvent the legal immigration processes. The legislative amendments to the IRPA by the BRRA and the PCISA address these differences, primarily as a policy decision to deter those who would use the refugee determination system for immigration rather than for protection purposes, but also as a government cost-cutting measure (fewer claims and quicker removals are supposed to reduce the overall cost of the refugee system and the costs of related medical, educational, and social assistance. Consequently, amendments to the statute and its regulations set out different timelines for processing claims; limit the right to appeal to certain claimants; and, in some cases, impose restrictions for applying for permanent residence even if a claimant is successful in having his refugee claim accepted.

Designated Country of Origin

Legislative amendments to the IRPA will grant the minister of CIC the authority to create a list of "designated countries of origin" (DCOs). Generally, DCOs will be those countries that have a high number of claims and low acceptance rates, or high withdrawal and abandonment rates. When the new provisions come into effect, the IRPA will require the minister to take the following criteria into consideration when making a DCO designation:

- the human rights record of the country in question as it relates to the factors found in the definitions of a Convention refugee and a person in need of protection, and in other international human rights instruments;
- the availability in the country in question of mechanisms for seeking protection and redress;
- the number of refugee claims made by claimants from the country in question;
- the acceptance rate by the RPD and the rate of appeals allowed by the RAD; and
- any other criteria set out in the regulations.

A DCO claim must be processed according to separate and faster timelines set out in the IRP Regulations. As a matter of policy, the quicker processing times serve to deter others who are considering using Canada's refugee determination process for immigration rather than for protection purposes, and provide for earlier removal of failed refugee claimants. A DCO claimant will not be allowed to apply for a work permit until after his claim has succeeded.

A failed DCO claimant cannot appeal his decision to the Refugee Appeal Division (RAD). He is not eligible to apply for a pre-removal risk assessment (PRRA) until 36 months have passed since the negative determination of his claim. He can, however, apply for a judicial review in the Federal Court but there will be no stay of his conditional removal order.

Designated Foreign National

Refugees sometimes arrive as part of a smuggled group of people. While some of the smuggled are legitimate refugees, others are economic migrants who do not qualify for either Canada's immigration programs or under Canada's refugee protection laws. The latter have been given the false promise by human smugglers that they will be allowed to stay in Canada and that they will be able to benefit from Canadian health care, education, and social assistance systems.

The minister of public safety has the discretion to confer the status of **designated irregular arrival** on a group (two or more individuals). Unless a foreign national can prove he has the appropriate visa—which most refugee claimants do not—a foreign national who is part of a designated irregular arrival group will also be designated and known as a **designated foreign national (DFN)** (IRPA, s. 20.1(2)).

Section 20.1(1)of the IRPA gives the minister the authority in the public interest to designate a group of persons as irregular arrivals if the minister:

> (a) is of the opinion that examinations of the persons in the group, particularly for the purpose of establishing identity or determining inadmissibility—and any investigations concerning persons in the group—cannot be conducted in a timely manner; or
>
> (b) has reasonable grounds to suspect that, in relation to the arrival in Canada of the group, there has been, or will be, a contravention of subsection 117(1) for profit, or for the benefit of, at the direction of or in association with a criminal organization or terrorist group.

A DFN is subject to automatic detention upon arrival. The review into the reason for the detention (and consequently the release from detention) is also subject to case differentiation (see Chapter 10.) Detention is mandatory for a refugee claimant over the age of 16 years. Briefly, a foreign national with a DFN designation will be held in detention until her refugee claim is finalized, or she is released by order of the Immigration Division (under IRPA, s. 58) or by order of the minister (under IRPA, s. 58.1).

The designation may also be made retroactively to March 31, 2009. You may recall the arrival by boat of two groups of refugee claimants: the *Ocean Lady*, which arrived in October 2009, and the *Sun Sea*, which arrived in August 2010. Refugee claimants who arrived on these boats may be affected should the government decide to retroactively designate these two groups as DFNs.

A DFN whose claim is positively determined will need to wait five years before being able to apply for permanent residence and will not be able to sponsor her family members until after she acquires her permanent residence status. If a DFN's refugee claim is rejected by the RPD, she has no right to appeal to the RAD. Although, a DFN may apply to the Federal Court for a judicial review, there would be no stay of her conditional removal order (we will explore this in further detail below.)

No Credible Basis

A refugee claim that is found to have *no credible basis* is a claim that is rejected by the RPD because the member found that there was no credible or trustworthy evidence on which the claim could have been accepted (IRPA, s. 107(2)). Such a finding is stated in the member's reasons for a negative determination decision. In accordance with the IRP Regulations, the failed refugee claimant does not have the right to appeal the decision to the RAD and may be subject to other restrictions on any future applications to remain in Canada.

Manifestly Unfounded Claim

The manifestly unfounded claim (MUC) label is for refugee claimants whose claims were rejected by the RPD because the member was of the opinion that the claimant was clearly fraudulent and states so in his reasons for the negative determination decision (IRPA, s. 107.1). According to the IRP Regulations, an MUC finding means that the failed refugee claimant does not have the right to appeal the decision to the RAD and is subject to other restrictions on any future applications to remain in Canada.

Front-End Process

Consider the following case scenario:

> Mr. M arrives by air at one of Canada's international airports on a cold day in February. He hasn't slept in 48 hours—he is too nervous, too afraid he will be sent back. From his window in the airplane, he can see that the ground is covered in white but it isn't sand like back home; the ground staff wear ear muffs and large mitts—he can see their breath. He is confident he knows what he's doing; leaving was the only way to save his life. Soon, he hopes he can send for his wife and children. He practised for hours the only words he knows in English: "Please give me asylum. I am a refugee." Mr. M follows the passengers off the plane, finally arriving in a large room where line-ups form in front of officials in booths. Mr. M suddenly feels weak and begins perspiring. He clutches the passport he bought from "an uncle," some man named Mak, who got it from someone else; it cost nearly a month's wages. When it is his turn at the booth, he hands the passport, the customs declaration card, and his ticket stub to the official, a woman in a dark uniform. The woman looks at Mr. M then back at the photo; she doesn't smile; she says something but Mr. M doesn't understand. A woman, he thinks, what does she know? I need to talk to a man. The officer is staring at him coldly now, so Mr. M moves in closer and quietly says, "Please, asylum, refugee." The woman is talking again; she doesn't smile. Mr. M just shakes his head, not understanding; he wonders whether he should give her some money; he has a little. Then he notices that she is directing him to another official. He is escorted to a bright, windowless room. Mr. M. knows he broke some rules to get to Canada—but isn't that how it's done? How else was he supposed to escape safely?

Consider a refugee like Mr. M who flees his homeland because his life is at risk. Somehow he chooses Canada—he might have relatives or friends here; he might have heard that it is a safe haven; he may have paid a smuggler and "ended up here." Or he may have come here as a temporary resident and then learned that the conditions in his country of origin have changed, causing him to fear returning (in which case he is a refugee *sur place*).

Although the port-of-entry officials do not decide the legitimacy of a refugee claim, they do have the authority to manage access to the refugee determination process: not every person is allowed to make a claim to protection in Canada.

The front-end stage serves to screen people early in the determination process to control who may have his claim heard by the IRB's Refugee Protection Division (RPD) and who will be denied access; furthermore, it serves to filter out potential security and criminal cases. Officers assess admissibility and eligibility and decide who should have access to the RPD. Security screening is initiated at the time that a claim is made. CBSA officials work with the Canadian Security Intelligence Service (CSIS) to conduct security screening and criminality checks. How does the process of making a refugee claim begin?

Front-End Stage Processes

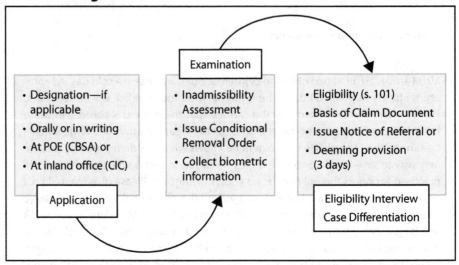

Initial Application

In all cases, the process of making a refugee claim begins with an initial application submitted to an officer. Unlike many of CIC's application processes, which are done through mail-in services, the refugee determination process must be initiated in person. Refugee claimants apply at a port of entry or at an inland office to provide information to an officer in one of the following manners:

- orally, in an interview;
- in writing, by application form; or
- through a combination of oral interview and written application form.

To prevent the refugee system from being used by non-refugees as a last-ditch effort to avoid removal, a refugee claim may not be initiated after a removal order is made. However, a claim may be made at any point in the immigration process in Canada up to the time that a removal order is made. The processing varies slightly for refugee claims according to whether the claim is made in one of the following ways:

- at a port of entry—for example, land border or airport (CBSA); or
- by notifying an immigration officer at an inland immigration office (CIC).

Generally, at the port of entry, the application process commences at the time of the examination by an officer (oral interview). The purpose of the oral application is to provide "tombstone" information about the claimant, such as name, date of birth, country of origin, telephone number, address, language spoken, and other background information. When the new refugee determination process is implemented in early 2013, new procedures will require new refugee claimants to complete the Generic Application Form for Canada (IMM 0008) at this stage.

If the claimant does not speak English or French, the officer will attempt to find an interpreter so that the refugee claimant will be able to communicate during the officer's examination. Generally, refugee claimants are not represented by counsel[1] at this stage of the process.

In the scenario, Mr. M made an oral application at a port of entry—an airport.

In Mr. M's case, after all his information has been taken by the officer, his application will be considered complete. The process starts when the "application" is received by the officer (IRPA, s. 99(3)).

The process may be different at an inland office. A person may be a legal visitor or may be without any legal status when she appears at the CIC office to make a claim for protection. Generally, the refugee claimant will be provided with the application form and interviewed or asked to report back to the office at a later date with the completed forms.

Examination

Refugee claimants must undergo an examination by the officer to determine the following:

- identity;
- inadmissibility; and
- eligibility.

The officer creates a file and assigns a Client ID number, which must be used when communicating with CIC about any matter related to the file.

Generally, at the port of entry and during the interview, the officer considers both inadmissibility and eligibility at the same time. The claimant, such as Mr. M, is photographed and fingerprinted. The officer conducts a search in various databases for information (for example, previous immigration file, criminality checks, and outstanding warrants for arrest) as a part of the preliminary background and criminality checking processes. Mr. M must surrender all identity documents, including passport and travel documents. He will receive certified copies if his documents are legitimate. Otherwise, the documents are seized and may become the subject of a forensic analysis.

Typically, when a refugee claimant makes a claim at a port of entry, he is considered inadmissible because he came to Canada with the intent of remaining in Canada without obtaining a visa. An inadmissibility report (A44(1)) is prepared and a **conditional removal order** is issued (for more information about inadmissibility see Chapter 3, Inadmissibility).

When a claim is made inland, however, the officer must consider whether the claimant is inadmissible or still *in status*, meaning that the refugee claimant may be in Canada as a temporary resident.

The conditional removal order comes into effect in any of the following circumstances:

- the claim is refused and all further steps have been exhausted;[2]
- the claimant abandons the claim; or
- the claimant withdraws the claim.

The conditional removal order may also specify terms and conditions (such as a requirement to report a change of address or to appear for all hearings and other matters, or a prohibition against working). The removal order is "conditional" upon the outcome of the claim for protection. When the refugee claimant is granted protected status, the conditional removal order has no force or effect. Should the claimant be refused refugee protection, the removal takes effect and the claimant must leave Canada.

The officer also considers whether to detain a refugee claimant, generally when the claimant does not have any identity documents or when there are "reasonable grounds to believe" that the claimant is inadmissible because of serious criminality or security reasons, or because he is a DFN. A refugee claimant who is detained must be advised of the right to counsel. If the officer decides to detain Mr. M—for example, because the officer believes that his passport is not legitimate or his identity is in question—it is at this point that he would be informed of his right to counsel.

According to s. 103 of the IRPA, if there are allegations that a refugee claimant is inadmissible because of criminality or a security risk, the case is "suspended," either because the allegations need to be argued before a member of the Immigration Division (ID) or because the officer considers it necessary to await a decision of a court. (See Chapter 10, General In-Canada Enforcement and Removal Procedures, for further details about the ID hearing process.)

Eligibility Interview

Determination of eligibility answers the questions, "Will this claim be referred to the RPD for consideration?" or "Is there some reason to bar the claimant from a refugee determination hearing?" It is not a decision about whether the claim is valid or whether the claimant is in need of protection. The IRPA does not give such decision-making powers to officers of CIC or CBSA. The officer has authority to decide only whether the claimant may seek a hearing before the RPD. As in all immigration matters, the refugee claimant is duty bound to answer all questions truthfully and produce all documents and information as requested (IRPA, ss. 16 and 100(4)). The onus is on the claimant to show that he should have access to the RPD.

Mr. M's claim will be referred to the RPD after the officer finds that he is "eligible." Under the IRPA, officers have three working days to make their eligibility decision; otherwise, the claim is deemed to be referred to the RPD, although these time standards may change when Bill C-31 is fully implemented.

Claims that are ineligible to be referred to the RPD fall under one of the following criteria listed in s. 101 of the IRPA:

- the claimant has been determined to be inadmissible on grounds of security, violating human or international rights, serious criminality, or organized criminality;
- the claimant has been recognized as a refugee under the 1951 Refugee Convention (Convention refugee) by a country other than Canada and can be sent or returned to that country;
- the claimant came to Canada through a third country designated by the regulations as a "safe third country"[3] (see below); or
- the claimant made a previous refugee claim in Canada and that claim was either accepted, rejected, deemed ineligible, withdrawn, or abandoned.

Refugee claimants whose claims are ineligible will not be referred to the RPD. For example, if Mr. M is found to be inadmissible on grounds of security, violating human or international rights, serious criminality, or organized criminality, this would preclude him from eligibility according to the criteria above and he would not be permitted to take his case for refugee status to the RPD.

When a claimant is found to be ineligible, the immigration officer issues an *ineligibility notice* and provides the refugee claimant with a removal order to initiate removal.

Although few refugee claimants exercise this right, in some circumstances claimants may apply to the Federal Court to seek leave for judicial review of an unfavourable eligibility decision on the basis of procedural unfairness.

Referral to the Refugee Protection Division

Returning to our scenario, if Mr. M is found to be eligible, he will be referred to the RPD to have his case for refugee status heard. Refugee claimants who are found eligible or deemed eligible (automatic after three working days) are referred to the RPD. The immigration officer issues the "eligibility notice" and provides the refugee claimant with a number of documents such as the following:

- a copy of the admissibility report (A44(1));
- a copy of the removal order, along with any conditions;
- a copy of the officer's notes relating to personal information about the claimant;
- certified copies of any travel or identity documents that were seized and a "seizure" form;
- a notice to appear for a hearing at RPD;
- medical forms and instructions (to complete medical examinations);
- an interim federal health letter and instructions.[4]

The claimant is also given an information package that is related to preparing for his refugee hearing, which may include the following:

- *For backlog cases:* a personal information form (PIF) with instructions to complete and send to the RPD within 28 days,[5] the port of entry (POE) or CIC officer's interview notes, and a photocopy of any written declaration by the refugee claimant; or
- *For Bill C-31 cases:* a basis of claim (BOC) form; the new process eliminates the PIF and replaces it with the BOC form with instructions to complete and send it to the RPD within 15 days if the claim was made at a port of entry; if the claim was initiated at an inland office, the claimant must complete the BOC and provide it to the CBSA or CIC officer who submits it directly to the RPD along with the referral;
- a list of immigrant and community services; and
- a list of non-governmental organizations (NGOs) that assist refugee claimants.

Basis of Claim Form

POE	• Officer provides BOC form at Eligibility Interview • Claimant submits BOC form directly to RPD (e.g., within 15 days)
Inland	• Claimant completes BOC and submits to officer at Eligibility Interview • CBSA/CIC submits BOC to RPD

These documents (the PIF or the BOC) are provided to the refugee claimant in English or French. In some regions of Canada, however, the lists of services and NGOs may be available in English, French, or selected foreign languages.

Occasionally, after the claim has been referred to the RPD, CIC will become aware of information that would have made the claimant ineligible to proceed with the claim. In such cases, proceedings before the RPD are terminated or, if a determination has already been made, it is nullified (IRPA, s. 104(2)).

At the time of referral, an officer of the CBSA (or CIC) will also schedule the first hearing date with the RPD. When scheduling the hearing, the officer will identify designated country of origin (DCO) claims for earlier hearing dates; the first date of hearing must be no later than:

- 30 days after the DCO claim was referred from an inland office;
- 45 days after the DCO claim was referred from a POE; and
- 60 days after the claim was referred for all non-DCO claimants.

Safe Third Country Agreement

The Safe Third Country Agreement rests on the general principle that a refugee claimant should make a claim in the first safe country in which she is physically present, unless she qualifies for an exception to the Agreement.[6] The United States is the first country to be designated as a **safe third country** for the purposes of

s. 101(1)(e) of the IRPA. This is because Canada and the United States signed the *Agreement Between Canada and the United States of America for Cooperation in the Examination of Refugee Status Claims from Nationals of Third Countries* on December 5, 2002 (commonly referred to as the Safe Third Country Agreement). (Final Canadian regulations relating to this Agreement were published in Part II of the *Canada Gazette* on November 3, 2004.)

The Agreement covers refugee claimants who are seeking entry to Canada from the United States at Canada–US land border crossings by train or at airports (for example, if the person is a failed refugee claimant in the United States who is in transit through Canada after being deported from the United States). As a result, most refugee claimants who pass through the United States on their way to Canada are not eligible to make a claim in Canada. Instead, they must make their refugee claim in the United States. CBSA officers who examine such claimants at the POE are obliged to carry out the provisions of the Agreement.

On November 29, 2007, the Federal Court ruled that the December 2004 Safe Third Country Agreement between Canada and the United States violated refugee rights and made an order quashing the designation of the United States as a safe third country. The Canadian Federal Court of Appeal, on June 27, 2008, reversed the Federal Court decision.

Security Screening

Security screening is conducted for all refugee claimants. Front-end security screening is used to identify people who pose potential security and criminal risks to Canada and restrict their access to the refugee determination system. In our example, Mr. M is fingerprinted and photographed and his travel and other identity documents are seized: this is part of the security screening process.

Security screenings are conducted in partnership with the CBSA and CSIS. The CBSA is responsible for coordinating and informing the IRB when security screenings are completed.

Accommodation, Work, and Study

Mr. M's next step while awaiting his hearing date is to find accommodation. If he does not have a place to live with relatives or community members, the officer will make a referral to local social service agencies. Refugees without funds are entitled to social assistance. (DCO and DFN cases will generally not be entitled to the same assistance.)

Most refugee claimants want to work; however, to be authorized to work they must be in need of a job—that is, they must not be economically self-sufficient—and they must meet the following criteria:

- complete and pass medical examinations;
- complete and file the PIF, on time, with the RPD (for older claims);
- comply with all notices; and
- apply for authorization to work as described in Chapter 4, Temporary Entry.

Refugee claimants who wish to study must apply for a student authorization; they are not exempt from the obligation to have a study permit, even for a short-term course or program of study. To secure a study authorization, the claimant must obtain a letter of acceptance from the educational institution and apply as described in Chapter 4. Note, however, that refugee claimants do not have to pay processing fees to CIC.

Refugee claimants from DCO countries will not be allowed to work or apply for benefits until their claim is accepted or their refugee claim has been in the system for more than 180 days with no decision.

Determination Process and the Refugee Protection Division

The refugee determination process begins at the tribunal when the Refugee Protection Division (RPD) receives a notice of referral from CIC. This referral gives the RPD the jurisdiction to hear the claim and starts the clock for counting the number of days that the claim is with the RPD. In our scenario, the RPD must also wait for notification from the CBSA that Mr. M has been cleared by the front-end security screening process, before it can proceed with his hearing.

When the RPD receives a referral from either an officer of the CBSA or CIC, the registrar creates a file and issues a file ID number that is unique to the claimant. The RPD file number is the reference to be used in all communications with the RPD about matters related to the case. Note that the RPD file number is *not* the same as the Client ID number issued by CBSA/CIC. Legal professionals should always use the appropriate case file number when communicating with CBSA/CIC or the RPD on behalf of the refugee claimant.

Overview of Refugee Determination Processes

Referral to RPD
- Receives Notice of Referral
- Prepares Tribunal Record
- Receives BOC Form:
  - from claimant within 15 days of referral for POE initiated claims; or
  - from officer for inland claims, together with notice of referral.

Tribunal Review and Case Preparation
- Identify Issues
- Research
- Claim Preparation
- Hearings Scheduled According to Case Differentiation:
  - 30 days for inland DCO
  - 45 days for POE DCO
  - 60 days for all non-DCO

Hear and Decide
- Member—Public Servant
- Determination
- Notice of Decision
- Reasons

Knowing and Following the Division Rules and Policies

Major changes made under the BRRA and the PCISA to the refugee determination system affect the RPD's structure and processes; the tribunal was required to review and update its rules. As noted in Chapter 2, Decision-Makers, the chairperson has the authority, as provided in s. 161 of the IRPA, to make rules relating to the RPD's activities, practices, and procedures, in consultation with the deputy chairperson, and subject to the approval of the governor in council. These rules are binding and it is important to know them well. Failure to comply with the rules may have severe consequences to claimants and their counsel.

The division has found that sometimes a flexible, non-binding approach to following procedures is more appropriate where a claimant may not be able to comply with a rule for valid reasons, rather than having rigid rules that must be followed in all circumstances. Policy instruments, as described in Chapter 1, Introduction, serve this purpose by providing guidance to those who need it, while not demanding compliance. Legal professionals are wise to familiarize themselves with these policy instruments, despite their non-binding nature. An awareness of policies will better able legal professionals to serve their clients efficiently and effectively.

Refugee Protection Division Rules

Each Division of the IRB has a distinct set of rules. The *Refugee Protection Division Rules* are regulations under the IRPA that set out roles and responsibilities and govern practices and procedures in matters brought before the RPD. The RPD Rules are a "how to" for processing a claim, from the time of referral to the resolution and closing of the file. For example, the rules require that applications and most communications be made in writing, within time limits, and that the claimant has been copied.

Legal professionals who represent claimants in RPD proceedings must have a thorough knowledge of the rules, in addition to knowing the provisions of the IRPA that set out the jurisdiction of the IRB and the RPD to hear and decide cases for refugee protection. The rules are listed in the IRPA's table of contents under "Related Regulations," and may be accessed at various websites including the IRB website, the Department of Justice website, and the CanLII website. A legal professional who is unsure about the meaning or application of a particular rule may direct questions and requests for clarification to the tribunal's registrar at the nearest business office of the IRB.

Compliance with the RPD Rules by everyone involved is intended to lead to the fair and consistent resolution of matters before the RPD. It is recommended that you obtain a current copy of the RPD Rules and write in the specific rule number next to the rule described below.

Before examining the Rules, note that it is not possible to predict every possible scenario that might arise in the future, so there is a general rule (usually found under general provisions) that provides the RPD with the necessary flexibility to address new concerns, to change the requirement of a rule, or excuse a person from the requirement of a rule. Consider the following examples where, in the absence of a provision in the Rules:

WEBLINK

There are several ways to find the RPD Rules, including searching on the CanLII website at www.canlii.org; searching on the IRB website at http://www.irb-cisr.gc.ca under "Legal and Policy References, Act, Rules and Regulations"; or from an electronic version of the IRPA, in the Table of Contents, http://laws-lois.justice.gc.ca/eng/acts/I-2.5/index.html.

- the RPD may do "whatever is necessary" to deal with a matter (s. 72, new RPD Rules);
- members of the RPD may act on their own initiative to change a rule, to excuse a person from a rule, or to extend or shorten time limits (s. 73, new RPD Rules); and
- failure to follow a rule in a proceeding does not, in itself, make the proceeding invalid (s. 74, new RPD Rules).

In this way, the rules attempt to strike a balance between the value of predictability and consistency, and the need to make adjustments to meet the particular needs of individual cases. Given that the rules have yet to be formalized, rules are referenced generally. It will be up to you to ensure that you work with the current rules and to review and understand all the rules before representing a client before the RPD. What follows is an overview of some of the key procedures.

Definitions

Important key terms are defined in rule 1 of the division's rules. Legal professionals—referred to as counsel by the IRB—demonstrate professionalism by understanding and using relevant and appropriate terminology while presenting refugee claims. For example, counsel must understand that a "proceeding" may refer to a claim that is decided with or without a hearing, a conference, or an application. The refugee claimant may need to participate in one or more of the following proceedings:

- **Conference.** At a conference, the claimant (and/or counsel) meets with the RPD member before the hearing to discuss issues, relevant facts, and any other matter for the purpose of making the hearing more fair and efficient.
- **Application.** On an application before the RPD, prior to or during the main hearing, the claimant (or counsel) asks the RPD to make a decision on a specific matter—for example, on a request for additional time for some compelling reason, or to change the date or time of a hearing.
- **Hearing.** At a hearing, the claimant appears in person before a member of the division (with or without counsel) to present evidence and testimony and to answer questions related to his claim.

Under former rules, the interview was part of a less formal and more expeditious process wherein an interview with a tribunal officer was used instead of a hearing before a member of the RPD. The interview process is not contemplated under the new tribunal procedures.

Scheduling a First Hearing

Tribunals do not generally wish to fix a date on their calendar if a case is not going to proceed. However, under the new refugee determination system, all claims will be referred with a first hearing date at the time of referral. According to a CIC backgrounder, three time frames will be set out in the regulations for refugee protection hearings: upon a finding of eligibility at the time of referral, hearings would be held within 30 days for claimants from designated countries of origin (DCOs) who make their claim inland; 45 days for claimants from DCO claimants who make their claims at ports of entry (POEs); and 60 days for all non-DCO claimants.[7]

In the event that the claimant and his counsel need additional time to gather information and prepare for the hearing, you may need to ask for a postponement or file an application to change the date or time of a proceeding, and the rules serve to assist you to do this.

Claimant Information

The rules define "contact information" as a person's name, postal address, telephone number, and fax number and email address, if any. Contact information for both the claimant and counsel must be provided to the RPD so that the division can serve notices about proceedings and other matters.

If notices, such as a notice to appear, are not received because the RPD does not have the proper address, the claimant might fail to show up for the proceeding, leading to a final determination that the claim has been abandoned. There are also rules that require that the RPD be notified of changes to the claimant's information without delay.

The RPD rules also require the claimant to provide documents that establish his identity, including a copy of identity and travel documents, genuine or not, and a copy of any other relevant documents in the claimant's possession. Identity is especially problematic for the RPD because many claimants arrive in Canada using fraudulent documents to gain entry to Canada.

Counsel of Record Information

The RPD Rules require counsel of record to provide contact information, regardless of whether counsel is considered an authorized representative (see Chapter 12, Regulating the Practice of Immigration and Refugee Law).

Unrepresented claimants who wish to be represented are expected to retain counsel without delay. If the claimant has already agreed to a hearing date, a counsel who is available to appear on that date should be chosen. It is a matter of professional ethics that an authorized representative—that is, a member of the Immigration Consultants of Canada Regulatory Council (ICCRC) (see Chapter 12)—not undertake representation unless he has the ability and capacity to deal adequately with the matters to be undertaken, and this would include being available.

Once retained, counsel must inform the RPD without delay. In some cases, counsel may wish to be removed from the record—for example, if the claimant refuses to pay or is very difficult. The rules direct counsel to seek permission from the RPD to withdraw from a case. If, on the other hand, the claimant wishes to remove counsel, the claimant must generally provide written notice to the RPD and to the minister (if the minister is a party to the proceeding). The regulator of immigration consultants—the ICCRC—also has rules about the circumstances and steps that a licensed immigration consultant must adhere to when withdrawing from representation (see article 14, *Code of Professional Ethics* in the appendix to Chapter 12, Regulating the Practice of Immigration and Refugee Law).

Counsel must complete the Counsel Contact Information form (IRB/CISR 687), available on the IRB website at http://www.irb-cisr.gc.ca/Eng/tribunal/form/Documents/IRB687.pdf and provide his or her membership identification number for either the ICCRC or the provincial law society to which he or she belongs.

Any counsel who represents a client and is not charging a fee should use the Notice of Representation Without a Fee form (IRB/CISR 692), also available on the IRB website at http://www.irb-cisr.gc.ca/Eng/tribunal/form/Documents/IRB692.pdf.

Notice to Appear

The RPD is responsible for notifying the claimant and the minister of the date, time, and location of a proceeding in accordance with its rules. This communication is usually done in writing in a notice to appear. The RPD must also provide a copy to the claimant of any notice or information that the division provides to the minister (for example, notice of possible exclusion issue at a hearing, or notice of minister's intervention.)

Communicating with the Decision-Maker

The claimant and counsel must never directly communicate with the member decision-maker, but rather must direct all communication through the division's registry or business office. This applies to all communication, both oral and written, including questions about the process, documents, or a particular proceeding. A listing of registries may be found in the appendix at the end of this chapter.

In order to avoid suspicions of bias or influence, communicating through a registry is an important procedure to follow. All parties must be aware of all information being passed on to the decision-maker, so that they have the opportunity to respond. Applications and other communications must be made in writing within prescribed time limits.

Interpreters

The claimant must choose a language of record, either English or French.

Only **accredited interpreters** are used by the IRB for hearings in any division. IRB-accredited interpreters have undergone security checks, passed a language exam, and have undergone an orientation and training period. IRB-accredited interpreters are not employees of the IRB; rather, they have a personal services contract with the board and are hired on a case-by-case basis. They are permanently bound by their promise to interpret accurately once they take an oath or make a solemn affirmation to do so. Generally, at the beginning of the proceeding, the interpreter confirms that she used a standardized script to ensure that she and the party or witness understands each other. The interpreter may not guide, provide advice, or offer an opinion.

In cases where the claimant has experienced a traumatic event such as rape or torture, the presence of family members or friends may inhibit the claimant from describing the event. It is important to reassure the refugee claimant that information will be kept confidential; that their case, including the file and hearing, are closed to the public; and that the RPD will not share the information with representatives of their country of nationality.

At the time of referral of the claim to the RPD, the claimant will be directed to community organizations, such as community legal clinics, and settlement and newcomer agencies, which provide referrals, advice, and language assistance. Many community organizations have interpreters on staff or as volunteers in order to assist with the variety of linguistic skills required by refugee claimants.

Most refugee claimants do not speak English or French, so unless you speak the claimant's language, you should conduct your business with the claimant through an interpreter. It is preferable not to use a family member or friend for this purpose, because they will not likely understand the legal terminology, or the consequences of omitting or embellishing information, and they may paraphrase or put their own spin on the claimant's statements.

When meeting with the refugee claimant, the legal professional should ensure that the interpreter is not providing information to the claimant, but rather translating only the information you present and interpreting it as accurately as possible.

When an interpreter is used to help translate the PIF/BOC and other documents for the refugee claimant, the interpreter must sign and date the "interpreter's declaration."

If the refugee claimant's language and dialect are different from what has already been provided to the RPD, you must notify the RPD in writing before the hearing. The RPD Rules will specify the time frame in which you must do this. The rules require that the RPD be notified if an interpreter will be required to enable a witness to testify on behalf of the claimant. At the beginning of a proceeding, the interpreter must take an oath or make a solemn affirmation to interpret the proceedings accurately and in accordance with the rules.

Documents

There are several kinds of documents relevant to refugee claim proceedings. These documents include identity documents and medical reports. Documents are important evidence at refugee proceedings, and the rules for filing documents are similar for all of the board's divisions. Because of the importance of documents to a fair resolution of the claim, there are rules regarding preparation and filing documents, rules regarding disclosure ensuring that everyone has a copy of the documents well before the hearing, as well as timelines for filing and replying to disclosed documents.

The legal professional must use appropriate forms and adhere to the following general rules:

- all documents provided to the RPD must be provided to the division registry; and
- any document provided to the minister must be provided to the claimant.

As counsel, you will want to provide organized and professional-looking documents. All documents intended for use at a proceeding must comply with the rules. The requirements for handling documents are similar for each of the board's divisions:

- *Format.* Documents must be typewritten using one side only of 216 mm by 279 mm (8½" × 11") paper, with pages numbered. If the document is a photocopy, it must be clear and legible. If you file more than one document, a numbered list of all such documents must also be filed.
- *Language.* Documents must be submitted in either English or French, which may require translation.
- *Method of service.* Documents may be provided by a number of methods: by hand, by regular or registered mail, by courier or priority post, by fax (for documents no more than 20 pages long), and sometimes by electronic mail. Otherwise, a request must be made to the division to provide it in an alternative format (or not at all.)
- *Computation of time.* A document is considered received by the division on the day that the document is date stamped.

When a document is provided by regular mail to the claimant or the minister, it is considered to be received seven days after the day that it was mailed. If day 7 falls on a Saturday, Sunday, or statutory holiday, then the document is considered received on the next working day.

General Procedures for Applications

There are many issues that may require resolution before a refugee hearing can even begin. Such issues include a change to the date or location of the hearing, reinstatement of a claim, or cancellation of a summons to witness. If counsel wants a decision on such a matter, the general procedure for making applications are set out in the Rules, generally in the following manner:

- in writing (although oral applications are sometimes accepted) and without delay;
- stating the outcome sought;
- providing the reasons for the request;
- stating (if known) whether the other party agrees to the application (in the case where the minister intervenes);
- including any evidence that the party wants considered, in an affidavit or statutory declaration; and
- with a statement of how and when a copy of the application was sent to the other party.

If the minister is intervening, then the minister and the refugee claimant—as parties to the proceedings—are given an opportunity to respond within time limits (generally, within seven days of receiving a copy of the application). The response must be provided in the following manner:

- in writing;
- stating the outcome sought;

- providing the reasons for the seeking of that outcome;
- including any evidence that the party wants considered, in an affidavit or statutory declaration; and
- providing a statement of how and when a copy of the written response was sent to the other party.

The applicant then has an opportunity to reply to the response. Generally, the applicant must do so within five days after receiving a copy of the written response.

Changing the Location

A request to change the location of a proceeding as specified in the notice to appear may be made by application to the RPD. This situation may arise if the claimant wishes to transfer the case to another office. The application must follow the general application procedures. Generally, such a request must be made no later than 20 days before the proceeding. If the application is not allowed, the claimant is expected to appear for the proceeding at the location fixed by the RPD.

The RPD will consider several factors when deciding an application to change the location of a proceeding, including the following:

- whether the claimant is living in the same location as the proceeding;
- whether a change of location would allow the proceeding to be full and proper; and
- whether a change would delay the proceeding.

Requesting a Public Hearing

Proceedings in the RPD are generally private and closed to the public. However, from time to time, someone may wish to make the proceeding open to the public. This typically occurs when there is media interest in a claim.

In accordance with the Rules, any person may make an application to have the hearing held in public. A public hearing application must provide the following:

- a request for a public hearing;
- reasons why the RPD should agree to a public hearing; and
- any evidence that the applicant wants the RPD to consider in deciding the application.

The original application and two copies must be provided to the RPD, and a copy must be provided to each of the parties (that is, the claimant and the minister).

Policy Instruments

When circumstances arise that are not addressed by the *Immigration and Refugee Protection Act*, its regulations, or the RPD Rules, the board and its chairperson have authority under the IRPA to address these gaps through policy instruments. There are several types of policy instruments that guide RPD procedures, in addition to the binding RPD Rules, such as chairperson's guidelines, policies, chairperson's instructions, policy notes, jurisprudential guides, and identified persuasive decisions. All policy instruments are available on the IRB website. Some policy instruments are general in application and others are specific to the RPD. Familiarity with policy instruments will provide the legal professional with confidence when navigating RPD processes.

Chairperson's Guidelines

The chairperson's guidelines are a source of guiding principles for members to manage cases. The chairperson has issued seven separate guidelines for the RPD, which can be reviewed on the IRB website. Examples include:

- Guideline 4—Women Refugee Claimants Fearing Gender-Related Persecution;
- Guideline 6—Scheduling and Changing the Date or Time of a Proceeding in the Refugee Protection Division;
- Guideline 7—Concerning Preparation and Conduct of a Hearing in the Refugee Protection Division; and
- Guideline 8—Guideline on Procedures with Respect to Vulnerable Persons Appearing Before the Immigration and Refugee Board of Canada.

Guidelines are not binding and members are not specifically directed to follow the guidelines. This is important to preserve the independent nature of the member's role in making decisions. However, members are expected to consider the guidelines and either apply them or provide a reason for not doing so.

Policies

Unlike the chairperson's guidelines, RPD policies are used to communicate with claimants and their counsel about initiatives of the RPD. Examples of policies governing the practices of the RPD are as follows:

- Policy for Handling IRB Complaints Regarding Unauthorized, Paid Representatives;
- Policy on the Transfer of Files for Hearings by Videoconference (Refugee Protection Division); and
- Policy on Country-of-Origin Information Packages in Refugee Protection Claims.

Chairperson's Instructions

Chairperson's instructions are formal instructions to IRB personnel about a specific practice and/or organizational concern. There are currently three sets of instructions that direct the actions of the Refugee Protection Division and one set of instructions that are applicable to the board generally:

- Instructions for Gathering and Disclosing Information for Refugee Protection Division Proceedings;
- Instructions Governing the Management of Refugee Protection Claims Awaiting Front-End Security Screening;
- Instructions Governing Communication in the Absence of Parties Between Members of the Refugee Protection Division and Refugee Protection Officers and Between Members of the Refugee Protection Division and Other Employees of the Board; and
- Instructions Governing Solicitor–Client Privilege and the Confidentiality of Legal Advice at the Immigration and Refugee Board of Canada.

Policy Notes

A policy note is the same as a memorandum and it is generally issued by a single business office to communicate with the members, staff, and the public (claimants and counsel) about a particular operational matter in that local office.

Jurisprudential Guides

The chairperson has the authority to issue jurisprudential guides for the RPD, pursuant to s. 159(1)(h) of the IRPA. Jurisprudential guides are issued as a tool to build a source of jurisprudence, based on member decisions that the RPD considers well reasoned. Jurisprudential guides serve to assist the members in adjudicating cases that share essential similarities and to encourage consistency in decision making. However, members are not bound by them. Although members are expected to provide an explanation if they choose not to follow these cases, the cases are not binding precedents.

Persuasive Decisions

Persuasive decisions are similar to jurisprudential guides. A decision that is designated as a "persuasive decision" is selected for its value to assist other members to consistently apply questions of law or of mixed law and fact. The difference is that a member is not required to explain why he is not applying a persuasive decision in his own reasons for his decision.

Before the Proceeding

Important Time Frames

The RPD Rules require that certain activities occur within certain time limits. Before taking on a refugee case, counsel must first consider both the time requirements of the RPD and the time necessary to carefully go over the client's information. For example, Mr. M's counsel must consider the many issues to overcome, such as communication barriers, the time needed to gather documents and information related to Mr. M's claim, and even Mr. M's ability to relive events, before deciding to take on Mr. M's case.

BACKLOG CASES

Counsel is expected to comply with the filing provisions of 28 days for the Personal Information Form (PIF), so it is important to determine when "the clock started" on the case—that is, the date of receipt of the blank PIF by the claimant. There are three immediate and important deadlines that must be met, as follows:

1. *10 days after receiving PIF—claimant contact information form.* The claimant contact information form must be filed with the IRB's registry no later than 10 days after the refugee claimant received the blank PIF. This ensures that the RPD is able to contact the claimant for any matter, including notices, interviews, and hearings.

2. *28 days after receiving PIF—personal information form.* The original and two copies of the PIF must be filed within 28 days of the claimant receiving the form, according to s. 6 of the RPD Rules (pre-Bill C-31 claims). Failure to file the PIF may result in the claim being declared abandoned. However, if the PIF cannot be completed within the 28 days, an application may be made for an extension of time.

3. *20 days before hearing—changes to PIF.* Any changes to the PIF must be submitted 20 days before the hearing, in three copies and underlined, in accordance with the RPD Rules.

BILL C-31 CASES

Bill C-31 replaces the PIF with a Basis of Claim form (BOC).[8] For refugee claims made at a port of entry (POE), claimants must provide the necessary documentation to the RPD within the time frames set out in the IRP Regulations, which is anticipated to be within 15 days (not yet in force at the time of writing; see Bill C-31, s. 56). For claims made at an inland office in Canada, refugee claimants provide necessary documentation to an immigration officer at their eligibility interview (Bill C-31, s. 33). It is essential for counsel to learn about where and when their clients made their refugee claim in order to comply with the deadlines.

The Record

The RPD opens a claimant's file with the notice of referral and adds the BOC form (or copies of the port of entry or officer's interview notes for backlog cases). Documents are added to the file as they are received by the RPD, and comprise the **record**. The record may include any or all of the following documents:

- claimant contact information form;
- change of address notifications, if any;
- notice of representation without a fee or counsel contact information form (from counsel);
- personal information form or basis of claim form (as applicable);
- list of claimant's documents form;
- list of minister's documents form (from the minister's representative, if the minister is intervening in the case);

- copies of any notices sent by the CBSA, CIC, and RPD;
- copies of any other correspondence; and
- any documents disclosed.

Like Mr. M, many refugee applicants do not communicate well in English or French and need help to understand the numerous forms and documents. One of the important roles of counsel is to take the time to explain the purpose and importance of the various documents and forms, especially the PIF or BOC—the most important form.

It is also counsel's role to identify those documents required as evidence to support the claims made, and to double-check facts as much as possible to ensure that they support the claims made.

THE PERSONAL INFORMATION FORM

The personal information form (PIF) was the key document used under the former refugee regime and will continue to be used by any claimant who was referred to the RPD prior to the implementation of the new refugee determination system, in early 2013. The PIF presented the RPD with the first glimpse of the claimant's case. In our example, Mr. M was required to complete the PIF and file it with the RPD before he can apply for a work or student authorization. He was given 28 days to complete and submit the form to the RPD. This provided him with the opportunity to seek assistance in completing the form (for example, at a legal clinic, at a non-governmental organization, or through his own representative). The RPD used the information in the PIF to achieve the following objectives:

- identify the key issues in the case;
- make decisions about scheduling the claim (conference, interview, or hearing);
- collect information about the claimant's country conditions;
- disclose any required information or documents to the minister of CIC; and
- provide information at the hearing.

The PIF was used together with the *port-of-entry notes* or the *officer's notes*.

Mr. M's counsel can help Mr. M develop a complete background, including family history, education, employment, and military service; and a logical and chronological history of events that gave rise to his fear and flight, such as dates of activities, arrests, travel history within the country, departure, and travel outside the country, for his PIF.

BASIS OF CLAIM FORM

When Mr. M met with his counsel, he was resentful and impatient about having to provide such personal details. He couldn't understand why the people at the refugee board wanted to know the same information he'd already given the other officials at CIC. He was also worried about what the Canadian government officials would do with the information. Would it be shared with officials of his country?

The BOC replaces the PIF and will be similarly used to gain information about the claimant's reasons for seeking refugee protection. As noted by Mr. M, the PIF was lengthy and duplicated much of the same information that was collected by immigration officials in the front-end process (the IMM 5601) and so it will be much shorter than the PIF. Its use will streamline the collection of information about the claimant and focus on specific aspects of the claim for protection.[9] Another difference is that the form may be completed either by an officer at the eligibility interview (DCO claims) or by the claimant at a later date. Much of the content of the BOC will not duplicate other information collected—such as personal information solicited in the Generic Application for Permanent Residence (IMM 0008) and any accompanying forms required by the CBSA or CIC. The content of the BOC will be set out in Schedule 1 to the new RPD Rules and, as noted above, there will be new timelines established for completing the form set out in the IRP Regulations.

Refugee claimants already face language and cultural barriers; they are not expected to be experts on refugee law; and so these documents (PIF or BOC) can be confusing for them. Consequently, the assistance provided by counsel to complete these and other important documents is invaluable to the refugee claimant. It remains to be seen to what extent counsel will be able to provide such help to refugee claimants given the strict time frames imposed under the new refugee determination system.

Refugee claimants will not necessarily understand that the RPD is separate and independent from other government departments and officials; so it is important for counsel to reassure clients such as Mr. M about the confidentiality of the process, at least with regard to sharing his information with officials from his country of origin.

Types of Documents

Consider the following types of documents, which are important to establish the facts of the case and to support the testimony of witnesses:

1. **Identity documents.** It is important that the refugee claimant provides acceptable documents to establish his identity and other elements of the claim, or provide a credible explanation as to why such documents are not available, and what steps were taken to obtain them. Identity documents may include:

   - birth certificate,
   - passport,
   - marriage certificate,
   - divorce certificate,
   - voter registration,
   - driver's licence,
   - police records, and
   - university transcripts.

   The existence of these kinds of documents bolsters the claimant's credibility and helps to establish the claimant's identity.

2. **Corroborative documents.** Documents that corroborate a claimant's allegations are a boost to his credibility, and may replace the need to relive traumatic events at the hearing. For example, if the claimant has been tortured, medical or psychiatric reports may be available to corroborate the claim. Examples of useful corroborative evidence that may be filed include:

   - references to the claimant or associates of the claimant in any high-profile human rights reports;

   - newspaper references to the claimant's involvement in incidents or activities, such as demonstrations;

   - evidence of the claimant's membership in a political party or social or religious group; and

   - objective evidence, including background research.

3. **Country information.** Information on the country of reference, such as country-of-origin information, is provided by the RPD. This means that every case will have some basic documentary evidence, which becomes part of the exhibit list used at the hearing. Counsel may already be familiar with the country conditions and human rights violations in the country of origin if they have represented other clients from the same place. Counsel should review the country information with the claimant to address any inconsistencies with the claimant's own personal experience.

In our scenario, Mr. M's counsel should review the copies of his client's identity documents provided to the officer at the front-end stage. In preparing for Mr. M's hearing, counsel should ask whether the claimant can obtain legitimate identity documents such as a passport, birth certificate, voter registration card, or domicile registration card, without putting relatives at risk, because Mr. M had used fraudulent documents to get to Canada. If documents cannot be safely obtained, are there any witnesses who can testify as to the claimant's identity?

Counsel should make a list of any evidence needed to confirm the facts of Mr. M's allegations. It is crucial that counsel be prepared to deal with discrepancies between information given at the eligibility interview, in the PIF or BOC, and during Mr. M's testimony at the hearing. Too many discrepancies may lead to a finding of "no credible basis" or that the allegations are based in fraud and are "manifestly unfounded."

FILING DOCUMENTS

As counsel, you must use appropriate forms and follow the rules for filing documents. Generally, the rules concerning documents can be applied to any document, notice, or request. You will want to provide organized and professional-looking documents to the RPD. All documents intended for use at the hearing must comply with the rules.

If the claimant files more than one document to be included in the record, a numbered list of all such documents must also be filed. The List of Claimant's Documents form (RPD.05.1) should be used for this purpose, and is available on the IRB website under the "Forms" tab.

DISCLOSURE AND PROVISION OF DOCUMENTS

Documents are exchanged before the hearing to ensure that all participants have an opportunity to review them, and respond if necessary, in preparation for the hearing. To ensure that this happens, the RPD Rules require **disclosure** of documents to the RPD, and to the minister (if the minister is intervening), and impose requirements for providing copies of the documents to those entitled to have them.

Consider the following general criteria regarding disclosure:

- Observe time limits for disclosing documents, so that they are received before a proceeding.

- Disclose any documentary evidence to be used in support of a client's claim to the RPD by listing the documents on the List of Claimant's Documents form, filed within the time limits set out in the Rules (at least 10 days before the hearing, under the new RPD rules).

- The RPD may refuse to use or allow documents that are not produced within the time limits.

- Consider the progress of the claim because, generally, if the hearing has already started, the member can consider whether to allow admission of the documents on the basis of the document's relevance and probative value, what new evidence the document brings to the hearing, and whether there was a reasonable effort made to provide the document on time.

It would be perceived as unfair and inefficient if documents were withheld until the last minute.

In managing its claim load, the RPD has used its own case management system to differentiate among claims that are manifestly founded, claims with multiple issues, and claims where the minister was intervening. Under the former refugee determination system, staff and members reviewed the PIF to identify the main issues that were central to the claim and used them to "stream" cases accordingly into a fast track or hearing process. The notice to appear identified the stream for counsel and the refugee claimant.

Case differentiation is part of the new refugee determination system and begins with the front-end stage, where cases are referred with a first-hearing date. Case differentiation, however, is based on where the claimant is from (for example, a DCO) or how the claimant came to Canada (for example, irregular arrival) and the timelines will be dictated by the IRP Regulations. The tight time frames of the new refugee determination process will not generally permit the RPD to screen files, conduct pre-hearing conferences, or do expedited interviews. Members will receive the record within days after it is referred to the RPD and they will be responsible for preparing it for the hearing.[10] Because there is a transition period for the coming into force of new the RPD rules and IRP regulations, backlog cases will continue to be processed using the PIF under the former refugee determination system, and so the case management strategies for the former process are noted briefly below.

Hearing Streams Under the Former Refugee Determination System

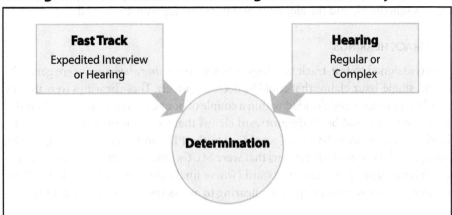

Fast-Track Process

Claims under the refugee determination system, which are assigned to the fast-track process are further subcategorized into either an expedited interview or a fast-track hearing.

FAST-TRACK EXPEDITED PROCESS: INTERVIEW

Under the former regime, the RPD Rules allowed for accepting a claim without a hearing and provided for an interview. In practice, this was called the expedited process, and, as the name suggests, it was a shorter process used to quickly decide claims. Rather than participating in a hearing, the claimant was interviewed by an officer—a public servant employed as staff at the RPD. The setting was informal—typically, an office consisting of a table and chairs, and the interview generally lasted 30 to 90 minutes.

Claims streamed into this process were generally considered to be *manifestly founded* cases—the RPD had a high acceptance rate for the country of reference. The fast-track expedited process was used in the following circumstances:

- the claimant's identity is established;
- no issues of credibility arise from the PIF or POE notes;
- the minister is not intervening in the case; and
- the case is supported by known human rights violations in the reference country.

The member was not present for the interview and based his decision, instead, on the officer's interview notes and recommendations and could make a final positive determination without a hearing. In this way, when a claim was manifestly founded, the RPD was able to finalize many cases in a day and expend fewer resources. With the final positive determination, claimants had their claims decided relatively earlier compared with those who were scheduled into the hearing process. If the officer or the member decided that the claim could not be determined positively, then a hearing was scheduled, and the elements of natural justice were preserved.

FAST-TRACK HEARINGS

Claims assigned to fast-track hearings, also known as *short hearings*, were generally simple, single-issue claims that could be decided quickly. These hearings were usually heard by a member and decided within a couple of hours. Claims that were scheduled to this process could be straightforward claims that were not suitable for the expedited process, or were baseless (according to the PIF) and needed to be dealt with promptly. The mix included claims that were MUCs (and were finalized with a negative determination) or straightforward (where final determinations could be either positive or negative) and required a hearing to assess the claimant's credibility.

Full Hearings

To manage its claim load by apportioning the appropriate amount of hearing time and resources to each claim, the RPD created two different types of hearings within the full-hearings stream under the former refugee determination process. It remains to be seen whether the RPD will continue to use different hearing types under the new system.

Regardless of the hearing type, hearings are usually held in private and are conducted in an informal and non-adversarial manner. In a limited number of cases, the minister, represented by counsel, may intervene to argue against the claim—for example, because the minister believes that the claimant should be excluded from protection (see below). The hearing may be conducted publicly in rare cases where the media takes an interest and brings an application for the hearing to be held in public.

The two hearing types are as follows:

1. *Regular hearings.* Claims scheduled as regular, full hearings usually involve more than two issues and require about a half day.

2. *Complex hearings.* Complex hearings are held for claims that have multiple issues, and may include issues about the claimant's identity, credibility, or other serious matters where the minister will be a party to the proceeding because he would intervene in the claim. When the minister intervenes, the hearing becomes adversarial and generally requires more hearing time. These cases may be scheduled for a half day or longer.

Ministerial Intervention

The minister may choose to intervene at the refugee protection hearing, rather than suspend it. When the minister intervenes, he or she is represented by "minister's counsel"—a public servant from the CBSA. The refugee hearing becomes adversarial because the minister's counsel will argue against the claim in the following areas:

- credibility (issues about the honesty and accuracy of the claimant's statements and/or authenticity of documents);

- exclusion under s. 98 of the IRPA (for example, to exclude a refugee claimant because she already has protection according to article 1E of the Refugee Convention or article F of the Convention, which excludes those who have been in the role of persecutor from later being granted protection). Exclusions are set out in ss. E and F of article 1 of the *United Nations Convention Relating to the Status of Refugees* (located in the Schedule to the IRPA, s. 2(1)) and essentially bar a refugee claimant from refugee protection because of alleged war crimes, crimes against humanity, serious non-political crimes, or acts contrary to the United Nations principles. (Exclusion is more fully discussed in Chapter 7, Refugees and Protected Persons.)
- inadmissibility (on grounds of security, violating human or international rights, serious criminality or organized criminality, or on the ground that there is an outstanding charge against the refugee claimant); or
- ineligibility (when the minister receives information after the claim has been referred and now wishes to argue that the claimant is ineligible according to the criteria provided at s. 101 of the IRPA, that there is misrepresentation according to s. 104(1)(c), or that the claim is not a first claim, as provided in s. 104(1)(d)).

Cases involving credibility issues and the exclusion clause of the Convention refugee definition are better suited to a ministerial intervention because these issues are refugee matters related to the application of the Convention refugee definition.

It is important that the RPD provide the claimant with a copy of the minister's notice of intervention and any accompanying information that was provided to the tribunal. Should the minister decide to intervene in a case, either as a result of the RPD's notice or acting on the minister's own information, the Rules require the minister to give notice to the RPD of the minister's intention to intervene in a claim. The notice sets out how the minister will intervene, the minister's counsel contact information, and proof of notifying the refugee claimant. The notice must be given to the RPD, generally no later than 20 days before the hearing. The minister must also serve the refugee claimant with a written copy of the notice of the minister's intention to intervene.

Refugee Hearings

Prior to a hearing, counsel must be familiar with the RPD Rules that relate to such things as document disclosure, and with the relevant legislation and case law. Counsel must have a clear understanding of the legal issues in the particular case. Common legal issues that frequently require hearings to resolve include:

- identity/nationality;
- existence of other claims;
- delay in making the claim;
- credibility assessment;
- nexus to the grounds (which grounds apply);

- the agents of persecution;
- objective evidence to support the claim; and
- what the claimant fears if he were to be returned.

Counsel must be aware of all the pertinent facts of the case, and what to expect from witness testimony. Finally, counsel must be able to apply the facts to the law, and formulate persuasive arguments to make at the hearing. For further information, see Guideline 7: Preparation and Conduct of a Hearing in the Refugee Protection Division, at http://www.irb-cisr.gc.ca/eng/brdcom/references/pol/guidir/Pages/preparation.aspx.

Consider the experience of Mr. M, when he appears for his hearing and interacts with his counsel, his interpreter, and the RPD member:

> Mr. M received a notice to appear for a hearing. On the day of his hearing, Mr. M arrived half an hour early to meet his counsel and go over last minute details. His counsel warned him not to be late because if the member is kept waiting for more than 15 minutes, she might conclude that Mr. M has abandoned his claim. This also gave him time to meet with the interpreter for his hearing, who asked him some questions to establish that they could understand each other. Mr. M bought a suit at a second-hand store for this day and he is very nervous. It has been so hard living in this new country, and he has had difficulty making new friends; he misses his family. He reminds himself that this is his only chance to convince the decision-maker that he cannot return home, and that he needs to get his family out of that country.
>
> When it is time to start the hearing, Mr. M's counsel leads him down a hall and they stop at a hearing room. He recognizes the Canadian flag at the front of the room, behind a long desk. There are three long tables, each with a microphone: one on each side of the desk and one at the back of the room facing the desk. There are some chairs around the room's perimeter. Mr. M is seated next to the interpreter, sitting facing the desk. His counsel takes a seat at one of the tables.
>
> The RPD member walks in from the front of the room a few minutes later, turns on the recording device, and introduces herself as the member in his case. From this point on, everything said in the room is translated into Mr. M's language so that he can understand, and everything he says is translated into English. Mr. M is given the choice of taking an oath or making a solemn affirmation at the beginning of the hearing. He hesitates, wondering what would please the lady member the most, and then decides he needs all the help of greater powers, so he chooses to swear on his holy book. The next part is confusing; he is feeling nauseous but tries to smile and nods when the interpreter asks whether he understands. The interpreter is translating something about "the order of the proceeding" and who will start the questioning first.

Changing the Hearing Date

Under the new refugee determination process, the timelines for the hearing will be specified in the IRP Regulations. Refugee advocates have signalled to the minister that the proposed time frames may not be sufficient for counsel to fully prepare a case and to properly represent a refugee claimant. Counsel could therefore apply for a request to change the date and time of a proceeding as specified in the notice to appear. This situation may arise if the claimant wishes to postpone a hearing to provide for more time to gather documents. The application must follow the general application procedures of the Rules.

An application to change the date must provide substitute dates and provide the reasons for the request. The Rules list several factors that may be considered by the RPD when deciding an application to change the date or time of a proceeding, including:

- whether the party has counsel;
- whether counsel is knowledgeable and experienced;
- the time already afforded to the party to prepare;
- the party's efforts to prepare; and
- previous delays.

Persons in Attendance

There are a number of people who must be present at a hearing, such as the claimant and the RPD member. Other persons are likely to be present, such as the claimant's counsel, and an interpreter. Still others may be present, such as witnesses, a designated representative, and the minister's counsel. Occasionally, a representative of the United Nations High Commissioner for Refugees may also be present.

RPD MEMBER

The RPD member would have reviewed his claim file within a few days of Mr. M's claim having been referred. The panel comprises a single decision-maker who has the authority to hear a refugee claim. The authority of the member has been extended to include the specific authority to question witnesses and the refugee claimant (IRPA, s. 170(1)). At the hearing, the member is therefore actively involved in the RPD's inquiry process and has the authority to tell the hearing participants how to present their cases.

Case law has established that the RPD has control of its own procedures.[11] The division decides and gives directions on how a hearing is to proceed. A member is a specialist in refugee law and is well informed about human rights abuses and other conditions and events in the country presented. Therefore, the member may inquire into anything considered relevant to establish whether a claim is well founded. The member will study the case file prior to a proceeding to become familiar with the issues that require resolution. Members must assess the credibility of the claimant's testimony and the veracity of his documentary evidence. The nature of the inquisitorial process permits the member to directly question the claimant and witnesses, even if it requires an in-depth examination of the allegations in order to derive a determination. Members also write reasons if they render a negative determination.

CLAIMANT

The claimant must be personally in attendance at the hearing.

Refugee Claimant's Rights and Responsibilities

When working with refugee clients, it is important that counsel review the clients' rights and responsibilities. Clients must understand that they have the following rights:

- the right to counsel;
- the right to an interpreter;
- the right to present evidence and call witnesses; and
- the right to be present at their own case before an impartial and independent decision-maker.

Clients must also understand that they have the following responsibilities:

- the responsibility to provide credible and trustworthy information and testimony; and
- the responsibility to meet the burden of proof—that suffering persecution upon return to one's own country is probable, not merely possible.

CLAIMANT'S COUNSEL

Counsel's role is essentially to protect the claimant's interests and right to a fair hearing. Counsel explains the process, provides advice, and presents the case in an efficient manner, within the limits set by the member.

The refugee claimant may choose to be represented by either an unpaid trusted adviser, such as a family member or clergy, or a paid consultant or lawyer. As of 2011, the IRP regulations require that non-lawyers who practise immigration law must be members in good standing of the Immigration Consultants of Canada Regulatory Council (ICCRC—"the Council") as Regulated Canadian Immigration Consultants (RCICs); members in good standing of a provincial or territorial law society, including licensed paralegals who are regulated by a provincial law society; or members of the Chambres des notaires. Any counsel who represents the claimant must provide contact information in writing to the RPD and the minister, including the membership identification number for the relevant professional regulatory body.

INTERPRETER

Only accredited interpreters are used for refugee hearings. At the beginning of the proceeding, the interpreter confirms that she used a standardized script to ensure that she and the refugee claimant understand each other. The interpreter may not guide, provide advice, or offer an opinion to the claimant.

WITNESSES

If counsel wishes to call a witness other than the claimant, he must comply with the Rules. For example, the witness's contact information, counsel's reasons for calling the witness, and an estimate of the amount of time needed at the hearing for the witness's testimony must be provided in writing to the RPD and to the other party if the minister is intervening within the time limits set out in the Rules (no later than 10 days before the hearing).

To reduce the risk of the witness failing to appear, it is prudent to request the RPD to issue a summons to order a witness to testify. The summons must be provided to the summoned witness, and the RPD notified of this in writing. Witness fees and travel expenses are also the responsibility of the claimant. Should a summoned witness fail to appear, the Rules set out the process for making a request to the RPD to issue a warrant for that person's arrest.

DESIGNATED REPRESENTATIVE

There are situations where the refugee claimant is not capable of making decisions, such as in the case of an unaccompanied minor or a person deemed mentally incompetent or unable to understand the proceedings.[12] In these instances, the division appoints a person to act and make decisions on behalf of the claimant. The **designated representative** may be a relative or a professional, such as a lawyer or social worker. Counsel is permitted to take on the role of designated representative.

MINISTER'S COUNSEL

Although most refugee hearings proceed without intervention from the minister, the RPD is required to notify the minister when it has information (found in the PIF or BOC, for example) that might be of interest to the minister for the purpose of intervening in a case, such as the claimant's military, which might indicate he was part of a regime that carried out human rights abuses. The Rules require the RPD to give written notice to the minister when the RPD has this kind of information, and to provide the minister with the related information.

REPRESENTATIVE OF THE UNITED NATIONS
HIGH COMMISSIONER FOR REFUGEES

A representative of the United Nations high commissioner for refugees is entitled to observe any refugee claimant's proceeding, according to s. 166(e) of the IRPA.

Refugee Protection Officer

Although the role of the refugee protection officer (RPO) has been eliminated by legislative amendments to the IRPA by the BRRA and PCIS, it is a role that is worth noting for its uniqueness within a tribunal system. Since the inception of the IRB in 1989, officers (career public servants known under such titles as refugee hearing officers, refugee protection officers, or tribunal officers) performed various critical functions within the non-adversarial refugee determination system. The RPO worked alongside members in the pre-hearing stage to identify issues in a refugee claim, to make recommendations for claim-specific research, and to prepare the claim with the requisite research (country and claim-specific) in time for the hearing. The officer conducted expedited interviews and made recommendations for the positive determination in a number of claims—this was not only expeditious for the claimant, but also an efficient case-management strategy to deal with mani-festly founded claims. Refugee hearings are inquisitorial in nature so the officer played a unique "neutral" role in the hearing room by ensuring that all evidence was presented and evaluated by the member. The officer could also question a claimant and other witnesses "vigorously," which is especially important when there are issues of credibility. Officers were equally talented in focusing on relevant issues when the minister intervened and the hearing became adversarial. The of-ficer role was built into the RPD Rules and included a provision to "do any other thing that is necessary to ensure a full and proper examination of a claim or other matter" (former RPD rule 16(g)).

Evidence

During the hearing, Mr. M must answer questions about the information he pro-vided on the PIF/BOC and about any documents he provided to the RPD. He is also given the opportunity to tell the member what he fears about returning to his home-land. He will explain why he is making a claim for refugee protection and provide details about his persecution or cruel treatment along with the facts that support his allegations. He will be expected to describe the actions he took to seek protection in his country of nationality, including steps to move to another part of his country.

The RPD is not bound by any legal or technical rules of evidence and may base its decision on evidence that is considered credible or trustworthy in the circum-stances, provided that the evidence is presented in the proceedings. The RPD must also deal with all proceedings that are before it, as informally and quickly as the circumstances and requirements of fairness and natural justice permit, according to s. 162(2) of the IRPA.

The RPD may take **judicial notice** of any generally recognized facts, or informa-tion or opinion within its specialized knowledge, providing that it gives notice to the refugee claimant that it is doing so, according to s. 170 of the IRPA. This means that it is unnecessary to bring evidence to prove a fact that is generally known. For example, it would not be necessary to prove that student protesters in Beijing's Tiananmen Square were massacred in June 1989 because this event is now generally known.

Oral Representations

After all questioning of Mr. M and any other witnesses is complete, and the member is satisfied that all the evidence has been heard, counsel has the opportunity to de-liver **oral representations**—that is, make a final statement.

Decisions and Reasons

The RPD member does not decide whether or not Mr. M would make a good permanent resident or Canadian citizen or whether he can remain in or must leave Canada. Rather, the member decides only whether Mr. M has established his claim under one of the following grounds:

- persecution under a Convention refugee ground,
- danger of torture, or
- risk to life or risk of cruel and unusual treatment or punishment.

There are five possible outcomes, as follows:

1. the claim is allowed because the claimant is found to be a Convention refugee;
2. the claim is allowed because the claimant is found to be a person in need of protection;
3. the claim is rejected because the claimant is not a Convention refugee and is not a person in need of protection;
4. the claim is rejected because the claimant is not a Convention refugee and is not a person in need of protection and there is no credible basis; or
5. the claim is rejected because the claimant is not a Convention refugee and is not a person in need of protection and the claim is manifestly unfounded.

Wherever practicable, the RPD member renders the decision and reasons orally at the end of the hearing, which means that the majority of refugee claimants will know the outcome of their claim at the end of the hearing. A copy of the written reasons and the **notice of decision** will generally follow by mail.

The division is required by the Rules to issue a written decision, called a notice of decision, to the claimant and to the minister, whether the minister intervened or not.

In the case of a rejected claim, written reasons for the decision must accompany the notice of decision. Furthermore, s. 107(2) of the IRPA stipulates that if the claim is rejected because there was no credible or trustworthy evidence, or if the claim is a manifestly unfounded claim (MUC) (IRPA, s. 107.1), the member must include this finding in the reasons for rejecting the claim. The purpose of the "no credible basis" and the "manifestly unfounded claim" labels is to identify these cases to immigration officials (because the conditional removal order will take effect). This is an immigration policy that is intended to discourage frivolous and non-genuine claimants by restricting their access to post-determination processes such as appeals, thereby providing for their speedier removal.

If the claim is successful, the claimant or the minister may request written reasons as long as the request is in writing and is made within ten days of notification of the decision, in accordance with the Rules and s. 169 of the IRPA.

Post-Determination Stage Under the PCISA

Claim Accepted

If Mr. M's claim is allowed, the conditional removal order issued by the CBSA officer during the front-end process does not take effect. As a successful claimant, Mr. M's next step, whether as a Convention refugee or as a person in need of protection, is to apply for permanent resident status for himself and his spouse and dependent children who are abroad.

Application information will normally accompany the notice of decision from the IRB. Under the former IRP regulations at s. 175, the successful claimant had 180 days to apply for permanent residence (check the new IRP regulations for updates to the requirements). Applications are processed in Canada for Mr. M and by the visa office for his family. Although there are processing fees for the application process, the right of permanent residence fee is waived for protected persons. In the interim, CIC issues a "protected person status document" (PPSD) to confirm the successful refugee claimant's status in Canada.

Mr. M may have to undergo security screening and medical examinations again, if the initial security checks and medical examinations have expired.

Designated Foreign National

If Mr. M had arrived as part of a group that was designated as an irregular arrival—for example, on a boat whose passage was arranged by human smugglers—then he would not be able to apply for permanent residence for five years after receipt of his determination by the RPD. Instead, Mr. M would be allowed to remain in Canada on a temporary resident permit (TRP), and the consequence of this is that Mr. M. would not have any right to sponsor his family members. Mr. M's family would not be able to join him in Canada as permanent residents.

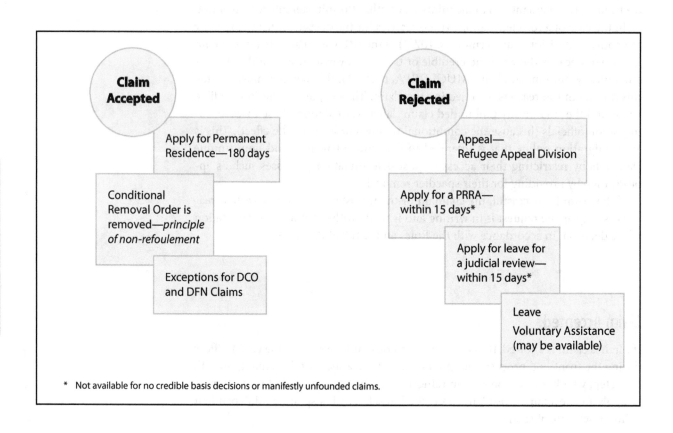

Claim Accepted
- Apply for Permanent Residence—180 days
- Conditional Removal Order is removed—*principle of non-refoulement*
- Exceptions for DCO and DFN Claims

Claim Rejected
- Appeal— Refugee Appeal Division
- Apply for a PRRA— within 15 days*
- Apply for leave for a judicial review— within 15 days*
- Leave Voluntary Assistance (may be available)

*   Not available for no credible basis decisions or manifestly unfounded claims.

Not Eligible for Permanent Residence

Under ss. 114(3), 108(2), and 109(3) of the IRPA, a successful refugee claimant is not eligible to apply for permanent residence in any of the following situations:

- *A misrepresentation has been discovered.* The protection was granted because of misrepresentation—for example, the claimant provided false information.
- *Protection has ceased.* For example, as a result of a newly elected government in the claimant's country of origin.
- *Protection has been vacated.* For example, further to an application by the minister, the RPD vacates its decision and nullifies refugee protection.

For each of the above situations, the minister must apply to the RPD to request a hearing into the matter to argue cessation or vacation.

Cessation

The cessation clause of the refugee definition is embedded in the IRPA at s. 108. As noted in Chapter 7, the provision exists so that the RPD may terminate refugee status when protection is no longer needed (if the refugee has signalled he no longer fears persecution because he has renewed his passport, and/or voluntarily returned to the country where he originally feared persecution for extended visits, or he obtained citizenship from a country other than his country of nationality, or the country conditions that gave rise to his fear of persecution have changed). The process requires the minister to file an application for cessation in accordance with the RPD rules. Although the provision has existed in Canadian immigration law for a long time, it was rarely used by the minister.

The PCISA amends the IRPA by adding a new section that states that when a permanent resident loses his refugee status, he automatically loses his permanent resident status, unless refugee protection ceased because of a change in country conditions (Bill C-31, s. 18; IRPA, ss. 40.1(1) and 40.1(2)). The effect of this new provision is that the permanent resident will be deemed "inadmissible" and thereby liable to removal from Canada. Moreover, the permanent resident has no right to appeal the decision to the RAD.

Claim Rejected

If Mr. M's claim is rejected, the removal order will come into effect. However, before removal takes place, the unsuccessful refugee claimant may have the following options:

- voluntary departure;
- appeal of the RPD determination to the Refugee Appeal Division (RAD);
- application for leave for judicial review by the Federal Court (the removal order may be stayed); or

- application to CIC for a pre-removal risk assessment (unless there was a "no credible basis" or "MUC" stipulation) within 15 days from the date of the notice of decision.

Instructions for applying for leave for judicial review, and for a pre-removal risk assessment, are sent to the rejected claimant by the RPD with the notice of decision.

Voluntary Departure

The unsuccessful refugee claimant must leave Canada within 30 days from the date of the notice of decision because the conditional removal takes effect. To encourage refugees to leave voluntarily, the government created the Assisted Voluntary Return and Reintegration (AVRR) pilot program, which commenced on June 29, 2012 and is expected to run for four years. The pilot program is only for unsuccessful refugee claimants who initiated their claims in the Greater Toronto Area and meet certain eligibility criteria (did not withdraw or abandon their claim, have no criminal record, are not inadmissible on any of the more serious grounds, or have not applied to be sponsored by a spouse).

The goal of the pilot program is to ensure that failed refugee claimants leave Canada shortly after they receive a final negative determination from the RPD. In exchange for agreeing to leave Canada immediately, the unsuccessful refugee claimant receives a return plane ticket and up to $2,000 "reintegration money." However, if the unsuccessful refugee claimant wishes to exercise any post-determination rights (such as an appeal to the RAD, an application for leave to the Federal Court, or an application for a pre-removal risk assessment), the sum will be reduced according to a descending sliding scale (see Chapter 10 for further discussion related to removals).

Appeal to the RAD

There is limited access to the Refugee Appeal Division. Only claimants who made claims under the new refugee determination system will be able to appeal their decision. Some, such as the following, will be barred from appealing to the RAD:

- claimants from designated countries of origin (DCOs);
- claimants who have manifestly unfounded claims or claims with no credible basis; and
- claimants who are exempted from the safe third country agreement.

See Chapter 11, Appeals, for a complete discussion of the RAD and refugee appeals.

Judicial Review by Federal Court

For refugee claims made prior to the implementation of the RAD, claimants have no right to appeal to the RAD. Claimants can, however, apply for a judicial review by the Federal Court. An applicant for judicial review must first seek leave of the Federal

Court, requesting the court to hear the case. This must occur within 15 days from the later of the notice of the decision or the issuance of written reasons by the RPD. The application requirements (such as the use of Form IR-1) and the procedures for applying for leave are set out in the Federal Court's Immigration and Refugee Protection Rules. The claimant's application for leave must also be served on the minister, who may decide to oppose it.

In our example, the effect of Mr. M's application is that there will be a stay of the conditional removal order that was issued against him, allowing him to remain in Canada pending the decision on his application for leave (in accordance with the IRP Regulations). However, if Mr. M's claim was rejected with a finding of "no credible basis" or if it was a "manifestly unfounded claim," then he would not be entitled to a stay of removal.

If the Federal Court grants leave, the stay of the removal will be extended to allow Mr. M to remain in Canada for the judicial review.

A judicial review is not an appeal on the merits of a claim or a rehearing of the claim. There are six grounds set out in s. 18.1(4) of the *Federal Courts Act* on which a judge may grant a judicial review. For example, if there was an error of law or of fact in the decision of the RPD, or if there was a failure to observe a principle of natural justice. If an application for judicial review is allowed, the Federal Court will normally set aside the decision of the RPD and send the case back to the IRB to be reconsidered.

Pre-Removal Risk Assessment

The pre-removal risk assessment (PRRA) is a program intended for people (not just failed refugee claimants) who are about to be removed from Canada and who are desperate to stay, because one of the following circumstances exists:

- a well-founded fear of persecution, according to the Convention refugee definition; or
- a risk of torture, risk to life, or risk of cruel and unusual treatment or punishment, according to the Convention Against Torture.

The PRRA program is managed by CIC, but is expected to be transferred to the RPD two years after all other changes to the refugee determination system come into force. CIC will continue to process the backlog of PRRA cases until the transfer of the function to the RPD. The new RPD Rules will be further amended (2013-2014 is the anticipated date of transfer) to provide for the changes required by the transfer function from CIC to the RPD as outlined in the BRRA and the PCSIA.[13]

The PRRA program is another example of Canada's commitment to the principle of *non-refoulement*. However, it is important to remember that the PRRA is not an appeal or review of a negative decision by the RPD.

Generally, a successful PRRA applicant will be granted refugee protection, will not be removed, and may apply for permanent residence. However, a negative decision on the application means removal arrangements will proceed, and the applicant must leave Canada.

WHO MAY APPLY

The PRRA is for people who are **removal ready**, meaning that they are subject to a removal order that is in force or that a security certificate has been issued against them (IRPA, s. 112(1)), and they are in possession of a valid passport or travel document. There are several circumstances under which an applicant may generally not apply for a PRRA, pursuant to s. 112 of the IRPA:

- the person is subject to extradition under s. 15 of the *Extradition Act*;
- the person's claim to refugee protection was determined ineligible because she came directly or indirectly from a designated country, other than a country of her nationality or former habitual residence;
- less than 12 months have passed since the person's refugee claim in Canada was rejected, withdrawn, or abandoned by the RPD or the RAD (under s. 112(2)(b.1));
- in the case of a failed DCO refugee claimant, the person cannot apply for 36 months; however, the minister has the discretion to exempt claimants from that bar if there is a sudden change in country conditions that could lead to a personal risk if the clamant returned to his country of origin (a DCO claimant whose claim was rejected on the basis of an exclusion—s. E or F of article 1 of the Refugee Convention—is not eligible to apply); or
- the claim was rejected because it was vacated or falls under the exclusion provisions (that is, rejected on the basis of s. E or F of article 1 of the Refugee Convention).

There is another list of categories under s. 112(3) of the IRPA. Applicants for a PRRA who fall under the s. 112(3) restrictions (for example, found to be inadmissible on grounds of security, violation of human or international rights, serious criminality, or organized criminality) are still entitled to have their applications considered for a risk assessment on the grounds of the Convention Against Torture, but they will not be assessed against the Refugee Convention. They will not be granted refugee status in keeping with the principle of the definition's exclusion clauses, and they will not be able to apply for permanent residence.

In assessing the application, the PRRA officer must take into account whether the applicant is a danger to the public in Canada. Section 112(3) stipulates that refugee protection may not be granted to a PRRA applicant if the applicant

- is determined to be inadmissible on grounds of security, the violation of human or international rights, or organized criminality;
- is determined to be inadmissible on grounds of serious criminality with respect to a conviction in Canada punished by a term of imprisonment of at least two years or with respect to a conviction outside Canada for an offence that, if committed in Canada, would constitute an offence under an Act of Parliament punishable by a maximum term of imprisonment of at least ten years;
- made a claim for refugee protection that was rejected on the basis of s. F of article 1 of the Refugee Convention, because those who have been in the role of persecutor are excluded from later being granted protection; or

- is named in a **security certificate** referred to in s. 77(1) of the IRPA; a security certificate is issued in exceptional circumstances where a person is deemed inadmissible for reasons of national security, for violating human or international rights, or for involvement in organized or serious crimes.

EVIDENCE CONSIDERED

A person who has been permitted to apply for a PRRA is allowed to remain in Canada until such time as the circumstances change—for example, there is a change in country conditions. Such changes would trigger a re-examination by the minister of the grounds on which the application was allowed and may lead to a cancellation of a stay and the execution of a removal order. Until this happens, the applicant is allowed to remain in Canada in a kind of legal limbo: she cannot apply to sponsor family members; if she leaves Canada, she most likely will not be able to return; and although she is allowed to work, her work permit is issued for a short period of time.

The PRRA is an administrative process conducted by officers with specialized knowledge, called PRRA officers. Generally, applications are decided without a hearing, although there are exceptions. PRRA officers process applications through a paper review of the application, consider documentary evidence and written submissions from the applicant and the minister, and assess whether there are any new facts or evidence to decide whether there is a risk in removing and returning a person subject to a removal order. Applicants may present only evidence that arose after the rejection of their claim or that the applicant could not reasonably have been expected in the circumstances to have presented at the time of the rejection. PRRA officers have the statutory authority to decide whether an oral hearing is warranted in exceptional cases. In rendering their decisions, PRRA officers assess applications against the requirements of the Refugee Convention (for the granting of refugee status) and the Convention Against Torture (for the granting of protection as "a person in need of protection").

In the case of unsuccessful refugee claimants, the PRRA provides the applicant with the opportunity to give new evidence only—that is, evidence that could not reasonably or possibly have been provided at the refugee hearing. An example is a change in the applicant's country that puts the applicant at risk, such as a new political party coming to power, a new law being passed that seriously violates the applicant's human rights, or the outbreak of a civil war; evidence may also include documentation that was not available at the hearing.

TIMELINES

A person who has an enforceable removal order issued against him (that is, a person found ineligible by the CBSA/CIC to make a refugee claim at the front-end stage, or a foreign national who is inadmissible) will be notified in an "advanced information notice" that he has 15 days to decide to apply for a PRRA; in the interim, the removal order is suspended. In the case of a failed refugee claimant, the clock starts ticking on the date of a negative determination by the RPD. Failed refugee claimants also have 15 days to decide to apply for a PRRA and the claimant is notified by the RPD about this option at the time of receiving the notice of decision.

At the point of receiving either the "advanced information notice" or the "notice of decision," the applicant has 15 days to complete the PRRA application form and return it to CIC. Once the application is submitted, the claimant cannot be removed until the PRRA officer makes a decision on the application. There is also an additional 15 days available for submitting evidence to support the application. Failure to submit the PRRA application by the 15-day deadline can result in the removal of the PRRA applicant.

DECISION

If the PRRA application is accepted, the applicant is usually granted status as a "protected person." Such applicants may then apply for permanent residence.

PRRA applicants who are successful in their request not to be removed, but who are ineligible for refugee determination (because of inadmissibility on grounds of security, violating human or international rights, serious or organized criminality, or because they are named in a security certificate further to s. 77(1) of the IRPA), may not apply for permanent residence. Instead, the successful outcome of the PRRA application has the effect of a stay of the execution of the removal order, and the applicant is not removed from Canada. The person is allowed to remain in Canada under a temporary resident permit until such time as the circumstances change—for example, there is a change in country conditions. Such changes would trigger a re-examination by the minister of the grounds on which the applicant was allowed to stay in Canada, and may lead to a cancellation of a stay of the removal order, and the subsequent execution of the removal order.

PRRA applicants who are rejected must generally be removed from Canada. There is, however, the possibility of applying to CIC to remain in Canada on humanitarian and compassionate grounds (see Chapter 5, Permanent Entry).

APPENDIX: IMMIGRATION AND REFUGEE BOARD REGIONAL OFFICES

The following are the business offices, also known as the "registries," for the purpose of contacting the Immigration and Refugee Board. All communication (oral or written) with the board's divisions must be made through a registry.

Eastern Region

Montreal (Divisions: ID, RPD, IAD)	Ottawa (Divisions: ID, RPD, IAD, RAD)
Registrar	Registrar
Immigration and Refugee Board of Canada	Immigration and Refugee Board of Canada
200 René-Lévesque Boulevard West	Minto Place, Canada Building
Guy Favreau Complex	344 Slater Street, 11th Floor
East Tower, Room 102	Ottawa, Ontario K1A 0K1
Montreal, Quebec H2Z 1X4	Tel.: (613) 943-8630
Tel.: (514) 283-7733	Fax: (613) 943-1550
Fax: (514) 283-0164	

Central Region

Toronto (Divisions: ID, RPD, IAD)	Niagara Falls (Division: ID)
Registrar	Registrar
Immigration and Refugee Board of Canada	Immigration and Refugee Board of Canada
74 Victoria Street	6080 McLeod Road
Suite 400	Unit #15
Toronto, Ontario M5C 3C7	Niagara Falls, Ontario L2G 7T4
Tel.: (416) 954-1000	Tel.: (416) 954-1000
Fax: (416) 954-1165	

Western Region

Vancouver (Divisions: ID, RPD, IAD)	Calgary
Registrar	225 Manning Rd NE
Immigration and Refugee Board of Canada	Suite 201
Suite 1600, Library Square	Calgary, Alberta T2E 2P5
300 West Georgia Street	Telephone : (403) 292-6620
Vancouver, British Columbia V6B 6C9	Fax : (403) 292-6116
Tel.: (604) 666-5946	
Fax: (604) 666-3043	

KEY TERMS

REVIEW QUESTIONS

Introduction

1. What is a spontaneous arrival?

2. What separate government organizations are involved in the refugee protection claim process in Canada?

Front-End Process

Under what circumstances is a refugee claim ineligible to be referred to the Refugee Protection Division?

Refugee Determination Processes

1. Name the key document that is relevant to a refugee claim. Outline the requirements for the claimant to submit this document for review by the Refugee Protection Division.

2. As counsel, you should be able to explain the refugee determination process in full and prepare your client for a refugee hearing. Answer the following questions for your client:

   a. What forms and documents must be provided to the RPD?

   b. What is the nature of the proceedings?

   c. What are a refugee claimant's rights and responsibilities at a proceeding before the Refugee Protection Division?

   d. Who is present at a typical regular refugee hearing where the minister is not intervening? What are the roles of each person present?

   e. What are all possible determinations that a Refugee Protection Division member can make?

Post-Determination Processes

1. Explain the options available to the refugee claimant if his claim is accepted.

2. Explain the options available to the refugee claimant if his claim is rejected.

DISCUSSION QUESTION

Refugee claimants are duty bound to answer all questions truthfully and produce all documents and information as requested. Imagine someone who has fled for her safety, who is fearful of government officials, and who cannot understand or speak either of our official languages. Would that person trust the immigration officer in an interview and answer all questions truthfully? Discuss.

ACTIVITY

1. Find out what resources exist in your community to assist newcomer immigrants and refugees. Together with your classmates, compile a list of agencies and the services provided to refugees in your community.

2. The refugee claimant will be nervous on the day of the interview or hearing. Counsel can make the event more comfortable by managing the claimant's expectations. With a partner, assume the roles of counsel and client. As counsel, describe and explain to your client:

   • the physical layout of a hearing or interview room and the fact that counsel may not be sitting next to the claimant;

- that the proceedings are private (generally closed to the public to protect the confidentiality of the claimant);

- that the proceedings will be recorded;

- that the proceedings will be held in English or French, although an interpreter will be provided;

- the type of proceeding—will it be an interview (expedited), a pre-hearing conference, or a hearing?—as well as what to expect during the proceeding;

- who will be present and what their roles are;

- that the proceedings will be non-adversarial unless the minister's representative is intervening; and

- the order of questioning.

NOTES

1. Counsel may be either legal counsel (member of a law society or membres des Chambre des notaires) or lay counsel; however, if lay counsel is representing the refugee claimant for a fee, counsel must be a licensed member in good standing of the Immigration Consultants of Canada Regulatory Council (ICCRC).

2. In certain cases, after a claim is refused by the RPD, the claimant may not be immediately removed should she appeal to the RAD or apply for a judicial review or a preremoval risk assessment (PRRA). The removal order comes into effect only after the claimant has exhausted all legal options available to her.

3. Section 102 of the IRPA and s. 159.3 of the *Immigration and Refugee Protection Regulations* (IRP Regulations).

4. The interim federal health letter provides coverage of emergency health services until the refugee claimant is eligible for provincial health coverage.

5. It is important to note the date when the refugee claimant receives the PIF because it is used by the RPD in calculating timelines.

6. Exceptions are outlined in the IRP Regulations (s. 159.5) and, generally, safeguard the principles of family reunification, the best interests of the child, and no return to a country where a person faces the death penalty.

7. See Citizenship and Immigration Canada, "Backgrounder— Summary of Changes to Canada's Refugee System," June 29, 2012, regarding the proposed regulatory changes, http://www.cic.gc.ca/english/department/media/backgrounders/2012/2012-06-29b.asp.

8. Ibid.

9. At the time of writing, the proposal for the new RPD Rules was available for review: "Refugee Protection Division Rules: Regulatory I, *Canada Gazette*, archived, vol. 146, no. 32, August 11, 2012, http://www.gazette.gc.ca/rp-pr/p1/2012/2012-08-11/html/reg1-eng.html#rias.

10. You can receive frequent updates from the IRB about the implementation of the new refugee determination system by clicking on the home page. Available at the time of writing, Immigration and Refugee Board, "Frequently Asked Questions—Bill C-31," October 18, 2012, http://www.irb-cisr.gc.ca/eng/reform/pages/faqreform.aspx.

11. *Rezaei v. Canada (Minister of Citizenship and Immigration)* (T.D.), [2003] 3 F.C. 421, which refers to the powers of administrative tribunals according to *Prassad v. Canada (Minister of employment and immigration)*, [1989] 1 S.C.R. 560.

12. Section 167(2) of the IRPA; rule 20 of the new RPD Rules.

13. Above note 9.

REFERENCES

Béchard, J., and S. Elgersma. Legislative Summary of Bill C-31: An Act to Amend the Immigration and Refugee Protection Act, the Balanced Refugee Reform Act, the Marine Transportation Security Act and the Department of Citizenship and Immigration Act, Library of Parliament Research Publications, 41-1-C31-E, revised June 4, 2012. http://www.parl.gc.ca/About/Parliament/LegislativeSummaries/bills_ls.asp?Language=E&ls=c31&Parl=41&Ses=1&source=library_prb#txt2.

Canada Gazette. "Refugee Protection Division Rules, Regulatory Impact Analysis Statement," archived, vol. 146, no. 32, August 11, 2012. http://www.gazette.gc.ca/rp-pr/p1/2012/2012-08-11/html/reg1-eng.html#rias.

Canada. Parliament, House of Commons, *An Act to Amend the Immigration and Refugee Protection Act, the Balanced Refugee Reform Act, the Marine Transportation Security Act and the Department of Citizenship and Immigration Act* (short title: *Protecting Canada's Immigration System Act*), Bill C-31, 41st Parl., 1st sess., 60-61 Eliz. II, 2011–2012, assented to June 28, 2012. http://www.parl.gc.ca/HousePublications/Publication.aspx?Docid=5697417&file=4.

Canada. Parliament, House of Commons, *An Act to amend the Immigration and Refugee Protection Act and the Federal Courts Act* (short title: *Balanced Refugee Reform Act*), Bill C-11, Third Session, Fortieth Parliament, 59 Elizabeth II, 2010, assented to June 29, 2010. http://www.parl.gc.ca/HousePublications/Publication.aspx?Language=E&Mode=1&DocId=4644728&File=14.

Coakeley, Simon. "New Developments in the Refugee Determination System: Presentation to the Canadian Council for Refugees, Hamilton," May 26, 2011. http://www.irb-cisr.gc.ca/Eng/media/newsnouv/2011/Pages/ccrsn.aspx.

Criminal Code. R.S.C. 1985, c. C-46.

Extradition Act. S.C. 1999, c. 18.

Federal Courts Act. R.S.C. 1985, c. F-7.

Federal Courts Immigration and Refugee Protection Rules. S.O.R./93-22.

Immigration and Refugee Board. "Instructions Governing the Management of Refugee Protection Claims Awaiting Front-End Security Screening," November 23, 2011. http://www.irb-cisr.gc.ca/eng/brdcom/references/pol/instructions/Pages/securit.aspx.

Immigration and Refugee Protection Act. S.C. 2001, c. 27.

Immigration and Refugee Protection Regulations. S.O.R./2002-227.

Legal Services, Immigration and Refugee Board. *Consolidated Grounds in the Immigration and Refugee Protection Act: Persons in Need of Protection—Danger of Torture.* May 15, 2002: www.irb-cisr.gc.ca/en/references/legal/rpd/cgrounds/torture/index_e.htm.

Legal Services, Immigration and Refugee Board. "Consolidated Grounds in the Immigration and Refugee Protection Act: Persons in Need of Protection—Risk to Life or Risk of Cruel and Unusual Treatment or Punishment," May 15, 2002. http://www.irb-cisr.gc.ca/Eng/brdcom/references/legjur/Pages/ProtectTorture.aspx.

Legal Services, Immigration and Refugee Board. "Interpretation of the Convention Refugee Definition in the Case Law," December 2002, Addendum #1—December 2003.

Canada Gazette. "Refugee Appeal Division Rules," vol. 135, no. 50, December 15, 2001. http://www.gazette.gc.ca/archives/p1/2001/2001-12-15/html/reg3-eng.html.

Refugee Protection Division Rules. S.O.R./2002-228.

Security Intelligence Review Committee. "SIRC Report 2003-2004: An Operational Review of the Canadian Security Intelligence Service," September 30, 2004. http://www.sirc-csars.gc.ca/anrran/2003-2004/index-eng.html.

United Nations High Commissioner for Refugees. Handbook on Procedures and Criteria for Determining Refugee Status Under the 1951 Convention and the 1967 Protocol Relating to the Status of Refugees, HCR/IP/4/Eng/REV.1, re-edited, Geneva, January 1992, UNHCR 1979.

Recommended Reading

Canadian Heritage. Human Rights Program. Describes the UN human rights system, UN instruments, and how Canada is involved in this area; provides a glossary of specialized terms and weblinks to related sites. http://www.pch.gc.ca/ddp-hrd/index-eng.cfm.

Hathaway, James C. "Rebuilding Trust: Report of the Review of Fundamental Justice in Information Gathering and Dissemination at the Immigration and Refugee Board of Canada," Ottawa: Immigration and Refugee Board, 1993. Accompanied by "Action Plan: Response of the Immigration and Refugee Board to the Report of Professor James Hathaway."

Hathaway, James C. *The Law of Refugee Status.* Toronto: Butterworths, 1991.

Hathaway, James C. *The Rights of Refugees Under International Law.* Cambridge, UK and New York: Cambridge University Press, 2005.

Office of the United Nations High Commissioner for Human Rights. http://www.ohchr.org/EN/Pages/WelcomePage.aspx.

Statutes of the Office of the United Nations High Commissioner for Refugees

Convention Relating to the Status of Refugees. 189 U.N.T.S. 150, entered into force April 22, 1954. http://www1.umn.edu/humanrts/instree/v1crs.htm.

Protocol Relating to the Status of Refugees. 606 U.N.T.S. 267, entered into force October 4, 1967. http://www1.umn.edu/humanrts/instree/v2prsr.htm.

Convention Against Torture and Other Cruel, Inhuman or Degrading Treatment or Punishment. Can. T.S. 1987 no. 36; G.A. res. 39/46 (annex, 39 U.N. GAOR Supp. (no. 51) at 197, U.N. Doc. A/39/51 (1984)). http://www1.umn.edu/humanrts/instree/ainstls1.htm.

International Covenant on Civil and Political Rights. G.A. res. 2200A (XXI), 21 U.N. GAOR Supp. (No. 16) at 52, U.N. Doc. A/6316 (1966), 999 U.N.T.S. 171, entered into force March 23, 1976. http://www1.umn.edu/humanrts/instree/b3ccpr.htm.

Universal Declaration of Human Rights. G.A. res. 217A (III) U.N. Doc. A/810 at 71 (1948). http://www.un.org/en/documents/udhr/index.shtml.

Human Rights Organizations

Amnesty International. An international organization whose mission is to conduct research and promote action to prevent human rights abuses. http://www.amnesty.org.

Canadian Council for Refugees. A non-profit umbrella organization that promotes the rights and protection of refugees, both in Canada and internationally; composed of organizations that aid in the settlement, sponsorship, and protection of refugees and immigrants. http://ccrweb.ca.

Human Rights Watch. An organization dedicated to protecting the human rights of people around the world and investigating human rights violations. http://www.hrw.org.

Centre for Refugee Studies (York University). For research on refugee issues; an organized research unit of York University, founded in 1988. http://crs.yorku.ca.

Refugee Forum (Human Rights Research and Education Centre of the University of Ottawa). For research and information on Canadian refugee law; the Forum enjoys a broad mandate to study and comment on Canada's asylum system. http://www.cdp-hrc.uottawa.ca.

Refugee Studies Centre (Oxford Department of International Development, Queen Elizabeth House, University of Oxford). Founded in 1982, the Centre's purpose is to build knowledge and understanding of the causes and effects of forced migration in order to help improve the lives of some of the world's most vulnerable people. http://www.rsc.ox.ac.uk.

Country-Specific Sources for Research Purposes

This is a small selection of credible sources where you can begin your research on background country conditions.

Amnesty International. For country reports and special studies. http://www.amnesty.org.

Human Rights Watch Country Reports. http://www.hrw.org/publications/reports.

Immigration and Refugee Board. Check out the "research tab" on the IRB website; the research database contains papers on a variety of countries. http://www.irb-cisr.gc.ca/eng/resrec/respro/Pages/index.aspx.

Journal of Refugee Studies. http://jrs.oxfordjournals.org/content/by/year.

United Nations High Commissioner for Refugees

Main website. http://unhcr.org.

UNHCR in Canada. http://unhcr.ca.

United States

US State Department Country Reports on Human Rights Practices. http://www.state.gov/j/drl/rls/hrrpt.

PART V

Enforcement

General In-Canada Enforcement and Removal Procedures

10

LEARNING OUTCOMES

After reading this chapter you should be able to:

- Describe general control and enforcement activities.

- Explain the process for causing immigration enforcement proceedings.

- Describe the reasons for detaining and releasing a person from immigration detention.

- Describe the role of participants at Immigration Division proceedings.

- Find your way around the Immigration Division Rules.

- Distinguish among the various removal orders.

Introduction

This chapter will help you gain basic knowledge about how officers enforce the IRPA and its regulations when someone becomes inadmissible, including general removal procedures. It also provides an overview of the role of the Immigration Division (ID) of the Immigration and Refugee Board (IRB) in hearing and deciding immigration hearings and detention reviews.

You learned in previous chapters that foreign nationals must apply for a visa before arriving in Canada (although there are some exceptions to this general rule that allow a foreign national to apply orally at a port of entry (POE)). Everyone who arrives at a POE must submit to an examination by an officer who decides whether or not an individual has an automatic right to enter (such as in the case of Canadian citizens) or whether he will be admitted with temporary or permanent resident status, along with any conditions the officer may impose before admitting an individual.

Enforcement Activities

As discussed in Chapter 2, the Canada Border Services Agency (CBSA) reports to the minister of public safety and has the responsibility for border management and enforcement activities; it is the agency that is primarily responsible for carrying out the enforcement provisions of the IRPA.

After being admitted to Canada, both temporary and permanent residents do not have any absolute right to remain here. A person who violates a Canadian law, such as the *Criminal Code* or the IRPA, may become inadmissible, triggering enforcement activities such as their removal from Canada. The general process includes an allegation by the minister's representative (an officer who has the delegated authority) of a breach of the law, and a process that may lead to removal. This process may include a referral to the tribunal for a decision about admissibility and a removal order. The CBSA may also detain a person under the IRPA (for reasons discussed later in this chapter) or this decision can be made by the tribunal.

Overview of the Inadmissibility and Removal Process

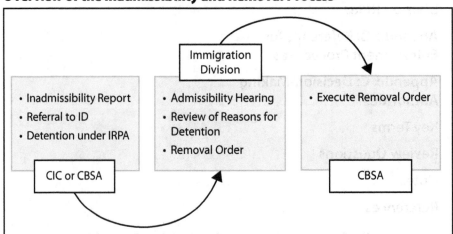

Key immigration enforcement and control activities include the following:[1]

- carrying out **interdiction** functions, or control activities that prevent illegal travellers and criminals from reaching Canada;
- conducting background checks and other observations before visas are issued;
- gathering information on activities such as human smuggling and illegal migration;
- gathering intelligence on activities such as the creation, use, and distribution of fraudulent documents;
- cooperating with other enforcement agencies, both domestic and international;
- performing examinations abroad and at ports of entry;
- conducting investigations and appearing at admissibility hearings;
- issuing removal and exclusion orders;
- creating and implementing measures to deal with dangerous criminals, security and safety risks, and war criminals;
- arresting and detaining foreign nationals who pose a security or safety risk;
- enforcing penalties for illegal activities;
- streamlining the appeal process; and
- removing foreign nationals who are illegally in Canada.

This chapter examines the general enforcement activities that lead to admissibility hearings and/or detention reviews before the Immigration Division.

Case Differentiation

Human Smuggling and Designated Foreign Nationals

On June 29, 2012, Bill C-31—*Protecting Canada's Immigration System Act*—received royal assent. Under new rules, the minister has the authority to confer the status of **designated foreign national (DFN)** on a person who arrives in Canada as part of a group of human smuggled persons who were also conferred special legal status as **designated irregular arrivals**.

Human smuggling is a criminal activity when it is carried out for the purpose of profit rather than for saving lives. Those who engage in human smuggling do so for a material gain by facilitating the illegal entry of foreign nationals. Human smuggling includes facilitating illegal migration and counselling smuggled persons—who are not refugees—to make claims for refugee status in Canada, usually for a substantial amount of money.

The smuggled arrive spontaneously—sometimes as a large group—without having followed the application procedures or without any proof that they are not ineligible and not inadmissible. Although some of the smuggled are legitimate refugees, others are economic migrants who could neither qualify for Canada's immigration programs nor under Canada's refugee protection laws. The latter have been given the false hope by human smugglers that they will be allowed to stay in Canada and, that even if they will eventually be removed, that they will be able to benefit from Canadian health care and other social assistance systems until removal.

Bill C-31 amends the IRPA with provisions to differentiate between cases of foreign nationals who follow the appropriate immigration and refugee application procedures and those who arrive as part of a group that is a designated irregular arrival. New ministerial authorities under Bill C-31 include:

- the authority to designate a group of persons as irregular arrivals;
- the authority to prosecute human smugglers and impose minimum mandatory prison sentences (see Chapter 3); and
- the authority to hold ship owners and operators to account for allowing the use of their vessels to smuggle human beings.

Section 20.1(1) of the IRPA gives the minister the authority, in the public interest, to designate a group of persons as irregular arrivals if the minister:

> (a) is of the opinion that examinations of the persons in the group, particularly for the purpose of establishing identity or determining inadmissibility—and any investigations concerning persons in the group—cannot be conducted in a timely manner; or
>
> (b) has reasonable grounds to suspect that, in relation to the arrival in Canada of the group, there has been, or will be, a contravention of subsection 117(1) for profit, or for the benefit of, at the direction of or in association with a criminal organization or terrorist group.

Unless a foreign national can prove he has the appropriate visa, a foreign national who is part of a group that is a designated irregular arrival will also be designated and known as a designated foreign national (DFN) (IRPA, s. 20.1(2)). There will be different requirements for in-person reporting to immigration officials for DFNs and also different rules for holding a DFN in detention if the DFN is 16 years of age or older.

Inadmissibility Reports

An officer who believes that a permanent resident or foreign national who is already in Canada has become inadmissible may prepare a report setting out the relevant facts to be reviewed by the minister, according to s. 44(1) of the IRPA. This may be a CIC officer or a CBSA officer.

The **inadmissibility report**, often referred to as a **s. 44(1) report**, sets out the grounds of inadmissibility alleged by the officer, with the related sections of the IRPA and the evidence in narrative form. The person may in some circumstances be detained under the IRPA pending a hearing.

Authority to Write Report

Generally, it is CIC officers who have the designated authority to write inadmissibility reports. However, if the grounds of inadmissibility are security, violations of human or international rights, or organized criminality, the cases are managed by the CBSA.

Inadmissibility

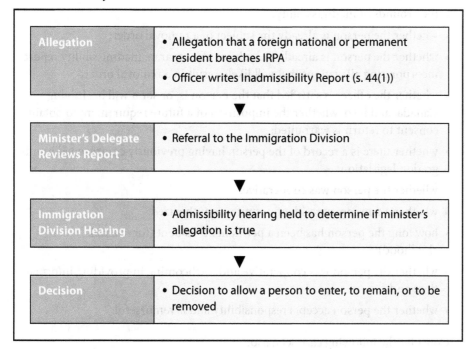

Discretion to Write Report

When an officer believes that a permanent resident has failed to comply with residency obligations and has lost permanent residence status as a result, the officer *must* write an inadmissibility report. However, in other cases, writing the report is at the discretion of the officer.

When the matter involves the more serious reasons for a finding of inadmissibility (that is, security, violations of human or international rights, serious criminality, or organized criminality), an officer will usually prepare an inadmissibility report, which initiates the removal process.

For matters involving less serious, non-criminal matters, an officer considers a number of options. For example, at a *port-of-entry examination* of a foreign national, an officer may take any of the following actions:

- inform the person that she is inadmissible and is allowed to leave Canada voluntarily—the person will be given an Allowed to Leave Canada form (IMM 1282B);
- write the s. 44(1) report and detain the person pending an admissibility hearing; or
- write the s. 44(1) report and allow the person to enter temporarily to attend an admissibility hearing.

CIC's *Enforcement (ENF)* operations manual on writing s. 44(1) reports lists several factors that officers may consider when deciding whether to write a report:[2]

- the length of time the person has been in Canada and her status;
- the grounds of inadmissibility;
- whether the person is already the subject of a removal order;
- whether the person is already the subject of a separate inadmissibility report incorporating allegations that will likely result in a removal order;
- whether the officer is satisfied that the person is, or soon will be, leaving Canada, and if so, whether the imposition of a future requirement to obtain consent to return is warranted;
- whether there is a record of the person having previously contravened immigration legislation;
- whether the person was cooperative;
- whether a temporary resident permit was authorized;
- how long the person has been a permanent resident (for example, since childhood);
- whether the person was cooperative and forthcoming in providing information; and
- whether the person accepts responsibility and is remorseful.

Consider the following case scenario:

Eunice is a 22-year-old citizen of Jamaica. Eunice applied for and obtained a temporary resident visa as a visitor so she could visit her older sister, Nadine, and Nadine's family in Toronto. Eunice had not seen Nadine since Nadine left for Canada over ten years ago. She was happy to get reacquainted with her older sister and to become acquainted with Nadine's two school-aged children and husband. Eunice was provided with her own room in Nadine's home, shown around the city, and given new clothes (so she could face the Canadian cold). Eunice adored her niece and nephew and played with them often. This caught the attention of a next-door neighbour, who asked if Eunice could watch over her children one day, while she went shopping. One of the neighbour's children was knocked down while playing with Eunice's nephew and got a bump on the head. This upset the neighbour, who thought Eunice too lenient about the ordeal. She also suspected that Eunice was an "illegal," seeing as she had been living next door for almost a year now. The neighbour—jealous about Nadine having the extra hands at home and offended by Eunice's attitude—decided to call the police and falsely accused Eunice of hitting her child. After investigating the incident, the police determined that none of the children had been abused and did not charge Eunice. However, they informed immigration authorities. It turns out the neighbour was right about one thing: Eunice overstayed her temporary visa.

In this scenario, Eunice will be interviewed about her immigration status by an immigration investigator at the local immigration office. If the officer has reasonable grounds to believe that Eunice is inadmissible because her temporary resident visa expired and consequently no longer has authorization to be in Canada, the officer has no discretion and must write an inadmissibility report.

Contents of Report

The officer must complete the s. 44(1) report in writing and include the following information:

- the date of the report and place of issue;
- basic information about the person (for example, full and correct name, date of birth, marital status, contact information, and immigration status);
- information about when the temporary resident visa was issued and when it expired;
- the allegation—in Eunice's case, that she failed to leave Canada by the end of the authorized period of stay;
- the exact section of the IRPA—in Eunice's case, s. 41(a) ("Non-compliance with the Act"); and
- the facts in the narrative of the report that amount to why the officer has reasonable grounds to believe that the person is inadmissible—in Eunice's case, the address where she is staying, the date and place her visa was issued, the date and place where she was admitted to Canada, the date her temporary visa expired, and any other details to support the allegation.

There is no information to support the neighbour's allegation that Eunice committed a crime, so the officer does not include this information in her report or base her finding of inadmissibility on criminal grounds.

The officer must address the report to the minister for review and sign the report.

Review and Referral

The minister is authorized under s. 44(2) to take one of the following actions:

- allow the person to stay in Canada, if the minister concludes that the report is not well founded;
- issue a removal order, if the minister concludes that the report is well founded and that it falls within the jurisdiction of the officer who wrote the report; or
- refer the case to the Immigration Division of the Immigration and Refugee Board, if the minister concludes that the report is well founded, but that it does not fall within the jurisdiction of the officer who wrote it.

If the minister (in practice, it is the officer's supervisor who is the officer with the delegated authority) is of the opinion that the report is well founded, the minister may issue a removal order in certain cases.

Alternatively, depending on the grounds of inadmissibility, the minister may refer the report to the ID for a hearing. In Eunice's case, the minister will refer the matter to the ID for a hearing because Eunice was already legally admitted to, and living, in Canada.

The officer will tell Eunice at the time of the interview that she is not under arrest and that there is no reason to detain her. She is free to return to Nadine's home to await her admissibility hearing. The officer explains that Eunice will be sent a notice of admissibility hearing by mail, that she must attend that hearing, and that she may make her case for staying in Canada. However, if the ID member finds that Eunice is inadmissible, an exclusion order will be issued and she will be required to leave Canada.

Onus of Proof

The onus of proof is the burden of proving facts, such as proving inadmissibility. In a criminal trial, the onus is on the prosecution to prove guilt. In a civil trial, the onus is generally on the plaintiff to prove that the defendant caused harm or breached a contract.

At an admissibility hearing, the onus of proof depends on whether or not the person concerned has legal status in Canada. If she was denied the right to enter Canada, and therefore has no legal status, the onus is on the person concerned to prove that she is not inadmissible.

However, if the person concerned was allowed to enter Canada and is alleged at a later time to have become inadmissible, then the onus is on the hearings officer to prove those allegations.

Standard of Proof

The standard of proof is the degree of proof necessary to satisfy the onus of proof. At an admissibility hearing, this means the degree or amount of proof necessary for a decision on inadmissibility to be made. It also applies to the decisions of a visa officer abroad or a CBSA officer at a port of entry.

Reasonable Grounds

The standard of proof varies depending on the ground of inadmissibility at issue. However, in most cases the decision-maker must have reasonable grounds for believing that some act has taken place, is taking place, or may take place that leads to the conclusion of inadmissibility.

Reasonable grounds involve more than a mere suspicion that a person is inadmissible; rather, there must be an objective basis for the allegation. The decision-maker must have credible information that is sufficiently specific and reliable to support the allegation that a person is inadmissible.

Consider another scenario relating to the minister's authority to make decisions that could lead to a foreign national's removal from Canada. As in the earlier case scenario, the minister's authority has been delegated to officers who carry out the immigration functions.

Jose Rodriguez came to Canada as a temporary resident to visit his uncle Juan, who owns a small restaurant called Mama Rosa's. Jose has been living with Juan, his wife Maribella, and their two young children in a small apartment over the restaurant. All of the signature dishes are based on Maribella's grandmother Rosa's recipes and she does most of the cooking and looks after their two young children while Juan manages the restaurant. One of Juan's employees quit suddenly so he asked Jose to help him out until he could find a replacement. Jose agreed and over a period of several weeks pitched in as a waiter and bus boy, and even helped his aunt in the kitchen to give her a break. Jose was having fun learning about running a restaurant. One slow day at the restaurant, Uncle Juan gave Jose the day off and gave him some cash to "go have some fun" in the city.

Jose came to the attention of immigration officials when officers conducted a raid of restaurants in the neighbourhood. Jose was allowed entry to Canada as a temporary visitor but had no authorization to work. The officer alleges that Jose was working illegally and wrote an inadmissibility report for being in a state of non-compliance (see IPRA, s. 41)—namely, not in possession of a work authorization. The way the officer sees it, there are too many illegals working in the restaurant district and this is just another example of a foreign national who violated the terms of his visitor visa and has become inadmissible.

In Jose's case, the minister's delegate will review the officer's admissibility report to ensure there are sufficient details to establish a case against Jose and make a decision that will also lead to an admissibility hearing and the potential order for Jose to leave Canada. What do you think? Does the officer have reasonable grounds to believe that Jose was working illegally? Who has the onus of proof at Jose's admissibility hearing: Jose or the minister?

Probable Grounds

The standard of proof is higher with respect to serious criminal acts under s. 36 of the IRPA.

For these cases, the decision-maker must have probable grounds for believing that some act has taken place, is taking place, or may take place that leads to the conclusion of inadmissibility. In other words, the facts must be proven on a balance of probabilities. This means that the decision-maker must believe that the allegations are more probable than not. In practice, the officer would attempt to obtain evidence such as the record of conviction; however, it is not always possible to do so.

Detention

The CBSA has the authority under the IRPA to arrest and detain permanent residents and foreign nationals at a port of entry, or after the person is in Canada. Detention may also be ordered by a member of the Immigration Division at an admissibility hearing following submissions by an officer. Depending on the risk posed by the person in detention, she may be held at a local jail, a correctional facility, or a CBSA immigration holding centre.

When a person is arrested or detained, the *Canadian Charter of Rights and Freedoms* requires the officer to inform that person of her rights, including:

- the right to know the reason for the arrest and detention;
- the right to counsel; and
- the right to notify her government representative of the arrest or detention.

Detention of Children

According to s. 60 of the IRPA, children under 18 should be detained only "as a measure of last resort." The best interests of the child must be taken into account generally when considering detention, as well as the following specific criteria from s. 249 of the IRP Regulations:

- the availability of alternative arrangements with local childcare agencies;
- the anticipated length of detention;
- where human smugglers brought the children to Canada, the risk of continued control by those smugglers;
- the type of detention facility that would be used;
- the availability for segregation of the children from adults; and
- the availability of educational, counselling, and recreational services.

Detention at a Port of Entry

At the port of entry (POE), an officer may arrest and detain a permanent resident or foreign national to ensure that the person will be available for examination. The officer can also arrest and detain a permanent resident or foreign national at a POE if the officer has reasonable grounds to believe that the person is inadmissible on any of the most serious grounds of admissibility, such as a threat to security, violation of human or international rights, serious criminality, or organized criminality (IRPA, s. 55(3)(b)). The officer must also notify the Immigration Division so that a detention review can be held within 48 hours.

Detention Within Canada

An officer may arrest and detain a permanent resident or foreign national after the person has been admitted to Canada. Generally, there is the requirement for an officer to obtain an immigration warrant for arrest and detention where the person is a permanent resident or a foreign national and there are reasonable grounds to believe that the permanent resident or foreign national is a danger to the public; or is unlikely to appear for examination, for an admissibility hearing, for removal from Canada, or at a proceeding that could lead to that person's removal from Canada because of a removal order issued by the minister (IRPA, s. 55(1).)

Within 48 hours of a detention, an officer may review the reasons for the detention and may exercise her authority under s. 56(1) of the IRPA to release the person if the reason for detention no longer exists. Otherwise, the officer must notify the ID about the detention, without delay, so that a hearing into the reasons for the detention may be reviewed by the ID (IRPA, s. 55(4)). There are exceptions to this procedure if the foreign national is a designated foreign national (see "Detention Reviews" later in this chapter.)

Detention at Admissibility Hearings

A person appearing at an admissibility hearing may already be in detention, or may later be detained at the end of the hearing. For example, a hearings officer may make a submission to the ID member to order the detention of a person at the end of the admissibility hearing. This will be discussed in more detail below.

The Immigration Division

The Immigration Division (ID) of the Immigration and Refugee Board (IRB) functions as an independent decision-making body with the jurisdiction to hear and decide immigration cases referred to it by the minister and to decide whether a person is inadmissible (and consequently should be removed from Canada); it also holds review hearings into the reasons for the detention under the IRPA. These proceedings are called:

- **Admissibility hearings.** The ID has the authority under s. 45 of the IRPA to hear and decide whether permanent residents and foreign nationals alleged to have contravened the IRPA should be allowed to enter or remain in Canada, or should be ordered removed.

- **Detention reviews.** The ID has the authority under s. 54 of the IRPA to review the reasons for the immigration detention of permanent residents, foreign nationals, and designated foreign nationals to decide whether to release them or whether there are sufficient reasons to continue the detention.

Proceedings Before the Immigration Division

Hearings before an ID member are quasi-judicial proceedings and are adversarial. The ID member is expected to hear and decide the matter in an impartial and unbiased manner. As explained in Chapter 2, according to s. 162(2) of the IRPA, the ID is not bound by formal rules of evidence and procedures. It may deal with matters more informally and efficiently than a court within the principles of natural justice.

Given the seriousness of the outcome of an immigration matter—namely, that the client can be removed—the client may have a high level of anxiety. To reduce the risk that this may interfere with the client's ability to answer questions clearly and credibly, it is important for counsel to prepare the client for the hearing by describing and explaining it and by answering any questions that the client may have. Below is a list of typical questions that clients may ask (or may want to know the answers to even if they do not ask), organized by topic. Selected sample answers are provided in parentheses.

- *Type of hearing.* What can the client expect during the hearing? What are the time frames? Is it possible that the client will be removed immediately after the admissibility hearing? (No, this will not happen immediately.) What happens if the client is not released from detention? Is the matter expected to take all day? (We must arrange for alternatives to detention. Do you have someone who can post a bond?)

- *Hearing room.* What is the physical layout of the hearing room? Will the proceeding be held via videoconferencing—for example, if the client is being held in a local jail or immigration holding centre? In that case, where will counsel be? (Counsel will be with the client.)

- *Public or private hearing.* Will the hearing be open to the public? (The proceedings are public, which means there could be observers. However, there are some exceptions—for example, if a refugee claimant or protected person is involved.)

- *Hearing recorded.* Will the hearing be recorded? (Yes. A transcript of the proceeding can be produced for appeal purposes, for example.)

- *Language.* In what language will the hearing be held? (The hearing will be held in English or French, and an interpreter will be provided if requested.)

- *Nature of the proceeding.* Will the hearing be adversarial? (Yes, the nature of the hearing is adversarial and involves the minister's counsel who will question the client and any witnesses, and argue that the client should be removed and/or detained, depending on the type of hearing.)

- *Consequences to family members.* If the client is ordered to be removed, will her family members be removed as well? (Family members who are included in the inadmissibility report may be subject to the same removal order, if one is made.)

  Clients who are being detained will have many questions about getting released or moved to a more comfortable facility, such as an immigration holding facility rather than a jail. It is also important to explain the difference between a criminal incarceration and an immigration detention.

- *Participants.* Who will be present and what is the role of each person? (The ID member, the hearings officer, counsel, the client, and possibly witnesses will be present).

Persons in Attendance

There are a number of people who must be present at an ID hearing, including the person concerned, the minister's counsel, and the ID member. Other persons, such as the claimant's counsel, are likely to be present. Still others may be present—for example witnesses.

IMMIGRATION DIVISION MEMBER

Each case is heard by only one member of the ID, who is a public servant. The member has the authority to hear and decide immigration matters of inadmissibility and reasons for detention. The member will also hear and decide any applications that are made orally at the hearing.

PERSON CONCERNED

The person concerned (PC) must be personally in attendance at the hearing. This can be physically or by videoconference, for example.

MINISTER'S COUNSEL

Minister's counsel is a public servant who works for the CBSA with the title of hearings officer. A hearings officer represents the minister of PSEP at ID proceedings. Prior to the hearing, the hearings officer reviews the report and prepares the case. At the hearing, the hearings officer examines and cross-examines witnesses and presents evidence.

COUNSEL

The legal professional who has the role of counsel is present to protect the interests and right to a fair hearing of the person concerned. Counsel explains the process, provides advice, and presents the case in an efficient manner, within the limits set by the ID member.

The person concerned may choose to be represented by either an unpaid, trusted adviser, such as a family member or clergy, or a paid, legal professional. An unpaid adviser who represents a client and is not charging a fee should use the Notice of Representation Without a Fee or Other Consideration form (IRB/CISR 692), available on the IRB website under the "Forms" tab.

All paid counsel must be members in good standing of the Immigration Consultants of Canada Regulatory Council of Canada (ICCRC) or a provincial or territorial law society (including licensed paralegals), or of the Chambres des notaires du Québec. Counsel who represent a person concerned for a fee must provide their contact information and membership identification number in writing to the ID; otherwise, the ID may consider the client as unrepresented. If counsel is charging a fee, the appropriate form to complete is the Counsel Contact Information form (IRB/CISR 687), available on the IRB website under the "Forms" tab.

According to the ID Rules, counsel is deemed counsel of record once a date for a proceeding is set. In some cases, counsel may wish to be removed from the record—for example, if the client refuses to pay or is very difficult. The rules provide that counsel must seek permission from the ID to withdraw from a case, and also provide for situations where the client wishes to remove the representative as counsel of record.

INTERPRETER

Only interpreters accredited by the IRB are used for hearings, which means they have undergone security checks and passed a language examination. They are not employees of the ID but are contracted for on a case-by-case basis. They are permanently bound by their promise to interpret accurately once they take an oath or make a solemn affirmation to do so. At the beginning of the proceeding, the interpreter confirms that she has used a standardized script to ensure that the interpreter and person concerned understand each other. The interpreter may not guide, provide advice, or offer an opinion to the person concerned.

The ID rules require that if a client or witness requires an interpreter, counsel must notify the ID in writing and specify the language and dialect needed before the hearing.

WITNESSES

If counsel wishes to call a witness other than his client, he must fulfill the requirements of the ID rules. Information such as the reason for calling the witness, the party's relationship to the witness, the amount of time required at the hearing for the witness's testimony, and whether the testimony is by videoconference or telephone must be provided in writing to the ID and copied to the other party. The timelines are set out in the ID rules.

To reduce the risk of the witness failing to appear, it is prudent to request that the ID issue a summons to order a witness to testify, in accordance with the ID rules either in writing or orally at a proceeding. The party is responsible for providing the summons to the summoned person by hand, for notifying the ID in writing of this, and for paying witness fees and travel expenses. In the request, counsel must set out the factors to be considered in issuing the summons, such as the importance of the testimony of a witness and the witness's ability to provide such information.

A witness may apply to the ID to cancel the summons. If the witness is unsuccessful with the application and subsequently fails to appear, a request may be made to the ID to issue a warrant for her arrest, pursuant to the ID rules.

The hearings officer may request that witnesses be excluded from the hearing room during the PC's testimony. A witness is not allowed to share any testimony given at the hearing with any other witness.

DESIGNATED REPRESENTATIVE

There are situations where the person concerned is not capable of making decisions, such as in the case of an unaccompanied minor, or a person deemed mentally incompetent or unable to understand the proceedings (IRPA, s. 167(2)). In these instances, the ID Rules provide that the ID appoint a person to act and make decisions on behalf of the person. Where counsel for either party believes that a designated representative is required, counsel must, without delay, notify the ID. The designated representative may be a relative, or a professional such as a lawyer or social worker. Alternatively, counsel may choose to take on the role of designated representative.

Immigration Division Rules

Legal professionals who represent persons who are subject to a proceeding in the ID must have a thorough knowledge of the ID Rules, in addition to the provisions of the IRPA that set out the jurisdiction of the IRB and the ID to hear and decide matters. The Immigration Division Rules are discussed in Appendix A to this chapter.

Chairperson's Guidelines

The chairperson's guidelines pertain to ID procedures. Familiarity with the chairperson's guidelines will further provide counsel with confidence when navigating ID processes.

Although the majority of the chairperson's guidelines apply to the Refugee Protection Division, there are guidelines issued that have a general application to all divisions, including the ID:

- Guideline 2—Guidelines on Detention—deals specifically with detention;
- Guideline 6—Scheduling and Changing the Date or Time of a Proceeding; and
- Guideline 8—Guideline on Procedures with Respect to Vulnerable Persons Appearing Before the Immigration and Refugee Board of Canada.

All may be useful when appearing before the ID.

As explained in Chapter 1, the guidelines are not binding and members are not specifically directed to follow them. However, they are a source of guiding principles. This is important to preserve the independent nature of the member's role in making decisions while balancing the need for consistency in the treatment of particular issues. The guidelines can be viewed on the IRB website, http://www.irb-cisr.gc.ca/eng/brdcom/references/pol/guidir/Pages/index.aspx.

Admissibility Hearings

Whereas reports regarding admissibility are called "inadmissibility reports," hearings on the same subject are referred to as "admissibility hearings." The inadmissibility report is used as the basis of the minister's allegations against the PC and is filed as part of the record at the admissibility hearing.

The minister's referral under s. 44(2) of the IRPA gives the ID jurisdiction to hold an admissibility hearing. The document is a Request for Admissibility Hearing form (IMM 5245B). In addition to providing the inadmissibility report to the ID, as required by s. 44(1), the minister is compelled by the ID Rules to provide other specific information, such as basic data about the person concerned (including name, contact information, date of birth, immigration status, and marital status), language of record, language of the interpreter if one is required, and other details.

The minister's representative—the hearings officer—presents a case for the inadmissibility of the person concerned whose admissibility is in question. The PC may be represented at the hearing by a member in good standing of the ICCRC or of a provincial or territorial law society (as discussed above and in Chapter 12). A member of the ID conducts the hearing, listens to both sides, and renders a decision.

Hearing Procedures

The ID member begins by making an opening statement. Then, the member has the parties and their counsel identify themselves for the record, and confirms that the PC can understand the interpreter (if one is required), swears in the interpreter, and deals with other matters such as witnesses.

The hearings officer reads the inadmissibility report into the record and asks to file it as the minister's evidence. The member then explains the possible outcomes of the hearing to the person concerned.

Generally, the hearings officer then calls the person concerned, who is sworn in and examined. The hearings officer files evidence and calls any other witnesses with information that supports the case for inadmissibility.

The PC (or her counsel, if represented) may then examine witnesses and file evidence. She may argue that the inadmissibility report is incorrect for technical, legal, or factual reasons. For example, she may argue that dates and names are wrong, signatures are missing, the grounds of inadmissibility do not apply, or the facts are inaccurate.

After all the evidence has been heard, counsel must be prepared to make a final oral statement, called representations, at the end of the hearing.

Consider the following scenario:

Frederico came to Canada on a student visa from Colombia. Shortly after his arrival, Frederico discovered a print shop not far from his apartment off campus, which was owned by Antonio and Maria. Antonio was an old friend of Frederico's father from Colombia, and Frederico often visited the print shop for his photocopying needs, to visit, and to get a "taste of home." When Antonio asked Frederico if he could help out a little on weekends, informing him that he would be paid cash "under the table," Frederico was happy to help, even though he already had enough money to pay his tuition, books, accommodation, and food expenses. However, an ex-girlfriend of Frederico spotted him working there. Upset over the recent breakup, she informed immigration that Frederico was working in the print shop without authorization.

Frederico's case would not be easy for a hearings officer to prove at an admissibility hearing. Are there reasonable grounds for believing that Frederico "worked" without authorization and was therefore in non-compliance with the IRPA? What credible information is available to support the allegation? Would testimony from an ex-girlfriend who was angry with him be credible?

The officer would have to prove that Frederico was working, and would use the IRP Regulations for the legal definition of "work." The onus is on the officer to prove that Frederico engaged in "an activity for which wages are paid or commission is earned, or that is in direct competition with the activities of Canadian citizens or permanent residents in the Canadian labour market." Were wages paid? How could you prove this? In this case would you like to be Frederico's representative, or the officer—how would you argue your side of the case?

Decision on Admissibility

Generally, following recommendations and oral representations, the ID member orally delivers the decision at the end of the hearing. A decision rendered orally takes effect at the time that it is stated (IRPA, s. 169.) If the hearing is adjourned for a decision to be made in writing, the decision takes effect on the date that the member signs and dates the decision.

In accordance with s. 45 of the IRPA, the ID member may make any of the following decisions:

- recognize the right of the person to enter Canada where the person is a Canadian citizen within the meaning of the *Citizenship Act*, a person registered as an Indian under the *Indian Act*, or a permanent resident;

- grant permanent resident status or temporary resident status to a foreign national if the member is satisfied that the foreign national meets the requirements of the IRPA;

- authorize a permanent resident or a foreign national, with or without conditions, to enter Canada for further examination; or

- make the applicable removal order (a) against a foreign national who has not been authorized to enter Canada, if the member is not satisfied that the foreign national is not inadmissible; or (b) against a foreign national who has been authorized to enter Canada or a permanent resident, if the member is satisfied that the foreign national or the permanent resident is inadmissible.

If the decision is in favour of the person concerned, the member signs and dates a notice of decision and provides the minister's counsel with a copy. In accordance with the ID rules, if the decision is unfavourable to the person concerned, the member must do the following:

- sign and date a notice of decision;

- issue a removal order, signed and dated; and

- advise the person concerned of the right to an appeal before the IAD or of the right to a judicial review by the Federal Court.

Counsel may make an oral request for written reasons at the end of the hearing, or later in writing, in accordance with rule 7(2), provided that the request is made within ten days of the date of the decision.

Types of Removal Orders

There are three types of removal orders that the ID member can make as follows:

- departure orders—reference IRP Regulations, s. 224;
- exclusion orders—reference IRP Regulations, s. 225; and
- deportation orders—reference IRP Regulations, s. 226.

Each removal order has a different consequence as discussed later under "Removal."

Inadmissibility on Serious Grounds

Canada is strictest about the entry of persons who are inadmissible based on the most serious grounds, as follows:

- security;
- the violation of human or international rights;
- serious criminality; or
- organized criminality.

Where there is a finding of inadmissibility on one or more of these serious grounds, the person concerned has fewer rights. For example, there is no right to appeal the member's decision, and no right to make a refugee claim.

Refugee Claimants

According to s. 101 of the IRPA, a person who is found inadmissible on any of the most serious grounds is barred from making a refugee claim. However, there is a strict time frame provision to process refugee claimants soon after a person asks to make a claim. As a result, it is not always possible to obtain the results of the security and background checks within this time frame. Consequently, the deeming provisions to refer claimants take effect and refugee claims that otherwise should have been stopped may slip through and proceed to a refugee hearing. This was discussed in Chapter 9.

Where information that the claimant is ineligible is received by the minister too late—that is, after a claim was referred to the RPD—the minister may choose to deal with the matter in one of two ways. The minister may suspend the refugee proceedings and hold an admissibility hearing, where issues of inadmissibility will be fully examined. (In this case, the RPD hearing will be held only if the claimant is successful at the admissibility hearing.) Alternatively, the minister may intervene and make arguments at the Refugee Protection Division.

SUSPENSION

The minister may serve notice to suspend a refugee claim at the RPD, according to s. 103 of the IRPA. The matter of inadmissibility is then argued by a hearings officer at an admissibility hearing before a member of the ID. If the member finds the claimant inadmissible on security grounds, the claimant is consequently ineligible to make the refugee claim. Under s. 104 of the IRPA, the proceedings at the RPD are then terminated.

Officers must consider the alleged grounds of inadmissibility when opting to suspend refugee proceedings and hold an admissibility hearing, according to CIC's *Enforcement (ENF)* operations manual on ministerial interventions.[3] For example, cases involving security, criminality, or new trends in the movement of refugees, such as fraud and trafficking, are better suited to an admissibility hearing before the ID than to ministerial intervention at an RPD hearing. This is because the ID member can issue the appropriate removal order at the end of the proceeding and then consider the issue of detention, both of which are immigration matters, not refugee matters.

Right to Appeal a Removal Order

Where there is a finding of inadmissibility on any of the most serious grounds, there is no right to appeal. This may result in earlier removal, because there will be no delay to await the outcome of further immigration processes.

Also, there is no right of appeal to the Refugee Appeal Division for a foreign national who has been classified as a designated foreign national.

Detention Reviews

The ID has jurisdiction to review the reasons for detention when it receives a request for a detention review by the minister. The CBSA provides the ID with a *request for detention review*, which generally contains the original grounds for detention and basic information about the person concerned. The ID Rules require the minister to provide the date, time, and place of detention and the type of review (48-hour review, 7-day review, or 30-day review) as well as basic information about the person concerned (including name, contact information, date of birth, immigration status, and marital status); the language of record and language of the interpreter, if one is required; and other details. Sections 57(1) and (2) of the IRPA set out specific time limits for detention reviews.

However, the issue of detention may also arise at the end of the admissibility hearing and counsel must be prepared to address the issue of detention pending removal (IRPA, s. 58).

Timing of Detention Reviews

There is no limit to the amount of time that a person may be in immigration detention as long as there is a periodic review. This principle was upheld by the Supreme Court of Canada when it stated that "extended periods of detention" are constitutionally valid so long as they are "accompanied by a process that provides regular opportunities" for "judicial review of the continued need for and justice" of the detention.[4]

The timing of reviews is set out in s. 57 of the IRPA. Reviews must be conducted

- within 48 hours after the person is detained;
- at least once during the seven days following the first detention review; and
- at least once during each 30-day period following each of the previous reviews.

Within 48 hours of a permanent resident's or foreign national's detention, an officer must review the reasons for the detention and has the authority (IRPA, s. 56) to release the person if the reason for the detention no longer exists. The officer may release the person with or without such conditions as the payment of a deposit or the posting of a guarantee.

Detention reviews for permanent residents who are being held under a security certificate are conducted by the Federal Court (IRPA, s. 82). Detention reviews for permanent residents must be conducted

- not later than 48 hours after the permanent resident is taken into detention;
- at least once in the six-month period following each preceding review; and
- at any other times that the judge authorizes.

The purpose of a hearing is to review the reasons for a continued detention. A party may make a written request for an early detention review, in accordance with the ID rules, if evidence to be produced could lead to release.

Detention Reviews for Designated Foreign Nationals

Designated foreign nationals are subject to different detention rules. In matters involving a designated foreign national (DFN), the ID may not consider any other factor than identity and the grounds of inadmissibility (IRPA, s. 58(1.1)).

In the case of a DFN, the detention review process is as follows:

- *the initial review*: held within 14 days of being detained (IRPA, s. 57.1(1));
- *the second and subsequent reviews*: to review the reasons for the continued detention, on the expiry of six months following the conclusion of the previous review (IRPA, s. 57.1(2)).

Detention will continue until a final positive decision is made by the Refugee Protection Division, when the DFN has made a refugee claim or until release is ordered by the ID or the minister (IRPA, s. 56(2)).

These time frames are in place to give the CBSA time to determine the real identity of the DFN, and to investigate whether the DFN is inadmissible for the more serious grounds of inadmissibility such as security, the violation of human or international rights, serious criminality, or organized criminality.

Upon release, a DFN must comply with any conditions imposed, such as in-person reporting to immigration officials, the payment of a deposit, or the posting of a guarantee for compliance.

A foreign national who is under 16 years of age is excluded from the detention provisions of the IRPA.

Detention Review Hearings

A CBSA officer must bring the detainee to the ID, or to a place specified by it, to argue and provide evidence why she should be released. This means that the person concerned might stay in the detention facility and be brought to a room with video-conferencing equipment or, alternatively, be physically transported to the ID (IRPA, s. 57(3)). The location will be specified in the notice to appear.

Detention reviews before the ID are adversarial hearings. A hearings officer attends at the hearing to argue why the detention should be continued or to make recommendations about conditions for release. The detainee has the right to counsel, although the proceeding is not generally adjourned for this purpose. In some provinces, *duty counsel* may assist the detainee. Where the detainee has no counsel, the hearings officer will also provide information about the hearing process and rights.

The ID member may make an opening statement; have the parties and counsel identify themselves for the record; confirm that the detainee can understand the interpreter, if one is required; swear in the interpreter, and deal with other preliminary matters. The member explains the purpose of the detention review and the possible outcomes.

The hearings officer then begins by submitting facts and arguments concerning the detention. The hearings officer will also make a recommendation to continue the detention or to release the person concerned with conditions. Counsel also has the opportunity to provide facts and arguments to have the client released. After all the evidence has been heard, counsel must be prepared to make a final oral statement—called oral representations—at the end of a hearing.

Prescribed Factors

There are a number of factors that must be considered by the ID member when she determines whether a person should be detained. The prescribed factors are set out in the IRP Regulations, in four categories:

1. flight risk;
2. danger to the public;
3. identity not established; and
4. other factors.

Consider the following scenarios with respect to these factors:

Shauna showed up for the admissibility hearing, but she has a history of staying in Canada after the expiry of her temporary resident visa. Five years ago, Shauna overstayed her visa and was brought before the ID; at that hearing, she cried on record, apologized, and claimed that she forgot about applying to extend her stay. She was issued a departure order and left Canada. This time, the evidence suggests that Shauna has done exactly the same thing: overstayed her status and failed to apply to extend the terms and conditions of her stay. After hearing the allegations, Shauna realizes their serious nature and asks for time to obtain counsel to assist her with her case. The hearing is adjourned; however, the officer wishes to ensure that Shauna will appear for the continuation of the proceeding. The officer is concerned that if Shauna is not detained, she may simply disappear. The officer will argue that Shauna is a **flight risk** and should therefore be detained.

Jerome has several convictions for assault in another country and entered Canada illegally using an alias. He was arrested in a drug raid by Canadian police. It was only after he was fingerprinted that Jerome's true identity was discovered, along with information about his prior foreign convictions. Police believe that Jerome has ties to organized crime, and although the case is part of a larger, ongoing investigation, they were only able to charge him with a minor offence for which he was convicted. As soon as Jerome was released from jail, however, he was immediately detained by the CBSA as a risk to public safety. While he waits for his admissibility hearing, Jerome is brought before an ID member to review the reasons for his detention. Since Jerome's last review (the seven-day detention review), the officer has learned that Jerome may be wanted on outstanding charges back home. The officer is waiting for confirmation of this information from foreign authorities. This is Jerome's first 30-day review and the officer asks for the detention to continue. Jerome has no family in Canada.

With these scenarios in mind, we can now consider each of the prescribed factors in more detail:

1. *Flight risk.* There are a number of factors set out in s. 245 of the IRP Regulations that will be considered by the ID when determining whether a person is a flight risk:

    - Is the person a fugitive from justice in another country?

    - Has the person previously complied with a departure order and appeared for any immigration hearing or criminal proceeding?

    - Has the person previously complied with any immigration conditions imposed when he was admitted to Canada, previously released from detention, or granted a stay of removal?

    - Does the person have a history of avoiding examination or escaping from custody or attempting to do so?

    - Does the person have any involvement in people smuggling or human trafficking?

    - Does the person have strong ties to a community in Canada?

    In the scenario involving Shauna, the officer will argue that Shauna is a flight risk because she did not comply with immigration conditions—for example, she did not leave Canada by the expiry of her visa, she did not extend her visa, and she has a history of overstaying. The officer could also seek alternatives to detention, such as the posting of a cash bond (see below under the heading "Release from Detention"), because although there are some factors of flight risk, they are not so great as to require detention. Shauna, on the other hand, does not wish to be detained. She will remind the ID member that she complied with a previous departure order and will promise to appear for the resumption of her hearing.

    Jerome's case is more complex and serious than Shauna's; the officer will do everything to make the case to keep Jerome in detention. Usually when an officer asks for the detention to be continued, it is for the same reasons as the original detention. In Jerome's case, the officer will also present the latest information. The officer will ask that the detention be continued not only because Jerome is a danger to the public but also because he is a flight risk. To support the latter claim, the officer will point to the following facts:

- Jerome has prior convictions and may be fleeing prosecution. The officer will inform the ID member that he is still waiting to hear from foreign authorities about whether Jerome has any outstanding charges against him because of his ties to organized crime.

- Jerome entered Canada illegally and under an alias in an effort to avoid detection.

- The only ties that Jerome appears to have with Canada are with criminal elements, possibly an organized drug ring.

2. *Danger to the public.* Being detained as a danger to the public is serious because it means that the person has likely engaged in or will likely engage in serious criminal acts. The hearings officer will provide evidence related to the grounds of inadmissibility. A member of the ID will hear arguments from both parties when considering whether to order the detention to continue or to order release. The member considers the following factors, set out in s. 246 of the IRP Regulations:

- Is the person inadmissible on grounds of security, the violation of human or international rights, or serious criminality? Criminal convictions outside or in Canada considered to be serious crimes include sexual offences, violent offences, weapons offences, and drug trafficking.

- Has the person engaged in people smuggling or human trafficking?

   In the scenario involving Jerome, the officer will also renew the argument that Jerome is a danger to the public because

- he is alleged to be inadmissible on several grounds, including serious criminality;

- he has criminal convictions outside Canada considered to be serious crimes, including drug-related convictions; and

- he is currently under investigation for engaging in organized crime.

3. *Identity not established.* There are a number of reasons why a person might conceal his identity from Canadian authorities. Consider the following examples:

- A person may be evading prosecution in his home country and be avoiding returning, such as in the case of Jerome.

- A person may have been previously deported from Canada.

   When the detainee is a foreign national whose identity is not confirmed or in situations where the person is uncooperative in proving his identity, the hearings officer will argue to keep the person in detention. In making a decision, the ID member will consider whether or not the person was cooperative in providing:

- evidence of his identity (to determine whether his identity documents are legitimate or false);

- information about his date and place of birth, as well as the names of his mother and father; and
- detailed information about his travel itinerary to Canada or in completing an application for a travel document, or in assisting to obtain evidence of identity.

Note that the above factors do not have an adverse effect on special considerations for minor children. Additional questions asked include the following:

- Has the person destroyed identity or travel documents, or travelled with fraudulent documents?
- Has the person lied or provided contradictory information about identity?
- Are there any documents that contradict information provided by the person about identity?

As a result of experiences with corrupt and violent government officials in their country of origin, many refugee claimants may be afraid to divulge personal information to government officials for the purpose of obtaining identity documents. They may also be reluctant to be completely candid with Canadian officials, because of a general distrust of authority. Although this may pose a challenge for legal professionals, clients are required to co-operate in obtaining identity documents or information.

4. *Other factors.* Other factors to be considered are set out in s. 248 of the IRP Regulations, including the following:

- the reasons for detention;
- the length of time already spent in detention, in cases where the person was previously detained;
- whether there are any elements that can assist in determining the length of time that detention is likely to continue and, if so, that length of time;
- any unexplained delays or unexplained lack of diligence caused by the department, the CBSA, or the person concerned; and
- the existence of alternatives to detention.

At the admissibility hearing, the ID member will ask the hearings officer to make a recommendation about any *aggravating circumstances* that the ID ought to consider, because s. 229(3) allows a deportation order to be made against a person instead of the prescribed removal order if the person concerned meets any of the following criteria:

- the person was previously subject to a removal order and is now inadmissible on the same grounds as in that order;
- the person failed to comply with any condition or obligation imposed under the IRPA or prior legislation, unless the failure is the basis for the removal order; or
- the person was convicted in Canada of an offence under an Act of Parliament punishable by way of indictment or of two offences under any Act of Parliament not arising out of a single occurrence, unless the conviction or convictions are the grounds for the removal order.

Decision on Detention Reviews

The decision at a detention review hearing is usually rendered orally at the end of the hearing, and takes effect immediately. On rare occasions, the hearing may be adjourned for a decision to be rendered in writing, in which case it takes effect on the date the ID member signs and dates the decision. The member must do one of the following in accordance with the ID rules:

- sign either an order for release or an order for detention, and provide a copy to the parties; or
- advise the person concerned of her right to a judicial review by the Federal Court (in cases where the person concerned does not have appeal rights).

An order for release may contain conditions, such as the payment of a deposit or the posting of a guarantee for compliance with the conditions (IRPA, s. 58(3)). Counsel may make an oral request for written reasons at the end of the hearing or later in writing as long as the request is made within ten days of the date of the decision.

Release from Detention

A person may be released from detention, either by an officer or a member of the Immigration Division. Conditions may be imposed, including the payment of a cash bond and/or the posting of a *performance bond* (written guarantee).[5]

According to s. 45(2) of the IRP Regulations, the cash bond may be paid by the detainee or by a third person. The amount of the bond is based on the following:

- the person's financial resources;
- the obligations that result from the conditions imposed;
- the costs that would likely be incurred to locate, arrest, detain, and remove the person; and
- in the case of a guarantee, the costs that would likely be incurred to enforce it.

If a third person or group acts as guarantor, it must, under s. 47 of the IRP Regulations, satisfy the decision-maker of the following:

- it is not in default of another guarantee;
- it is a Canadian citizen or permanent resident;
- it is physically present and residing in Canada;
- it can ensure that the detainee obeys any conditions imposed; and
- it has the ability to fulfill the obligation if the person fails to comply with conditions imposed, and must provide evidence of this ability (s. 47(2)).

Also, if there are reasonable grounds to believe that the guarantor's money was obtained illegally, it must be refused (IRP Regulations, s. 47(3)). Both the detainee and guarantor must notify CIC or the CBSA, as directed, of any change of address and must appear for any matter as directed by an officer or the ID, according to s. 48 of the regulations. If any conditions are broken, the cash bond is forfeited. In the case of a guarantee, the signing person is required to pay the specified amount of money. The CBSA, and not the ID, is responsible for the administration and enforcement of cash bonds.

Consider again the example of Eunice:

> The officer decided that a detention was not warranted, so when Eunice appeared for her admissibility hearing she was not "on immigration hold." Eunice chose to have legal representation at her admissibility hearing and felt well prepared; she knew there was a possibility that she could be detained after her hearing. But her counsel is confident he can show that Eunice is not a flight risk. Eunice does not have a criminal record outside Canada and has not committed any crimes while in Canada, so she would not be considered a danger to the public. All of Eunice's identity and travel documents are in good order and Eunice has complied with police and immigration authorities, so her identity is not in question.
>
> At the admissibility hearing, it was clear from the evidence presented by the hearings officer that Eunice had, in fact, overstayed her visit. The ID member found Eunice to be inadmissible for "failing to comply" and issued an exclusion order.
>
> After the order was made, the hearings officer made submissions that Eunice was a flight risk because she was close to her family members in Canada and overstayed her visit to be with them. Eunice's counsel proposed, as an alternative to detention that Nadine act as a bondsperson to ensure that Eunice leaves Canada. (Before Eunice's hearing, her counsel explained the conditions of release and arranged for Nadine to attend the hearing just in case.)
>
> The hearings officer recommended an appropriate sum as a deposit, which the member accepted. Nadine was able to answer questions to show she met the regulatory requirements of a bondsperson. The member ordered Eunice's release with conditions. Before Eunice was free to go, Nadine posted the deposit. When Nadine paid the sum of money as a guarantee (to a CBSA official), she was given a copy of a security deposit form. She and Eunice were also required to sign an acknowledgment of conditions form as proof they both understood the conditions imposed.

Had Eunice's counsel not been adequately prepared for this situation, it is possible that Eunice would have been detained pending removal.

Removal

Canadian citizens are not subject to removal even if they do something that would make a foreign national inadmissible (for example, commit a crime). The only situation in which a citizen may be removed from Canada is if citizenship is first revoked. This may happen only in rare circumstances such as where citizenship was granted on the basis of a misrepresentation or fraud.

Foreign nationals and permanent residents who stay in Canada lawfully generally need not be concerned about removal. However, when a non-citizen is found to be inadmissible in Canada either at the port of entry or after being admitted (such as in the case of Eunice, above), the person may be ordered removed. As noted earlier, a **removal order** may be made in either of the following circumstances:

- following an examination, in which case the minister issues the removal order; or
- at an admissibility hearing, in which case a member of the Immigration Division issues the removal order.

Any family members in Canada who are dependants of a person who is the subject of a removal order may also be included in the order as long as the family member is not a Canadian citizen or permanent resident 19 years of age or over (IRP Regulations, s. 227).

Removal Orders

Let's examine in detail the three different types of removal orders, because each has a different consequence for the person against whom the order is made.

Departure Orders (Section 224)

A **departure order** generally requires a person to leave Canada within 30 days of the departure order coming into effect, and to obtain a certificate of departure as part of the criteria for removal (IRP Regulations, ss. 240(1)(a) to (c)).

A departure order is usually issued for a less serious violation of immigration law. A person may successfully request a departure order at an admissibility hearing if voluntary compliance can be shown. As counsel, you can prepare your client by providing proof of the client's ability and willingness to leave Canada. Proof may include a valid passport or travel document, an ability to pay for travel arrangements with a return ticket, a letter of resignation from the employer, or arrangements to terminate a lease or the sale of a house.

A person who leaves Canada on a departure order may apply to return to Canada as long as a *certificate of departure* was obtained from CBSA officials at the port of entry just prior to departure. Although Canada does not have exit controls, the certificate of departure is a type of control that serves as proof that the person complied with the order by leaving for a country of destination that allowed lawful entry.

If a person fails to leave Canada within the 30-day time period, or leaves and fails to obtain a certificate of departure, the departure order is automatically deemed to be a deportation order, according to s. 224(2) of the IRP Regulations. This has serious consequences should the person ever wish to return to Canada.

Additionally, if immigration officials cannot locate the person, they may issue an *immigration warrant* for the person's arrest. The immigration warrant can be viewed in the Canada-wide Canadian Police Information Centre (CPIC), a computerized information system that provides Canadian law enforcement agencies with information about crime and criminals. A person for whom an immigration warrant has been issued usually comes to the attention of CBSA or CIC officials after apprehension by police—for example, after being stopped by police for a minor traffic violation.

When the person who has not left Canada is eventually arrested, he will likely be detained pending removal. It may be difficult for counsel to arrange for the person's release from detention given his previous failure to appear for removal.

EXCEPTIONS TO THE 30-DAY RULE

There are several exceptions to the 30 days allowed for departure under a departure order, as follows:

1. **Conditional removal order.** A conditional removal order, or removal order with conditions, is a departure order with conditions attached. It is issued pending the outcome of a refugee claim, for example.

2. **Stay of removal.** A stay of removal is an order that freezes the removal order temporarily, and allows the person to remain in Canada until the removal order becomes enforceable.

3. **Detention.** When a foreign national is detained within the 30-day period, such as for arrest on a criminal charge, the 30-day period is suspended until either the foreign national is released or the removal order becomes enforceable.

Exclusion Orders (Section 225)

The **exclusion order** differs from the departure order in that it bars a foreign national from returning to Canada for a specified period of time—either for one year or for two years.

The one-year ban is generally issued when a foreign national has committed a minor offence, such as trying to enter at a port of entry with incomplete documentation. The two-year ban is reserved for more serious offences. For example, if the person engaged in misrepresentation, an exclusion for two years must be issued (IRP Regulations, s. 225(3)).

A person against whom an exclusion order has been issued may not return to Canada for the duration of the ban without the written authorization of an officer. The person must apply for an *authorization to return to Canada.*

Deportation Orders (Section 226)

The **deportation order** permanently bars a person from future admission to Canada unless that person obtains the written consent of the minister. A deportation order may be issued in the following circumstances:

- the person has been found inadmissible to Canada on serious grounds;
- the person has committed a serious violation of Canadian law; or
- a departure order issued against the person has been turned into a deportation order.

If the deportation order is made against an accompanying family member of an individual who was found inadmissible, that family member may return to Canada without written authorization.

The following chart summarizes the grounds of inadmissibility and the related removal orders that can be made, by type of decision-maker.

Removal Orders

Person against whom the removal order is made	Grounds of inadmissibility	Action taken by minister's delegate	Prescribed removal order
Refugee claimant	At the time the claimant makes the claim: • reasons of health • financial grounds • non-compliance.	Issues removal order	Departure[a]
Foreign national	The foreign national is: • an unaccompanied minor or • a person unable to appreciate the nature of the proceedings. For any ground of inadmissibility (IRP Regulations s. 28(4)).	Refers case to ID	Order depends on ground of inadmissibility
Foreign national or permanent resident	Security risk (IRPA s. 34(1)).	Refers case to ID	Deportation
Foreign national or permanent resident	Violating human or international rights (IRPA s. 35(1)).	Refers case to ID	Deportation
Foreign national	Serious criminality in case where the evidence is straightforward and does not require extensive analysis or weighing (IRPA s. 36(1)(a) or 36(2)(a)).	Issues removal order	Deportation
Foreign national	Serious criminality (IRPA s. 36(1)(b) or (c), or s. 36(2)(a), (b), (c), or (d)).	Refers case to ID	Deportation
Permanent resident	Serious criminality (IRPA s. 36(1)).	Refers case to ID	Deportation
Foreign national or permanent resident	Organized criminality (IRPA s. 37(1)).	Refers case to ID	Deportation
Foreign national	Health grounds (IRPA s. 38).	Refers case to ID	Exclusion[b]
Foreign national or permanent resident	Financial grounds (IRPA s. 39).	Refers case to ID	Exclusion[c]
Foreign national	Misrepresenting or withholding material facts (IRPA s. 40(1)(a)). Being sponsored by a person who is determined to be inadmissible for mis-representation (IRPA s. 40(1)(b)).	Refers case to ID	Exclusion[d]

Person against whom the removal order is made	Grounds of inadmissibility	Action taken by minister's delegate	Prescribed removal order
Permanent resident	Misrepresenting or withholding material facts (IRPA s. 40(1)(a)).	Refers case to ID	Exclusion
Permanent resident	Being sponsored by a person who is determined to be inadmissible for mis-representation (IRPA s. 40(1)(b)).	Refers case to ID	Departure
Foreign national	On a final determination to vacate a decision to allow the claim for refugee protection by the permanent resident or the foreign national (IRPA s. 40(1)(c)).	Issues removal order	Deportation
Foreign national or permanent resident	On ceasing to be a citizen (IRPA s. 40(1)(d) and *Citizenship Act* s. 10).	Refers case to ID	Deportation
Foreign national	Non-compliance: • failing to appear for an examination or an admissibility hearing.	Issues removal order	Exclusion
Foreign national	Non-compliance: • failing to appear for examination (IRPA s. 41(a)).	Refers case to ID	Exclusion[e]
Permanent resident	Non-compliance: • failing to comply with any conditions imposed under the regulations, or • failing to comply with residency obliga-tions (IRPA s. 41(b), 27(2), or 28).	Refers case to ID	Departure
Permanent resident	Non-compliance: • failing to establish permanent residence (IRPA s. 41(a)).	Refers case to ID	Exclusion[f]
Foreign national or permanent resident	Non-compliance: • failing to comply with any other section of the Act (IRPA s. 41(a)).	Refers case to ID	Exclusion[g]
Foreign national	Non-compliance: • failing to leave Canada by the end of the authorized period of stay (IRPA s. 41(a)).	Refers case to ID	Exclusion[h]
Foreign national	Non-compliance: • failing to obtain the authorization to return to Canada (IRPA ss. 41 and 52(1)).	Issues removal order	Deportation

Person against whom the removal order is made	Grounds of inadmissibility	Action taken by minister's delegate	Prescribed removal order
Foreign national	Non-compliance: • failing to establish that they hold a visa (IRPA ss. 41 and 20).	Issues removal order	Exclusion
Foreign national	Non-compliance: • failing to leave Canada by the end of the authorized period of stay (IRPA ss. 41 and 29(2)).	Issues removal order	Exclusion
Foreign national	Non-compliance: • failing to comply with any conditions on the visa (IRPA ss. 41, 29(2), and 184).	Issues removal order	Exclusion
Permanent resident	Non-compliance: • failing to comply with a residency obligation (IRPA ss. 41 and 28).	Issues removal order	Departure
Foreign national	Inadmissible family member (IRPA s. 42).	Issues removal order	Same removal order as issued to the inadmissible family member

Notes

The chart is based on ss. 228 and 229 of the IRP Regulations. For a complete list and explanation of exceptions, consult part 13 of the IRP Regulations.

a Exception: Departure order is stayed and is conditional upon the outcome of the matter: the claim is ineligible; has been decided by the RPD and is rejected; or is withdrawn, abandoned, or terminated.

b Exception: A departure order to be issued for undecided refugee claims on health grounds and for persons who were previously removed for the same reasons.

c Exception: A departure order to be issued for undecided refugee claims for financial reasons and for persons who were previously removed for the same reasons.

d Exception: A departure order to be issued for persons who were previously removed for the same reasons of misrepresentation.

e Exception: A departure order to be issued for undecided refugee claims for failing to appear for an examination and for persons who were previously removed for the same reasons.

f Exception: A departure order to be issued for persons who are inadmissible for reasons of failing to establish permanent residence if the person was previously removed for failing to establish permanent residence.

g Exception: A departure order to be issued for undecided refugee claims if inadmissible for reasons of failing to comply; or for persons who are inadmissible for failing to comply with the Act if the person was previously removed for the same reasons, or the person failed to comply with conditions under the previous Act, or the person has been convicted of an indictable offence or two offences in Canada, unless the grounds for removal are the convictions.

h Exception: A departure order to be issued for undecided refugee claims if inadmissible for reasons of overstaying a temporary visa.

Types of Stays of Removal

Enforcement of a removal order may be stayed pending some other action or outcome. Specifically, there are five ways in which a removal order may be stayed:

1. by the minister;
2. by application for leave for a judicial review;
3. by application for a pre-removal risk assessment (PRRA);
4. by application for humanitarian and compassionate considerations; or
5. by appeal to the Immigration Appeal Division.

Each of these is discussed below.

1. Minister's Stay

According to s. 230(1) of the IRP Regulations, the minister has discretion to stay a removal order in situations where the person would be sent to a country engaged in an armed conflict, or a country dealing with a serious environmental disaster or other situation that poses a risk to the civilian population there. However, the minister's discretion is limited by the need to protect Canadian society. The minister may not issue a stay where

- the person is inadmissible on grounds of security, the violation of human or international rights, serious criminality, or organized criminality;
- the person is a refugee claimant who is ineligible because of s. F of article 1 of the Refugee Convention (crimes against peace, war crimes, or crimes against humanity); or
- the person has consented in writing to her removal (IRP Regulations, s. 230(3)).

A minister's stay is cancelled when the minister is satisfied that the circumstances in the country no longer exist and the person under removal order would not be at risk if removed to that country (IRP Regulations, s. 230(2)).

2. Stay Pending Judicial Review

An unsuccessful refugee claimant may obtain a stay of removal under s. 231 of the IRP Regulations if the claimant applied for a judicial review at the Federal Court within the permitted time limit unless the claim was rejected by the Refugee Protection Division with a finding of "no credible basis." This finding removes the claimant's appeal rights.

3. Stay Pending Pre-Removal Risk Assessment

The pre-removal risk assessment (PRRA) program is available to certain persons considered to be "at risk" who are about to be removed from Canada. The PRRA is a program intended for people who are desperate to stay. For a person to be eligible, one of the following conditions must exist:

- the person must have a well-founded fear of persecution in the country to which he would be returned, according to the Convention refugee definition; or

- if the person were returned to that country, one of the following risks would exist: a risk of torture, a risk to life, or a risk of cruel and unusual treatment or punishment, according to the Convention Against Torture.

This program and its procedures are discussed in Chapter 9, In-Canada Refugee Determination Process. When a person applies for a PRRA within the appropriate time limits, and in accordance with s. 232 of the IRP Regulations, the removal order is stayed pending the decision on the application.

4. Stay Pending Humanitarian and Compassionate Considerations

A removal order may be stayed if the minister is of the opinion that humanitarian and compassionate considerations or public policy considerations exist. The stay will be granted under s. 233 of the IRP Regulations until a decision is made whether to grant permanent resident status. Humanitarian and compassionate grounds are explored fully in Chapter 5, Permanent Entry.

5. Stay Pending Appeal

Where the right to appeal exists, a person may appeal the removal order to the Immigration Appeal Division. Pursuant to s. 68 of the IRPA, the removal order may be stayed until the appeal is heard, if the person satisfies the IAD member that, taking into account the best interests of a child, or humanitarian and compassionate considerations, the decision ought to be stayed.

A more detailed discussion about the IAD is provided in Chapter 11; however, it is important to note here that the IAD can impose certain conditions attached to decisions to stay removal orders.

Conditions and Review of a Stay

A stay does not make the removal order go away—in a sense it buys the person time to prove that he can stay out of trouble and comply with the IRPA. One way of ensuring this is through the imposition of conditions. Under s. 68(2)(a) of the IRPA, the IAD must impose mandatory conditions, such as the following set out in s. 251 of the IRP Regulations:

- provide current address information in writing;
- provide a copy of a valid passport or travel document;
- not commit any criminal offence;
- if charged with a criminal offence, immediately report to the CBSA or as instructed by the IAD in writing; and
- if convicted of a criminal offence, immediately report to the CBSA or as instructed by the IAD in writing.

The IAD also has the discretion to impose "any condition that it considers necessary" under s. 68(2)(a) of the IRPA, such as the following:

- report in person to the CBSA as determined by the IAD;
- submit to drug testing;
- attend meetings of Alcoholics Anonymous; or
- attend drug or alcohol rehabilitation programs or counselling.

The IAD does not monitor compliance with stay conditions. This is the responsibility of the CBSA (for example, for criminality cases) or CIC (for example, for monitoring compliance in entrepreneurial cases).

A *review of a stay* of a removal order may occur if there is a concern regarding compliance with the conditions. A person who breaches any condition must appear before the IAD to speak to the matter of the breach.

The IAD may, on application by the minister or on its own initiative, reconsider the appeal, pursuant to s. 68(3) of the IRPA. A *reconsideration of the appeal* is made to determine whether the person is complying with the conditions of the stay of the removal order. At the review, the IAD hears recommendations by the minister and makes a decision to do one of the following:

- maintain the stay for an additional amount of time, and maintain conditions or issue new or additional conditions;
- cancel the stay, dismiss the appeal, and order the removal to be enforced; or
- cancel the stay, allow the appeal, and quash the removal order (very unlikely if conditions have been breached).

However, in cases where a person who was inadmissible on the ground of criminality is subsequently convicted of a serious offence, the stay is cancelled by operation of law and the appeal is terminated.

Timelines for Removal

Removal from Canada is an important enforcement activity that is carried out by the CBSA and authorized under the IRPA. In some cases, people leave voluntarily after being issued a removal order; in other cases, CBSA officers must enforce removal orders by physically removing those persons.

Depending on the type of removal order, the person may be allowed time to prepare and arrange for leaving. The length of time allowed may vary. Or, according to s. 49 of IRPA, a removal order may be enforceable on the day that it is made when any of the following conditions exist:

- the person has no right to appeal the order;
- the person has a right to appeal but has not appealed the order; or
- in the event of an appeal, a final determination has been made by the Immigration Appeal Division.

However, where refugee claimants and protected persons are subjected to a removal order, the removal is conditional on the outcome of the claim. This is important because the consequences of removal may be life threatening. Generally, the order takes effect as follows:

- 7 days after a person is determined ineligible;
- 15 days after the claim has been decided by the Refugee Protection Division (RPD) and is rejected;
- 15 days after the claim has been decided as withdrawn, abandoned, or terminated; or
- 15 days after the claim has been decided by the Refugee Appeal Division (RAD) and is rejected.

A removal order may be enforceable immediately in some cases. For example, when a foreign national arrives at a port of entry, the CBSA may issue a removal order against him and enforce it on the same day if he waives or exhausts any legal right to remain in Canada.

However, the removal process is not often such a simple process. After the removal order is issued, a person may seek a judicial review of the matter before the Federal Court of Canada and this decision may be appealed to the Federal Court of Appeal. In some cases, it may even reach the Supreme Court of Canada. The removal order takes effect when the person either does not pursue any further legal recourse or has exhausted these avenues.

Before the CBSA may carry out the removal order, however, there are a number of activities that must be attended to which may also prolong or further delay removal, especially if the individual being removed is not cooperative:

- instruct the individual for removal to ensure that he understands his responsibilities, such as the requirement to prepare for removal within the stipulated time frame and the need to report to an immigration officer before leaving;
- confirm the identity of the person (who may conceal his identity to avoid being returned);
- obtain travel documents such as passports and visas from the person's country of destination (made more difficult if there is a situation of general unrest in the country or if the person is concealing his identity); and
- issue an immigration warrant for arrest and detention under the IRPA, if the person fails to appear for removal.

For the actual removal of a person, such as boarding the person on a plane destined for another country, the CBSA may assign escorts if any of the following concerns exist: the person will not obey the removal order, the person poses a risk of violence to himself or others, or the person poses a threat to the health or safety of other travellers. Generally, CBSA officers carry out removals but, in some cases, they may be assisted by the Royal Canadian Mounted Police (RCMP), if there are safety or security concerns, or by medical personnel, if there are health-related concerns. Furthermore, the airline may refuse to transport the person without an escort.

The function of removing a person from Canada is further complicated by the fact that the country of destination must be willing to allow the person to return. Generally, Canada removes persons to one of the following countries:

- the country from which they came to Canada;
- the country in which they last permanently resided before coming to Canada;
- the country in which they are a national or citizen; or
- their country of birth (IRP Regulations, s. 241).

However, if these countries are not willing to accept the person, the minister may select another country that is willing to allow the legal entry of the person.

Removal Costs

Removal costs may be paid by the person being removed (usually when the person leaves voluntarily), by the airline, or at the government's expense. In cases where the foreign national arrives at an airport and is not allowed to enter Canada, the airline must cover the cost. It is the airline's responsibility to ensure that travellers hold the proper documentation. If the airline transported the person without proper documentation, the airline is responsible for returning the person and also incurs the cost of an administrative fee.

The government has estimated the cost for removal to be in the range of $1,500 to $15,000, but it can go as high as $300,000 if a chartered aircraft is used. Detention is estimated to cost $200 per day.[6]

A person who is removed at the expense of the government is not allowed to return to Canada until the removal costs are paid back. These costs are prescribed under s. 243 of the IRP Regulations.

Assisted Voluntary Return and Reintegration

In a background paper in 2010, CIC reported that it takes an average of 4.5 years from the time a rejected refugee claim makes his claim to the time he is removed from Canada, and that there are reportedly cases that take more than 10 years. Assisted voluntary return and reintegration (AVRR) is a pilot program that began on June 29, 2012 and is expected to run for four years.

The goal of the program is to ensure that failed refugee claimants leave Canada shortly after they receive a decision from the Refugee Protection Division. In exchange for leaving Canada, the failed refugee claimant would receive a return plane ticket and up to $2,000 "reintegration money." However, if the failed refugee claimant wishes to exercise any post-determination rights (such as an application for leave for a judicial review by the Federal Court, or an application for a pre-removal risk assessment), the sum will be reduced according to a descending sliding scale (that is, use more Canadian resources, receive less money).

The pilot program is only for failed refugee applicants who initiated their claims in the Greater Toronto Area and meet certain eligibility criteria (did not withdraw or abandon their claim, have no criminal record, are not inadmissible on any of the more serious grounds, have not applied to be sponsored by a spouse, etc.).

The application process requires the failed refugee applicant to appear in person at an enforcement office and to meet with a CBSA officer. If the applicant qualifies for the AVRR program, her departure will be coordinated with the International Organization for Migration (IOM).

APPENDIX A: IMMIGRATION DIVISION RULES

The Immigration Division Rules are the division's regulations, established to set out roles and responsibilities, and govern practices and procedures in proceedings before the ID.

Section 16(1) of the IRPA gives the chairperson of the IRB the authority to make rules related to the ID's activities, practices, and procedures, in consultation with the director general of the Immigration Division, subject to the approval of the governor in council. The ID Rules are binding, and it is important to know them well. Failure to comply with the Rules may have severe consequences to both clients and counsel.

The Rules are part of the regulations under the IRPA and may be accessed at various websites, including the IRB website, the Department of Justice website, and the CanLII website. Requests for clarification about the meaning or application of a particular rule may be made to the registrar's staff at the nearest business office of the IRB.

The Rules are divided into three parts:

- Part 1—Rules Applicable to Admissibility Hearings;
- Part 2—Rules Applicable to Detention Reviews; and
- Part 3—Rules That Apply to Both Admissibility Hearings and Detention Reviews.

In addition to the binding ID Rules, there are important policy instruments— namely, chairperson's guidelines and policy notes (see Chapter 1).

> **WEBLINK**
>
> The Rules are part of the regulations under the IRPA and may be accessed at various websites, including the IRB website, under the "Legal and Policy References" tab (http://www.irb-cisr .gc.ca/eng/brdcom/references/pol/ Pages/index.aspx); the Department of Justice website (http://laws-lois .justice.gc.ca/eng/regulations/SOR -2002-229/index.html); and the CanLII website (http://www.canlii.org/en/ca/ laws/regu/sor-2002-229/latest/ sor-2002-229.html).

Rules: Before the Proceeding

Compliance with the ID Rules by everyone involved is intended to lead to a fair and consistent approach. However, when the Rules were drafted, it was not possible to predict all potential scenarios that might arise in future cases, so rule 49 provides the ID with the flexibility to "do whatever is necessary to deal with the matter" should a procedural problem arise during a proceeding. Consider the following examples:

- ID members may act on their own initiative to change a rule, to excuse a person from a rule, and to extend or shorten time limits, according to rule 50; and
- failure to follow a rule in a proceeding does not, in itself, make the proceeding invalid, according to rule 51.

In this way, the Rules attempt to strike a balance between the value of predictability and consistency, and the need to make adjustments to meet the particular needs of individual cases. The following is an overview of those ID Rules that counsel will work with most often in a proceeding before the ID. However, it is important to review and understand all the Rules before representing a client before the ID.

Definitions

It is very important to know the meaning of key terms, which are defined in rule 1 of the ID Rules. Counsel demonstrate their professionalism when they understand and use relevant and appropriate terminology while presenting immigration cases.

For example, "detention review" is defined as a "forty-eight hour review, a seven-day review and a thirty-day review," and then each of these terms is further defined. Check for updates, because this rule may be amended following the coming into force of Bill C-31, *Protecting Canada's Immigration System Act*.

Time Limits

The ID Rules require that certain activities occur within certain time limits. The time limits are included in the Rules for specific actions, as follows:

- holding detention reviews—rules 8(2) and 9;
- disclosing documents—rules 26(a) and (b);
- providing witness information—rule 32(2);
- making applications—rule 38(2);
- responding to applications—rule 39(3);
- responding to written responses—rule 49(3);
- making applications to conduct a proceeding in private—rule 45(4);
- making applications to conduct a proceeding in public—rule 46(4); and
- providing a notice of constitutional question—rule 47(4).

A document is considered received by the division on the day that the document is date-stamped, according to rule 31(1). When counsel sends a document to the minister's counsel by regular mail, it is considered received seven days after the day it was mailed, according to rule 31(2). If day seven falls on a Saturday, Sunday, or statutory holiday, the document is considered received on the next working day.

Scheduling a Hearing and Notice to Appear

According to rule 21, the ID must "fix the date for a hearing and any other proceeding relating to the hearing." The ID may "require the parties to participate in the preparation of a schedule of proceedings by appearing at a scheduling conference or otherwise providing information."

According to rule 22, the ID is responsible for notifying both the person concerned and the minister of the date, time, and location of a hearing. This may be done orally—for example, at a proceeding—or in writing, in a notice to appear document.

Communicating with the Decision-Maker

The parties and their representatives must never directly communicate with the decision-maker, but rather must direct all communication through the registry, according to rule 2 of the ID Rules. This applies to all communication, both oral and written, including questions about the process, documents, or a particular proceeding.

It is very important that rule 2 be followed in order to avoid suspicions of bias or influence. All parties must be aware of all information being passed on to the decision-maker, so that they have the opportunity to respond. Applications and other communications must be made in writing, within the time limits, and generally with proof that all parties have been served.

Contact Information

"Contact information" is defined in rule 1 of the ID Rules as a person's name, postal address, telephone number, and fax number and electronic mail address, if any.

Contact information for both the person concerned and counsel must be provided to both the ID and the minister. This is necessary to ensure that notices of proceedings and other matters can be communicated. Rule 12 requires counsel of record to provide this information.

If notices, such as a notice to appear for a hearing, are not received because the ID does not have the proper address, the person concerned might fail to show up for the proceeding, leading to the issue of a warrant for the person's arrest. According to rule 4, changes to contact information must also be provided to the ID and the minister without delay, unless the person is detained.

Interpreter Services

According to rule 17 of the ID Rules, if an interpreter is needed by the person concerned or any witness, the party must notify the ID of this. Notice to the ID should be given as soon as possible in the case of a 48-hour or 7-day review or an admissibility hearing held at the same time, and in all other cases at least 5 days before the hearing.

Documents

Documents are important evidence at ID proceedings. There are several kinds of documents, such as documents that show the identity of the client, travel documents, documents that show the client's willingness to leave Canada, court documents, and conviction records. Because of the importance of documents to a fair resolution of the case, there are rules regarding filing documents with the ID, disclosing documents to the opposing side, and ensuring that everyone has a copy of the documents well before the hearing.

The rules concerning documents apply to any document, notice, written request, or application, according to rule 27 of the ID Rules. The timing for providing documents to the registry and parties is set out in rule 28. Any document provided to a party must also be provided to the party's counsel.

As counsel, you will want to provide organized and professional-looking documents to the ID. All documents intended for use at the proceeding must comply with the following requirements:

- *Format.* According to rule 24, documents must be typewritten using one side only of 21.5 cm by 28 cm ($8\frac{1}{2} \times 11''$) paper, with pages numbered. If the document is a photocopy, it must be clear and legible. If more than one document is filed, a numbered list of all the documents must also be filed.
- *Language.* According to rule 25, documents must be submitted in either English or French, which may require translation.
- *Method of service.* According to rule 39, documents may be provided by a number of methods: by hand, by regular or registered mail, by courier or priority post, by fax (for documents no more than 20 pages long), and sometimes by electronic mail.

Documents are exchanged before the hearing to ensure that all parties have an opportunity to review them, and respond if necessary, in preparation for the hearing. If counsel plans to provide documentary evidence at a client's hearing, the evidence must be disclosed to the opposing side before the proceeding.

The time limits for disclosing documents are set out in rule 26 as follows: as soon as possible, in the case of a 48-hour or 7-day review or an admissibility hearing held at the same time; and in all other cases, at least 5 days before the hearing.

Rules: Application Procedures

There are many issues that may require resolution before the hearing can begin. If a party wants a decision on a matter, such as a change to the date or location of the hearing, an application must be brought.

There are general procedures that apply to all applications, and other procedures that apply for each kind of application. The general procedures are set out in rules 38 to 40 of the ID Rules and apply to all of the following matters:

- changing the location of a hearing—rule 42;
- changing the date or time of a hearing—rule 43;
- joining or separating hearings—rule 44; and
- making oral representations—rule 48.

Each type of application is also governed by its own rule, as shown above.

General Procedures

According to rule 38 of the ID Rules, applications must be provided to the ID in the following manner:

- orally or in writing and as soon as possible or within the time limit in the IRPA or the ID Rules;

- stating the outcome sought;
- providing the reasons for the request;
- including any evidence that the party wants considered;
- including supporting evidence in an affidavit or statutory declaration, if the application is not specified in the ID Rules; and
- with a statement of how and when a copy of the application was sent to the other party.

The opposing party has the opportunity to respond to the application under rule 39, as soon as possible in the case of a 48-hour or 7-day review or an admissibility hearing held at the same time, and in all other cases no later than 5 days. The response must be provided in the following manner:

- in writing;
- stating the outcome sought;
- providing the reasons for seeking that outcome;
- including any evidence that the party wants considered;
- including supporting evidence in an affidavit or statutory declaration, if the application is not specified in the ID Rules; and
- providing a statement of how and when a copy of the written response was sent to the opposing party.

According to rule 40, the applicant then has an opportunity to reply to the response.

Specific Applications

Below is a description of the rules that apply to each type of application, in addition to the general procedures in rule 38 of the ID Rules, which also apply.

CHANGE OF DATE AND TIME

A request to change the date and time of a proceeding as specified in the notice to appear may be made by application to the ID, according to rule 43 of the ID Rules. This situation may arise if, for example, the person concerned wishes to postpone or adjourn a hearing to provide for more time to gather evidence. Rule 43 also provides several factors that may be considered by the ID when deciding an application to change the date or time of a proceeding, including the following:

- when the application was made;
- whether the party was consulted about the date and time;
- the time already afforded to the party to prepare;
- the party's efforts to prepare;
- whether there have been exceptional circumstances;

- whether there are previous delays;
- the nature and complexity of the matter to be heard;
- whether the party has counsel;
- whether the time and date fixed for the hearing was peremptory; and
- whether allowing the application would unreasonably delay the proceeding or likely cause an injustice.

It is important for counsel to address these factors when arguing for a change of date or time, because they will be considered by the ID member when she makes her decision.

CHANGE OF VENUE

A request to change the location of a proceeding as specified in the notice to appear may be made by application to the ID, according to rule 42 of the ID Rules. This may arise if the client wishes to transfer the case to another IRB business office.

Rule 42 also provides several factors that may be considered by the ID when deciding an application to change the location of a proceeding, including the following:

- whether a change of venue would allow the proceeding to be full and proper;
- whether a change would delay the proceeding; and
- whether the change would endanger public safety.

If the application is not allowed, the person concerned is expected to appear for the proceeding at the fixed location.

PUBLIC AND PRIVATE HEARINGS

According to s. 166(a) of the IRPA, proceedings before the ID that do not concern a refugee claimant are generally required to be held in public. Proceedings that concern a refugee claimant or protected person are generally held in private. From time to time someone may wish to make a public proceeding private, or a private proceeding public. In such a case, an application must be brought under rule 45 or rule 46 of the ID Rules, respectively.

APPLICATION FOR A PRIVATE HEARING

An application to make a public hearing private may be brought under rule 45 of the ID Rules in the following circumstances:

- there is a serious possibility that the life, liberty, or security of a person will be endangered;
- there is a real and substantial risk to the fairness of the proceeding; or
- there is a real and substantial risk that matters of public security will be disclosed.

According to rule 45, a request to have the proceeding conducted in private must provide the following:

- a statement of the desired outcome;
- reasons why the ID should agree to make the hearing private; and
- any evidence that the applicant wants the ID to consider in deciding the application.

APPLICATION FOR A PUBLIC HEARING

Although proceedings before the ID are generally held in public, matters concerning a refugee claimant or a protected person are generally held in private. From time to time someone may wish to make the private proceeding open to the public, such as when there is media interest in a claimant or protected person.

According to rule 46 of the ID Rules, any person may make an application to have the hearing held in public. The application must provide the following:

- a request for a public hearing;
- reasons why the ID should agree to a public hearing; and
- any evidence that the applicant wants the ID to consider in deciding the application.

NON-DISCLOSURE OF INFORMATION

Occasionally, the minister may have information that must remain confidential because its disclosure could be injurious to national security or endanger the safety of any person. In such circumstances, s. 86 of the IRPA allows the minister to make an application for non-disclosure to exclude information from the person concerned.

In accordance with rule 41 of the ID Rules, before the admissibility hearing or before a detention review, the minister must make the application for non-disclosure. A member of the ID will hold a meeting with the hearings officer *ex parte*, meaning privately and in the absence of the person concerned and counsel, and before the immigration matter has commenced.

If the minister makes the application at the admissibility hearing or before a detention review, rule 41(2) requires the member to exclude the person concerned and counsel from the hearing room before hearing the application.

According to rule 41(3), if the member decides that the minister's information is relevant to the matter and requires non-disclosure, the member writes a summary of the excluded material without disclosing it, a copy of which is provided to the person concerned and the minister. The member may then consider all the non-disclosed information when determining the immigration matter.

APPENDIX B: REFERENCE FOR ENFORCEMENT PROCEDURES

Provision	IRPA and IRP Regulations
Removals	IRP Regulations, Part 13
Removal orders	IRP Regulations, ss. 223 to 225 and 228 to 229
Removal orders stayed	IRP Regulations, ss. 230, 231, 232
Removal orders—minors	IRP Regulations, s. 249
Entry requirements	IRPA, ss. 11, 16
Examinations	IRPA, ss. 15, 18
Right of entry	IRPA, s. 19
Temporary resident status and permits	IRPA, ss. 22 to 24
Detention and release	IRPA, ss. 54 to 61, IRP Regulations Part 14
Inadmissibility	IRPA, ss. 33 to 43
Admissibility hearings	IRPA, ss. 44, 45

APPENDIX C: DECISION-MAKING AUTHORITIES

The following table summarizes the various decisions that the minister or ID member can make for admissibility and detention review hearings, the provisions that grant jurisdiction, and the associated appeal rights to the Immigration Appeal Division.

Admissibility Hearings

Decision-makers and their powers	Essential features of the proceeding	Provisions granting jurisdiction	Nature of the proceeding	Decisions/Reasons	Possible outcomes	Appeal
Director general (manager): authority as designated by the minister ID member: public servant, employed in accordance with *Public Service Employment Act*. The ID member has the power and authority of a commissioner (*Inquiries Act*) to • administer an oath • issue a summons (rule 33 of the ID Rules).	Held to determine whether the person is inadmissible to and removable from Canada. Inadmissibility and removal are assessed on the following grounds: • security: espionage, subversion, terrorism • human or international rights: war crimes, crimes against humanity • serious criminality convictions inside or outside Canada • criminality/organized criminality • health grounds • financial reasons • misrepresentation • non-compliance with the IRPA.	The manager must "refer" the case to the ID under s. 44(2) of the IRPA. The ID member has jurisdiction to hear a matter when a referral for an admissibility hearing is received from the minister (rule 3 of the ID Rules).	Quasi-judicial Adversarial Proceedings generally held in public Parties are the subject of the proceeding and include • person concerned (PC); • counsel for the PC, who may be a lawyer or member of the CSIC, or other counsel if not paid; • hearings officer as the minister's counsel (PSEP/CBSA). Conducted before a single member. Not bound by any legal or technical rules of evidence. Decision based on evidence considered credible or trustworthy.	The ID member must give reasons for her decision. The decisions may be given orally or in writing. At the request of the PC or the minister, the ID member must provide written reasons within ten days of the Notice of Decision.	Recognize right to enter Canada. Grant permanent or temporary resident status. Permit entry to Canada for further examination. Make one of the following removal orders: • departure order • exclusion order • deportation order.	If the PC has the right to appeal, he may appeal to the Immigration Appeal Division. If the PC has no right of appeal, he may file an application for judicial review to the Federal Court (IRPA s. 64). The PC has no right to appeal to the IAD if he is inadmissible on one of the following grounds: • security • violating human or international rights • serious criminality (punished in Canada; imprisonment of at least two years) • organized criminality.

Admissibility Hearings

Decision-makers and their powers	Essential features of the proceeding	Provisions granting jurisdiction	Nature of the proceeding	Decisions/Reasons	Possible outcomes	Appeal
Same as above.	Applies to most persons detained under the IRPA. Timing of detention reviews (IRPA s. 57): • within 48 hours after the person is detained; • at least once during the seven days following the first detention review; and • at least once during each 30 day period following each previous review.	A referral for detention review from the minister (IRPA ss. 57(1) and (2); rules 3 and 8 of the ID Rules).	Same as above.	The decision may be given orally or in writing. The ID member must give reasons for her decision. At the request of the PC or the minister, the ID member must provide written reasons within ten days of the Notice of Decision.	Release, with or without conditions. Continue detention on one of the following grounds: • danger to public • unlikely to appear • flight risk • identity not established • other factors.	The PC has the right to file an application for judicial review to the Federal Court.

KEY TERMS

admissibility hearing, 377

conditional removal order, 394

departure order, 393

deportation order, 394

designated foreign national (DFN), 369

designated irregular arrival, 369

detention, 394

detention review, 377

exclusion order, 394

flight risk, 387

inadmissibility report, 370

interdiction, 369

removal order, 393

s. 44(1) report, 370

stay of removal, 394

REVIEW QUESTIONS

This chapter covered CIC/CBSA's responsibilities for admissibility, detention and removals, and the ID's admissibility hearings process, detention reviews process, and rules. You should now be able to answer the following questions:

1. List and briefly describe the three types of removal orders.

2. List and briefly describe the prescribed factors that must be considered for detaining a person.

3. What is the purpose of an admissibility hearing?

4. What are a person's rights and responsibilities at a proceeding before the Immigration Division?

NOTES

1. Office of the Auditor General of Canada, "Chapter 5: Citizenship and Immigration Canada—Control and Enforcement," in *2003 April Report of the Auditor General of Canada*, 2003, http://www.oag-bvg.gc.ca/internet/English/parl_oag _200304_05_e_12911.html.

2. Citizenship and Immigration Canada, "ENF 5: Writing 44(1) Reports," in *Enforcement (ENF)*, s. 8, May 20, 2011, http://www.cic.gc.ca/english/resources/manuals/ enf/enf05-eng.pdf.

3. Citizenship and Immigration Canada, "ENF 24: Ministerial Interventions," in *Enforcement (ENF)*, s. 5.4, December 2, 2005, http://www.cic.gc.ca/english/resources/manuals/enf/ enf24-eng.pdf.

4. *Charkaoui v. Canada (Citizenship and Immigration)*, 2007 SCC 9, [2007] 1 S.C.R. 350, at paras. 110 and 123.

5. Section 58(3) of the IRPA and s. 45 of the IRP Regulations.

6. Backgrounder—Detention, Removals and the New Assisted Voluntary Returns Program, March 30, 2010, http://www.cic .gc.ca/english/department/media/backgrounders/2010/ 2010-03-30c.asp.

REFERENCES

Canada Border Services Agency. "Assisted Voluntary Return and Reintegration Pilot Program: About the AVRR Pilot Program," May 9, 2012. http://www.cbsa-asfc.gc.ca/prog/avrr-arvr/ menu-eng.html.

Canada Border Services Agency. "Fact Sheet: Arrests and Detentions," August 7, 2009. http://www.cbsa-asfc.gc.ca/media/ facts-faits/007-eng.html.

Charkaoui v. Canada (Citizenship and Immigration). 2007 SCC 9, [2007] 1 S.C.R. 350.

Citizenship Act. R.S.C. 1985, c. C-29.

Citizenship and Immigration Canada. "Backgrounder—Detention, Removals and the New Assisted Voluntary Returns Program, March 30, 2010. http://www.cic.gc.ca/english/department/ media/backgrounders/2010/2010-03-30c.asp.

Citizenship and Immigration Canada. "Backgrounder—Overview: Ending the Abuse of Canada's Immigration System by Human Smugglers," June 29, 2012. http://www.cic.gc.ca/english/ department/media/backgrounders/2012/2012-06-29i.asp.

Citizenship and Immigration Canada. "ENF 1: Inadmissibility," in *Enforcement (ENF)*, August 8, 2008. http://www.cic.gc.ca/ english/resources/manuals/enf/enf01-eng.pdf.

Citizenship and Immigration Canada. "ENF 2/OP 18: Evaluating Inadmissibility," in *Enforcement (ENF)*. May 1, 2012. http://www.cic.gc.ca/english/resources/manuals/ enf/enf02-eng.pdf.

Citizenship and Immigration Canada. "ENF 5: Writing 44(1) Reports," in *Enforcement (ENF)*, May 20, 2011. http://www.cic .gc.ca/english/resources/manuals/enf/enf05-eng.pdf.

Citizenship and Immigration Canada. "ENF 24: Ministerial Interventions," in *Enforcement (ENF)*, December 2, 2005. http://www.cic.gc.ca/english/resources/manuals/enf/ enf24-eng.pdf.

Citizenship and Immigration Canada. "News Release—Legislation to Protect Canada's Immigration System Receives Royal Assent," Ottawa, June 29, 2012. http://www.cic.gc.ca/english/ department/media/releases/2012/2012-06-29.asp.

Crimes Against Humanity and War Crimes Act. S.C. 2000, c. 24.

Criminal Code. R.S.C. 1985, c. C-46.

Immigration Division Rules. S.O.R./2002-229.

Vinokur, David. "An Introduction to the Immigration Division of the Immigration and Refugee Board," April 8, 2004. Notes from address at the Canadian Bar Association, Citizenship & Immigration Law Conference, IRPA: The Continuing Evolution, April 30 and May 1, 2004, Toronto, Ontario.

PART VI

Appeals

CHAPTER 11   Appeals

Appeals

11

LEARNING OUTCOMES

After reading this chapter you should be able to:

- Identify general Immigration Appeal Division rules.
- Identify the four types of immigration appeals.
- Understand the role of participants at immigration appeal proceedings.
- Describe who has the right to appeal a decision to the Refugee Appeal Division.
- Identify the basis for appealing a decision from the Refugee Protection Division
- List the basic procedures for appealing a decision from citizenship applications.

Introduction

What happens next? An application for sponsorship is denied by a visa officer; a refugee claimant's claim is rejected; a permanent resident's application for citizenship is denied. Generally in administrative law, when an applicant is denied the right of benefit sought, she may challenge the decision. Depending on the statutory framework, this challenge may include the right to be heard at an administrative tribunal or a judicial review at the Federal Court. Under the IRPA most administrative decisions made by the CBSA, CIC, and citizenship judges may be judicially reviewed by the Federal Court, while most tribunal decisions from the Immigration Division or the Refugee Protection Division may be appealed to either the Immigration Appeal Division or the Refugee Appeal Division. IRPA ss. 62 through 71 specify the right to appeal on immigration matters (sponsors and permanent residents); s. 72 provides for the right to a judicial review of any decisions, determination, or order relating to immigration and refugee protection matters (where no statutory right of appeal exists or those rights have been exhausted); and s. 110 confers specific jurisdiction on the Refugee Appeal Division to hear appeals related to refugee claims, when that section comes into force in early 2013.

The parties to an appeal are called the appellant and the respondent. The *appellant* is the party requesting that the appeal be heard, and the *respondent* is the party arguing that the lower decision should stand. In most cases, the minister is the respondent. At the Immigration and Refugee Board, a member of the IAD hears immigration appeals and a member of the RAD hears appeals from rejected refugee claimants. Individuals who have a right to appeal at the IRB have the right to counsel, the right to an interpreter, the right to present and call witnesses, and the right to be heard (which is not the same as the right to a hearing) before an independent and impartial decision-maker.

There is no citizenship appeal tribunal. The *Citizenship Act* (s. 14(5)) allows both the minister and citizenship applicants the right to appeal the decision of a citizenship judge to the Federal Court for grant, retention, renunciation, and resumption applications.

This chapter examines the appeal processes before the Immigration Appeal Division, the Refugee Appeal Division, and briefly the judicial review process for citizenship matters.

Immigration and Refugee Board Divisional Rules

Each division of the IRB has a distinct set of rules. The divisional rules are the division's regulations established to set out roles and responsibilities, and govern practices and procedures in proceedings before the division. The IRPA gives the chairperson of the IRB the authority under s. 161 to make rules related to each division's activities, practices, and procedures, in consultation with the deputy chairpersons, and subject to the approval of the governor in council.

Legal professionals who represent persons who are subject to a proceeding in any of the divisions must have a thorough knowledge of that division's rules, in addition to the provisions of the IRPA that set out the jurisdiction of the IRB and the division to hear and decide matters. The rules are binding, so it is important to know them well. Failure to comply with the rules may have severe consequences for your client.

The Rules are part of the regulations under IRPA and may be accessed at various websites including the IRB website, the Department of Justice website, and the CanLII website. A legal professional who is unsure about the meaning or application of a particular rule may direct questions and requests for clarifications to the tribunal's registrar at the nearest business office of the IRB.

WEBLINK

There are several ways to find the divisional rules, including searching on the CanLII website at http://www.canlii.org; searching on the IRB website at http://www.irb-cisr.gc.ca under "Legal and Policy References Act, Rules and Regulations"; or from an electronic version of the IRPA, in the Table of Contents, http://laws-lois.justice.gc.ca/eng/acts/I-2.5/index.html.

Knowing and Following the Rules

Definitions

Important key terms are generally defined in rule 1 of each division's rules. Legal professionals—referred to as counsel by the IRB—demonstrate professionalism by understanding and using relevant and appropriate terminology while arguing appeals. For example, counsel must understand that a "proceeding" may refer to an appeal that is decided with or without a hearing, a conference, an application, or an alternative dispute resolution process. It is also important that counsel be able to distinguish the terms "appellant" and "respondent" and understand what "contact information" entails (see below).

Scheduling a Hearing

Tribunals do not generally wish to fix a date on their calendar if a case is not going to proceed; and so the rules serve to ensure that the parties are prepared and will be ready to proceed. Appeals are scheduled when the case is considered *ready to be heard*, meaning that the appeal record and/or the required documents have been received, documents have been exchanged pursuant to the rules of disclosure, and witnesses are available.

Generally, the parties may be required to participate in a scheduling conference. For example, the IAD holds *assignment court*, which is a formal proceeding that is recorded and presided over by a member for the purpose of setting a hearing date pursuant to IAD rule 22. In this example, assignment court is held so that the parties can speak to the matter of readiness to proceed. The parties have the opportunity to agree to a hearing date or, alternatively, explain why they are not ready to proceed. For example, the IAD member presiding at assignment court can remind unrepresented appellants of their right to counsel, explain the hearing process, and describe what is expected of them. Where the record has not been received on time pursuant to the IAD Rules, or where there is reason to believe that one of the parties is delaying the hearing, the member may decide to proceed peremptorily by setting a date for a hearing.

Notice to Appear

The Division is responsible for notifying the parties of the date, time, and location of a hearing in accordance with its rules. This may be done orally—for example, at assignment court or another proceeding before the IAD—or in writing in a notice to appear—for example, within a specific time frame in a case before the RAD.

Contact Information

Divisional rules define "contact information" as a person's name, postal address, telephone number, and fax number and electronic mail address, if any.

Contact information for both the appellant and counsel must be provided to the division so that the division can serve notices about proceedings and other matters.

If notices, such as a notice to appear, are not received because the division does not have the proper address, the appellant might fail to show up for the proceeding, leading to dismissal of the appeal. Also, changes to the appellant's or counsel's contact information must be provided to the division and the other party without delay.

Counsel of Record Information

The divisions have rules that require counsel of record to provide contact information, regardless of whether counsel is considered an authorized representative or not (see Chapter 12, Regulating the Practice of Immigration and Refugee Law).

Unrepresented appellants who wish to be represented are expected to retain counsel without delay. If the appellant has already agreed to a hearing date, counsel who is available to appear on that date should be chosen. (It is a matter of professional ethics that an authorized representative—that is, a member of the ICCRC [see Chapter 12]—not undertake representation unless she has the ability and capacity to deal adequately with the matters to be undertaken, which includes being available).

Once retained, counsel must inform the division without delay. In some cases, counsel may wish to be removed from the record—for example, if the client refuses to pay or is very difficult. The divisions have rules that direct that counsel must seek permission from the division to withdraw from a case. If, on the other hand, the client wishes to remove counsel, the client must generally provide written notice to the division, to counsel, and to the minister. The regulator of immigration consultants—the ICCRC—also has rules about the circumstances and steps that a licensed immigration consultant adhere to when withdrawing from representation (see the appendix to Chapter 12, Article 14, *Code of Professional Ethics*).

Counsel must complete the counsel contact information form (IRB/CISR 687), available on the IRB website at http://www.irb-cisr.gc.ca/Eng/tribunal/form/Documents/IRB687.pdf, and provide his or her membership identification number for either the Immigration Consultants of Canada Regulatory Council (ICCRC) or the provincial law society to which he or she belongs.

Any counsel who represents a client and is not charging a fee should use the notice of representation without a fee form (IRB/CISR 692), also available on the IRB website at http://www.irb-cisr.gc.ca/Eng/tribunal/form/Documents/IRB692.pdf.

Communicating with the Decision-Maker

The parties and their representatives must never directly communicate with the decision maker, but rather must direct all communication through the registry. This applies to all communication, both oral and written, including questions about the process, documents, or a particular proceeding.

This is an important procedure to be followed in order to avoid suspicions of bias or influence. All parties must be aware of all information being passed on to the decision-maker, so that they have the opportunity to respond. Applications and other communications must be made in writing, within time limits, and generally with proof that all parties have been served.

Interpreters

The appellant must choose a language of record, either English or French, no later than 20 days after filing a notice of appeal with the IAD, pursuant to rule 17.

Only **accredited interpreters** are used by the IRB for hearings in any division. An IRB-accredited interpreter has undergone security checks, passed a language exam, and attended an orientation and training period. An IRB-accredited interpreter is not an employee of the IRB, but rather has a personal services contract with the board, and is hired on a case-by-case basis. Interpreters are permanently bound by their promise to interpret accurately once they take an oath or make a solemn affirmation to do so. Generally, at the beginning of the proceeding, the interpreter confirms that she used a standardized script to ensure that she and the party or witness understand each other. The interpreter may not guide, provide advice, or offer an opinion.

Documents

There are several kinds of documents relevant to appeal proceedings, such as financial statements or medical reports and documents that show the client's relationship to family members in a sponsorship appeal, or new information, such as identity documents or country-specific information at a refugee appeal. Documents are important evidence at appeal proceedings, and the rules are similar for both divisions. Because of the importance of documents to a fair resolution of the case, there are rules regarding filing documents, ensuring that everyone has a copy of the documents well before the hearing, and timelines.

As counsel, you must use appropriate forms and follow these rules for filing documents:

- all documents provided to the IAD or the RAD must be provided to the division registry;
- any document provided to the minister must be provided to the minister's counsel; and
- any document provided to a person other than the minister must be provided to that person's counsel if the person is represented.

As counsel, you will want to provide organized and professional-looking documents. All documents intended for use at a proceeding must comply with the rules. The requirements for handling documents are similar for the IAD and the RAD—with only minor variations between the divisions:

- *Format.* Documents must be typewritten using one side only of 21.5 cm by 28 cm (8½ × 11″) paper, with pages numbered. If the document is a photocopy, it must be clear and legible. If you file more than one document, a numbered list of all such documents must also be filed.
- *Language.* Documents must be submitted in either English or French, which may require translation.
- *Method of service.* Documents may be provided by a number of methods: by hand, by regular or registered mail, by courier or priority post, by fax (for documents no more than 20 pages long), and sometimes by electronic mail. Otherwise, a request must be made to the division to provide it in an alternative format (or not at all).
- *Computation of time.* A document is considered received by the division on the day that the document is date-stamped.

When a document is provided by regular mail to the appellant or respondent, it is considered to be received seven days after the day that it was mailed. If day 7 falls on a Saturday, Sunday, or statutory holiday, then the document is considered received on the next working day.

The IAD rules provide for situations where, if the document was mailed to or from outside Canada, it is considered received 20 days after the day that it was mailed. If day 20 falls on a Saturday, Sunday, or statutory holiday, then the document is considered received on the next working day.

The Immigration Appeal Division

The Immigration Appeal Division (IAD) has jurisdiction to hear and decide certain types of appeals on immigration matters, pursuant to s. 62 of the *Immigration and Refugee Protection Act* (IRPA). In this section we discuss who may appeal to the IAD, the different types of immigration appeal, how to initiate an appeal, and a brief overview of the related processes.

The right to appeal an immigration decision is not available in all cases, but only in circumstances described in s. 63 of the IRPA, as follows:

- sponsorship appeals by Canadian citizens and permanent residents, whose applications to sponsor close family members to Canada have been refused (IRPA, s. 63(1));
- removal order appeals by permanent residents, foreign nationals with a permanent resident visa, and protected persons who have been ordered removed from Canada (IRPA, ss. 63(2) and (3));[1]

- Loss-of-permanent-residence appeals (also called residency obligation appeals) by permanent residents who have been determined not to have fulfilled their residency obligation by an immigration officer outside Canada (IRPA, s. 63(4));[2] and

- minister's appeals.

Usually, the appellant is an individual, such as a sponsorship applicant, the subject of a removal order, or a failed permanent resident applicant. However, the minister too (of public safety, who has responsibility for the Canada Border Services Agency) has a right to appeal a decision made by a member of the IRB's Immigration Division (ID) at an admissibility hearing (IRPA, s. 63(5)).

A person may not have the right to appeal according to s. 64 of the IRPA if he is found inadmissible for serious reasons, such as security, violation of human or international rights, serious criminality, or organized criminality. The loss of appeal rights for reasons of serious criminality requires that the person must have been sentenced in Canada to two years or more of imprisonment for a single sentence. Furthermore, a person has no right to appeal if found inadmissible for misrepresentation unless that person is the sponsor's spouse, common-law partner, or child.

Notice of Appeal

In all cases, the process begins with a notice of appeal, generally filed at the registry (IRB business office) closest to the appellant's residence. The notice of appeal must meet the following criteria:

- it must be made by a person who has the right to appeal;
- it must be filed on time; and
- it must be filed in accordance with the rules of procedure specific to the type of appeal.

The IAD must then notify either the minister or the ID of the appeal so that the record can be prepared.

Time Limits for Filing Appeals

The time requirements for filing appeals are very important. If the notice of appeal is filed out of time, the minister may dispute the appellant's appeal right and make an application to dismiss the appeal on the basis that the IAD does not have jurisdiction to hear it. Time limits may differ depending on the type of appeal, as noted below.

Sponsorship Appeals

A refused sponsorship application may be appealed. The appellant must provide the notice of appeal to the IAD, together with the visa officer's written reasons for the refusal, no later than 30 days after the sponsor received the written reasons for refusal, according to rule 3 of the IAD Rules.

Removal Order Appeals

Removal orders may be issued by a member of the Immigration Division at an admissibility hearing or by an officer at examination. The person against whom a removal order is made may appeal in either situation. The time limits for appeal in each situation are discussed below.

DECISION AT ADMISSIBILITY HEARING

If the appellant is subject to a removal order made at an admissibility hearing, then rule 5 of the IAD Rules provides two options, as follows:

1. the appellant may provide the Notice of Appeal by hand at the end of the admissibility hearing to the member of the ID who made the removal order, in which case it is the ID member's responsibility to provide the Notice of Appeal to the IAD without delay; or

2. the appellant may provide the Notice of Appeal directly to the IAD, together with the removal order, no later than 30 days after the appellant received the removal order.

DECISION AT EXAMINATION

If the appellant is subject to a removal order made by an officer at an examination, rule 7 of the IAD Rules requires the person to provide the notice of appeal to the IAD together with the removal order, no later than 30 days after receiving the removal order. In this situation, the IAD must notify the minister of the appeal with the removal order, without delay.

Residency Obligation Appeals

A permanent resident outside Canada may appeal an officer's decision that permanent residence status was lost. To do so, the appellant must provide a notice of appeal to the IAD along with the officer's written decision to the registry closest to where the appellant last resided in Canada, within 60 days after receiving the written decision, according to rule 9 of the IAD Rules.

The longer time limit for this type of appeal (60 days rather than 30 days) is intended to accommodate the fact that the appellant is located outside Canada. The IAD must notify the minister of the appeal with the written decision, without delay.

If the appellant wishes to be physically present in Canada for the appeal hearing, this must be indicated in the notice of appeal and the appellant must formally make a request under rule 46 of the IAD Rules (see below under the heading "Return to Canada—Rule 46").

Minister's Appeals

The minister of public safety, as a party to the admissibility hearing, also has the right to appeal the decision of a member of the ID. To initiate the appeal, the minister must provide a notice of appeal to the respondent (the subject of the admissibility hearing), to the ID, and to the IAD, in accordance with rule 11 of the IAD rules, no later than 30 days after the ID decision was made.

The Appeal Record

After receiving a notice of appeal, the IAD verifies that it has jurisdiction to hear the matter. If the IAD is satisfied that the notice of appeal complies with all requirements, the IAD notifies the respondent (the minister or the ID, depending on the type of appeal), without delay. It is then the responsibility of the respondent to prepare and serve a group of documents, known as the *appeal record*, in accordance with the IAD Rules.

Time Limits for Serving the Appeal Record

The IAD may not commence a hearing until the appeal record is received. In the past, the time limitation afforded to the minister to prepare the record was problematic, generally because of operational demands such as heavy workload of visa offices and transfer of personnel. Consequently, appellants were kept waiting for lengthy periods for their appeal to be scheduled and heard. To shorten these delays, the IAD created rules to address situations where the record is not received on time. These are discussed below with respect to each type of appeal.

Sponsorship Appeals

Generally, the visa office is informed of a sponsorship appeal and this triggers the preparation of the appeal record by the officer who refused the sponsorship. The following documents comprising the record must be prepared, according to rule 4 of the IAD Rules:

- a table of contents;
- the application for permanent residence that was refused;
- the sponsor's application and undertaking;
- documents that were considered in the application; and
- the written reasons for refusal.

The record must be provided to both the IAD and the appellant no later than 120 days after the minister is served with the notice of appeal.

If the record is not received within the 120 days, rule 4(5) compels the minister to explain the delay and provide reasons to wait for the record, or provides the IAD with the option to start the appeal hearing with a partial record or no record.

Removal Order Appeals

DECISION MADE AT AN ADMISSIBILITY HEARING

The ID is responsible for preparing the appeal record, which is composed of the following documents in accordance with rule 6 of the IAD Rules:

- a table of contents;
- the removal order;
- the transcript of the admissibility hearing;
- documents admitted into evidence at the admissibility hearing; and
- the ID's written reasons for the removal order.

The record must be provided to the IAD, the appellant, and the minister no later than 45 days after the ID received the notice of appeal. Unlike sponsorship appeals, there is no rule dealing with non-receipt of the record, because the ID is a division of the same tribunal as the IAD and internal procedures are in place to meet the 45-day time frame. Rule 6 is silent, however, on the issue of non-compliance from the ID for providing the record within this time frame. The record in these situations is prepared by the registrar, who is responsible for providing support to both the ID and the IAD.

DECISION MADE AT AN EXAMINATION

For appeals relating to a decision made at an examination, the minister is responsible for preparing the appeal record no later than 45 days after the minister received the notice of appeal. In accordance with rule 8 of the IAD Rules, the record must consist of the following:

- a table of contents;
- the removal order;
- any document relevant to the removal order; and
- the written reasons for the minister's removal order.

The record must be provided to the IAD and the appellant. Rule 8(5) provides the IAD with a process for dealing with late receipt of the record: if the record is not received within the 45 days, the IAD may compel the minister to explain the delay and provide reasons to wait for the record, or it may start the appeal hearing with a partial record or no record.

Residency Obligation Appeals

The minister of Citizenship and Immigration Canada (CIC) is responsible for preparing the appeal record, which is composed of the following documents in accordance with rule 10 of the IAD Rules:

- a table of contents;
- any document relevant to the decision on the residency obligation; and
- the visa officer's written decision and reasons.

The minister must provide the record to the IAD and the appellant no later than 120 days after the minister received the notice of appeal. Rule 10(5) provides the IAD with a process for dealing with late receipt of the record: if the record is not received within the 120 days, the IAD may compel the minister to explain the delay and provide reasons to wait for the record, or it may start the appeal hearing with a partial record or no record.

Minister's Appeals

The ID is responsible for preparing the appeal record, which consists of the following documents in accordance with rule 12 of the IAD Rules:

- a table of contents;
- the removal order;
- the ID's decision;
- the transcript of the ID admissibility hearing;
- any document accepted into evidence at the hearing; and
- any written reasons for the ID's decision.

The ID must provide the record to the IAD, the respondent, and the minister, no later than 45 days after the ID receives the notice of appeal.

Knowing and Following the IAD Rules

The IAD Rules set out the applicable procedures first by appeal type, such as sponsorship appeals or removal order appeals, then by rules that apply to all immigration appeals. There are 60 rules in all, governing practices and procedures before the IAD.

Rule 57 of the IAD Rules provides the IAD with the flexibility to "do whatever is necessary to deal with the matter" should a procedural problem arise during a proceeding. Consider the following situations:

- According to rule 58, IAD members may act on their own initiative to change a rule, to excuse a person from a rule, and to extend or shorten time limits.
- According to rule 59, failure to follow a rule in a proceeding does not, in itself, make the proceeding invalid.

Although there are many similarities between the rules of the divisions, it is important to review and understand all the IAD Rules before representing a client before this division.

The following are some of the key rules that guide the legal professional in his or her presentation of immigration appeal cases.

Disclosure of Documents

Documents are exchanged before the hearing to ensure that all parties have an opportunity to review them, and respond if necessary, in preparation for the hearing. If counsel plans to provide documentary evidence, the evidence must be disclosed to the opposing side before the proceeding, together with a copy to the IAD, and a written statement of how and when the copy was provided to the other party, according to rule 30. If a document is not disclosed before the hearing, the IAD may not use it at the hearing, according to rule 31.

Disclosure of documents must occur at least 20 days before the hearing, unless the documents are in response to another document provided by the other party, in which case disclosure must occur at least 10 days before the hearing.

There is a separate rule for the disclosure of medical documents related to an appeal based on inadmissibility on health grounds: these documents must be disclosed no later than 60 days before the hearing, unless the document is in response to another medical document, in which case the time limit is 30 days before the hearing.

Application Procedures

There are many issues that may require resolution before a hearing can even begin, such as a change to the date or location of the hearing. If a party wants a decision on such a matter, an application must be brought. There are general procedures, which apply to all applications, and other procedures that apply for each kind of application. The general procedures are set out in rule 42 of the IAD Rules and apply to all the following matters:

- a request to return to Canada to appear for an appeal hearing—rule 46;
- an application to change the location of a hearing—rule 47;
- an application to change the date or time of a hearing—rule 48; and
- a notification to withdraw an appeal—rule 50.

Each type of application is also governed by its own rule, as shown above.

General Procedures

Applications must be provided to the IAD and in the following manner, according to rule 43 of the IAD Rules:

- orally or in writing and as soon as possible or within the time limit in the IRPA or IAD Rules;
- stating the outcome sought;
- providing the reasons for the request;
- including, if known, whether the other party agrees to the application;
- including supporting evidence in an affidavit or statutory declaration, if the application is not specified in the IAD Rules; and
- with a statement of how and when a copy of the application was sent to the other party.

The opposing party has the opportunity to respond to the application under rule 44, no later than seven days after receiving the application. The response must be provided in the following manner:

- in writing (if the application was made in writing);
- stating the outcome sought;
- providing the reasons for seeking that outcome;

- including supporting evidence in an affidavit or statutory declaration, if the application is not specified in the IAD Rules; and
- providing a statement of how and when a copy of the written response was sent to the opposing party (the applicant).

The applicant then has the opportunity to reply to the response according to rule 45, no later than five days after receiving the copy of the response.

Specific Applications

Below is a description of the rules that apply to each type of application, in addition to the general procedures under rule 43 of the IAD.

RETURN TO CANADA—RULE 46

A request to return to Canada to appear for an appeal hearing may be made to the IAD according to rule 46. This may arise if the client is appealing an officer's decision that he has lost his permanent resident status because he did not meet the residency obligation of residing in Canada for two years out of a five-year period. Documents must be provided to the IAD no later than 60 days after the Notice of Appeal was filed on the IAD. If the application is accepted and the IAD orders the person to physically appear for his hearing, CIC must issue a travel document for that purpose according to s. 175(2) of the IRPA.

CHANGE THE DATE AND TIME—RULE 48

A request to change the date and time of a proceeding as specified in the notice to appear may be made by application to the IAD, according to rule 48 of the IAD Rules. This situation may arise if, for example, the person concerned wishes to postpone a hearing to provide for more time to gather evidence. The application must be received at least two working days before the proceeding, and must include at least six alternative dates. If the application is not allowed, the client is expected to appear for the proceeding at the fixed date and time.

Rule 48 provides several factors that may be considered by the IAD when deciding an application to change the date or time of a proceeding, including:

- whether the party was consulted about the date and time;
- when the application was made;
- the time already afforded to the party to prepare;
- the party's efforts to prepare;
- whether the party needs more time to obtain information and whether proceeding in the absence of such information would cause an injustice;
- the knowledge and experience of counsel representing the party;
- whether there have been previous delays;
- whether the time and date fixed for the hearing was peremptory;

- whether allowing the application would unreasonably delay the proceeding or likely cause an injustice; and
- the nature and complexity of the matter to be heard.

CHANGE OF VENUE—RULE 47

A request to change the location of a proceeding as specified in the notice to appear may be made by application to the IAD according to rule 47 of the IAD Rules. This situation may arise if the client wishes to transfer the case to another office. Documents must be provided to the IAD no later than 30 days before the proceeding. If the application is not allowed, the client is expected to appear for the proceeding at the fixed location.

Rule 47 provides several factors that may be considered by the IAD when deciding an application to change the location of a proceeding, including:

- whether the client is residing in the location where she wants the proceeding to take place;
- whether a change of venue would allow the proceeding to be full and proper;
- whether a change would delay or slow the proceeding;
- whether the change would affect the operation of the IAD; and
- whether the change of venue would affect the parties.

PUBLIC VERSUS PRIVATE HEARINGS—RULE 49

The IRPA requires that proceedings before the IAD be held in public (IRPA, s. 166(a)). However, from time to time someone may wish to make the proceeding private. This typically occurs when

- there is a serious possibility that the life, liberty, or security of a person will be endangered;
- there is a real and substantial risk to the fairness of the proceedings; or
- there is a real and substantial risk that matters of public security will be disclosed.

A request to have the proceeding conducted in private must be made no later than 20 days before the proceeding. Any person may respond in writing to the request.

NON-DISCLOSURE OF INFORMATION

Occasionally, the minister may have information that must remain confidential because its disclosure could be injurious to national security or endanger the safety of any person. In such circumstances, s. 86 of the IRPA allows the minister to make an application for non-disclosure to exclude information from the person concerned.

Before the hearing, the minister must make the application for non-disclosure in accordance with the general application rules. A member of the IAD will hold a meeting with the hearings officer *ex parte*, meaning in the absence of the appellant and counsel, and before the appeal hearing has commenced.

If the minister makes the application at the appeal hearing, the IAD member adjourns the hearing before holding the *ex parte* meeting.

If the member decides that the minister's information is relevant to the appeal and requires non-disclosure, the member writes a summary of the information and gives it to the minister. If the minister agrees with the summary, the summary is provided to the appellant. The member may then consider all the non-disclosed information when deciding the appeal. Should the minister disagree with the summary, in whole or in part, the minister has the option of withdrawing the application or the information, and then the member's decision shall not take into consideration any of the information.

Immigration Appeal Hearings

Counsel can prepare the client for the appeal process by describing and explaining it and by answering any questions that the client may have. Below is a list of typical questions that clients may ask (or may want to know the answers to even if they do not ask), organized by topic. Selected sample answers are provided in parentheses.

- *Type of hearing.* What can the client expect during the appeal hearing? What are the time frames? Is the matter expected to take all day? (The length of the hearing depends on the number of witnesses and other factors. It is important to set out which issues will be examined and cross-examined.)
- *Hearing room.* What is the physical layout of the hearing room?
- *Public or private hearing.* Will the hearing be open to the public? (The proceedings are public, which means there could be observers.)
- *Hearing recorded.* Will the hearing will be recorded? (Yes. The hearing will be recorded.)
- *Language.* In what language will the hearing be held? (The hearing will be held in English or French, and an interpreter will be provided if requested.)
- *Participants.* Who will be present and what is the role of each person?
- *Nature of the proceeding.* Will the hearing be adversarial in nature? (Yes. The hearing is adversarial and involves the minister's counsel questioning the client and any witnesses, and arguing against the appellant's appeal.)
- *New evidence.* Can new evidence be presented during the appeal hearing? (Yes. Information that wasn't presented or available at the time that the decision was made may be presented during the appeal hearing.)

Generally, after the appellant and any witnesses are sworn in, the appellant's counsel will begin the examination, followed by the minister's counsel.

Jurisdiction

IAD hearings are *de novo* (Latin for "anew") and therefore the IAD member is not limited strictly to reviewing the evidence that led up to the refusal or removal order, but must also consider any additional facts as they exist at the time of the hearing.

The IAD has jurisdiction to hear appeals from decisions of the Canada Border Services Agency (CBSA), CIC, or ID, and may consider whether the decision was wrong in law or wrong in fact, whether the decision was wrong in mixed law and fact, or whether there was a breach of natural justice.

For sponsorship appeals, the IAD may consider humanitarian and compassionate reasons as long as the sponsor meets the definition of "sponsor" and the person whose application was refused meets the definition of "member of the family class" as described in s. 65 of the IRPA.

Persons in Attendance

There are a number of people who must be present at an appeal, including the appellant, the minister's counsel, and the IAD member. Other persons are likely to be present, such as the appellant's counsel. Still others may be present, such as witnesses.

Appellant

The appellant must be personally in attendance at the appeal.

Counsel

Counsel's role is to protect the appellant's interests and right to a fair hearing. Counsel explains the process, provides advice, and presents the case in an efficient manner, within the limits set by the IAD.

The appellant may choose to be represented by either an unpaid trusted adviser, such as a family member or clergy, or a paid consultant or a member in good standing of a law society, such as a lawyer or licensed paralegal, or a member of the Chambres des notaires du Québec. An unpaid adviser who represents a client and is not charging a fee should use the notice of representation without a fee form (IRB/CISR 692).

Minister's Counsel

Minister's counsel is a public servant who works for the CBSA with the title of hearings officer. A hearings officer may represent the minister of PSEP or the minister of CIC depending on the decision being appealed. For example, for sponsorship appeal or residency obligation appeal hearings, a hearings officer represents the minister of CIC; for any other appeal, the hearings officer represents the minister of PSEP.

At the hearing, the hearings officer's role is generally to defend the decision against which the appeal is made, such as a visa officer's refusal of a sponsorship application or the minister's or the ID member's decision to issue a removal order. However, a hearings officer may in some cases consent to allow the appeal, if the hearings officer agrees with the appellant that there was an error in law or fact or a breach of natural justice.

Immigration Appeal Division Member

Generally, only one decision-maker, a member of the IAD, has the authority to hear and decide appeals. The member will also hear and decide any applications that are made orally at the hearing.

Interpreter

If a client or witness requires an interpreter, rule 18 of the IAD Rules requires that counsel notify the IAD in writing and specify the language and dialect needed no later than 20 days before the hearing.

Witnesses

If counsel wishes to call a witness other than her client, she must fulfill the requirements of rule 37 of the IAD by informing the opposing party and the IAD in writing no later than 20 days before the hearing. The following information must be provided:

- the witness's contact information;
- the amount of time required at the hearing for the witness's testimony;
- the party's relationship to the witness;
- whether the testimony is by videoconference or telephone; and
- a signed report with qualifications and summary of evidence for any expert witness.

If counsel does not make the request in writing, she faces the risk that her witness may not be allowed to testify under rule 37(4).

To reduce the risk of the witness failing to appear, it is prudent to request that the IAD issue a summons to order a witness to testify, according to rule 38, in writing or orally at a proceeding. The party is responsible to provide the summons to the summoned person by hand, to notify the IAD in writing of this, and to pay witness fees and travel expenses. In the request, counsel must set out the factors to be considered in issuing the summons, such as the importance of the testimony of a witness and the witness's ability and willingness to provide such information. Under rule 39, the witness may apply to the IAD to cancel the summons.

Rule 40 sets out the process for making a request to the IAD to issue a warrant for the arrest of a summoned witness who fails to appear.

Witnesses testify following the appellant's testimony. While the appellant testifies, witnesses stay in the waiting room. A person is not allowed to share any testimony given at the hearing with any witness who was excluded from the hearing room until after the witness has testified, according to rule 41.

Designated Representative—Rule 19

There are situations where the person concerned is not capable of making decisions, such as in the case of an unaccompanied minor, or a person deemed mentally incompetent or unable to understand the proceedings (IRPA, s. 167(2)). If counsel for either party believes that a designated representative is required, counsel must notify the IAD without delay, according to rule 19 of the IAD Rules. The IAD may then appoint a person to act and make decisions on behalf of the person concerned. The designated representative may be a relative, or a professional such as a lawyer or social worker. Alternatively, counsel may be permitted to take on the role of designated representative.

Decisions

A final disposition of an appeal is communicated to the parties by way of a **notice of decision**, according to rule 54(1) of the IAD Rules. Sponsorship appeals and any decision to stay a removal order also require written reasons for the decision. The decision may be one of the following:

1. *Appeal allowed.* The appeal may be allowed pursuant to s. 67 of the IRPA, if the appellant satisfies the IAD member that the minister's decision was wrong for any of the following reasons:

   - there was an error in law;
   - there was an error in fact;
   - there was an error in mixed fact and law;
   - there was a breach of the principles of natural justice; or
   - taking into account the best interests of a child or humanitarian and compassionate considerations, the appeal ought to be allowed.

   If the appeal is allowed, the original decision is set aside and the IAD may substitute its own decision, such as to admit the person to Canada, or refer the matter to the appropriate decision-maker for reconsideration. For example, if the appeal of a decision in a sponsorship case is allowed, the sponsorship application may be returned for further processing and assessment.

2. *Stay of the removal order.* A stay of a removal order may be granted pursuant to s. 68 of the IRPA, if the appellant satisfies the member that, taking into account the best interests of a child, or humanitarian and compassionate considerations, the original decision ought to be stayed. If the member stays the removal order, conditions may be attached. Some conditions are mandatory, as found in s. 251 of the IRP Regulations (discussed in Chapter 10 under the heading "Conditions and Review of a Stay").

3. *Dismiss the appeal.* The appeal may be dismissed pursuant to s. 69 of the IRPA, if the appellant does not satisfy the member that the appeal ought to be allowed or a removal order ought to be stayed.

The IAD is required to provide written reasons for all decisions regarding an appeal by a sponsor and for decisions that stay a removal order. For all other decisions, the person concerned or the minister must request written reasons within ten days after the day that person receives the decision, according to rule 54(2).

Alternative Dispute Resolution

Alternative dispute resolution (ADR) in the context of immigration appeals involves mediation and negotiation, as provided by rule 20(1) of the IAD Rules. In many cases it is successful at quickly resolving the appeal without a hearing.

ADR brings the parties together in an informal meeting to explore opportunities to negotiate and settle the appeal. The process is much shorter than a hearing, often lasting about an hour. Generally, sponsorship appeals are suitable for the ADR process.

In addition to the appellant and counsel, and the minister's counsel, a dispute resolution officer (DRO) attends the meeting to facilitate the process. The DRO is a specially trained tribunal officer or a member of the IAD (IAD Rules, rule 20(2)). The DRO is not a party and does not decide the outcome of the appeal. The DRO is neutral and does the following:

- makes an opening statement;
- if desired, meets with the parties separately;
- asks questions about why the appeal should be allowed;
- provides an opinion about the strengths and weaknesses of the appeal;
- prepares a summary statement if the minister consents to allowing the appeal, or, if the appeal cannot be settled, prepares an objective assessment for consideration by the appellant in deciding whether to proceed to a hearing or to withdraw the appeal; and
- sets a date for a hearing, if required.

During the meeting, the parties may also ask each other questions and provide information and evidence. The process is confidential. Possible decisions arising from the ADR meeting include:

- *Appeal **allowed on consent**.* The appeal may be allowed on consent, if the minister concedes to the appellant's position.
- *Appeal **withdrawn**.* The appeal may be withdrawn by the appellant, if the appellant concedes to the minister's position.
- *Appeal referred to a hearing.* The appeal may be referred to a hearing if it is unresolved—that is, if neither party is willing to concede.

Even when the minister consents to an appeal, a member of the IAD must approve the settlement. A notice of decision will be issued thereafter, and, in the case of a sponsorship appeal, the minister will advise the visa office to process the sponsorship application.

If the appeal cannot be settled, the appellant maintains the right to be heard by a member at a hearing or may withdraw the appeal. Under rule 20(4), any information, statement, or document that was used at the ADR meeting generally remains confidential and does not appear on the hearing file unless it is disclosed in accordance with the IAD Rules.

The Refugee Appeal Division

Jurisdiction

When the IRPA came into force in June 2002, the sections that would have given appeal rights to refugee claimants (ss. 110 and 111) were never proclaimed into law. Bill C-11, the *Balanced Refugee Reform Act* (BRRA), received royal assent on June 29, 2010, and created a new structure of the IRB (see Chapter 2), most significantly including the Board's fourth division—the Refugee Appeal Division (RAD). The BRRA was to be implemented within two years, or on any earlier day or days that may be fixed by order of the governor in council. However, before the provisions of the BRRA could come into force, the government introduced Bill C-31, *Protecting Canada's Immigration System Act* (PCISA). The PCISA amended both the IRPA and the BRRA but delayed the implementation of the RAD and required a revision of the rules; at the time of this text's publication, the division's rules were not yet finalized. What follows, therefore, is a general description of the refugee appeal process.

In most cases, appeals to the RAD will be from a refugee claimant whose claim was negatively determined. However, the minister may also appeal a decision made from a member of the RPD. As with the IRB's other tribunals, appellants will have the right to counsel, the right to present evidence, and the right to be heard—generally through the submission of a memorandum.

The appeal may be made against a decision of the RPD to allow or reject a claim for refugee protection (IRPA, s. 110(1)):

- on a question of law,
- on a question of fact, or
- on a question of mixed law and fact.

Most RAD appeals will be decided by a single member through a paper review (the right to be heard) with a right to an oral hearing permitted in exceptional cases. The RAD will allow new evidence to be introduced that was not reasonably available at the time of the refugee's hearing at the RPD; therefore, the RAD member is not strictly limited to reviewing the evidence that led to a negative determination.

Right to Appeal

There are a number of claimants who will not have the right to appeal pursuant to the IRPA, s. 110, as follows:

Right of Appeal to the RAD

Right of Appeal	No Right of Appeal
All claimants that do not fall into one of the categories on the right	• DCO claimant* • DFN claimant (designated irregular arrival—IRPA, s. 110(2)(a)) • Manifestly unfounded claimant (IRPA, s. 110(2)(c)) • No credible basis claimant (IRPA, s. 110(2)(c)) • Claimants who withdrew or abandoned their claim (IRPA, s. 110(2)(b)) • Safe third country agreement claimant (IRPA, s. 110(2)(d)) • Claims referred before coming into force of the PCISA (Bill C-31) • Cessation decisions of protected person status (IRPA, s. 110(2)(e)) • Vacation decisions of protected person status (IRPA, 110(2)(f))

* Citizenship and Immigration Canada, "Backgrounder—Overview of Canada's New Refugee System," June 29, 2012, http://www.cic.gc.ca/english/department/media/backgrounders/2012/2012-06-29c.asp.

Notice of Appeal and Time Limits

Generally, the appellant must submit a written notice of appeal no later than 15 working days after the day on which the person or the minister receives written reasons for the decision by the RRD (you should check the IRP Regulations and the RAD Rules for the up-to-date timelines after the coming into force date.) The notice must be filed at the registry that is located in the same region as the RPD office where the refugee claim was originally decided and serve the minister with a copy.

The Refugee Appeal Record

The appellant must provide a memorandum that sets out the details of the appeal (for example, the grounds and/or errors) and the outcome sought along with the following documents:

- the notice of decision, written reasons for the RPD decision, and the transcript of the RPD proceedings;
- any documents that were refused as evidence by the RPD;
- any documents, law, case law, or other legal authority.

The appellant is permitted to present only evidence that arose after the rejection of his claim or that was not reasonably available at the time of his RPD hearing, or that he could not reasonably have been expected in the circumstances to have presented at the time of the rejection (IRPA, s. 110(4)).

If the appellant is requesting an oral hearing, he should explain why the RAD should hold a hearing. The RAD Rules will set out other requirements for the memorandum (for example, format and content).

Overview of the Refugee Appeal Process

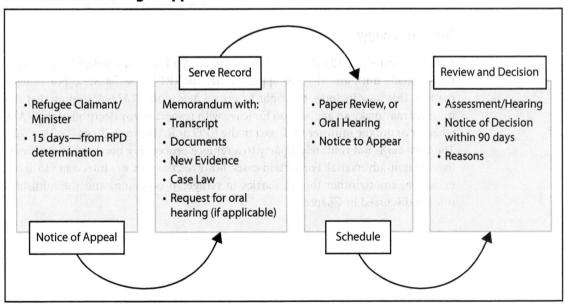

Refugee Appeal Hearings

The government has signalled that the appeal process must be efficient and that decisions on most appeals are expected within 90 days unless an oral hearing is required.[3]

According to IRPA s. 110(3), the RPD member must decide an appeal

on the basis of the record of the proceedings of the Refugee Protection Division, and may accept documentary evidence and written submissions from the Minister and the person who is the subject of the appeal and, in the case of a matter that is conducted before a panel of three members, written submissions from a representative or agent of the United Nations High Commissioner for Refugees and any other person described in the rules of the Board.

The RAD may hold a hearing if there is documentary evidence that

- raises a serious issue about the claimant's credibility;
- is central to the decision with respect to the refugee protection claim;
- if accepted would have justified allowing or rejecting the refugee protection claim (IRPA, s. 110(6)).

Decisions

Section 111(1) sets out the options for deciding appeals:

- confirm the determination of the RPD;
- set aside the determination of the RPD and substitute it with the determination that should have been made; or
- refer the matter back to the RPD with directions for a re-determination.

Judicial Review

Note that under s. 72(2)(a) of IRPA, applications for leave for a judicial review may not be made until any right of appeal under the IRPA is exhausted. For refugee matters, this now includes the right to appeal before the RAD. Also note that the minister may make an application for leave with respect to any decision of the RAD, whether or not the minister took part in the RPD or RAD proceedings (IRPA, s. 73). The minister is not routinely a party to a refugee proceeding because refugee hearings are non-adversarial. For certain cases, however, the minister intervenes to argue exclusion, among other things. Parties in refugee proceedings and the minister's role are discussed in Chapter 9.

Citizenship Appeals

There is no citizenship appeal tribunal. Section 14(5) of the *Citizenship Act* allows both the minister and citizenship applicants to appeal the decision of a citizenship judge to the Federal Court for grant, retention, renunciation, and resumption applications. The minister is represented by a lawyer who is a public servant in the federal Department of Justice (DOJ.) A person whose citizenship application was not approved may appeal the citizenship judge's decision because she believes there was an error in the decision or because the citizenship judge did not take all of the evidence into account.

Federal Court Rules

The Federal Court has its own set of rules, called the Federal Court Rules. The Rules are the court's regulations, established to set out roles and responsibilities, and govern practices and procedures in proceedings before the court. They are extensive and far more complex than the rules for the IRB.

The parties and their representatives must never directly communicate with the judiciary, but rather must direct all communication through the registry of the Courts Administrative Services (CAS). This applies to all communication, both oral and written, including questions about the process, documents, or a particular proceeding.

WEBLINK

Federal Court Rules

There are several ways to find the Federal Court Rules, including searching on the CanLII website at http://www.canlii.org; the Federal Court website at http://cas-ncr-nter03.cas-satj.gc.ca/portal/page/portal/fc_cf_en/Rules; or the Department of Justice website at http://laws-lois.justice.gc.ca/eng/regulations/SOR-98-106/index.html.

Overview of the Citizenship Appeal Process

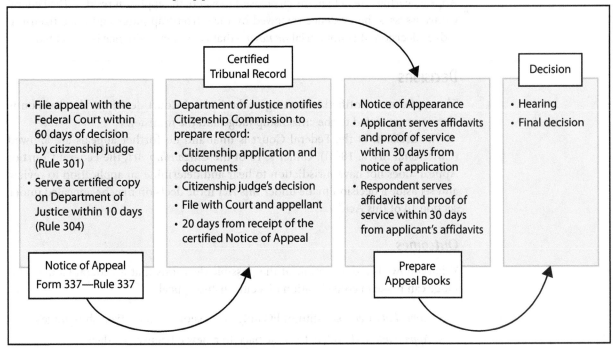

Certified Tribunal Record

Decision

- File appeal with the Federal Court within 60 days of decision by citizenship judge (Rule 301)
- Serve a certified copy on Department of Justice within 10 days (Rule 304)

Notice of Appeal
Form 337—Rule 337

Department of Justice notifies Citizenship Commission to prepare record:
- Citizenship application and documents
- Citizenship judge's decision
- File with Court and appellant
- 20 days from receipt of the certified Notice of Appeal

- Notice of Appearance
- Applicant serves affidavits and proof of service within 30 days from notice of application
- Respondent serves affidavits and proof of service within 30 days from applicant's affidavits

Prepare Appeal Books

- Hearing
- Final decision

General Application Procedures

Applicants must file a notice of appeal with the Federal Court within 60 days of the date that the citizenship judge's decision was mailed, together with a $50 filing fee. The court certifies the notice of appeal and then it is up to the applicant to serve it on the respondent. In citizenship matters before the Federal Court, the respondent is the DOJ, which acts as the Citizenship Commission's counsel. The Federal Court Rules set out very detailed procedures for filing and service of the notice and other documents required for the appeal process.

The Record

The Citizenship Commission is responsible for preparing the record—called a certified tribunal record (CTR)—for the court, which generally contains:

- a copy of the applicant's citizenship application;
- a copy of all the applicant's supporting documents;
- a copy of all the documents the citizenship judge examined;
- a copy of the citizenship judge's decision (for example, Notice to the Minister of the Decision of the Citizenship Judge form) and refusal letter.

The applicant may submit a request for a copy of the record within 20 days of filing her notice to appeal.

Hearings

Appeal hearings are held in the city closest to where the applicant resides. The Federal Court assesses the evidence reviewed by the citizenship judge and the citizenship judge's decision. It is not a trial *de novo*—that is, no new evidence is presented.

Decisions

The applicant is notified in writing of the Federal Court decision. The decision is also communicated to the citizenship judge and the minister.

The decision of the Federal Court is final and no further appeals are allowed (*Citizenship Act*, s. 18(3)). Under s. 16 of the *Citizenship Act*, the Federal Court of Appeal "does not have jurisdiction to hear and determine an application to review and set aside a decision made under this Act if the decision may be appealed under section 14 of this Act."

Outcomes

What follows is a description of the possible decisions that a Federal Court (FC) judge can make in consideration of a citizenship appeal:

- *Appeal allowed*: substitutes FC judge's decision for the citizenship judge's;
- *Appeal allowed*: refers the case back to a new citizenship judge;

- *Appeal allowed*: refers the case back to the original citizenship judge for a redetermination;
- *Appeal dismissed*: refunds right of citizenship fee; or
- *Appeal dismissed*: for reconsideration under s. 5(3) (compassionate grounds) or a discretionary grant by the minister, s. 5(4):
  - refers the case back to a new citizenship judge; or
  - refers the case back to the original citizenship judge; or
  - refers the case back to the minister.

When an appeal is allowed in cases of grant and resumption of citizenship cases, the applicant must take the oath of citizenship to complete the process. For retention and renunciation appeal cases, applicants are issued a citizenship certificate or a renunciation certificate, instead of taking the oath of citizenship.

APPENDIX

Reference for the Immigration Appeal Division

Provision	IRPA and IRP Regulations
Removal orders stayed	IRP Regulations, ss. 230 to 234
Right to appeal	IRPA, ss. 63 to 64
Decision on appeals	IRPA, ss. 66 to 69

Provision	IAD Rules
Definitions	rule 1
Communicating with the division	rule 2
Sponsorship appeal	rules 3, 4
Removal order appeals	rules 5 to 8
Residency obligation appeal	rules 9, 10
Minister's appeal	rules 11, 12
Contact information	rule 13
Counsel of record	rules 14 to 16
Language of record	rules 17, 18
Designated representative	rule 19

Provision	IRPA and IRP Regulations
Alternative dispute resolution	rule 20
Conferences	rule 21
Scheduling	rules 22, 23
Stay of removal order	rules 26, 27
Documents	rules 28 to 36
Witnesses	rule 37
Applications	rules 42 to 48
Withdraw appeal	rule 50
Decisions	rules 53 to 56
General provisions	rules 57 to 59

Reference for the Refugee Appeal Division

Provision	IRPA
Right to appeal	IRPA, s. 110(1)
Exceptions to the right to appeal	IRPA, s. 110(2)
Decision on appeals	IRPA, s. 111

KEY TERMS

accredited interpreter, 421

allowed on consent, 435

notice of decision, 434

withdrawal, 435

REVIEW QUESTIONS

This chapter covered the process for appealing immigration decisions. You should now be able to answer the following questions:

1. List and briefly describe the four types of immigration appeals before the Immigration Appeal Division.

2. What types of admissibility cases do not have a right to an immigration appeal?

3. Discuss the advantages and disadvantages of a scheduling conference.

4. What is the nature of a hearing before the Immigration Appeal Division?

5. What are the appellant's rights at a proceeding before the Immigration Appeal Division and the Refugee Appeal Division?

6. What are the advantages of alternative dispute resolution as an immigration appeal process? What type of appeal is suited to this process?

7. What are the grounds for appealing a decision by the Refugee Protection Division?

8. Who does not have the right to appeal a decision by the Refugee Protection Division?

9. Can a person appeal a decision on a citizenship application made by a citizenship judge? If so, which tribunal hears the appeal?

NOTES

1. There is no right to appeal a removal order if the person was found inadmissible on the grounds of security, violations of human or international rights, serious criminality, or organized criminality.

2. In Canada, a removal order is issued against a permanent resident who loses her permanent resident status; that person can appeal the minister's decision to issue the removal order. The difference is that there is no removal order made against a person outside Canada who loses her status.

3. Citizenship and Immigration Canada, "Backgrounder—Overview of Canada's New Refugee System," June 29, 2012, http://www.cic.gc.ca/english/department/media/backgrounders/2012/2012-06-29c.asp.

REFERENCES

Canada, Parliament, House of Commons. *An Act to amend the Immigration and Refugee Protection Act, the Balanced Refugee Reform Act, the Marine Transportation Security Act and the Department of Citizenship and Immigration Act* (short title, *Protecting Canada's Immigration System Act*), Bill C-31, First Session, Forty-first Parliament, 60-61 Elizabeth II, 2011-2012, assented to June 28, 2012. http://www.parl.gc.ca/HousePublications/Publication.aspx?Docid=5697417&file=4.

Canada, Parliament, House of Commons. *An Act to amend the Immigration and Refugee Protection Act and the Federal Courts Act* (short title, *Balanced Refugee Reform Act*), Bill C-11, Third Session, Fortieth Parliament, 59 Elizabeth II, 2010, assented June 29, 2010. http://www.parl.gc.ca/HousePublications/Publication.aspx?Language=E&Mode=1&DocId=4644728&File=14.

Citizenship and Immigration Canada. ENF 24: Ministerial Interventions, December 2, 2005. http://www.cic.gc.ca/english/resources/manuals/enf/enf24-eng.pdf.

Federal Court. "How to Appeal a Decision of a Citizenship Judge?" August 23, 2012. http://cas-ncr-nter03.cas-satj.gc.ca/portal/page/portal/fc_cf_en/Appeal_citizenship.

Federal Courts Act. R.S.C. 1985, c. F-7.

Federal Courts Immigration and Refugee Protection Rules. S.O.R./93-22.

Immigration and Refugee Protection Act. S.C. 2001, c. 27.

Immigration Appeal Division Rules. S.O.R./2002-230.

Canada Gazette. "Refugee Appeal Division Rules, Part I: Notices and Proposed Regulations," archived, vol. 146, no. 32, August 11, 2012. http://www.gazette.gc.ca/rp-pr/p1/2012/2012-08-11/html/reg2-eng.html.

Citizenship and Immigration Canada. CP 8: "Appeals," in *Operational Manual Appeals* (CP), April 8, 2009. http://www.cic.gc.ca/english/resources/manuals/cp/cp08-eng.pdf.

PART VII

Legal Professionals

CHAPTER 12   Regulating the Practice of Immigration
and Refugee Law

Regulating the Practice of Immigration and Refugee Law

12

LEARNING OUTCOMES

After reading this chapter you should be able to:

- Identify which level of government regulates immigration consultants.

- Describe how a non-lawyer can be authorized to act in immigration matters.

- Apply the code of professional ethics of regulated immigration consultants.

- Distinguish between professional misconduct and conduct unbecoming an immigration consultant.

- Apply the profession's code of ethics to the operation of an immigration consultant's practice.

- Understand the process for dealing with a claim of misconduct against an immigration consultant and the discipline measures that may be taken.

Introduction

This chapter provides an overview of the need to protect consumers of immigration and refugee services and to protect the public interest through the regulation of the practice of immigration and refugee law in Canada by non-lawyers who practise immigration law.

In other fields of law, non-lawyers who provide legal services are called *independent paralegals*. In the field of immigration law, non-lawyers who provide legal services are called *immigration consultants*. Both are licensed to work independently and must be distinguished from *law clerks*, who also provide legal services, but who are employed and supervised by lawyers.

In the past, there have been highly publicized instances of non-lawyers involved in immigration work committing frauds on their clients and the Canadian government and engaging in shoddy work; they did so in the absence of any control over their education, their qualifications, their competence, and their probity as providers of immigration legal services. Governments use regulation as a policy tool to benefit consumers of legal services and to protect the public interest, as in the case of lawyers who are regulated by their law societies. In 2003, the federal government decided to regulate the business of immigration consulting. As of 2011, the IRP regulations require that non-lawyers who practise immigration law must be members in good standing of the Immigration Consultants of Canada Regulatory Council (ICCRC—the council) as Regulated Canadian Immigration Consultants (RCICs), or licensed paralegals who are regulated by a provincial law society.

Background: Regulation of Immigration Consultants

Regulating the business of immigration consulting was first introduced in 2003 when the government established the Canadian Society of Immigration Consultants (CSIC) as the regulator. The CSIC was a self-regulating, professional organization that determined the requirements for entry to practise, set rules for the professional conduct of its members, and imposed discipline or other corrective measures if those rules were disregarded. Many of the unethical and prohibited activities addressed by the CSIC *Rules of Professional Conduct* were identified by the government in its reasons for regulating immigration consultants:

> Most representatives conduct their work in an ethical, professional and effective manner. However, there were persistent and credible reports that some unscrupulous immigration consultants, both in Canada and abroad, facilitated people smuggling and fabricated documents permitting foreign nationals to enter this country illegally. Certain consultants who held themselves out as experts had no training or experience handling complex files. Others promised the impossible and failed to deliver, and charged exorbitant fees for their services. In a number of reported cases, consultants had charged fees for an unfulfilled promise to file

immigration applications, while providing bogus file reference numbers and advising clients that the Canadian government refused their application.[1]

Consider the following examples of the types of conduct engaged in by unscrupulous immigration consultants, found in the news media:

1. Gideon McGuire Augier was convicted of defrauding would-be immigrants because of his bogus scheme to get immigrants into Canada. Some of his clients lost their life savings. It is alleged that he cheated hundreds of people in Russia and the Ukraine. He sold desperate families the dream of job opportunities and new lives in Canada. He collected fees, in some cases $5,000, from people abroad by promising to expedite their work permits for Canada, often when no application was made. He also charged families to be sponsored under a non-existent family sponsorship scheme, and accepted consulting fees from people in Russia and the Ukraine, knowing their applications to enter Canada on humanitarian and compassionate grounds could not be made from outside the country. (*Hamilton Spectator*, May 21, 2006)

2. Mr. Zhang immigrated to Canada in 1991. He returned to China and married his high school sweetheart. He paid a $2,000 fee for an immigration consultant to help him sponsor his new bride and her son from a previous marriage into Canada. The consultant filed the application but did not complete the required documentation. The sponsorship application was dismissed and the consultant did not inform Mr. Zhang, so the time period for filing an appeal expired. As a result, Mr. Zhang had to engage in the lengthy process of getting the decision judicially reviewed. (*Toronto Star*, April 13, 2004)

3. An immigration consultant was charged with nine counts of fraud totalling $100,832. The consultant advised clients to pay between $3,000 and $28,000 to buy businesses or real estate because they were told such investments would improve their chances of being accepted as immigrants. These purchases had no impact on their applications. (*Toronto Star*, May 5, 1987)

There were many other reported instances of misconduct by immigration consultants, but it took several years for the profession to be regulated. The failure of government to legislate was a result, in part, of uncertainty as to whether the federal or provincial level of government had jurisdiction. This constitutional issue was resolved by the Supreme Court of Canada in 2001 in *Law Society of British Columbia v. Mangat*.

Federal Jurisdiction: Law Society of British Columbia v. Mangat

The Supreme Court of Canada, in the case of *Law Society of British Columbia v. Mangat*, determined that the federal government and not the provincial government had jurisdiction to regulate immigration consultants. The *Mangat* case arose when the Law Society of British Columbia claimed that only lawyers could legally provide paid immigration services. Mr. Mangat, an immigration consultant, was charged with the provincial offence of conducting an unauthorized legal practice, because he was not a lawyer yet he provided immigration services to clients for a fee.

The services provided by Mr. Mangat included appearing on behalf of clients at the Immigration and Refugee Board (IRB), drafting immigration documents for clients, and giving clients advice about Canada's immigration laws. There was no evidence that the services he provided were below the standard that would have been provided by a lawyer.

The Supreme Court decided that because immigration was a federal matter according to the *Constitution Act, 1867*, it was the responsibility of the federal government, not British Columbia, to decide who may practise immigration law. The Court found that the provincial statute governing the practice of law in British Columbia did not apply to the practice of immigration law.

The *Immigration Act*, which was in force at the time, permitted representation by a barrister or solicitor or other counsel. This was broad enough to allow non-lawyers to act on behalf of clients on immigration matters. There were no restrictions on how immigration law was practised by non-lawyers. Anyone could open up a business and call himself an "immigration consultant." This total lack of regulation led to many instances of incompetence and fraud.

The *Mangat* case clarified that it was the federal government that had the power to restrict the practice of immigration law. The federal government chose not to prohibit practice by non-lawyers, as the BC government had attempted to do; instead, it set up a regulatory regime to ensure the ability and integrity of immigration consultants and the quality of their services.

Legal Challenges to Regulation

In its first few years of existence, the CSIC was challenged by immigration consultants who did not wish to be regulated, and by the Law Society of Upper Canada (LSUC) in Ontario, which would have preferred to take over that regulatory role itself.

In *Chinese Business Chamber of Canada v. Canada*, several organizations and some individuals challenged the power of the government to regulate and restrict immigration practice. They challenged the creation of a regulatory scheme that requires all immigration consultants to be members of the CSIC, and applied to the court for an order preventing CIC and the IRB from refusing to deal with immigration consultants who were not members of the CSIC.

The court rejected these claims and stated the following:

> The immigration consultant regulations are aimed at the protection of vulnerable persons and the preservation of the integrity of the immigration process, both of which are clearly in the public interest. Indeed, all of the parties agree that regulation in this area is both necessary and long overdue.[2]

The court found that the applicants had failed to demonstrate that they would suffer irreparable harm as a result of regulation.

In *Law Society of Upper Canada v. Canada (Citizenship and Immigration)*, the LSUC contested the CSIC's authority to regulate immigration consultants. The court confirmed that the CSIC did have authority: it is an independent body separate from CIC. It further found that delegation of regulatory powers to the CSIC was authorized by s. 91 of the IRPA and that investigation by the CSIC of complaints against consultants employed at law firms did not pose a risk of breach of solicitor–client privilege.

In its reasons, the court reaffirmed the importance of immigration consultants and the valuable role they play in helping individuals navigate the immigration system.

Bill C-35: Cracking Down on Crooked Immigration Consultants Act

Despite the establishment of CSIC, there continued to be a number of complaints from the public and from within the profession that unacceptable practices by immigration consultants continued. In 2008, the House of Commons Standing Committee on Citizenship and Immigration ("standing committee") heard representations from a wide range of stakeholders including CIC, the Canadian Bar Association, immigration practitioners, the LSUC, the RCMP, and the public. Complaints concerning CSIC's governance and accountability framework raised concerns that immigration consultants were not adequately regulated in the public interest with respect to the provision of professional and ethical consultation, representation, and advice. Consequently, the standing committee made a number of recommendations that led to the introduction of Bill C-35, *An Act to Amend the Immigration and Refugee Protection Act* (originally called the *Cracking Down on Crooked Immigration Consultants Act*). Bill C-35 was introduced June 8, 2010, received royal assent on March 23, 2011, and came into effect on June 30, 2011.

Amendments to the IRPA provide for more government oversight in order to improve the way in which immigration consultants are now regulated. Bill C-35 grants the minister the authority to make regulations to designate or revoke the designation of a body responsible for the regulation of immigration consultants under s. 91(5) of the IRPA and to provide for transitional measures, by regulation, in relation to the designation or revocation of the body responsible for regulating immigration consultants under s. 91(7).

The federal government may also make regulations, in accordance with s. 91 of IRPA, to license immigration consultants under a regulatory body that is accountable to the minister. Section 13.2 of the IRP Regulations defines an authorized representative and prohibits any person who is not an authorized representative from acting for a fee. The most notable change to the regulation of immigration consultants was the government's selection of a new regulatory body, the Immigration Consultants of Canada Regulatory Council (ICCRC).

Other Amendments

In May 2012, amendments were made to the IRP Regulations that authorize government officials (from CIC, CBSA, and the IRB) to disclose information to the regulating body—the ICCRC or a law society—about an immigration representative's professional or ethical conduct (IRP Regulations, s. 13.1).

Authorized Practitioners

Although individuals with an immigration or refugee matter can seek the help of unpaid third parties, such as family members, friends, and non-governmental or religious organizations to act on their behalf, many choose to obtain assistance from knowledgeable and experienced representatives; regulation serves to protect the consumer of immigration and refugee services.

It is an offence for anyone other than a lawyer, an authorized immigration consultant, other representative, or authorized entity to charge a fee for immigration advice or representation *at any stage* of an application or proceeding. This includes

> representing or advising persons for consideration—or offering to do so—to all stages in connection with a proceeding or application under the IRPA, including before a proceeding has been commenced or an application has been made.[3]

Those who are authorized in IRPA to represent individuals for a fee include lawyers and paralegals in good standing of a provincial or territorial law society, notaries in Quebec (members of Chambre des notaires du Québec), and authorized immigration consultants.

Unauthorized Representation

There are penalties for unauthorized representatives who provide, or offer to provide, advice or representation for a fee, at any stage of an immigration application or proceeding, *including the period before a proceeding begins or an application is submitted.*[4]

The indictable offence of providing unauthorized representation carries a penalty of $100,000 and/or up to a two-year term of imprisonment; a summary conviction carries a fine of $20,000 and the possibility of a term of imprisonment of up to six months.

A non-lawyer, such as a licensed paralegal or an immigration consultant, must be a "member in good standing" of the regulatory body to

- provide direct or indirect representation;
- advise a person for consideration; or
- offer to advise or represent a person in connection with a proceeding or application under the IRPA.

This requirement applies to all matters before the following decision-makers:

- the minister responsible for Citizenship and Immigration Canada (CIC);
- the minister responsible for the Canada Border Services Agency (CBSA);
- immigration officers; and
- the Immigration and Refugee Board.

The regulatory scheme does not extend to citizenship applications, because citizenship is governed by the *Citizenship Act* and not the IRPA.

Paralegals

Under s. 91(2)(b) of the IRPA, Bill C-35 also recognizes paralegals who are members in good standing of a provincial or territorial law society as authorized representatives. As of December 2012, however, the only law society to regulate paralegals in Canada is the Law Society of Upper Canada (LSUC), in Ontario. Under the LSUC's regulatory scheme, paralegals are required to have minimum education credentials, pass a licensing examination, and meet good character requirements.[5] The LSUC also accredits private and public colleges in Ontario and is therefore responsible for determining the educational competencies for paralegals. Those educational credentials do not currently include the requirement for specialized knowledge in immigration or refugee law. It is still too early to know how paralegals are expected to acquire such specialized knowledge if their educational institutions do not offer such courses or how they will be able to demonstrate their competence in the fields of immigration and refugee law.

Immigration Consultants of Canada Regulatory Council and Regulated Canadian Immigration Consultants

The minister revoked CSIC's designation as regulator and, as of June 30 2011, designated the Immigration Consultants of Canada Regulatory Council (ICCRC, or the Council) as the new self-regulated body.

There was a 120-day transitional period ending on October 28, 2011, during which time, to provide for continuity, members in good standing with CSIC were permitted to continue to represent clients and were required to register with the ICCRC to become members in good standing of the new regulatory body. Members of ICCRC are called Regulated Canadian Immigration Consultants (RCICs) to distinguish them from ghost consultants—those who are not authorized to practise.

Members in good standing of the ICCRC are listed on that organization's website.[6]

Most regulated professions require specialized education, knowledge, and skill, and usually employ a code of ethics to govern the conduct of members in their relationships with clients, employees, colleagues, and the public, as well as some system of accountability.[7] In the case of RCICs, regulation has the features of a professional organization, including licensing, which will grant entry into the immigration profession. To be admitted as a member of the ICCRC, and thus be permitted to practise as an RCIC, an applicant must satisfy the following criteria:

- be at least 18 years old and a Canadian citizen, permanent resident, or registered Indian under the *Indian Act*;
- have post-secondary education, defined as a college diploma/certificate/degree or university degree, or comparable work experience; work experience assessments may be an option for some applicants (check with the regulator);
- pass a "full skills exam" on immigration and practice management, consisting of a three-hour set of one-hundred scenario-based multiple-choice questions. Up to three attempts are permitted;

- pass a practice management skills test to demonstrate competency in the preparation of standard immigration applications;

- be of good character, as shown by police certificates from all countries, in accordance with the requirements set by the Admissions Committee of the ICCRC; and submit sworn statements regarding countries of residence, police certificates, and criminal record; bankruptcy; suspension or expulsion from another regulatory body; practising immigration law for a fee while unauthorized, contrary to the IRPA prior to admission; and, on an annual basis, provide a statutory declaration regarding criminal charges, bankruptcy, and suspension or expulsion from any other regulatory body; and

- show the ability to carry on business in English or French by having successfully completed an accredited language test within the past two years.

Full Skills Exam

The ICCRC provides a study guide for the full-skills exam online, at https://www.iccrc-crcic.ca/admin/contentEngine/contentImages/file/Study%20Guide_Dec2011_ENG.pdf.

Members of the ICCRC maintain their membership by

- fulfilling annual continuing professional development requirements;

- fulfilling mandatory practice management and education requirements;

- paying membership dues and a liability insurance fee for errors and omissions insurance (see http://www.iccrc-crcic.ca for up-to-date fees); and

- abiding by the regulator's *Code of Professional Ethics*.

A persistent but illegal practice is that of *ghost consulting*. In this practice, a person who is not authorized to practise as an immigration consultant completes the application forms on behalf of a client, but then has the forms submitted as if they were personally completed by the applicant. Fake consultants pass themselves off as legitimate immigration professionals, but do not have a licence to provide assistance on any immigration matter, and are therefore unauthorized. The unauthorized person then charges a fee for the work done. Ghost consulting is a breach of the IRPA and may be subject to an investigation by the RCMP. Ghost and fake consulting also carries a risk for the client. If a client has difficulties with a non-authorized consultant, he will have no access to the complaint procedures of the ICCRC because the council has no power to deal with the practices of ghost consultants. The ICCRC will investigate the situation and, where necessary, pass the information along to the RCMP, CBSA, a provincial or territorial law society, or any other authority.

Consider the following scenario:

> Joe is a permanent resident from Mexico and works at a travel agency.
>
> Joe is sometimes approached by visitors from Mexico for advice and assistance about extending their visits, particularly those who have a limited ability to read and write in English. Joe wants to help his clients, so he explains Canada's immigration laws and advises them about alternatives, such as first applying as a student. Joe has even helped some of his clients to fill out immigration application forms, but he does not sign them. In return for his trouble, Joe has received free dinners, drinks, and other gifts.

If dinner, drinks, and gifts qualify as a "fee," Joe may be in violation of the rule against ghost consulting. A number of industry-related professionals may find that their work may place them in a position where they wish to dabble in immigration law. The ICCRC provides a series of immigration advisories for various industries that set out the type of activities that may not be performed by unauthorized representatives. For example, travel agents, recruiters, human resource professionals, and educational representatives are not authorized to explain or provide advice about completing immigration forms or to communicate with CIC or CBSA on behalf of a client; recruiters may not represent employers in an arranged employment opinion or labour market opinion application; and adoption agencies are not allowed to advertise that they can provide immigration advice for compensation or represent clients in an immigration application or proceeding.

ICCRC Structure

The ICCRC is governed by an elected board of directors consisting of seven directors from which a chairperson is elected. Members are elected based on regional representation (Ontario—4; Quebec—2; Western Canada—4; Other—2) and 3 others are elected as public interest directors for a total of 15 directors. Directors receive $2,500 per month for their services, and the chairperson is entitled to an additional $2,500 per month. In addition to usual directors' responsibilities, directors are responsible for operating the council.

The ICCRC has enacted a set of bylaws to govern the operation of the organization. These bylaws include rules for the election of directors and conduct of directors' meetings, rules for the establishment of standing committees (Admissions Committee, Appeal Committee, Communications Committee, Complaints Committee, Discipline Committee, Finance and Audits Committee, Governance and Nominating Committee, Human Resources and Compensation Committee, Outreach Committee, Practice Management and Education Committee, Practice Quality Review Committee, and the Review Committee), and rules to determine the conditions that must be satisfied for entry to practise as a regulated immigration consultant.

Code of Professional Ethics

The Code of Professional Ethics is intended to protect the public from unprofessional, unethical, incompetent practice by the ICCRC members and students (article 1). A regulated Canadian immigration consultant (RCIC) who fails to comply with the Code may face disciplinary measures, including the revocation of membership from the ICCRC.

The Code provides guidelines on how to run an immigration consulting practice in a proper manner. Note that minimal compliance with the strict letter of the Code may not be sufficient because the immigration professional is expected not only to comply with the minimum set of specific situations detailed in the Code but to live up to the "spirit of the Code," especially in situations that are not specifically dealt with under it.

The Code is organized into 20 separate articles as follows:

Article 1. Intention of Code

Article 2. Interpretation

Article 3. Ethical Practice

Article 4. Professionalism

Article 5. Competence

Article 6. Quality of Service

Article 7. Advising Clients

Article 8. Confidentiality

Article 9. Conflicts of Interest

Article 10. Preservation of Client Property

Article 11. ICCRC Member as Advocate

Article 12. Retainer and Fees

Article 13. Joint Retainers

Article 14. Withdrawal from Representation

Article 15. Outside Interests

Article 16. Advertising, Solicitation and Making Services Available

Article 17. Discrimination and Harassment

Article 18. Errors and Omissions

Article 19. Disciplinary Authority

Article 20. Responsibility to ICCRC and Others

These topics are explained briefly below; however, RCICs should be familiar with the *Code of Professional Ethics* in their entirety. The Code is reproduced in the appendix to this chapter, and is also available on the ICCRC website at http://www.iccrc-crcic .ca/admin/contentEngine/contentImages/file/Code_of_Professional_Ethics__ Sept_2011.pdf.

Conduct Unbecoming (Interpretation, Article 2)

Conduct unbecoming refers to improper conduct that occurs in the member's personal or private capacity. Generally, it does not directly affect a client. The rationale behind prohibiting such conduct is that any improper conduct by a person identified with the profession might discredit the profession in the eyes of the public. This could undermine the public's confidence in the integrity of all immigration consultants.

Examples of the types of conduct that are prohibited and will likely result in discipline include:

- participating in criminal activity, such as fraud, that brings into question the member's integrity, honesty, trustworthiness, or fitness;
- committing a breach of this Code;
- taking improper advantage of a person in a vulnerable situation, such as people who are young, ill, unsophisticated, poorly educated, inexperienced, or lacking in business savvy;
- engaging in conduct involving dishonesty; and
- failing to abide by a fee dispute resolution resolved by the ICCRC or a court of competent jurisdiction.

A purely private indiscretion on the part of a member that does not bring into question the consultant's integrity should not cause the ICCRC to impose discipline, but it is left to the ICCRC to determine the boundaries between conduct unbecoming and purely private conduct.

Professional Misconduct (Interpretation, Article 2)

Professional misconduct is any improper action of an immigration consultant during the course of conducting business that tends to discredit the profession. It is professional misconduct for the RCIC to

- violate or attempt to avoid or violate the bylaws, rules, regulations, code, or policies of ICCRC, or knowingly assist or induce another member, employee, or agent to do so;
- violate or attempt to violate any requirement of IRPA; or
- engage in conduct that undermines the integrity of Canada's immigration system.

It is also professional misconduct for an RCIC to misappropriate or deal dishonestly with another person's money, including any of the client's money deposited with the consultant. This prohibition is so important that it is addressed again in Article 10: Preservation of Client Property and in Article 12: Retainer and Fees.

It goes without saying that an RCIC may not bribe or attempt to bribe a government official to ignore immigration rules or give preferential treatment to a client. It is also professional misconduct for an RCIC to state or imply that he or she is engaged in this type of activity.

Consider the following scenario:

> Lara is a licensed immigration consultant. She has been working in this field for many years and is familiar with many immigration officials and tribunal members. When a prospective client comes into her office, she promotes herself by emphasizing that she "knows everyone in this business" and "knows how to get her clients through the red tape." "It is all about who you know and keeping them happy," she says.

Lara's statements could be interpreted as meaning that she knows how to get preferential treatment for her clients. Even if she has never actually bribed any officials, intimating that she does constitutes professional misconduct.

Competence (Article 5) and Quality of Service (Article 6)

An RCIC must be diligent, efficient, and conscientious. Unprofessional habits, such as poor record keeping, disorganization, shoddy work, or failing to respond to phone calls and correspondence, are unacceptable. Members must have an effective **tickler system** in place for reminding them of deadlines. Missing a deadline for the filing of information, where the consequences to the client may be severe, is a particularly serious transgression.

The standard of competence and quality of service demanded is objective—based on what could be expected of a reasonably competent immigration professional in similar circumstances. The standard is not perfection—reasonable people are not perfect. However, it does not allow for personal circumstances or disability, such as addiction or depression, to excuse poor performance. Members have a responsibility to keep abreast of changing laws, regulations, and policies affecting their practice, and must continue to develop their knowledge and skills in compliance with the continuing education policies of the ICCRC.

Professional Responsibility for Agents and Staff (Article 6)

A member may hire employees to perform tasks such as record-keeping, reception, and interviewing clients. A licensed immigration consultant may also hire agents to perform functions such as delivering documents. A member may not hire any person who has previously been removed from membership or suspended by the ICCRC or any designated legal regulatory body as a result of disciplinary action. It is important that the duties of employees and agents do not involve advising, consulting with, or representing clients, unless the agent or employee is also a member of the ICCRC. It is not sufficient to have an RCIC member supervise an agent or employee who is not a member of the ICCRC.

As noted above, it is professional misconduct if a member knowingly assists or induces an agent or employee to violate any of the bylaws, rules, regulations, code, or policies of ICCRC. Thus, an RCIC member cannot try to avoid the consequences of breaching the rules of the ICCRC by having someone else do the improper actions on his or her behalf. Immigration professionals should also be aware that they may be held personally responsible for the actions of agents or employees, according to the principle of **vicarious responsibility**.

Advising Clients (Article 7)

Immigration consultants must provide *proper advice* to their clients, meaning they must be "honest and candid." To enable the client to make appropriate decisions and give directions to the consultant, a consultant must explain the case in a manner that the client understands. If the consultant does not speak the client's language, an interpreter should be used.

The Code states that the consultant must take reasonable steps to avoid becoming "the tool or dupe of an unscrupulous" client. The consultant must be careful never to "knowingly assist in or encourage" dishonesty, omission of relevant information, provision of misleading information, fraud, crime, or illegal conduct. The consultant may advise a client on how to comply with immigration law and regulations, but must not advise on how to violate the law. For example, a client sponsoring a spouse who is a resident in a foreign country should be encouraged to collect and maintain all records of contact with the spouse, such as letters and phone records, but it would be improper to encourage the client to fabricate such records.

The consultant must be very cautious in providing services, especially when dealing with clients outside the country and when providing advice and completing documents based on documents produced outside the country. The IRPA makes misrepresentation an offence, and if the consultant suspects that the client's documents are false, they should not be used.

Confidentiality (Article 8)

An immigration consultant is required to keep client information and communications confidential, and generally must obtain the client's permission before disclosing any such information, even after the termination of the retainer. However, the consultant may be compelled by a court to disclose *confidential information* in a legal proceeding or by order of a tribunal. For example, if a client is charged with an IRPA or *Criminal Code* offence, or there is a lawsuit against the client, the immigration consultant can be subpoenaed and be required to attend court and answer questions related to the legal proceeding.

Also, according to bylaw 27, in the course of an investigation, the ICCRC may demand information—including a client file—from an immigration consultant. This obligation overrides the duty of confidentiality owed to clients. By contrast, client information and communications shared in the context of a lawyer–client relationship are protected by **solicitor–client privilege**. A court may not compel the disclosure of such information against the wishes of the client. This may be an important advantage to clients in some cases. Therefore, immigration consultants should explain their duty of confidentiality, and how it differs from solicitor–client privilege, at the time of the initial interview with the client. It is important that the clients of immigration consultants be aware that they are not protected by solicitor–client privilege, before they divulge information.

Avoiding Conflicts of Interest (Article 9)

A **conflict of interest** occurs where a consultant represents clients with incompatible interests. In other words, the best course of action for one client may harm the interests of another.

A situation may also arise where there is a potential for a conflict, but no actual conflict. For example, a consultant may represent both an employer and a foreign worker that the employer wants to hire. In these circumstances the consultant must inform both the employer and foreign worker of the potential for a conflict of interest. Should an actual conflict arise, such as the foreign worker obtaining a job offer from another employer, the consultant must cease representation of one or both parties.

Preservation of Client Property (Article 10)

Immigration consultants must be very careful with property belonging to clients. Meticulous records must be kept, and a trust account designated so that client property does not find its way into the general business account. (For details, see article 12 of the Code, discussed below.) Funds held in trust on behalf of a client should be limited to an amount reasonably necessary for payment of the consultant's fees and disbursements, any agent's fees, and CIC fees. Funds for other purposes, such as those required for entry under the investor class, should not be in the possession of the consultant.

ICCRC Member as Advocate (Article 11)

Members may appear before government officials or the Immigration and Refugee Board to advocate for clients. The duty of a member is to represent the client's interests resolutely, fearlessly raise every issue, and advance every argument to support the client's position. However, the member must do so while treating board members, the minister, and other parties with candour, courtesy, and respect. The member must act legally and ethically. For example, the member must not counsel a witness to lie or make claims that are clearly unsupported or false.

The member has an absolute duty to abide by the rules of procedure of the IRB.

Retainer and Fees (Article 12)

A member must provide a written *retainer* agreement or engagement letter to a client to account for funds paid in advance of services. Retainers must be deposited in a separate trust account at a financial institution, and be transferred into the business account only after services are rendered on the client's behalf and the client is billed.

The retainer agreement must indicate the reason that the member is being hired, and set out the fair and reasonable fees for services and *disbursements* (out-of-pocket expenses, such as photocopying) that will be charged by the member. Terms and conditions, such as a statement that interest will accrue on unpaid accounts, should also be specified. The agreement must also inform the client of how to contact the member and the ICCRC in the event of a disagreement over fees.

Withdrawal from Representation (Article 14)

Once a member has accepted a client, the member is generally obliged to maintain the relationship. There are, however, exceptions that allow the member to terminate the relationship, and in a few circumstances the member is required to do so.

A member must withdraw his or her services when

- the client discharges the member;
- the client instructs the member to violate the law or contravene the code of professional ethics; or
- the consultant will be placed in a conflict of interest by continuing to represent the client.

Situations may arise in which there is a serious loss of confidence between the ICCRC member and a client, making withdrawal optional, as when the client

- deceives the member;
- fails to give adequate instructions to the member; or
- refuses to take advice on a significant matter.

An ICCRC member may sever the professional relationship with the client only for a proper purpose and if it is not unfair or prejudicial to the client.

The Code also provides for situations where a member may end the relationship with a client who has failed to provide funds on account of disbursements or fees.

A member who wishes to withdraw representation must ensure that the client has sufficient opportunity to seek the assistance of new counsel in time for any upcoming hearing dates. The member must return the client's papers and information on the case; return any retainer funds held in trust (less the amount of any outstanding fees); account for fees and disbursements; cooperate with any new representative hired by the client; and inform CIC, CBSA, and/or the IRB. Terminating the relationship for the purpose of delaying a hearing to allow the client to stay in Canada longer is an improper purpose, even if it is the client's wishes.

There are no restrictions on a client's ability to "fire" a member. The client may end the relationship at any time, without explanation. However, the client does remain responsible for payment of any outstanding fees.

If you are taking over a case from another ICCRC member, it is prudent to contact the former consultant and confirm that she is no longer handling the case.

Advertising, Solicitation, and Making Services Available (Article 16)

Advertising must be in good taste and not bring the profession, the ICCRC, or the laws of Canada into disrepute. Advertising may not be false or misleading. In particular, advertising should not guarantee results or guarantee maximum times for completing processing of applications, nor should it be expressed or implied that the member has special access or influence with the minister or government officials, or that the member is a lawyer. The member must be careful that any foreign credentials listed, such as a foreign law degree, do not suggest to the public that the consultant is a lawyer in Canada.

A member of the ICCRC may advertise the fact of ICCRC designation and use the ICCRC logo. A member may use endorsements and testimonials in advertisements as long as consent has been obtained from the client and is true and accurate.

Discrimination and Harassment (Article 17)

A member of the ICCRC is not permitted to discriminate against clients on the basis of age, gender, sexual orientation, same-sex partnership status, marital status, family status, national or ethnic origin, ancestry, race, colour, religion, creed, citizenship, physical or mental disability, political affiliation, record of offences, or socio-economic status. Discrimination may include charging more or refusing to represent. Consultants will often target their marketing efforts at certain groups by noting that they are able to speak certain languages, by advertising in specific community newspapers, and by getting referrals from contacts within a certain community. This is acceptable and not considered to be discrimination. It is also possible, and in fact required, to refuse clients on the basis that the service requested is outside the area of expertise of the member. However, it is not permissible to refuse clients based on their ethnicity or indicate that you will only represent people of a particular religion, gender, or ethnic group.

A member of the ICCRC is not permitted to engage in sexual or other forms of harassment of a colleague, a staff member, client, or any other person, including electronic harassment by sending unsolicited electronic messages that are abusive, offensive, intrusive, unprofessional, or unwanted.

Consider the following scenario:

> Gita is a qualified ICCRC member and an immigrant herself. She has a law degree from her native country and she speaks four languages—English and three other languages from her country of birth. She is very connected to her ethnic community here in Canada, and her clients are exclusively from that community. Gita writes a column in her local ethnic newspaper, which lists her law degree and membership in the ICCRC. Gita also advertises in this newspaper and sometimes includes words of praise from well-known members of her community who were former clients.

This scenario raises a number of issues. Gita must be careful when referencing her foreign law degree. She must not misrepresent herself as a lawyer in Canada. There is nothing wrong with promoting herself to her own ethnic community, but she must be careful not to refuse service to a client who does not belong to her ethnic group.

Errors and Omissions (Article 18)

Members of the ICCRC must purchase *liability insurance*, also called *errors and omissions insurance*. This insurance protects clients by providing funds for compensating clients for any successful professional negligence or fraud claim against a regulated immigration consultant. For example, if a member of the ICCRC defrauds a client of $100,000 by telling him that the money will be used for a qualifying investment under the investor class, the insurer will pay the money back to the client. This is important, because the money may have disappeared and not be retrievable.

Errors and omissions insurance also protects regulated immigration consultants— without it, a member could be forced to use personal assets, such as a family home, to pay a damages award. Consider a regulated immigration consultant who misses a deadline and thereby causes a client to expend an additional $60,000 in legal fees. The consultant would benefit from the insurer paying the amount of the damages award, rather than being required to cash in a registered retirement savings plan in order to pay it.

Disciplinary Authority (Article 19)

An unsatisfied client of a member of the ICCRC must submit a complaint in writing to the ICCRC (the specific form can be found on the ICCRC website). The member must be informed of the complaint and be given 30 days to respond to the allegations. If the complaint is groundless, no action will be taken. However, if an investigation discloses that the claim is credible, the ICCRC may negotiate a settlement, caution or admonish the member, or refer the complaint to the Discipline Committee to commence discipline procedures.

The member has a right to appeal to the Appeal Committee of the ICCRC.

Certain complaints cannot be resolved by the ICCRC because it has authority only to discipline a member for professional misconduct or for conduct unbecoming an ICCRC member. If the investigation discloses that the complaint relates to negligence, the matter may be referred to the errors and omissions insurance company or to the civil courts. If the complaint is against an individual who is not a member of the ICCRC, the issue is referred to the police for prosecution pursuant to the IRPA (see ss. 126 and 127 for offences and penalties related to counselling and misrepresentation). In this case, the ICCRC cannot resolve the issue; it is a matter for the courts.

If the Discipline Committee finds the member guilty of professional misconduct, it may make an order to do one or more of the following actions:

- revoke membership;
- suspend membership;
- reprimand the member;
- direct the member to refrain from using any ICCRC designation or logo, or to return her certificate of membership;
- direct the member to take any specific rehabilitative measure (for example, professional development training, counselling, and treatment); or
- direct the member to pay a fine.

The ICCRC's responsibility is limited to enforcement of the Code and the bylaws, and the remedies it may impose are limited to discipline and costs.

APPENDIX

IMMIGRATION CONSULTANTS OF CANADA REGULATORY COUNCIL

CODE OF PROFESSIONAL ETHICS

June 2012

ARTICLE 1. INTENTION OF CODE

1.1 Standard of Professional Conduct
This Code establishes high standards of professional conduct for ICCRC members and provides guidance for their practice.

1.2 Primary Purpose
The primary purpose of this Code is to protect the public from unprofessional, unethical, incompetent practice by the ICCRC members and students.

1.3 Code Binding
This Code is binding on all ICCRC members and, with necessary variations, to all ICCRC students.

1.4 Following Spirit Required
ICCRC members must endeavour to follow the spirit of this Code. This Code cannot address every potential situation or impropriety, but provide principles that govern all conduct.

1.5 Discipline upon Breach
ICCRC members or students who breach this Code are subject to disciplinary proceedings.

ARTICLE 2. INTERPRETATION

2.1 Interpretation Consistent with Bylaws
This Code shall be interpreted in a manner consistent with the Bylaws of ICCRC unless the context otherwise requires.

2.2 Defined Terms
In this Code:
    2.2.1 "Agent" means a person who:
        (i) does not provide immigration advice for a fee in contravention of IRPA;
        (ii) represents an ICCRC member in furtherance of the member's practice;
        (iii) solicits or facilitates business in connection with the ICCRC member's practice;

(iv) is registered, or required to be registered, as an Agent pursuant to ICCRC's Bylaws;

and for greater certainty, "Agent" does not include an individual who merely refers a Client to a member but does not otherwise take any part in a proceeding or application, or potential proceeding or application, under the IRPA;

2.2.2 "Board" means the Immigration and Refugee Board and any of its staff, branches or divisions;

2.2.3 "Bylaws" mean the bylaws of ICCRC;

2.2.4 "Canadian Society of Immigration Consultants" (and the acronym "CSIC") means the body incorporated under the Canada Corporations Act and previously designated by the Minister pursuant to section 91 of the Immigration and Refugee Protection Act, S.C. 2001, c. 27, as amended, (IRPA) as a regulatory body for immigration consultants;

2.2.5 "CBSA" means Canada Border Services Agency, and any successor agency;

2.2.6 "CIC" means Citizenship and Immigration Canada;

2.2.7 "Client" means a person whose interests the ICCRC member undertakes to advance, for a fee or otherwise, regarding a proceeding or application, or potential proceeding or application, under the IRPA;

2.2.8 "Conduct Unbecoming an ICCRC member" means conduct in the member's personal or private capacity that tends to bring discredit upon the profession including, but not limited, to:

(i) committing a criminal act that reflects adversely on the member's integrity, honesty, trustworthiness, or fitness as an ICCRC member;

(ii) committing a breach of this Code;

(iii) taking improper advantage of a person's youth, age, inexperience, lack of education, lack of sophistication, ill health, or un-businesslike habits;

(iv) engaging in conduct involving dishonesty; or

(v) failing to abide by a fee dispute resolution resolved by the ICCRC or a court of competent jurisdiction.

2.2.9 "Designated Legal Regulatory Body" means a law society of a province or territory or the Chambre des notaires du Québec;

2.2.10 "Employee" means a person who is in an employee/employer relationship with an ICCRC member, excluding another ICCRC member;

2.2.11 "Firm" means a firm as defined in the Bylaws;

2.2.12 "IRPA" means the Immigration and Refugee Protection Act, S.C. 2001, c. 27, as amended, and includes all Regulations made pursuant to it;

2.2.13 "ICCRC" means Immigration Consultants of Canada Regulatory Council;

2.2.14 "ICCRC member means a person who is a member of ICCRC;

2.2.15 "Minister" means the Minister or Ministers responsible for the administration of IRPA; namely the members of the Queen's Privy Council designated as such by the Governor-in-Council;

2.2.16 "Officer" means any person or class of person designated as Officers by the Minister to carry out any purpose or any provision of IRPA;

2.2.17 "Practice" means professional work undertaken by an ICCRC member in connection with any application or proceeding, or potential application or proceeding, under IRPA;

2.2.18 "Professional Misconduct" means conduct in the ICCRC member's practice that tends to discredit the profession including:

(i) violating or attempting to avoid or violate the Bylaws, Rules, Regulations, Codes or policies of ICCRC, or knowingly assisting or inducing another ICCRC member to do so;

(ii) violating or attempting to violate any requirement of IRPA;

(iii) knowingly assisting or inducing an Employee or Agent to engage in conduct prohibited by clause 2.2.18(i) or clause 2.2.18(ii);

(iv) engaging in conduct that undermines the integrity of Canada's immigration system;

(v) misappropriating or otherwise dealing dishonestly with money or property in connection with a member's practice;

(vi) stating or implying an ability to influence improperly any government agency or official; or

(vii) engaging in conduct prejudicial to the administration of justice.

2.2.19 "Student" means a student registered with ICCRC.

ARTICLE 3. ETHICAL PRACTICE

3.1 Serve Honourably

An ICCRC member has a duty to provide immigration services honourably, and to discharge all responsibilities to Clients, government agencies, the Board, colleagues, the public and others affected in the course of the member's practice with integrity.

3.2 Privileged Role

An ICCRC member, as an authorized representative of individuals in the immigration and refugee system, has a privileged role to play in maintaining the integrity of Canada's immigration system and the administration of justice. Despite any request or demand to the contrary received from any person, an ICCRC member must uphold the rule of law and act at all times honestly and in good faith towards immigration officials, without intent to deceive or undermine the integrity of the system, or assist others to do so.

ARTICLE 4. PROFESSIONALISM

4.1 Maintain Integrity

An ICCRC member shall act in such a way as to maintain the integrity of the profession of immigration practice.

4.2 Courtesy and Good Faith

An ICCRC member shall be courteous and civil, and shall act in good faith, in all professional dealings. An ICCRC member should avoid maligning the reputation of colleagues for personal motives.

4.3 No Offensive Communications

An ICCRC member shall not send correspondence or otherwise communicate with the ICCRC, a Client, another ICCRC member, a government official or any other person in a manner that is abusive, offensive or otherwise inconsistent with the proper tone of professional communication from an ICCRC member.

4.4 Report of Breaches of This Code

Subject to the duty of Client confidentiality, an ICCRC member should report to the appropriate authority any unprofessional, illegal or unethical conduct by colleagues or others. Wherever possible, the ICCRC member should request an explanation first from this individual to assist in determining whether there is any obligation to report the conduct.

4.5 No Misconduct or Conduct Unbecoming

An ICCRC member shall not engage in professional misconduct or conduct unbecoming an ICCRC member.

4.6 No Breach of Bylaws

An ICCRC member shall not engage in conduct that is a violation of the Bylaws.

ARTICLE 5. COMPETENCE

5.1 Nature of Competence

To be competent includes knowing and applying the relevant legal rules, policies and practices appropriate to the matter undertaken on behalf of a Client.

5.2 Duty of Competence

An ICCRC member owes duty to be competent to perform any services undertaken for a Client in connection with the member's practice.

5.3 Standard of Service

An ICCRC member shall perform any services undertaken on behalf a Client to the standard of a competent ICCRC member.

5.4 Not Practice if Not Competent

An ICCRC member shall be alert to recognize any lack of competence for a particular task and the disservice that could be done to the Client by undertaking that task, and shall not undertake a matter without being competent to handle it or being able to become competent without undue delay or expense to the Client.

5.5 Obligation if Not Competent

An ICCRC member who discovers a lack competence to complete a retainer, shall either decline to act or obtain the Client's consent to retain, consult or collaborate with another person who is competent and licensed to perform that task.

5.6 Maintenance of Skills and Knowledge

An ICCRC member has a responsibility to adapt to changing laws and policies affecting professional practice, as well as requirements and policies of the ICCRC. The member must keep up-to-date on the skills and knowledge needed for competent practice and comply with the requirements and the spirit of the Continuing Education policies of ICCRC.

ARTICLE 6. QUALITY OF SERVICE

6.1 Maintenance of Quality Service

An ICCRC member must conduct all elements of practice in a conscientious, diligent and efficient manner, and provide a quality of service at least equal to that which ICCRC members generally would expect of a competent member in a similar situation. The ICCRC member must at all time use best efforts to:

6.1.1 meet all applicable deadlines;

6.1.2 conduct Client affairs in an efficient, cost-effective manner;

6.1.3 communicate with the Client at all stages of a matter in a timely and effective way;

6.1.4 engage the services of an interpreter when necessary;

6.1.5 answer reasonable Client requests in a timely and effective manner;

6.1.6 apply intellectual capacity, judgment, and deliberation to all functions;

6.1.7 pursue appropriate training and development to maintain and enhance knowledge and skills;

6.1.8 adapt to changing laws, requirements, standards, techniques and practices; and

6.1.9 comply in letter and in spirit with this Code.

6.2 Professional Responsibility for Agents and Staff

The ICCRC member is responsible for the acts or omissions of the member's Agents and Employees, and must ensure that all Agents and Employees conduct themselves in accordance with this Code.

6.3 Supervision of Agents and Staff

An ICCRC member must assume complete professional responsibility for all work entrusted to the member and adequately supervise Employees and Agents who have been assigned specific tasks.

6.4 Registration of Agents

An ICCRC member must register with ICCRC the names of all Agents, and ensure that any registered Agents are de-registered when no longer engaged. Application for registration or de-registration shall be made promptly after it occurs, but in every instance, within thirty (30) days after the event.

6.5 Prohibited Employees and Agents

Except with the written permission of ICCRC, an ICCRC member may not employ or retain in any capacity having to do with the member's practice a person whose membership or registration has been removed or suspended by ICCRC or any Designated Legal Regulatory Body as a result of a disciplinary action, or share space or be a partner or associate of such a person.

6.6 Mandatory Assistance When Required
An ICCRC member should seek help from colleagues and appropriately qualified professionals for personal problems that adversely affect either professional practice or responsibilities to ICCRC.

ARTICLE 7. ADVISING CLIENTS

7.1 Honesty and Candour Required
An ICCRC member must be honest and candid when advising Clients.

7.2 Restricted to Scope of Practice
An ICCRC member shall not undertake or provide advice with respect to a matter that is outside the member's permissible scope of practice.

7.3 Avoid Corrupt Associations
An ICCRC member shall take all reasonable measures to avoid becoming the tool or dupe of an unscrupulous Client, person or persons associated with same.

7.4 Cheating Prohibited
An ICCRC member must exercise due care and not knowingly assist in or encourage:

7.4.1 any dishonesty, fraud, crime or illegal conduct,

7.4.2 the provision of misleading information,

7.4.3 the omission of any required relevant information,

7.4.4 counselling of a Client on how to violate the law or

7.4.5 counselling of a Client on how to avoid punishment, but this shall not preclude the provision of information as to mitigation of possible sentence for breach of IRPA.

7.5 Response to Illegality
When an ICCRC member is employed or retained by a person or organization to act in a matter the ICCRC member knows is dishonest, fraudulent, criminal or illegal with respect to that matter, then in addition to any obligations above, the ICCRC member shall:

7.5.1 advise the person or organization from whom the ICCRC member takes instructions that the proposed conduct would be dishonest, fraudulent, criminal or illegal, and should be stopped; and

7.5.2 if the person or organization, despite the advice, intends to pursue the proposed course of conduct, withdraw from acting in the matter in accordance with Article 14.

7.6 Translation Services Required
When advising a Client who does not speak English or French, or another language in which the ICCRC member is fluent, the ICCRC member must make a reasonable effort to engage the services of an interpreter when communicating with the Client.

7.7 Availability of ICCRC Language Services

An ICCRC member shall, where the Client speaks French but not English, inform the Client in writing in the French language of the contact information and French services of ICCRC; and reciprocally, where the Client speaks English but not French, an ICCRC member shall inform the Client in writing in the English language of the contact information and English services of ICCRC.

ARTICLE 8. CONFIDENTIALITY

8.1 Maintenance of Confidentiality

An ICCRC member has a duty to hold in strict confidence at all times all information concerning the personal and business affairs of a Client acquired during the course of practice, and should not disclose such information unless disclosure is expressly or impliedly authorized by the Client, required by law or by a tribunal of competent jurisdiction, or is otherwise permitted by this Code.

8.2 Confidentiality Survives Retainer

The duty of confidentiality under Section 8.1 continues indefinitely after the ICCRC member has ceased to act for the Client, whether or not differences have arisen between them. For greater clarity, an ICCRC member, subject to being compelled by law or legal process, shall preserve the Client confidential information even after the termination of the retainer.

8.3 Protection of Confidential Information

An ICCRC member shall take all reasonable steps to ensure the privacy and safekeeping of a Client's confidential information. The ICCRC member shall keep the Client's papers and other property out of sight, as well as out of reach, of those not entitled to see them.

8.4 Disclosure Prohibited

An ICCRC member shall not disclose the fact of having been consulted or retained by a person unless the nature of the matter requires such disclosure.

8.5 Application to Employees and Agents

An ICCRC member should ensure that their Employees and Agents maintain and preserve the Client's confidential information.

8.6 Exception When Required By Law

Notwithstanding the above, an ICCRC member may disclose confidential information when required by law or by order of a tribunal of competent jurisdiction.

8.7 Exception for Defence of Allegations

In order to defend against allegations, an ICCRC member may disclose confidential information if it is alleged that the ICCRC member or the member's Agents or Employees are:

    8.7.1 guilty of a criminal offence involving a Client affairs;

    8.7.2 civilly liable with respect to a matter involving a Client's affairs; or

    8.7.3 guilty of a breach of this Code.

8.8 Exception for Collections

An ICCRC member may disclose confidential information in order to establish or collect professional fees or disbursements.

8.9 Limits on Exceptions

An ICCRC member shall not disclose more information than is necessary when disclosing confidential information required or permitted by Sections 8.6, 8.7 or 8.8.

ARTICLE 9. CONFLICTS OF INTEREST

9.1 Prohibition Where Conflict

An ICCRC member shall not represent parties with potentially conflicting interests in an immigration matter, unless after adequate disclosure to and with the consent of the parties, and shall not act or continue to act in a matter where there is or is likely to be a conflict of interest.

ARTICLE 10. PRESERVATION OF CLIENT PROPERTY

10.1 Safekeeping of Client Property

An ICCRC member owes a duty to the Client to ensure the safekeeping of the Client's property in accordance with the law and with the same care of such property as a careful and prudent owner would when dealing with property of like description.

10.2 Notification of Safekeeping

An ICCRC member shall promptly notify the Client of the receipt of any money or other property of the Client, unless satisfied that the Client is aware that the property has come into the member's custody.

10.3 Segregation of Client Property

An ICCRC member shall clearly label and identify the Client's property and place it in safekeeping, distinguishable from the ICCRC member's own property.

10.4 Safekeeping Records Required

An ICCRC member shall maintain such records as necessary to identify Client property that is in the ICCRC member's custody.

10.5 Accounting for and Return of Client Property

An ICCRC member shall account promptly for any Client property that is in the member's custody and shall, upon request, deliver it to the order of the Client.

ARTICLE 11. ICCRC MEMBER AS ADVOCATE

11.1 Twin Responsibilities

When representing the Client before government officials or the Board, the ICCRC member should resolutely, and honourably, within the limits of the law, represent the Client's interests while treating the Board members, the Minister, Officers and other parties with candour, courtesy and respect.

ARTICLE 12. RETAINER AND FEES

12.1 Content of Retainer Generally

The ICCRC member must provide the Client with a written retainer agreement or engagement letter that:

12.1.1 clearly states the matter and scope of services for which the ICCRC member is retained;

12.1.2 fully discloses

(i) the fees payable, such fees to be fair and reasonable in the circumstances;

(ii) the disbursements to be charged;

(iii) the payment terms and conditions:

a) by the hour or

b) flat fee billing with payment by milestones or by predetermined date;

(iv) schedule of payments.

12.1.3 identifies the nature but not the amount of any other remuneration, such as but not limited to a referral fee, being or to be received by the ICCRC member in connection with the matter;

12.1.4 discloses that the ICCRC member is a member of ICCRC; and

12.1.5 provides sufficient details as to how to contact ICCRC.

12.2 Specific Content of Retainer

The retainer agreement shall provide a written complaint procedure regarding Client fee disputes, the failure to respond to requests for information, and the return of Client's property. The retainer agreement shall provide that any complaint be made in writing to the ICCRC member, and that the member will address the concerns of the Client within a specified time period.

12.3 Application of Trust Money

An ICCRC member must not appropriate any money or property of a Client held in trust or otherwise under the ICCRC member's control for or on account of fees or disbursements without the express or implied authority of the Client.

12.4 Certain Prohibition

An ICCRC member may not hold Client money for the benefit of a third party except for money to pay the ICCRC member's fees, including Agent's fees, CIC fees and disbursements related thereto. For greater clarity, the prohibition on holding Client monies applies to money the Client needs to qualify for any eligibility program under the IRPA.

ARTICLE 13. JOINT RETAINERS

13.1 Initial Obligation

Before agreeing to act for more than one Client in a matter, an ICCRC member shall advise the Clients that:

13.1.1 no information received in connection with the matter from one Client can be treated as confidential so far as any of the others are concerned; and

13.1.2 if a conflict develops that cannot be resolved, the ICCRC member cannot continue to act for both or all of them and may have to withdraw completely.

13.2 Where Continuing Relationship with One

If an ICCRC member has a continuing relationship with a Client for whom he or she acts regularly, before agreeing to act for that Client and another Client in a matter or transaction, the ICCRC member shall advise the other Client of the continuing relationship and recommend that the Client obtain independent legal advice about the joint retainer.

13.3 When Avoid Joint Retainer

Although all parties concerned may consent, an ICCRC member shall avoid acting for more than one Client if it is likely that an issue contentious between them will arise or their interests, rights, or obligations will diverge as the matter progresses.

ARTICLE 14. WITHDRAWAL FROM REPRESENTATION

14.1 When Withdrawal Required

Withdrawal is obligatory, and an ICCRC member shall sever the professional relationship with the Client or withdraw as the representative, if:

14.1.1 discharged by the Client;

14.1.2 instructed by the Client to do something illegal or in contravention of professional obligations or this Code;

14.1.3 the ICCRC member's continued involvement will place the ICCRC member in a conflict of interest; or

14.1.4 the ICCRC member is not competent to handle the matter.

14.2 When Withdrawal Optional

Withdrawal is optional and an ICCRC member may, but is not required to, sever the professional relationship with the Client or withdraw as representative if there has been a serious loss of confidence between the ICCRC member and Client, such as where:

14.2.1 the Client has deceived the ICCRC member;

14.2.2 the Client has refused to give adequate instructions to the ICCRC member; or

14.2.3 the Client has refused to accept and act upon the ICCRC member's advice on a significant point.

14.3 Withdrawal on Other Basis

In situations not covered by Sections 14.1 and 14.2, an ICCRC member may sever the professional relationship with the Client or withdraw as representative only if the severance or withdrawal:

14.3.1 will not be unfair to the Client; and

14.3.2 is not done for an improper purpose.

14.4 Withdrawal on Failure to Pay

Where, after reasonable notice, the Client fails to provide funds on account of disbursements or fees, an ICCRC member may withdraw for non-payment of fees or disbursements unless serious prejudice to the Client would result.

14.5 Member Action Required on Withdrawal

When an ICCRC member withdraws, the ICCRC member should try to minimize expense and avoid prejudice to the Client and should do all that can reasonably be done to facilitate the orderly transfer of the matter to a successor. Upon discharge or withdrawal, an ICCRC member should:

14.5.1 deliver to or to the order of the Client all papers and property to which the Client is entitled;

14.5.2 give the Client all information that may be required in connection with the case or matter;

14.5.3 account for all funds of the Client held or previously dealt with, and refund of any funds not earned during the retainer;

14.5.4 promptly render an account for outstanding fees and disbursements;

14.5.5 co-operate with the successor so as to minimize expense and avoid prejudice to the Client; and

14.5.6 notify in writing any government agency, such as Citizenship and Immigration Canada, CBSA or the Board where the ICCRC member's name appears as representative for the Client that the ICCRC member has withdrawn.

14.6 Obligation of Successor Member

Before agreeing to represent a Client, a successor ICCRC member should be satisfied that the former ICCRC member, or other representative authorized by law to represent the Client, has withdrawn, or has been discharged by the Client.

14.7 Where Withdrawal Threat Prohibited

An ICCRC member shall not use the threat of withdrawal as a device to force a hasty decision by the Client on a difficult question.

ARTICLE 15. OUTSIDE INTERESTS

15.1 Other Work Not to Compromise Member's Obligations

An ICCRC member who engages in another profession, business, occupation or other outside interest, or who holds public office concurrently in addition to practice, shall not allow the outside interest or public office to jeopardize the member's integrity, independence, or competence.

15.2 Maintenance of Independence

An ICCRC member shall not allow any involvement in an outside interest or public office to impair the exercise of independent judgment on behalf of a Client.

ARTICLE 16. ADVERTISING, SOLICITATION AND MAKING SERVICES AVAILABLE

16.1 Quality of Service Availability

An ICCRC member should make professional services available to the public in an efficient and convenient manner that will command respect and instil confidence, and by means that are compatible with the integrity, independence and effectiveness of the profession and the integrity of Canada's immigration program.

16.2 Quality of Holding-out

An ICCRC member, or Employees and Agents of members, shall not engage in false or misleading advertising or representations or misrepresent or mislead a Client as to the member's qualifications, services, fees, available programs or benefits or provide false or unrealistic expectations regarding potential results, or processing times. An ICCRC member, or Employees or Agents of members, may not hold themselves out as having special access or influence with respect to the Minister, an Officer, or the Board.

16.3 Endorsements and Testimonials

An ICCRC member may use endorsements or testimonials or both in the member's advertising and promotion provided that the nature of the form and content of any such endorsement or testimonial conforms to the policies of ICCRC, unless and until otherwise determined by ICCRC, any such endorsements or testimonials or both shall conform to the following:

16.3.1 any such endorsement or testimonial has actually been given by a Client or former Client; [and]

16.3.2 any such endorsement or testimonial is true and accurate;

16.3.3 the Client or former Client has given to the member written permission for the exact content of any such endorsement or testimonial.

16.4 Good Taste

In all instances, advertising should be in good taste and is not such as to bring the profession, ICCRC or the laws of Canada into disrepute.

16.5 Use of ICCRC Designation and Logo

An ICCRC member shall only use the ICCRC designation and the logo of ICCRC in compliance with ICCRC's policies.

ARTICLE 17. DISCRIMINATION AND HARASSMENT

17.1 No Discrimination

An ICCRC member shall not discriminate against any person in the course of their practice on such grounds as age, gender, sexual orientation, same-sex partnership status, marital status, family status, national or ethnic origin, ancestry, race, colour, religion, creed, citizenship, physical or mental disability, political affiliation, record of offences, or socio-economic status.

17.2 Respect for All

An ICCRC member shall respect the dignity and integrity of all individuals and ensure fair and equitable treatment in all aspects of the provision of immigration services.

17.3 No Denial of Service

An ICCRC member shall ensure that no one is denied services or receives inferior service on the basis of the grounds set out in this Article 17. This does not affect the ICCRC member's right to refuse to accept a Client for legitimate reasons.

17.4 No Harassment

An ICCRC member shall not engage in sexual or other forms of harassment of a colleague, a staff member, a Client or any other person on the ground of race, ancestry, place of origin, colour, ethnic origin, citizenship, creed, sex, sexual orientation, age, record of offences, marital status, family status or disability.

17.5 Use of Electronic Medium

An ICCRC member shall not engage in electronic harassment by sending unsolicited email messages of an abusive, offensive, intrusive, unprofessional or unwanted nature to another ICCRC member or a member of the public, in particular where the recipient has expressly requested to be removed from the sender's list.

17.6 Employment Practices Included

An ICCRC member's employment practices may not offend this Article 17.

ARTICLE 18. ERRORS AND OMISSIONS

18.1 Errors and Omissions Insurance Required

Every ICCRC member shall maintain the errors and omissions insurance in the minimum amount as prescribed by ICCRC from time to time.

18.2 Required Action upon Discovery of Error or Omission

If the ICCRC member discovers, in connection with a matter for which the ICCRC member was retained, an error or omission that is or may be damaging to the Client and that cannot be rectified readily, the ICCRC member shall:

18.2.1 promptly and fully inform the Client of the error or omission, being careful not to prejudice any rights of indemnity that either of them may have under an insurance, Clients' protection or indemnity plan, or otherwise;

18.2.2 seek advice from the ICCRC's Practice Management Unit where needed;

18.2.3 recommend that the Client obtain legal advice elsewhere concerning any rights the Client may have arising from the error or omission;

18.2.4 advise the Client that in the circumstances, the ICCRC member may no longer be able to act for the Client;

18.2.5 promptly inform his or her errors and omissions insurance provider; and

18.2.6 promptly inform ICCRC that the errors and omissions insurance provider has been informed.

ARTICLE 19. DISCIPLINARY AUTHORITY

19.1 ICCRC Impose Discipline

ICCRC may discipline an ICCRC member for Professional Misconduct or Conduct Unbecoming an ICCRC member.

19.2 Location of Conduct Irrelevant

An ICCRC member is subject to the disciplinary authority of ICCRC regardless of where the conduct occurred that is alleged to be a breach of this Code, or where the person resides.

19.3 Conduct Before Becoming ICCRC Member

An ICCRC member who was a CSIC member immediately before joining ICCRC is subject to the disciplinary authority of ICCRC for conduct which occurred during the period of CSIC membership which constitutes a breach of this Code.

19.4 Liability for Costs

An ICCRC member who is subject to discipline may also be required to pay all or a portion of the costs associated with the investigation and discipline hearing.

ARTICLE 20. RESPONSIBILITY TO ICCRC AND OTHERS

20.1 Maintenance of Contact Information

An ICCRC member shall immediately notify ICCRC and Clients of any changes in contact information, including but not limited to home and business address, telephone, fax and email address.

20.2 Obligation to Respond to ICCRC

An ICCRC member shall reply promptly to any communication from ICCRC.

20.3 Restriction on Communicating with Complainant

An ICCRC member shall not communicate with a person who has made a complaint to ICCRC unless the complainant has otherwise requested.

KEY TERMS

conduct unbecoming, 457
conflict of interest, 460
professional misconduct, 457
solicitor–client privilege, 459
tickler system, 458
vicarious responsibility, 459

REVIEW QUESTIONS

1. List the steps that a person must take to become a member of the ICCRC.

2. What is the difference between a regulated immigration consultant and a law clerk?

3. Compare and contrast professional misconduct and conduct unbecoming a regulated immigration consultant.

4. What is ghost consulting and why would Canadian officials want this practice stopped?

5. Describe the types of advertising that are acceptable to the ICCRC.

6. How should a consultant deal with money paid to the consultant in order to pay fees to CIC?

7. What is the obligation of a consultant acting as an advocate in a hearing before the IRB?

8. What organization can impose discipline on a regulated immigration consultant? What reasons will motivate that organization to impose discipline and what forms of discipline is that organization authorized to impose?

9. If a regulated immigration consultant operates more than one business, what must the consultant do in order to avoid improper practices?

10. What is a conflict of interest? How can a regulated immigration consultant avoid getting into a conflict of interest, or resolve a conflict of interest if one arises?

NOTES

1. Regulatory Impact Analysis Statement, *Canada Gazette*, Extra, vol. 138, no. 4, Part II, April 14, 2004, http://www.gazette.gc.ca/archives/p2/2004/2004-04-14-x/html/sor-dors59-eng.html.
2. *Chinese Business Chamber of Canada v. Canada*, 2005 FC 142, aff'd. 2006 FCA 178.
3. Citizenship and Immigration Canada, "Coming Into Force of Bill C-35, An Act to Amend the Immigration and Refugee Protection Act (Authorized Representatives)," *Operational Bulletin* 317, June 30, 2011, http://www.cic.gc.ca/english/resources/manuals/bulletins/2011/ob317.asp.
4. Canada News Centre, "Legislation Targeting Crooked Immigration Consultants Receives Royal Assent," March 23, 2011, http://news.gc.ca/web/article-eng.do?nid=598969.
5. Set out in s. 27(2) of the *Law Society Act* and bylaw 4, s. 8(1)3.
6. See "Who Can Represent You?" on the ICCR website, http://www.iccrc-crcic.ca/public/advisories.cfm.
7. Canadian Network of National Associations of Regulators, FAQ web page, http://www.cnnar.ca/FAQs.html.

REFERENCES

Chinese Business Chamber of Canada v. Canada, 2005 FC 142, aff'd. 2006 FCA 178.

Citizenship and Immigration Canada. "Coming Into Force of Bill C-35, An Act to Amend the Immigration and Refugee Protection Act (Authorized Representatives)," Operational Bulletin 317, June 30, 2011. http://www.cic.gc.ca/english/resources/manuals/bulletins/2011/ob317.asp.

Canada News Centre. "Legislation Targeting Crooked Immigration Consultants Receives Royal Assent," March 23, 2011. http://news.gc.ca/web/article-eng.do?nid=598969.

Constitution Act, 1867. (U.K.), 30 & 31 Vict., c. 3.

Immigration and Refugee Protection Act. S.C. 2001, c. 27; 2011, c. 8, s. 1.

Immigration and Refugee Protection Regulations. S.O.R./2002-227; S.O.R./2012-77, s. 1.

Immigration Consultants of Canada Regulatory Council. Code of Professional Ethics, June 2012. http://www.iccrc-crcic.ca/admin/contentEngine/contentImages/file/Code_of_Professional_Ethics__Sept_2011.pdf.

Law Society of British Columbia v. Mangat. 2001 SCC 67, [2001] 3 S.C.R. 113.

Law Society of Upper Canada v. Canada (Citizenship and Immigration). 2008 FCA 243.

Glossary

A

accredited interpreter an interpreter used in a refugee hearing who has undergone a security check and has passed a language exam

acquittal a finding of not guilty

administrative tribunal a specialized governmental agency established under legislation to implement legislative policy—for example, the Immigration and Refugee Board is an administrative tribunal established under the IRPA

admissibility hearing the hearing that is held at the Immigration Division when a person allegedly breaches Canadian immigration laws pursuant to s. 44 of the IRPA, where an officer is of the opinion that a permanent resident or foreign national is inadmissible

alienage being outside one's country of nationality or citizenship

allowed on consent an appeal that may be allowed if the minister concedes to the appellant's position

application in the immigration and refugee context, a request that can be made orally or in writing to an officer or other decision-maker by a person seeking a government action; for example, a person may make an application for permanent residence

arrest to take a person into legal custody

B

balance of probabilities the standard of proof in civil matters, determined on the basis of whether a claim or a fact as alleged is more probably true than not true; this is a much lower standard of proof than that required in criminal court, where the evidence must establish "beyond a reasonable doubt" that an accused is guilty

bridge extension an interim work permit for a live-in caregiver that is valid for a period of two months

business person a person who seeks entry to Canada through some sort of pre-arrangement, such as an employment contract or under NAFTA or GATS

business visitor under NAFTA, a citizen of the United States or Mexico who seeks admission to Canada to engage in certain international business activities, and whose primary source of remuneration remains outside Canada

C

Canadian Orientation Abroad (COA) program a one-to five-day program designed to help integrate refugees into Canadian society

case law created by courts and other adjudicators in their judgments; case law includes the common law as well as the interpretation of statutes and regulations

cessation clause a clause that provides the framework for when protection may lawfully cease under s. 108 of the IRPA

citizen a person who has the right to live in a country by virtue of birth or by legally acquiring the right

citizenship the full political and civil rights in the body politic of the state

citizenship judges quasi-judicial decision-makers who have the authority to decide citizenship applications

codified formalized and clarified in writing in the form of binding legislation

common law a body of legal principles and rules that trace back to Britain and which are found in court judgments; a category of case law

community sponsor organizations, associations, and corporations that sponsor refugees

conditional removal order a departure order with conditions attached; issued pending the outcome of a refugee claim

conduct unbecoming improper conduct that occurs outside the immigration consultant's practice

conference a proceeding at which the refugee claimant (and/or counsel) meets with an RPD member before a hearing to discuss issues, relevant facts, and other matters to make the hearing more fair and efficient

conflict of interest occurs where a consultant represents clients with incompatible interests

constituent group (CG) a group authorized by a sponsorship agreement holder to sponsor refugees on its behalf

Constitution the basic framework under which all other laws are created, establishing the basic principles to which all other laws must conform

convention an agreement that obliges countries under international law to conform to its provisions

Convention refugee a person who has been granted protection under the refugee definition in the 1951 Convention Relating to the Status of Refugees

corroborative documents documents that corroborate a claimant's allegations

co-signer a person who co-signs with a sponsor who does not have the necessary financial means to be an approved sponsor

country information for a refugee claimant, information on the country of reference, such as country-of-origin information, as provided by the RPD

crimes against humanity any inhumane acts or omissions that are committed against any civilian population or any identifiable group

criminality domestic crime, as opposed to crimes against humanity or war crimes; the IRPA defines three categories of criminality: serious criminality under s. 36(1), criminality under s. 36(2), and organized criminality under s. 37

customary international law law customs and practice that take on the force of law over time

D

deemed rehabilitated an exemption from criminal inadmissibility; a person who was convicted outside Canada and who meets the criteria under s. 18(2) of the IRP Regulations may be deemed rehabilitated and permitted to enter Canada

delegation of authority the giving of decision-making power to someone else; for example, a minister may delegate authority to an immigration officer

departure order type of removal order that generally provides a person with 30 days in which to leave Canada

deportation order type of removal order that bars re-entry to Canada indefinitely

derogable rights human rights that can be temporarily suspended by a state in a time of public emergency; for example, freedom of movement may be temporarily restricted or removed

designate choose someone for a position, duty, or responsibility

designated foreign national (DFN) a person (generally a refugee claimant) who was part of a group of smuggled persons into Canada whom the minister has designated as an irregular arrival (see specific definition in IRPA, s. 20.1)

designated irregular arrival a group (generally of refugee claimants) that the minister has reasonable grounds to believe was part of a human smuggling operation and is so designated in the public interest

designated representative person chosen by the RPD to act and make decisions on behalf of a refugee claimant

detain keep a person in legal custody, such as in a prison or immigration holding centre, prior to a hearing on a matter

detention when a foreign national is detained within the 30-day period, such as for arrest on a criminal charge, the 30-day period is suspended until either the foreign national is released or the removal order becomes enforceable

detention review hearing before the Immigration Division for the purpose of reviewing the reasons for a permanent resident's detention under the IRPA

disclosure the release of documents to the opposing side in a proceeding

dual intent intention to become first a temporary resident and then a permanent resident

durable solution a lasting solution to a refugee's temporary status: local integration in the country of asylum, voluntary return to the refugee's home country (repatriation), or resettlement in another country

E

educational credential any diploma, degree, or trade or apprenticeship credential issued on completion of a program of study or training at an educational or training institution recognized by the authorities responsible for registering, accrediting, supervising, and regulating such institutions in the country of issue

eligible in an immigration context, the applicant is not inadmissible

exclusion order type of removal order that includes a one-year or two-year ban from re-entering Canada

F

federal system of government a division of law-making powers between the national (federal) and provincial governments according to subject matter

flight risk a person who is likely to fail to appear at an immigration proceeding in order to stay in Canada illegally

foreign national a person who is neither a Canadian citizen nor a permanent resident in Canada

full-time equivalent in reference to part-time or accelerated studies, the period that would have been required to complete those studies on a full-time basis

full-time studies a program of study leading to an educational credential, consisting of at least 15 hours of instruction per week during the academic year

G

GATS professional a person who seeks to engage in an activity at a professional level in a designated profession, and meets the GATS criteria

genocide an act or omission committed with intent to destroy, in whole or in part, an identifiable group of persons

Government-Assisted Refugee (GAR) program a program that applies only to the sponsorship of members of the Convention refugees abroad class, including special needs cases

governor in council the governor general acting with the advice and consent of Cabinet; formal executive authority is conferred by the statutes on the governor in council

Group of Five (G5) a group of five or more people who join together to sponsor one or more refugees

H

hearing a proceeding at which a refugee claimant appears in person before a member of the RPD to present evidence and testimony and to answer questions related to his claim

home study an assessment of the prospective parents with respect to their suitability to adopt

hybrid or dual procedure offences offences for which the Crown prosecutor chooses to proceed either by summary conviction or by indictment

I

identity documents lawfully obtained documents designed to prove the identity of the person carrying them (for example, a passport or birth certificate)

immigrant a person who wishes to settle (or has settled) permanently in another country (as opposed to a refugee, who is forced to flee)

immigration the movement of non-native people into a country in order to settle there

Immigration and Refugee Board (IRB) an independent, quasi-judicial tribunal whose mission is "to make well-reasoned decisions on immigration and refugee matters—efficiently, fairly and in accordance with the law"

Immigration Loans Program (ILP) special federal fund available to indigent refugees and immigrants who qualify

immigration resettlement plan plan tabled by the CIC minister each year that includes the number and types of foreign nationals who can come to Canada as permanent residents

immigration visa officer a public servant working in a Canadian consulate or visa office abroad

inadmissibility hearing adversarial hearing to determine whether or not an applicant is inadmissible

inadmissibility report a report that sets out the grounds of inadmissibility alleged by the officer, with the related sections of the IRPA and the evidence in narrative form

indictable offences serious offences such as murder, with longer periods of imprisonment and more complex prosecution procedures than those for summary conviction offences

individual rehabilitation a method of removing a ground of inadmissibility (criminality) that requires the applicant to apply to a visa officer, who will then consider whether certain criteria have been met

interdiction control activity that prevents illegal travellers and criminals from reaching Canada

Interim Federal Health Program (IFHP) essential and emergency health care coverage for refugees in need of assistance before provincial health care is available

International Organization for Migration (IOM) an intergovernmental organization that works with partners in the international community to assist in meeting the operational challenges of migration, advance understanding of migration issues, encourage social and economic development through migration, and uphold the human dignity and well-being of migrants

intra-company transfer a category of work permit designed to assist multinational businesses to move executives temporarily to Canada, when required for business

intra-company transferee a US or Mexican citizen who is admitted to Canada under NAFTA for the purpose of assisting in the operations of a foreign company's Canadian parent, subsidiary, branch, or affiliate company

J

Joint Assistance Sponsorship (JAS) program a refugee sponsorship program that involves both CIC and a private sponsor

jointly and severally liable refers to the legal doctrine that either partner in a relationship may be required to pay the full amount of a financial obligation—for example, where a sponsor takes on a co-signer, both may be liable for the full amount in the event of a default

judicial notice a rule of evidence that allows a decision-maker to accept certain commonly known, indisputable, and uncontentious facts without requiring that they be proven with evidence

jus sanguinis citizenship based on blood ties

jus soli citizenship based on the land of birth

L

labour market opinion (LMO) an HRSDC document obtained by a Canadian employer in order to employ a foreign worker; also known as an HRSDC confirmation

language in an immigration context, the ability to speak, read, write, and listen in either French or English

letter of acceptance document that indicates that a foreign student has been accepted into a Canadian educational institution

letter of no-involvement a letter that may be accepted instead of a home study where a private adoption takes place outside Canada and in a state that is not a signatory to the Hague Convention

letter of no-objection a written statement from the province or territory where the child will live, stating that the province or territory does not object to the adoption (IRP Regulations, ss. 117(1)(g)(iii)(B) and 117(3)(e))

letter (or notice) of agreement a letter or notice of agreement required in Hague Convention adoption cases, indicating that the province and adoptive parents agree to the adoption (IRP Regulations, ss. 117(1)(g)(ii) and 117(3)(f) and (g)). It is sent by the receiving provincial or territorial authorities to the visa office, with a copy to the central authority of the adopted child's country of residence

low income cut-off (LICO) minimum income requirement for sponsors of permanent residents

Low Skill Pilot Project (LSP) an HRSDC program designed to meet the labour market demand for temporary foreign workers in low-skill jobs

M

medical surveillance a designation by the designated medical officer that provides for monitoring of an applicant's medical condition

member the title given to a decision-maker in the Refugee Protection Division, Immigration Division, or Immigration Appeal Division of the Immigration and Refugee Board

misrepresentation a ground of inadmissibility under the IRPA that involves misstating facts or withholding information

multiple citizenships a situation where a person who becomes a citizen of Canada can retain any previous citizenships

multiple-entry visa a document that allows a foreign national to enter Canada from another country multiple times during the validity of the visa

N

named cases sponsor-referred refugee cases

nationality refers to a person's citizenship, and also a person's ethnic or linguistic group, and so may sometimes overlap with race

naturalization the process by which a foreign national, after being admitted to Canada as a permanent resident, applies for and obtains Canadian citizenship

non-derogable right a person's core human rights, which must be respected and cannot be taken away or suspended for any reason (for example, the right to life, and freedom from torture)

non-political crimes an act committed for personal gain with no political end or motive involved

non-state agent persecutors of the refugee claimant who are not members of the state—for example, rebels or warlords

notice of arrival notice of a refugee's arrival into Canada that is sent to the sponsor

notice of decision a written decision by the decision-maker, issued to those involved in the case, such as by the RPD to the refugee claimant and the minister

O

officers under s. 6(1) of the IRPA, a person or class of person designated by the minister as an officer to carry out any purpose of any provision of the IRPA and who is given specific powers and duties

open work permit a document possessed by a foreign student enabling her to work for any employer for a specific time period

oral representation an argument that is made orally, such as at the end of a refugee hearing

orders in council administrative orders that serve notice of a decision taken by the executive arm of government

P

panel physician a local physician, authorized by the Canadian government; formerly known as a "designated medical practitioner"

parallel processing processing the permanent residence application of the main applicant and those of sponsored family members at the same time, such as is allowed under the Live-In Caregiver Program

paramountcy a principle providing that if a law falls within the jurisdiction of both the federal and provincial governments, the federal government takes jurisdiction

pardon a grant under the *Criminal Code* resulting in an offence being deemed not to have occurred

peace officer a law enforcement officer having the power to examine people and perform searches and seizures

permanent residence application process under the family class the process whereby an applicant becomes a permanent resident

permanent resident a person who has been granted permanent resident status in Canada and who has not subsequently lost that status under s. 46 of the IRPA; also known as a "landed immigrant" under older legislation

permanent resident card (PR card) a card issued to permanent residents after their arrival in Canada showing proof of immigration status

permanent resident status the enjoyment of most of the same rights and responsibilities guaranteed to Canadians under the *Canadian Charter of Rights and Freedoms*

permanent resident visa a document allowing a foreign national to travel to Canada and, after a successful examination at a port of entry, to enter Canada as a permanent resident

persecution sustained and systematic violation of basic human rights

person in need of protection a person who has been granted refugee protection under the IRPA because of a danger of torture or because of risk to life or cruel and unusual treatment or punishment; used when the refugee claim does not fall within the scope of the Refugee Convention

policy non-binding guidelines created by agencies to support the administration of statutes and regulations, and reflecting the government and agency's agenda

precedent a court ruling on a point of law that is binding on lower courts

prescribed senior official as referenced under s. 35(1)(b) of the IRPA, a senior official in the service of a government that has been designated by the minister as a perpetrator of terrorism, human rights violations, genocide, war crimes, or crimes against humanity

principle of *non-refoulement* a rule of international law that obliges countries to provide protection to refugees against return to the country where they face a risk of persecution, or where their life or freedom would be threatened because of their race, religion, nationality, membership in a particular social group, or political opinion

professional under NAFTA, a citizen of the United States or Mexico who has pre-arranged employment with a Canadian employer and whose occupation is listed in NAFTA

professional misconduct any improper action of an immigration consultant during the course of conducting business that tends to discredit the profession

R

ratification a confirmation to abide by an international agreement

reasonable grounds a set of facts and circumstances that would satisfy an ordinarily cautious and prudent person, and that are more than mere suspicion; a lower standard of proof than a balance of probabilities

record the collection of documents received by the RPD from a refugee claimant before there is a decision to hold a hearing

refugee a person who is forced to flee from persecution (as opposed to an immigrant who chooses to move)

refugee claimant a person who has made a refugee protection claim where the decision is yet to be made; this term is used in Canada and is equivalent to "asylum seeker"

refugee *sur place* a person who did not initially flee the home country, but while in another country became a refugee in need of protection because of changed country conditions or circumstances in the home country

refusal letter document sent to a permanent resident applicant outlining the reasons for the application's refusal

regulations additional rules created pursuant to a statute by the governor in council and that fill in practical details for the administration and enforcement of the statute

removal order an order issued either after an examination or at an admissibility hearing instructing the person to leave Canada

removal ready refers to people who are subject to a removal order that is in force or to a security certificate that has been issued against them

resettlement in the context of refugee law, the relocation and integration of a refugee or person in a refugee-like situation from a camp or other temporary situation to another country where he can reside on a permanent basis; this option may be used when the refugee cannot return to his country of origin because of a risk to life or other serious problems

Resettlement Assistance Program (RAP) program that provides financial and immediate essential services to government-assisted refugees

residence in Canada a requirement for citizenship

residency calculator CIC website tool for timing citizenship applications

residual power power that is not otherwise delegated elsewhere; the federal government has a residual power to legislate in all subject areas that are not specifically assigned to the provinces

risk of cruel and unusual treatment or punishment and risk to life ill-treatment causing suffering that is less severe than torture

rules a category of regulation that has the purpose of establishing practices and procedures for the presentation of cases

S

s. 44(1) report *see* inadmissibility report

safe third country a receiving country that is any country, other than the country of origin, in which a refugee enjoys protection

Seasonal Agricultural Worker Program (SAWP) a program that allows the entry of foreign nationals to work in the agricultural sector in Canada

security certificate a document providing for a removal hearing in the absence of the person named, where information must be protected for reasons of public safety

settlement plan details of a refugee sponsor's commitment to provide basic financial support and care for a sponsored refugee

significant benefit a ground of exemption from the usual requirement of foreign workers to obtain an HRSDC confirmation; the exemption applies to foreign workers whose presence in Canada will likely result in a significant benefit to the country and permits them to apply for a work permit without first obtaining the HRSDC confirmation

single-entry visa a document that allows a foreign national to enter Canada only once, usually only for six months

solicitor–client privilege the protection of client information and communication shared in the context of a solicitor–client relationship

special advocate a person who must be appointed to act on behalf of a person who is subject to a closed security certificate hearing process to protect his or her interests

sponsorship agreement holder (SAH) an established, incorporated organization that has signed an agreement with the minister of CIC to facilitate refugee sponsorship

sponsorship application process under the family class, the process whereby an approved sponsor may apply to be reunited with a family member

state agent authority of the refugee claimant's country of origin—for example, police and members of the military

statutes the written codes of law passed by legislatures, which typically deal with a particular subject matter—for example, the IRPA is a statute dealing with immigration and refugee matters

stay of removal usually refers to a decision by a member of the Immigration Appeal Division where the member decides not to continue with an appeal against a removal order; the appellant is allowed to remain in Canada but must abide by certain conditions imposed by the member; if there is no breach of the conditions within the ordered period of time, the appeal is allowed, the removal order quashed, and the person permitted to remain in Canada; however, proceedings could be resumed at some future time if conditions are breached

summary conviction offences less serious offences with a maximum sentence of six months in jail and prosecuted using streamlined procedures

Super Visa a document that allows the foreign national to re-enter Canada for up to two years without the need to renew her visa

T

temporary resident a person who has permission to remain in Canada on a temporary basis (the main categories are students, temporary workers, and visitors)

temporary resident permit (TRP) a permit for temporary residence issued at the discretion of an officer to a foreign national who is inadmissible or does not meet the requirements of the IRPA; for example, a TRP may be issued to a foreign national for medical treatment in Canada in certain circumstances

temporary resident visa (TRV) a document authorizing a person to board an airplane or ship to travel to Canada

terrorist group as defined under s. 83.01 of the *Criminal Code*, "an entity that has as one of its purposes or activities facilitating or carrying out any terrorist activity … and includes an association of such entities"

tickler system a reminder system for deadlines

torture the infliction of severe bodily pain, especially as a punishment or a means of interrogation or intimidation

transit visa a document that allows travel through Canada to another country by anyone who would need a temporary resident visa to enter Canada and whose flight will stop here for less than 48 hours

U

ultra vires outside the jurisdiction of the government that passed it

undertaking a promise or agreement to do something

unnamed cases refugee sponsorship requests referred to the CIC Matching Centre, which attempts to find a suitable match for a would-be sponsor

urgent need of protection a term that describes, in respect of a member of the Convention refugees abroad class, the country of asylum class, or the source country class, a person whose life, liberty, or physical safety is under immediate threat and who, if not protected, is likely to be (a) killed; (b) subjected to violence, torture, sexual assault, or arbitrary imprisonment; or (c) returned to her country of nationality or former habitual residence (IRP Regulations, s. 138)

V

vacate nullify, such as may occur to a refugee determination that was obtained fraudulently

vicarious responsibility a principle that can lead to immigration professionals being held personally responsible for the actions of agents or employees

visa a document that permits the holder to enter Canada for a specific purpose either temporarily or permanently.

visa officers officers who work abroad processing immigration applications

visitor visa a temporary resident visa issued under the visitor class

visitor's record a record of information documented by a port-of-entry officer, stapled to the holder's passport; additional information may be kept on computer and referenced in the visitor's record

voluntary repatriation in the context of refugee law, the return of a refugee to her country of origin, of her own free will, once conditions have become safe

vulnerable a term describing Convention refugees or persons in similar circumstances who have a greater need of protection than other applicants for protection abroad because their particular circumstances give rise to a heightened risk to their physical safety (s. 138 of the IRP Regulations)

W

war crime an act or omission committed during an armed conflict

well-founded fear one of the four inclusion elements of the definition of a Convention refugee, assessed by the Refugee Protection Division in a refugee claim; the RPD member assesses whether a well-founded fear of persecution exists

withdrawal refers to an appeal that may be withdrawn by the appellant if she concedes to the minister's position

withholding to hold back from doing or taking an action

Women at Risk Program a program to resettle women who are members of the Convention refugees abroad class or humanitarian-protected persons abroad class

Index